Twelfth Edition

PREBLES' ARTFORMS

Patrick Frank

VP, Portfolio Management: Dickson Musslewhite
Portfolio Management Specialist: Ed Parsons
Marketing Managers: Nicholas Bolt, Wendy Albert
Managing Content Producer: Donna DeBenedictis
Project Coordination, Text Design, and
Electronic Page Makeup: Laurence King Publishing Ltd
Design Lead: Kathryn Foot
Manufacturing Buyer: Mary Ann Gloriande
Printer/Binder: LSCC/Kendallville
Cover Printer: Phoenix Color

Team at Laurence King Publishing:
Commissioning Editor: Kara Hattersley-Smith
Senior Editor: Deborah Hercun
Production Manager: Simon Walsh
Cover and Page Designer: Ian Hunt
Picture Researcher: Julia Ruxton and Cheryl Thomas
Copy Editor: Rosie Fairhead
Indexer: Vicki Robinson

Cover Image: *Autoconstrucción Suites* by Abraham Cruzvillegas. Courtesy of the artist, Walker Art Center, Minneapolis and kurimanzutto, Mexico City. Photo © Walker Art Center.

Acknowledgments of text and images reproduced by permission of third-party sources appear on the appropriate page in this textbook.

Library of Congress Cataloging-in-Publication Data

Names: Frank, Patrick, 1953- author. | Preble, Duane. Artforms.
Title: Prebles' artforms / Patrick Frank.
Description: Twelfth edition. | Upper Saddle River : Pearson, 2019. |
Includes bibliographical references and index.
Identifiers: LCCN 2017060257| ISBN 9780134791364 (pbk.) | ISBN 0134791363
   (pbk.)
Subjects: LCSH: Composition (Art) | Visual perception. | Art--History.
Classification: LCC N7430 .P69 2019 | DDC 701/.8--dc23
LC record available at https://lccn.loc.gov/2017060257

1 18

Rental Edition
ISBN 10: 0-13-479136-3
ISBN 13: 978-0-13-479136-4

À la Carte Edition
ISBN 10: 0-13-479312-9
ISBN 13: 978-0-13-479312-2

Instructor's Review Copy
ISBN 10: 0-13-489742-0
ISBN 13: 978-0-13-489742-4

www.pearsonhighered.com

BRIEF CONTENTS

CONTENTS

Part Three
ART AS CULTURAL HERITAGE

DEAR READER

I'm a visual person; I have two Instagram accounts. I love looking at things and thinking about them. For me, art from any period or culture is just about the most interesting thing on the planet. This is because art is a human product, made by people just like us. Looking at a work of art instantly leads me to imagining the mindset and working methods of whoever made it. Then I start comparing it, in my mind, with similar things that I have seen; and then I am hooked.

We form art. Art forms us. The title of this book has a dual meaning. As humans form works of art, we in turn are formed by what we have created. Such human creativity influences and stimulates us. Several editions ago, this book's title was changed to Prebles' *Artforms*, acknowledging the pioneering contribution of the original authors, Duane and Sarah Preble. They first posited the emphasis on our two-way interaction with works of art, and that emphasis continues to inform every page of this book.

Why study art? Because artists have dealt at one time or another with nearly every aspect of the human experience, from the common to the forbidden, the mundane to the sacred, the repugnant to the sublime. Artistic creativity is a response to being alive, and by experiencing such creativity, we enrich our experience of life. This is especially true of today's creations, which are more wide-ranging than ever before, and sufficiently accessible to almost any curious person. Artistic creativity is a human treasure, and in art we can see it in a very pure form.

From my post here in southern California, I try to keep up with what's going on in the art world; I also travel a lot. My notebook tells me that in just the last year, I saw 220 art exhibitions. These ranged from Native American rock art sites to the latest London galleries. (To see what I am enthused about lately, visit my Instagram feed @PatrickFrankAuthor.) From all of that looking I select the best for inclusion in *Artforms*. Behind all of the learning objectives, new terms, quizzes, flashcards, and writing prompts that accompany this book, there is a wealth of visual creativity that has constantly informed, surprised, inspired, challenged, or thrilled me. If some of that enthusiasm of mine comes through in this text, I will count it a success.

Patrick Frank
Venice, California

WHAT'S NEW

This New Edition Enhances Learning for Students:

To facilitate student learning and understanding of the arts, this twelfth edition is centered on **Learning Objectives** that introduce each chapter. These learning objectives are tailored to the subheadings so that the student will be continually reminded of the goals and objectives of study as they progress through each chapter.

The art world is changing, and *Artforms* is changing with it. The twelfth edition of this book is a deep and thorough revision which unveils a great deal of new content. I have bought **a record 196 new pictures**, adding new works in the vast bulk of the cases.

New Content in the 12th Edition:

- Following up on the discussions of creativity introduced in the last edition, a new essay feature in each chapter called **Creators** highlights the contributions of key artists. Many classic artists are featured, such as Michelangelo and Vincent Van Gogh, but 13 of the 25 essays discuss female creators, and eleven of them discuss creators of color.

- The interaction of **art and the digital world** has driven new content in several chapters, for example: Chapter 6 on Drawing has expanded treatment of interactive comics and digital drawing. Chapter 9 on Photography has expanded discussion of digital cameras and artists' use of software editing. Digital creativity is now a special focus in Chapter 10 on Cinema and Digital arts, with increased treatment of special effects, virtual reality cinema, and high-tech artists such as Lynn Hershman Leeson. The section on Interactive Design in Chapter 11 has been rewritten and expanded.

- Chapter 2 has been rewritten to deepen the focus on the **social functions of art**.

- The chapter on Craft Media (Chapter 13) has been rewritten to focus specifically artistic objects **meant for use**.

- The last section of Chapter 14 has been revamped to increase treatment of **contemporary sustainable architecture**.

- New dating of some cave paintings in Indonesia makes them the **world's oldest painted art**, older than European work by several thousand years. They are discussed in Chapter 15.

- Through a new subheading in Chapter 19, *Artforms* is now also the only book of its kind to include discussion of **Muslim modern art**.

- The final chapter on Contemporary Art is one of the most revised, with 17 new images along with discussion of **new topics** such as relational aesthetics, Post-Internet art, and a biographical essay on Ai Weiwei.

New to the Revel Edition of *Artforms*

All of the new material cited above is included in the Revel edition as well, but Revel's cross-platform digital environment allows us to offer many more aids to student learning in an interactive, engaging way.

- **Pan/zooms** appear with a simple click for almost all of the figures, allowing students to zoom in and examine details with high clarity and resolution, and then return to the overall view of the work of art, so they can relate these details to the whole.
- The pan/zooms' **scale feature** opens a window where works of art appear next to a scaled human figure (or, for small works, a scaled human hand), giving students an instant sense of the size of what they are studying.
- **3D animations of architectural and art historical techniques** depict and explain processes and methods that are difficult for students to grasp simply through narrative text.
- **Panoramas from global sites** have been integrated into the design, bringing students into the setting, both inside and out, of major buildings and monuments such as the Taj Mahal, Great Zimbabwe, and Frank Lloyd Wright's Fallingwater.
- **The Closer Looks** been transformed into Revel video presentations, where students are guided through a detailed examination of key works.
- A new series of **Explore** videos go into further detail on select topics in each chapter. The topics run a wide gamut, including political art, the stages of construction at Stonehenge, why some artists opted for the radicalism of Dada, and the latest innovations in photography.
- The entire text is available on **streaming audio**, read by the author.

In addition a variety of self-tests, review features, and writing opportunities have been built into the platform. These are all designed to ensure the student's mastery of the material.

- **Multiple-choice self-tests**, at the conclusion of each major section of a chapter, allow the student to assess quickly how well they have absorbed the material at hand.
- **Interactive learning tools**, in a variety of formats, review key terms and ideas, and make use of flashcards to test student retention.
- Each chapter contains three kinds of **writing prompts**. All are keyed to specific works of visual art and appear in conjunction with figures that illustrate the works. **Journaling** prompts focus on building skills of visual analysis; **Shared Writing** responses relate the material in the chapter to today's world; and **Writing Space** prompts encourage students to engage in cross-cultural thinking, often across chapters.

ACKNOWLEDGMENTS

I greatly appreciate the help and encouragement of the many people who have been directly involved in the writing of this twelfth edition. Several deserve special mention for their contributions: Picture researcher Julia Ruxton tirelessly tracked down images and fulfilled the increasingly complex legal requirements of today's copyright-sensitive age. Helen Ronan, Melissa Danny, and Deborah Hercun served as project managers, keeping us all on track while preserving a wonderfully civilized attitude.

This book also benefited from assistance in specialized content areas from Elizabeth East, Charles James, and Ken Smith. Many artists opened their studios to me as I was researching this book; I greatly appreciate their generosity, just as I hope that I have communicated the vigor and inspiration of their creativity.

I also express my sincere appreciation to the instructors who use this textbook as well as the following reviewers. All offered exceedingly valuable suggestions that were vital to the revising and updating of this edition:

Rabea Ballin, Lone Star College North-Harris
Paul Benero, Tarrant County College South
Paul Berger, Modesto Junior College
Ingrid Cartwright, Western Kentucky University
Russell Cook, Georgia Highlands College
Judith Dierkes, Dyersburg State Community College
Kurt Dyrhaug, Lamar Univeristy
Bobette Guillory, Carl Albert State College
Pamela Harris, University of North Texas – Dallas
Shawnya Harris, Tidewater Community College
Beth Hinte , San Jacinto College – South
Kenyon Holder, Troy University
Timothy Jones, Oklahoma City Community College
Vincent Lardieri, Palm Beach State College
Paul Levitt, Hawaii Pacific University
Scott McRoberts, Nashville State Community College
Maya Stanfield-Mazzi, University of Florida
Jason Sweet, Atlanta Metro College

ABOUT THE AUTHOR

Patrick Frank has taught in many higher education environments, from rural community colleges to public and private research universities. Most recently, he was Regents' Lecturer at the University of California, Los Angeles. His specialty as a scholar is modern art of Latin America, and he has authored or co-authored six books in this field. Most recently, he edited and translated *Manifestos and Polemics in Latin American Modern Art*, published in 2017 by University of New Mexico Press. He earned M.A. and Ph.D. degrees at George Washington University in Washington, DC.

ABOUT THE COVER

Autoconstrucción Suites by Abraham Cruzvillegas. At first glance the installation seems like a highly disorderly scene. Wooden scaffolds dominate the view, with shirts tied together spanning the distance between them. A few television sets, primitive stairs, metal frameworks, a wheelbarrow, and other seemingly miscellaneous junk populate the gallery space. Cruzvillegas gathered these objects from the immediate neighborhood. Yet behind all of this apparent chaos is a story that relates to his personal history and, by extension, to most of us as viewers. The construction of the artwork parallels the story of the construction of Cruzvillegas's family home on the outskirts of Mexico City. There, in a neighborhood outside the reach of most city services, the artist's relatives built the house he grew up in, room by room, floor by floor, by themselves, using whatever they could find or buy.

Courtesy of the artist, Walker Art Center, Minneapolis and kurimanzutto, Mexico City. Photo © Walker Art Center.

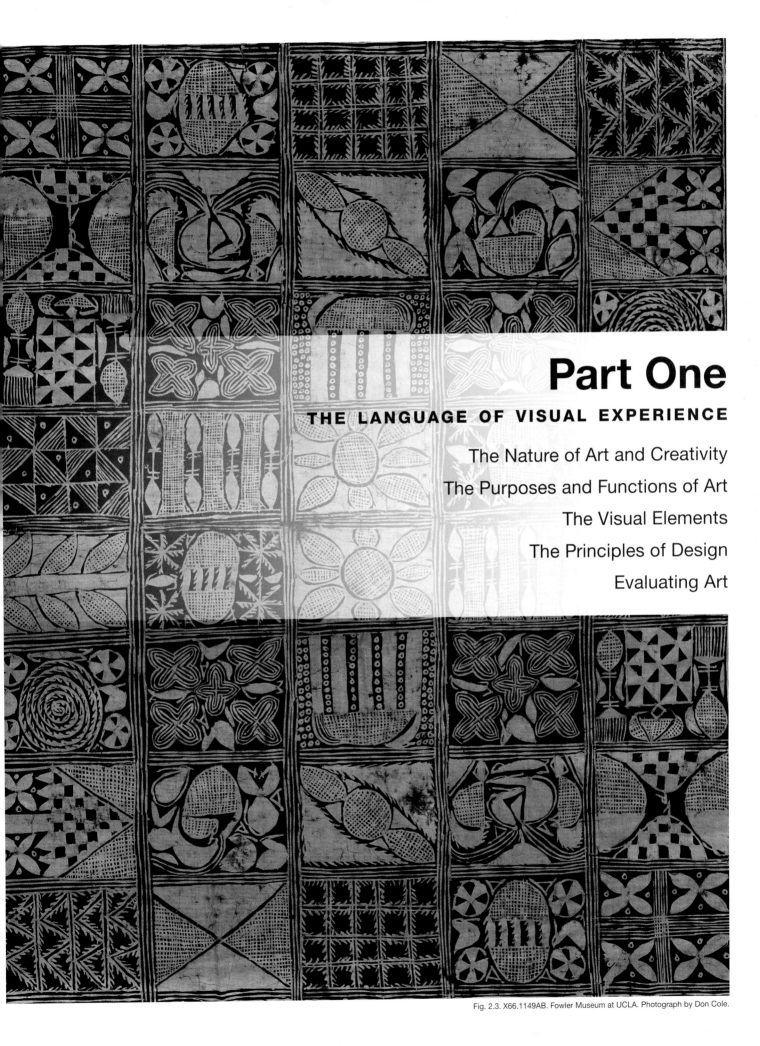

Part One

THE LANGUAGE OF VISUAL EXPERIENCE

The Nature of Art and Creativity

The Purposes and Functions of Art

The Visual Elements

The Principles of Design

Evaluating Art

Fig. 2.3. X66.1149AB. Fowler Museum at UCLA. Photograph by Don Cole.

1

THE NATURE OF ART AND CREATIVITY

LEARNING OBJECTIVES

1.1 Describe art as a means of visual expression that uses various media and forms.

1.2 Explain what is meant by creativity.

1.3 Discuss the role creativity plays in the work of trained and untrained artists.

1.4 Assess the ways in which representational, abstract, and non-representational art relate to reality.

1.5 Contrast the terms looking and seeing.

1.6 Differentiate between form and content, and show how artists may use iconography to communicate the latter.

Is it necessary for us to give visual form to things we feel, think, and imagine? Must we gesture, dance, draw, speak, sing, write, and build? To be fully human, it seems we must. In fact, the ability to create is one of the special characteristics of being human. The urge to make and enjoy what we call art has been a driving force throughout human history. Art is not something apart from us. It grows from common—and uncommon—human insights, feelings, and experiences.

Art does not need to be "understood" to be enjoyed. Like life itself, it can simply be experienced. Yet the more we understand what art can offer, the richer our experience of it will be.

For example, when Janet Echelman's huge artwork *Her Secret Is Patience* (**fig. 1.1**) was hoisted into the air above Phoenix, Arizona, in mid-2009, even most of the doubters became admirers once they experienced this stunning work. Suspended from three leaning poles between 40 and 100 feet above the ground, its colored circles of netting appear both permanent and ever changing, solid yet spacious, defying gravity as they dance and wave slowly in the breeze.

The artist chose the cactus-flower shape to symbolize the desert city of Phoenix. She was inspired by the patience of the saguaro cactus, she said, "a spiny cactus putting down roots in search of water in the desert, saving up every ounce of energy until, one night, in the middle of the cool darkness, it unfurls one succulent bloom."[1] The work also refers to the character of nature itself. Echelman took her title from the words of American poet and philosopher Ralph Waldo Emerson, who wrote, "Adopt the pace of nature; her secret is patience."

The citizens who advocated the piece during the extended waiting time between conception and completion were patient as well. Doubters objected to the price tag ($2.4 million), the shape (one said it resembled a giant jellyfish), and the artist's origins (she is not from Arizona). Those misgivings and a few technical problems kept *Her Secret Is Patience* on the drawing board for a year and a half. But today most Arizonians look on the work with pride: This unique visual delight has become a landmark for the city of Phoenix just as the Eiffel Tower became one for Paris. The *Arizona Republic* editorialized: "This is just what Phoenix needs: a distinctive feature that helps create a real sense of place."[2]

The creation and the reception of *Her Secret Is Patience* embody an important idea: artistic creation is a two-way street. That is, we form art, and then the art forms us by enriching our lives, teaching us, commemorating our human past, touching our spirits, and inspiring or

1.1 Janet Echelman. *Her Secret Is Patience*. 2009. Fiber, steel, and lighting. Height 100′ with a top diameter of 100′.

Civic Space Park, Phoenix, AZ. Courtesy Janet Echelman, Inc. Photograph: Will Novak.

persuading us (see Chapter 2). It can also challenge us to think and see in new ways, and help each of us to develop a personal sense of beauty and truth.

While *Her Secret Is Patience* may not resemble the type of artwork that you are familiar with—it is not a painting, and it is not in a museum—it is art. In this chapter we will explore some definitions of what is meant by "art" and "creativity," and look at how creativity is expressed through different types of art and through its form and content.

What is Art?

When people speak of the arts, they are usually referring to music, dance, theater, literature, and the visual arts. Our senses perceive each artform differently, yet all art comes from a common need to give expressive substance to feelings, insights, and experiences. The arts communicate meanings that go far beyond ordinary verbal exchange, and artists use the entire range of thought, feeling, and observation as the subjects of their art.

The visual arts include drawing, painting, sculpture, film, architecture, and design. Some ideas and feelings can best be communicated only through visual forms. American painter Georgia O'Keeffe said: "I found that I could say things with colors and shapes that I couldn't say in any other way—things I had no words for."[3]

In this book, a **work of art** is the visual expression of an idea or experience, formed with skill, through the use of a **medium**. A medium is a particular material, along with its accompanying technique. (The plural is *media*.) Artists select media to suit the function of the work, as well as the ideas they wish to present. When a medium is used in such a way that the object or performance contributes to our understanding or enjoyment of life, we experience the final product as art.

For *Her Secret Is Patience*, Echelman sought to create a work that would say something about the Phoenix area, in a way that harmonized with the forces of nature. Thus, she chose flexible netting for the medium because it responds gracefully to the wind. She similarly chose the size, scale, shape, and color of the work that would best support and express her message.

Media in use for many centuries include clay, fiber, stone, wood, and paint. By the mid-twentieth century, modern technology had added new media, including video and computers, to the nineteenth-century contributions of photography and motion pictures. Many artists today combine media in a single work.

What is Creativity?

The source of all art, science, and technology—in fact, all of civilization—is human imagination, or creative thinking. But what do we mean by this talent we call "creativity"?

Creativity is the ability to bring forth something new that has value. Mere novelty is not enough; the new thing must have some relevance, or unlock some new way of thinking.

Creativity also has the potential to influence future thought or action, and is vital to most walks of life. In 2010, the IBM corporation interviewed 1,500 chief executive officers (CEOs) from 60 countries, asking them what was the most important leadership skill for the successful

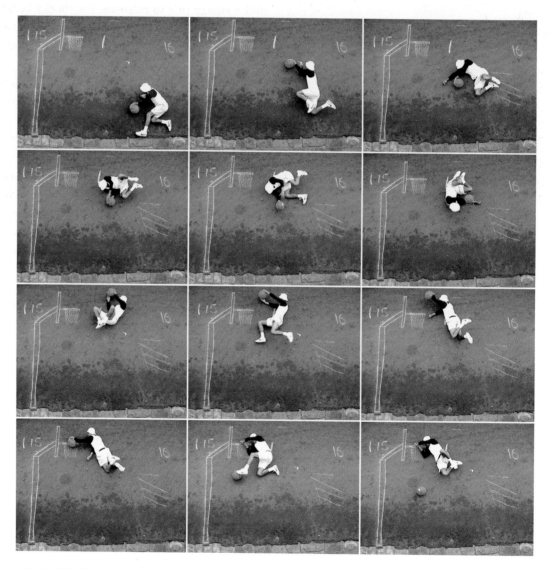

1.2 Robin Rhode. *He Got Game*. 2000. Twelve color photographs.
Lehmann Maupin, New York and Hong Kong. © Robin Rhode.

businesses of the future. Their answer was not economic knowledge, management skills, integrity, or personal discipline, but creativity.

While studying creative people in several disciplines, the authors of the 2011 book *Innovator's DNA*[4] found five traits that seem to define creativity:

1. Associating. The ability to make connections across seemingly unrelated fields.
2. Questioning. Persistently challenging the status quo, asking why things function as they do now, and how or why they might be changed.
3. Observing. Intently watching the world around, without judgment, in search of new insights or ways of operating.
4. Networking. Being willing to interact with others, and learn from them, even if their views are radically different or their competencies seem unrelated.
5. Experimenting. Exploring new possibilities by trying them out, building models and then taking them apart for further improvement.

Creativity can be found in most human endeavors, but here we focus on artistic creativity, which can take many forms. A film director places actors and cameras on a sound stage in order to emphasize a certain aspect of the script. A Hopi potter decorates a water jar by combining traditional designs in new ways. A graphic designer seated at a computer creates an arrangement of type, images, and colors in order to communicate a message. A carver in Japan fashions wood into a Buddha that will aid meditation at a monastery. Most of us have at some time arranged images on our walls or composed a picture for a photograph. All these actions involve visual creativity, the use of imagery to communicate beyond what mere words can say.

Hi Got Game (**fig. 1.2**) is a good example of visual creativity using simple means. Contemporary South African artist Robin Rhode drew a basketball hoop on the asphalt surface of a street, then photographed himself lying down in 12 positions as if he were flipping through the air performing an impossible slam dunk. The artist here imitates the slow-motion and stop-motion photography often seen in sports television to create a piece with transcendent dramatic flair. The work cleverly uses low-tech chalk drawing and a slangy title to celebrate the cheeky boastfulness of street culture. As it clearly shows, creativity is an attitude, one that is as fundamental to experiencing and appreciating a work of art as it is to making one.

Twentieth-century American artist Romare Bearden showed a different type of creativity in his depictions of the daily life he witnessed in the rural South. In *Prevalence of Ritual: Tidings* (**fig. 1.3**) he created a work using borrowed picture fragments with a few muted colors to portray a mood of melancholy and longing. In the work, a winged figure seems to comfort an introspective woman who holds a flower, suggesting the story of the Christian Annunciation; a train implies departure, perhaps from this world or simply to a better life in the North. In this work, as in many of his others, Bearden was concerned with the effectiveness of his communication to the viewer, but equally important was his own inner need for creative expression.

1.3 Romare Bearden. *Prevalence of Ritual: Tidings*. 1967. Photomontage. 36″ × 48″.

Trained and Untrained Artists

Most of us tend to think of "art" as something produced only by "artists"—uniquely gifted people—and, because art is often separated from community life in contemporary society, many people believe they have no artistic talent. Yet we all have the potential to be creative.

In the past, the world's trained artists generally learned by working as apprentices to accomplished masters. (With a few notable exceptions, women were excluded from such apprenticeships.) Through practical experience, they gained necessary skills and developed knowledge of their society's art traditions. Today most art training takes place in art schools, or in college or university art departments. Learning in such settings develops sophisticated knowledge of alternative points of view, both contemporary and historical, and often trained artists show a self-conscious awareness of their relationship to art history. Romare Bearden, for example, learned his skills at the Art Students League in New York and the Sorbonne in Paris; Janet Echelman earned a Master of Fine Arts degree at Bard College, New York.

While training, skills, and intelligence are helpful in creativity, they are not always necessary. The urge to create is universal and has little to do with art training. Those with a small amount of or no formal art education—usually described as untrained artists or **folk artists**—and children can be highly creative. Art by untrained artists, also called **outsider artists**, is made by people who are largely unaware of art history or the art trends of their time. Unlike folk art, which is made by people working within a tradition, art by outsider artists is personal expression created apart from any conventional practice or style.

Outsider Art

One of the best-known (and largest) pieces of outsider art in the United States is *Nuestro Pueblo* (*Our Town*), more commonly known as the Watts Towers (**fig. 1.4**). Its creator, Sabatino "Simon" Rodia, exemplifies the artist who visualizes new possibilities for ordinary materials. He worked on his cathedral-like towers for 33 years, making the fantastic structures from cast-off materials such as metal pipes and bed frames held together with steel reinforcing rods, mesh, and mortar. Incredibly, he built the towers without power tools, rivets, welds, or bolts.

As the towers rose in his triangular backyard, he methodically covered their surfaces with bits and pieces

1.4 Sabatino "Simon" Rodia. *Nuestro Pueblo.*
Top: distant view. Bottom: detail of enclosing wall with construction tool impressions. 1921–54. Mixed media. Height 100´. Watts, California.
Photographs: Duane Preble.

of broken dishes, tile, melted bottle glass, shells, and other colorful junk from the vacant lots in his neighborhood. Rodia's towers are testimony to the artist's creativity and perseverance. He said, "I had it in mind to do something big, and I did it."[5]

Some creative people are so far outside the art world that even their names are unknown to us. In 1982, an art

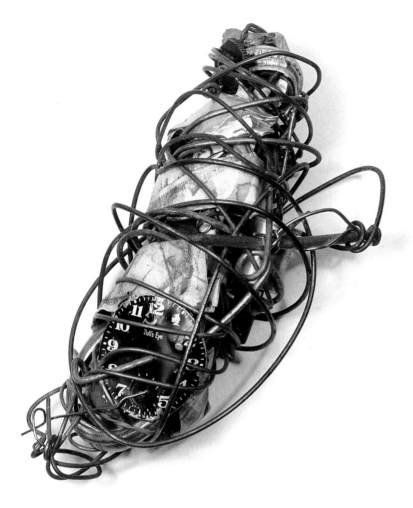

student in Philadelphia found several boxes of hand-sized sculptures that had been set out among the trash in a run-down neighborhood. Numbering more than a thousand, the sculptures were collections of refuse and other small objects, all wrapped in wire (**fig. 1.5**). Dubbed the Philadelphia Wireman, the creator of these works is still unknown, as no one has yet claimed authorship after several exhibitions of the works. Because of the force required to bend the wire, the artist is generally thought to have been male. In any case, he created compelling conglomerations of debris that stir memory and imagination.

Folk Art

In contrast to outsider artists, folk artists are part of established traditions of style, theme, and craftsmanship. Simply put, folk art is art by the folks. Most folk artists have little systematic art training, and their work often shows great enthusiasm or devotion to tradition. Folk art can take many forms, including quilts, embroidered handkerchiefs, decorated weather vanes, sculptures, or customized cars.

In many areas of the United States, quilting has long been a flourishing form of folk art, usually practiced by women. Often working together, the women embellish bed covers to make them into finely crafted and eye-catching works, as we see in *Peony* (**fig. 1.6**). In this quilt the decorations are made from fabric overlays that the artist stitched down. Often the imagery is traditional to the culture or region; this work shows influence from Pennsylvania German pottery. The artist suggested the bright, many-petaled blooms of peonies in the design, which she abstracted to six-pointed star shapes.

1.6 Mary Wallace. *Peony.* Quilt: pieced, appliquéd, and quilted cotton. 100¾″ × 98″.
Los Angeles County Museum of Art. Gift of Rhea Goodman (M.75.133)

1.7 *Retablo.* 1915. Paint on tin. 9″ × 11″.
Fowler Museum at UCLA. Photograph by Don Cole.

In Mexico and the American Southwest, the folk art of *retablo* painting is a customary way of giving thanks to God when someone escapes from danger or recovers from an illness. Such paintings generally depict the scene of salvation along with a narrative of the events. In this example (**fig. 1.7**), a man falsely accused of a crime escaped execution and created the painting. The inscription credits the "fervent prayers of my dear parents and my aggrieved wife" for saving him from the ultimate punishment. The spelling errors in the inscription combine with the sincere and charming painting style to yield a highly attractive work.

Children's Art

Children use a universal visual language. All over the world, drawings by children aged 2–6 show similar stages of mental growth, from exploring with mark-making, to inventing shapes, to symbolizing things seen and imagined. Until they are about 6 years old, children usually depict the world in symbolic rather than realistic ways. Their images are more mental constructions than records of visual observations. The drawing *Grandma* (**fig. 1.8**) by 3-year-old Alana shows enthusiasm and self-assurance in the repeated circles of green and brown. She found a rhythm in the eyes and the head, and she followed it exuberantly out to the sleeves.

Young children often demonstrate an intuitive ability to combine diverse elements into a whole. Unfortunately, much of this intuitive sense of balanced design is lost when they begin to look at the world from a

1.8 Alana, age 3. *Grandma.*

conceptual and self-conscious point of view. Most children who have been given coloring books, workbooks, and pre-drawn printed single sheets become overly dependent on such impersonal stereotyped props. In this way, children often lose the urge to invent unique images based on their own experiences. Recent research shows that many children begin to doubt their creativity at about the age of 9 or 10 years. But creative people, be they artists or CEOs, retain their creativity into adulthood.

Whether trained, outsider, or folk, the most interesting artists are independent thinkers who have the courage to go beyond group mentality. In this way artists can offer fresh insights that extend the experiences of viewers.

Art and Reality

Artists may depict what they see in the physical world, they may alter appearances, or they may invent something that no one has yet seen. Regardless of their approach, most artists invite viewers to see beyond mere appearances. The terms **representational**, **abstract**, and **nonrepresentational** are used to describe an artwork's relationship to the physical world.

Representational Art

Representational art depicts the appearance of things. (When the human form is the primary subject, it is called **figurative art**.) It represents—or "presents again"—objects we recognize from the natural, everyday world. Objects that representational art depicts are called **subjects**.

There are many ways to create representational art. The most "real"-looking paintings are in a style called *trompe l'oeil* (pronounced "tromp loy")—French for "fool the eye." Paintings in this illusionistic style impress us because they look so "real." In William Harnett's painting *A Smoke Backstage* (**fig. 1.9**), the assembled objects are close to life-size, which contributes to the illusion. We almost believe that we could touch the pipe and match.

Belgian painter René Magritte shows a different relationship between art and reality (**fig. 1.10**). The subject of the painting appears to be a pipe, but written in French on the painting are the words, "This is not a pipe." The viewer may wonder, "If this is not a pipe, what is it?" The answer, of course, is that it is a painting! Magritte's title, *The Treachery of Images* (*La Trahison des Images*), suggests the visual game that the artist had in mind.

California artist Ray Beldner further complicated the relationship between art and reality. He created a reproduction of Magritte's painting out of sewn dollar bills, and

1.10 René Magritte. *La Trahison des Images (Ceci N'est Pas une Pipe)*. 1929. Oil on canvas. 25⅜″ × 37″.
Los Angeles County Museum of Art (LACMA). Purchased with funds provided by the Mr. and Mrs. William Preston Harrison Collection (78.7). © 2018 Digital image, The Museum of Modern Art, New York/Scala, Florence. © 2018 C. Herscovici, London/Artists Rights Society (ARS), New York.

called it *This Is Definitely Not a Pipe* (**fig. 1.11**). Modern artists are so famous these days, and their work sells for such high prices, that they may as well be "made of money," just as this work is. Beldner's point is that even representational art has a complex relationship to reality; artists almost never merely depict what they see. Rather, they select, arrange, and compose reality to fit their personal vision. The process can take them several steps away from the fact of a pipe on a tabletop.

1.9 William Harnett. *A Smoke Backstage*. 1877. Oil on canvas. 7″ × 8½″.
Honolulu Museum of Art, Gift of John Wyatt Gregg Allerton, 1964 (32111).

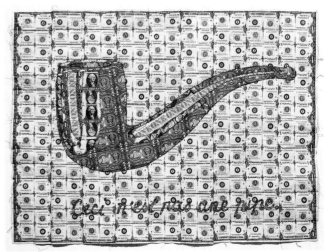

1.11 Ray Beldner. *This Is Definitely Not a Pipe*. 2000. After René Magritte's *The Treason of Images* (1929). Sewn US currency. 24″ × 33″.
Courtesy of the artist.

Abstract Art

The verb "to abstract" means "to take from"; it means to extract the essence of an object or idea. In art, the word "abstract" can mean either (1) works of art that have no reference at all to natural objects, or (2) works that depict natural objects in simplified, distorted, or exaggerated ways. Here we use abstract in the second sense.

In abstract art the artist changes the object's natural appearance in order to emphasize or reveal certain qualities. Just as there are many approaches to representational art, there are many approaches to abstraction. We may be able to recognize the subject matter of an abstract work quite easily, or we may need the help of a clue such as a title. The interaction between how the subject actually looks and how an artist presents it is part of the pleasure and challenge of abstract art (see *Alma Thomas: Devoted to Abstraction*, opposite).

Abstraction in one form or another is common in the art of many cultures. The chief's stool (**fig. 1.12**) from Cameroon shows repeated abstractions of the human form. We still recognize, of course, that the principal subject of the sculpture is people. They symbolize the community of the Cameroon grasslands that supports the chief who sits on this stool. This piece was regarded as the chief's "seat of power." No one else was allowed to use it, and when he died, according to custom, the stool was buried or thrown away.

Early modern artists in Europe also embraced abstraction. We see stages of abstraction in Theo van Doesburg's series of drawings and paintings, *Abstraction of a Cow* (**fig. 1.13**). The artist apparently wanted to see how far he could abstract the cow through simplification and still have his

1.12 Chief's stool. Late 19th–early 20th century. Wood plant fiber. Height 16½".
Western Grasslands, Cameroon.
Fowler Museum at UCLA. Photograph by Don Cole.

image symbolize the essence of the animal. He used the subject as a point of departure for a composition made up of colored rectangles. If we viewed only the final painting and none of the earlier ones, we would probably see it as a nonrepresentational painting.

1.13 Theo van Doesburg (born C.E.M. Küpper). *Abstraction of a Cow* series.
Museum of Modern Art (MoMA). Purchase 227.1948.1 (a.), 227.1948.6 (b.), 226.1948 (c.), and 225.1948 (d.).
© 2018 Digital image, The Museum of Modern Art, New York/Scala, Florence.

a. *Composition (The Cow).* c.1917. Pencil on paper. 4⅝″ × 6¼″.

b. *Study for Composition (The Cow).* 1917. Pencil on paper. 4⅝″ × 6¼″.

c. *Study for Composition (The Cow).* c.1917 (dated 1916) Tempera, oil, and charcoal on paper. 15⅝″ × 22¾″.

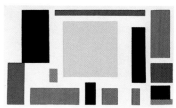

d. *Composition VIII (The Cow).* c.1917. Oil on canvas. 14¾″ × 25″.

CREATORS

Alma Thomas: Devoted to Abstraction

1.14 Alma Thomas at an opening at the Whitney Museum of American Art, New York, 1972.

Alma Thomas papers, 1894–2000, bulk 1936–1982. Archives of American Art, Smithsonian Institution

When asked if she saw herself as a black artist, Alma Thomas (1891–1978) replied, "No, I do not. I am an American."[6] Through a lifelong devotion to abstraction, her creativity reached beyond accepted definitions, and it also unfolded in an unusual way. She was born in western Georgia into a middle-class home. Racial prejudice motivated her father to uproot the family and settle in Washington, D.C., in 1907. There she obtained a teaching degree and taught kindergarten for several years before realizing a dream to study art. She was the first graduate of the Howard University art program in 1924, and for the next 60 years she taught art in a junior high school in the nation's capital.

Thomas painted on the side, exhibiting her representational watercolors only occasionally. But she played an active part in the art scene in Washington; in 1943, she became the founding vice-president of the first private gallery in that city to show work by artists of all races. Further study at American University in the late 1950s exposed her to recent currents in modern art.

Only after her retirement from teaching in 1960 did Thomas begin to devote herself full-time to her art. She also had her first solo exhibition in that year, at age 69. Then her work progressed quickly toward the abstract style that she practiced for the rest of her life.

Thomas said she was inspired by the flickering movement of leaves and flowers under differing light conditions in her garden, and she titled many of her paintings after such observations. Small strokes or patches of paint, rhythmically set down, in mostly brilliant colors, became her signature style. Sometimes these strokes resemble stones in a mosaic, as we see in *White Roses Sing and Sing* (**fig. 1.15**). Although the work seems nonrepresentational at first, the title gives the key to its inspiration: roses moving on their stems in a light breeze. Aerial vantage points also inspired the artist to avoid detailed depictions. She told an interviewer, "I began to think about what I would see if I were in an airplane. You look down on things. You streak through the clouds so fast, you don't know whether the flower below is a violet or what. And so I began to paint as if I were in that plane."[7]

Further recognition came in the 1970s, when Thomas became the first African-American woman to have a solo exhibition at the Whitney Museum of American Art in New York. President Jimmy Carter invited her to the White House. She remarked on her success in museums, comparing it to her earlier life under segregation, when "the only way to go in there as a Negro would be with a mop and bucket."[8]

Thomas always believed that creativity was a human universal, not bound by race or nation. She said, "We artists are put on God's green earth to create. Some of us may be black, but that's not the important thing. The important thing is for us to create, to give form to what we have inside us. We can't accept any barriers, any limitations of any kind, on what we create or how we do it."[9]

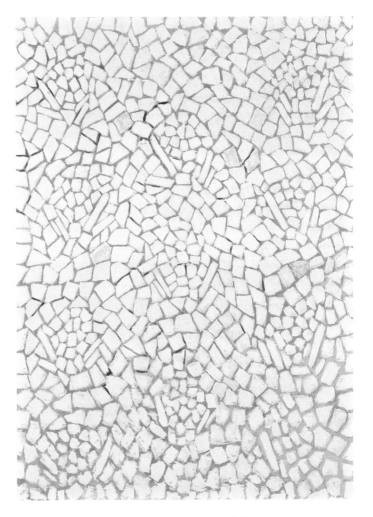

1.15 Alma Thomas. *White Roses Sing and Sing*. 1976. Acrylic on canvas. 72½″ × 52⅜″

National Museum of American Art, Washington, D.C. 1980.36.3. © 2018. Photo Smithsonian American Art Museum/Art Resource/Scala, Florence

Nonrepresentational Art

A great deal of the world's art was not meant to be representational at all. Amish quilts, many Navajo textiles, and most Islamic wood carvings consist primarily of flat patterns that give pleasure through mere variety of line, shape, and color. Nonrepresentational art (sometimes called nonobjective or nonfigurative art) presents visual forms with no specific references to anything outside themselves. Just as we can respond to the pure sound forms of music, so we can respond to the pure visual forms of nonrepresentational art.

The following two contrasting works show that in nonrepresentational art, a wide variety of forms, compositions, moods, and messages is possible. The Pair of Doors (**fig. 1.16**) from an Egyptian mosque is a dazzling piece of wood carving that is centered on two twelve-sided stars. Radiating out we see a web of carved straight lines that ricochet off the edges and cross each other to create an array of polygonal panels. Curving symmetrical designs within these panels, carved of wood and ivory, interweave and overlap. Without representing anything or telling any story, the doors draw and hold our attention for the virtuosic display of skill and the tremendous intricacy of the lines, shapes, and patterns.

The Pair of Doors is symmetrical and obviously handcrafted of natural materials, but *Yellow and Black* by Carmen Herrera (**fig. 1.17**) is asymmetrical and sleek, while also nonrepresentational. We may see a hint of a subject in this work (a lightning bolt?), but the artist was only experimenting with the juxtaposition of two strong colors. The work communicates vigorous energy and an agitated state of mind. This impact is strengthened by the work's large size, 6 feet across.

While nonrepresentational art may at first seem more difficult to grasp than representational or abstract art, it can offer fresh ways of seeing and new visual experiences. In the absence of subject matter, we can direct our attention to the shapes and forms before us in themselves. Once we learn how to read this language of vision, we can respond to both art and the world with greater understanding and enjoyment.

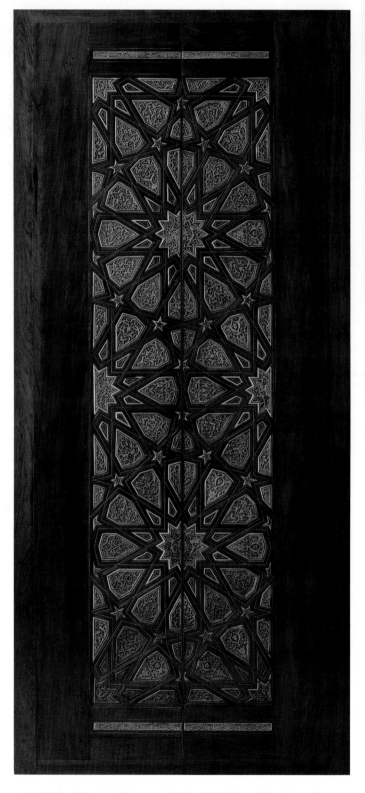

1.16 Pair of doors. Egypt, c.1325–1330. Wood (rosewood and mulberry); carved, inlaid with carved ivory, ebony, and other woods. 77¼″ × 35″ × 1¾″, encased in weighted freestanding mount.
Metropolitan Museum of Art, New York. 91.1.2064.

1.17 Carmen Herrera. *Yellow and Black*. 2010. Acrylic on canvas. 36″ × 72″.
© Carmen Herrera; Courtesy Lisson Gallery. Photographer: Ken Adlard.

Looking and Seeing

Whether a work of art is representational, abstract, or non-representational, we access it primarily through our eyes; thus we must consider how we use them.

The verbs "look" and "see" indicate varying degrees of visual awareness. Looking is habitual and implies taking in what is before us in a generally mechanical or goal-oriented way. If we care only about function, we simply need to look quickly at a doorknob in order to grasp and turn it. But if we find ourselves excited about the shape and finish of a doorknob, or of the bright quality of a winter day, or we empathize with the creator of an artwork, we go beyond simple, functional looking to a higher level of perception; this is "seeing."

Seeing is a more open, receptive, and focused version of looking. In seeing, we look with our memories, imaginations, and feelings attached. We take in something with our eyes, and then we remember similar experiences, or we imagine other possible outcomes, or we allow ourselves to feel something about it. We are doing more than looking.

The twentieth-century French artist Henri Matisse wrote about how to see intently:

To see is itself a creative operation, requiring an effort. Everything that we see in our daily life is more or less distorted by acquired habits, and this is perhaps more evident in an age like ours when cinema, posters, and magazines present us every day with a flood of readymade images which are to the eye what prejudices are to the mind. The effort needed to see things without distortion takes something very like courage.[10]

Because words and visual images are two different languages, talking about visual arts with words is always an act of translation one step removed from actually experiencing art. In fact, our eyes have their own connections to our minds and emotions. By cultivating these connections, we can take better advantage of what art has to offer.

Ordinary things become extraordinary when we see them deeply. Is Edward Weston's photograph of a pepper (**fig. 1.18**) meaningful to us because we like peppers so much? Probably not. To help us truly see, Weston created a memorable image on a flat surface with the help of a common pepper. A time exposure of over two hours gave *Pepper #30* a quality of glowing light—a living presence that resembles an embrace. Through his sensitivity to form, Weston revealed how this pepper appeared to him. Notes from his *Daybook* communicate his enthusiasm about this photograph:

> August 8, 1930
> I could wait no longer to print them—my new peppers, so I put aside several orders, and yesterday afternoon had an exciting time with seven new negatives.
>
> First I printed my favorite, the one made last Saturday, August 2, just as the light was failing—quickly made, but with a week's previous effort back of my immediate, unhesitating decision. A week?—Yes, on this certain pepper,—but twenty-eight years of effort, starting with a youth on a farm in Michigan, armed with a No. 2 Bull's Eye [Kodak] 3½ × 3½, have gone into the making of this pepper, which I consider a peak of achievement.
>
> It is a classic, completely satisfying—a pepper—but more than a pepper: abstract, in that it is completely outside subject matter . . . this new pepper takes one beyond the world we know in the conscious mind.[11]

1.18 Edward Weston. *Pepper #30*. 1930. Gelatin silver print. 9 ⁷⁄₁₆″ x 7 ½″.

Photograph by Edward Weston. Museum of Modern Art , New York. Gift of David H. McAlpin (1913.1968) © 2018. Digital image, The Museum of Modern Art, New York/Scala, Florence © 2018 Center for Creative Photography, Arizona Board of Regents/Artists Rights Society (ARS), New York.

Weston's photograph of a seemingly common object embodies a particularly intent way of seeing. The artist was uniquely aware of something in his surroundings; indeed, he seems to have gazed at the pepper for a long time. He worked over an extended period (perhaps 28 years!) to achieve the image he wanted. The photograph that he created communicates a sense of wonder about the natural world. It may also stimulate us to participate in his prolonged seeing.

Finally, seeing is a personal process. No two people will see the same thing in the same way, because each of us brings our own background, temperament, and feelings to bear. Confronted with the same visual information, different people will evaluate it differently, and come to differing conclusions about its meaning, worth, or importance (see Chapter 5).

Form and Content

In Weston's *Pepper #30* the texture, light, and shadow, and shape of the pepper is the form that we see, and the content is the meaning (or meanings) the work communicates—for example, a sense of wonder about the natural world. **Form** thus refers to the total effect of the combined visual qualities within a work, including such components as materials, color, shape, line, and design. **Content** refers to the message or meaning of the work of art—what the artist expresses or communicates to the viewer. Content determines form, and form expresses content; thus the two are inseparable.

1.20 Constantin Brancusi. *The Kiss.* 1916. Limestone. 23″ × 13″ × 10″.
Photograph: The Philadelphia Museum of Art/ Art Resource/Scala, Florence. © Succession Brancusi – All rights reserved (ARS) 2018.

One way to better understand the relationship is to compare works that have the same subject but differ greatly in form and content. *The Kiss* (**fig. 1.19**) by Auguste Rodin and *The Kiss* (**fig. 1.20**) by Constantin Brancusi show how two sculptors interpret an embrace. In Rodin's work, the life-size human figures represent Western ideals of the masculine and the feminine. Rodin captures the sensual delight of that highly charged moment when lovers embrace. We may remember or hope for such encounters ourselves. Our emotions are engaged as we overlook the hardness of the marble from which he carved it. The natural softness of flesh is heightened by the rough texture of the unfinished marble supporting the figures.

In contrast to Rodin's sensuous approach, Brancusi used the solid quality of a block of stone to express lasting love. Through minimal cutting of the block, Brancusi symbolized—rather than illustrated—the concept of two becoming one. He chose geometric abstraction rather than representational naturalism to express love of a solid, enduring kind. We might say that Rodin's work expresses the *feelings* of love, while Brancusi's expresses the *idea* of love.

1.19 Auguste Rodin. *The Kiss.* 1886. Marble. 5′11¼″.
Musée Rodin, Paris. Photograph akg-images / Erich Lessing.

Seeing and Responding to Form

Obviously, artists expend effort to produce a work of art; less obvious is the fact that responding to a work of art also requires effort. The artist is the source or sender of any work put on view; the work itself is the means of carrying the message. We viewers must receive and experience the work to make the communication complete. In this way, we participate in the creative process.

Learning to respond to form is part of learning to live in the world. We guide our actions by "reading" forms of people, things, and events that make up our environment. Even as infants, we have an amazing ability to remember visual forms such as faces, and all through life we interpret events based on our previous experiences with these forms. Every form can evoke some kind of response from each of us.

Subject matter can interfere with our perception of form. One way to learn to see form without subject is to look at pictures upside down. Inverting recognizable images frees the mind from the process of identifying and naming things. Familiar objects become unfamiliar.

When confronted with something unfamiliar, we often see it freshly only because we have no idea what we are looking at. For example, when we see the twisting, curving green and rust-red shapes in Georgia O'Keeffe's painting (**fig. 1.21**), we may not at first realize that the work depicts a jack-in-the-pulpit flower. The artist greatly enlarged it to 4 feet in height, and she focused closely on the flower, omitting nearly all else. We may wonder for a moment if we are looking at abstract or representational art.

O'Keeffe hoped that her way of seeing would cause us to sense the natural rhythms present in a flower. She said of this painting:

Everyone has many associations with a flower—the idea of flowers. Still—in a way—nobody sees a flower—really—it is so small—we haven't the time—and to see takes time, like to have a friend takes time. If I could paint the flower exactly as I see it, no one would see what I see because I would paint it small like the flower is small.
So I said to myself—I'll paint what I see—what the flower is to me but I'll paint it big and they will be surprised into taking time to look at it.[12]

1.21 Georgia O'Keeffe. *Jack-in-the-Pulpit No. V.* 1930. Oil on canvas. 48″ × 30″.
Alfred Stieglitz Collection, Bequest of Georgia O'Keeffe, National Gallery of Art, Washington, D.C. 1987.58.4. Photograph: Malcolm Varon.

Iconography

As we have noted, form conveys content even when no nameable subject matter is represented. But when subject matter is present, meaning is often based on traditional interpretations.

Iconography refers to the subjects, symbols, and motifs used in an image to convey its meaning (from the Greek *eikon*, meaning image or picture). Not all works of art make use of iconography. In those that do, it is often the symbolism (rather than the obvious subject matter) that carries the deepest levels of meaning. Iconography is a set of customs or conventions that cue us about the meanings in a work of art. For example, if we are seeing a painting of a mother and child, its iconography will tell us whether it is Mary and the baby Jesus.

An artist's use of iconography can reveal a wealth of cultural information. For example, the Peruvian painting *The Virgin of Carmel Saving Souls in Purgatory* (**fig. 1.22**) contains many iconographic details that enrich its meaning. Some of these are obvious to those familiar with Christian iconography: The two winged figures standing in the foreground are angels; at the top is God the Father holding the orb of the world; below him is a dove that represents the Holy Spirit; Mary wears a crown to show that she is the Queen of Heaven. People emerge from a flaming pit that is purgatory, led by an angel. In the left corner, another angel holds a cross that symbolizes the sacrifice of Christ; he also holds a balance, symbolizing the weighing of souls that takes place in purgatory. The meaning of these details is established by convention and long use.

Other details might be less familiar but equally meaningful. *The Virgin of Carmel* refers to an appearance of Mary that took place in the thirteenth century; at that time she promised that anyone who wore a special garment called a scapular would not suffer the fires of hell. Both Mary and the child Jesus carry purselike objects that represent the scapulars that people wore or carried for protection. In this painting, Mary makes a special effort to save from

1.22 Circle of Diego Quispe Tito. *The Virgin of Carmel Saving Souls in Purgatory*. Late 17th century. Oil on canvas. 41″ × 29″.
Brooklyn Museum of Art, New York, USA/Bridgeman Images.

purgatory the souls who may not have owned the protecting scapular. Thus the work was a sign of hope.

Asian traditions also use a rich iconographic language, which makes the Amida Buddha (**fig. 1.23**) easily distinguishable from a portrait of any other seated person. He has a topknot that symbolizes his enlightenment. The long earlobes show that he was a wealthy prince who wore heavy earrings before he sought religious truth. His garment is simple, as after enlightenment he lived by begging. His hands are folded in the traditional position of meditation. His lotus-flower throne symbolizes the fact that enlightenment can come in the midst of life, just as a lotus flower may bloom on the surface of a stagnant pond. The degrees of abstraction in the hands, chest, and face point to a twelfth-century date for this work, but the iconographic details that mark him as the Buddha had already been in use for more than 1,000 years.

In our time, artists often mash up and quote from various iconographic traditions. Rashaad Newsome, for example, borrowed from art history, hip-hop, and heraldry for his collage piece *Saltire Compton* (**fig. 1.24**). The frame is one that might normally surround a precious historical painting, but he had it sprayed with radiant gold enamel at an auto body shop. Within the frame are scanned photos of jewelry, necklaces, and brooches from fashion magazines—"bling," in other words—objects that might be worn by a hip-hop artist or someone going out for a night of vogue dancing. A saltire is an X-shaped motif commonly found in

1.23 Amida Buddha (wood). Japanese school (17th century).
San Diego Museum of Art, USA/Bequest of Mrs. Cora Timken Burnett/ Bridgeman Images.

flags, family crests, and heraldry. The X at the center of this work is almost swallowed in the symmetrically arranged bling that surrounds it. In the lower center is a black T-shirt showing the word Compton, the name of a historically African-American city just south of Los Angeles, a center of hip-hop culture. Newsome, who is himself African American, walks a fine line in this work between celebrating and satirizing that culture.

As we have seen from the works illustrated in this chapter alone, art is produced in a range of media and for different reasons. Artists, whether trained or untrained, may use their creativity to bring forth something new of value that can enrich and inform our lives.

1.24 Rashaad Newsome. *Saltire Compton*. 2011. Collage in customized antique frame. 17¼″ × 14¾″ × 1½″.
© Rashaad Newsome Studio

KEY TERMS

abstract art – art that depicts natural objects in simplified or exaggerated ways which may not be recognizable at first

content – the meaning or message communicated by a work of art, including its emotional, intellectual, symbolic, thematic, and narrative connotations

figurative art – representational art in which the human form (rather than the natural world) plays a principal role

folk art – art of people who have had no formal, academic training, but whose works are part of an established tradition of style and craftsmanship

form – the total effect of the combined visual qualities within a work, including such components as materials, color, shape, line, and design

iconography – the symbolic meanings of subjects and signs used to convey ideas important to particular cultures or religions

medium (plural: media) – a particular material along with its accompanying technique

nonrepresentational art – art without reference to anything outside itself (also called "nonobjective")

outsider art – art produced by those with no formal training, outside the established channels of art exhibition

representational art – art that recognizably represents or depicts a particular subject

subject – in representational art, what the artist chooses to depict

work of art – what the artist makes or puts in front of us for viewing

2

THE PURPOSES AND FUNCTIONS OF ART

LEARNING OBJECTIVES

2.1 Explain the ways in which artists transform objects for daily use.

2.2 Describe how design and embellishment create visual delight in art.

2.3 Compare the different ways in which art can function as a means of communicating information.

2.4 Discuss the use of art for both public and personal expression.

2.5 Demonstrate how art can be used to meet religious and spiritual needs.

2.6 Explain how art can be used for political purposes.

Art forms us by meeting our needs. Not our most basic needs for food or shelter, but deeper and more subtle ones that define us as people and as members of a society. These needs vary with time and cultural setting. In a culture in which religion is very important, for example, a great deal of art answers that need. In our own society, which emphasizes individual achievement, much of our art is devoted to self-expression. Note that here we are considering purposes and functions of art in the lives of viewers, not as they may meet the needs of artists themselves. Thus, in this chapter we consider art in its social and cultural context, as it relates to six functions in the following general areas: daily use, delight, communicating information, public and personal expression, religion, and politics.

As we begin this discussion, we will quickly see that a given work may well address more than one function or need. A piece of political art might also delight us with its beauty; an item for daily use may also express something about its creator. And if one purpose for art seems to dominate in one culture, this does not mean that other possible functions go unfilled or are ignored. Viewing art from the perspective of its purpose or function shows us commonalities among people across different time periods and civilizations, from ancient times to the present. This is because most human needs that art meets have remained relatively constant throughout history. On the other hand, artists' methods of meeting those needs vary greatly. Thus art embraces many of the shared traits, and all of the diversity, of humanity itself.

Art for Daily Use

Objects of all kinds, from ancient carefully crafted flint knives to today's personal digital devices, have been conceived to delight the eye as well as to serve more obviously useful functions. Well-designed utilitarian objects and spaces—from spoons to cities— bring pleasure and efficiency into our daily lives. Artists transform objects for daily use by either designing them in new ways or by embellishing them; sometimes both.

Designing for Everyday

Objects that we use every day can be designed artfully for greater enjoyment. This is what Eva Zeisel did in the 1950s with a common sauce ladle and its accompanying boat (**fig. 2.1**). She brought the ends of the boat together at the top, and put a hole in the ladle that echoes that shape. She created the design in clay and then glazed it a creamy, deep white. This color highlights both the contents of the boat and the graceful lines that enliven both pieces. If the united tips of the boat have a somewhat playful look,

2.1 Eva Zeisel. *Sauce Boat with Ladle*. c.1949–50.
Glazed earthenware. Sauce boat: 6¼″ × 6½″ × 5¼″.
Ladle: 4″ × 4½″ × 1⅞″.

2.2 George Nakashima. *Conoid Chair*. 1971.
Black walnut and hickory. Height 35⅜″.

there is a reason for this. Zeisel once described her life's mission as "a playful search for beauty."[1] Molds were made for these shapes, and they are still being produced for wide distribution.

George Nakashima gave a radical shape to a common seat with his *Conoid Chair* (**fig. 2.2**). The design may appear unstable but in fact it balances well, and its two legs facilitate moving it over carpeted areas. Unlike the gravy ensemble above, this is a uniquely crafted object. The natural wood medium has special significance for Nakashima. He said, "I find it impossible to try to design a chair out of plastic or metal . . . in producing a fine piece of furniture, the spirit of the tree lives on and I can give it a second life."[2] Thus he carefully sanded and finished the chair to highlight its warm color and pleasing texture.

Embellishment

Most societies value the artistic embellishment of everyday things. Do you have a cell-phone case? If so, why did you choose that particular one? Maybe there was a practical reason (perhaps to protect the phone), but other factors in the choice would probably relate to your desire to embellish the phone, or to have it coordinate with other items you own. Embellishment of a useful object was probably an important factor in your choice.

The urge to embellish has motivated a great deal of creativity throughout history. For example, the Yoruba peoples of West Africa have for centuries used deep-blue dye from indigo plants to embellish practical items of clothing (**fig. 2.3**). The patterns on this cloth were created by women who applied a thick starch made from cassava flour to one side of the sheet before immersing the whole in a dye bath. The intricate designs that they painted in the flour paste resisted the penetration of the dye, leaving those areas a lighter shade of blue. The designs in this cloth are particularly detailed, and they repeat around the two central rectangles that show a sunburst. The dye process here yields an absorbing design in a rich blue color.

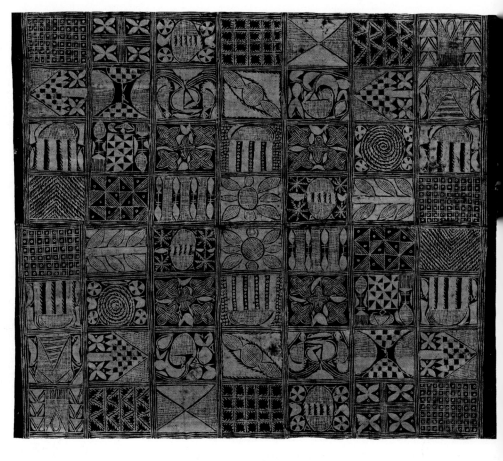

2.3 Resist-dyed cloth (*adire eleko*). Mid-twentieth century. Indigo dye on cotton.

X66.1149AB. Fowler Museum at UCLA. Photograph by Don Cole.

Shelter is a basic need, but architects and designers can improve our surroundings and make them distinctive, as early twentieth-century American architect Frank Lloyd Wright did with Hollyhock (Barnsdall) House in Hollywood (**fig. 2.4**). The decoration scheme is based on repeated hollyhock flowers, the favorite plant of the house's first owner, Alice Barnsdall, who commissioned the building. Hollyhock flowers bloom on stalks, without branches; the band of decoration at the base of the roofline represents abstract versions of these. Wright also designed this house with the warm and dry local climate in mind: Each room opens onto an accompanying outdoor patio, and the flat roof has several terraces for indoor-outdoor living.

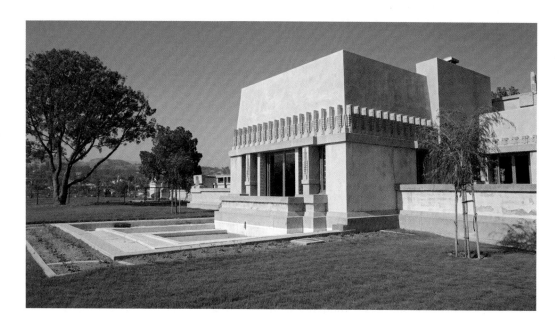

2.4 Frank Lloyd Wright. Barnsdall House, Los Angeles. 1919–1921. Exterior view.

Citizen of the Planet/Alamy Stock Photo.

Art for Visual Delight

Many of us probably think of delight as the principal goal of art. Why create art after all, if not for someone's pleasure or enjoyment? We need delight, enjoyment, pleasure, decoration, amusement, and embellishment in our lives to "lift us above the stream of life," as a noted art critic wrote.[3] Absorbed in contemplating a work, we forget where we are for a moment.

Visual delight happens when we are captivated by a work of art, and we enjoy it aside from practical or moral or political considerations. **Aesthetics** refers to the branch of philosophy that studies how and why artworks are considered beautiful. Most cultures that have a definition of "beautiful" define it as something pleasing to the eye and agreeable to the mind. However, what is pleasing to the eye or mind (and hence to the sense of beauty) varies considerably across cultures. Here we will consider two pathways to beauty: idealism and harmony.

Idealism

In some cultures, something beautiful must also exhibit a certain idealism. In other words, beauty is not found in the everyday but rather in something that is ideal or close to perfection. This belief animated much of the art of ancient Greece, which has influenced Western artists for centuries.

We see this idealism at work in the sculpture known as the Charioteer (**fig. 2.5**). This charioteer has won the race, but he remains alertly calm rather than jubilant. The sculpture personifies balance and quiet dignity; it shows "noble simplicity and calm grandeur," as a critic once wrote. This work is not a portrait—portraiture was rare in ancient Greece—because real people are too often imperfect in their looks and fallible in their deeds. Rather, this work represents the ideal charioteer, in the prime of life and blemish-free. The beauty in this work might therefore inspire others to similar deeds and attitudes.

In our own times, art has been far less often concerned with idealistic beauty. Rather, we are more likely to find such idealistic standards illustrated in fashion magazines or sports photography.

Harmony

Another common definition of beauty includes a pleasing balance or harmonious proportions. In Western art, many regard the landscape paintings of the seventeenth-century French artist Claude Lorrain as exemplifying these virtues.

2.5 Charioteer. c.470 BCE. Bronze. Height 5´11˝.
Archaeological Museum, Delphi. © Craig & Marie Mauzy, Athens.

The composition of *Ascanius Shooting the Stag of Silvia* is very harmonious in its colors (**fig. 2.6**). Blues and blue-greens dominate the sky, the foliage, and the draperies of Ascanius as he holds his bow. Ascanius has not actually shot the stag yet, so any violence is only possible. The buildings on the left are balanced by the trees and cliffs on the right. This balance is not symmetrical, but then nature rarely is. Light is evenly diffused throughout, with just enough contrasting dark zones. The work does not depict an actual place; the artist invented it from the volumes of sketches he made on trips through the Italian peninsula. The storyline of the painting is mythological, remote from most viewers; most likely it engages the imagination for that reason. Claude Lorrain was so well known for painting such pleasant views that his works influenced landscape gardening in Britain. Some wealthy landowners in the late

2.6 Claude Lorrain. *Ascanius Shooting the Stag of Silvia*, 1682. Oil on canvas, 48″ × 60″.

Ashmolean Museum, University of Oxford, UK/Bridgeman Images.

lines of poetry say, we can appreciate the contained energy of the strokes as they make up the ten well spaced characters. This piece was created in 1261 by the emperor Lizong, who was more devoted to art than to governing during his rule. His calligraphy is still highly valued for its union of close detail, vigorous execution, and harmonious arrangement.

Peter Behrens, an early twentieth-century German designer, created a harmonious decorative scheme for his porcelain plate (**fig. 2.8**). The green arcs resemble ripples that we might see after dropping a stone in a still pond. They also echo the shape of the plate as a whole, in thin lines that required careful painting. The outermost arcs converge in a curving square motif at the center, suggesting the sort of embroidered napkin that might accompany this plate in an elegant table service. Such visual pleasure can prepare us for the other pleasures of the table, such as dining and companionship.

eighteenth century attempted to reproduce the harmonious effect of his paintings on their properties. Such landscapes were termed **picturesque**, meaning like a picture by Claude Lorrain. The term survives to this day.

A graceful arrangement of well-proportioned forms is basic to beauty, be it in a human face or an artwork. These same traits are also highly valued in the ancient Chinese artform of **calligraphy**, or the art of beautiful handwriting (**fig. 2.7**). Even without knowing what these two vertical

2.7 Emperor Lizong. Couplet from a poem by Han Hong. 1261. Song Dynasty. Fan mounted as an album leaf. Ink on silk. 8³⁄₁₆″ × 8¹¹⁄₁₆″.

Metropolitan Museum of Art, New York. Bequest of John M. Crawford Jr., 1988 (1989.363.23a).

2.8 Peter Behrens. Porcelain plate. British Museum, London.

Photograph: © The Trustees of the British Museum. © 2018 Artists Rights Society (ARS), New York.

Art for Communicating Information

Because art makes a statement that can be understood by many people, it has often been used to impart information and ideas. Indeed, before the invention of photography in the nineteenth century, artists and illustrators were our only source of information about the visual appearance of anything. During the Middle Ages in Europe, the stained-glass windows and stone sculptures of the cathedrals taught Bible stories to a largely illiterate population. By providing a visual account of a story or an event, or by expressing an opinion, artists have shaped not only the way people understand their own world but also how their culture is viewed by others.

Storytelling

A great deal of art tells stories. These can be personal, moral, or historical. Today, we satisfy our desire for stories primarily through television and movies, but before the advent of mass media, artists had principal responsibility for the task. Stories of any sort can move us or teach us or merely interest us.

How about this for a fascinating story: It comes from the literature of ancient Rome. The princess Ariadne had helped Theseus to free her father, King Minos, from the monstrous Minotaur. Theseus then took Ariadne with him to the island of Naxos, but soon tired of her and cruelly abandoned her there in the wild. As she lamented her fate and plotted her next move, help arrived from an unexpected source. This is the moment we see in the painting *Bacchus and Ariadne* (**fig. 2.9**) by the sixteenth-century Italian artist Titian. Bacchus, the god of wine, has arrived in his chariot at the head of a procession of drunken revelers. Instantly enamored of the beautiful Ariadne, he leaps from his chariot and promises her the entire sky. Bacchus' glance leads our eyes to Ariadne at the left; she looks back at him with a mixture of hope and fear. The stars in the sky at the upper left form the constellation Corona Borealis, or Northern Crown, referring both to Ariadne's royal status and to the promise Bacchus made.

In contrast to Titian's recounting of a mythological story, some artworks tell stories of everyday life that can help to broaden our perspective by showing us how others live.

2.9 Titian. *Bacchus and Ariadne*, 1520–3. Oil on canvas. 5'9" x 6'3".
National Gallery, London/akg

2.10 Abraham Cruzvillegas, *Autoconstrucción Suites*. 2013. Installation view at Walker Art Center, Minneapolis.

Courtesy of the artist, Walker Art Center, Minneapolis and kurimanzutto, Mexico City. Photo © Walker Art Center

We see a contemporary example of this in *Autoconstrucción Suites* (**fig. 2.10**) by Abraham Cruzvillegas. At first glance the installation seems like a highly disorderly scene. Wooden scaffolds dominate the view, with shirts tied together spanning the distance between them. A few television sets, primitive stairs, metal frameworks, a wheelbarrow, and other seemingly miscellaneous junk populate the gallery space. Cruzvillegas gathered these objects from the immediate neighborhood. Yet behind all of this apparent chaos is a story that relates to his personal history and, by extension, to most of us as viewers. The construction of the artwork parallels the story of the construction of Cruzvillegas's family home on the outskirts of Mexico City. There, in a neighborhood outside the reach of most city services, the artist's relatives built the house he grew up in, room by room, floor by floor, by themselves, using whatever they could find or buy. Cruzvillegas described the process in an essay:

> The materials and techniques they used were completely improvised, depending on the specific circumstances and immediate surroundings, in the midst of widespread social and economic instability in Mexico and probably across the world. Every solution answered a pressing situation or need, such as how to add a new room; to modify a roof; or to improve, alter, or eliminate a certain space. Because its construction lacked both a budget and input from architects, the house today looks chaotic and almost useless; however, every corner and detail has its reason for being there. The house is an authentic labyrinth, polished to a sheen by simultaneous construction, use, and destruction.[4]

Carrie Mae Weems created a remarkable series of photos, titled *The Kitchen Table Series* (**fig. 2.11**), that reveal the lives of other people to us. She installed a camera at one end of her kitchen table, under a hanging lamp, and took dozens of photos of life events that happened around it for

2.11 Carrie Mae Weems, *Man Reading Newspaper* from *The Kitchen Table Series*. Photograph. 1990.

Courtesy of the artist and Jack Shainman Gallery, New York.

several months. She used herself and her friends, neighbors, and relatives as actors in constructed scenes, some invented and some real, which she imagined and then shot, as a film director might. When she reduced the series to just 20 images in 1990, she found that she had told a story of the ups and downs of a relationship with a man and the birth of their daughter. In the photos reproduced here, we see a rather tense moment, as the man reads the newspaper while the artist herself smokes distractedly, eyes askance, before retreating into the background. The series depicts the course of a relationship, which viewers may recognize from their own lives. Weems said of the series, "Even though it's anchored around a black woman, my hope was always that it would be understood as a condition of women. And it exceeded my expectations, because women around the world relate to that piece, as do men; they see themselves in it."[5]

Commentary

Artists who fulfill our need for commentary often speak in a language that is easy to understand; they view art's primary purpose as communication between artist and viewer by means of subject matter. British artist William Hogarth took on the difficult subject of alcohol consumption in *Gin Lane* (**fig. 2.12**) in 1751. This memorable work urges moderation by exposing the horrors of excess. The dominant figure in the lower center is a drunken woman who reaches for a pinch of snuff as her baby tumbles from her lap. In the lower right corner, a cadaverous figure holds the fatal cup in one hand and a jug in the other. At the right edge, the distiller is doing a thriving business. The sign above shows that the company is called Kilman, an obvious reference to the work's message. Also open for business is the pawn shop at the left, where people hock their possessions to buy more liquor. Death haunts the work in two other places: At the upper right, a man has killed himself by hanging, and in the center, above the drunken woman, a partially dressed cadaver is laid in a coffin that probably came from the coffin shop just to the right. Hogarth made this print during a true binge of gin consumption in eighteenth-century London; he hoped, by telling many cautionary tales in this one work, to curb the habit. He made this print in a large edition and sold it for low prices in an effort to encourage sobriety.

Many artists have used photography to capture the grandeur and wonder of nature, but today's photographers

2.12 William Hogarth, *Gin Lane*. 1751.
Etching and engraving. Plate: 14¼″ × 12″.
National Gallery of Art, Washington D.C. Rosenwald Collection.

are more likely to use their art to inform us about some of the ways that humans have impacted and even spoiled the landscape. Chris Jordan documents this grim reality in color photographs that give a visual jolt. For his recent series "Midway: Message from the Gyre" (**fig. 2.13**), he

2.13 Chris Jordan. *CF000668*, from the series "Midway: Message from the Gyre". 2009.
Photo by Chris Jordan.

traveled to Midway Island in the Pacific and photographed the decaying bodies of dead fledgling albatrosses. This island is a nesting ground for seagoing birds, and it is located at the center of a gyre, or circular pattern of ocean currents. The currents bring great deal of floating plastic waste matter toward the island's shores. The albatrosses frequently mistake the smaller pieces for food, which they then give to their young with often fatal results. Jordan cuts open the bodies, revealing the ingested colored pieces of waste that humans across the Pacific Rim have discarded inappropriately. At the time of writing, Jordan was editing his photographic journeys into a documentary movie about the island to help spread his message further.

Art for Public and Personal Expression

Sometimes a human life is so notable or an event so momentous that a monument is created to help us remember it. At other times self-expression by artists builds bridges of empathy to individual viewers.

Commemoration

Visual imagery can serve as an aid to our memories. Many of us carry photos of loved ones with us, or we take pictures

2.14 Taj Mahal. Agra, India. 1632–48.
Mazzzur. Shutterstock.

to remember where we have been. When such commemoration becomes public, artists enter the process. Public commemoration connects us with the chain of humanity that stretches back millennia, making human life seem more significant and valuable.

Many of the monumental works of art in the ancient world had a commemorative function. The pyramids of ancient Egypt, for example, are tombs of rulers. The best-known work in the Islamic tradition, the Taj Mahal (**fig. 2.14**), commemorates the seventeenth-century ruler Shah Jahan's favorite wife, who died in childbirth. It sits at one end of a four-part paradise garden that recalls the description of paradise in the Qur'an. The surface of the white marble exterior seems to change color by catching sunlight at various angles. The proportions of the bulb-shaped dome make the building appear light in weight, as if it barely touches the ground. The Taj Mahal's testament to romantic love and devotion, and its combination of otherworldliness and beauty, draws visitors from across the world.

In many traditional societies of Africa, much art has a commemorative aspect. This carving (**fig. 2.15**) represents Shyaam the Great, the founder and most important king of the Kuba peoples of the Congo. He holds a ceremonial weapon in his left hand as he sits, cross-legged and aloof, the picture of quiet detachment. His headdress is traditional royal regalia, a hoe-shaped cap that alludes to his introduction of iron smelting and his encouragement of agriculture as the basic economic activity of the region. His eyes are shaped like cowrie shells, a symbol of wealth. The oval-shaped box at his feet represents the strategic board game known as *mankala* that he invented in order to improve the intellectual abilities of his subjects. While Shyaam was alive, this statue was kept in the quarters of his wives, to increase their fertility. On Shyaam's death, his successor slept with the statue in order to facilitate the transmission of wisdom between generations. Thereafter, the statue was stored as part of a commemorative altar, and regularly rubbed with oil, which gives this work its rich glow. If a royal portrait statue of this type is ever damaged, Kuba artists create a replica to prolong the memory; this work is an eighteenth-century copy of a seventeenth-century original.

Closer to our own time, many public spaces contain commemorative statues honoring heroes who are deemed worthy, or memorials to individual victims of warfare or atrocities. One distinctive war monument is the Vietnam

Veterans Memorial (**fig. 2.16**) in Washington, D.C., by Maya Lin. Arousing controversy when it was completed in 1982, the almost 250-foot-long, V-shaped wall bears the names of the nearly 60,000 American servicemen and women who died or are missing from the time of that controversial war. The style of the monument, with its simple chronological list, was unprecedented among the monuments on the National Mall. The initial resistance to the work was so great that a further monument was commissioned, a statue of a group of three soldiers, for a nearby location. But the Vietnam Veterans Memorial soon attracted thousands of visitors, who appreciated the solemnity of the black granite walls and the personal attention involved in the recording of every lost soldier's name. The monument has also influenced many other public memorials since, as inscribing the names of all commemorated people has become a more common practice.

Self-Expression

For most of human history, self-expression has not been a primary reason for creating art. Other social and cultural needs, such as those discussed in this chapter, more fully engaged the talents of artists. In more recent times, however, particularly when a great deal of art is sold as a private possession, self-expression has increasingly become one of art's most common functions.

Art fulfills an expressive function when an artist conveys information about his or her personality or feelings or worldview. Such art becomes a meeting site between artist and viewer, through which the viewer feels empathy and gains an understanding of the creator's personality. We all derive comfort from the fact that others in the world are similar to ourselves, and artists' various modes of self-expression reach out to us in hopes of establishing a bond.

Such bridges of empathy may also extend among viewers. If you have ever discussed with a friend or relative the feelings that you found in an expressive work, you have extended the chain of empathy that the artist initiated. Self-expression has been a fairly common theme in Western art for about 200 years.

2.16 Maya Lin. Vietnam Veterans Memorial. The Mall, Washington D.C. 1980–82. Black granite. Each wall 10′1″ × 246′9″.

Photograph: Duane Preble.

2.17 Frida Kahlo. *The Broken Column*. 1944.
Oil on canvas. 15¹¹⁄₁₆″ × 12¹⁄₁₆″.

Museo Dolores Olmedo, Xochimilco, Mexico City, Mexico. Photograph akg-images/Album. © 2018 Banco de México Diego Rivera Frida Kahlo Museums Trust, Mexico, D.F. / Artists Rights Society (ARS), New York.

Some of the most self-expressive work of the twentieth century was created by the Mexican artist Frida Kahlo. At the age of 18, Kahlo suffered a severe internal injury in a bus accident. This led to a lifetime of surgical operations and medical treatments, which left her in nearly constant pain. Her 1944 work *The Broken Column* (**fig. 2.17**) is a confrontational self-portrait. Her body is split open at the core, revealing a shattered column. The brace that enfolds her torso is similar to one that she wore for most of her life. Nails pierce her flesh, a symbol of the injections and medical proddings she endured. Just as Kahlo exposes herself to us, so her body is exposed in a barren and gouged landscape. The artist seems to stare mutely back at us, eyes flowing with tears. Her firm yet impassive face enhances the emotional intensity of the work she created.

Not all self-expression tells stories of anguish, or even uses self-portraiture. Wassily Kandinsky, a leader in the Expressionist movement of early modern Germany, reached out to viewers by beginning with his inner feelings. He wrote that he hoped to create art only in response to what

he called "inner necessity," or the emotional stirrings of his soul, rather than in response to what he saw in the world. He created nonrepresentational works in which he attempted to translate the swirl and surge of inner spiritual energies into color and form. *Composition VI* (**fig. 2.18**) renders a restless inner state, an experience probably not unknown to most viewers. Kandinsky often named his works after musical forms, because he wanted them to communicate as immediately as music does: "Color directly influences the soul," he wrote; "Color is the keyboard, the eyes are the hammers, the soul is the piano with many strings. The artist is the hand that plays, touching one key or another purposefully, to cause vibrations in the soul."[6] He hoped that the souls of viewers would resonate with the rhythms and colors of his paintings, and that his works would infect viewers with the same emotions that he felt while creating them.

Self-expressive art is less common outside the modern Western world, but we see one of the more distinctive manifestations of it in the totem poles of the native peoples of the Pacific Northwest. Artists carved poles on commission from families, and these poles illustrate the crests or legends associated with a family's history. Many tribal groups in that region organize themselves by family clans that are named after the animals from which they trace their heritage. This pole (**fig. 2.19**) has a complex mixture of large and small figures, starting at the top with three watchers who constantly scan the horizon for approaching danger.

2.18 Wassily Kandinsky. *Composition VI*. 1913.
Oil on canvas. 76¾″ × 118″.

The State Hermitage Museum, St. Petersburg, Russia. akg-images/Album/VEGAP © Vassily Kandinski/Prisma © 2018 Artists Rights Society (ARS), New York.

2.19 Bill Reid. House Frontal Totem Pole. 1959.
Museum of Anthropology. Werner Forman Archive/University of British Columbia, Vancouver, Canada.

Below them is a raven with a smaller human-bird hybrid face beneath its beak. Next is a bear with a raven between its legs, above the face of a frog. The largest eyes near the bottom are those of a bear, with a frog in its mouth, a wolf between its legs, and a cub between its ears. As with most such poles that survive today, the specific stories that it tells are lost, but the expressive intent is present, just as it is in many cultures that value family crests. The carver of this work wrote of totem poles, "Like heraldic crests, these poles told of the mythological beginnings of the great families, at a time before time, when animals and mythic beasts and men lived as equals."[7]

Art for the Spirit

Another function of art has been to enhance religious contemplation, and most of the world's religions have found ways to incorporate artists' creativity into their sacred rituals, places, and ceremonies. Sometimes this art serves the ritualistic needs of an established faith; other faith expressions in art are more personal, inward, or spiritual.

Worship and Ritual

Many religious buildings intended for gathering the faithful have a striking visual aspect that helps to induce a feeling of wonder or sublimity. One of the most remarkable of these is the Sainte-Chapelle in Paris (**fig. 2.20**). King Louis IX of France commissioned this building to serve as a personal prayer chapel and also to hold his collection of relics, which included what he regarded as the original crown of thorns from Christ's trial and crucifixion. The walls of the chapel consist almost entirely of stained glass, which floods the interior with colored light. This visual effect is probably about as striking to visitors now as it was in 1248, when the chapel was consecrated. The intricately designed stained-glass windows may seem at first to be a welter of color, but in fact they tell stories from the Bible and from the later discovery of the relics and their transportation to this site by the king. Statues of saints and martyrs mark the major

2.20 Sainte-Chapelle, Paris. Upper chapel, interior view.
Photograph: akg-images/A.F. Kersting.

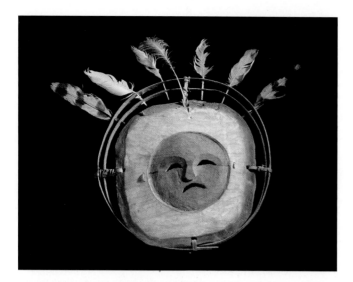

2.21 Moon Mask. Eskimo, village of Andreofsky. Collected 1893. Height 13 ½", width 13".
Werner Forman Archive/ Sheldon Jackson Museum, Sitka, Alaska.

vertical supports. The Sainte-Chapelle overall resembles a giant jewel-box, appropriate to its original function as a storehouse for precious relics.

Other religious traditions show less interest in special buildings and focus their visual creativity instead on ritual tools. Such a case is the Eskimo peoples of the Arctic region. One of their creation stories tells of a mythical sister and brother who became the sun and the moon, respectively. The girl/sun chases her brother/moon across the sky daily, bearing a torch, which is the sun's light. This Moon Mask (**fig. 2.21**) represents the moon in the sky, with two outer rings that symbolize levels of the cosmos. The feathers are sparks from the sister's torch that became stars. This mask was used in ceremonies by a shaman, or person who serves as an intermediary between people and spiritual beings. Accompanied by the appropriate chants and dances, the shaman wore the mask in order to embody the moon in all of its mythical meaning.

Spirituality

Contemporary spirituality can take many forms, and art assists some of them. Shirazeh Houshiary was born in Iran and learned early about the mystical traditions of the Sufi branch of Islam; it influenced her work, along with other contemplative traditions that she blends together in paintings such as *Ancient Light* (**fig. 2.22**). Asked about her artistic goals, she said, "This work is about presence. Presence is like light—how can you describe light? Light can be only experienced, it has a presence. This work also has a presence and has only to be experienced." At approxi-

mately 6 by 9 feet, the work fills our visual field with a white glow of light that the artist has called an "energy field." She begins with small adjacent calligraphic pencil strokes, repeated hundreds of times like a meditation exercise. These combine into softly rippling lines that she compares to breaths or musical vibrations. She created the deep radiance with numerous layers of water-based paint, which gives the sensation of looking into a bottomless yet textured space. She said, "White is an experience of boundlessness, it opens in front of you," helping viewers to experience infinity. We could be staring into a microcosm of atoms, or a boundless expanse of space. But the artist does not mind the contradiction, because she hopes to reach the widest possible audience. She said, "I would like my work to be open and generous, different for every person who sees it."[8]

Nancy Holt was born in Massachusetts, but when she first experienced the flat, open expanses of nature in the desert West, she immediately felt at home and made this the subject of several artworks. "It seemed to me that I had this Western space that had been within me. That was my inner reality. I was experiencing it on the outside, simultaneously with my spaciousness within. I felt at one." She created *Sun Tunnels* (**fig. 2.23**) in 1976 on empty land in western Utah to express and represent the vastness of the landscape.

Contracting with various specialists, including an astrophysicist and various construction firms, Holt installed four huge concrete pipes, each 9 feet high and 18 feet long. These tubes form sight lines that viewers can look through to see the sunrise and sunset at each

2.22 Shirazeh Houshiary. *Ancient Light*. 2009. Pencil, aquacryl, and pigment on canvas. 74¾" × 106¼".
Courtesy of the artist.

2.23 Nancy Holt. *Sun Tunnels*, 1973–76. Concrete, steel, and earth. Great Basin Desert, Utah. Overall dimensions: 9' 3" x 68' 6" x 53'; diagonal length: 86'; each tunnel: 18' 1" x 9' 3" diameter.

Utah Museum of Fine Arts. © Holt-Smithson Foundation/Licensed by VAGA, New York, NY.

winter and summer solstice. The effect is like seeing the desert through a telescope. She drilled holes in the pipes in arrangements that picture four different celestial constellations that hover over the site at night. The holes channel light from the sun and moon to re-create constellations on the floor of the pipes. She said of this work, "The tunnels orient you out in space and frame the view. It brings the landscape back to human scale."[9]

Art for Political Purposes

Just as art has often served religious needs, so at times it has been used to express political goals or ideals. Artists throughout history have worked on both sides of the most basic political equation: Some have attempted to persuade us to submit to authority; others have expressed protest or even encouraged revolt.

Persuasion

Many artforms have a persuasive purpose. Splendid government buildings, public monuments, television commercials, and music videos all harness the power of art to influence action and opinion. They invite and urge us to do or think things that we may not have otherwise.

To begin with expressions of authority, the rulers of the West African region of Benin commissioned skilled metalworkers to create brass plaques to decorate their palaces

(**fig. 2.24**). This one depicts the king, or Oba as he is known, as a supernatural strongman. He wears ceremonial clothing, with a high helmet and neck rings. His all-seeing eyes glare back at us. From his belt hang two mudfish, showing the royal kinship with the gods of water, which nourish all of life. In a gesture of power, he raises two leopards by their tails, showing his rulership over nature. Both the king's garments and the background are finely textured, showing excellent workmanship. The technology of brass casting was reserved for use only by the royal family of Benin, and this plaque in its prominent location on the exterior of the palace showed to passersby the divine powers of the ruler who lived within.

Modern governments do not claim divine power, but they do use the arts to express their authority as well; the United States Supreme Court building in Washington,

2.24 Plaque Showing the Oba Holding Leopards. c.1700. Benin. Brass. 19½" × 13½" × 2½".

The British Museum, London. Af1898,0115.31 © The Trustees of the British Museum.

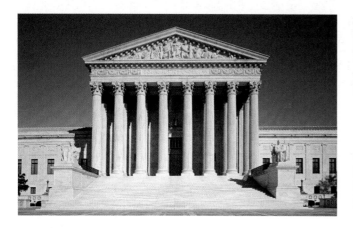

2.25 Carol Highsmith. U.S. Supreme Court Building. Photograph. 1980.

Library of Congress, Carol Highsmith Archive, 2011632073.

2.26 Rodney McMillian. *Untitled (The Supreme Court Painting)*. 2004–2006. Poured acrylic on cut canvas, 216″ × 216″.

Inventory #MCR130. Courtesy of the artist and Susanne Vielmetter Los Angeles Projects. Photo credit: Gene Ogami.

D.C., is a case in point (**fig. 2.25**). The style of this marble-clad building is derived from the ancient Roman Republican period, during which citizens also enjoyed the right to vote. It is massive and symmetrical, communicating balance, order, stability, and continuity with the past. The scale of the building is intended to correspond with that of the Capitol building across the street, where the Congress meets; this relationship shows the Court as an equal branch of government. The decorations on the outside of the building help to communicate the purposes and methods of the Court. Above the columns on a central panel we read "Equal justice under law." On either side of the inscription are garlands that symbolize the abundance and plenty that flow from justice. Above the inscription is a triangular sculpture group titled *Enthroned Liberty Guarded by Order and Authority*. Flanking the steps at the left and right are figures representing the contemplation of justice and the authority of law. The goal in designing this building, which was completed in 1936, was to house the justices in a building that communicates an image of the power of law in governing the country, as well as the dignity and serenity of the justices working therein.

Protest

Many artists use their creativity in the service of protest, involving themselves in the politics of the day (see *Käthe Kollwitz: Art of Human Concern*, opposite). We get a completely different view of the Supreme Court, for example, from contemporary African-American artist Rodney McMillian in his work *Untitled (The Supreme Court Painting)* (**fig. 2.26**). The piece protests against certain court decisions in the areas of voting rights and election districting that McMillian saw as harmful to African Americans. He made

the painting on canvas in the shape of the façade of the building, but he removed the framework so that it sags and buckles. He mixed the colors and applied them to the canvas by pouring; this gives the work the look of fake marble. The central panel above the columns is blank, as if its inspiring inscription about equal justice has been erased. On either side we see that the garlands on the original building have been supplanted by smiley faces. What should be an inspiring symbol here becomes a tumbledown and phony-looking monument to lazy disorder. The artist created this work because he felt that the Court was moving in an unfruitful ideological direction; he felt that it had supported individual liberty and the quest for civil rights in the past, but that the justices were backing away from those commitments.

As we have seen, many works of art may fulfill more than one purpose; art that is persuasive may also delight with its beauty; a religious work may express the creator's personal quest for transcendence; a commemorative piece may also inform us. Yet all art meets one human need or another, and has the power to shape our lives in many ways.

KEY TERMS

aesthetics – the philosophy of art focusing on questions regarding what art is, how it is evaluated, the concept of beauty, and the relationship between the idea of beauty and the concept of art

calligraphy – the art of beautiful writing; broadly, a flowing use of line, often varying from thick to thin

picturesque – used to describe natural landscapes that are attractively poetic, rather than dramatic; original meaning is traced to the paintings of Claude Lorrain and other landscape painters

CREATORS

Käthe Kollwitz: Art of Human Concern

2.27 Käthe Kollwitz. *Self-Portrait*. 1904. Color lithograph. 16¼″ x 12½″.
Photograph akg-images. © 2018 Artists Rights Society (ARS), New York.

An artist who devoted her career to art that took political positions was the German printmaker and sculptor Käthe Kollwitz (1867–1945). Born into a middle-class family in Prussia, she showed artistic talent at an early age and took drawing classes at local women's colleges. At the age of 24, she married a physician and went to live in a poor neighborhood of Berlin. There her husband treated the local population as she took an interest in the lives of workers. She wrote, "I was powerfully moved by the fate of urban workers and everything connected with their way of life."[10]

Kollwitz made several series of prints that encouraged workers and peasants to attempt to improve their lot by protest and struggle. Her series *The Peasants' War* was based on her reading of a book about the event; she felt that workers in her times could learn from the struggles of the past. One of the prints from this series is *The Outbreak* (**fig 2.28**), which illustrates a rebellion by rural agricultural workers in Germany from 1522 to 1525. Kollwitz learned that one of the instigators of the revolt was a woman known as Black Anna, so she depicted her with arms raised, shouting encouragement to the peasants as they surge forward in a hunched, huddled mass. Kollwitz once stated that she identified with Black Anna; both devoted their lives to improving the lot of disadvantaged people. This work lacks color because it was created as a print on paper; this was the artist's preferred medium because she could sell the sheets at relatively low prices to more people and thereby spread her message.

When Kollwitz made art that directly depicted the difficult living conditions of Berlin's working classes, she often faced controversy or censorship. For example, in 1906 she made a poster promoting an art exhibition that showed an accurate but unvarnished image of a destitute woman; the Empress of Germany refused to allow the exhibition to open until every poster had been whitewashed.

Soon after her son died in battle in the early days of World War I, Kollwitz became a pacifist, opposing all wars on principle. In 1924, on the tenth anniversary of the outbreak of World War I, she released a print series on the human cost of war, printing on large, poster-size sheets for greater impact. She wrote of her hopes for the work in a letter to a friend, "These sheets should travel throughout the entire world and should tell all human beings comprehensively: that is how it was—what we have all endured throughout these unspeakably difficult years."[11]

The controversy that Kollwitz at times created added to her growing reputation among fellow artists. She was elected to the executive committee of the Berlin Secession, an artists' exhibition society. She was also the first woman ever elected to membership in the Prussian Academy of Fine Arts, where she also became a professor of printmaking.

Kollwitz's art of social commitment continued. In later life she began to focus her art on the particular problems that women face. She never joined any political party, attempting instead to speak to and for humanity as a whole.

She wrote in her diary, "I am horrified and shaken by all the hatred in the world. I long for the kind of socialism that lets people *live*, and find that the earth has seen *enough* of murder, lies, misery, distortion."[12]

When the Nazis took power in Germany in 1933, Kollwitz was forced out of her teaching position and forbidden from exhibiting in public. Yet she continued to make her prints and to sell them to an ever-wider audience through private sales. In 1936 the Gestapo political police threatened to send her to a prison camp, but her international reputation likely prevented them from carrying out the threat. She left Berlin in 1943 for the rural city of Moritzburg; soon after, her house and studio were hit by Allied bombing, which led to the loss of many works. She died in 1945, just before the end of the hostilities.

2.28 Käthe Kollwitz. *The Outbreak*. From the series *The Peasants' War*. 1903. Etching, engraving, and aquatint on paper. 19½″ × 23″. Sheet 5 of the series: Bauernkrieg.
Hanover, Sprengel Museum Photograph akg-images.
© 2018 Artists Rights Society (ARS), New York.

THE VISUAL ELEMENTS

LEARNING OBJECTIVES

3.1 Describe the characteristics of line.

3.2 Identify the two general categories of shapes and their different qualities.

3.3 Differentiate between two-dimensional and three-dimensional depictions of mass.

3.4 Summarize how technical devices such as implied depth and linear perspective are used to render space in two-dimensional works of art.

3.5 Discuss how visual artists can express or embody the passage of time and the concept of motion in their work.

3.6 Explain the characteristics of light and how it is used as a medium in the work of contemporary artists.

3.7 Describe the physical properties and relationships of color.

3.8 Discuss how texture aids the expressive quality of an artwork.

Edward Hopper's 1939 painting *New York Movie* (**fig. 3.1**) depicts a movie theater with a few people in the audience and an usher standing just outside in the lobby. More important, this work also shows the artist's use of several visual elements that play key roles in most works of art. On the right, thickly painted *lines* separate the walls and ceiling. The lamps above the theater seats reveal dimly lit suspended *shapes* that suggest the *mass* of the rows of balcony seats above. The work includes two *spaces*, theater and lobby, which seem to recede from us. Movies take place over *time*, and this movie is probably about to end, as the usher waits for the crowd to exit. *Motion* is suggested by the partial, blurred movie screen and by the expectation that the audience will soon be leaving. *Light*, coming from the overhead lamps in the theater and the three wall lamps in the lobby, helps to clarify the spaces in the work; it is particularly important in establishing the pensive presence of the usher. The deep blue *color* of her uniform contrasts with the pale colors of the walls. The artist also suggested smooth

3.1 Edward Hopper. *New York Movie*. 1939.
Oil on canvas. 32″ × 40″.

Museum of Modern Art, (MoMA). Given anonymously. Acc. n.: 396.1941.© 2018.
Digital image, The Museum of Modern Art, New York/Scala, Florence.

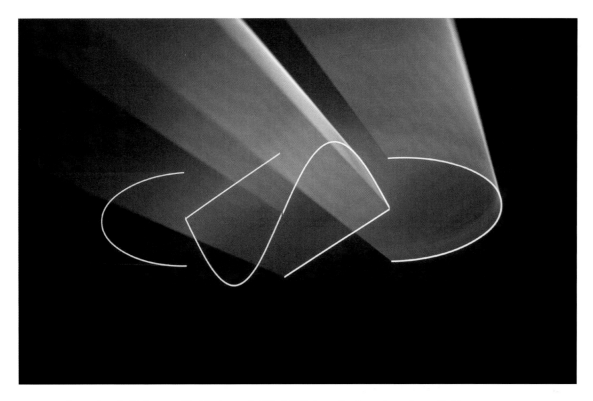

3.2 Anthony McCall. *You and I, Horizontal (III)*. 2007. Installation view, Sean Kelly Gallery, New York, 2007.

Photograph by Steven Harris. © the artist, courtesy: Sean Kelly, New York.

and rough *textures* in the red velvet theater seats, the flat plaster walls, and the carved wood column at the center.

This chapter introduces the visual elements identified in *New York Movie*: line, shape, mass, space, time, motion, light, color, and texture. Not all these elements are important, or even present, in every work of art; many works emphasize only a few of them. To understand their expressive possibilities, we will examine some of the expressive qualities of each of these visual elements and the way in which artists use them.

Line

We write, draw, plan, and play with lines. Our individuality and feelings are expressed as we write our one-of-a-kind signatures or make other handmade lines. Line is our basic means of recording and symbolizing ideas, observations, and feelings; it is a primary means of visual communication.

A **line** is a long, narrow mark, usually made by drawing with a tool or brush. Lines can be of various thickness, but length always predominates over height or depth. Wherever we see an edge, we often perceive the edge as

a line—the place where one object or plane appears to end and another object or space begins. In a sense we often "draw" with our eyes, converting edges to lines. In *New York Movie*, this happens at the joints between the theater and lobby spaces, and where the lobby floor meets the wall.

In art and in nature, lines can appear to be paths of action—records of the energy left by moving points. Lines in space are the principal elements in Anthony McCall's *You and I, Horizontal (III)* **(fig. 3.2)**. We can imagine that moving points of light may have made the lines that make up this work. McCall set up projectors that send bright images of lines onto sloping dark screens. When viewers pass through the space, they interrupt the lines and thereby alter them at will. Viewers thus help to draw the lines that this work features.

Characteristics of Line

Lines can be active or static, aggressive or passive, sensual or mechanical. Lines can indicate directions, define boundaries of shapes and spaces, imply volumes or solid masses, and suggest motion or emotion. Lines can also be grouped to depict light and shadow and to form patterns

3.3 Line Variations.

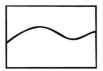

a. Actual line.

b. Implied line.

c. Actual straight lines and implied curved line.

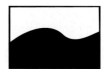

d. Line created by an edge.

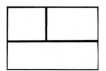

e. Vertical line (attitude of alert attention); horizontal line (attitude of rest).

f. Diagonal lines (slow action, fast action).

g. Sharp, jagged line.

h. Dance of curving lines.

i. Hard line, soft line.

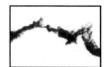

j. Ragged, irregular line.

and textures. Note the line qualities shown in the Line Variations diagram (**fig. 3.3**).

Consider the range of uses artists found for lines in the works pictured here. The two Japanese prints have similar subjects, but use line in radically different ways. *Kabuki Actor* (**fig. 3.4**) is curvy and suggests slow, rhythmic motion. Torii Kiyotada's *Actor* (**fig. 3.5**), in contrast, uses angular lines to express swift and violent motion.

The Venezuelan artist Gego took lines into the third dimension in her room-size work *Reticulárea* (**fig. 3.6**).

3.4 Far left: Attributed to Torii Kiyonobu I. *Kabuki Actor*. c.1708. Woodblock print. 21¾″ × 11½″.

The Metropolitan Museum of Art, Harris Brisbane Dick Fund and Rogers Fund, 1949. (JP 3098).

3.5 Left: Torii Kiyotada. Ichikawa Danjūrō II in the Scene 'Wait a Moment' (Shibaraku). *An Actor of the Ichikawa Clan in a Dance Movement of Violent Motion*. c.1715. Hand-colored woodcut. 11¼″ × 6″.

The Metropolitan Museum of Art, Harris Brisbane Dick Fund and Rogers Fund, 1949. (JP 3075).

3.6 Gego. *Reticulárea (Environment)*. 1969. Aluminum and stainless-steel wire. Dimensions variable.
Fundación Gego.

She created this field of lines by linking segments of stainless-steel wire into a disorienting welter. As viewers move through the space, they see short lines in varying degrees of density that proceed in every direction. Fred Sandback also put lines into our space (**fig. 3.7**), but he used black yarn in a much more organized array to suggest elegant open rectangles. The shapes that the lines create alternate between only two orientations; three of the rectangles lie at 90-degree angles from the other three, creating a rather stately procession. The widely differing mood of these two room-sized works depends entirely on the artists' use of line.

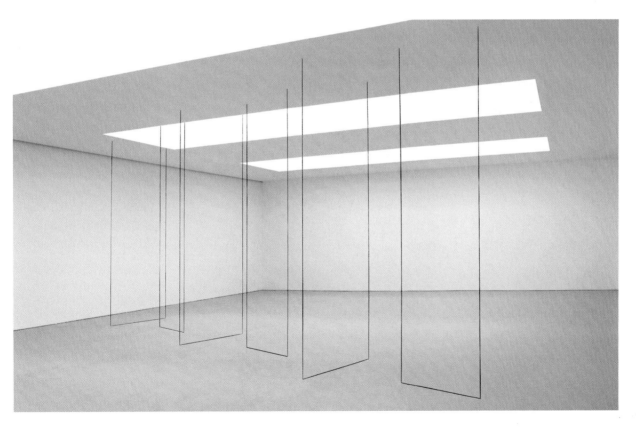

3.7 Fred Sandback. *Untitled (Sculptural Study, Six-Part Construction)*. 1977/2008. Black acrylic yarn. Dimensions variable.
Glenstone Museum, Potomac, Maryland. Photo by Cathy Carver © 2017 Fred Sandback Archive; courtesy of David Zwirner, New York/London.

Many types of prints are made up almost entirely of lines, with little shading or color. Kiki Smith etched lines in a metal plate to create *Ginzer* (**fig. 3.8**), a depiction of her cat. She painstakingly drew one line for each of Ginzer's hairs. The eyes and foot pads are slightly shaded, but all else was done with line. She successfully captured the cat's flexible limbs and back as Ginzer reclined, but she also showed a hint of the animal's wild side in the mouth and alert eyes.

Implied Line

Implied lines suggest visual connections. Andrea di Lione used several of these in his painting *Tobit Burying the Dead* (**fig. 3.9a**); a diagram (**fig. 3.9b**) separates them out for clarity. Implied lines that form geometric shapes can serve as an underlying organizational structure. The figures in the lower foreground form a triangle with the head of the white-clad Tobit as its apex. One side of this triangle is the implied line from Tobit's head downward toward the right, through a head, back, and leg each belonging to other figures. Part of this triangle's other side is formed by the

3.8 Kiki Smith. *Ginzer*. 2000. Etching, aquatint, and drypoint on mold-made paper. 22½″ × 31″.
Published by Harlan & Weaver, New York.

3.9a Andrea di Lione. *Tobit Burying the Dead*. 1640s. Oil on canvas. 50¼″ × 68½″.
Metropolitan Museum of Art, New York, 1989.225.

b Implied lines in Andrea di Lione. *Tobit Burying the Dead*.

sightline of the dog as it looks upward at Tobit. Painters often use such sightlines as implied lines. The figures above form another triangle over a baseline consisting of the floor of the building they stand in. One side of this triangle is implied by the head and pointing arm of the figure in the rear. Another comes from the sightline of the white-turbaned figure; his sightline extends downward to the burial scene below, thus helping to unify the two groups.

Shape

The words *shape*, *mass*, and *form* are sometimes used interchangeably, but they mean different things in the visual arts. **Shape** is the area within the outline of an object or figure, whether **two-dimensional** or **three-dimensional**. When we see a three-dimensional object in natural light, we see that it has mass, or volume; it has height, width, and depth. If the same object is silhouetted against a sunset, we may see it only as a flat shape. Enclosing a shape inside of lines or making it a different color sets the shape apart from its surroundings so that we recognize it.

We can group the infinite variety of shapes into two general categories: geometric and organic. **Geometric shapes**—such as circles, triangles, and squares—tend to be precise and regular. They are most often made with the help of tools such as rulers or a compass. The shapes in Torii Kiyotada's *Actor* (see fig. 3.5) are geometric. **Organic shapes** are irregular, often curving or rounded, and seem more relaxed and informal than geometric shapes. The shapes in the Japanese print *Kabuki Actor* (see fig. 3.4) are predominantly organic. The most common shapes in the human-made world are geometric: the edges of a computer screen, the steering wheel of a car. Although some geometric shapes exist in nature—in such forms as crystals and snowflakes—most shapes in nature are organic, such as

stones, ocean waves, or bending branches. A related term with a similar meaning is **biomorphic**, which also suggests shapes based on natural forms.

When a shape appears on a **picture plane** (the flat picture surface), it simultaneously creates a second shape out of the background area. The dominant shapes are referred to as **figures** or **positive shapes**; background areas are **ground** or **negative shapes**. The figure–ground relationship is a fundamental aspect of perception; it allows us to sort out and interpret what we see. Because we are conditioned to see only objects, and not the spaces between and around them, it takes a shift in awareness to see the white negative shapes in *A Shape of Space* (**fig. 3.10**). Most artists consider both positive and negative shapes simultaneously and treat them as equally important to the total effectiveness of a composition.

Paul D'Agostino used simple means to create an absorbing game of positive and negative shapes in his pair of gently humorous works titled *The Rarely Glimpsed Junkfish*. The sculpture (**fig. 3.11**) is a fish shape worked in synthetic clay and painted solid black. From across the room it appears as an organic shape against the white background of the wall. It is irregular but recognizable because of the gaping mouth and tailfin. A closer approach reveals its lumpy surface in three dimensions, and also brings its eye into view. To assist us in viewing it as a positive shape, the artist placed it on a wire support over a base. In the drawing (**fig. 3.12**), the fish emerges from areas of the paper that the artist left blank. The fish is still recognizable from the mouth, eyes, and tail. The shape of the fish is thus a negative space against a black background that the artist applied to the paper with charcoal. He also left two other areas as negative spaces and filled them with a handwritten storyline; a final negative space represents food.

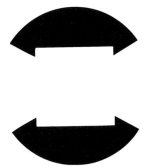

3.10 *A Shape of Space.*
Implied space.

3.11 Paul D'Agostino. Floor Translations, Sculpture 3: *The Rarely Glimpsed Junkfish*. Acrylic and polymer medium on resin with wire, wood and shellac. Dimensions variable, 2013.

Collection Armin Kunz. Photograph by Vincent Romaniello.

3.12 Paul D'Agostino. Floor Translations 3: *The Rarely Glimpsed Junkfish* (page 1 of 3). Charcoal and ink on cream wove paper. 6″ × 4½″. 2012.

Collection Armin Kunz. Image courtesy C.G. Boerner Gallery.

Mass

A two-dimensional area is called a shape, but a three-dimensional area is called a **mass**: the physical bulk of a solid body of material that has height, width, and depth. When mass encloses space, the space is called **volume**. The word *form* is sometimes used instead of mass to refer to physical bulk.

Mass in Three Dimensions

Mass is often a major element in sculpture and architecture. The sculpture in Paul D'Agostino's *Rarely Glimpsed Junkfish* (see fig. 3.11) is also a three-dimensional mass. The contemporary sculptor Fernando Botero created a bronze horse of immense mass for a public monument in Mexico (**fig. 3.13**). The bulging legs and neck are intensified by the

3.13 Fernando Botero. *The Horse*. 2008. Bronze. Height 134″. Plaza Centenario, Monterrey, Mexico.

Photograph: Patrick Frank.

horse's short backbone, bringing the four legs together like strong pillars. The mass of this horse goes far beyond what mere muscle could produce, giving the body an inflated look. The legs are in a position of rest, and the head points toward the ground, yielding a form that does not openly interact with the surrounding space. *The Horse* is thus a good example of **closed form**.

In contrast to the hulking mass of Botero's horse, the slight mass of Alberto Giacometti's *Man Pointing* (**fig. 3.14**) conveys a sense of fleeting presence rather than permanence. The tall, thin figure appears eroded by time and barely existing. Because Giacometti used little solid material to construct the figure, we are more aware of a linear form in space than of mass. If Botero's *Horse*

represents closed form, the *Man Pointing* is an **open form**: The figure reaches out; its arms are spread wide; the face seems to peer into the distance, and the feet point outward. The open form of this work interacts with the surrounding space, which seems to overwhelm it, suggesting the fragile, impermanent nature of human existence.

Mass in Two Dimensions

Paula Modersohn-Becker implied mass in both of the figures in her painting *Mother and Child* (**fig. 3.15**). She filled the picture plane so that they occupy most of it with their shapes. She also shaded the figures in light and dark to suggest bulging, curving flesh. Thus, she used both composition and shading to imply mass.

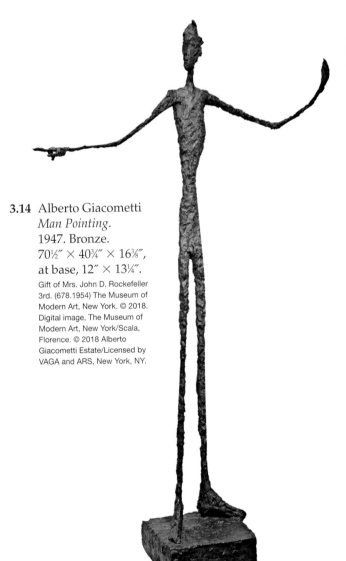

3.14 Alberto Giacometti *Man Pointing*. 1947. Bronze. 70½″ × 40¾″ × 16⅜″, at base, 12″ × 13¼″.

Gift of Mrs. John D. Rockefeller 3rd. (678.1954) The Museum of Modern Art, New York. © 2018. Digital image, The Museum of Modern Art, New York/Scala, Florence. © 2018 Alberto Giacometti Estate/Licensed by VAGA and ARS, New York, NY.

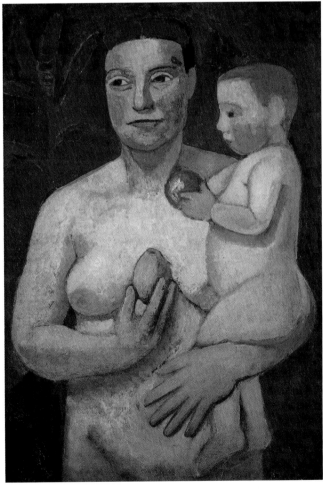

3.15 Paula Modersohn-Becker. *Mother and Child*. 1906/07. Oil on canvas, 32″ × 23″.

Ostwall Museum, Dortmund. Photograph: akg-images/Erich Lessing.

Space

Space is the indefinable, general receptacle of all things—the seemingly empty space around us. How artists organize space in the works they make is one of their most important creative considerations.

Space in Three Dimensions

Of all the visual elements, space is the most difficult to convey in words and pictures. To experience three-dimensional space, we must be in it. We experience space beginning with our own positions in relation to other people, objects, surfaces, and voids at various distances from ourselves.

Each of us has a sense of personal space—the area surrounding our body—that we like to protect, and the extent of this invisible boundary varies from person to person and from culture to culture.

Architects are especially concerned with the qualities of space. Imagine how you would feel in a small room with a very low ceiling. What if you raised the ceiling to 15 feet? What if you added skylights? What if you replaced the walls with glass? In each case you would have changed the character of the space and, by doing so, would have radically changed your experience.

Whereas we experience the outside of a building as mass in space, we experience the inside as volume and as a sequence of enclosed spaces. Cesar Pelli's design for the North Terminal at Ronald Reagan Washington National Airport (**fig. 3.16**) takes the passenger's experience of space into account. Large windows offer views of the runways and also of the Potomac River and the nearby Washington Monument. The architect divided the huge interior space into smaller modules to give the concourse a more domestic feel: "The module has an important psychological value in that each one is like a very large living room in size," the architect said. "It's a space that we experience in our daily life.... The domes make spaces designed on the scale of people, not on the scale of big machines."[1]

3.16 Cesar Pelli and Associates. North Terminal, Ronald Reagan Washington National Airport. 1997.
Alamy.

3.17 Doug Wheeler. *SA MI 75 DZ NY 12*. 1975/2012. Reinforced fiberglass, LED lights, high-intensity fluorescent lights, UV fluorescent lights, quartz halogen lights, DMX control, architecturally modified space. 564″ × 702″.
© 2012 Doug Wheeler. Photo: Tim Nighswander. Courtesy David Zwirner, New York/London.

3.18 *Pool in the Garden.* Wall painting from the tomb of Nebamun. Egypt. c.1400 BCE. Paint on dry plaster.

Doug Wheeler creates a feeling of infinite space in many of his immersive installations. Viewers who enter his piece *SA MI 75 DZ NY 12* (**fig. 3.17**) are confronted with a space that appears to be divided in two by a wall of light. Closer approach through the diffused "membrane" slowly reveals a room that seems to be of infinite dimensions. Carefully controlled light sources and featureless construction create the optical effect, as the lighting changes slowly from blinding white to near-darkness over a 32-minute period. The artist has referred to this work as a "Continuous Atmospheric Environment."

Space in Two Dimensions

With three-dimensional objects and spaces, such as sculpture and architecture, we must move around to get the full experience. With two-dimensional works, such as drawing and painting, we see the space of the surface all at once. In drawings, prints, photographs, and paintings, the actual space of each picture's surface (picture plane) is defined by its edges—usually the two dimensions of height and width. Yet within these boundaries, a great variety of possible pictorial spaces can be implied or suggested, creating depth in the picture plane.

Paintings from ancient Egypt, for example, show little depth. Early Egyptian painters made their images clear by

portraying objects from their most easily identifiable angles and by avoiding the visual confusion caused by overlap and the appearance of diminishing size. *Pool in the Garden* (**fig. 3.18**) demonstrates this technique. The pool is shown from above, while the trees, fish, and birds are all pictured from the side.

Implied Depth

Almost any mark on a picture plane begins to give the illusion of a third dimension: depth. Clues to seeing spatial depth are learned in early childhood. A few of the major ways of indicating space on a picture plane are shown in the diagrams Clues to Spatial Depth (**fig. 3.19**).

3.19 Clues to Spatial Depth.

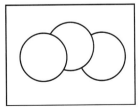

a. Overlap.

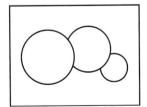

b. Overlap and diminishing size.

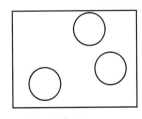

c. Vertical placement.

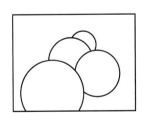

d. Overlap, vertical placement, and diminishing size.

3.20 Paul Cézanne. *Still Life with Apples.* c.1890. Oil on canvas. 13¾″ × 18⅛″.

State Hermitage Museum, St. Petersburg/ Bridgeman Images

When shapes overlap, we immediately assume from experience that one is in front of the other (diagram a). Overlapping is the most basic way to achieve the effect of depth on a flat surface. (Note that *Pool in the Garden* uses very little overlapping.) The effect of overlap is strengthened by diminishing size, which gives a sense of increasing distance between each of the shapes (diagram b). Our perception of distance depends on the observation that distant objects appear smaller than near objects. A third method of achieving the illusion of depth is **vertical placement**: Objects placed low on the picture plane (diagram c) appear to be closer to the viewer than objects placed high on the plane. This is the way we see most things in actual space. Creating illusions of depth on a flat surface usually involves one or more such devices (diagram d).

When we look at a picture, we may be conscious of both its actual flat surface and the illusion of depth that the picture contains. Artists can emphasize either the reality or the illusion, or strike a balance between these extremes. Paul Cézanne suggested depth in various ways in his small work *Still Life with Apples* (**fig. 3.20**). The basic subject is a dark tabletop against a pale background. We see the "horizon line" of the tabletop at either end of the picture, but the artist left an intriguing gap in the middle. On the tabletop, he created pictorial depth both by overlapping and by vertical placement of the fruit. The lemon is both closer to us and lower in the picture. Note also that the three fruits on the tabletop seem to inhabit a different space from the apples on the dish. The space before the dish seems flat, parallel to the picture surface. Cézanne also flattened the overall space by placing patches of parallel brushstrokes in both background and tabletop; this encourages us to read both spaces as "surface." Finally, the space behind the tabletop is unclear; it could be a fraction of an inch deep, or several feet. These suggestions and denials of space create an absorbing and unstable visual experience, a set of subtle optical illusions.

Linear Perspective

In general usage, the word perspective refers to point of view. In the visual arts, **perspective** is any means of representing three-dimensional objects in space on a two-dimensional surface. Japanese prints (see figs. 3.4 and 3.5) and Egyptian murals (see fig. 3.18) have their perspective systems, although neither of these systems is similar to the **linear perspective** system, which was perfected during the fifteenth century in Italy. In the West, we have become accustomed to artists' use of linear perspective (also called simply *perspective*) to depict the way objects in space appear to the eye. Different traditions and intentions, rather than mere skill, give us various ways of depicting depth.

Linear perspective is based on the way we see. We have already noted that objects appear smaller when seen at a distance than when viewed close up. Because the spaces between objects also appear smaller when seen at a distance, parallel lines appear to converge as they recede into the distance, as shown in the first of the Linear Perspective diagrams (**fig. 3.21a**). Intellectually, we know that the edge lines of the road must be parallel, yet they seem to converge, meeting at last at what is called a **vanishing point** on the horizon—the place where land and sky appear to meet. On a picture surface, the horizon (or **horizon line**) also represents your eye level as you look at a scene.

Eye level is an imaginary plane, the height of the artist's eyes, parallel with the ground plane and extending to the horizon, where the eye level and ground plane appear to converge. In a finished picture, the artist's eye level becomes the eye level of anyone looking at the picture. Although the horizon is frequently blocked from view, it is necessary for an artist to establish a combined eye-level/horizon line to construct images using linear perspective.

With the linear perspective system, an entire picture can be constructed from a single, fixed position called a **vantage point**, or viewpoint. Diagram (a) shows **one-point perspective**, in which the parallel sides of the road appear to converge and trees in a row appear smaller as their distances from the vantage point increase.

Diagram (b) shows cubes drawn in one-point perspective from different vantage points. The cubes at the left are at eye level; we can see neither their top nor their bottom surfaces. We might imagine them as buildings.

The cubes in the center are below eye level: we can look down on their tops. These cubes are drawn from a high vantage point: a viewing position above the subject. The horizon line is above these cubes, and their perspective lines go up to it. We may imagine these as boxes on the floor.

The cubes at the right are above our eye level; we can look up at their bottom sides. These cubes are drawn from a low vantage point. The horizon line is below these cubes and their perspective lines go down to it. Imagine that these

3.21 Linear Perspective.

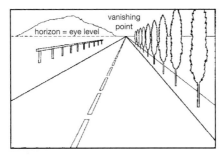

a. One-point linear perspective.

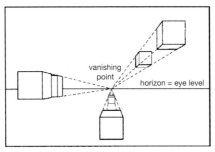

b. One-point linear perspective. Cubes above eye level, at eye level, and below eye level.

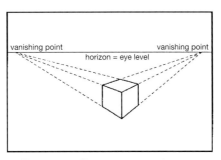

c. Two-point linear perspective.

boxes are sitting on a glass shelf high above our heads.

In one-point perspective, all the major receding edges of the subject are actually parallel, yet visually they appear to converge at a single vanishing point on the horizon line. In two-point perspective, two sets of parallel lines appear to converge at two points on the horizon line, as in diagram (c). When a cube or any other rectilinear object is positioned so that a corner, instead of a side, is closest to us, we need two vanishing points to draw it. The parallel lines of the right side converge to the right; the parallel lines of the left side converge to the left. Complex works with several geometric figures in them may require many vanishing points.

In *The School of Athens* (**fig. 3.22**), Raphael invented a grand architectural setting to provide an appropriate space for his depiction of the Greek philosophers Plato and Aristotle and other important thinkers. The size of each figure is drawn to scale according to its distance from the viewer; thus the entire group seems natural. Lines superimposed over the painting reveal the basic one-point perspective system Raphael used (**fig. 3.23a**). However, the cube in the foreground is not parallel to the picture plane or to the painted architecture, and is in **two-point perspective**.

Raphael used perspective for emphasis. We infer that Plato and Aristotle are the most important figures in this painting because of their placement at the center of receding archways in the zone of greatest implied depth.

If the figures are removed, as shown in the study of *The School of Athens* (**fig. 3.23b**), our attention is pulled right through the painted setting into implied infinite space. Conversely, without their architectural background defined by perspective, Plato and Aristotle lose importance; picking them out from the crowd becomes difficult.

3.22 Raphael. *The School of Athens*. 1508. Fresco. Approximately 18´ × 26´.
Stanza della Segnatura, Vatican, Rome. Photograph: akg-image/Erich Lessing.

3.23a Perspective lines in *The School of Athens*.
Stanza della Segnatura, Vatican, Rome. Photograph: akg-image/Erich Lessing.

3.23b Raphael. Study of *The School of Athens*. 1508. Fresco. Approximately 18´ × 26´.
Stanza della Segnatura, Vatican, Rome. Photograph: akg-image/Erich Lessing.

Atmospheric Perspective

Atmospheric (aerial) perspective is a nonlinear means for giving an illusion of depth. In atmospheric perspective, the illusion of depth is created by changing color and detail. In visual experience of the real world, as the distance increases between the viewer and faraway objects such as mountains, the increased quantity of air, moisture, and dust causes the distant objects to appear increasingly blue and less distinct. Color intensity is diminished, and contrast between light and dark is reduced.

Asher Brown Durand used atmospheric perspective in his painting *Kindred Spirits* (**fig. 3.24**) to provide a sense of the vast distances in the North American wilderness. The illusion of infinite space is balanced by dramatically illuminated foreground details, by the figures of the men, and by Durand's lively portrayal of trees, rocks, and waterfalls. We identify with the figures of painter Thomas Cole and poet William Cullen Bryant as they enjoy the spectacular landscape. As in *The School of Athens*, the implied deep space appears as an extension of the space we occupy.

Traditional Chinese landscape painters have another way of creating atmospheric perspective. In Shen Zhou's painting *Poet on a Mountaintop* (**fig. 3.25**), near and distant mountains are suggested by washes of ink and color on white paper. The light gray of the farthest mountain at the upper right implies space and atmosphere. Traditional Chinese landscape paintings present poetic symbols of

3.24 Asher Brown Durand. *Kindred Spirits*. 1849. Oil on canvas. 44″ × 36″.
Courtesy of Crystal Bridges Museum of American Art, Bentonville, Arkansas. Photography by The Metropolitan Museum of Art.

3.25 Shen Zhou. *Poet on a Mountaintop*. c.1500. From the series *Landscape Album: Five Leaves*. Album leaf mounted as a handscroll. Ink and watercolor on paper on silk mount. 15¼″ × 23¾″ overall.
The Nelson-Atkins Museum of Art, Kansas City, Missouri. Purchase: William Rockhill Nelson Trust, 46-51/2. Photo: John Lamberton.

landforms rather than realistic representations. Whereas *Kindred Spirits* draws the viewer's eye into and through the suggested deep space, *Poet on a Mountaintop* leads the eye across (rather than into) space.

Time and Motion

Time is the fourth dimension, in which events occur in succession. Because we live in an environment combining space and time, our experience of time often depends on our movement in space, and vice versa. Although time itself is invisible, it can be made perceptible in art. Time and motion become major elements in visual media such as film, video, and some works of sculpture.

The Passage of Time

Many traditional non-Western cultures teach that time is cyclic. The Aztecs of ancient Mexico, for example, held that the Earth was subject to periodic cycles of destruction and re-creation, and their calendar stone embodies this idea. At the center of the Aztec Calendar Stone (**fig. 3.26**) is a face of the sun god representing the present world, surrounded by four rectangular compartments that each represent one previous incarnation of the world. The whole stone is round, symbolizing the circular nature of time.

3.27 Sassetta. *The Meeting of Saint Anthony and Saint Paul.* c.1440. Tempera on panel. 18⁵⁄₁₆″ × 13⅛″.
The National Gallery of Art, Washington. 1939.1.293.(404). Samuel H. Kress Collection.

3.26 Aztec Calendar Stone. 1479. Diameter 141″.
National Anthropological Museum, Mexico.

The Judeo-Christian tradition of Western culture teaches that time is linear—continuously moving forward. The fifteenth-century painter Sassetta implied the passage of time in his painted narration *The Meeting of Saint Anthony and Saint Paul* (**fig. 3.27**). The painting depicts key moments during Saint Anthony's progression through time and space, including the start of his journey in the city, which is barely visible behind the trees at the top center. He first comes into view as he approaches the wilderness in the upper left; we next see him encountering the centaur at upper right; finally, he emerges into the clearing in the foreground, where he meets Saint Paul. The road on which he travels implies continuous forward movement in time.

Comics also generally express a linear conception of time, as we read the frames from top to bottom and left to right. In this early strip (**fig. 3.28**), the main character Krazy Kat appears in a movie as a singer and is rewarded with a thrown brick.

In both film and television, the impression of time need not be linear but can be manipulated so that past, present, and future are intermixed, and events that occur too quickly or too slowly to be perceived can be made visible by slowing them down or speeding them up. The impression of time can thus be compressed, expanded, run backward, and rerun. Contemporary music videos often present widely disparate moments of time in quick succession, as if time moves in a series of sudden jumps of unpredictable length. This creates a feeling of disjunction from the passage of clock time.

While most movies compress time to varying degrees, Christian Marclay in 2010 created a riveting meditation on time that actually passes in real time. His video *The Clock* (**fig. 3.29**) lasts 24 hours, and is assembled from thousands of film clips in which characters look at their watches or discuss what time it is. The snippets are perfectly coordinated to the time of day, so that viewers will see dozens of film clips of clocks and watches, all registering the correct time. In *The Clock* we see time pass, but through a dizzying variety of moments captured from jarringly unpredictable scraps pulled from the entire history of film.

3.28 Gilbert Herriman. *Krazy Kat*. October, 1916. Newspaper comic strip.

3.29 Christian Marclay. *The Clock*. 2010. Single-channel video with stereo sound. 24 hours, looped. Installation view.

Implied Motion

To give lifelike feeling, artists often search for ways to create a sense of movement. Sometimes movement itself is the subject or a central quality of the subject. An appealing depiction of movement, the dancing Krishna (**fig. 3.30**) portrays the Hindu god as a playful child who just stole

3.30 Dancing Krishna. Tamil Nadu, South India. Chola dynasty. c.1300. Bronze. Height 23⅝″.

Honolulu Museum of Art. Partial gift of Mr. and Mrs. Christian H. Aall; partial purchase, The Jhamandas Watumull Family Fund, 1997. (86401) Photograph by Shuzo Uemoto.

his mother's butter supply and now dances with glee. The cast-bronze medium provides the necessary strength to hold the dynamic pose as the energy-radiating figure stands on one foot, counterbalancing arms, legs, and torso.

Artists of the Futurist movement in the early twentieth century found innovative ways to depict motion and speed, which they regarded as the most important new subjects for art. Umberto Boccioni made many drawings of racing cyclists before painting *Dynamism of a Cyclist* (**fig. 3.31**). The curving lines near the center describe a cyclist hunched over the machine as it hurtles from right to left. The inclination and angle of the straight lines implies speed, just as the dabs of color suggest our blurred vision as we watch the cyclist sail by. Rather than capturing a frozen moment, the artist rendered the dynamism of the moving air and straining muscles that power the passing bicycle.

Contemporary artist Jenny Holzer made clever use of implied motion in an untitled work (**fig. 3.32**), in which she installed light boards on the inner edge of the spiral ramp in the Guggenheim Museum in New York. These boards

3.31 Umberto Boccioni. *Dynamism of a Cyclist.*

Milan. Private Collection. © 2018. Photograph: Scala, Florence.

are commonly used for advertising, but she populated this extended helix with sayings of her own invention. The sayings seem to progress down the ramp in a continuous flow, but in reality the lights go on and off only at carefully programmed intervals. In this welter of constantly shifting slogans, Holzer hoped to show how the mass media bombard us with input.

Actual Motion

Before the advent of electric motors, artists created moving sculpture by harnessing the forces of wind and water. Fountains, kites, banners, and flags have been popular since ancient times.

Alexander Calder's mobiles, such as his large work in the National Gallery (**fig. 3.33**) in Washington, D.C., rely on air movement to perform their subtle dances. As viewers enter and leave the galleries of the East Building, the sculpture slowly moves in space. Calder, a leading inventor of **kinetic art**, or art that moves, was one of the first twentieth-century artists who made actual motion a major feature of their art.

3.32 Jenny Holzer. *Untitled (Selections from Truisms, Inflammatory Essays, The Living Series, The Survival Series, Under a Rock, Laments, and Child Text).* 1989. Extended helical tricolor L.E.D. electronic display signboard. Site-specific dimensions: height 16½″, length 162′.

Solomon R. Guggenheim Museum, New York. Partial gift of the artist, 1989; Gift, Jay Chiat, 1995; and purchased with funds contributed by the International Director's Council and Executive Members: Eli Broad, Elaine Terner Cooper, Ronnie Heyman, Dakis Joannou, Peter Norton, Inge Rodenstock, and Thomas Walther, 1996. 89.3626 © 2018 Jenny Holzer, member Artists Rights Society (ARS), New York.

3.33 Alexander Calder. *Untitled.* 1972. Aluminum and steel. Overall: 358⅜″ × 911⅜″.

National Gallery of Art, Washington. 1977.76.1. Gift of the Collectors Committee. © 2018 Calder Foundation, New York/Artists Rights Society (ARS), New York.

Light

Our eyes are light-sensing instruments. Everything we see is made visible by the radiant energy we call light. Sunlight, or natural light, although perceived as white or clear, actually contains all the colors of light that make up the visible part of the electromagnetic spectrum. Light can be directed, reflected, refracted, diffracted, or diffused. The source, color, intensity, and direction of light greatly affect the way things appear; as light changes, surfaces illuminated by it also appear to change.

Seeing Light

The way light falls on a subject powerfully influences how we see it. A simple shift in the direction of light dramatically changes the way we perceive the sculpture of Abraham Lincoln (**fig. 3.34**) by Daniel Chester French. When the monumental figure was first installed in the Lincoln Memorial in Washington, D.C., the sculptor was disturbed by the lighting. Sunlight reflected off the floor (left) made Lincoln seem like a frightened man. The problem was corrected by placing spotlights in the ceiling above the statue (right). This made him seem decisive and thoughtful. Because the spotlights are stronger than the natural light reflected from the white marble floor, they illuminate the figure with the kind of overhead light that creates an entirely different impression. Rendering mass or solid form as revealed by light is a predominantly Western preoccupation that began with Italian artists in the fifteenth century.

Most of us have some experience in managing light if we take pictures outdoors: Light coming from a source directly in front of or behind objects seems to flatten three-dimensional form and emphasize shape. Light from above or from the side, and slightly in front, most clearly reveals the form of objects in space.

In the terminology of art, **value** (also called *tone*) refers to the relative lightness and darkness of surfaces. Value ranges from white through various grays to black. Subtle relationships between light and dark tones determine how things look. To suggest the way light reveals form, artists use changes in value. A gradual shift from lighter to darker values can give the illusion of a curving surface, while an abrupt change in value usually indicates an abrupt change in surface direction.

Implied Light

The diagram Dark/Light Relationships (**fig. 3.35**) shows that we perceive value as a relationship rather than an isolated form: The gray bar has the same gray value over its entire length, yet it appears to change from one end to the other as the value of the background changes.

When François Bonvin sketched his *Self-Portrait* (**fig. 3.36**) in black chalk, he set himself a challenge. He posed in a dark room with only one light source, so that all the values from light to dark would fall on his face. The brightest part is at the upper right corner of his forehead, where he left no marks on the paper. The darkest spot is at his ear on the left. Between these two zones, his charcoal strokes grew ever denser across his forehead and cheek. This technique of shading from light to dark is called **chiaroscuro**, from the Italian *chiaro* for light and *oscuro* for dark. This technique makes it possible to create the illusion that figures and objects depicted on a flat surface have roundness and bulk.

3.34 Daniel Chester French. Lincoln Memorial (detail). 1911–22. Historical professional composite photograph (1922) of full-sized plaster model of head (1917–18). 50½″ tall.
Far left: As originally lit by daylight.
Left: With the addition of artifical light.
Chapin Library, Williams College; gift of the National Trust for Historic Preservation Chesterwood Archive. Photographer: De Witt Ward.

3.35 Dark/Light Relationships. Value scale compared to uniform middle gray.

Paul Chan uses light from a digital projector to display his haunting creations (**fig. 3.37**). For his series of seven works called *The 7 ~~Lights~~*, he installed the projector at various angles so that it sent an irregular window of light onto the floor or wall of the gallery space. Over each work's 14-minute duration, a bewildering variety of objects seems to tumble or glide or fall through the projected field of light. We see shadows of all kinds of things, from pets to people, from luggage to locomotives. These shadows are "light that has been struck out," said the artist, and thus the word Lights of the title has been struck through. It looks as if we are witnessing some silent catastrophe, as the laws of gravity are suspended and everything has come loose from its moorings.

3.36 François Bonvin. *Self-Portrait*. 1846-47. Fabricated black chalk with scratching. 13¾₆″ × 9⅞₆″.
The J. Paul Getty Museum, Los Angeles.

Light as a Medium

Some contemporary artists use artificial light as their medium. They enjoy using light because it gives pure, intense colors that radiate into the viewer's space. Others who use light are drawn to the idea of making electric power into art.

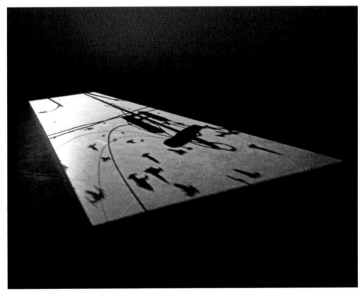

3.37 Paul Chan. *1st ~~Light~~*. 2005. Digital video projection. 14 minutes.
Courtesy of the artist and Greene Naftali, New York. Photograph: Jean Vong.

3.38 Keith Sonnier. *Motordom.* 2004. Light installation at Caltrans District 7.

Photograph: Roland Halbe © 2018 Keith Sonnier/Artists Rights Society (ARS), New York.

Keith Sonnier used the intense colors provided by light when he placed an array of neon tubes in the outdoor lobby of a new government building in Los Angeles. He called the work *Motordom* (**fig. 3.38**), to express the reality of car culture that Southern Californians live with. The neon tubes slowly flicker in a pattern that repeats every five minutes, as if tail lights are passing along the sides of the walls and around the lobby. At different moments, the quality and color of light influence the volume that viewers perceive. Because the light seems to shape the surrounding space, viewers do more than merely look at the work; they enter it. The agency that commissioned the building operates the state's roads and bridges, making *Motordom* particularly appropriate for that space (see *Keith Sonnier: Turning Light into Art*, opposite).

Color

A component of light, color affects us directly by modifying our thoughts, moods, actions, and even our health. Psychologists, as well as designers of schools, offices, hospitals, and prisons, understand that colors can affect work habits and mental conditions. People surrounded by expanses of solid orange or red for long periods often experience nervousness and raised blood pressure. In contrast, some blues have a calming effect, causing blood pressure, pulse, and activity rates to drop to below normal levels.

Dressing according to our color preferences is one way we express ourselves. Designers of everything from clothing and cars to housewares and interiors recognize the importance of individual color preferences, and they spend considerable time and expense determining the colors of their products.

Most cultures use color according to established customs. Leonardo da Vinci was influenced by earlier European traditions when he wrote, "We shall set down for white the representative of light, without which no color can be seen; yellow for earth; green for water; blue for air; red for fire; and black for total darkness."[2] Between the fifteenth and nineteenth centuries, color was used in limited, traditional ways in Western art, as Leonardo indicated. In traditional painting in North India, however, flat areas of color are used to suggest certain moods, such as red for anger and blue for sexual passion. A modern artist may paint the sky or the ground with a bright shade that relates not to the appearance of the area, but to the feeling appropriate to the work. In Austrian slang, yellow describes a state of envy or jealousy, while blue means intoxicated.

Keith Sonnier: Turning Light into Art

3.39 Keith Sonnier. 2012.
Photograph by Jason Schmidt, courtesy of the artist and Pace Gallery.

It may have been the electric fences in the region of rural Louisiana where Keith Sonnier (b. 1941) grew up that led to his fascination with electricity. He told an interviewer, "When I was a kid in the country, we had electric fences and we were always getting shocked. We loved getting shocked—you know, there are very few thrills out in the country."[3] Sonnier's early interest in electricity evolved into pioneering artworks that use light as a medium.

After studies at Rutgers University, Sonnier settled in New York in the late 1960s, a time when many artists were abandoning oil painting, some moving to video, others toward large-scale sculpture. He recalled, "Our type of work was somehow counterculture. We chose materials that were not 'high art'; we weren't working in bronze, or paint, even. We were using materials that weren't previously considered art materials. They were deliberately chosen to psychologically evoke certain kinds of feelings."[4]

Sonnier wanted to create works that involved the viewer more directly than mere looking at a work on the wall. "When I began to work in light, I began to think about an artwork being interactive with an audience, meaning how it affects the audience physically when they look at an artwork.... When you stand in front of the work, you are in the work, and I wanted artworks that forced the audience to be a part of the work.... One is physically and psychologically cut by the materials that you move through."[5]

Colored light tends to move outward from its source, projecting into the viewer's space; thus it can seem to take on volume. As Sonnier has explained: "When color becomes that intense and physical, you begin to think of color as a material. There is a density to color, and color becomes a volume in fact."[6] We see this effect with *Motordom* (**fig. 3.38**), in which light invades the space of the outdoor lobby, and it changes as the lights flicker.

In his light works for galleries, Sonnier generally includes the transformers and wiring in the work, so that the electric sources remain obvious. We see this in his more recent work *Hartebeest* (**fig. 3.40**). This work has a human scale, confronting viewers with an electrical, stick-figured person with huge blue horns. The upward sweep of blue lights is based on drawings that Sonnier made during a trip to Africa, where he saw wildebeest and other long-horned animals.

Sonnier's use of neon is related only to its color properties, not to its possible uses in lettered signs. He said, "I love light in my work but I was never influenced by neon signage in itself, rather its effect on nature and architecture."[7] His pieces give us a sense of what light can do in art, as it both illuminates the surroundings and creates colored volumes in space.

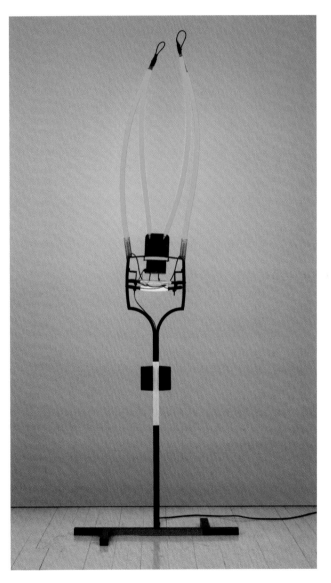

3.40 Keith Sonnier. *Hartebeest*. 2008. Steel, neon paint, neoprene, rubber, and transformer. 10´2″ × 3´6″ × 1´10″.
Photography by Genevieve Hanson, courtesy Pace Gallery.
© 2018 Keith Sonnier/Artists Rights Society (ARS), New York.

The Physics of Color

What we call "color" is the effect on our eyes of light waves of differing wavelengths or frequencies. When combined, these light waves make white light, the visible part of the spectrum. Individual colors are components of white light.

The phenomenon of color is a paradox: color exists only in light, but light itself seems colorless to the human eye. Objects that appear to have color are merely reflecting the colors that are present in the light that illuminates them. In 1666, British scientist Isaac Newton discovered that white light is composed of all the colors of the spectrum. He found that when the white light of the sun passes through a glass prism, it is separated into the bands of color that make up the visible spectrum, as shown in the diagram White Light Refracted by a Prism (**fig. 3.41**).

Because each color has a different wavelength, each travels through the glass of the prism at a different speed. Red, which has the longest wavelength, travels more rapidly through the glass than blue, which has a shorter wavelength. A rainbow results when sunlight is refracted and dispersed by the spherical forms of raindrops, producing a combined effect like that of the glass prism. In both cases, the sequence of spectral colors is: red, orange, yellow, green, blue, and violet.

Pigments and Light

Our common experience with color is provided by light reflected from pigmented surfaces. Therefore, the emphasis in the following discussion is on pigment color rather than on color coming from light alone.

When light illuminates an object, some of the light is absorbed by the surface of the object and some is reflected. The color that appears to our eyes as that of the object (called **local color**) is determined by the wavelengths of light being reflected. Thus, a red surface illuminated by white light (full-spectrum light) appears red because it reflects mostly red light and absorbs the rest of the spectrum. A green surface absorbs most of the spectrum except green, which it reflects, and so on with all the hues.

When all the wavelengths of light are absorbed by a surface, the object appears black; when all the wavelengths are reflected, the surface appears white. Black and white are not true colors: white, black, and their combination, gray, are **achromatic** (without the property of hue) and are often referred to as **neutrals**.

Each of the millions of colors human beings can distinguish is identifiable in terms of just three variables: hue, value, and intensity.

- **Hue** refers to a particular wavelength of spectral color to which we give a name. Colors of the spectrum—such as yellow and green—are called hues.
- **Value** refers to relative lightness or darkness from white through grays to black. Pure hues vary in value. On the color chart shown in The Three Dimensions of Color (**fig. 3.42**), hues in their purest state are at their usual values. Pure yellow is the lightest of hues; violet is the darkest. Red and green are middle-value hues. Black and white pigments can be important ingredients in changing color values. Adding black to a hue produces a **shade** of that hue. For example, when black is added to orange, the result is a brown; when black is mixed with red, the result is maroon. White added to a hue produces a **tint**. Lavender is a tint of violet; pink is a tint of red.
- **Intensity**, also called saturation, refers to the purity of a hue or color. A pure hue is the most intense form of a given color; it is the hue at its highest saturation, in its brightest form. With pigment, if white, black, gray, or another hue is added to a pure hue, its intensity diminishes and the color is thereby dulled.

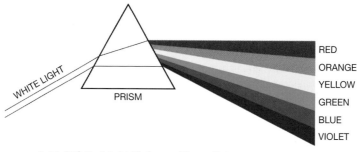

3.41 White Light Refracted by a Prism.

3.42 The Three Dimensions of Color.

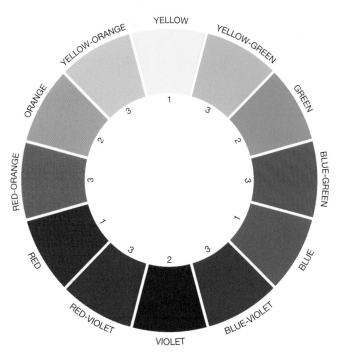

a. Hue—the color wheel.

b. Value—from light to dark. Value scale from white to black.

+WHITE　　　　PURE HUE　　　　+BLACK

c. Value variation in red.

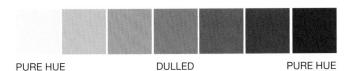

PURE HUE　　　　DULLED　　　　PURE HUE

d. Intensity—from bright to dull.

Most people are familiar with the three pigment primaries: red, yellow, and blue (**fig. 3.43**). Mixtures of these are what we usually experience as local color when we look at a leaf, a wall, or a painting. When the pigments of different hues are mixed together, the mixture appears duller

3.43 Pigment Primaries: Subtractive Color Mixture.

and darker because pigments absorb more and more light as their absorptive qualities combine. For this reason, pigment mixtures are called **subtractive color mixtures**. Mixing red, blue, and yellow will produce a dark gray, almost black, depending on the proportions and the type of pigment used.

A lesser-known triad is the three light primaries: red-orange, green, and blue-violet (**fig. 3.44**). These are actual electric light colors that produce white light when combined; they are the colors that our televisions and computer screens use, along with certain light artists such as Sonnier (see fig. 3.38). Such mixtures are called **additive color mixtures**. Combinations of the light primaries produce lighter colors: Red and green light, when mixed, produce yellow light.

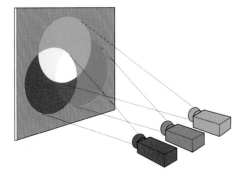

3.44 Light Primaries: Additive Color Mixture.

Color Wheel

The color wheel (see fig. 3.42) is a twentieth-century version of a concept first developed in the seventeenth century by Isaac Newton. After Newton discovered the spectrum, he found that both ends could be combined into the hue red-violet, making the color wheel concept possible. Numerous color systems have followed since that time, each with its own basic hues. The color wheel shown here is based on twelve pure hues and can be divided into the following groups:

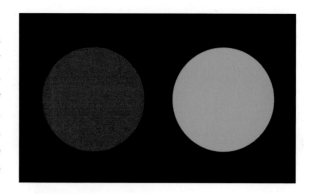

3.45 Warm/Cool Colors.

3.46 Color Printing.

a. Yellow.

b. Magenta.

c. Yellow and magenta.

d. Cyan.

e. Yellow, magenta, and cyan.

f. Black.

g. Yellow, magenta, cyan, and black.

h. Color printing detail of Sandro Botticelli's *Birth of Venus*.

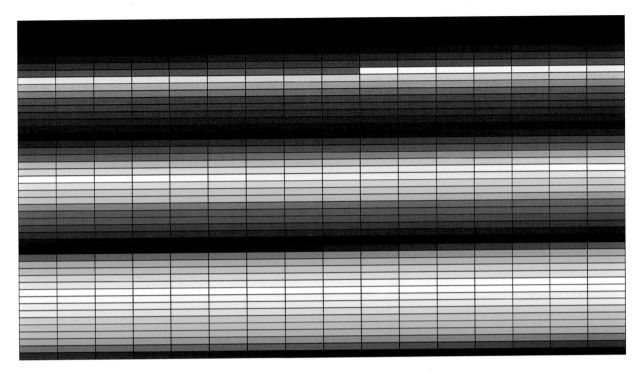

3.47 Red, Blue, and Green color palettes from Gimp, an image-editing application.

- **Primary hues** (see 1 on the color wheel): red, yellow, and blue. These pigment hues cannot be produced by an intermixing of other hues. They are also referred to as primary colors.
- **Secondary hues** (see 2 on the color wheel): orange, green, and violet. The mixture of two primaries produces a secondary hue. Secondaries are placed on the color wheel between the two primaries of which they are composed.
- **Tertiary hues** (see 3 on the color wheel): red-orange, yellow-orange, yellow-green, blue-green, blue-violet, and red-violet. Each tertiary is located between the primary and the secondary of which it is composed.

The blue-green side of the wheel seems **cool** in psychological temperature, and the red-orange side **warm**. Yellow-green and red-violet are the poles dividing the color wheel into warm and cool hues. The difference between warm and cool colors may come chiefly from association. Relative warm and cool differences can be seen in any combination of hues. Color affects our feelings about size and distance as well as temperature. Cool colors appear to contract and recede; warm colors appear to expand and advance, as in the Warm/Cool Colors diagram (**fig. 3.45**).

The most vibrant color sensations come not from blending colors, but from placing tiny dots of purer hues next to each other so that they blend in the eye and the mind. This is what happens in modern four-color printing, in which tiny dots of ink in the printer's three primary colors—magenta (a bluish red), yellow, and cyan (a greenish blue)—are printed together in various amounts with black ink on white paper to achieve the effect of full color. For example, in the color printing separations and the enlarged detail of Botticelli's *Birth of Venus* (**fig. 3.46h**), the eye perceives subtle blends as it optically mixes tiny dots of intense color.

Today, many computer users employ color pickers or on-line palettes (**fig. 3.47**) in the way that painters use the color wheel. In this example, we see the various shades and tints of the light primaries, which are arrived at by adding small increments of white or black to the pure hue. Digital designers and some computer artists choose colors by merely clicking on a region; they can combine and further shade their choices using sliders. Because computer screens use the light primaries rather than the pigment primaries, their color mixtures retain a high level of brightness; this effect is visible with every Web page or phone application that we open.

Color Schemes

Color groupings that provide distinct color harmonies are called **color schemes**.

Monochromatic color schemes are based on variations in the value and intensity of a single hue. In a monochromatic scheme, a pure hue is used alone with black and/or white, or mixed with black and/or white. Artists may choose a monochromatic color scheme because they feel that a certain color represents a mood. Other artists adopt the monochromatic color scheme as a kind of personal discipline, in order to experiment with the various gradations of a relatively narrow band of the spectrum. An extreme example of such an artist is Mary Corse, who for many years has been making only white paintings. She creates them by embedding tiny spheres of glass into their surfaces in patterned zones. These white areas reflect surrounding light, and even change as the viewer walks past them. In *Untitled (White multiple inner band, beveled)* (**fig. 3.48**), the spheres form four vertical stripes.

Analogous color schemes are based on colors adjacent to one another on the color wheel, each containing the same pure hue, such as a color scheme of yellow-green, green, and blue-green. Tints and shades of each analogous hue may be used to add variations to such color schemes.

Jennifer Bartlett often uses analogous colors in her work. Her large oil painting *Path* (**fig. 3.49**) is a two-panel work that depicts a stone path from above. Most of the colors in this work come from the blue, blue-violet, and blue-green sectors of the color wheel. Because these sectors all border each other on the color wheel, the colors seem to harmonize, as analogous colors usually do.

Complementary color schemes emphasize two hues on opposite sides of the color wheel, such as red and green. When actually mixed together as pigments in almost equal amounts, complementary hues form neutral grays, but when placed side by side as pure hues, they contrast strongly and intensify each other. Such sharp contrasts are often used in football jerseys, for example, in order to highlight the players' numbers and to contrast opposing teams. Complementary hues red-orange and blue-green tend to "vibrate" more when placed next to each other than do other

3.48 Mary Corse. *Untitled (White multiple inner band, beveled).* 2009. Glass microspheres in acrylic on canvas. 90″ × 60″.
Courtesy of Lehmann Maupin Gallery.

3.49 Jennifer Bartlett. *Path*. 2011. Oil on canvas, diptych. Each panel: 60″ × 60″. Overall: 60″ × 120″
© Jennifer Bartlett. Courtesy Paula Cooper Gallery, New York.

complements because they are close in value and produce a strong warm/cool contrast. The complements yellow and violet provide the strongest value contrast possible with pure hues. The complement of a primary is the opposite secondary, which is obtained by mixing the other two primaries. For example, the complement of blue is orange.

Keith Haring often used complementary color schemes for their clashing effects. His untitled work (**fig. 3.50**) is painted in only green and red, which are opposites on the color wheel. The sheer intensity of these contrasting colors makes the image seem to vibrate. This is because our eyes generally dart across the surface of whatever we are looking at, rather than focusing for an extended period on one spot. Each of these momentary glances loads the eye with one color before moving on to the next, which loads an opposite color. Haring began his career making graffiti, where such visual impact is prized.

These examples provide only a basic foundation in color theory. In fact, most artists work intuitively with color harmonies more complex than the schemes described above.

3.50 Keith Haring. *Untitled (Square head with three eyes)*. 1982. Oil on canvas.
© Keith Haring Foundation.

3.51 Meret Oppenheim. *Object (Breakfast in Fur)*. 1936. Fur-covered cup, saucer, and spoon. Saucer diameter 9⅜″.

Museum of Modern Art (MoMA) Purchase. Acc. n.: 130.1946.a-c. © 2018 Digital image, The Museum of Modern Art, New York/Scala, Florence. © 2018 Artists Rights Society (ARS), New York/ProLitteris, Zurich.

Texture

In the visual arts, **texture** refers to the tactile qualities of surfaces, or to the visual representation of those qualities. As children, we explored our surroundings by touching everything within reach, and we learned to equate the feel with the look of surfaces. As adults we know how most things feel, yet we still enjoy the pleasures that touching gives; we delight in running our hands over the fur of a pet or the smooth surface of polished wood.

All surfaces have textures that can be experienced by touching or through visual suggestion. Textures are categorized as either actual or simulated. Actual textures are those we can feel by touching, such as polished marble, wood, sand, or swirls of thick paint. Simulated (or implied) textures are those created to look like something other than paint on a flat surface. A painter can simulate textures that look like real fur or wood, but to the touch would feel like smooth paint. Artists can also invent actual or simulated textures. We can appreciate most textures even when we are not permitted to touch them, because we know, from experience, how they would feel.

3.52 Man's Bodice. Native American, Northern Plains. 1835. Buckskin, buffalo hide, deer fur, beads, porcupine quills. Length 27½″; width 21¼″.

Plains Indian Museum, Buffalo Bill Center of the West, Cody, Wyoming, USA. Chandler-Pohrt collection. Gift of Mr. William D. Weiss. NA.202.348

3.53 Vincent van Gogh. *The Starry Night*. 1889. Oil on canvas. 29″ × 36¼″.

The Museum of Modern Art, New York. Acquired through the Lillie P. Bliss Bequest. (472.1941). © 2018. Digital image, The Museum of Modern Art, New York/Scala, Florence.

Meret Oppenheim's fur-covered teacup, titled *Object* (**fig. 3.51**), is a rude tactile experience. She presented an intentionally contradictory object designed to evoke strong responses ranging from revulsion to amusement. The actual texture of fur is pleasant, as is the smooth texture of a teacup, but the idea of touching one's tongue to fur rather than porcelain is startling.

Sculptors and architects make use of the actual textures of their materials and the relationships between them. They can also create new textures in the finishing of surfaces. For example, Giacometti's *Man Pointing* (see fig. 3.14) uses eroded surfaces to heighten emotional impact.

Combining textures in one object is typical of the art of many traditional Native American cultures. In the man's bodice pictured here (**fig. 3.52**), the basic fabric is deerskin, painted in the upper part, with sleeves of buffalo hide and fringes made from those materials. The round motif at the center is crafted from porcupine quills dyed in three colors in a nonrepresentational design. Beads decorate the shoulder stripes and sleeves. These varied textures make our experience of this object multisensory.

A painter may develop a rich tactile surface as an expressive device. We can see actual texture on a two-dimensional surface in the detail of Vincent van Gogh's *The Starry Night* (**fig. 3.53**). With brushstrokes of thick paint, Van Gogh invented textural rhythms that convey his intense feelings. Such texture is a vivid sign of the artist's presence.

3.54 Alê Abreu. *Boy and the World*. Movie still. 2013.
Filme de Papel, producer. Collection Christophel/Alamy Stock Photo.

Today's digital animators have tools at their disposal to simulate a wide variety of textures that we see in video games and animated features. In *Boy and the World* (**fig. 3.54**), animator Alê Abreu tells a contemporary story of a rural Brazilian family on a failing farm. After the father is forced to migrate to the city for industrial work, the boy follows in search of him. Much of the movie shows the texture of hand-drawn lines, but as the boy approaches the urban center, Abreu begins to incorporate more digital rendering to help capture the texture of industrial surfaces such as cars, clothing, and waste material. The movie's deft blending of media and at times stunning beauty earned it an Academy Award nomination.

In this chapter we have explored how artists use some of the expressive qualities of line, shape, mass, space, time, motion, light, color, and texture in their works. As we have seen, not all these visual elements are present in every artwork, but each can be a valuable tool for conveying ideas, emotions, and atmosphere—creating art that can inform, inspire, and delight us.

KEY TERMS

achromatic – having no color (or hue)

additive color mixture – the mixture of colored light

analogous colors – colors that are adjacent to each other on the color wheel, such as blue, blue-green, and green

atmospheric (aerial) perspective – a type of perspective in which the illusion of depth is created by changing color, value, and detail

biomorphic shape – a shape in a work of art that resembles a living organism or an organic shape

chiaroscuro – the gradations of light and dark values in two-dimensional images

closed form – a self-contained or explicitly limited form that has a resolved balance of tensions

color scheme – a set of colors chosen for a work of art in order to promote a specific mood or effect

complementary colors – two hues directly opposite one another on a color wheel, such as red and green, that, when mixed together in proper proportions, produce a neutral gray

cool colors – colors whose relative visual temperatures make them seem cool

eye level – in linear perspective, the presumed height of the artist's eyes; this becomes the presumed height of the viewer standing in front of the finished work

figure – separate shape(s) that seem to lie above a background or ground

geometric shape – any shape enclosed by square or straight or perfectly circular lines

ground – the background in a two-dimensional work; the area around and between figure(s)

horizon line – in linear perspective, the implied or actual line or edge placed on a two-dimensional surface to represent the place in nature where the sky meets the horizontal land or water plane

hue – that property of a color identifying a specific, named wavelength of light such as green, red, blue, and so on

implied line – a line in a composition that is not actually drawn; it may be a sight line of a figure in a composition, or a line along which two shapes align with each other

intensity – the relative purity or saturation of a hue (color), on a scale from bright (pure) to dull

kinetic art – art that incorporates actual movement as part of the design

line – a long, narrow mark; usually made by drawing with a tool or a brush, but may be created by placing two forms next to each other

linear perspective – a system of perspective in which parallel lines appear to converge as they recede into the distance, meeting at a vanishing point on the horizon

local color – the color of an object as we experience it, without shadows or reflections

mass – the physical bulk of a solid body of material

monochromatic – a color scheme limited to variations of one hue

negative shape – a background or ground shape seen in relation to foreground or figure shapes

neutrals – not associated with any single hue; can be made by mixing complementary hues

one-point perspective – a perspective system in which all parallel lines converge at a single vanishing point

open form – a form whose exterior is irregular and which has a sense of growth, change, or unresolved tension

organic shape – an irregular, non-geometric shape

perspective – a system for creating an illusion of depth or three-dimensional space on a two-dimensional surface

picture plane – the two-dimensional picture surface

positive shape – a figure or foreground shape, as opposed to a negative ground or background shape

primary hues (also referred to as primary colors) – red, yellow, and blue; these pigment hues cannot be produced by an intermixing of other hues

secondary hues – orange, green, and violet; the mixture of two primaries produces a secondary hue

shade – a hue with black added

shape – a two-dimensional or implied two-dimensional area defined by line or changes in color

subtractive color mixture – mixture of colored pigments in the forms of paints, inks, pastels, and so on

tertiary hues – red-orange, yellow-orange, yellow-green, blue-green, blue-violet, and red-violet; each hue is located between the primary and the secondary hue of which it is composed

texture – the tactile qualities of surfaces, or the visual representation of those qualities

three-dimensional – having height, width, and depth

tint – a hue with white added

two-dimensional – having the dimensions of height and width only

two-point perspective – a perspective system in which two sets of parallel lines appear to converge at two points on the horizon line

value – the relative lightness and darkness of surfaces

vanishing point – in linear perspective, the point on the horizon line at which lines or edges that are parallel appear to converge

vantage point – the position from which the viewer looks at an object or visual field

vertical placement – a method for suggesting the third dimension of depth in a two-dimensional work by placing an object above another in the composition

volume – the space enclosed or filled by a three-dimensional object or figure

warm colors – colors whose relative visual temperature makes them seem warm

THE PRINCIPLES OF DESIGN

LEARNING OBJECTIVES

4.1   Define the concepts of unity and variety in works of art.

4.2   Differentiate between symmetrical and asymmetrical design.

4.3   Describe how artists use emphasis and subordination to direct the attention of viewers.

4.4   Identify directional forces in a work of art and explain how artists use them.

4.5   Discuss how artists use repetition and rhythm in their designs.

4.6   Explain how scale and proportion affect our interpretation of works of art.

4.7   Illustrate how Matisse used the principles of design to change the composition of *Large Reclining Nude*.

In 1928, American artist Charles Demuth set out to make a portrait of his friend the poet William Carlos Williams. Demuth visualized a poem that Williams wrote after seeing a fire engine with the numeral 5 on its side, racing through city streets on a rainy night with its siren blaring. He titled the painting *I Saw the Figure 5 in Gold* (**fig. 4.1**). To Demuth, that moment seemed to both symbolize the poet and provide a compelling subject for an artwork.

The process of creation involves choosing which visual elements to use. It also involves organizing those elements so that the final arrangement best conveys the artist's intention. In two-dimensional arts, such as painting and photography, this organization of the visual elements is usually called **composition**, but a broader term that applies to the entire range of visual arts is **design**. The word *design* indicates both the process of organizing visual elements and the product of that process.

In creating *I Saw the Figure 5 in Gold*, Demuth used the important principles of design. He used the large numeral 5 to *unify* the composition, bringing together a *variety* of colors. Although the work is not symmetrical, it seems *balanced*. The other inscriptions on the work, such as "Bill" at the top for William Carlos Williams, are *subordinated* to the central figure 5, which the artist *emphasized*. The diagonals

4.1   Charles Demuth. *I Saw the Figure 5 in Gold*. 1928. Oil on cardboard. 35½″ × 30″.
The Metropolitan Museum of Art, Alfred Stieglitz Collection, 1949 (49.59.1).

in the work suggest slanting raindrops, establishing a strong *directional force*. The numeral 5 is repeated in a visual *rhythm* that suggests the approach and passing of the truck. We see the numeral in various *scales* of size, though each numeral shows the same *proportions*.

Demuth thus used in this work the most important principles of design:

> unity and variety
> balance
> emphasis and subordination
> directional forces
> repetition and rhythm
> scale and proportion

Artists do not use all the design principles in every work of art. But in this chapter we will explore each one in more detail because they provide an understanding not only of how artists work, but also of how design affects us.

Unity and Variety

Unity and **variety** are complementary concerns lying at opposite ends of a spectrum. Unity is the appearance or condition of oneness. A cube painted all one color has absolute unity without variety. Very few artworks are absolutely unified into one homogeneous thing. John McCracken came close when he created this untitled work (**fig. 4.2**). Its yellow color is unvaried throughout. There is some variety in the difference between its height and its thickness, but overall this work is an extreme example of unity. It could seem boring for that reason. Standing just over 8 feet tall, it leans quietly and anonymously against the wall, as the artist specified.

Variety, on the other hand, provides diversity. Variety acts to counter unity. The more variety we see in an artwork, the less orderly it seems. An example of extreme variety is the outdoor installation by Sarah Sze, *Triple Point* (**fig. 4.3**). She used stones, aluminum tubing, and rectangular panels across the façade of the building, on the ground before it, and in the air above it. At first it looks varied enough to seem completely chaotic. Yet the artist introduced orderly elements. Note the circle of fragments in the foreground. The aluminum tubes form diagonals that lead the eye toward the top of the building. Oval rocks and rectangular panels punctuate the design. The work seems to have been created by improvisation, a sense that is important to the artist.

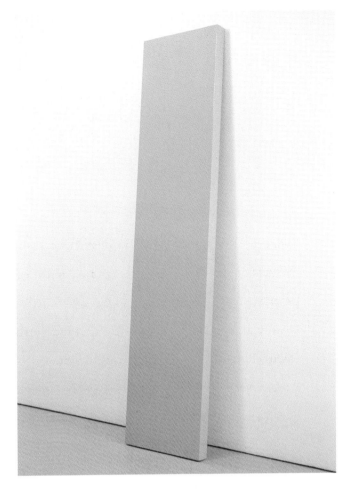

4.2 John McCracken. *Untitled*. 1970. Polyester resin, fiberglass, and plywood. 96″ × 22″ × 3″.
© The Estate of John McCracken. Courtesy of David Zwirner, New York/London.

4.3 Sarah Sze. *Triple Point (Gleaner)*. 2013 Photograph of rock printed on Tyvek, trees, moss, rocks, aluminum, wood, steel, bricks, stone, sandbags, outdoor pump, outdoor lights, mixed media. Dimensions variable. Installation in Venice Biennale 2013.
Courtesy of the artist and Tanya Bonakdar Gallery, New York.

4.4   Jacob Lawrence. *Going Home.* 1946. Gouache. 21½″ × 29½″.

Private collection, courtesy of DC Moore Gallery, New York. © 2018 The Jacob and Gwendolyn Knight Lawrence Foundation, Seattle/Artists Rights Society (ARS), New York.

The sameness of too much unity can be boring, and the diversity of uncontrolled variety may be chaotic; most artists strive for a balance between unity and variety that can yield interesting compositions.

In his painting *Going Home* (**fig. 4.4**), Jacob Lawrence balanced unity and variety. He established visual themes with the lines, shapes, and colors of the train seats, figures, and luggage, and then he repeated and varied those themes. Notice the varied repetition in the green chair seats and window shades. As a unifying element, the same red is used in a variety of shapes. The many figures and objects in the complex composition form a unified design through the artist's skillful use of abstraction, theme, and variation. The diagram of this work shows some of its more prominent structural elements.

Lawrence was known for the lively harmony of his distinctive compositions. Although he worked in a manner that may seem unsophisticated, he was always resolving his designs through adjustments of unity and diversity. Lawrence studied other artists' work, and he was influenced by painters who were design problem-solvers. He said, "I like to study the design to see how the artist solves his problems and brings his subjects to the public."[1]

Pieter de Hooch's *Interior of a Dutch House* (**fig. 4.5**) balances unity and variety through different means. The artist enclosed all of the action within one room, which enhances the unity of the composition. It is not overly crowded, and the interactions between the people are relatively easy to understand through their glances and gestures. Furthermore, the artist made liberal use of squares and rectangles in the floor, in the decorations on the rear wall, and in the ceiling. The diagram shows some of the more prominent of these. These rectangles vary in shape, size,

4.5 Pieter de Hooch. *Interior of a Dutch House.* 1658.
Oil on canvas. 29″ × 35″.

Acc.n.: 1734 © 2018. Copyright The National Gallery, London/Scala, Florence.

and orientation, providing variety, but their regular recurrence provides a structure that promotes unity. The rectangles also echo the format of the work as a whole. Unity and variety are thus in harmony here.

Balance

Balance is the achievement of equilibrium, in which acting influences are held in check by opposing forces. We strive for balance in our lives, and may lack peace of mind in its absence. The dynamic process of seeking balance is equally basic in art, and here our instinct for physical balance finds its parallel in a desire for visual balance (although some artists seek lack of balance in their work for one expressive reason or another). Balance may be achieved through either **symmetry** or **asymmetry**.

Symmetrical Balance

Symmetrical balance is the near or exact matching of left and right sides of a three-dimensional form or a two-dimensional composition. Such works have symmetry.

Architects often employ symmetrical balance to give unity and formal grandeur to a building's façade or front side. For example, in 1792 James Hoban won a competition for his *Design for the President's House,* a drawing of a symmetrical, Georgian-style mansion. The central part of the design is united under a triangular pavilion, and the windows are identical and evenly divided on each side. Today, two centuries and several additions later, we know this building as the White House (**fig. 4.6**).

4.6 James Hoban. *Design for the President's House.* 1792.

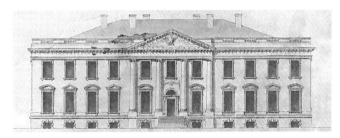

a. Elevation.

Courtesy of the Maryland Historical Society. Item ID # 1976.88.3.

b. The White House. Washington, D.C. Front view. 1997.

Albert de Bruijn/Shutterstock.

Few works of art are perfectly symmetrical, but *Posterity – The Holy Place* (**fig. 4.7**) by Damien Hirst is one. The artist formed it entirely out of butterfly wings (sourced from a farmer who raises them), and it is symmetrical at every level: each butterfly, each unit of the composition, and the work as a whole. It resembles a stained-glass window, but is even more symmetrical than most of those. The stability of symmetry is a useful tool for religious art, which suggests the divine. But the sheer luminosity of *Posterity – The Holy Place* exceeds even that of a stained-glass window because butterfly wings do not depend on direct sunlight to show brilliance. Because the work is made up of so many small parts, the levels of symmetry help to structure the composition.

Asymmetrical Balance

With **asymmetrical balance**, the left and right sides are not the same. Instead, various elements are balanced, according to their size and meaning, around a felt or implied center of gravity. For example, in *Noli Me Tangere* by Lavinia Fontana (**fig. 4.8**), the composition as a whole seems balanced, but

4.7 Damien Hirst. *Posterity – The Holy Place*. 2006. Butterflies and household gloss on canvas. 89⅝″ × 48″.

Courtesy of Gagosian Gallery. Photographed by Prudence Cuming Associates, Inc. © Damien Hirst and Science Ltd. All rights reserved/DACS, London/ARS, NY 2018.

Symmetrical design is useful in architecture because it is easier to comprehend than asymmetry, in which the halves of a composition are not the same. Symmetry imposes a balanced unity, making large, complex buildings comprehensible at a glance. Symmetry connotes permanence and poise. We generally want our symbolically important buildings to seem motionless and stable. All the qualities that make symmetry desirable in architecture make it generally less desirable in sculpture and two-dimensional art. Too much symmetry can be boring. Although artists admire symmetry for its formal qualities, they rarely use it rigidly. Artists usually do not want their work to seem static.

4.8 Lavinia Fontana. *Noli Me Tangere*. 1581. Oil on wood. 47⅜″ × 36⅜″.

Galleria degli Uffizi. Photograph: akg-images/Erich Lessing.

only because dramatic imbalances are held in check. The painting illustrates a New Testament story in which Mary Magdalene went to the empty tomb of Jesus and saw the risen Christ, whom she at first took for the gardener. The story thus requires two people in the foreground, one of them prostrate.

This presents a difficult balancing problem, but Fontana solved it with a few ingenious steps. First, she gave the center of the composition strong weight, with Mary's large figure dressed in warm colors; above Mary is a glow in the sky. These anchor the composition. Christ occupies the right foreground, but he does not disrupt the equilibrium of the whole, because he is balanced by the higher and more massive tomb on the left. The small figure in red just outside the tomb also helps to balance the strong figure of Christ.

If we look at a different version of *Noli Me Tangere* (**fig. 4.9**), we can compare how two artists painting the same subject arrived at balance. In both cases, Mary Magdalene kneels before the newly risen Christ. Titian's version, which was painted about 67 years earlier than Fontana's, shows a more subtle approach, closer to symmetry than the Fontana work, with more delicate balances. Christ outweighs Mary because he is standing, and Titian put yet more weight on that half of the canvas by placing the tree above him. This tree also serves to mark Christ as the more important figure in the encounter. The central group forms an irregular triangle whose three points are Christ's head and foot, and the red tip of Mary's garment. These elements create a great deal of weight on the left half of the work, but Titian balanced it skillfully. Mary's head, left arm, and hand seem to continue the vertical line of the central tree, establishing an axis in the lower portion of the work. On the right side, Titian created balance by giving Mary a red dress, a warm color that advances toward the viewer. The green bush also helps to balance Christ's fleshy body. Above, the artist placed a distant village whose high position and solid masses further counteract the weight of Christ and the tree. The jagged pathway to this village roughly balances the leaning tree with its protruding lower branch. As a final touch, Titian painted the remote landscape in blue, a cool color that recedes, reducing its influence. Titian here shows himself an adept composer of pictorial dynamics; viewers who take a long look at this work can enjoy the effortless quality of good asymmetrical balance.

An extreme case of dynamic balancing is *Jockeys Before the Race* by Edgar Degas (**fig. 4.10**). The artist boldly located the center of gravity on the right. To reinforce it, he drew it in as a pole. At first glance, all our attention is drawn to our extreme right, to the nearest and largest horse. But the solitary circle of the sun in the upper left exerts a strong

fascination. The red cap, the pale pink jacket of the distant jockey, the subtle warm/cool color intersection at the horizon, and the decreasing sizes of the horses all help to move our eyes over to the left portion of the picture, where a barely discernible but very important vertical line directs our attention upward.

In this work a trail of visual cues moves our attention from right to left. If we are sensitive to them, we will perform the act of balancing the painting. If we are not, the painting will seem forever unbalanced. Degas, who was known for his adventurous compositions, relied on the fact that seeing is an active, creative process and not a passive one.

A good way to explore a picture's balance is to imagine it painted differently. Cover the jockey's red cap in the Degas, or mentally remove the small tree below the sun, and you will see a spark of life go out of the painting.

Besides whatever visual balance the creator may seek, works of sculpture and architecture need structural balance or they will not stand up. Mark di Suvero's *Declaration*

4.10 Edgar Degas. *Jockeys Before the Race.* c.1878–79. Oil essence, gouache, and pastel. 42½″ × 29″.

The Barber Institute of Fine Arts, University of Birmingham/ Bridgeman Images.

4.11 Mark di Suvero. *Declaration*. 1999–2001.

© Mark di Suvero, courtesy of the artist and Spacetime C.C.

Through **subordination**, an artist creates neutral areas of lesser interest that keep us from being distracted from the areas of emphasis. We have seen them at work in the paintings we have just examined.

In *Noli Me Tangere* (see fig. 4.9), Titian emphasized the figures by placing them near the center, the strongest location in any visual field. The bodies of both are lighter in color than their immediate surroundings. Their interaction becomes the focal point. In the *Noli Me Tangere* by Fontana (see fig. 4.8), the focal point is less clear. Led by Christ's arm and a vertical above, our eyes naturally go to the center of the work, to Mary's face. This leaves Christ relatively subordinated. There is also a secondary focal point in the empty tomb in the upper left, created by the angel at the center of the dark rectangle and the two figures facing it. In *Jockeys Before the Race* (see fig. 4.10), Degas took a different approach, using size, shape, placement, and color to create areas of emphasis *away* from the center. The sun is a separate focal point created through contrast (it is lighter than the surrounding sky area and the only circle in the painting) and through placement (it is the only shape in that part of the painting). Sky and grass areas, however, are muted in color with almost no detail, so that they are subordinate to, and thus support the areas of emphasis.

(**fig. 4.11**) was erected in 2001 on a spot near the beach in Venice, California. As a work of public art, *Declaration* required a building permit and official structural checks to ensure its safety in earthquakes and tsunamis. The artist used his engineering ability to balance the long V-shaped wings that seem to leap out from the three-legged base. The artist described the work as "a painting in three dimensions with the crane as my paintbrush." Originally intended for a four-month viewing period, the dynamic geometries of *Declaration* have remained on the site ever since.

Emphasis and Subordination

Artists use **emphasis** to draw our attention to an area. If that area is a specific spot or figure, it is called a **focal point**. Position, light-dark **contrast** (the juxtaposition of strongly dissimilar elements), color intensity, and size can all be used to create emphasis.

Directional Forces

As with emphasis and subordination, artists use **directional forces** to influence the way we look at a work of art. Directional forces are paths for the eye to follow, provided by actual or implied lines. Implied directional lines may be suggested by a form's axis, by the imagined connection between similar or adjacent forms, or by the implied continuation of actual lines. Studying directional lines and forces often reveals a work of art's underlying energy and basic visual structure.

Looking at *Jockeys Before the Race* (see fig. 4.10), we find that our attention is pulled to a series of focal points: the horse and jockey at the extreme right, the vertical pole, the red cap, the pink jacket, and the blue-green at the horizon. The dominant directional forces in this work are diagonal. The focal points mentioned above create an implied directional line that runs from right to left and foreground to background. The face of the first jockey is included in this line.

The implied diagonal line created by the bodies of the three receding horses acts as a related directional force. As our eyes follow the recession, encouraged by the attraction of the focal points, we perform the act of balancing the composition by correcting our original attraction to the extreme right.

Just as our physical and visual feelings for balance correspond, so do our physical and visual feelings about directional lines and forces. The direction of lines produces sensations similar to standing still (|), being at rest (—), or being in motion (/). Therefore, a combination of vertical and horizontal lines provides stability. For example, the horizon line in Titian's *Noli Me Tangere* (see fig. 4.9), crossed by the tree, stabilizes that composition. The vertical pole and the horizon also provide stability in *Jockeys Before the Race*.

Francisco Goya's print *Bullfight* provides a fascinating example of effective design based on a dramatic use of directional forces (**fig. 4.12**). To emphasize the drama of man and bull, Goya isolated them in the foreground as large, dark shapes against a light background. He created suspense by crowding the spectators into the upper left corner.

Goya evoked a sense of motion by placing the bullfighter exactly on the diagonal axis that runs from lower left to upper right (**fig. 4.12a**). He reinforced the feeling by placing the bull's hind legs along the same line. He further emphasized two main features of the drama by placing the man's hands at the intersection of the image's most important horizontal and vertical lines. He also directed powerful diagonals from the bull's head and front legs to the pole's balancing point on the ground. The resulting sense of motion to the right is so powerful that everything in the rest of the etching is needed to balance it.

By placing the light source to the left, Goya extended the bull's shadow to the right, to create a relatively stable horizontal line. The man looks down at the shadow, creating a directional force that causes us also to look. When we do, we realize that the implied lines reveal the underlying structure to be a stable triangle (**fig. 4.12b**). Formally, the triangle serves as a balancing force; psychologically, its missing side serves to heighten the tension of the situation.

The dynamism of the man's diagonal axis is so strong that the composition needed additional balancing elements; thus, Goya used light to create two more diagonals in the opposite direction (**fig. 4.12c**). The area of shadow in the background completes the balance by adding visual weight and stability to the left.

It has taken many words and several diagrams to describe the visual dynamics that make the design of Goya's etching so effective. However, our eyes take it in instantly. Good design is efficient; it communicates its power immediately.

4.12 Francisco Goya. *Bullfight: The Agility and Daring of Juanito Apinani.* Plate 20. c.1815. Etching with aquatint. 9½″ × 14″.
Yale University Art Gallery, The Arthur Ross Collection 2012.159.38.20

a.

b.

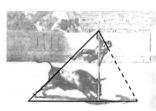

c.

Repetition and Rhythm

The **repetition** (regular recurrence) of visual elements can give a composition unity, continuity, flow, and emphasis. As we saw earlier, *Interior of a Dutch House* (see fig. 4.5) is organized around the repetition of rectangular shapes. And *Going Home* by Jacob Lawrence (see fig. 4.4) achieves its harmony in part through the repeated use of the green seat-backs.

Pattern refers to an all-over design created by the repetitive ordering of elements. Patterning is a common design strategy in many of the world's textile art traditions. In Afghanistan, weavers have for centuries made carpets that include imagery from their lives. Since the Afghan War broke out in 2001, weavers have even begun including imagery of war in their carpets, repeated in patterns following traditional practice (**fig. 4.13**). In this rug, inside the rectangular border (itself a pattern) the weaver embedded repeated images of helicopters, hand grenades, and automobiles. Each of those items takes form in the carpet as a memorized sequence of stitches. This becomes a pattern that the weaver varies slightly in color.

4.13 War rug. Afghanistan. 1990–2000. Medium: wool. Technique: knotted pile. 32½″ × 25¼″.

Rhythm refers to any structure of dominant and subordinate elements in sequence. We generally associate rhythm with temporal arts such as music, dance, and poetry. In the visual arts, rhythm is created through the regular recurrence of elements with related variations. Artists often use this principle as an organizational and expressive device.

The simplest way to create rhythm is by repetition; this is what Wallace Berman did in his untitled collage (**fig. 4.14**). He found a photo in a magazine advertisement of a hand holding a transistor radio, and he used a Verifax – an early version of a photocopy machine – to reproduce that shape exactly, varying the exposure slightly each time. He anchored the composition with the rhythm of the hands and repeated rectangular radio and then attached photographs and Hebrew letters to each to provide more variety.

Japanese artist Ogata Korin used rhythm to charming effect in *Cranes* (**fig. 4.15**), one of a pair of folding screens. The birds are severely simplified, their bodies and legs forming a shape that is repeated with variations. The heads

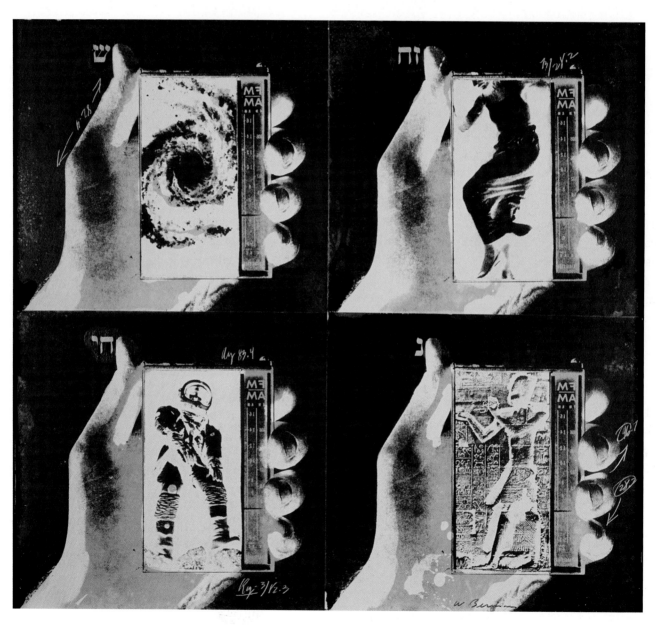

4.14 Wallace Berman. *Untitled (A1-Nebulae)*. 1970. 4-images positive Verifax collage. 12″ × 13″.
Courtesy of the Estate of Wallace Berman and Kohn Galley, Los Angeles.

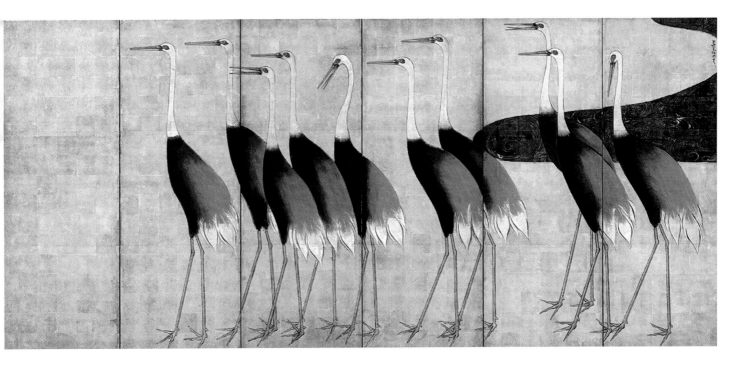

4.15 Ogata Korin. *Cranes.* c.1700. Japanese, Edo period (1615–1868). Ink, color, gold, and silver on paper. 65⅜″ × 146⅛″.

and beaks of the cranes create a strong directional force toward our left, leading the eye to an ironically empty rectangle. The heads are held high, and their location near the top of the composition enhances this loftiness, making the birds seem just a bit pretentious. Their rhythmic procession in marching steps in a seemingly straight line supports this note of humor. The background landscape is a flat yet opulent background of gold leaf, interrupted only by a suggestion of a curving stream at the right.

Scale and Proportion

Scale is the size relation of one thing to another. **Proportion** is the size relationship of parts to a whole.

Scale is one of the first decisions an artist makes when planning a work of art. How big will it be? We experience scale in relation to our own size: Things larger than ourselves, either actual or depicted, help to induce feelings of wonder, awe, or even fear. In contrast, small-scale things are more approachable and more likely to be pleasing and agreeable. This experience of scale constitutes an important part of our response to works of art.

It is difficult to get a sense of the scale of a work in photographs, because a book such as this must distort the scale of nearly every work reproduced in it. To fully grasp an

artist's intent and message, it is far better to see works "in the flesh" at their original scale.

We see many relationships in terms of scale. You have probably noticed that when a short person stands next to a tall person, the short one seems shorter and the tall one taller. Their relationship exaggerates the relative difference in their heights. In the diagram Scale Relationships (**fig. 4.16**), the inner circles at the center in both groups are the same size, but the center circle at the right seems much larger.

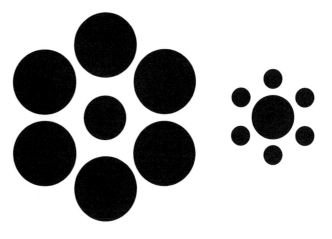

4.16 Scale Relationships.

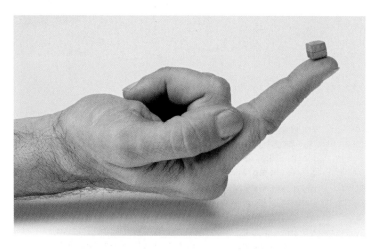

4.17 Cildo Meireles. *Cruzeiro do Sul (Southern Cross)*. 1969–70. Wooden cube, one section pine, one section oak. ⅜″ × ⅜″ × ⅜″.

© Cildo Meireles. Courtesy of Galerie Lelong, New York.

Many artists since the twentieth century have distorted scale for visual effect. One of the smallest-scale works ever created was *Cruzeiro do Sul (Southern Cross)* by Brazilian artist Cildo Meireles (**fig. 4.17**). Photographs of this work usually include the hand, to give viewers a sense of its unique scale, which the artist used to help make a political point. The work consists of two tiny, joined blocks of wood less than a half-inch across. The artist made it to comment on the lack of importance that most people attribute to Southern Hemisphere countries, which produce many natural products such as lumber. This work is so small in scale that exhibiting it is a challenge because most viewers miss it, just as many of them skip the news from Brazil. The small scale of this work thus serves the artist's intent to comment on common attitudes toward his country.

Claes Oldenburg and Coosje van Bruggen use scalar distortion of the opposite kind in a humorous way (see *Claes Oldenburg and Coosje van Bruggen: Distorting Scale*, opposite). In *Shuttlecocks* (**fig. 4.18**) the artists arrayed four huge metal shuttlecocks on the lawns outside the north and south façades of the Nelson-Atkins Museum of Art in Kansas City, Missouri. Each shuttlecock is an outlandish 18 feet high and weighs over 5,000 pounds. Because badminton is played on grass, it appears that the shuttlecocks fell during a game between giants who used the museum as a net. *Shuttlecocks* thus uses distortion of scale to poke gentle fun at the museum, mocking its rather prim look with a playfully irreverent attitude. The work was, however, resisted by many because this frivolousness was felt to be out of keeping with the serious purpose of the museum. The city's principal newspaper editorialized against it. Members of the board of the city Department of Parks and Recreation, which controls the land, tried to block it. Museum curators received hate mail. Yet *Shuttlecocks* stands today, much beloved.

Proportion and Composition

The term **format** refers to the size and shape—and thus to the scale and proportion—of a two-dimensional picture plane, such as a piece of paper, a canvas, a book page, or a digital screen. For example, the format of the paper version of this book is a vertical 8½ by 11-inch rectangle, the same format used for photocopy paper and most notebooks.

The format an artist chooses strongly influences the total composition of a particular work. Henri Matisse made this clear in his *Notes of a Painter*:

> Composition, the aim of which should be expression, is modified according to the surface to be covered. If I take a sheet of paper of a given size, my drawing will have a necessary relationship to its format. I would not repeat this drawing on another sheet of different proportions, for example, rectangular instead of square.[2]

4.18 Claes Oldenburg and Coosje van Bruggen. *Shuttlecocks* (one of four). 1994. Aluminum, fiberglass-reinforced plastic, and paint. 215¾″ × 209″ × 191¾″.

The Nelson-Atkins Museum of Art, Kansas City, Missouri. Purchase: acquired through the generosity of the Sosland Family, F94-1/1. Photograph: Jamison Miller © 1994 Claes Oldenburg and Coosje van Bruggen.

CREATORS

Claes Oldenburg and Coosje van Bruggen: Distorting Scale

signs. He frequently enlarged the scale of his subjects to help viewers see them afresh. A case in point is *Floor Cone* (**fig. 4.20**), a rendition of an ice-cream cone that he created out of roughly painted canvas and stuffing. The work stretches out longer than 11 feet. Its companions at *The Store* included a *Floor Burger* and a *Floor Cake*, the latter a bulging slice of chocolate cake measuring 5 by 9 feet.

Oldenburg's quest was to make art that was not precious, not autobiographical, and based on everyday things. The works he created were both comforting and surprising, both recognizable and unfamiliar. He wrote that he wanted to create artworks that could be used as furniture, or eaten like an ice cream cone, or smelled like an old pair of shoes, or sounded like a refrigerator

opening and closing. In other words, he wanted to take art off the museum walls and into people's lives.

Moving outside the gallery was the next logical step: creating work that lived outdoors where people pass by every day. Out in public, people encounter art without intending to. This was potentially an entirely new arena for Oldenburg's visual surprises. In 1977, he married the Dutch art historian Coosje van Bruggen (1942–2009), and they became collaborators, jointly signing their public projects after 1981. They made many large-scale projects together besides the *Shuttlecocks* (see fig. 4.18), including a giant saw, a flashlight, and a huge knife cutting through the exterior wall of a building. The partnership between the two artists lasted until Van Bruggen's death.

4.19 Photo of Claes Oldenburg and Coosje van Bruggen.
Photograph by Jesse Frohman © 1992.
Artwork © 1992 Claes Oldenburg and Coosje van Bruggen.

4.20 Claes Oldenburg. *Floor Cone.* 1962. Synthetic polymer paint on canvas filled with foam rubber and cardboard boxes. 53¾″ × 136″ × 56″.
Gift of Philip Johnson. Acc. n.: 425.1981 © 2018. Digital image, The Museum of Modern Art, New York/Scala, Florence. © 1962 Claes Oldenburg.

Claes Oldenburg (b. 1929) was born in Sweden to a diplomatic family who took him to Chicago as a child. After art studies at Yale University, he settled in New York in 1956. Soon he became an activist in the cause of de-mystifying art by mixing it with real life in new ways. He achieved some of his surprising impact on the public by exploiting distortions of scale.

Oldenburg drew a great deal of attention as a young artist with his solo exhibition called *The Store*, which he displayed on two separate occasions in 1961 and 1962. By stitching together old pieces of canvas and splashing paint on quickly shaped plaster, he created worn-looking sculptures based on everyday objects that most people would not think of as art: pastries, electric fans, shop

4.21 Michelangelo Buonarroti. *Pietà*. c.1498–1500. Marble. Height 5′ 8½″. St. Peter's, Vatican, Rome. Photograph akg-images/De Agostini Picture Lib./ G. Cigolini.

edges, omitting visual material that the artist positioned. Just as it is important to view artworks at their original scale, it is important to view screen-based media in the intended aspect ratio.

A change in proportion can make a major difference in how we experience a given subject. This becomes apparent when we compare two *pietàs* (*pietà*, Italian for "pity," refers to a depiction of Mary holding and mourning over the body of Jesus).

Creating a believable composition with a fully grown man lying on his mother's lap is difficult. In his most famous *Pietà* (**fig. 4.21**), Michelangelo solved the problem by dramatically altering the human proportions of Mary's figure. Michelangelo made the heads of the two figures the same size but greatly enlarged Mary's body in relation to that of Christ, disguising her immensity with deep folds of drapery. Her seated figure spreads out to support the almost horizontal curve of Christ's limp body. Imagine how the figure of Mary would appear if she were standing. Michelangelo made Mary's body into that of a giant; if she were a living human being rather than a work of art, she would stand at least 8 feet tall!

Because the proportions of the figure of Christ are anatomically correct and there are abundant naturalistic details, we overlook the proportions of Mary's figure, yet the distortion is essential to the way we experience the content of the work.

Formats of movies and videos are conventionally determined by the technology used to produce them, but they have evolved over time. The format of a movie or video is expressed as the aspect ratio of screen width to height. Early films were created at a more or less 4:3 aspect ratio. HD video and today's digital broadcast television have an aspect ratio of 16:9 or 1.78:1. Widescreen cinema can go as high as 2.39:1. This matters because some computer and television screens alter the format of older material played on them. Such alterations in format can sometimes lead to distortion of the artist's composition of a scene by stretching or compression. Some reformatting simply cuts off

4.22 *Roettgen Pietà*. 1300–25. Painted wood. Height 34½″.
LVR-Landesmuseum Bonn.

Compare Michelangelo's work with the *Roettgen Pietà*, created about two centuries earlier (**fig. 4.22**). Unlike the Renaissance work, the German sculptor carved both figures of similar height. Making Christ bony and emaciated helped to alleviate the problem of how Mary can support a person of similar size; Christ's gaunt body also expresses the truth of his suffering in a way that Michelangelo avoided. The anonymous creator of the *Roettgen Pietà* also carved both heads larger, out of proportion to the sizes of their bodies. These distortions help to heighten the expressiveness of the work.

Design Summary

A finished work affects us because its design seems inevitable, but design is not inevitable at all. Faced with a blank piece of paper, an empty canvas, a lump of clay, or a block of marble, an artist begins a process involving many decisions, false starts, and changes, in order to arrive at an integrated whole. This chapter has presented some of the principles of design that guide the creation of artworks.

By photographing the progress of his painting *Large Reclining Nude*, Henri Matisse left us a rare record of the process of designing (**fig. 4.23**). He took 24 photographs over a period of four months; three of them are reproduced here.

The first version (State I; **fig. 4.23a**) is by far the most naturalistic: The proportions of the model's body on the couch and the three-dimensional space of the room seem ordinary. This stage of the work shows the use of various principles of design discussed in this chapter, but this is only the start of a fascinating journey.

By State IX (**fig. 4.23b**), Matisse had introduced a number of bold changes. Because the model's head and crooked right arm did not give the proper weight to that side of the composition, he greatly enlarged the arm. He added more curves to the torso, and he put the legs together to provide a balancing element on the left side. The space of the room now has a new look because he removed the diagonal that runs from the model's upper torso to the flowers; this change flattened the composition, highlighting its two-dimensional design. The model's left arm is now closer to a 90-degree angle, which makes it seem to support more weight; this is a stronger effect than that of the rubbery arm in the first photo. The boldest change involves the couch. Now it is far larger, with vertical white stripes in a rhythmic pattern. Because the stripes are nearly parallel, they do not function as perspective lines; rather, the couch appears to be tipped toward us. This change helps to emphasize the model by pushing her toward the picture surface. Matisse kept the potted flowers and the chair, but he simplified the chair and placed the flowers on the couch; this reduces the emphasis on the chair.

By the time the artist took our third photograph (State XIII; **fig. 4.23c**), he had introduced even more changes, to compensate for some of the bold effects he had introduced earlier. The model's head is larger and placed upright, so that it fits better into the shape of the raised arm. Her larger arm and more direct gaze create a stronger focal point there. He simplified the curves of the torso and created a new position for the left arm, a compromise between its position in the first photo and the second one. The legs are now almost a unit, their bulky mass balancing the verticals

4.23 Henri Matisse. Photographs of three states of *Large Reclining Nude*.

a. State I, May 3, 1935.

b. State IX, May 29, 1935.

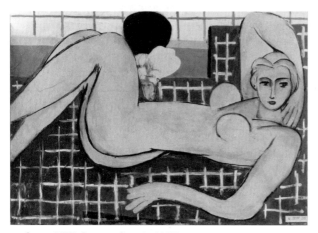

c. State XIII, September 4, 1935.

and diagonals on the right. He added horizontal lines to the couch, making a pattern of squares that parallel the framing edges of the painting. This netlike motif is repeated in the larger squares on the back wall of the room, becoming a visual rhythm that helps to unify the composition. The work is already interesting, but Matisse did not stop here.

The final version (**fig. 4.24**) shows further refinements and a few discoveries. Because the model's left arm probably still seemed weak, Matisse finally fixed it in the corner of the work at a strong angle aligned with the picture frame. This creates a downward directional force. The head is smaller, because the new position of the arms provides enough visual weight on that side of the work. His suppression of the fingers of both hands eliminates a small-scale design element, thus helping to unify the whole. He intensified the pattern on the back wall, so that it now serves as a variation of the motif on the couch. He gave new functions to the shapes and lines of the chair back and flowers by emphasizing their curves. They now echo the shapes of the body and balance the rigidity of the squares in the couch and wall. The position of the legs is the biggest change. By moving one of them down, he created a "pinwheel" effect that the arms carry through, adding a new circular element to the design of the whole. The rhythmic curves of the arms and legs lead our eye naturally around the composition. Finally, he repositioned the model's entire body at a slight angle from the horizontal.

Matisse's keen sense of design and restless experimentation produced a work in which powerful forces in the composition are balanced with seemingly simple means. He wrote that the expressiveness of a work does not rest merely on facial expressions or gestures of figures:

> The entire arrangement of my picture is expressive: the place occupied by the figures, the empty spaces around them, the proportions, everything has its share.[3]

As we have seen in the works illustrated in this chapter, artists organize visual elements in order to create meaningful and interesting form—a process known as design. While there are no absolute rules for good design, there are a number of key principles. Studying these not only gives us a vocabulary for talking to one another about what we see, but also increases our sensitivity to the expressive and relational possibilities of art.

4.24 Henri Matisse. *Large Reclining Nude.* 1935. Oil on canvas. 26⅛″ × 36¾″.

The Baltimore Museum of Art: The Cone Collection, formed by Dr. Claribel Cone and Miss Etta Cone of Baltimore, Maryland, BMA 1950.258. Photography by: Mitro Hood © 2013 Succession H. Matisse/Artists Rights Society (ARS), New York.

KEY TERMS

asymmetrical balance – the various elements of a work are balanced but not symmetrical

asymmetry – lack of symmetry

balance – an arrangement of parts achieving a state of equilibrium between opposing forces or influences

composition – the organization of visual elements in an artwork

contrast – the juxtaposition of strongly dissimilar elements; dramatic effects can be produced when dark is set against light, large against small, bright colors against dull

design – the process of organizing visual elements and the product of that process

directional forces – pathways that the artist embeds in a work for the viewer's eye to follow

emphasis – a method an artist uses to draw attention to an area; may be done with central placement, large size, bright color, or high contrast

focal point – the principal area of emphasis in a work of art; the place to which the artist directs the most attention through composition

format – the shape or proportions of a picture plane

pattern – all-over design created by the repetitive ordering of design elements

proportion – the size relationship of parts to a whole and to one another

repetition – the recurrence of visual elements

rhythm – the regular or ordered repetition of dominant and subordinate elements or units within a design with related variations

scale – the size relation of one thing to another

subordination – technique by which an artist ranks certain areas of a work as of lesser importance; areas are generally subordinated through placement, color, or size

symmetrical balance – the near or exact matching of left and right sides of a three-dimensional form or a two-dimensional composition

symmetry – a design (or composition) with nearly identical form on opposite sides of a dividing line or central axis

unity – the appearance of similarity, consistency, or oneness

variety – the opposite of unity; diverse elements in the composition of a work of art

5

EVALUATING ART

LEARNING OBJECTIVES

5.1 Explain how the evaluation of an artwork can change over time and across cultures.

5.2 Compare formal, contextual, and expressive approaches used in art criticism.

5.3 Describe the relationship between cash value and artistic quality.

5.4 Demonstrate an understanding of the factual, analytical, and evaluative steps required when writing about an artwork.

5.5 Explain censorship as a type of evaluation, based on religious, moral, or political values.

How do we tell whether a work of art is good? Is it innovative? Does it move us? Is it skillfully done? Which criteria do we use in judging art? As we consider answers to these questions, we will find that there are many ways of judging the quality of art. Further, we will see that our assessments of quality are usually connected to other values that we also hold about the function of art in society; hence our preferences about art are often connected to our other deeply held beliefs.

Evaluation

Have you ever heard someone say, "I don't know anything about art, but I know what I like"? We all express our own likes or dislikes many times a day. When we select one thing over another, or appreciate the specialness of something, we are evaluating.

The creative experience is also a process of selecting and evaluating. For the artist the creative process involves selecting and evaluating each component before deciding if or how to include it in the final form. After the work is complete, the viewer's enjoyment comes from recognizing the quality that has been achieved. How do viewers evaluate art to determine whether it has quality?

Quality is relative. How a work of art is evaluated varies from person to person, from culture to culture, and from age to age. In some cultures, adherence to past standards matters most. In Mexico before the Spanish conquest, the Aztec writers judged art to be good if it resembled the style of the Toltecs, an ancient neighboring people that the Aztecs admired. In other cultures, communicating an intangible spirit takes priority over other skills. In traditional Chinese art criticism, an artist who showed mere skill in representation generally received poor evaluations. A superior artist could communicate the inner spirit or "life breath" of a subject. To call an artist or artwork "skillful" was to give it faint praise.

In the European tradition, few famous artists or styles have had unchanging reputations. For example, the Impressionist painters of the late nineteenth century were ridiculed by most critics, museum curators, and the public of the time. Critics alleged that these artists chose seemingly trivial subjects and painted them so quickly that they resembled mere sketches (see fig. 21.18). In other words, the Impressionists' style differed too radically from that of their predecessors. Today, because we now value innovation more highly, Impressionist paintings have an honored place in museums and are eagerly sought by the public. Conversely, many artists who were celebrated in their own time are forgotten today; they are victims of changing standards.

Value judgments about art necessarily involve subjectivity; it is not possible to measure artistic quality objectively. In this regard, let us compare *Shy Glance* by

5.1 Dawn Marie Jingagian. *Shy Glance.* 1976. Acrylic on canvas. 24″ × 18″.

With permission, Museum of Bad Art, www.museumofbadart.org

5.2 Elisabeth Vigée-LeBrun. *Self-Portrait in a Straw Hat.* 1782. Oil on canvas. 38½″ × 27¾″.

The National Gallery, London. NG1653. © 2018. © The National Gallery, London/ Scala, Florence.

Dawn Marie Jingagian (**fig. 5.1**) with *Self-Portrait in a Straw Hat* by Marie Louise Elisabeth Vigée-LeBrun (**fig. 5.2**). The former work was recovered from a trash bin; the latter was created by a leading painter of the late eighteenth century. The painter of *Shy Glance* lacks skill in many areas: color shading (the cheek is blotchy), anatomy (the eyebrow is too narrow and the forehead bulges), composition (it is difficult to tell positive from negative space), and brushwork (the hair and eyelashes!). The feeling it communicates is almost embarrassingly sweet. In contrast, *Self-Portrait* shows great assuredness in the use of paint to show anatomy. The light seems to fall naturally over the subject's face and shoulder. The eyes and face show a relaxed, confident gaze. The two artists are poles apart in level of traditional skill.

Yet today's viewers might find *Shy Glance* at least as interesting as the other work. *Self-Portrait,* for all its skill, looks conventional, even ordinary. In contrast, *Shy Glance* has an obvious sincerity and enthusiasm that may be infectious. The painter of *Shy Glance* showed great boldness in even bringing forth this work, which shows no training.

Hence the level of traditional skill that an artist shows may be relevant to a judgment of quality, but rarely gives the final answer.

When we look at a work of art and feel pleased or displeased, asking ourselves why we respond in that way is an excellent exercise. What we find in a work of art depends on what we are looking for. Do we like art to dazzle our senses? Show great skill? Move our feelings? Show a vision of a better world? Bare the artist's soul? These are personal value orientations that will lead us to make judgments about the works of art we encounter.

Each of us applies these value-based assumptions about art each time we look at a work. If we hope that art will divert us from our daily problems and routines, then we will favor certain kinds of creation. If we want art to build understanding between people, we will likely favor other sorts of work. Expressing our taste in art involves our personality and our values more than other kinds of judgment. The type of art that we prefer reveals far more about us than does our selection from a dinner menu, for example.

Whether you are approaching art for your own enjoyment or for a class assignment, it is most rewarding to begin with an open, receptive mind, and go beyond snap judgments. Give yourself time to get acquainted and to respond. Practice seeing rather than merely looking (see Chapter 1).

Art Criticism

The term **art criticism** refers to making discriminating judgments, both favorable and unfavorable. We all do art criticism, but professional critics writing in newspapers and magazines tend to follow one or more of three basic theories:

- **Formal theories**, which focus attention on the composition of the work and how it shows originality, how it may have been influenced by other works, or how it influences other artists
- **Contextual theories**, which consider art as a product of a culture and value system
- **Expressive theories**, which pay attention to the artist's expression of a personality or worldview

These theories emphasize the work, the culture, and the artist, respectively. Let us consider each in turn, as they might be used to analyze three paintings that are pictured in this chapter.

Formal Theories

Critics who use formal theories look carefully at how a work is made: how the parts of the composition come together to create a visual experience that may interest us, or not. They generally believe that the most important influence on a work is other works that the artist has seen or studied. Because the formal organization of the work is the most important factor in evaluating it, the theories are called *formal*. The subject or theme of the work is less important than how the artist presented it. Formalist critics value innovation in style above all; thus they always want to know when a work was done, so that they can compare it (at least mentally) with its predecessors and contemporaries. They value such stylistic innovation because they believe that art can be an important source of visual refreshment, unconnected to our complicated and strife-torn world. All three of these works show formal innovation in different ways.

From a formal perspective, Titian's *Pietà* (**fig. 5.3**) is very innovative in its brushwork. Titian's immediate predecessors in Italian art were the Renaissance masters Raphael, Michelangelo Buonarroti, and Leonardo da Vinci, among others. See, for example, *Paul Preaching at Athens* by Raphael (fig. 17.12). Titian understood the painting methods that they used, but he went beyond them by making his brushwork more loose and painterly, adding a new element of expressiveness to painting that would influence artists for generations to come. The work also uses an innovative composition: The center is an empty niche surrounded by a diagonal row of heads that is

5.3 Titian. *Pietà*. 1576. Oil on canvas. 149″ × 136″.
Accademia, Venice. © Cameraphoto Arte, Venice.

5.4 Sonia Delaunay-Terk. *Simultaneous Contrasts.*
1913. Oil on canvas. 18½″ × 21½″.
Museo Thyssen-Bornemisza, Madrid. 518 (1976.81). © 2018 Museo
Thyssen-Bornemisza/Scala, Florence. © Pracusa 2017637.

balanced by the two figures at the upper right. This emptiness at the center is a bold compositional device for that time.

Sonia Delaunay-Terk also innovated when she painted *Simultaneous Contrasts* (**fig. 5.4**) in 1913. The work was influenced by the early twentieth-century art movement Cubism, which represented subjects as flattened, geometric shapes (see Chapter 22). Delaunay-Terk did not, however, overlap the planes as earlier Cubists did; the elements of this work fit together like a jigsaw puzzle. Yet she used shading to shape each zone, as if the zones were curved surfaces. The work is innovative in the way it suggests and denies a third dimension at the same time. This painting is also more innovative in its color than most early Cubist works, and explores how one bright color can have an impact on our perception of a neighboring one. The work is also a novel treatment of the landscape as a subject. In sum, the way this work revises and expands on the Cubist style is its most interesting formal characteristic.

A more recent work, *Horn Players* (**fig. 5.5**) by Jean-Michel Basquiat, also presents interesting formal innovations. First, he created it using techniques he learned from making graffiti, something few other artists were doing at the time. Second, the division into three vertical panels is interesting because the artist successfully avoided the pitfall of making the work seem like three separate paintings. He counteracted the division, and held the work together, by repeating certain motifs across the panels, such as heads, patches of white, and words in boxes. The work's roots in graffiti may make it look improvised at first glance; yet he brought discipline to the work, creating a knowing balance between unity and variety.

Contextual Theories

Critics who use these theories tend to look first at the environmental influences on a work of art: the economic system, the cultural values, and even the politics of the time; because the context matters a great deal, they are termed *contextual theories*. Just as formalist critics will want to know the date of a work, contextual critics are likely to ask, "What else was going on in the culture at that time?" Contextual critics tend to favor works that either cogently embody important cultural values, or memorably express resistance to them. These three works are not all equally interesting from a contextual standpoint.

Titian's *Pietà* is an altarpiece, destined for public viewing in a chapel at a church in Venice; altarpieces generally took up important Christian themes, and this one is no exception. However, Titian painted it during an epidemic of the plague, and its theme of mortality and grief takes on added meaning in that context. The vacant niche probably symbolizes death, and Titian's eloquent depiction of the dead Christ must have given comfort to the many Venetians who lost relatives in the epidemic. The work expresses grief over current events, but Titian has successfully taken it out of its time, so that even today we can still appreciate its mournful aspect.

Simultaneous Contrasts by Sonia Delaunay-Terk is less interesting from a contextual perspective because its subject seems to be a simple sunlit landscape. The work tells us very little about its time (the early twentieth century). The work refers to an optical theory that many artists studied in those days, which dealt with the interaction of colors. The nineteenth-century scientist Michel-Eugène Chevreul researched the ways in which our perception of one color influences how we see a neighboring one. He called this visual effect the "Law of Simultaneous Contrasts," a phrase that the artist borrowed for the title of this work. Delaunay-Terk also did fabric designs, and she used her discoveries in fabrics and painting to fertilize each other (see *Sonia Delaunay-Terk: Innovator in Art and Fashion* on p. 91).

5.5 Jean-Michel Basquiat. *Horn Players*. 1983.
Acrylic and oil paintstick on three canvas panels.
Overall 8′ × 6′5″.

The Broad Art Foundation, Santa Monica. Photograph: Douglas M. Parker
Studio, Los Angeles. © The Estate of Jean-Michel Basquiat/ADAGP, Paris/
ARS, New York 2018.

In contrast, *Horn Players* is filled with contextual information. Basquiat admired the leaders of the bebop movement in jazz, which originated in the 1940s, and this work is a homage to them. Saxophonist Charlie Parker is at the upper left, red musical notes pouring out of his instrument. The ear that seems about to be cut off may refer to the late nineteenth-century painter Vincent van Gogh, an artist of similar innovative power, who indeed cut off his own ear. (Both Parker and Van Gogh died young, "cut off" in their prime.) We can make out the name of trumpeter Dizzy Gillespie at the top center, and see him pictured at the right. The word "ornithology" refers to one of Parker's musical compositions, which he and Gillespie recorded in a famous track. Together they must have created the "alchemy"

(magically transformative mixture) that the artist scrawled at the lower right. In this work Basquiat affirmed an important African-American musical movement.

Expressive Theories

All artworks are made by people. The skill level, personal intent, emotional state, mindset, and gender of the creator must play a role in the creative process. Artist-centered theories are thus termed *expressive theories*. If formalists want to know about dates of creation and contextualists want to know about the background culture, an expressive critic will want to know, "Who made it? And who is she or he?" Critics who favor this approach tend to look for powerful personal meanings, deep psychological insight, or profound human concern. These types of critical theory have been strongly influenced by psychoanalysis and by gender studies. Each of our three paintings is quite expressive, but in different ways.

Titian painted the *Pietà* in the last year of his life; hence its somber reflection on death expresses the artist's own thoughts about mortality. Indeed, the figure at the lower right in the red shawl is Titian himself (we know this from other self-portraits). Anyone who has ever mourned can probably identify with Mary's grieving attitude in this painting. The brushwork here is loose and expressive: Many critics believe that this represents an "old-age style" in which the artist cast off the restraint of his younger days, and painted with greater freedom.

Contemporaries attested to Sonia Delaunay-Terk's ebullient personality, and it comes across in *Simultaneous Contrasts*. No clouds darken its sunlit skies. Her bright and exuberant color palette comes from her memories of brightly colored folk costumes in her native Ukraine, especially wedding costumes that were festooned with ribbons. This work's vivid and expressive qualities are infectious.

Critics of an expressive bent tend to like Jean-Michel Basquiat because his works are full of personal meaning. Most interesting is his use of line: It is a personal style that seems both intent and intense, characteristics that the artist also displayed in life. That intensity contrasts nicely with the seemingly casual arrangement of the figures and script. The painting seems to have come together like a three-verse song. This work also explores the artist's personal history as an African American by upholding examples from the music world, and sharing with us some people who are important to him.

Sonia Delaunay-Terk: Innovator in Art and Fashion

5.6 Sonia Delaunay-Terk. *Simultaneous Dresses (Three Women, Forms, Colors).* 1925. Oil on canvas, 57½" × 43¾".
Thyssen-Bornemisza Collection. Inv. No. 519. © Pracusa 2017637.

When modern art in Europe exploded in the early twentieth century, Sonia Delaunay-Terk (1885–1979) not only participated in some of its innovations, but also took them into the fashion world. She was thus a twofold pioneer.

Born in the Ukraine, the artist was adopted at the age of 5 by well-to-do relatives with the surname Terk, in St. Petersburg, Russia. The family noticed her artistic aptitudes early, and, when she was 18, sent her to a drawing school in Germany. Two years later, in 1905, she moved to Paris, drawn by the climate of artistic innovation.

A brief marriage, arranged for immigration purposes, ended in 1910 when she met Robert Delaunay (1885–1941), a young painter of increasing renown. Together the two of them explored radical juxtapositions of color in abstract and nonrepresentational paintings. The Delaunay-Terks called their style "Simultaneism," after the simultaneous contrasts that characterized their bold use of color. They intended the style to evoke the speed and vividness of modern urban life.

Delaunay-Terk made her first nonrepresentational artwork when she made a quilt out of brightly colored fabrics for her newborn son in 1911. Its bold colors and vibrant patterns encouraged her to think of making more artworks with fabrics. Within two years she was making revolutionary women's dresses with the same ideas. Gone were the traditional patterns that many women then wore, based on flowers or twining vegetation. Her *Simultaneous Dresses* (**fig. 5.6**) put her at the leading edge of fashion and still look audacious today.

World War I drove Delaunay-Terk and her husband to neutral Spain. There she opened her first shop, selling fashions and accessories. With the close of hostilities, she established the shop in Paris under the name "Simultaneous Boutique." For most of the 1920s she was one of Europe's trendsetters. She created clothing and set designs for ballet, and for two silent films. A cover for *Vogue* magazine followed in 1926. She even extended her inspiration to automobile exteriors (**fig. 5.7**). Unfortunately, only black-and-white photos exist of this car, but we can imagine how eye-catching it must have been.

The depression of the 1930s and war in the 1940s somewhat curtailed Delaunay-Terk's designing activities; instead she worked on paintings. When the histories of modern art began to be written in the postwar years, her parallel work in the fashion world caused many (mostly male) art historians to neglect her contributions in favor of her husband's. This was unfair, because the two of them worked equally. Her neglect was caused in part by simple sexism and also by a dominant belief that involvement in fashion meant a lack of seriousness about art. Attitudes changed in the 1960s, when artists and critics began to take more interest in popular culture. In 1964, Delaunay-Terk was the first living woman artist to have a solo exhibition at the Louvre museum in Paris. Today, many fashion designers also inhabit the art world, and some artists also design fashions. Many such designers and artists now look to Sonia Delaunay-Terk for inspiration.

5.7 Sonia Delaunay-Terk. Clothing and Customized Citroën B-12. 1925.
© Pracusa 2017637

What Makes Art Great?

The most obvious answer is, "It's great if you think it is!" And everyone has their own personal list of great artworks. However, with our three theories in hand, we can now say how a work of art comes to be regarded as a "masterpiece," and commands the place of honor in a museum (or appears in a book such as this): Some degree of innovation, important contextual meanings, and a recognizable personal statement are key ingredients. Not all three are necessary, but at least one must be strongly present.

Cash value correlates poorly with artistic importance or quality. Artworks are bought and sold every day in our world, and every few months some work makes news because of its price at auction. At the time of writing, a portrait of Christ by Leonardo da Vinci holds the record for a public auction price, $450.3 million. However, several art historians found invasive restorations and overpainting by later hands. A record price did not buy a work in excellent condition. Generally speaking, the art market can tell us only what a certain group of collectors is willing to pay for a work at a given time.

In addition, the cash value of a great many artworks cannot be known with certainty because they are outside of the marketplace for one reason or another. Most works now in museums, for example, will never be sold. In addition, some artists purposely create works that are difficult to sell because they are too massive or too controversial or destined for a public place. Thus, dollar values have little bearing on either the historical importance of an artwork or its degree of innovation.

Most works hanging in museums have been selected by the specialists on the staff because they embody at least one of the three theories. Your judgments may not agree with theirs, and that is fine.

But to go deeper is rewarding. The three theories of art criticism presented here give us three standards of quality, and three ways of judging artworks. Often we apply one or more of these without thinking, and we say something like, "I like art that I can relate to." Well, why do you relate to it? What are you looking for? A little self-examination should help you to uncover what values are motivating your choices, and can help to open an interesting discussion about art with other viewers.

Evaluating Art with Words

Writing about art is an excellent way to understand it, because writing can channel our thoughts and clarify our beliefs. Writing about art also involves us more deeply in the process of creation. Here is a three-step method that can serve for almost any work.

1. Get the facts. These include the name of the creator, title, date, subject, medium, size, and location of the work. (Not all of these may be knowable for every work.) Describe the work using as many of the facts as you can find. If you are looking at a reproduction of a work, it is especially important to clarify its original medium, size, and texture.

2. Analyze. Look at the parts of the work and how they fit together. How does the choice of medium affect the work (see Chapters 6 to 14)? What formal elements did the creator use (see Chapter 3)? Assess the work in its context: Does it fit into a movement or time period? Does it lead the way to a new movement, or follow behind? Consider also its place in the artist's overall output. If the work was created years ago, how was it received at that time?

3. Evaluate. Use one of the three types of art criticism discussed above to assess the quality or historical importance of the work. Is it innovative? Does it affect your feelings? Does it express a particular time period or artist's personality? Does it communicate a social vision or cause? Is it ravishingly beautiful, or challenging to the eyes? What message does the work convey, and how effectively does it accomplish this?

An essay on a work should include all three steps, seamlessly blended together. Steps 1 and 2 should be fairly objective; Step 3 should lead you to a debatable thesis or position on the work. The three steps are not equal in weight or difficulty. Step 1 should be the easiest. Step 2 requires study and background knowledge. Step 3, the most important, requires practice and careful seeing.

Censorship: The Ultimate Evaluation

Simply defined, **censorship** is the alteration or removal of works of art from public view. Censorship may be carried out for moral, political, or religious reasons, when civil authorities decide that the artist's freedom takes a back seat to other important values.

Censoring art is not a recent practice. In sixteenth-century Italy, Michelangelo painted *The Last Judgment*, with a great many nude figures, on the end wall of the Sistine

Chapel (see fig. 17.9). The work aroused no controversy at the time, but later popes found the figures too revealing and ordered loincloths to be painted over their genitals; several of these survive to this day.

On political grounds, many dictatorial regimes have censored art production. In 1937, the Nazis in Germany confiscated more than 16,000 pieces of modern art that did not conform to their party goals. Nazi theoreticians believed that most modern art, especially abstract art, was not sufficiently nationalistic. The artists who had made the confiscated pieces were banned from working, and many emigrated. Artists who glorified the German people in acceptable ways were widely exhibited.

In many countries where Islam is the dominant religion, any depiction of the Prophet Muhammad is frowned upon or even forbidden. Muhammad prohibited pictures of himself during his life because he considered himself only a messenger of the one true God. Muslims everywhere generally accept this, and many especially take offense at drawings or cartoons that satirize him. A few have at times used violence in order to protest against and suppress such depictions. In 2011 and 2015, for example, Muslim militants attacked the office of the French satirical magazine *Charlie Hebdo* with bombs and guns, protesting against the cartoons it published that lampooned the Prophet and Muslim worship practices.

Artists in the United States today usually enjoy wide latitude to create as they please. This right was best codified in a 1973 Supreme Court case, *Miller* v. *California*, which held that a work may be censored only if it is demonstrably obscene; that is, if the "average person, applying contemporary community standards," finds it obscene, and if "the work taken as a whole lacks serious literary, artistic, political or scientific value." Thus our society, which places high value on individual achievement and personal self-expression, seems to tip the balance in favor of freedom for artists. However, when an exhibition benefits from public funds, or it gives rise to protests, or an official finds it inflammatory, attempts to censor often ensue.

Consider the following recent cases, which show that artistic creation is often contested territory in which wider struggles over values resonate. The three cases illustrate attempts to censor based on religious, moral, and political grounds.

In the fall of 1999, New York City mayor Rudolph Giuliani tried to close the Brooklyn Museum because of the painting *The Holy Virgin Mary* by Chris Ofili (**fig. 5.8**).

5.8 Chris Ofili. *The Holy Virgin Mary*. 1996. Acrylic, oil, polyester resin, paper collage, glitter, map pins, and elephant dung on linen. 96" × 72".
© Chris Ofili. Courtesy of Victoria Miro, London.

Giuliani found the work offensive to Roman Catholics because of the way it portrayed Mary, and because the work had pieces of elephant dung attached to it. The museum operates in a city-owned building, so the mayor went to court to try to evict it and cut off its maintenance funds if the directors did not remove the work from view. The artist and the museum claimed that elephant dung is an art medium in certain African cultures, and that Ofili has the right to interpret the Christian religion, in which he was also raised, as he chooses. The court sided with the artist and the museum. Far from suppressing Ofili's work, the mayor's lawsuit brought record-breaking crowds.

The social media sites Facebook and Instagram are often in the news because they suppress or remove imagery for alleged sexual content. In early 2016, the Philadelphia Museum of Art found its Facebook page censored because it posted an image of *Ice Cream 1* by the Belgian artist Evelyne Axell (**fig. 5.9**). The museum had already used the work in billboards and publications to promote an exhibition that contained it. But Facebook censored the picture because, it said, the work violated its standards regulating

5.9 Evelyne Axell. *Ice Cream 1*. 1964. Oil on canvas.
31½″ × 27½″. Unique.

Courtesy of BROADWAY 1602 HARLEM, New York EA/P 3534. © 2018
Artists Rights Society (ARS), New York/ADAGP, Paris.

"suggestive content." The museum protested the removal
and pointed out that Facebook standards specifically allow
photos of artworks even if they depict suggestive subjects.
Facebook relented several weeks later and allowed the
museum to repost.

An example of political censorship occurred in late
2011 when the governor of Maine removed a mural from
the headquarters of the state's Labor Department, claiming
that it showed bias toward organized labor, and implied
a bias against business. The 36-foot mural was installed
in 2007, and depicted the history of workers in the state
(**fig 5.10**). In defending the removal, the governor's press
secretary said, "The Department of Labor is a state agency
that works very closely with both employees and employ-
ers, and we need to have a décor that represents neutrality."
The artist responded, "I don't agree that it's one-sided. It's
based on historical fact. I'm not sure how you can say history is one-sided." After the artist and some union activists
sued to have the work put back on view, a district judge
ruled that because the government paid for the mural, it
could dispose of it. State workers removed the work to an
undisclosed location.

As we have seen in this chapter, although we can
describe, analyze, interpret, and appraise art, there is no
single correct way to evaluate it. All three approaches discussed have enjoyed favor at one time or another. But the
process of evaluation is rewarding from any viewpoint
because it draws the viewer into the creative process.

KEY TERMS

art criticism – the process of using formal analysis,
description, and interpretation to evaluate or explain the
quality and meanings of art

censorship – the alteration of works of art, or their removal
from public view

contextual theory – a method of art criticism that focuses
on the cultural systems behind works of art; these may be
economic, racial, political, or social

expressive theory – a method of art criticism that
attempts to discern personal elements in works of art,
as opposed to formal strategies or cultural influences

formal theory – a method of art criticism that values
stylistic innovation over personal expression or cultural
communication

5.10 Judy Taylor. *History of Labor in Maine*. 2007. Oil on particle board, eleven joined panels. 8′ × 36′.
Courtesy of Judy Taylor Studio.

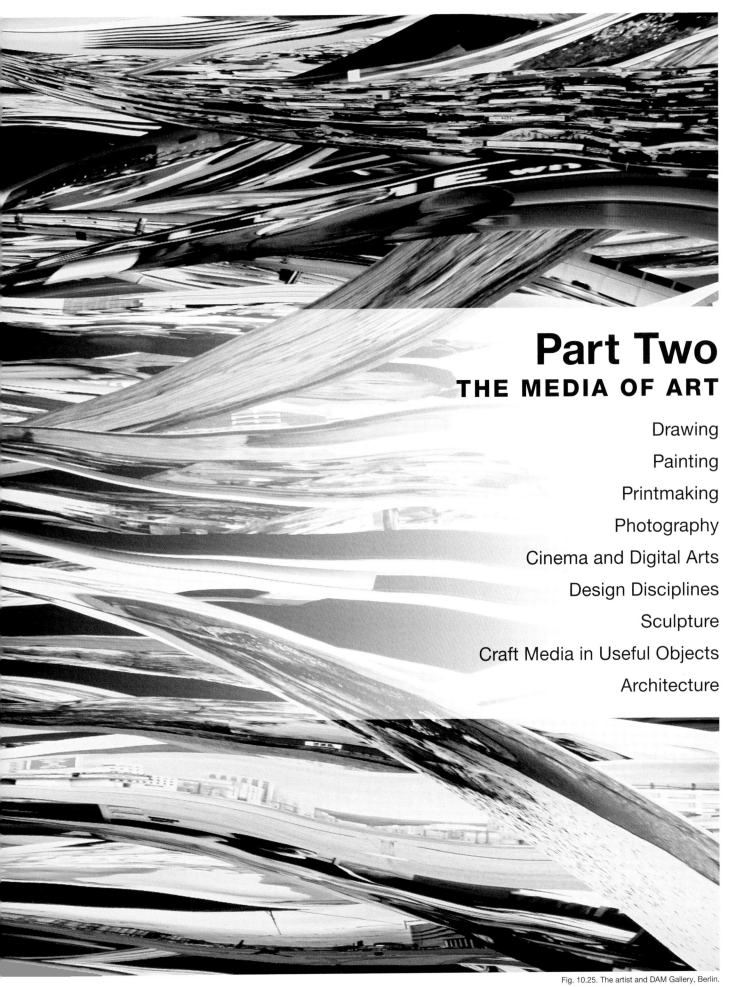

Part Two
THE MEDIA OF ART

Drawing

Painting

Printmaking

Photography

Cinema and Digital Arts

Design Disciplines

Sculpture

Craft Media in Useful Objects

Architecture

Fig. 10.25. The artist and DAM Gallery, Berlin.

6 DRAWING

LEARNING OBJECTIVES

6.1 Describe how artists use drawing as an important tool for recording events and developing ideas.

6.2 Distinguish the use of drawings to record ideas, as preliminary studies, and as independent works of art.

6.3 Discuss drawing tools and techniques used with dry and liquid media.

6.4 Explain the role of drawing in comics and graphic novels.

6.5 Discuss contemporary drawing techniques and technologies.

Drawing is an immediate and accessible way to communicate through imagery. When the British government appointed Henry Moore an Official War Artist in 1940, he made dozens of drawings of Londoners sheltering from the Nazi bombing raids (**fig. 6.1**). His official status gave him a pass to the basements and subway tunnels where thousands sought refuge. Moore made his drawings later from notes taken on the spot. This drawing shows a mostly illegible inscription that begins "Rows . . ." along with the words "tunnel shelterers," above a receding subway tunnel crowded with tensely reclining figures. He suppressed details of each person's appearance, which helped to transform a scene of immense fear into one of stoic endurance. Because most cameras do not function in such dimly lit spaces, Moore's *Shelter Drawings* are among the few records we have of these episodes.

Through his drawings Moore not only provided a valuable record of events but also shared with us his feelings about and experiences of war. In the Western world especially, drawing has often been a key medium for recording events and improving skills. In this chapter we will explore the various types and purposes of drawing and the tools and techniques artists use to draw. We also consider comics and graphic novels, artforms in which drawing takes a predominant role. We will conclude with more contemporary pieces that take new approaches to drawing by involving the use of diverse media.

6.1 Henry Moore. *Study for Tube Shelter Perspective: The Liverpool Street Extension.* Pencil, wax crayon, colored crayon, watercolor, wash, pen and ink, Conté crayon on wove paper. 8″ × 6½″

The Drawing Process

The desire to draw is as natural as the desire to talk. As children, we draw long before we learn to read and write. (In fact, handwriting is a kind of drawing.) Some of us continue to enjoy drawing; others return to it as adults. Those who no longer draw probably came to believe they did not draw well enough to suit themselves or others. Yet drawing is a skill that can be perfected through practice. It is also a way of seeing and communicating, a way of paying attention.

In the most basic sense, to draw means to pull, push, or drag a marking tool across a surface to leave a line or mark. Most people working in the visual arts use drawing as an important tool for visual thinking—for recording and developing ideas.

Many people find it valuable to keep a sketchbook handy to serve as a visual diary, a place to develop and maintain drawing skills and to note whatever catches the eye or imagination. From sketchbook drawings some ideas may develop and reach maturity as finished drawings or complete works in other media. Leonardo da Vinci, for example, was a restless draftsman who used sketches as a type of scientific research. His drawing *Facial Proportions of a Man in Profile* (**fig. 6.2**) shows him measuring the various ratios in a human face, as he also sketches figures on horseback. Today we have drawing applications for our digital devices that allow us to create drawings on a screen and alter, save, or share them.

Guillermo del Toro, director and producer of *Pacific Rim*, *Crimson Peak*, and other films, keeps a sketchbook for jotting notes and ideas. The pages reproduced here (**fig. 6.3**) show his musings about the desire for fame, meeting other directors, and sketches of some strange beings that found their way into his 2006 feature *Pan's Labyrinth*.

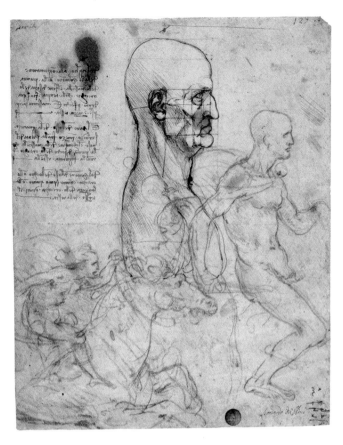

6.2 Leonardo da Vinci. *Facial Proportions of a Man in Profile*. 1490–95. Brown ink, charcoal, and red chalk. 11″ × 8¾″.

Gallerie dell'Accademia, Venice. © 2018. Photograph: Scala, Florence. Courtesy of the Ministero Beni e Att. Culturali.

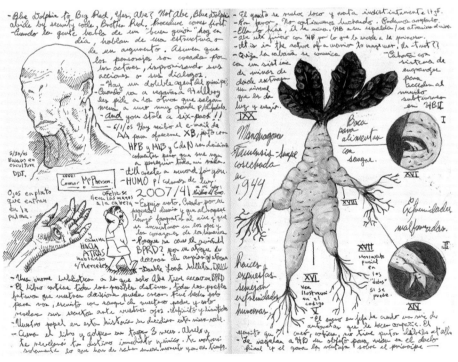

6.3 Guillermo del Toro. Pages from sketchbook. *Pan's Labyrinth*. 2006.

© MMVI. New Line Productions Inc. Photo appears courtesy of New Line Cinema/Time Warner.

Receptive and Projective Drawing

A great deal of drawing is receptive; that is, we use it to attempt to capture the physical appearance of something before us. Many people use drawing in this way, as they take up a pencil or pen or chalk to render the fall of light on a jar, the leaves of a tree, the arrangement of a landscape, the roundness of a body, or their own reflection in a mirror. The nineteenth-century artist Mary Cassatt, for example, took a sketchbook onto public transportation and captured a family group (**fig. 6.4**). One woman looks intently ahead as another tends to a small child. Drawings such as this can be a professional necessity for an artist, or recreation for the rest of us.

Other drawings, in contrast, are projective: We may draw something that exists only in our minds, either as a memory of something we have seen or a vision of something we imagine. Some of the most compelling projective drawings were created by the Mexican-American artist Martín Ramírez, who lived most of his life in a mental hospital. His imaginary scenes resound with fantasy and vision. In this untitled drawing (**fig. 6.5**), four animals inhabit shelves in

6.5   Martín Ramírez. *Untitled*. c.1953. Gouache, colored pencil, and graphite on pieced paper. 36″ × 24″.
NU 285.327. Courtesy Ricco of Maresca Gallery, New York. © Estate of Martín Ramírez.

the midst of a landscape that he created from parallel curving lines and dash marks. The empty background adds to the strong fantasy element of this work, making the entire composition seem to hover in space. Artists whose work is based on imagination often use this sort of drawing, as do architects when they plan new structures. Leonardo's drawings are more often projective than receptive; del Toro's *sketchbook* likewise combines projective and receptive approaches. The general tendency among today's artists in Europe and the United States seems to be toward projective types of drawing. These artists are also expanding the definition of the medium, as we shall see at the end of this chapter.

Drawing and the Creative Process

Many artists regard drawing as deeply important to their creative process. Contemporary sculptor Richard Serra, for example, said, "It's a place where I can get lost, and a place where I can throw out work, and a place where I don't have to worry about what it is I'm up to."[1] Keith Haring, in contrast, valued the immediacy: "Drawing is still the same as it has been since prehistoric times. It brings together man and the world. It lives through magic."[2]

6.4   Mary Cassatt. *In the Omnibus*. c.1891. Black chalk and graphite on paper.
National Gallery of Art, Washington, DC. 1948.11.51a.

6.6 Vincent van Gogh. *Carpenter.* c.1880.
Black crayon. 22″ × 15″.
Kröller-Müller Museum, Otterlo, Netherlands.

6.7 Vincent van Gogh. *Old Man with His Head in His
Hands.* 1882. Pencil on paper. 19¹¹⁄₁₆″ × 12³⁄₁₆″.
Van Gogh Museum, Amsterdam (Vincent van Gogh Foundation).

Some artists, such as Pablo Picasso, demonstrated exceptional drawing ability as young children. Others, such as the nineteenth-century artists Paul Cézanne and Vincent van Gogh, did not start out with obvious drawing ability; they developed skills through diligent effort. In spite of early difficulties, both succeeded in teaching themselves to draw. Their examples show that seeing and drawing are learned processes, not just inborn gifts.

Van Gogh learned a great deal about both seeing and painting through his practice of drawing (see *Vincent van Gogh: Mastering Drawing*, p. 100). He was just beginning his short career as an artist when he made the drawing *Carpenter* (**fig. 6.6**). Although the figure is stiff and clumsy in proportion, the drawing reveals van Gogh's careful observation and attention to detail. His letters to his brother Theo show how he struggled to render the world with pencil and crayon. In one of these notes, he recalled the difficulty and a breakthrough:

I remember quite well, now that you write about it, that at the time when you spoke of my becoming a painter, I thought it very impractical and would not hear of it. What made me stop doubting was

reading a clear book on perspective . . . and a week later I drew the interior of a kitchen with stove, chair, table, and window—in their places and on their legs—whereas before it had seemed to me that getting depth and the right perspective into a drawing was witchcraft or pure chance. If only you drew one thing right, you would feel an irresistible longing to draw a thousand other things.[3]

Old Man with His Head in His Hands (**fig. 6.7**), made two years after *Carpenter*, shows that van Gogh made great progress in seeing and drawing during those two years. By this time he was able to portray the old man's grief, as well as the solidity of the figure, and to give a suggestion of his surroundings. The groups of parallel lines appear to have been drawn quickly, with sensitivity and self-assurance.

Good drawing may appear deceptively simple, yet it can take years of patient work to learn to draw easily and effectively. According to one account, a person viewing a drawing by Constantin Brancusi with only a few quick lines asked the artist with some disgust, "How long did it take you to do this?" Brancusi replied, "Forty years."[4]

CREATORS

Vincent van Gogh: Mastering Drawing

6.8 Vincent van Gogh. *Self-Portrait with Felt Hat.* 1888. Oil on canvas. 17¼″ × 14¾″.

Van Gogh Museum, Amsterdam (Vincent van Gogh Foundation).

Vincent van Gogh (1853–1890) took up art not because he possessed any obvious talent, but because he saw art as a means of communication with others. Although he was determined to be a painter, he believed that he had to master drawing before he allowed himself to use color. His letters to his brother Theo show both the effort that he expended, and a certain rebellious attitude that he had toward the drawing methods of his day.

After attempting the careers of art dealer and lay preacher, van Gogh enrolled in a private drawing school where traditional techniques were taught. These included drawing from plaster casts of human body parts, which most art schools then used as teaching tools. Van Gogh disliked this routine:

> I utterly detest drawing from plaster casts—yet I had a couple of hands and feet hanging in the studio, though not for drawing. Once he [the teacher] spoke to me about drawing from plaster casts in a tone that even the worst teacher at the academy wouldn't have used, and I held my peace, but at home I got so angry about it that I threw the poor plaster moldings into the coal-scuttle, broken. And I thought: I'll draw from plaster casts when you lot become whole and white again and there are no longer any hands and feet of living people to draw.[5]

Once van Gogh started drawing from life, he found it so interesting that he kept it up for hours at a time:

> In these new drawings I'm starting the figures with the torso, and it seems to me that they're fuller and broader as a result. If 50 aren't enough, I'll draw 100 of them, and if that's still not enough, even more, until I've got what I want solidly, that's to say that everything is round, and there is, as it were, neither beginning nor end anywhere on the form, but it constitutes a single, harmonious, living whole.[6]

He hoped to go beyond mere photographic accuracy to capture moods and energies in the moments that he sketched: "What I'm trying to get with it is to be able to draw not a hand but the gesture, not a mathematically correct head but the overall expression. . . Life, in short."[7]

In 1888, van Gogh moved to southern France, where in little more than two years he produced most of the paintings for which he is now known. Parallel with his paintings, he also drew continually. His drawing *Trees with Ivy in the Garden of the Asylum* (**fig. 6.9**) is based on a painting that he completed in 1890. He described the subject of this drawing to his brother: "Thick tree trunks covered with ivy, the ground also covered with ivy and periwinkle; a stone bench and a bush with roses that have paled in the cool shadow. In the foreground a couple of plants with white calyces. It is green, violet and pink."[8] The drawing's distinctly busy welter of pen strokes and its crowded composition express some of the urgency that he felt when depicting the scene.

Van Gogh admired more simple styles of drawing, and the ability to capture a subject quickly (see fig. 6.23): "I envy the Japanese the extreme clarity that everything in their work has," he wrote in late 1888. "It's never dull, and never appears to be done too hastily. Their work is as simple as breathing, and they do a figure with a few confident strokes with the same ease as if it was as simple as buttoning your waistcoat. Ah, I must manage to do a figure with a few strokes."[9]

Although van Gogh struggled with drawing, he always believed in its importance for an artist. In 1888 he wrote to Theo: "What's always urgent is to draw, and whether it is done directly with a brush, or with something else such as a pen, you never do enough."[10] While most of his contemporaries could not see the value of his art, van Gogh's drawings and paintings are displayed today in major museums worldwide.

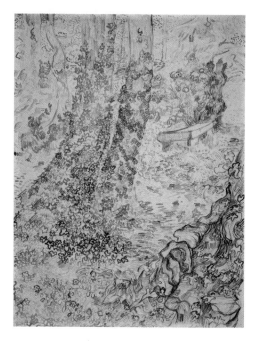

6.9 Vincent van Gogh. *Trees with Ivy in the Garden of the Asylum.* 1890. Reed pen and pen and ink on cream wove paper. 24½″ × 18½″.

Van Gogh Museum, Amsterdam (Vincent van Gogh Foundation).

Purposes of Drawing

A drawing can function in three ways:

- as a notation, sketch, or record of something seen, remembered, or imagined
- as a study or preparation for another, usually larger and more complex work
- as an end in itself, a complete work of art

We see examples of the first case in Henry Moore's *Study for Tube Shelter Perspective*, which began this chapter, and in the Vincent van Gogh drawings just examined. The second case, drawing as preparatory tool, is traditional in Western art. For example, Michelangelo made detailed studies of a *Reclining Male Nude* (**fig. 6.10**) for his finished painting of the figure on the ceiling of the Sistine Chapel (see fig. 17.9).

Michelangelo's studies are a record of exploration and discovery as he carefully drew what he observed. His knowledge of anatomy helped him to define each muscle. The flow between the head, shoulders, and arms of the figure is based on Michelangelo's feeling for visual continuity as well as his attention to detail. The parts of the figure that he felt needed further study he drew repeatedly, as we see in the hands. To achieve the dark reds, Michelangelo evidently licked the point of the chalk.

6.10 Michelangelo Buonarroti. *Study of a Reclining Male Nude.* c.1511. Red chalk over stylus underdrawing. 7⅞″ × 10¼″.

6.11 Pablo Picasso. First Composition Study for *Guernica*. May 1, 1937. Pencil on blue paper. 8¼″ × 10⅝″.

Museo Nacional Centro de Arte Reina Sofia, Madrid, Spain.
© 2018 Estate of Pablo Picasso/Artists Rights Society (ARS), New York.

6.12 Pablo Picasso. Composition study for *Guernica*. May 9, 1937. Pencil on white paper. 9½″ × 17⅞″.

Museo Nacional Centro de Arte Reina Sofia, Madrid, Spain.
© 2018 Estate of Pablo Picasso/Artists Rights Society (ARS), New York.

6.13 Pablo Picasso. *Guernica*. 1937. Oil on canvas. 11′6″ × 25′8″.

Museo Nacional Centro de Arte Reina Sofia, Madrid, Spain.
Art Resource/Scala, Florence/John Bigelow Taylor.
© 2018 Estate of Pablo Picasso/Artists Rights Society (ARS), New York.

A simple, tiny sketch, quickly done, is often the starting point for a far larger and more complex work. In such drawings an artist can work out problems of overall design or concentrate on small details. For example, Picasso did many studies in preparation for his major painting *Guernica* (**figs. 6.11–13**), a huge work measuring more than 11 by 25 feet. Forty-five of Picasso's studies are preserved and dated; they show the evolution of this important work.

The first drawing for *Guernica* shows a dark form at the top center; this later became a woman with a lamp, apparently an important symbol to Picasso. The woman leans out of a house in the upper right. On the left appears a bull with a bird on its back. Both the bull and the woman with the lamp are major elements in the final painting. The first drawing was probably completed in a few seconds, yet its quick, gestural lines contain the essence of the large, complex painting.

Although artists do not generally consider their preliminary sketches as finished pieces, studies by leading artists are often treasured both for their intrinsic beauty and for what they reveal about the creative process. Picasso recognized the importance of documenting this process from initial idea to finished painting:

> It would be very interesting to preserve photographically, not the stages, but the metamorphoses of a picture. Possibly one might then discover the path followed by the brain in materializing a dream. But there is one very odd thing to notice, that basically a picture doesn't change, that the first "vision" remains almost intact, in spite of appearances.[11]

Another type of preparatory drawing is the **cartoon**. The original meaning of cartoon, still used by art professionals, is a full-sized drawing made as a guide for a large work in another medium, particularly a mural, mosaic, or tapestry. In making the final work, artists often use such cartoons as overlays for tracing.

In today's common usage, the word *cartoon* also refers to a narrative drawing emphasizing humorous or satirical content. Cartoons and comics are among the most widely enjoyed drawings, and will be discussed later in this chapter.

Many artists today view drawing as a medium in itself, and drawings as finished works of art. Among these are several in this chapter, such as the works by William Kentridge (see fig. 6.25) and Julie Mehretu (see fig. 6.30).

Tools and Techniques

Each drawing tool and each type of paper has its own characteristics that influence the nature of the resulting drawing. The illustration Drawing Tools and Their Characteristic Lines (**fig. 6.14**) shows the different qualities of marks made by common drawing tools. Some of these tools give a dry, refined line; others are wet and more expressive. Note also how each tool responds to varying degrees of pressure; the ink brush in the middle is most responsive, the pen at the bottom, the least.

Artists often draw rows of parallel lines to suggest shadows or volumes. These lines are called **hatching**; each method is illustrated in the accompanying diagram, Types of Hatching (**fig. 6.15**).

The sixteenth-century Italian painter Bartolomeo Passarotti used all three of these methods in his sheet of studies (**fig. 6.16**). He used simple hatching in the small standing figure at the upper right. To render the look of a bulging, muscular arm, he used both **contour hatching** on the upper side and **cross-hatching** in the darker areas below. Printmakers often use all three types of hatching as well to suggest mass and shadow (see Chapter 8).

6.14 Drawing Tools and Their Characteristic Lines.

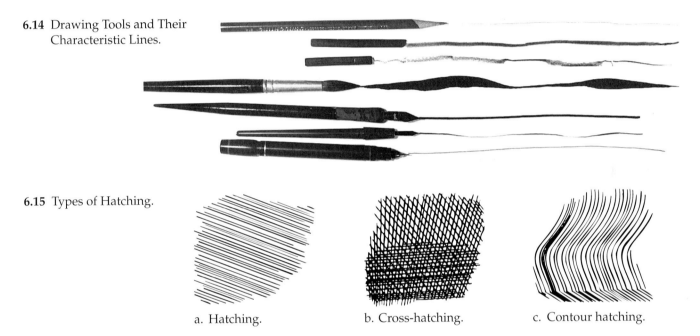

6.15 Types of Hatching.

a. Hatching.   b. Cross-hatching.   c. Contour hatching.

6.16 Bartolomeo Passarotti. *Studies of a Left Arm, a Young Woman,* etc. Undated 16th century. Pen and iron gall ink on laid paper. 7⅞″ × 11⅜″.
National Gallery of Art. 2000.124.1.a.

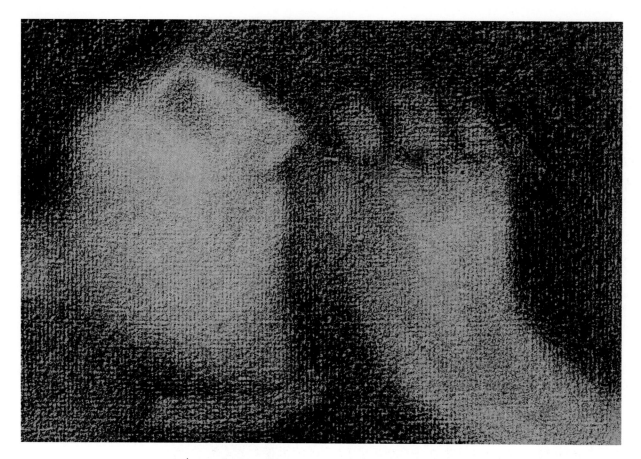

6.17 Georges Pierre Seurat. *L'Écho* (detail). 1883–84. Black Conté crayon on Michallet paper.
Yale University Art Gallery, New Haven, Connecticut, USA. Bequest of Edith Malvina K. Wetmore.

The quality and type of paper that an artist uses also have an important impact on the drawing. Most drawing surfaces are smooth, but some papers have **tooth**, a quality of roughness or surface grain that gives texture to a drawing. Georges Seurat worked on very toothy paper to draw the child's face and cupped hand in *L'Écho* (**fig. 6.17**); this detail from the larger work (**fig. 6.20**) shows the weave of the paper fibers.

Dry Media

Dry drawing media include pencil, **charcoal**, **Conté crayon**, and **pastel**. Most drawing pencils are made of graphite (a crystalline form of carbon). They are available in varying degrees of hardness; softer pencils give darker lines, and harder pencils give lighter ones.

Darkness and line quality are determined both by the degree of hardness of the pencil and by the texture of the drawing surface. Pencil lines can vary in width or length, can be made by using the side of the pencil point in broad strokes, and can be repeated as hatching. Artists create a considerable range of values by varying the pressure on a medium–soft drawing pencil.

Umberto Boccioni used a variety of tools and techniques to create his drawing *States of Mind: The Farewells* (**fig. 6.18**). We see sharp lines, strokes made with the side of the charcoal, parallel hatched lines, and shaded areas.

The sticks of charcoal used today are similar to those used by prehistoric peoples to draw on cave walls: Both are simply charred sticks of wood. With charcoal, dark areas can be drawn quickly. Charcoal produces a wide range of light to dark values, from soft grays to deep velvety blacks. The various hard-to-soft grades of charcoal provide a versatile medium for both beginning and advanced artists. Because not all charcoal particles bind to the surface of the paper, charcoal is easy to smudge, blur, or erase. This quality is both an advantage and a drawback: it enables quick changes, but finished works can easily smear. A completed charcoal drawing may be set or "fixed" with a thin varnish called a **fixative**, which is sprayed over it to help seal the charcoal onto the paper and prevent smudging.

We see many shades of gray in the remarkable drawing *Web #5* by Vija Celmins (**fig. 6.19**). The web emerges from darkness at the upper left, as the artist carefully shaded each concentric circle. She made only black marks, letting

the paper show through for the white portions. She even captured the web's flaws and incomplete parts.

Conté crayon is made from graphite that is mixed with clay and pressed into sticks. It can produce varied lines or broad strokes that resist smudging far more than charcoal. Wax-based crayons, such as those that children use, are avoided by serious artists; they lack flexibility, and most fade over time. Because the strokes of color do not blend easily, it is difficult to obtain bright color mixtures with wax crayons.

Georges Seurat used Conté crayon to build up the illusion of three-dimensional form through value gradations (chiaroscuro) in his drawing *L'Écho* (**fig. 6.20**). Seurat actually drew a multitude of lines, yet in the final drawing the individual lines are obscured by the total effect of finely textured light and dark areas. He selected Conté crayon on rough paper as a means of concentrating on basic forms and on the interplay of light and shadow.

Natural chalks of red, white, and black have been used for drawing since ancient times. Pastels, produced since the

6.21 Rosalba Carriera. *Portrait of a Girl with a Bussola.* 1725–30. Pastel on paper. 13⅜″ × 10½″.
Gallerie dell'Accademia, Venice. © Cameraphoto Arte, Venice.

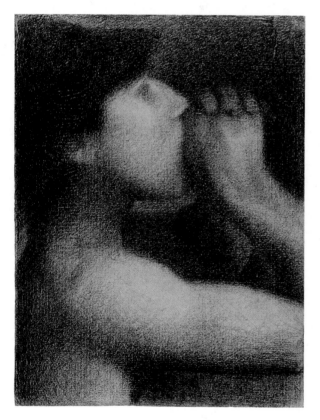

6.20 Georges Pierre Seurat. *L'Écho.* 1883–84. Black Conté crayon on Michallet paper. 12⅝₁₆″ × 9⁷⁄₁₆″.
Yale University Art Gallery, New Haven, Connecticut, USA. Bequest of Edith Malvina K. Wetmore.

seventeenth century, have characteristics similar to those of natural chalk. They have a freshness and purity of color because they are composed mostly of pigment, with very little binding material. Because no drying is needed, there is no change in color, as occurs in some paints as they dry. Soft pastels do not allow for much detail; they force the user to work boldly. Blending of strokes with fingers or a paper stump made for the purpose produces a soft blur that lightly mixes the colors. Pastels yield the most exciting results when not overworked.

Venetian portraitist Rosalba Carriera made dozens of works with pastels in the early eighteenth century. Her *Portrait of a Girl with a Bussola* (**fig. 6.21**) shows her sensitivity to the medium. The hard, fine-grained pastels in common use at that time give the finished work a smooth surface that makes possible fine color shadings. Because of the artist's light, deft touch with short strokes of the pastel, the work resembles an oil painting in its appearance, an effect promoted by the very smooth paper.

French artist Edgar Degas shifted his attention from oil painting to pastels in his later years, and occasionally he combined the two in a single work. He took advantage of the rich colors and subtle blends possible with pastel. Although carefully constructed, his compositions look like casual, fleeting glimpses of everyday life. In *Le Petit Déjeuner après le bain* (*Breakfast after the Bath*) (**fig. 6.22**), bold contours give a sense of movement to the whole design. He drew the work in pastels coarser than the fine-grained ones that Carriera used; we can see the difference by comparing the level of detail in each work.

Liquid Media

Black and brown inks are the most common drawing liquids. Some brush drawings are made with **washes** of ink thinned with water. Such ink drawings are similar to watercolor paintings. Felt- and fiber-tipped marker pens are widely used recent additions to the traditional pen-and-ink media.

Nineteenth-century Japanese artist Katsushika Hokusai, a skilled and prolific draftsman, is said to have created about 13,000 prints and drawings during his lifetime. In *Tuning the Samisen* (**fig. 6.23**), the expressive elegance of his lines was made possible by his control of the responsive brush. In Asia, the same brushes are used for traditional writing and for drawing. These brushes are ideal for making calligraphic lines because they hold a substantial amount of ink and readily produce lines thick and thin under varying pressure. Hokusai played the uniformly thin lines of head, hands, and instrument against the bold, spontaneous strokes indicating the folds of the kimono. We can follow some of his longer brushstrokes with our eyes, watching as the line grows thicker or thinner.

6.22 Edgar Degas. *Le Petit Déjeuner après le bain (jeune femme s'essuyant).* c.1894. Pastel on paper. 39¼″ × 23½″.
Private Collection/Photo © Christie's Images/Bridgeman Images.

6.23 Hokusai. *Tuning the Samisen.* c.1820–25. Brush drawing. 9¾″ × 8¼″.
Freer Gallery of Art and Arthur M. Sackler Gallery, Smithsonian Institution, Washington, D.C. Gift of Charles Lang Freer, F1904.241.

6.24 Rembrandt van Rijn. *Eliezer and Rebecca at the Well*. 1640s. Reed pen and brown ink
with brown wash and white gouache. 8¼″ × 13¹⁄₁₆″.
National Gallery of Art, Washington, D.C. Widener Collection 1942.9.665.

In *Eliezer and Rebecca at the Well* (**fig. 6.24**), the seventeenth-century artist Rembrandt van Rijn used liquid media to sketch quickly a compositional arrangement for a possible painting. Pens of varying widths yield ink strokes that show his speed of execution. He used parallel hatching lines for darker areas, and further darkened several of these regions with brown wash, especially in the right half of the page. In a few places—near the foot of the cliff, at Eliezer's knee, and near the top of the mountain at the right—he lightened his previous shadings by applying white **gouache**, a type of opaque watercolor. This drawing shows Rembrandt at his most spontaneous; he probably had little idea that we would be studying it centuries later. The inscriptions along the lower edge come from a later owner.

Some artists today create drawings and offer them as finished works because they value the immediacy and spontaneity of drawing. One of these is the South African William Kentridge. He created Drawing for "Lulu" (**fig. 6.25**) using both wet and dry media over pages of an obsolete dictionary. He told an interviewer that he enjoys working on such paper because it represents faded authority. This work is a portrait of the composer Alban Berg, whom the artist admired. The quick execution of the drawing finds a parallel in the casually slapped-together pages. He has also created drawings for animation, in which each drawing is photographed individually and projected in rapid succession, similar to movie frames.

Comics and Graphic Novels

A comic is a sequential artform based on drawing. Printed comics represent the culmination of a development that includes some ancient Egyptian murals, medieval

6.25 William Kentridge. Drawing for "Lulu". 2015. Indian ink and charcoal on
Shorter Oxford Dictionary pages. 22¼" x 33½".
Courtesy of the artist and Marian Goodman Gallery, New York.

tapestries, and some print series created in the 1730s. They have been a popular feature in newspapers for more than 100 years. One of the most imaginative of the early newspaper comics was *Little Nemo in Slumberland* (**fig. 6.26**), which narrated and illustrated a child's fantastic dreams. In the example shown here—the last line of a full-page comic—a tuba player loses control of his instrument as it lengthens with every note that he plays.

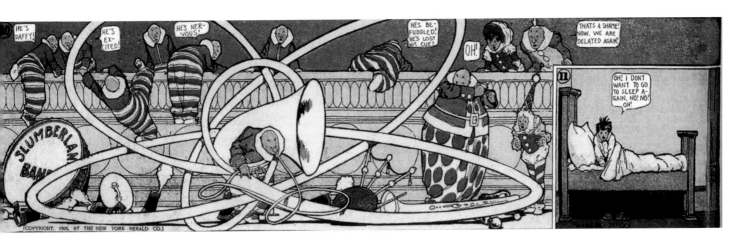

6.26 Windsor McCay. *Little Nemo in Slumberland* (detail).
New York Herald, 4 April 1906.

In recent years, comics have become a much more serious artform, as their creators take up unusual or important subjects. In the 1980s, Los Angeles-based Gilbert Hernandez teamed with his brothers Jaime and Mario to create *Love and Rockets*, one of the longest-running comics. This series dealt with gang life, love and romance, and social issues that the Southern California Mexican-American community faced. When the series came to an end in 1996, Gilbert began drawing highly imaginative short stories that were collected into the volume *Fear of Comics* (**fig. 6.27**) in 2000. These stories show a wide range of characters and themes (not all of them publishable in a text such as this). In one story, for example, Gilbert takes Herman Melville's classic novel *Moby-Dick* and boils it down to six crisply drawn frames.

6.27 Gilbert Hernandez. Cover of *Fear of Comics*. 2000.

6.28 Emily Carroll. *All Along the Wall*. Webcomic. 2014. Dimensions variable.

6.29 Richard McGuire. Excerpt from *Here*. 2015.

More ambitious are graphic novels, which resemble comic books but have book-length story lines. The increasing acceptance of this type of novel has led major publishers to seek out artists and produce their work for national distribution. One of the most successful such artists in recent years is the Canadian-born Emily Carroll. Her graphic novels and stories update ancient horror tales by locating them in contemporary situations. She also works frequently on the Internet, where she posts webcomics for all to see. For example, she created her recent story *All Along the Wall* (**fig. 6.28**) by scanning pen drawings and loading them into Photoshop for alteration and finishing. This story is about a girl who finds herself bored at a family holiday party, so she asks to hear a horror story. We access this work by clicking and scrolling instead of turning pages.

Graphic novelist Richard McGuire goes further into interactivity with his hand-drawn stories. His 2015 graphic novel *Here* was first published on paper in 1989 (**fig. 6.29**). It tells the story of one person's life as it progresses in a single house at various moments in time. In the interactive version, which is accessible on either a computer or a tablet screen, the various dates in each frame become "hot spots" for viewers to click on. They decide for themselves how to unfold the story. Different events at widely different times can share the same screen. This graphic novel reaches back into the ancient past and forward to the future, bending our sense of time.

Contemporary Approaches

Today's artists have considerably expanded the definitions and uses of drawing. Many use it in combination with other media in finished works. Some artists create works in new ways using new media, and label them drawings because no other name quite describes what they do. Julie Mehretu, for example, uses media from both drawing and painting in the same large works. Her *Back to Gondwanaland* (**fig. 6.30**) includes colored swatches of cut paper along with drawn ink lines. She makes abstract drawings, but the shapes she uses generally suggest the impersonal public spaces of today's mass-produced world: offices, classrooms, airports, and stadiums. If drawing has been traditionally an organic process, her works do not look entirely handmade.

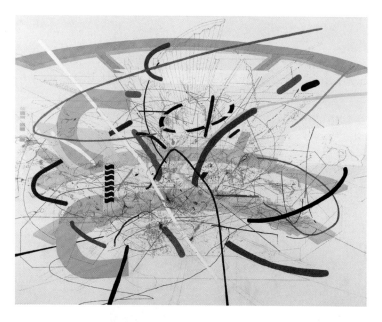

6.30 Julie Mehretu. *Back to Gondwanaland*. 2000. Ink and acrylic on canvas. 8′ × 10′.

Collection A & J Gordts-Vanthournout, Belgium. Courtesy of the artist and Marian Goodman Gallery.

Rather, they exist in a gap between the natural and the manufactured, and between drawing and painting.

Christine Hiebert makes lines directly on walls with the blue tape that painters use to mask negative spaces. In works that she creates specifically for each exhibition,

6.31 Christine Hiebert. *Reconnaissance* (detail view). 2009–10. Blue tape and glue on wall. Wall coverage approx. 110′ running wall length × approx. 35′ high.

Installation view from the Davis Museum at Wellesley College. Photograph © Christine Hiebert.

her lines affect our perception of the space. In her work *Reconnaissance* (**fig. 6.31**), for example, she interrupted the clean horizontals and verticals of a gallery with diagonals of varying thickness. Her lines resemble drawn lines, but in fact she has "drawn" the tape across the walls. When the show is over, the tape comes off without leaving a trace.

The drawings of Ingrid Calame begin as rubbings taken from highly textured surfaces. For *#334 Drawing, Babel in Wonderland* (**fig. 6.32**), she visited an abandoned steel plant in upstate New York, and the cement-lined pathway of the Los Angeles River. She selects and combines rubbings by overlaying them, and then she laboriously copies each layer with colored pencil. Each color in a final drawing comes from a different initial rubbing. These drawings render the most minute details of the floor beneath us, exactly and painstakingly, in images of eerie beauty.

An increasing (but still small) number of artists have begun to routinely employ digital screen-based drawing techniques and to create works with them. Carla Gannis, for example, makes self-portraits by taking selfies and then altering them using these new media. *The Selfie Drawings* is a series of 52 works that she created over the course of one year in 2015. She put her photographic self-portrait through all sorts of manipulations, adding text or drawing, adding layers or color, or cropping and duplicating. Many of these drawings refer to earlier works in the history of art. Number 41 in the series (**fig. 6.33**) shows her own body poking out of a Tower of Babel, which is based on a famous 1563 work with that title. Gannis created some of the clouds that roll by with the clone stamp tool in Photoshop. We see the artist herself doing financial calculations on a screen with a stylus. The numbers are backward, as if she were writing on the other side of the transparent screen. Artists throughout history have made self-portraits as vehicles for self-examination; Gannis sees herself in the latest media, filtering her identity through historic images.

At the time of writing, Google was introducing a digital system called Tilt Brush that enables drawing in three dimensions. By donning a virtual-reality headset and holding the proper tools, users can select colors and stroke styles from a digital palette in one hand and then draw in space with the other. Results are visible only through the headset, but the work can be saved for later use or for enjoyment by another viewer. We can only speculate about the possible uses for this technology.

6.32 Ingrid Calame. *#334 Drawing (Tracings from the L.A. River and ArcelorMittal Steel).* 2011. Colored pencil on tracing Mylar. 115¼″ × 75″ × 3¼″.

Courtesy of Susanne Vielmetter Los Angeles Projects and James Cohan Gallery, New York/Shanghai.

As we have seen in the examples in this chapter, drawing is an immediate way to communicate through imagery. It enables artists to share their ideas, feelings, experiences, and imaginings with us whether in a sketch, a preparatory study, or a finished work.

6.33 Carla Gannis. *Selfie Drawing #41, Babel in Wonderland.* 2015. Digital drawing. 40″ × 40″.

© Carla Gannis 2017. Courtesy of the artist.

KEY TERMS

cartoon – a full-size drawing made as a guide for a large work in another medium, particularly a fresco painting, mosaic, or tapestry; a humorous or satirical drawing

charcoal – a dry drawing medium made from charred twigs, usually vine or willow

Conté crayon – a drawing medium developed in the late eighteenth century; similar to pencil in its graphic content, includes clay and small amounts of wax

contour hatching – a set of parallel curved lines that suggest a volume in space

cross-hatching – drawing one set of hatchings over another in a different direction so that the lines cross

fixative – a light, liquid varnish sprayed over finished charcoal or pastel drawings to prevent smudging

gouache – an opaque water-soluble paint

hatching – a technique in which lines are placed in parallel series to darken the value of an area

pastels – sticks of powdered pigment held together with a gum binding agent

tooth – a quality of roughness or surface grain in paper that gives texture to a drawing

wash – a thin, transparent layer of paint or ink

7 PAINTING

LEARNING OBJECTIVES

7.1 Distinguish between the pigment, binder, vehicle, and support in paintings.

7.2 Explain the composition of watercolor and some reasons artists use this medium.

7.3 Summarize the process of creating a fresco.

7.4 Describe the composition and technique of encaustic.

7.5 Identify the characteristics of tempera.

7.6 Discuss the reasons for the popularity of oil paint.

7.7 Explain the recent rise in the use of acrylic paint.

7.8 Demonstrate knowledge of contemporary innovations in tools and supports for paint.

7.1 Gerhard Richter. *Abstract Painting.* 1984. Oil on canvas. 17″ × 23⅝″.
© Gerhard Richter 2018.

Drawing and painting are related, overlapping processes. Drawing is often a prelude to painting. Paint strokes often resemble drawing techniques. In Gerhard Richter's *Abstract Painting* (**fig. 7.1**), the medium (paint) and the process of its application are a major part of the message. Richter's invented landscape suggests rugged forms in the foreground and an open, distant sky. Large brushstrokes of thickly applied oil paint in the foreground contrast with the smooth gradations of tone in the sky area, showing us some of the range of textures possible with the medium.

For many people across the world, the word "art" means painting. The long, rich history of painting, the strong appeal of color, and the endless image-making possibilities have made painting a preferred medium for both artists and viewers for centuries.

In this chapter we will look at the process of making paintings, and then explore the unique characteristics, advantages, and disadvantages of the most common types of paint. We will conclude with a look at some of the ways in which contemporary artists are stretching the boundaries of the medium.

Ingredients and Surfaces

All paints consist of three ingredients: **pigment**, **binder**, and **vehicle**. The pigment provides color, usually in the form of a very fine powder. Some of the purest and most brilliant colors available to the human eye are in pigment powders. The people who made the earliest cave paintings used natural pigments obtained from plants and nearby deposits of minerals and clays. Pigments used in cave paintings at Pont d'Arc, France—including blacks from charred woods and earth colors—have lasted more than 30,000 years (see fig. 15.6).

Artists prefer pigment colors that remain stable during the execution of a work and resist fading over time. Ground minerals and dried plant juices were the most common of the many natural pigment sources in ancient times. More exotic pigments have included powdered animal urine and even dried insect blood. In the nineteenth and twentieth centuries, major advances in the chemical industry made it possible to produce synthetic pigments that extend the available range of stable colors. Since then, the durability of both natural and synthetic pigments has improved. Most of the same pigment powders are used in manufacturing the various painting and drawing media.

The binder is a sticky substance that holds the pigment particles together and attaches the pigment to the surface. Binders vary with the type of paint: Oil paint, for example, contains linseed oil as a binder, while traditional **tempera** uses egg yolk. By Rembrandt van Rijn's time, the seventeenth century, painters or their assistants mixed finely ground pigments with oil by hand until the paint reached a desirable fineness and consistency. The invention of tubes for oil paint in the nineteenth century made it possible for artists to take their work outdoors and paint on the spot. This helped to enable the Impressionist style.

The vehicle makes the paint a liquid, and can be added to the paint for thinning. In traditional oil paint, turpentine is the vehicle; watercolors, of course, use water.

Paint surfaces require a **support**, or structure to hold them. Wood panel, stretched canvas, and paper are common supports. Many of these supports require sealing, to lessen their absorptive qualities and to smooth them by filling in the pores of the material. Such sealant is usually called **sizing** or size, and is generally made from liquid clay, wax, or glue. Wood and canvas usually require sizing by artists (or their assistants), while paper used for watercolor is generally manufactured with a small amount of sizing included. Over the sizing (or instead of it), artists often apply a **primer** (usually white) in order to create a uniform surface. The sizing plus the primer creates the ground of a painting, and constitutes the surface preparation that artists generally do.

We will now consider the most common painting media in historical order of their appearance.

Watercolor

Artists have used water-based paint media for thousands of years. Paints very similar to modern watercolor appear in paintings from ancient Egypt, and also in ancient Chinese manuscripts.

In **watercolor**, pigments are mixed with water as a vehicle and gum arabic (sap from the acacia tree) as a binder. The most common support today is white rag paper (made from cotton rag), because of its superior absorbency and longevity. Such paper usually requires no priming; the paper itself is both the ground and the support. Watercolor was traditionally sold in solid blocks that the painter mixed with water to reach the desired thickness; today most professional watercolor is sold in tubes.

7.2 Winslow Homer. *Boys Wading*. 1873. Watercolor and gouache over graphite on wove paper sheet. 9¾″ × 13¾″.
National Gallery of Art, Washington, D.C. 2014.18.15.

Watercolor is basically a staining technique. The paint is applied in thin, translucent washes that allow light to pass through the layers of color and to reflect back from the white paper. Highlights are obtained by leaving areas of white paper unpainted. Opaque (nontranslucent) watercolor is sometimes added for detail. Watercolors are well suited to spontaneous as well as carefully planned applications. Despite the simple materials involved, watercolor is a demanding medium because the absorbency of the paper support does not permit easy changes or corrections. Moreover, if you overwork a watercolor, you lose its characteristic freshness.

Watercolor's fluid spontaneity makes it a favorite medium for painters who want to catch quick impressions outdoors. The translucent quality of watercolor washes particularly suits depictions of water, atmosphere, light, and weather.

Nineteenth-century American artist Winslow Homer was among the most devoted to watercolor. His 1873 work *Boys Wading* (**fig. 7.2**) shows many of watercolor's properties. Both the boys and the water seem quickly sketched; the background shapes are flatter, which reflects how things farther away appear to our eyes under bright light. The water and the foreground shoreline

7.3 Li Shida. *Five Deer Hermitage*. Not dated, early 17th century. Ink and color on gold-flecked paper. 12½ x 24".

are quickly brushed, with mostly horizontal strokes. In order to capture the dappled surface of the water, Homer used strokes of analogous colors. The brightness of the boys' shirts in the sunshine was easy to achieve with this transparent medium.

Homer created the highlights on the water after the first layer had dried by applying opaque watercolor, also known as **gouache**. We see these strokes most clearly at the left near the shoreline. Gouache is watercolor with small amounts of white chalk powder added for opacity. It was common in book illustration during the European Middle Ages, and also in traditional Persian art. It is popular in our times with designers and illustrators because of its ease of use and low cost.

In traditional Chinese watercolor technique, the artist employs water-based black ink as well as color, and often uses the ink without color. The Chinese regard painting as descended from the art of calligraphy, which is also done with black ink. In Asia, black ink painting is a fully developed artform, accorded at least as much honor as painting with color.

A good example of a traditional Chinese painting that uses both ink and watercolor is *Five Deer Hermitage* by Li Shida (**fig. 7.3**). The artist used ink for the black areas such as roof lines, with watercolor in the green and bluish areas. He also used many different types of brushstroke, most of them small in scale, which he learned by making calligraphy; we see this most clearly in the foliage.

Fresco

In true **fresco**, pigments suspended in water are applied to a damp lime-plaster surface. The vehicle is water, and the binder is the lime present in the damp plaster. The earliest true fresco paintings date from about 1800 BCE at a site in today's southwestern Turkey. The technique was also practiced in some cultures of pre-Columbian Mexico.

In Renaissance Italy, fresco was the favored medium for painting on church walls. Probably the best-known fresco paintings are those by Michelangelo on the Sistine Chapel ceiling in the Vatican (see fig. 17.9). His contemporary Raphael also created frescoes. We see a close-up of his technique in *Assumed Portrait of Francesco Maria della Rovere* (**fig. 7.4**). This is a detail of the much larger work *The School of Athens* (see fig. 3.22).

Most fresco painters first prepare a full-size drawing in the form of a cartoon, then transfer the design to the freshly laid plaster wall before painting. Because the plaster dries quickly, only the portion of the wall that can be painted in one day is prepared; joints between each day's work are usually arranged along the edges of major shapes in the composition.

The painter works quickly in a rapid staining process similar to watercolor. Lime, in contact with air, forms transparent calcium crystals that chemically bind the pigment to the moist lime-plaster wall. The lime in the plaster thus becomes the binder, creating a smooth, extremely durable surface. Once the surface has dried, the painting is part of the wall, rather than resting on its surface. Because lime-plaster walls are subject to mold infestations, fresco is most suitable to drier climatic zones.

The artist must have the design completely worked out before painting, because no changes can be made after

7.4 Raphael. *Assumed Portrait of Francesco Maria della Rovere*, detail from *The School of Athens*. c.1510–12. Fresco.
Vatican, Stanza della Segnatura. © 2018. Photograph: Scala, Florence.

7.5   Diego Rivera. Mural depicting *Detroit Industry*. 1932–33. Fresco.

the paint is applied to the fresh plaster. Fresco technique does not permit the delicate manipulation of transitional tones; but the luminosity, fine surface, and permanent color make it an ideal medium for large murals. (A **mural** is any wall-size painting; fresco is one possible medium for such a work.)

Fresco secco (dry fresco), another ancient wall-painting method, is done on finished, dried lime-plaster walls. With this technique, tempera paint is applied to a clean, dry surface or over an already dried true fresco to achieve greater color intensity than is possible with true fresco alone. Fresco painters often retouch their work, or put on finishing details, in *fresco secco* over the true fresco.

After the Renaissance and Baroque periods, fresco became less popular, being eclipsed by the more flexible oil medium. However, a revival of the fresco technique began in Mexico in the 1920s, encouraged by the new revolutionary government's support for the arts. A fresco mural is often a piece of public art that cannot be bought or sold; such a mural in a public place is available to all classes of people equally. This characteristic motivated the Mexican government in the 1920s to pay painters at union wages to decorate public buildings with murals, most of them in fresco. Diego Rivera was a leader in this movement, which influenced art in the United States. The Detroit Institute of Arts invited him to create *Detroit Industry* (**fig. 7.5**) in true fresco in the lobby. The largest panel of this large work depicts the manufacture of automobile engines. The panels above show raw materials in the earth; those at the wings depict scientific advances.

Encaustic

Encaustic was known to the ancient Greeks, and flourished in Egypt during the time when it was a Roman colony. Encaustic pigments are suspended in hot beeswax, resulting in lustrous surfaces that bring out the full richness of colors. The wax is both binder and vehicle. The Egyptian city of Fayum was a center of encaustic painting during the second century CE. Fayum portraits, such as *Portrait of a Boy* (**fig. 7.6**), were memorials to the deceased, painted directly on their wooden coffins. These are the earliest surviving encaustic works. In these portraits the sense of lifelike individuality remains strong, and colors have retained their intensity after almost 2,000 years.

Early practitioners found it difficult to keep the wax binder of encaustic at the right temperature for proper handling. Although modern electrical heating devices make such temperature maintenance easier, encaustic is less commonly used today.

One modern artist who made consistent use of encaustic was Jasper Johns. His encaustic works from the 1950s, such as *Three Flags* (**fig. 7.7**), show another characteristic of the medium: The waxy consistency of the paint easily yields a textured surface, because each brushstroke begins to harden immediately after application as the wax cools. Johns applied paint with a loaded brush, and as a result we can see nearly every stroke that he made. *Three Flags* consists of three canvases attached together. The artist used this common patriotic symbol in order to investigate what a painting is, because both a flag and a painting are colored canvases. The textured encaustic surface helps to highlight the difference between the two.

7.6 *Portrait of a Boy.* c.100–50 CE.
Encaustic on wood. 15″ × 7½″.
Metropolitan Museum of Art. Gift of Edward S. Harkness, 1918. (18.9.2).

Tempera

Tempera was also known to the Greeks and Romans, but was highly developed during the late Middle Ages, when it was used for small paintings on wood panels. Since those times the principal tempera medium has been egg tempera, in which egg yolk is the binder, mixed in equal parts with pigment powder and then thinned with water as a vehicle. Tempera is little used today, and as a result the word has changed its meaning. Today, "tempera" is often used for water-based paints such as poster paints or paints with binders of glue or milk protein.

Traditional egg tempera has a luminous, slightly **matte** (not shiny) surface when dry. Because it cannot be mixed after it is applied, artists generally apply tempera in thin layers to build up desired shades of color. The preferred ground for egg tempera is **gesso**, a chalky, water-based liquid that dries to a bright white.

Egg tempera is good for achieving sharp lines and precise details, and it does not darken with age. However, its colors change during drying, and blending and reworking are difficult because tempera dries rapidly.

7.7 Jasper Johns.
Three Flags. 1958.
Encaustic on canvas.
30⅝″ × 45½″ × 4⅝″.

Whitney Museum of American
Art, New York; purchase,
with funds from the Gilman
Foundation, Inc., The Lauder
Foundation, A. Alfred Taubman,
Laura Lee Whittier Woods,
Howard Lipman, and Ed Downe
in honor of the Museum's
50th Anniversary 80.32.
© Jasper Johns/Licensed
by VAGA, New York.

Tempera painting traditionally requires complete preliminary drawing and pale underpainting because of its translucency and the difficulty in making changes. Overpainting is done by applying layers of translucent paint in small, careful strokes. Because tempera lacks flexibility, movement of the support may cause the gesso and pigment to crack. Thus a rigid support, such as a wood panel, is required.

Most modern artists have found little use for tempera, but one who used it to good effect was George Tooker. The painstaking execution and high detail of a work such as *The Waiting Room* (**fig. 7.8**) enhance its haunted quality. This work is not based on direct observation, but most of us might recognize the oppressive atmosphere of a waiting room in it. The artist said that the slowness of working in tempera fit his way of thinking.

7.8 George Tooker.
The Waiting Room.
1959. Egg tempera
on wood. 24″ × 30″.

Smithsonian American Art
Museum. Gift of S.C. Johnson
& Son, Inc. 1969.47.43. ©
2018. Photograph: Smithsonian
American Art Museum/Art
Resource/Scala, Florence.
© Estate of George Tooker.
Courtesy of DC Moore Gallery,
New York.

Oil

In Western art, oil paint has been a favorite medium for five centuries. Pigments mixed with various vegetable oils, such as linseed, walnut, and poppyseed, were used in the Middle Ages for decorative purposes. But, beginning in the fifteenth century, oil painting flourished when Flemish painters perfected a recipe for paint made with a binder of linseed oil pressed from the seeds of the flax plant, mixed with turpentine as a vehicle. In this early period, artists applied oil paint to wood panels covered with smooth layers of gesso, as in the older tradition of tempera painting.

The brothers Hubert and Jan van Eyck were among the early leaders of European oil painting. They achieved glowing, jewel-like surfaces that remain amazingly fresh to the present day. Jan van Eyck's *Madonna and Child with the Chancellor Rolin* (**fig. 7.9**) is an example of his early mastery of the oil technique. Jan painted it on a small gesso-covered wood panel. After beginning with a brush drawing in tempera, he proceeded with thin layers of oil paint,

moving from light to dark and from opaque to translucent colors. The luminous quality of the surface is the result of successive oil glazes. A **glaze** is a very thin, transparent film of color applied over a previously painted surface. To produce glazes, oil colors selected for their transparency are diluted with a mixture of oil and varnish. Glazes give depth to painted surfaces by allowing light to pass through and reflect from lower paint layers.

In this painting, the sparkling jewels, the textiles, and the furs each show their own refined textures. Within the context of the religious subject, the artist demonstrated his enthusiasm for the delights of the visible world. Veils of glazes in the sky area provide atmospheric perspective and thus contribute to the illusion of deep space in the enticing view beyond the open window. The evolution in the new oil painting technique made such realism possible.

Oil has many advantages over other traditional media. Compared to tempera, oil paint can provide both increased opacity—which yields better covering power—and, when thinned, greater transparency. Its slow drying time is a distinct advantage, allowing artists to blend strokes of color and make changes during the painting process. Pigment colors in oil change little when drying; however, the binder (usually linseed oil) has a tendency to darken and yellow slightly with age. Because layers of dried oil paint are flexible, sixteenth-century Venetian painters who wished to paint large pictures replaced heavy wood panels with canvas stretched on wood frames. A painted canvas is not only light in weight but can also be unstretched and rolled for transporting if the paint layer is not too thick. Most oil painters today still prefer canvas supports.

Oil can be applied thickly or thinly, wet onto wet or wet onto dry. When applied thickly, it is called **impasto**, a variation of the word paste (oil paint works best for this technique). Artists use impasto when they feel that a richly textured surface is appropriate

7.9 Jan van Eyck. *Madonna and Child with the Chancellor Rolin.* c.1433–34. Oil and tempera on panel. 26″ × 24⅜″.
Louvre Museum, Paris. Photograph: akg-images/Erich Lessing.

7.10 Tom Wudl. *Rembrandt's Indulgence was Van Gogh's Dilemma*. 1991. Oil on canvas. 4″ × 3″.

for their message. When a work is painted wet onto wet and completed at one sitting, the process is called the **direct painting** method.

Tom Wudl used the direct method to create his small work *Rembrandt's Indulgence was Van Gogh's Dilemma* (**fig. 7.10**), shown here slightly larger than actual size. He created this work to test the properties of oil paint, and indeed it shows many traits of the medium. In this painting we see the texture of the canvas at the edges, covered with a white ground. The artist built up layers of impasto near the top of the work, showing the piled-up strokes that oil-based paint makes possible. The paint must be relatively thick, like paste, to create this effect. Below, curving strokes in shades of yellow swim around. Here he thinned the paint by adding turpentine. At the center is a meticulous depiction of a metal pitcher similar to one that the artist saw in a painting by Rembrandt. In that portion of the work, Wudl smoothed over his brushstrokes to heighten the *trompe l'oeil* qualities. He titled the work after two historical artists, Rembrandt and van Gogh, whose treatment of oil paint was innovative. This tiny work, alongside *Madonna and Child with the Chancellor Rolin,* shows us a wide range of the capabilities of the medium.

More recently, oil painters have broken out of the box of the rectangular canvas. Elizabeth Murray was a leader in this, as she painted on irregular shapes that she bolted together into whimsical and high-spirited creations (see *Elizabeth Murray: Paintings Let Out of the Zoo* on p. 124). *Bop* (**fig. 7.11**) is an array of jagged and irregular surfaces that the artist titled after a style of jazz music that she enjoyed listening to as she worked. She found the subject matter in something from her daily life. She said, "When you walk out of the studio, and you walk down the street, that's where you find art; you find it in the street. Or you find it at home, right in front of you. I paint about the things that surround me—things that I pick up and handle every day. That's what art is. Art is an epiphany in a coffee cup."[1]

7.11 Elizabeth Murray. *Bop*. 2002–3. Oil on canvas. 9′10″ × 10′10½″.

Elizabeth Murray: Paintings Let Out of the Zoo

7.12 Portrait of Elizabeth Murray.
Photograph by Ellen Page Wilson, June 1999. Courtesy of The Pace Gallery, New York.

"I never thought of myself as very talented," Elizabeth Murray (1940–2012) told an interviewer in 1991. "It's just that I found something that I really wanted to do."[2]

Murray was born in Chicago and grew up wanting to be a commercial artist. "All my ideas about art came from looking at comic books," she said.[3] She enrolled in the Art Institute of Chicago, but soon developed a somewhat rebellious attitude: "I went to art school in Chicago and took your basic art history courses and I was shocked at how boring it was. There wasn't any emotion or heart or a sense of where these things came from, why people did these paintings."[4] Exposure to early modern art from the turn of the twentieth century excited her interest enough that she continued her education in California, earning a Master of Fine Arts degree at Mills College.

Many artists during the 1960s regarded New York as the most important center of the art world, so Murray settled there after finishing her degree. There she found a scene basically controlled by men who seemed to promote one another. She crossed that hurdle by steady effort: "When I was young, the question was, 'How does a woman who wants to be an artist in the early 1960s find her voice when her teachers and heroes are men and all the art that she admires is by men?' I found the male-female thing tended to fall away the more deeply I studied their works."[5]

At that time many in the art world thought that painting as an art medium was exhausted and that nearly everything meaningful had already been said or done with paint. This also delayed recognition for Murray; her first solo exhibition came in 1976, when she was aged 36.

Murray's somewhat irreverent attitude was the key to her early success, as we see in *Falling*, a work from that period **(fig. 7.13)**. The canvas is divided into abstract shapes in which distinguishing positive from negative, foreground from background, is difficult. A jagged blue line like a lightning strike divides the canvas above a looping red-orange trail. The canvas is rectangular, but the artist hung it at an angle as if it were unstable, or perhaps falling as the title says.

The next step, which Murray took in the 1980s, involved shattering the canvas surface and painting onto irregularly shaped parts, which she then bolted together. In short, she bade farewell to the rectangle. Her working method was to make drawings of the shapes on large sheets of paper, and send them off to fabricators, who made wood silhouettes from them before covering them with canvas for her to paint on. Such a work is *Bop* (see fig. 7.11). This brash and exuberant work has many pieces, some of which have holes in them. Some of the shapes resemble motifs from comics, such as speech bubbles or explosions. Like many of Murray's works, *Bop* lies between abstract and representational art. It also lies between painting and sculpture, an idea that very few other artists had at the time.

Murray's principal contribution was to break painting out of the molds that people had put it into. Or, as she described it, "I want my paintings to be like wild things that just burst out of the zoo."[6]

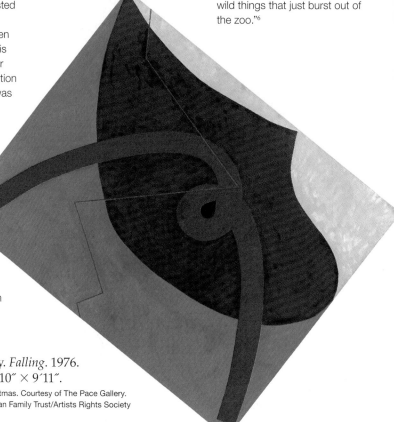

7.13 Elizabeth Murray. *Falling*. 1976. Oil on canvas. 9′10″ × 9′11″.
Photograph by G.R. Christmas. Courtesy of The Pace Gallery.
© 2018 The Murray-Holman Family Trust/Artists Rights Society (ARS), New York.

Acrylic

Many artists today use **acrylic** paint, an invention of the mid-twentieth century. The binder that holds the pigment is acrylic polymer, a synthetic resin that provides a fast-drying, flexible film. The vehicle is water. Acrylics adhere to a wider variety of surfaces than do traditional painting media. Because the acrylic resin binder is transparent, colors can maintain a high degree of intensity. Unlike oils, acrylics rarely darken or yellow with age. Their rapid drying time restricts blending and limits reworking, but it greatly reduces the time involved in layering processes such as glazing. Water thinning is also more convenient in the studio than the volatile and toxic turpentine of oil paint.

The paintings of Yunhee Min take advantage of the properties of the acrylic medium. A recent work is *Into the Sun #10* (**fig. 7.14**). Here she uses pure, bright shades, which may or may not come from nature. She generally lays large canvases down on a work table before applying the paint with a squeegee rather than a brush. She works this way in order to remove traces of the artist's hand and make the color the first object of our attention. Acrylic works well for laying down these flat areas, and its water-based translucency allows the layers to blend, creating mixtures that are sometimes accidental or arrived at during the process of creation. At 6 x 7 feet, the work nearly fills the viewer's eye, somewhat like looking into the sun.

Contemporary Approaches

Painting has had several "near-death experiences" over the last few decades, times when artists or specialists have wondered whether it might become obsolete. Yet painting survives and even flourishes still, as artists discover new types of paint and new means of applying it, and find ways to make it grapple with the digital world.

7.14 Yunhee Min. *Into the Sun #10*. 2013. Acrylic on linen. 72˝ × 84˝.
Inventory #MIN221. Courtesy of Susanne Vielmetter, Los Angeles Projects. Photo credit: Robert Wedemeyer.

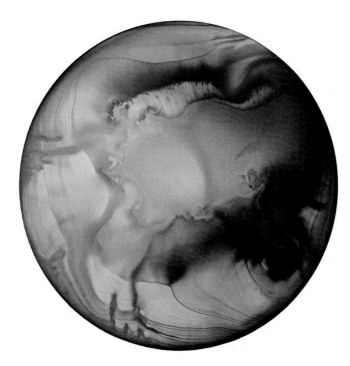

7.15 John Sabraw. *Chroma S1 17*. 2014. Mixed media on aluminum composite panel. 36″ × 36″.
McCormick Gallery, Chicago.

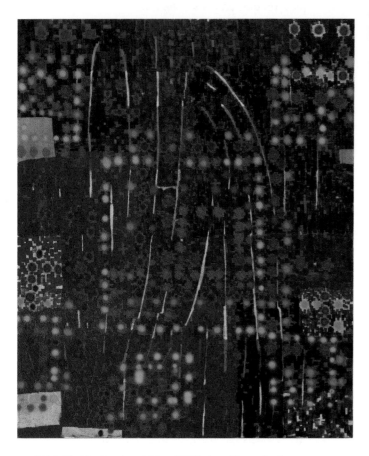

7.16 Keltie Ferris. *oRiOn*. 2015. Acrylic and oil on canvas. 72″ × 60″.
© Keltie Ferris. Courtesy of the artist and Mitchell-Innes & Nash, NY

7.17 Ken Okiishi. *Gesture/Data*. 2013. Oil paint on flatscreen monitor, VHS transferred to .mp4 (color, sound). 35⁵⁄₁₆″ × 21″ × 3¹¹⁄₁₆″.
Whitney Museum of American Art, New York; purchase, with funds from Richard Mishaan 2015.6. © Ken Okiishi. Photo credit: Ken Okiishi.

John Sabraw uses new pigments that create fresh meaning for the word "sustainable." In Ohio where he lives, there are many abandoned coal mines in rural areas that leach out highly toxic iron oxides, polluting nearby streams. Sabraw recovers this poisonous sludge and derives from it powdered pigments that he blends with the usual binders and vehicles to make oil and acrylic paints. The color palette that he achieves is limited but striking in its luminescence, as we see in *Chroma S1 17* (**fig. 7.15**). His compositions are mostly abstract, based on the flowing streams of water where he found the pigment, or landforms nearby. To complete the cycle, he has begun to make these paints in commercial quantities, which he sells, using the proceeds to subsidize environmental remediation in those very streams.

While traditional brushes are the most common tool for applying paint, in recent years many painters have used **airbrushes** to apply acrylics, oil, and other types of paint. An airbrush is a small-scale paint sprayer capable of projecting a fine, controlled mist of paint. It provides an even paint application without the personal touch of individual brushstrokes, and is therefore well suited to creating subtle gradations of color. Graffiti artists, of course, also favor airbrushes or spray cans because the high speed of execution reduces their exposure to law enforcement.

Keltie Ferris uses spray guns to finish most of her works. In her painting *oRiOn* (**fig. 7.16**), she created several layers of hand-brushed patches and sprayed dots along with a few thin, undulating strokes. The layers that she builds up do not necessarily harmonize in color or texture, creating jarring vertical mixtures. She also often mixes acrylic and oil in the same work. She told an interviewer: "To me, painting is most exciting when it has some notion of touch and texture. It's the human element of abstract work . . . By contrast spray paint is about a complete lack of touch. I'm painting with a machine on top of my more handmade marks."[7] This painting comes from a series that she titled after constellations in the night sky. The constellation Orion is bounded by an irregular rectangle of four bright stars; she created a similar constellation using sprayed yellow dots.

Other painters have used their venerable and handmade medium to engage with the digital world. Ken Okiishi uses digital television screens as support for his highly textured oil paintings. For the 2014 series *Gesture/Data* (**fig. 7.17**) he digitized an old VHS videocassette of television shows from the 1990s, and edited it to an endless loop, which plays on the screen. He then painted in oil in vigorous brushstrokes over the glass in contrasting colors. Thus, the artist's intervention becomes part of the screen through which we see a dimly visible mash-up of content from the mass media.

As we have seen, artists have found myriad ways to make a statement by applying colors to flat surfaces. These techniques can be grouped by medium, and each has its own unique strengths and characteristics.

KEY TERMS

acrylic – paint that uses an acrylic polymer (a synthetic resin that provides a fast-drying, flexible film) as the binder and water as the vehicle

airbrush – a small-scale paint sprayer that allows the artist to control a fine mist of paint

binder – the material used in paint that causes pigment particles to adhere to one another

direct painting – execution of a painting in one sitting, applying wet over wet colors

encaustic – a type of painting in which pigment is suspended in a binder of hot wax

fresco – a technique in which pigments suspended in water are applied to a damp lime-plaster surface

fresco secco – a technique in which tempera paint is applied to a dried lime-plaster surface or over an already dried true fresco to achieve greater color intensity

gesso – a mixture of glue and chalk, thinned with water and applied as a ground before painting with oil or egg tempera

glaze – a thin transparent or translucent layer brushed over another layer of paint, allowing the first layer to show through but enriching its color slightly

gouache – an opaque, water-soluble paint

impasto – thick paint applied to a surface in a heavy manner, having the appearance and consistency of buttery paste or of cake frosting

matte – a dull finish or surface

mural – any wall-size painting; fresco is one possible medium for such a work

pigment – any coloring agent, made from natural or synthetic substances, used in paints or drawing materials

primer – a primary layer of paint applied to a surface that is to be painted

sizing – any of several substances made from glue, wax, or clay, used as a filler for porous material such as paper, canvas, or other cloth, or wall surfaces

support – the physical material that provides the base for and sustains a two-dimensional work of art; canvas and panels are common supports for paintings

tempera – a water-based paint that uses egg yolk as a binder

vehicle – liquid emulsion used as a carrier or spreading agent in paints

watercolor – paint that uses water-soluble gum as the binder and water as the vehicle; characterized by transparency

PRINTMAKING

The first thing we might notice about the print *Quiver* (**fig. 8.1**) is its layering of images. A framed dragonfly hovers in a yellow-green square; a negative picture of a radio telescope seems to overlay a closer view of a similar device. Underneath all is a pattern of gray-green branches, silhouetted as if on a forest floor. Note that each layer has its color: gray, blue, brown, black, green. Overall, the work seems a meditation on fragile structures, which might "quiver" in a strong wind.

This layering of images resembles in some ways the process of memory: Each of our memories inhabits a layer of our minds, and each probably has its "color" of feeling or association. Such are the goals of the creator of *Quiver*, Tanja Softic, who said that she tries to make "visual poems." It is no mistake that she chose a print to realize this vision, because this type of layering is a technique uniquely suited to printmaking.

Because of their lower prices and wider distribution, prints are among the more accessible artforms. In this chapter we will define prints and consider some of the purposes behind their creation. We will then discuss the various traditional methods of printmaking: relief, intaglio, lithography, stencil. We will conclude with a look at how some artists today are breaking out of old boundaries and making prints in new ways.

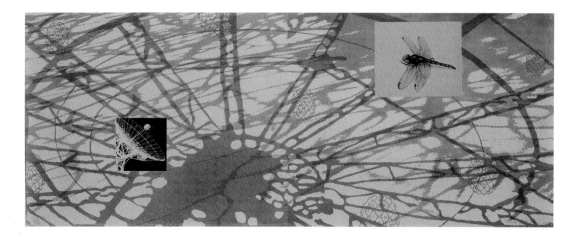

8.1   Tanja Softic. *Quiver.* 2008. Lithograph. 20″ × 52″.
University of Richmond.

Prints and Their Purposes

In the simplest terms, a **print** is an artwork that exists in multiple copies. A print is thus one of a series of nearly identical pieces, usually printed on paper. Prints are made from a **matrix** (the plural is matrices), which an artist may create of metal, wood, or stone. The matrix carries ink, and artists create prints by pressing or overlaying the matrix onto the print surface. Artists may supervise the printing process or do it themselves; in either case, a group of images from the same matrix is usually called an **edition**, and prints are often referred to as **editioned works**, as opposed to unique works in other media such as painting.

Nearly all prints are numbered to indicate the total quantity of prints pulled, or printed, in the edition, and to give the number of each print in the sequence. The figure 6/50 on a print, for example, generally indicates that it was the sixth print pulled from an edition of 50. Artists usually both sign and number prints created by them or under their supervision.

As part of the printmaking process, artists sometimes make prints called progressive proofs at various stages to see how the image on the matrix is developing. When a satisfactory stage is reached, the artist makes a few prints for his or her record and personal use. These are marked AP, meaning **artist's proof**.

One of the best definitions of an original print comes from artist June Wayne: "It is a work of art, usually on paper, which has siblings . . . They all look alike, they were all made at the same time from the same matrix, the same creative impulse, and they are all originals. The fact that there are many of them is irrelevant."[1] Another artist described print editions this way: "Prints mimic what we are as humans: we are all the same and yet every one is different."[2]

The technologies for both printing and papermaking came to Europe from China. By the ninth century, the Chinese were printing pictures from woodblock matrices; by the eleventh century, they had invented (but seldom used) movable type. Printmaking was developed in Europe during the fifteenth century—first in order to meet the demand for inexpensive religious images and playing cards, then to illustrate books printed with the new European movable type.

As recently as the late nineteenth century, printmakers were still needed to copy drawings, paintings, and even early photographs by making plates to be used, along with movable type, for illustrating newspapers and books. However, as photomechanical methods of reproduction were developed in the later nineteenth century, handwork played a decreasing role in the printing process.

Generally, artists make prints for one or more of the following reasons:

- They may wish to make multiple works that are less expensive than paintings or sculpture, so that their work will be available for purchase by a wider group of viewers.
- They may wish to influence social causes. Because prints are multiple works, they are easy to distribute far more widely than a unique work of art.
- They may be fascinated by the process of printmaking, which is an absorbing craft in itself.

Relief

We already know what a **relief print** is, if we think of how fingerprints, rubber stamps, and wet tires leave their marks. In a relief process the artist creates the matrix by cutting away all parts of the printing surface not meant to carry ink; this leaves the design "in relief" at the level of the original surface (see the Relief diagram, **fig. 8.2**). Tools for such carving include gouges of various widths, knives, and chisels. The surface is then inked, and the ink is transferred to paper with pressure. The design carved into the matrix is reversed on contact with the paper.

8.2 Relief.

Woodcut

The oldest relief prints are **woodcuts** (or *woodblocks*). The woodcut process lends itself to designs with bold black-and-white contrast. The image-bearing block of (usually soft) wood is a plank cut along the grain. Because the woodcut medium does not easily yield shades of color, artists who use it are generally drawn by the challenge of working

8.3 Utagawa Hiroshige. *Shono Hakuu* (*Light Rain at Shono*), number 46. 1832–33.
Full-color woodcut. 8⅞″ × 13¾″.

Collection of The Newark Museum, John Cotton Dana Collection. Inv.: 29.2081. © 2018. Photograph: The Newark Museum/Art Resource/Scala, Florence.

in black and white only. Others use woodcut because they enjoy the feel of carving a fresh block of wood. Woodcut editions are limited to a couple of hundred because the relief edges begin to deteriorate with repeated pressure.

Woodblock printing flourished in Japan in the seventeenth through the nineteenth centuries. Japanese woodblock prints were made through a complex process that included multiple blocks to achieve subtle and highly integrated color effects. Because they were much cheaper than paintings, these prints were the preferred artform for middle-class people who lived in the capital city of Edo (now known as Tokyo). Their subject matter included famous theater actors, nightlife, landscapes, and even erotic pictures. Japanese prints were among the first objects of Asian art to find favor among European artists, and many painters in the late nineteenth century were strongly influenced by them (see Chapter 21).

Color woodcuts, a Japanese specialty, are usually printed with multiple woodblocks. As with most printmaking techniques, when more than one color is used, individually inked blocks—one for each color—are carefully lined up to ensure that colors will be exactly placed in the final print; this is known as **registration**.

Utagawa Hiroshige's print *Shono Hakuu* (*Light Rain at Shono*; **fig. 8.3**) is a good example of Japanese printmaking at a high level. The print required four blocks, one for each color. The atmospheric effects of the rain and the distant forest are delicate and difficult to achieve, as the fine lines in this work require both careful carving and precise registration. The work is one of 53 that Hiroshige created that depict various stops on the road from Edo to Kyoto; it was his most popular series.

The detail in Hiroshige's print is quite different from the roughness of the woodcut *Port Scene* by Ernst Ludwig Kirchner (**fig. 8.4**). This image may even be indecipherable at first; it depicts a harbor with sailboats that cast large, dark, triangular shadows downward. We sense the texture of the matrix in this work, because the artist seems to have gouged or even hacked at the wood to make the white areas. Because most of the strokes go vertically, the grain

8.4 Ernst Ludwig Kirchner. *Port Scene*. 1908. Woodcut. 19⅜″ × 15⅞″.

National Gallery of Art, Washington, D.C. 1943.3.5181.

of the wood block was probably also vertical. Kirchner's direct and expressive approach amounted to a revolt against the highly polished and subtle effects that many other European printmakers were seeking in those days.

Wood Engraving

A related method that was commonly used in the nineteenth century for book illustration is **wood engraving**. In this method, the artist uses very dense wood (often boxwood) set on end rather than sideways. The hardness of the wood requires the use of metal engraving tools, but it also makes large editions possible, facilitating the use of wood engraving in publishing.

English artist William Blake was one of the early pioneers of this medium. He illustrated the book *Thornton's Pastorals of Virgil* in 1821 with a series of wood engravings. The book is a collection of ancient Roman poems extolling the virtues of rural life; one of Blake's illustrations is *Boy Returning Joyfully, with Plough and Oxen* (**fig. 8.5**). Here we see some herders going home at sunset; we also see the high detail that is possible through the use of engraving tools. The artist's fine white gouges go with nearly equal ease in all directions, showing the lack of grain in dense wood that is stood upright for carving. Blake made the brighter areas by carving deeper gouges.

8.5 William Blake. *Boy Returning Joyfully, with Plough and Oxen*. 1821. Wood engraving. 1½″ × 3¹⁄₁₆″.

Metropolitan Museum of Art. 31.87.29.

Linocut

The **linoleum cut** (or **linocut**) is a modern development in relief printing. The artist starts with the rubbery, synthetic surface of linoleum, and, just as in woodcut, gouges out the areas not intended to take ink. Linoleum is softer than wood, has no grain, and can be cut with equal ease in any direction. The softness of this matrix material makes fine detail impossible.

A good example of a linoleum cut is *I Have Special Reservations. . .* by Elizabeth Catlett (**fig. 8.6**). We see here the soft, relatively large gouges typical of this medium. The strokes also go in every direction, reflecting the lack of grain in linocut. This work is an example of socially conscious printmaking, as it highlights the issue of race segregation, which was still practiced when the artist made this print. The "special reservations" of the title refers to the segregation of public transportation that was legal in the United States until 1956. This work is one of a series that Catlett made called *The Negro Woman*, in which she attempted to counteract stereotypes by making serious and dignified images of women of her race.

A contemporary artist who uses relief techniques in an original way is Betsabeé Romero of Mexico City (**fig. 8.7**). She buys used tires with the tread almost gone, and she carves in them relief patterns that are based on traditional Mexican popular culture motifs, such as skeletons and flowers. The tires are easily inked for printing on long sheets, which she either sells by the yard or exhibits together with the tires.

8.6 Elizabeth Catlett. *I Have Special Reservations…*. 1946. Linocut. 10½″ × 9″.
Publisher: The artist, Mexico City. Printer: The Artist's Studio. Edition: 20. Leslie J. Garfield Fund. Acc. n.: 241.1991. © 2018. Digital image. The Museum of Modern Art, New York/Scala, Florence.

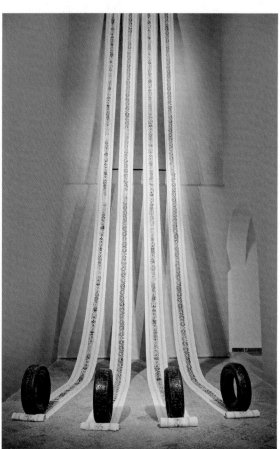

8.7 Betsabeé Romero, *Ciudades que se van* (*Cities on the Move*). 2004. Tires and relief prints. Installation view. Each tire 23⅝″ diameter × 6¹⁹⁄₆₄″ wide. Four prints on domestic fabric. Each 59′ × 19¹¹⁄₁₆″.
Museo Amparo, Puebla México.
Above: *Del otro lado de la velocidad* (*On the Other Side of Speed*). Tire. 51³⁄₁₆″ × 15¾″.
Courtesy of the artist.

Intaglio

Intaglio printing is the opposite of relief printing: Areas below the surface hold the ink (see the Intaglio diagram, **fig. 8.8**). The word *intaglio* comes from the Italian verb *intagliare*, "to cut into." The image to be printed is cut or scratched or etched into a metal surface. To make an intaglio matrix, the printmaker first daubs the plate with printer's ink, then wipes the surface clean, leaving ink only in the etched or grooved portions. Damp paper is then placed on the inked plate, which then passes beneath a press roller. A print is made when the dampened paper picks up the ink in the grooves. As in relief printing, the image in the matrix is reversed in printing on paper. The pressure of the roller creates a characteristic **plate mark** around the edges of the image. Intaglio printing was traditionally done from polished copper plates, but now zinc, steel, aluminum, and even plastic are often used. Engraving, drypoint, and etching are the principal intaglio processes.

Engraving

To make an **engraving**, the artist cuts lines into the polished surface of a metal plate with a **burin**, or engraving tool. This exacting process takes strength and control. Lines are made by pushing the burin into the metal to carve a groove, removing a narrow strip of metal in the process. A clean line is preferable; thus any rough edges of the groove must be smoothed down with a scraper. Engraved lines cannot be freely drawn because of the pressure needed to cut the grooves. Darker areas are shaded with various types of crosshatching. A successful engraving therefore requires precise, smooth curves and parallel lines. To see a good example of engraving, look at the United States currency; all the bills are engravings, made by experts.

We can also see the complex richness of engraved lines in Albrecht Dürer's engraving

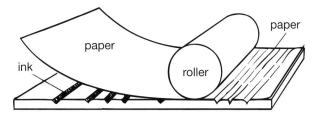

8.8 Intaglio.

The Knight, Death, and the Devil (**fig. 8.9**). Thousands of fine lines define the shapes, masses, spaces, values, and textures in this complex print. The precision of Dürer's lines seems appropriate to the subject—an image of the noble Christian knight moving with resolute commitment, unswayed by the forces of chaos, evil, and death that surround him.

8.9 Albrecht Dürer. *The Knight, Death, and the Devil.* 1513. Engraving. Plate 9⅝″ × 7½″.
National Gallery of Art, Washington, D.C. Rosenwald Collection 1943.3.3519.

Drypoint

Drypoint is similar to engraving. Using a pointed tool with a steel or diamond tip, the artist scratches shallow lines into a soft copper or zinc plate. The displaced metal leaves a **burr**, or rough edge, similar to the row of earth left by a plow. The burr catches the ink and, when printed, leaves a slightly blurred line (see the Drypoint Plate diagram, **fig. 8.10**). Because the burr is fragile and deteriorates rapidly from the pressure of the printing press rollers, drypoint editions are by necessity small and rarely done. Skillful draftsmanship is required, for drypoint lines are difficult to execute and almost impossible to correct. More often, artists use drypoint to put the finishing touches on already etched plates.

8.10 Drypoint Plate.

Etching

The process of making an **etching** begins with the preparation of a metal plate. The artist paints the surface of the copper or zinc plate with a coating of either wax or varnish that will resist acid. The artist then draws easily through this ground with a pointed tool, exposing the metal with each stroke. An etching tool may be as thick as a pen,

8.11 Rembrandt van Rijn. *Christ Preaching*. c.1652. Etching, engraving, and drypoint. Plate 6¹/₁₆″ × 8⅛″.
National Gallery of Art, Washington, D.C. Gift of W.G. Russell Allen. 1955.6.5.

8.12 Mary Cassatt. *The Letter.* 1891. Drypoint and aquatint, printed in color from three plates; fourth state of four. 13⅝″ × 8¹⁵⁄₁₆″.
National Gallery of Art, Washington.

but is more often closer to a needle. Finally, the plate is immersed in nitric acid. Acid bites into the plate where the drawing has exposed the metal, making a groove that varies in depth according to the strength of the acid and the length of time the plate is in the acid bath.

Because they are more freely drawn, etched lines are generally more relaxed or irregular than engraved lines. We can see the difference in line quality between an etching and an engraving—the freedom versus the precision—by comparing the lines in Rembrandt's etching *Christ Preaching* (**fig. 8.11**) with the lines in Dürer's engraving (see fig. 8.9).

In *Christ Preaching*, Rembrandt's personal understanding of Christ's compassion harmonizes with the decisive yet relaxed quality of the artist's etched lines. This etching shows Rembrandt's typical use of a wide range of values, mostly created through hatching. Skillful use of light and shadow draws attention to the figure of Christ and gives clarity and interest to the whole image. In a composition in which each figure is similar in size, Rembrandt identified Jesus as the key figure by setting him off with a light area below, a light vertical band above, and implied lines of attention leading to him from the faces of his listeners.

Etching yields only lines, but there is a way to create shaded areas in an intaglio matrix. **Aquatint** is an etching process used to obtain gray areas in black-and-white or color prints. The artist sprinkles acid-resistant powder on the plate over parts that need a gray tone. When the plate is bathed in acid, the exposed areas between the powder particles are eaten away to produce a rough surface capable of holding ink. Values thus produced can vary from light to dark, depending on how long the plate is in the acid and how thick the dusting of powder. Because aquatint is not suited to making thin lines, it is usually combined with a linear print process such as engraving or etching.

American artist Mary Cassatt combined a few intaglio techniques in her work *The Letter* (**fig. 8.12**). She made the colored areas with aquatint; she scratched the lines in the surface of the plates with drypoint. She used three plates, one for each color.

Because the acids used in intaglio printing are highly toxic and give off potent fumes, many contemporary intaglio artists are drawn to new nontoxic methods. Some of these involve using different chemicals, such as dry citric acid or ferric chloride powders, in place of the nitric acid bath. Another method is electroetching, in which a low-wattage electric current is passed through a solution of sulfate salts in water. This process yields a nonacidic bath that will etch a plate without endangering the health of the artist.

Lithography

Unlike relief and intaglio methods, **lithography** requires no cutting of the matrix. Thus, lithography is a surface or planographic printing process (**fig. 8.13**). Lithography lends itself well to a direct manner of working because the artist draws an image directly onto the surface of the stone or plate. This directness makes lithography faster and somewhat more spontaneous than other methods. A lithograph is often difficult to distinguish from a crayon drawing because many lithographic drawing tools resemble waxy pencils.

Using litho crayons, litho pencils, or a greasy liquid called tusche, the artist draws the image on flat, fine-grained Bavarian limestone (or on a metal surface that duplicates its character). After the image is complete, the stone is chemically treated with gum arabic and a small amount of acid to fix the drawing onto the stone. The surface is then dampened with water and inked. The oil-based ink is repelled by

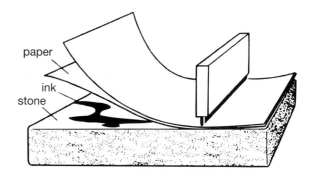

8.13 Lithography.

water in the blank areas, but it adheres to the greasy area of the image. As in other print processes, when the surface is covered with paper and run through a press, the image is transferred to the paper. Because the surface remains intact, lithographic stones or plates can be reused after the matrix surface is scraped and washed clean.

8.14 Honoré Daumier. *Rue Transnonain, April 15, 1834.* 1834. Lithograph. 11¼″ × 17⅜″.
National Gallery of Art, Washington.

Lithography was perfected in the early nineteenth century, and it soon had a major impact on society because prints could be produced quickly and easily. Before the development of modern photographic printing presses, lithographs provided the illustrations for newspapers, posters, and handbills. Honoré Daumier, one of the first artists who took lithography seriously, made his living drawing satirical and documentary lithographs for French newspapers. His fast but assured drawing style was well suited to the immediacy of the lithographic process.

In *Rue Transnonain, April 15, 1834* (**fig. 8.14**), Daumier carefully reconstructed a horrible event that occurred during a period of civil unrest in Paris in 1834. The militia claimed that a shot was fired from a building on Transnonain Street. Soldiers responded by entering the apartment and killing all the occupants, including many innocent people. Daumier's lithograph of the event was published the following day. The lithograph reflects the artist's feelings, but it also conveys information in the way television news programs and websites do today. Rembrandt's influence is evident in the composition of strong light and dark areas that increase the dramatic impact of Daumier's image.

The leading European printmaker of the late nineteenth century, Henri de Toulouse-Lautrec, created many of his most innovative works using lithography. The freedom and directness of the technique made it ideal for his spontaneous and witty approach to subjects. In the space of about ten years, he created hundreds of posters that advertised everything from nightclub acts to bicycles. His use of bright colors and flattened, modern compositions influenced graphic designers for several decades (see *Henri de Toulouse-Lautrec: Printing from Life* on p. 138).

Toulouse-Lautrec had a fruitful and long-lasting friendship with the cabaret singer Aristide Bruant. In this portrait print of his friend (**fig. 8.15**), we see the artist's creative use of the lithographic medium. He used crayons of various widths for the lines, and tusche for the solid dark areas. He created the white patches at the right by dropping melted wax on the stone, keeping ink away from that part. The speckles were created by spattering, as he flicked the bristles of an ink-laden brush.

Most books that have pictures are printed today with a version of lithography called **offset**. Each page image is burned onto a metal lithographic plate and then inked, but the ink is first transferred, or offset, onto a rubber cylinder before printing on paper. This method, which is suited to rotary presses, gives uniform ink depth across an entire printing. It is used to print this book and many others.

8.15 Henri de Toulouse-Lautrec.
Aristide Bruant. 1893.
Lithograph. 10½″ × 8¼″.
National Gallery of Art, Washington, D.C.
Rosenwald Collection 1947.7.169.

CREATORS

Henri de Toulouse-Lautrec: Printing from Life

8.16 Portrait photo of Henri de Toulouse-Lautrec in his studio.
Photograph courtesy of Patrick Frank.

Henri de Toulouse-Lautrec (1864–1901) was born into comfortable circumstances, but his parents were first cousins, which caused a genetic difficulty that left the future artist physically handicapped and under 5 feet tall. However, this lack of physical ability probably led him to focus more intently on art.

Private study with academic teachers left Toulouse-Lautrec sufficiently skilled in traditional drawing and perspective, but he set aside that knowledge and instead followed the style of the Impressionist Edgar Degas and other artistic rebels of the day. He also plunged heavily into the notorious nightlife of Paris, from which he drew his principal subjects.

When his friend Aristide Bruant opened his own cabaret in 1885, Toulouse-Lautrec became

one of its most devoted patrons; the following year, Bruant put the artist's work on permanent display at the club. By the early 1890s, Toulouse-Lautrec had pioneered a new style of lithographic poster, with a large format and innovative compositions that brought him wide renown.

When the upper-crust nightclub Les Ambassadeurs lured Bruant for an engagement in its fashionable area of Champs-Elysées, the singer commissioned Toulouse-Lautrec to design a poster (**fig. 8.17**). He responded with a rich creation in five colors, composed of a few, mostly flat, shapes in a larger-than-usual format. Each color required a separate lithographic stone. The deep-blue area at the upper right is a doorway where a sailor stands. Bruant's body fills most of the frame, bringing him close to the picture surface, overlapping the name of the club at the top. The two zones of the flaming-red scarf converge near Bruant's head, leading us to confront the singer's distant and somewhat haughty facial expression. Toulouse-Lautrec specialized in capturing such reserved emotional states. The poster also reflects Toulouse-Lautrec's careful study of the work of Japanese printmakers, who often used flat shapes in bright colors to depict nightlife scenes.

The Ambassadeurs manager disliked the bold design, which was novel for its day. But Bruant loved it: "Am I that grand?" he reportedly remarked.[3] He insisted that hundreds be printed and plastered across Paris.

Unfortunately, Toulouse-Lautrec's poor health, compounded by probable alcoholism, shortened his life. His family sent him to an asylum for two months in 1899; two

years later, at the age of 36, he suffered a stroke that proved fatal. But the bold design of his posters lived on, influencing graphic artists and designers in succeeding generations.

8.17 Henri de Toulouse-Lautrec. *Ambassadeurs: Aristide Bruant*. 1892. Color tusche and spatter lithograph. Sheet: 61″ × 39³⁄₁₆″. Image: 52¹⁵⁄₁₆″ × 36¼″.
Photograph: akg-images.

Stencil and Screenprinting

In simplest terms, a **stencil** is a sheet with a design cut out of it; painting or spraying over the sheet transfers the design to the picture surface. Stencils are a quick way to make lettering or repeated designs on walls, but here we will consider them as a method for making multiple works of art.

Stencils are a favored method of street artists who communicate political messages, because they permit fast fabrication without the need for redrawing each time. (One such work, by the well-known street artist Banksy, is pictured in fig. 25.17.) A few stencil artists make objects of more subtle design, however. One of these is Kim McCarthy, a Seattle-based artist who also uses the alias Urban Soule. Her *Urban Buddha* (**fig. 8.18**) shows many repeated patterns in the background that she achieved with stencils using blue and green paint. The black skulls and the dominant Buddha image were also sprayed through stencils. The drawback to using stencils is that only positive and negative spaces are produced; shading is not possible. McCarthy overcame this difficulty by adding many colors, brushstrokes, and paint drips. The trails of black and white paint suggest the quick execution of street art.

Screenprinting is a refinement of the technique of stencil printing. Early in the twentieth century, stencil technique was improved by attaching the stencil to a screen made of silk fabric stretched across a frame (synthetic fabric is generally used today). With a rubber-edged blade or a squeegee, ink is then pushed through the fabric in the open areas of the stencil to make an image of the stencil on the paper being printed (see the Screenprinting diagram, **fig. 8.19**). Because silk was the traditional material used for the screen, the process is also known as **silkscreen** or **serigraphy** (from the Latin for silk, *sericum*).

Screenprinting is well suited to the production of images with areas of uniform color. Each separate color requires a different screen, but registering and printing are relatively simple. There is no reversal of the image in

8.18 Kim McCarthy. *Urban Buddha.* 2009. Stencils and mixed media on canvas. 36″ × 48″.
Kim McCarthy.

8.19 Screenprinting.

screenprinting—in contrast to relief, intaglio, and lithographic processes, in which the image on the plate is reversed in the printing process. The medium also allows the production of large, nearly mass-produced editions without loss of quality.

Silkscreen printing thus lends itself to poster production, and many social movements have allied themselves with silkscreen artists to help spread the word about their causes. For example, residents of the low-lying Marshall Islands in the central Pacific have already been affected by climate change, as rising sea levels have washed away homes and businesses during high tides. One of the most prominent activists on this issue, Milañ Loeak, has drawn attention to the roots of climate change in various ways, from writing opinion pieces in newspapers to protesting the burning of coal to generate electricity. A poster workshop in California made a silkscreen (**fig. 8.20**) with a portrait of the activist along with a quote from one of her essays. This print is is both an excellent example of silkscreen art and a memorable summation of the the activist and her position.

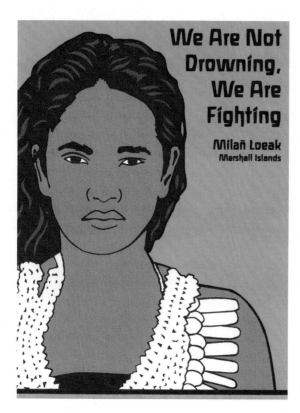

8.20 Jesús Barraza. *We Are Fighting!*
Screenprint. 9″ x 12″.
Dignidad Rebelde.

8.21 Andy Warhol. *Gangster Funeral*. 1963. Acrylic and silkscreen ink on canvas. 105″ × 75⅝″.

8.22 Michelle Murillo. *Adrift 1979 – Rosalba Llanos de Muñoz*. 2015.
Sandblasted kiln-formed glass, digital decal print. 21″ × 36″ × 2″.
Photograph by Sibilia Savage.

A more mechanical procedure in screenprinting is the photographic stencil, or **photo screen**, achieved by attaching light-sensitive gelatin to the screen fabric. This allows the transfer of a photograph to the screenprint stencil. Andy Warhol made such photo-based screenprints often in the 1960s and 1970s, such as *Gangster Funeral* (**fig. 8.21**), in which he reproduced a news photo of the subject five times onto the screen. In this cemetery scene, the two white masses in the photo are heaped-up piles of melting snow. Above each white mass is a group of mourners standing on either side of a casket decorated with flowers. Warhol caused the variations in the repetitions of this photo by varying the amount of ink that the squeegee pushed through the screen.

Contemporary Approaches

Experimental printmakers in recent years have taken on new types of printing materials, and digital technology.

More artists are also taking the idea of multiple artworks into the third dimension. Each of these has altered the boundaries of the medium.

Michelle Murillo uses printmaking processes in new ways. While doing personal genealogical research, she found some official identity documents belonging to her ancestors. She photographed these and printed them onto sheets of sandblasted glass that she made by hand (**fig. 8.22**). She used a photo-transfer process similar to silkscreening to embed the image onto the surface of blue glass. The overall effect thus resembles a faded ID card floating on the ocean, which is reflected in the title *Adrift*. This work, part of a series with that title, highlights the frequent ocean-crossing migrations that the artist's ancestors made.

Many printmakers today combine printmaking techniques with other media. One of these is Nicola López, who uses woodcut and lithography to create installations that

8.23 Nicola López. *Blighted*. 2006. Woodcut and lithography on Mylar. 20′ × 22′.
Caren Golden Fine Art/ Nicola Lopez.

are specific to each exhibition. In her 2006 work *Blighted* (**fig. 8.23**), she printed on Mylar, a transparent film. Her images of shattering buildings and tumbling structures are based on her memories of the attacks of September 11, 2001.

Digital technology has altered printmaking at a basic level by eliminating the tangible plate. A digital matrix is made not by hand but with a keyboard and mouse. Some artists make digital prints using painting and photo-editing programs, and then erase the matrix files when the "edition" is complete. This technology allows the creation of prints that are not original in the traditional sense because they are infinitely reproducible. In 2007, the English duo Gilbert and George (who do not use their last names) made a print available for free downloading on the Internet for 36 hours. The edition was limited not by the number of downloads, but by the clock.

The new technology of digital printing in three dimensions makes possible another sort of editioned work. In **3-D printing**, the artist creates a design in three dimensions using modeling software. A 3-D print is not a print

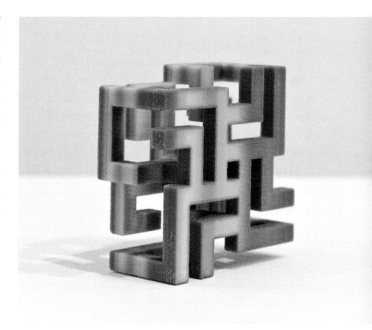

8.24 Brenna Murphy. *Rainbow Array 1*. 2015. 3-D printed sandstone, pigment. 2″ × 2″ × 1″. Edition of 4 plus 2 AP.
Photo by Mario Gallucci. Courtesy of Brenna Murphy and Upfor Gallery, Portland, OR.

in the traditional sense because it is not an impression, but we include it here because it is a limited edition made by an artist. Brenna Murphy's *Rainbow Array 1* (**fig. 8.24**) is such a work. She made it in an edition of four, which she sold online.

As we have seen in the examples in this chapter, prints have been used throughout the centuries to produce multiple copies of an image. Because printmaking is less expensive than other media, and can be more easily distributed, works can reach a wider audience.

KEY TERMS

3-D printing – printing in three dimensions from a design created using modeling software

aquatint – an intaglio printmaking process in which value areas rather than lines are etched on the printing plate; powdered resin is sprinkled on the plate, which is then immersed in an acid bath, and the acid bites around the resin particles, creating a rough surface that holds ink; also a print made using this process

artist's proof – a trial print, usually made as an artist works on a plate or block, to check the progress of a work

burin – a tool used in engraving

burr – the ridge left by scratching a drypoint line in a copper plate; the burr holds ink for printing

drypoint – an intaglio printmaking process in which lines are scratched directly into a metal plate with a steel needle; the scratch raises a ridge (burr) that takes the ink

edition – the total number of prints made and approved by the artist, usually numbered consecutively

editioned work – any work produced in an edition, such as a print; not unique as in the case of a painting

engraving – an intaglio printmaking process in which grooves are cut into a metal or wood surface with a sharp cutting tool called a burin or graver; also the resulting print

etching – an intaglio printmaking process in which a metal plate is first coated with acid-resistant wax or varnish, then scratched to expose the metal to the bit of nitric acid where lines are desired; also the resulting print

intaglio – any printmaking technique in which lines and areas to be inked are recessed below the surface of the printing plate

linoleum cut (or **linocut**) – a relief printmaking process in which an artist cuts away negative spaces from a block of linoleum, leaving raised areas to take ink for printing

lithography – a planographic printmaking technique based on the antipathy of oil and water; the image is drawn with a grease crayon or painted with tusche on a stone or grained aluminum plate; the surface is then chemically treated and dampened so that it will accept ink only where the crayon or tusche has been used

matrix – the block of metal, wood, stone, or other material that an artist works to create a print

offset lithography – lithographic printing by indirect image transfer from photomechanical plates; the plate transfers ink to a rubber-covered cylinder, which "offsets" the ink to the paper

photo screen – a variation of a silkscreen in which the stencil is prepared by transferring a photograph to the stencil

plate mark – an impression made on a piece of paper by pressing a printing plate onto it; usually a sign of an original print

print – a multiple original impression made from a plate, stone, woodblock, or screen by an artist or made under the artist's supervision; usually made in editions, with each print numbered and signed by the artist

registration – in color printmaking or machine printing, the process of aligning the impressions of blocks or plates on the same sheet of paper

relief printmaking – a technique in which the parts of the printing surface that carry ink are left raised, while remaining areas are cut away

screenprinting (silkscreen, serigraphy) – a technique in which stencils are applied to fabric stretched across a frame, and paint or ink is forced through the unblocked portions of the screen onto paper or another surface beneath

stencil – a sheet of paper, cardboard, or metal with a design cut out; painting or stamping over the sheet prints the design on a surface

wood engraving – a method of relief printing in wood; made with denser wood, cutting into the end of the grain rather than the side

woodcut, woodblock – a type of relief print made from a plank of relatively soft wood; the artist carves away the negative spaces, leaving the image in relief to take the ink for printing

PHOTOGRAPHY

LEARNING OBJECTIVES

9.1   Describe the early innovations that led to the development of photography.

9.2   Explain the mechanics of a camera and outline the key adjustments photographers make when taking a picture.

9.3   Discuss the influences on early art photography.

9.4   Compare the use of photography as art to its documentary function in society.

9.5   Explain why artists did not commonly use color photography before the 1970s.

9.6   Discuss experimental photographic processes used by contemporary artists.

9.7   Demonstrate the influence of digital technology on photography in the twenty-first century.

Jane and Louise Wilson's photograph *The Silence is Twice as Fast Backwards I* (**fig. 9.1**) captures a magical moment in a lush, green forest. It appears as if the artists went for a morning walk and stumbled upon a wooded glade, flooded with streaking sunlight. The picture they printed is 6 feet square, filling our entire field of vision. The image seems irresistible: Viewers may want to dive right into the scene.

The word *photography* literally means "light-writing," although a more accurate description would be "light-drawing." Like drawing, photography can be either a practical tool or an artform. Beyond its many uses in journalism, science, advertising, and personal record keeping, photography offers artists, such as Jane and Louise Wilson, a powerful means of expression.

Beyond selecting camera, lens, and film, a skilled photographer makes many choices about composition, angle, focus, distance, and light. The Wilson sisters carefully composed *The Silence is Twice as Fast Backwards I*. The three trees are perfectly positioned in the frame, and the branch that leads our eye in from the lower left points upward to connect with the foliage of the second tree. Note also how the branch at the lower right seems to parallel the one at lower left in a rhythmic repetition. These curving branches lie at

9.1   Jane and Louise Wilson. *The Silence is Twice as Fast Backwards I.* 2008. Photograph (C-print). 72″ × 72″.
© Jane and Louise Wilson. Courtesy of 303 Gallery, New York.

a roughly 90-degree angle to the sun's rays that stream in from the upper left. The artists seem to have set the exposure of the shot perfectly, as well, so that details are visible even in intense light and darkness. And one more fact completes this photo's contrivances: To create the effect of sunlight, the artists loosed some mist into the scene before shooting it.

In this chapter we will consider how photography has evolved since the mid-nineteenth century, from a tool for capturing the appearance of people and places into an established artform. We will also consider its use as a means of encouraging social change, and look at the impact of the digital revolution.

The Evolution of Photography

The basic concept of the camera preceded actual photography by many centuries. The forerunner of the modern camera was the **camera obscura**, literally "dark chamber" (**fig. 9.2**). Sunlight passing through a small hole in the wall of a darkened room projects onto the opposite wall an inverted image of whatever lies outside. In about 1000 CE, Muslim scientist Alhazen wrote of using one to view solar eclipses safely. In the fifteenth century, artist Leonardo da Vinci, who had read translations of Alhazen's work, described the device as an aid to observation and picture making. In about 1585 the Neapolitan mathematician Giambattista della Porta placed a lens in the hole, making the image sharper. Several artists in the seventeenth century used tabletop-size versions to aid in drawing. The camera obscura thus already functioned like a camera, but the means for preserving or copying its images was still lacking.

Photography became possible when scientists discovered that certain chemicals were sensitive to light. In about 1826, the first vague photographic image was made by Joseph Nicéphore Niépce. He recorded and fixed on a sheet of pewter an image he made by exposing the sensitized metal plate to natural light for almost an entire day of eight hours. During the next decade, the painter Louis-Jacques-Mandé Daguerre further improved Niépce's chemical process and produced some of the first satisfactory photographs, known as **daguerreotypes**. He made them by exposing iodized silver plates in the presence of mercury vapor; images were fixed on the plate with a mineral salt solution. Combining this light-sensitive chemistry with a box-sized camera obscura yielded the first camera that

9.2   Camera Obscura.

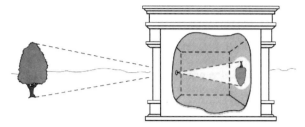

a. Sixteenth-century camera obscura.

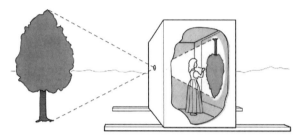

b. Portable camera obscura.

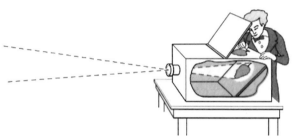

c. Table model camera obscura.

gave predictable results. Daguerre first publicized his work in 1839, a convenient date for the invention of photography.

At first, because the necessary exposure times were so long, photography could record only stationary objects. In Daguerre's photograph *Le Boulevard du Temple* (**fig. 9.3**), taken in Paris in 1839, the streets appear deserted because moving figures such as pedestrians and carriages made no lasting light impressions on the plate. The exposure time for this plate was about a half hour. However, one man, having his shoes shined, stayed still long enough to become part of the image. He is visible on the corner in the lower left, the first person ever to appear in a photograph. It was a significant moment in human history: At last images of people and things could be made without the hand of a trained artist.

The first common use of photography was portraiture. Before the development of the camera, only the wealthy could afford to hire artists to paint their portraits.

9.3 Louis-Jacques-Mandé Daguerre. *Le Boulevard du Temple.* 1839. Daguerreotype.
Bayerisches National Museum, Munich (R6312). Alamy.

But by the mid-nineteenth century most major cities had several portrait photographers. People of average means went in great numbers to photography studios to sit, stiff and unblinking, in bright sunlight for five to eight seconds to have their portraits made with the camera. As the nineteenth century progressed, shorter exposure times, less-toxic technology, and printing on paper all helped to popularize photography.

Techniques

A modern camera (**fig. 9.4**) still resembles a traditional camera obscura. The lens collects light from whatever is before it. This image passes through the dark chamber where it is collected, upside down, by the **image sensor**. In traditional cameras the sensor was either a chemically treated plate or chemical film. In today's digital cameras, the sensor converts the light into an electric charge, which the camera's software reconstitutes as a photograph for display on the camera's screen. This captured image can be stored in a memory card in the camera.

Photographers make three important adjustments as they take pictures. First, they adjust the **focal length**, or distance between the lens and the sensor (q in the diagram). This is done by physically moving the lens inward or outward (zooming), by changing the lens, or by digital means

in the software. This adjustment determines whether the camera takes in a wide view or a narrow one. Second, they adjust the **aperture**, or width of the opening that admits light. Aperture is expressed as an **f-stop**, which is the ratio of the focal length to the size of the opening. A narrow aperture that lets in little light is a high f-stop; typically this could be f-22, which might be commonly used in bright light. A wider aperture for lower-light conditions is a lower f-stop, perhaps as low as f-1.8. The f-stop determines the

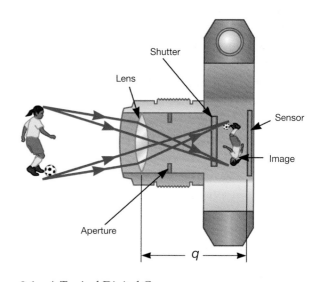

9.4 A Typical Digital Camera.

depth of field, or the depth of the area before the camera that will be in sharp focus in a photo. Low f-stops give a shallower field of focused material; higher ones can bring everything, near and far, into focus. The third principal adjustment is **shutter speed**, or the length of time the shutter is open; this too determines the brightness of the resulting photo. Typical shutter speeds range from 1/1000 of a second in bright light to about 1/60 in lower light. For handheld cameras, shutter speeds longer than about 1/60 run the risk of introducing hand movement, which would blur the photo. Putting the camera on a stand, of course, allows much longer exposures.

Most of today's popular cameras, such as those that are included with smartphones, automatically set an aperture and shutter speed, leaving the focal length for the user to adjust by zooming. Artists and specialists generally readjust all three settings for each new photo. These adjustments are the kinds of choices that make artistic expression possible.

Early Art Photography

For many years the public was reluctant to accept photography as an artform because of its reliance on a mechanical device. And, indeed, many early photographers were content merely to record visual information. Today, however, most people agree that the camera can be a vehicle for personal expression and symbolic communication.

From the beginning, portrait painting greatly influenced portrait photography. One of the very first portrait photographers to be regarded as an artist was Julia Margaret Cameron. By 1864, she had become an avid photographer,

creating expressive portraits. Cameron pioneered the use of close-ups and carefully controlled lighting to enhance the images of her subjects, who were often family members or famous friends. Her photo *Paul and Virginia* (**fig. 9.5**) shows many of her concerns. She finely crafted her exposure to allow enough light to perfectly define the children's round bodies and their disheveled clothing. She posed them off-center, and created a dynamic balance with the umbrella and its diagonal. The two children are known to us from other photos, but Cameron titled this work after a popular novel about a pair of shipwrecked children. She suggests the atmosphere of the novel in both the title and the poses.

9.5 Julia Margaret Cameron.
Paul and Virginia. 1864.
Albumen print. 10″ × 7⅞″.
The J. Paul Getty Museum, Los Angeles.
84.XZ.186.3.

9.6 Alfred Stieglitz. *Spring Showers, New York.* 1901. Photograph. 3¾″ × 1½″.
Getty Museum.

An early crusader in the art photography movement was the American Alfred Stieglitz, who opened a photography gallery in New York City in 1905. He also founded an influential magazine, *Camera Work*, which published photography along with essays about modern art and culture.

Stieglitz's own photography often showed influence from the delicate shadings of the paintings of his contemporaries. His 1901 photograph *Spring Showers, New York*

(**fig. 9.6**) is a superb exercise in tonal control because it effortlessly handles subtle gradations of texture and shade. The wet street looks different from the sidewalk, for example, as both differ from the misty sky with its looming buildings in the distance. The background is also out of focus, a product of intentionally shallow depth of field. Stieglitz created and exhibited photos to show that photographers could be as skilled as painters in capturing and interpreting the world around them. In early photographs such as this one, he revealed the poetry he found in everyday urban scenes.

French photographer Henri Cartier-Bresson captured a subtle moment of drama in *Place de l'Europe Behind the Gare St. Lazare, Paris* (**fig. 9.7**). Here he released the shutter at exactly the right moment, and at the perfect shutter speed,

9.7 Henri Cartier-Bresson. *Place de l'Europe Behind the Gare St. Lazare, Paris.* France. 1932.
© H. Cartier-Bresson/Magnum Photos.

9.8 Manuel Álvarez Bravo. *Two Pairs of Legs.* 1928–29. Gelatin silver print. 6½″ × 9½″.
© Colette Urbajtel/Archivo Manuel Álvarez Bravo SC.

9.9 Man Ray. *Rayograph.* 1927. Gelatin silver print. 11⁷⁄₁₆″ × 9⅛″.
Private Collection/The Stapleton Collection. © Man Ray Trust/Artists Rights Society (ARS), NY/ADAGP, Paris 2018.

to capture a man leaping over a puddle on a cloudy day. The man's shape is echoed in both his own reflection and that of the dancer in the poster behind, just as semicircular ripples find a parallel in the round shapes close by in the water. For Cartier-Bresson, good photography is a matter of capturing the decisive moment:

> To me, photography is the simultaneous recognition, in a fraction of a second, of the significance of an event as well as of a precise organization of forms which give that event its proper expression.[1]

If Stieglitz and Cartier-Bresson wake us up to everyday poetry that we might not otherwise notice, Manuel Álvarez Bravo photographs jarring surprises in his urban environment. His photo *Two Pairs of Legs* (**fig. 9.8**) combines a billboard and a building site. The subjects of this work seem

to ascend in pairs, starting with the legs from a shoe advertisement. Above that is a pair of lamps, and further up a pair of (doubled) windows from an office building under construction. Other pleasant revelations await the careful viewer: the parallel between the woman's skirt and the shadow of the awning, which creates a "skirt" on the man; the shadows of the lamps as they collide with the rectilinear pieces of the billboard; the way the bodies seem to disappear into the building above; and how the photographer's angle of vision makes room for the sign at the top.

Other photographers went beyond the camera itself to achieve more inventive effects. Man Ray made innovative photographs, which he called *rayographs*, by placing objects on light-sensitive paper and exposing them to sunlight. The rayographs are photographs in which no cameras or lenses are used; they are also visual inventions recorded on film. Sometimes, as in the work pictured here (**fig. 9.9**), it is not even clear what the original subject was.

Photography and Social Change

Each generation produces its own memorable photographs. Such photographs move us not only because of the way their subjects are presented, but also because we know the photographer was present at the scene, allowing us to join him or her as witnesses. The significance of such images lies not only in their ability to inform us, but also in their power to stir our emotions.

Only a few decades after the invention of photography, photographers began to bring public attention to suffering caused by war, poverty, hunger, and neglect. The new tool made visual statements believable in ways that no essay or drawing could. Of all the arts, photography is uniquely suited not only to documenting events and social problems, but also to bringing about empathetic awareness that can lead to reform.

An early leader in the use of photography for social change was the Danish-born American Jacob Riis. In the late nineteenth century, he photographed squalid living and working conditions in poor areas of New York and published them for the world to see. Photographs such as *Five Cents a Spot* (**fig. 9.10**) drew public attention that led to stricter housing codes and improved work safety laws. The vividness of this photo was made possible by the recent invention of flash photography, which allowed Riis to take his camera into previously unseen places. His most famous book, *How the Other Half Lives*, was a landmark in the social impact of photography.

For most of the twentieth century, photography enjoyed an unquestioned reputation as a vehicle of truth, giving rise to the saying, "The camera never lies." During the 1930s, Margaret Bourke-White introduced the concept of the photographic essay—an approach that other photographers soon adopted. A photo essay is a collection of photographs on a single subject, arranged to tell a story or convey a mood in a way not possible with a single photograph. Bourke-White documented construction projects, industrial plants, foreign customs, and Depression-era poverty in many such works. On assignment to document the effects of a flood in 1937, she created *African American Flood Victims Lined Up* (**fig. 9.11**), one of the more famous images of the Depression in the United States.

In addition to focusing on social problems, photography has aided the efforts of environmentalists. Ansel Adams often used his photographs to increase public awareness of the need for conservation of the natural environment. His *Clearing Winter Storm, Yosemite National Park, California* (**fig. 9.12**) reflects the symphonic grandeur of nature's design. It renders the cathedral-like Yosemite Valley as an orchestration in black and white, where stark rock mingles with soft mist. All is in perfect focus in an infinite depth of field, which Adams achieved by using a high f-stop. He also carefully adjusted the lighting during the development process by selectively exposing some parts of the picture to more light. Adams viewed aspects of nature as symbols of spiritual life, capable of transcending the conflicts of society. In his majestic black-and-white photographs, nature becomes a timeless metaphor for spiritual harmony.

9.10 Jacob A. (Jacob Augustus) Riis (1849–1914). *Five Cents a Spot.* Unauthorized lodging in Bayard Street Tenement. c.1890. Gelatin silver print. 6³⁄₁₆″ × 4¾″.
Museum of the City of New York, The Jacob A. Riis Collection (#155) (90.13.4.158).

9.11 Margaret Bourke-White.
*African American Flood Victims
Lined Up.* 1937.

Time & Life Pictures/Getty Images.

9.12 Ansel Adams. *Clearing Winter Storm, Yosemite National Park, California.* 1944.
© The Ansel Adams Publishing Rights Trust.

9.13 Chris Steele-Perkins. *Marshall Islands*. 2004.
© Chris Steele-Perkins/Magnum Photos.

Today's environmental photographers are more likely to focus on the serious human impact on our surroundings. For example, Chris Steele-Perkins traveled to the Marshall Islands in the Pacific in 2004, and he found that rising sea levels threaten the very existence of these islands. His photo from the series *Marshall Islands* (**fig. 9.13**) shows a makeshift sea wall created out of castoffs and junk, a desperate attempt to hold back rising tides. Steele-Perkins is one of ten photographers who collaborated on the book and exhibition *NorthSouthEastWest: A 360° View of Climate Change*, a worldwide compendium of views of the problem.

Color Photography

Photography began as a primarily black-and-white process. Indeed, for the first 100 years, black and white was the only practical option for photographers. Through much of the twentieth century, technical problems with color persisted: Film and printing papers were expensive, and color prints faded over time. Even when fairly accurate color became practical, many photographers felt that color lacked the abstract power of the black-and-white image.

The development of color photography began in 1907 with the invention of color transparencies. In 1932, the Eastman Kodak Company began making color film. The key invention came in 1936 with Kodachrome film, which substantially improved the versatility and accuracy of color photography. Later progress improved the relative permanence of color prints.

9.14 William Eggleston. *Untitled (Nehi Bottle on Car Hood)*. From *Los Alamos Portfolio*. 1965–74.
© Eggleston Artistic Trust. Courtesy of Cheim & Read, New York.

Through the 1960s, most art photographers disdained color film. At first they did so because the chemical development processes yielded unstable prints that faded or evolved toward red over time; later, because color photographs were associated with family snapshots and tourist photographs. But when William Eggleston exhibited his color work at the Museum of Modern Art, New York, in 1976, the world took notice and a new branch of art photography was born.

Eggleston's pictures from the *Los Alamos Portfolio* are elegant compositions of everyday things. In *Untitled* (*Nehi Bottle on Car Hood*; **fig. 9.14**), two cars block out an abstract composition of off-balance diagonals against a paved background darkened by wedges of shadow. The soda bottle seems perfectly positioned to both anchor the composition and capture the sunlight; its red color further lends it emphasis. The blue car, being a cool color, tends to recede. Besides the skillful arrangement, the photo rivets our attention because it immediately evokes a world: a casual social setting in some American rural area on a warm afternoon. To prove the validity of Eggleston's commitment to color photography, all we have to do is imagine this work in black and white.

Pushing the Limits

Artists have recently explored a variety of techniques to go beyond photography's assumed limits. British artist Susan Derges lays large sheets of photosensitive paper on the bottom of shallow ponds at night, and captures the look of the night sky through the water. She often shines a flashlight on the paper through surrounding bushes to compose ghostly night scenes with their shadows (**fig. 9.15**). She thus creates landscapes of a new kind, as if we were looking up from below the water's surface.

Trevor Paglen pushes the limits of the camera in a way that highlights contemporary questions about government secrecy. For his project called *Limit Telephotography*, he approached secret government installations, getting as close as he could legally as a private citizen. Many of these facilities are in remote locations in the desert West. He then photographed the secret sites with the best equipment commercially available. One work from this series is *Open Hangar, Cactus Flats, NV, Distance ~ 18 miles, 10:04 a.m.* (**fig. 9.16**). The results are unsurprisingly blurry, but still tantalizing because his cameras can see far better than the unaided eye. Cactus Flat is a secret military installation

9.15 Susan Derges. *Gibbous Moon Cloud*. 2009. Unique ilfochrome print. 66½″ × 36″.
© Susan Derges. Courtesy of Purdy Hicks Gallery.

where controllers pilot reconnaissance drones in war-torn or forbidden areas of the world. It is also part of the Tonopah Test Range, which is described rather mysteriously on its website as "the testing range of choice for all national security missions." Paglen's photo represents the citizen's eye, straining to learn even a bit of information about what our government is doing.

9.16 Trevor Paglen. *Open Hangar, Cactus Flats, NV, Distance ~ 18 miles, 10:04 a.m.* 2007. C-print. 30″ × 36″.
Courtesy of the artist and Metro Pictures, New York.

Vietnamese-born artist Binh Danh invented his own method of recording photographs onto plant material. He takes or borrows photographs and then attaches them to leaves from his garden. He then places the leaf and photo between layers of glass, and exposes them outdoors for up to several weeks on the roof of his house. The sunlight transfers the photographic images to the leaves, in a process he calls chlorophyll printing.

Danh most often uses images of the victims of warfare in Southeast Asia to create haunting works that memorialize the dead. The face that emerges from the leaf in *Iridescence of Life #7* (**fig. 9.17**) came from the Genocide Museum in Cambodia, which holds thousands of photos that the Khmer Rouge methodically took of their victims. In this work Danh embedded the printed leaves in resin, and paired them with butterfly specimens. The resulting work seems fragile, precious, and beautiful. Danh said, "I have tried to show how like plants humans are; we participate in the kinetics of events and the process of creating memories by absorbing the history around us—and, like leaves, we wither and eventually die. The residue of our existence nourishes the memories of the living like a decaying leaf nourishes the soil."[2]

Danh's interest in chemical photo processes also led him to explore the ancient medium of the daguerreotype (see *Binh Danh: Exhuming the Landscape* on p. 155).

9.17 Binh Danh. *Iridescence of Life #7.* 2008. Chlorophyll print, butterfly specimen, and resin. 14″ × 11″ × 2″.
Courtesy of the artist and Haines Gallery.

CREATORS

Binh Danh: Exhuming the Landscape

9.18 Photo of Binh Danh.
Courtesy of the artist and
Haines Gallery.

If a photograph is a repository for memories, then Binh Danh (b. 1977) is creating them for both himself and his viewers. At the time of his birth in Vietnam, the Khmer Rouge regime in neighboring Cambodia was eliminating dissidents of all kinds in a genocide that eventually claimed nearly two million victims. Danh migrated to the United States with his refugee parents in 1979. His unique versions of photography poetically reconstruct a difficult past.

"I am half Cambodian," Danh said. "My father is Cambodian and my mother is Vietnamese. The Khmer Rouge were pretty much exterminating any foreigners in the country, including people who wore glasses, who drank milk, who were artists, or Buddhist monks, Catholic nuns."[3] Because he has no memory of his homeland, he reconstructed it through the landscape. "You could call me a landscape photographer, because I'm looking at the landscape, but instead of just photographing the landscape, I'm looking into the landscape, into the earth, underneath the soil, into the cells of plants."[4]

Danh took an interest in the daguerreotype process, in which an image is exposed on a treated silver plate sensitized with vapor. "They called the daguerreotype a mirror with a memory; it is a mirror you hold up to yourself, and it remembers who you are; it has a ghostly quality to it."[5] He bought several antique box cameras, fitted them for daguerreotype plates, and took them to Yosemite National Park, where he resolved to photograph in the footsteps of Ansel Adams and others (**fig. 9.19**). Surprisingly, he is the first daguerreotypist to visit Yosemite.

The daguerreotype process is difficult to carry out in a remote location. Danh described it: "I go to Yosemite with a van, which I have converted to a darkroom. I call the van 'Louis' after Louis Daguerre. I'm in the van with a [silver] plate, which I have polished to a high finish. I sensitize the plate with iodine vapor. When the iodine comes into contact with the silver, the plate becomes light sensitive. From there I put it in a plate holder with my camera and go hiking. I'll find a spot and make an exposure, come back to the van and develop the plate."[6]

Exposures take between one and two minutes, so he has to avoid shooting on windy days.

Viewers who see these images, as with any daguerreotype, also see themselves reflected in the silver plate, placing themselves in the image. The plates that Danh uses are larger than most nineteenth-century plates, partly to facilitate this mirroring quality for viewers. Danh further explained, "These specific photographic processes allow me to exhume the landscape and all of its metaphors. I consider this work social documentary. For me, social documentary examines historical events and their relation to our contemporary lives."[7]

9.19 Binh Danh. *El Capitan, Yosemite, CA, May 22.* 2012. Daguerreotype, unique (in camera exposure). Plate 6½″ × 8½″. Frame 11½″ × 13″.
Courtesy of the artist and Haines Gallery.

The Digital Revolution

Near the end of the twentieth century, the chemical photographic negative began to go out of fashion under the impact of the new digital technology. While photochemical film is still manufactured and sold, the convenience of digital photography is causing the slow decline of the older process. Trevor Paglen, for example, uses only digital cameras. Now most cameras do not use film; rather, the lens focuses information onto sensors that translate light into digital files. Using photo-editing computer programs, these files can be manipulated in almost infinite ways, and reproduced endlessly.

The implications of these changes are profound. If a photo can be altered in almost any imaginable way, then its reputation as a vehicle of truth has expired, and the camera can indeed lie. Moreover, the reproducibility of images means that the specialness of a photograph is much reduced. Many contemporary photographers take advantage of these facts.

Jeff Wall, for example, calls himself a "near-documentary" photographer. He creates scenes that seem vividly "real," yet they retain a decidedly stagy quality. *Boy Falls from Tree* (**fig. 9.20**) seems a matter-of-fact photo of an unfortunate (but not entirely uncommon) event. Yet Wall created it at his computer by combining several related photos.

Photographing the falling boy in motion would require a fast shutter speed that would greatly limit the depth of field. But today's digital cameras enable such effects. Wall also takes full advantage of the high-resolution technology by blowing up his pictures to maximum size, in this case about 8 by 10 feet. We are left wondering what is real and what is manipulated in this too-perfect picture of a minor calamity.

If Jeff Wall hides his manipulation of the photos he takes to make them appear natural, other photographers explicitly maximize the editing potential of software to create vivid and complex images. One of these is James Welling, who began his career using film but eagerly embraced the new technology as it developed.

Welling's 2016 photo *9812* (**fig. 9.21**) is one of a series in which he layered together photos of modern dance companies, landscapes, and government buildings. This photo includes the Los Angeles Contemporary Dance Company, the *Nova* installation by Soft Lab in Madison Square Park, New York City, and the Orange County Government Center in Goshen, New York. Welling saturated each of the three source photos in red, green, and blue, the basic colors of digital photography; then he mixed them together as adjustment layers in Photoshop. The result is a highly dynamic collage of a figure in a dense backdrop with splashes of rich digital color. Welling uses software to create almost as a painter might, arranging forms in a constructed space with applied color. He prints his photos in high resolution and large format to increase the impact. When he exhibits the works from this series, he also makes available a booklet for viewers that sets forth all the steps he took to reach the final images.

9.20 Jeff Wall. *Boy Falls from Tree*. 2010. Color photograph. 92″ × 123″.
Courtesy of the artist and Marian Goodman Gallery, New York.

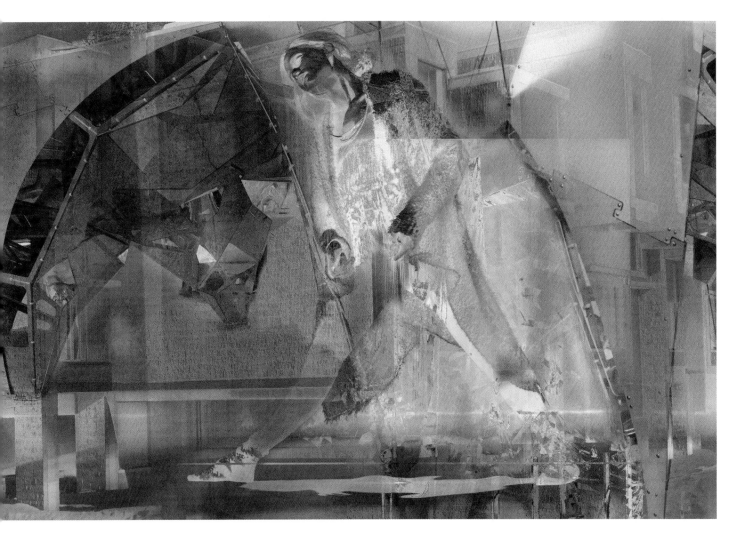

9.21 James Welling. *9812*. 2016. Inkjet on rag paper. 42″ × 63″.
© James Welling. Courtesy of Regen Projects, Los Angeles.

KEY TERMS

aperture – the width of the opening that admits light into a camera; a narrow aperture that lets in little light might be used in bright light and a wider aperture for lower-light conditions

camera obscura – the forerunner of the modern camera, a dark room (or box) with a small hole in one side, through which an inverted image of the view outside is projected onto the opposite wall, screen, or mirror, and then traced

daguerreotype – a photograph taken by an early photographic process developed in the 1830s, in which a treated metal plate was exposed to light, and the chemical reactions on the plate created the first satisfactory photographic images

depth of field – the depth of the area before the camera that will be in sharp focus in a photo

f-stop – the ratio of the focal length to the size of the opening (aperture); low f-stops give a shallower field of focused material and higher ones can bring everything, near and far, into focus

focal length – the distance between the lens and the image sensor

image sensor – the surface inside a camera where the image is collected, upside down; in traditional cameras the sensor was photographic film, but in digital cameras the sensor converts the light into an electric charge, which the camera's software reconstitutes as a photograph for display on the camera's screen

shutter speed – the length of time the camera shutter is open; this determines the brightness of the resulting photo

10 CINEMA AND DIGITAL ARTS

LEARNING OBJECTIVES

10.1 Trace the development of cinema from its origins in photography.

10.2 Describe early technical innovations and techniques in movies.

10.3 Discuss the types of movie that originated in Hollywood and internationally from the 1930s.

10.4 Explain the impact of the digital revolution on special effects and movie production.

10.5 Summarize the use of digital video as an art medium.

10.6 Discuss how artists today use computers to produce digital artworks.

The first experimental color movie seen in Germany had to be shown under false pretenses. The year was 1933 and the work was *Circles* by Oskar Fischinger (**fig. 10.1**). It was a nonrepresentational movie, composed of dancing and interlocking rings and circles that moved and evolved across the screen, accompanied by dramatic orchestral music. Only a few minutes in length, it was screened together with entertaining black-and-white features. The public seemed to enjoy Fischinger's experiment in color and form.

However, those were the years in which the Nazi party suppressed all forms of abstract and nonrepresentational art, which they regarded as "degenerate." In order to avoid such censorship, Fischinger made *Circles* as an advertisement for a public relations company; the last few moments of the movie display the name of the company and an advertising slogan. Finding Nazi browbeating intolerable, Fischinger left Germany for Los Angeles in 1936.

10.1 Oskar Fischinger. *Circles.*
1933–34. Film still.
© Center for Visual Music.

This story illustrates two important points about cinema: First, that it is a mass art closely monitored by those in authority; and second, that creative people have been making experimental cinema for generations. In this chapter we will examine the origins of cinema and trace the development of innovations and techniques through movies that have broken new creative ground, some in the mass market and others in smaller, more artistic circles. We will also look at the impact of new technology on special effects and production, and consider how the digital revolution has led to the creation of new artforms and new ways of presenting artworks.

The Birth of Cinema

Cinema, the production of movies as an art or an industry, is a logical extension of photography. If a camera takes a sufficiently rapid sequence of photos of a moving subject, and those photos are viewed in a quick enough succession, the appearance of movement is created in the viewer's eye and mind. This illusion of motion is made possible by **persistence of vision**, the brief retention of an image on the retina of our eyes after a stimulus is removed. This phenomenon was already known in children's flip books, which first appeared in 1868.

The roots of cinema lie in an experiment funded by Leland Stanford (Governor of California and founder of Stanford University). A devotee of horse racing, he wondered whether all four legs of a horse ever left the ground during a gallop. In 1872, he commissioned photographer Eadweard Muybridge to find a way to capture the animal's motion in pictures. Muybridge lined up a series of still cameras close together alongside a California racetrack; each camera shutter was fixed with a string that the horse's front legs tripped as it ran by. The resulting pictures of *The Horse in Motion* (**fig. 10.2**) conclusively proved that the horse was indeed airborne for a brief moment. After Muybridge later discovered a way to project his still photographs in rapid succession, he made the first primitive cinema. He called his invention a zoöpraxiscope (a name that did not survive, fortunately for all of us).

The first practical film camera was invented in 1891 at the Thomas Edison Laboratory in Menlo Park, California; it used a long strip of photographic **film**, which an electric motor fed through a camera capable of taking 16 frames per second. Projecting the developed film at the same rate yielded a movie.

By the late 1890s, cinema was a popular entertainment medium, as theaters in most major cities projected programs of short movies of usually less than ten minutes in length. In those early days, few people accepted cinema as an artform, for the same principal reason that photography was not accepted immediately: The film camera seemed like a mere mechanical recording device. And indeed, most early movies were brief narrations of stories told in pantomime. In order to gain public acceptance, early filmmakers tried to make their movies look like filmed theatrical performances. Actors made entrances and exits in front of a camera fixed in place, as though it too were a member of the audience at a stage play. Because the technology for recording sound on film was not perfected until the late 1920s, these early silent projections were accompanied by live music, usually a piano player.

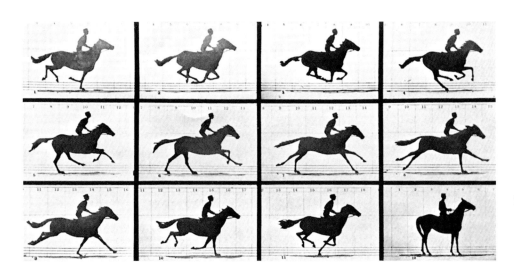

10.2 Eadweard Muybridge. *The Horse in Motion.* 1878. Photographs.
Courtesy of the Library of Congress. LC-USZ62-45683 DLC.

Silent Cinema: Innovations and Techniques

Much of the power of cinema comes from its ability to reconstruct time. A movie is not inhibited by the constraints of clock time; it can convincingly present the past, the present, and the future, or it can mix all three in any manner. Cinematic time can affect us more deeply than clock time, because sequences can be constructed to approximate the way we feel about time. In addition to editing, cinema can also manipulate time by slowing or accelerating motion. The director's control over time, sequence, light, camera angle, and distance can create a feeling of total, enveloping experience so believable that it becomes a new kind of reality.

One of the first important directors to pioneer certain effects of **cinematography** (the art of movie photography and camerawork) was the Frenchman Georges Méliès, who began his career as a magician. Between 1896 and 1913 he directed over 500 movies, most of them just a few minutes in length and based on narration of a single event. He built his movies from a succession of **shots**, which are brief unbroken sequences of recorded action. Between them he used dissolves (fading instead of rapid cutting). Showing his roots in the world of magic, he also perfected visual effects such as time-lapse photography (giving the illusion of very fast motion) and disappearances (freezing the shooting, removing an actor or item, and continuing). The fantasy *Le Voyage dans la lune* (*A Voyage to the Moon*)

(**fig. 10.3**) is among his most highly regarded movies. Four astronauts climb into a bullet-shaped projectile and are shot out of a huge cannon. On the lunar surface, they find a culture based on the popular conception of traditional Pacific Islanders. Because silent movies did not depend on spoken language, they were enjoyed across the Western world.

Between 1907 and 1916, American director D. W. Griffith helped to bring the motion picture from its infancy as an amusement to fuller stature as a means of artistic expression. Griffith introduced the moving camera by releasing it from its fixed, stagebound position in order to better express narrative content. The camera was placed where it would best reveal the dramatic meaning of each scene. A scene thus came to be composed of several shots taken from different angles, thereby greatly increasing the viewer's feeling of involvement.

Assembling a scene from several shots involves **film editing,** a process in which the editor selects the best shots from raw footage, then reassembles them into meaningful sequences and finally into a total, unified progression.

Later, Griffith used parallel editing to compare events occurring at the same time in different places or in different times, such as a person in danger and the approach of a would-be rescuer. He used this technique in his feature *Intolerance* (**fig. 10.4**), in which he cut back and forth among four stories about intolerance of various kinds set in four periods of history.

Griffith was the first to use the **close-up** and the **long shot**. Today, the close-up is one of the most widely used shots; but when Griffith first wanted to try a close shot, his cameraman balked at the idea of a head without a body! In a long shot the camera photographs from a distance to emphasize large groups of people or a panoramic setting.

Several other early shot innovations came from Russian directors. Director Lev Kuleshov, for example, discovered that viewers' emotions from one shot persist into the next, even if

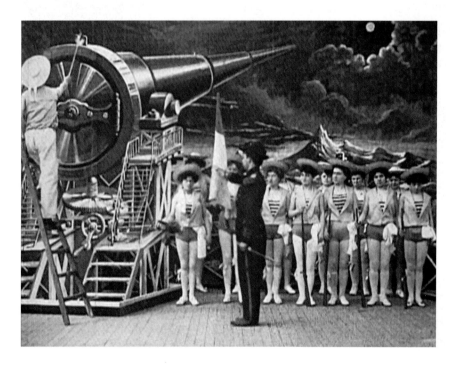

10.3 Georges Méliès. *Le Voyage dans la lune* (*A Voyage to the Moon*). 1902. Film still.

in the West as in Russia. Eisenstein greatly admired Griffith's directorial techniques, but he developed them further, becoming one of the first directors to produce epic features of high quality.

One of Eisenstein's major contributions was his skilled use of **montage** to heighten dramatic intensity. He adapted Griffith's editing technique of combining a number of very brief shots, representing distinct but related subject matter, in order to create new relationships, build strong emotion, or indicate the passage of time. With the use of montage, a great deal seems to happen simultaneously, in a short time.

In his movie *Battleship Potemkin* (**fig. 10.5**), Eisenstein created one of the most powerful sequences in cinema history: the terrible climax of a failed revolt as army troops crush a protest. The montage of brief shots, edited into a sequence of no more than a few minutes, effectively portrays the tragedy of the historic event. Rather than shoot

they are unrelated in content. A shot of a smiling actor followed by a shot of a plate of food will make the food seem attractive; if the actor is scowling or grimacing, the food will likely seem repugnant. This technique, still widely used in movies, is called the **Kuleshov effect**.

Another important innovative Russian director was Sergei Eisenstein. Following the Russian Revolution in 1917, he emerged as a major director, honored as much

10.5 Sergei Eisenstein. *Battleship Potemkin*. 1925. Selected frames from "Odessa Steps" sequence. Film stills.
The Museum of Modern Art/Film Stills Archive.

10.6 Salvador Dalí and Luis Buñuel. *Un Chien Andalou* (*An Andalusian Dog*). 1929. Film still.
AF archive/Alamy. © 2018 Salvador Dalí, Fundació Gala-Salvador Dalí, Artists Rights Society.

the entire scene with a wide-angle lens from a spectator's perspective, Eisenstein intermixed many close-ups to give viewers the sensation of being caught as participants in the middle of the violence. The juxtaposition of close-ups and long shots gives audiences a powerful sense of the people's fear and the tragedy that took place.

A movie resembles a collective dream, in which a group of people sitting in the dark experience the same vivid story. In 1929, Surrealist artists Salvador Dalí and Luis Buñuel took advantage of this fact when they made *Un Chien Andalou* (*An Andalusian Dog*) (**fig. 10.6**). Like our dreams, the movie is a sequence of seemingly unrelated and irrational events: Ants crawl out of a man's palm; two dead donkeys lie bleeding in a pair of grand pianos; a woman's eye is sliced open with a razor. The overall theme of the picture seems to be unrealized sexual desire, and at the end the man and woman are frozen half-buried in the soil like a pair of statues. The manifest illogic of *An Andalusian Dog* influenced the hallucinatory content of music videos decades later.

An Andalusian Dog is silent with a musical accompaniment, but in fact synchronized sound had been introduced two years earlier. By 1930, almost all movies had sound. "Talkies," as they were called, required subtitles for foreign audiences, making it less easy for the movies to cross international boundaries. Color was also introduced during the 1930s; the wide screen and three-dimensional images in the 1950s.

From the Talkies to the Seventies

Beginning in the 1930s, movie studios grew into larger companies, each contracting its own producers, directors, technicians, and actors. These firms would control most mass-market cinema through the 1960s.

Hollywood, with its large studios, became the production site for the vast majority of the world's movies in the 1930s. Beginning in mid-1934, the major Hollywood studios all adhered voluntarily to the Motion Picture Production Code, which attempted to regulate the moral content of movies. The Code forbade profanity in the script, as well as depictions of nudity, sexual activity, drug use, interracial romance, and ridicule of the clergy. It also prohibited the glamorization of crime, so that all criminals had to be arrested or killed in the end. Studios submitted scripts to the Code authorities prior to shooting, and any feature that lacked a Code seal of approval had no chance of wide distribution. At times, Code strictures were relaxed somewhat: Clark Gable's famous farewell to Vivien Leigh in *Gone With the Wind* ("Frankly, my dear, I don't give a damn") remained in the movie, but the producer paid

10.7 Orson Welles. *Citizen Kane.* 1941. Film still.
The Museum of Modern Art/Film Stills Archive.

10.8 Edgar G. Ulmer. *Detour*. 1945. Film still.

meaningful social message, *Citizen Kane* immediately set new standards for directing. The movie employs an unprecedented array of cinematic devices: dramatic lighting that communicates feeling, distorted lenses, dialog that bridges breaks between scenes, and clever editing to show the passage of time. Welles and his cinematographer, Gregg Toland, also pioneered the use of extreme camera angles. The low-angle camera presents Kane (Welles) as a towering presence; another such angle is the tilt, which emphasizes Kane's crooked politics. The movie is also important for the life that it portrays. Hearst was the prototype of the media mogul who achieves fame and wealth by selling sensational news ("If the headline is big enough, it makes the news big enough," he says).

During the 1940s, a new style called **film noir** originated in Hollywood. These dark and brooding black-and-white movies usually dealt with murder, sometimes committed by professional criminals, but more often by ordinary folks down on their luck who are tempted at the wrong moment. These movies depict the dark side of the American Dream, few of them more grimly than *Detour* (**fig. 10.8**), in which the main character tries to illicitly collect a dead man's large inheritance, but ends up as a suspect in two murders. The film noir genre is based primarily on American detective fiction, shot with expressive lighting and camera-angle techniques borrowed from *Citizen Kane* and the Europeans.

Despite Hollywood's numerical dominance in movie production in the postwar period, many foreign directors also made groundbreaking movies. Many of these international creations used more creative cinematography or told stories never made in Hollywood. One of the former was the Japanese director Akira Kurosawa, who often adapted

a fine of $5,000 for it. The Code's authority declined in succeeding decades, but remained in effect until 1968, when the Motion Picture Association of America introduced the ratings system that is still in force today.

In the 1930s and 1940s, animators from the Walt Disney studio meticulously explored the possibilities of **animation**, in which hand-drawn frames are photographed and projected in sequence to create the illusion of motion. Disney was the first to create an animated feature-length movie, *Fantasia*, in 1940. This was a new type of movie that integrated classical music, painting, dance, and drama with a mix of human cartoon characters as the stars.

Ideas for such animations were initially portrayed on **storyboards** (a series of drawings or paintings arranged in sequence), which were then used to visualize the major shots that make up a movie. Layout artists made the story come alive as the spatial relationships were worked out, and animators then dramatized individual characters in each action sequence. Disney's goal was always to create characters who gave the illusion—at 24 frames per second—that they were not just moving, but also thinking and feeling.

Many movie critics rank the 1941 movie *Citizen Kane* (**fig. 10.7**) as a landmark in cinema. Orson Welles co-wrote the script, directed, and played the leading role in the thinly disguised biography of the newspaper tycoon William Randolph Hearst. Because of its aesthetic quality and

stories was the Italian Federico Fellini. His 1961 movie *La Dolce Vita* (*The Sweet Life*) foreshadows many of today's critiques of the mass media (**fig. 10.10**). Marcello Mastroianni plays the lead character, a tabloid journalist (also named Marcello) who makes his career reporting on sensations, scandals, and celebrities.

The protagonist follows the lifestyles of the rich and famous, dutifully attending spectacles of all kinds, from the exploits of American movie stars to decadent parties to religious visions. He frolics in a fountain at 4 AM with a starlet. He joins the media circus as thousands throng to a small town where two children say they saw the Virgin Mary. One of these fellow travelers is a photographer friend nicknamed Paparazzo (after the "pop" of the camera flash), and, ever since this movie's release, intrusive photographers throughout the world have been called *paparazzi*. The movie's construction facilitates its message: The director criticizes the sweet life by plunging into it, with long and loosely connected scenes.

European plays and stories for filtering through his own vision. One of these works was *Throne of Blood* (**fig. 10.9**), in which he retold the story of Shakespeare's *Macbeth* in an ancient Japanese setting. The actors used techniques from traditional Japanese theater as they interpreted the tale. Kurosawa typically composed every shot very carefully, as if it were a painting. He frequently used long lenses, placing more than one camera at a distance from an actor in order to elicit a more natural performance. He also used wide-angle lenses to provide more scope for composition. Trained as a painter before becoming a director, he often drew and painted his own storyboards as he developed the various shots into a movie. His visual style owed more to such pictorial composition than to other factors such as montage. Western directors, in turn, have adapted or remade many of Kurosawa's movies; the plot of *Star Wars*, for example, owes a great deal to Kurosawa's 1958 action adventure feature *The Hidden Fortress*.

A leading international director who told non-Hollywood

10.10 Federico Fellini. *La Dolce Vita*. 1961. Film still.
© INTERFOTO/Alamy.

Experimental Cinema

Only occasionally did the careers of artists intersect successfully with those of Hollywood directors and studios. In the late 1930s, Walt Disney recruited Oskar Fischinger to collaborate on *Fantasia*, but the partnership was not a success because Disney opposed Fischinger's commitment to abstract art. In 1945, however, Alfred Hitchcock worked more fruitfully with Salvador Dalí to create a dream sequence for *Spellbound*, in which lead character Gregory Peck relates a dream that unlocks his amnesia. By the 1960s, the separation between artists and directors was as complete as it would ever be. Most artists who made movies considered their work "underground" and showed it mostly in galleries and art venues where such experimental cinema could flourish.

An early leader in the underground cinema movement was Stan Brakhage. In the late 1950s, he began painting directly on raw film and then scratching through it to create abstract movies. In 1959, he filmed the birth of his first child, a subject forbidden by the Production Code. His most famous movie is the feature-length *Dog Star Man* (**fig. 10.11**). A radical experiment in film editing, this movie combines shots of a man walking his dog in a snowy forest with shots of the night sky, the sun's surface, and other material. Some shots are hand-painted by the artist; others use distorting lenses. Although the movie has no clear plot, its theme of the creation of the universe slowly dawns on the viewer.

10.12 Kenneth Anger. *Scorpio Rising.* 1964. Film still.
Photofest.

Sometimes an artist's experimental movie influenced the mainstream, as happened with Kenneth Anger's *Scorpio Rising* (**fig. 10.12**). This 1964 work is in effect a documentary about the rituals of a Brooklyn motorcycle gang. They fix their bikes, go to parties, take drugs, and even suffer deadly crashes. Anger filmed it all in highly saturated color above a soundtrack of pop songs of the day. *Scorpio Rising* memorably creates a world, with intercut footage from other movies and music that comments on the main action. The movie strongly influenced the later idea of the "biker movie," and Hollywood directors such as Stephen Spielberg and Martin Scorsese have said that its mood-creating qualities also influenced their own work.

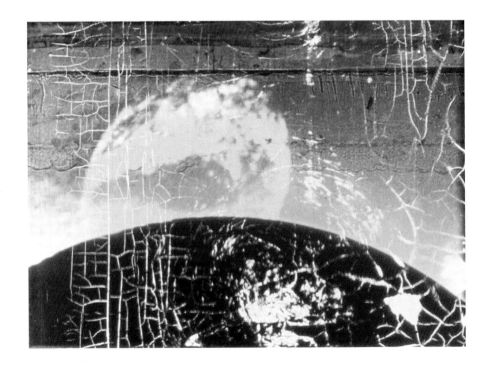

10.11 Stan Brakhage. *Dog Star Man.* 1964. Film still.
Courtesy of the Estate of Stan Brakhage and Fred Camper

The Seventies

Increasing competition from television took a toll on movie attendance, which decreased the power and influence of the studios. Moreover, the decline of the Production Code in the late 1960s released studio-based directors to explore formerly restricted story lines regarding relationships, race, violence, and sexuality. This led many of them to rethink the old movie types, experimenting with characters and plots in Westerns, thrillers, romances, and others. Robert Altman was a leader in this reconsideration with *The Long Goodbye* (**fig. 10.13**), a witty and knowing detective story adapted from a famous novel. The main character is Philip Marlowe, a hapless but hardworking private eye, set adrift in sunny and self-centered 1970s Los Angeles. He copes (barely) with several gangsters, a less-than-honest best friend, neighbors who meditate outdoors in the nude, and abusive police who suspect him of murder. Altman inserted many deft touches: Every time Marlowe appears in any scene, he lights a cigarette; the musical score consists of one song, played in myriad arrangements; numerous references to previous detective movies ricochet through the script. *The Long Goodbye* repays study of earlier movies, and awareness of cinematic conventions, because it satirizes or undercuts many of them.

10.13 Robert Altman. *The Long Goodbye*. 1973. Film still.
Photo 12/Alamy.

10.14 Gordon Parks. *Shaft*. 1971. Film still.
Entertainment Pictures/Alamy Stock Photo.

Another 1970s detective movie that innovated in a different direction was *Shaft*. As an outgrowth of the civil rights movement, ethnic minorities began to advance in Hollywood during that decade. This trend began with the **blaxploitation movement**, in which studios employed African-American directors and actors in action-adventure movies that were set mostly in urban neighborhoods.

Shaft was an early example of this new type of movie that proved successful with white audiences as well, much to the surprise of the producers. A black gang leader hires street-wise private investigator John Shaft to rescue his daughter, who has been kidnapped by the Mafia (**fig. 10.14**). The plot is basic to Hollywood but the movie, directed by well-known photographer Gordon Parks, shows gritty urban life in Harlem with new clarity. The Shaft character who navigates the stormy script is both well-dressed and ruthless; he gets the job done by allying with an African-American revolutionary group. The blaxploitation movement was controversial because it seemed at times to reinforce stereotypes. But this movie's visual style, magnetic lead character, and award-winning score by Isaac Hayes potently influenced later urban hip-hop culture. It also engendered several sequels, knock-offs, and remakes.

Special Effects and Digital Cinema

Special effects have been made possible in recent years by a merging of old techniques such as animation with the new technology of computers. Teams of artists and technicians work with producer-directors such as George Lucas, creator of the *Star Wars* series, to provide working sketches, models, animation, and sets that are fantastic yet believable. Industrial Light and Magic (ILM), the special effects division of Lucasfilm Ltd., was the leading special-effects studio of the late 1970s and 1980s. Lucas was also responsible for the increased use of computers to edit film.

A recent example of the use of digital special effects is *Pan's Labyrinth* (**fig. 10.15**) by Mexican director Guillermo del Toro. A joint Spanish-American production, the movie is also an example of international co-production, in which companies from several countries collaborate in financing and distribution so that the risk to any one of them is minimized. The movie shows what happens when imagination and reality intersect in the life of an 11-year-old girl in Spain of the 1930s. Her difficult life under a cruel stepfather leads her to take refuge in a fantasy world populated by tiny flying fairies and trees that move, led by a faun who represents a kingdom beyond this world.

In the scene pictured here, the monster at the right, a made-up human actor, is about to awaken from seated slumber by picking up the two eyeballs on the dish in front of him and inserting them into the palms of his hands. The use of computer graphics in this digitally shot movie enables the seamless joining of the made-up hands of a real actor with the digitally animated eyeballs, which glance around and express surprise on seeing the girl. Del Toro's principal theme is how imagination can help us to cope with adversity, and its many vivid sets and characters testify to the director's visual creativity (see some of his notebook pages at fig. 6.3). *Pan's Labyrinth* has moments of both stunning beauty and aching horror; del Toro refuses to tell us which is real and which imaginary, leaving the final decision to us.

In the new century, the gradual shift from traditional film to digital cinematography is nearly complete. The first all-digital feature-length movie was *Rainbow* (1996), but its digital files had to be converted to film to enable projection in theaters. Three years later, George Lucas's *Star Wars Episode I—The Phantom Menace* was the first movie to combine film and digital cinematography. Later movies in the series were shot with all digital cameras. The box-office power of the *Star Wars* movies strongly influenced the parallel gradual adoption of digital projection equipment in movie theaters. Aided by subsidies from studios, nearly

10.15 Guillermo del Toro. *Pan's Labyrinth*. 2006. Film still.
AF archive/Alamy.

10.16 Ridley Scott. *Prometheus*. 2012. Movie still.
Scott Free Prod/20th Century Fox/Photo 12/Alamy Stock Photo.

all movie theaters today project digitally. Only a handful of directors still shoot with film, and their work must be converted for digital projection.

This evolution has important implications for both the creation and the enjoyment of movies. Most major Hollywood studios are owned by large international media companies, and they have discovered that they can draw audience interest around the world with movies that employ luxurious special effects with a fast-moving story line. Digital production, with its speed of composition and editing, greatly facilitates this type of cinema. To boost international receipts, these "blockbusters" generally do not rely on character development, local cultural traditions, or divisive social comment for their success, and some are promoted together with merchandise based on the movie.

Digital projection also facilitates uniform worldwide distribution: Instead of heavy film cans, theaters now receive a DCP (Digital Cinema Package)—a 2-inch-thick hard drive sized about midway between a smartphone and a tablet—which a worker plugs into a projection device. Satellite transmission will soon replace the DCP for mass-market movies. Meanwhile, theaters that specialize in projecting vintage movies on traditional film are vanishing.

One of the more recent blockbusters, Ridley Scott's *Prometheus*, exemplifies many of these trends. It was shot using multiple digital cameras to enable 3-D

projection, and it opened in 49 countries over a ten-day period in mid-2012. It has many scenes that seamlessly blend human actors with digital animation (**fig. 10.16**). The crew of the spaceship *Prometheus* is multi-ethnic, and it includes a robot who seems as human as some of the other actors.

The most common way to achieve this effect is through **motion capture**. Actors wear special suits with several dozen markers attached to various parts of their bodies

10.17 Researcher wearing a full body suit "Ergomoven", designed for human motion capture.
AZTI-Tecnalia Marine and Food/age fotostock/Alamy Stock Photo.

10.18 Janicza Bravo. *Hard World for Small Things*. 2016. Still from VR movie.

Janicza Bravo and virtual reality company, Wevr.

(**fig. 10.17**). They go through the motions required for a scene on an empty stage as digital cameras record. Their marker motions are then plotted to 3-D software for animation. In this way an actor can become a digital monster, and can be easily inserted into other digitally shot scenes. Producers of video games make wide use of this technique as well. The technology for motion capture keeps improving, because markers can be cumbersome and limit resolution. The newest suits, for example, allow capture without markers, as we see here.

The latest technical innovation in cinema, and its most immersive form, is **virtual reality**, or VR. These movies are either animated or shot live with three-dimensional cameras. Viewers experience them by donning headsets that allow them to move their heads or bodies to see the action unfold around them in a complete panorama. Many of these movies are viewable by loading the movie onto a smartphone, which is then installed in a headset. This art-form emerged in gaming and music videos early in this century, but the arrival of consumer-friendly headsets in 2012 led to a boom in creativity. Some types of animated VR allow viewers to reach into a scene through hand-held devices and interact with characters.

A recent VR experience that makes a social comment through live action is *Hard World for Small Things* by Janicza Bravo (**fig. 10.18**). Bravo staged this six-minute short in South Central Los Angeles, putting the viewer in the back seat of a convertible as it drives through the neighborhood. After meeting and chatting with a handful of characters, the actors park outside a convenience store. Inside, an encounter with two plain-clothes policemen leads to a tragic and controversial conclusion. The movie vividly portrays a police-involved shooting, one of today's most contentious social issues.

Video Art

The Sony Corporation set the stage for the beginning of video art in 1965 when it introduced the first portable video recording camera, the Portapak. Although the camera was cumbersome, some artists were drawn to the new medium because of its unique characteristics: The instant feedback of video did away with development times necessary for film. Video works could be stored on inexpensive cassettes, erased and re-recorded. In addition, because a video signal could be sent to more than one monitor, it allowed flexibility of presentation.

Early videos by artists were relatively simple, consisting mainly of recordings of the artists themselves performing, or of dramatic scenes staged with only a few actors or props. Because no editing was possible, and the black-and-white image was incompatible with the color resolution of television broadcasts of the time, the medium was best suited to private screenings for small groups, a continuation of underground cinema. In 1972, the compatibility issue was resolved with the introduction of standardized ¾-inch tape; this allowed artists to work with television production equipment, and even to broadcast the results of their labors. The 1980s brought vast improvements in video technology in the form of color, lighter cameras, and computerized editing.

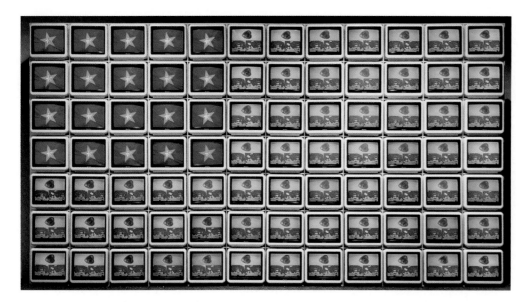

In the short history of video art, some artists have consistently tried to expand the limits of the medium's technical capacities. The Korean-born Nam June Paik frequently used the video medium in a slyly humorous fashion to comment on the role of television in our lives. His 1986 work *Video Flag Z* (**fig. 10.19**), for example, uses 84 television sets in an array that resembles the American flag. On each monitor, portions of old Hollywood features flicker endlessly across the screens, as if our very national identity is made up of what we see in movies.

Other video artists have used the medium to create and tell stories using themselves as actors. In *Volcano Saga* (**fig. 10.20**), Joan Jonas tells a story of a memorable trip to

Iceland. Caught in a fierce windstorm, she is blown off the road and loses consciousness. Awakened by a local woman who offers help, the artist is magically transported back to ancient times in the company of Gudrun, a woman from Icelandic mythology, who tells her dreams. The artist sympathizes with Gudrun's struggles in her ancient society, and returns to her New York home feeling kinship with women of the past. In the video, images move back and forth between past and present with the aid of overlays and an evocative musical score.

Digital Video Art

The cathode-ray television tube has now disappeared in favor of the flat-screen monitor, and videotape cassettes have given way to digital media and DVDs. Given the ease of shooting and editing digital video today, the line between video art and cinematography has blurred. The five movies of the *CREMASTER Cycle* by Matthew Barney were shot on digital video and are usually projected in art galleries, but part of *CREMASTER 3* (**fig. 10.21**) has been released on DVD as well.

These movies innovate in their elaborately symbolic story lines and expensive production values. Describing the plot of any of the *CREMASTER* movies is difficult, but plot is less important than the symbolic content of each movie. The portion released on DVD is called "The Order," and it recounts an endurance

10.20 Joan Jonas. *Volcano Saga*. 1987. Performance still.
The Performing Garage, NY. Courtesy of Gavin Brown's Enterprise.

10.21 Matthew Barney. *CREMASTER 3.* 2002. Production still.

© 2002 Matthew Barney. Photograph: Chris Winget. Courtesy of Gladstone Gallery, New York.

test that the Apprentice must undergo by passing four ordeals at various levels of the Guggenheim Museum. Allusions to Masonic Orders, Mormon theology, heavy metal music, and the once-famous convicted murderer Gary Gilmore only begin to describe the various layers of this video. The Apprentice passes through each obstacle, and thus gains the right to kill another character, called the Architect. The murder takes place at the Chrysler Building, but the building itself takes revenge by killing the Apprentice.

Many artists today combine digital video with other artforms into multimedia installations. Diana Thater, for example, created a dramatically lit installation for her video work *Science, Fiction* (**fig. 10.22**). In the center of one blue-lit room is a tall, rectangular box that seems to float above an intense yellow glow. The box houses a projector, which sends onto the ceiling a movie that depicts living dung beetles. These insects, which live and move chiefly in manure, guide their motions at night by the position of the Milky Way; they are the only animals known to do so. The next room houses large-format screens that show footage of the night sky shot through an observatory telescope. The installation brings together the most elemental (and odoriferous) world with the seeming infinity of the cosmos.

10.22 Diana Thater. *Science, Fiction.* 2014. Installation for two video projectors, media player, and lights. Dimensions vary with installation.

© Diana Thater. Courtesy of David Zwirner, New York/London.

Digital Artforms

The art-making capacity of computer-linked equipment ranges from producing finished art, such as color prints, movies, and videos, to generating ideas for works that are ultimately made in another medium. Computers are also used to solve design problems by facilitating the visualization of alternative solutions. The computer's capacity to store images in progress enables the user to save unfinished images while exploring ways of solving problems in the original.

The multipurpose characteristics of the computer have also accelerated the breakdown of boundaries between media specializations. A painter working with a computer can easily employ photo imaging or even add movement and sound to a work. A photographer can edit an image in almost any imaginable way.

Artists began using computers as soon as they came into wide use. The first exhibition of computer-generated digital imagery took place in a private art gallery in 1965. Few claimed that it was art. Most of the pioneering digital artists used computers to make drawings with a plotter, a small ink-bearing device that moves over a piece of paper drawing a line in one color according to programmed instructions. The computers that they used were so expensive that they were owned only by universities, large corporations, or research centers.

At a research lab in Paris, Vera Molnar made some of the most visually interesting of these early efforts, such as her digital 1976 work *Parcours* (**fig. 10.23**). The computer was programmed to create randomized variations on a basic set of plotter movements, yielding a work that resembles a drawing quickly done by hand. In many of these early types of computer art, the plotter's motions were not entirely predictable, a fact that added to the attractiveness of the images. The expense and complexity of computer technology in those years, however, kept all but a few artists away from the medium.

The advent of faster computers, color printers, and interactive graphics radically changed the scenario in the mid-1980s, and as the computer's capabilities grew, more artists began to take interest. Today, many photographers, directors, designers, sculptors, and architects use the computer to aid their projects. They may store and alter images, or they may use a 3-D modeling application to help visualize the shape of a design. For some artists, software and digital equipment are an essential part of their creative practice. Here are three recent projects that show some of the pathways artists are taking.

Rafael Lozano-Hemmer makes dramatic digitally based works that engage viewers directly in the creative process. His 1999 work *Vectorial Elevation* (**fig. 10.24**) was installed in the central square of Mexico City during the night of the change to the new millennium and for several nights thereafter. Viewers could program an array of powerful searchlights by visiting terminals at the square; viewers worldwide could do so by going to a website.

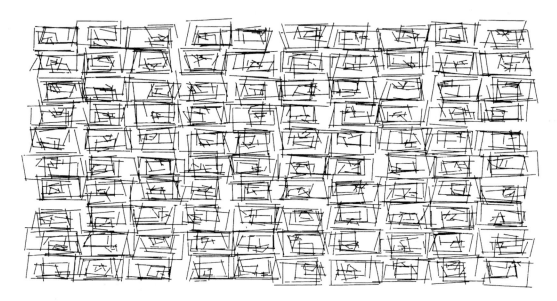

10.23 Vera Molnar. *Parcours (Maquette pour un Environment Architectural).* 1976.
Courtesy of the artist. © 2018 Artists Rights Society (ARS), New York/ADAGP, Paris.

10.24 Rafael Lozano-Hemmer. *Vectorial Elevation, Relational Architecture 4.* 1999. Zócalo Square, Mexico City, Mexico.

Courtesy of the artist. Photo by: Martin Vargas. © 2018 Artists Rights Society (ARS), New York/VEGAP, Madrid.

The programmed arrays were all placed in a queue and carried out in sequence. Each array was held for six seconds as the website displayed the name and location of that array's creator. The artist merely designed and set up the apparatus so that anyone could share the responsibility of creation.

Many digital artists also take advantage of the computer's ability to process massive amounts of data. Casey Reas, for example, created *Today's Ideology* (**fig. 10.25**) in 2015, a video screen connected to a database of one day's photos from the digital edition of the *New York Times.* The computer distorts and displays those photos by laying them out slowly across the screen in what appear to be animated paint strokes. The distended photos are stretched out thin, but the bright colors and contemporary content give viewers a new and unique perspective on contemporary events.

10.25 Casey Reas. *Today's Ideology (26 July 2015).* 2015. Computer code, digital images, computer, screen. 1080 x 1920 pixels.

The artist and DAM Gallery, Berlin.

Lynn Hershman Leeson confronted the issue of digital simulation when she created the video cyborg *DiNA* (**fig. 10.26**). (The title comes from the phrase "digital DNA.") *DiNA* appears on a video installation in which viewers walk up to a microphone and interact with the virtual woman on the screen before them. *DiNA* is running for the imaginary office of Telepresident, and in her slightly disembodied cybervoice she invites viewers to use the microphone to raise questions and concerns. *DiNA*'s responses sound surprisingly intelligent for a machine, but she is linked to the

10.26 Lynn Hershman Leeson. *DiNA*. 2004. Artificially intelligent agent, network connection, custom software, video, and microphone. Dimensions variable.

Courtesy of Lynn Hershman Leeson.

Internet and searches in real time for text to use in response to viewer input. After interacting with *DiNA* for a few minutes, viewers learn that she takes moderately liberal positions on abortion and capital punishment, for example. Most viewers conclude either that *DiNA* could indeed run for office, or that she seems more thoughtful than most politicians. Her campaign slogan is "Artificial intelligence is better than no intelligence."[1] In an age when telling the real from the pre-packaged is difficult, *DiNA* complicates the issue in a memorable way. The artist has used and discussed contemporary digital life and its human problems in several formats (see *Lynn Hershman Leeson: Interrogating Tech Life*, opposite).

As we have seen, cinema has progressed from a novel entertainment to an important artform capable of accommodating many types of experiment and thematic statement. The advent of accessible digital technology in the 1980s has not only led to a special effects revolution but also changed the way movies are shown and distributed around the world. Digital technology has also led to new artforms, as artists use software and digital equipment as part of their creative practice.

KEY TERMS

animation – the technique of photographing a series of hand-drawn or computer-generated frames of a movie to create the illusion of motion

blaxploitation movement – a cinema movement of the 1970s in which studios employed African-American directors and actors in action-adventure movies that were set mostly in urban neighborhoods

cinema – the production of movies as an art or industry

cinematography – the art of camerawork and photography in making movies

close-up – a shot taken when the camera is so close to a subject that it fills the frame

film – spooled photographic stock for the recording of movies

film editing – the process by which an editor compiles shots into scenes and into a movie

film noir – a genre of dark and brooding black-and-white movies originating in Hollywood in the 1940s

Kuleshov effect – an editing technique that takes advantage of the fact that viewers' emotional responses to one shot are transferred to the next

long shot – a camera shot taken at a distance from the subject; used to emphasize groups of people or a panoramic setting

montage – in motion pictures, the combining of shots into a sequence to portray the character of a single event through multiple views

motion capture – the process of digitally recording movements of actors for animation

persistence of vision – an optical illusion that makes cinema possible; the eye and mind tend to hold images in the brain for a fraction of a second after they disappear from view

shot – any uninterrupted run of a movie camera; shots are compiled into scenes, then into movies

special effects – the creation of illusions in cinema through the use of camerawork, models, animation, computer graphics, or other means

storyboard – a sequence of drawings prepared to guide camera shots in motion picture production

virtual reality – an immersive form of cinema in which viewers don headsets that allow them to move their heads or bodies to see the action unfold around them in a complete panorama

CREATORS

Lynn Hershman Leeson: Interrogating Tech Life

10.27 Photo of Lynn Hershman Leeson.
Courtesy of Lynn Hershman Leeson.

Exploring the human–tech interface has been a nearly lifelong quest for Lynn Hershman Leeson (b. 1941). After earning a Master's degree from San Francisco State University, she began creating wax human figures that she enlivened with sound and placed in installations. Even before digital technology became commonplace, she was investigating the difference between the real and the virtual.

When Hershman Leeson proposed an interactive self-portrait sculpture for a museum exhibition in 1968, the directors refused to exhibit it because it seemed more like a piece of technology than of art. Working on that boundary has been her preferred stance since then.

In 1984, Hershman Leeson created *Lorna*, a work that allowed viewers to intervene in the life of the title character, a lonely woman who feared leaving her home. It was the first artwork that used laserdisc technology, a predecessor of the

DVD. Hershman Leeson was on the Internet almost as soon as it came into use, using it in a work called *CybeRoberta* (1996). This was an interactive doll whose eyes were video cameras. Visitors to both CybeRoberta's website and to her physical exhibition in a gallery could interact with viewers in the other realm through the doll.

In the new century, Hershman Leeson continues her investigations in feature-length movies. Her best-known work to date is *Teknolust* (**fig. 10.28**), a science-fiction fable that sets forth some pitfalls accompanying our embrace of digital technology. The main character is a bio-geneticist named Rosetta Stone, who devises a method of downloading her own DNA into her computer. This fusion of the human and the technological is a current issue that lies at the root of this movie. Soon the computer generates three life-size half-human clones of Rosetta that resemble her exactly except for differing hair color. Rosetta names them Ruby, Olive, and Marinne after red, green, and blue, the three colors in RGB computer monitors. (Actress Tilda Swinton played all four roles.) These human-cyborg hybrids soon begin to take on more human traits, and this causes trouble when they venture out.

The three female clones in their increasing humanness resemble Frankenstein characters, a product of human invention gone wrong, but they are ingeniously updated for today's world and concerns. One of the three clones speaks lines that she downloaded from romance movies, a comment on how cinema influences people. Rosetta created the clones thinking that she could control them, but she comes to see that she can't, just as we cannot control the direction of technology in our culture. The movie shows little lust or sex; the title comes more from Hershman Leeson's belief that "as a culture we are continuously seduced by digital possibilities," as she put it on the director's voiceover on the DVD version of the movie. *Teknolust* thus provides a vehicle for thinking about the consequences of too eagerly embracing digital technology.

10.28 Lynn Hershman Leeson. *Teknolust*. 2002. Film still.
Entertainment Pictures/Alamy Stock Photo.

Design Disciplines

11.1 Discuss the use of graphic design in the visual communication of information and ideas.

11.2 Explain the rise of motion graphics as a design discipline.

11.3 Describe the uses of interactive design.

11.4 Assess industrial products that integrate utility, technology, and cutting-edge design.

The Saks Fifth Avenue department store had a problem as the twenty-first century dawned. Its brand name was already iconic, and it had stores in most large cities. Its reputation for quality and elegance was established. Its demographic of upscale shoppers was dependable, as it had been ever since the first store opened in 1924. The problem was this: How do you renew a brand, keeping the best of the old while you show the public that you can still innovate? How do you attract younger shoppers while keeping the (aging) old ones?

11.1 Michael Bierut. Saks Fifth Avenue logo. 2007.
Design Firm: Pentagram. Image courtesy of Saks Fifth Avenue.
HBC Corporate Collection.

Saks presented the situation to Michael Bierut of the graphic design firm Pentagram, and asked for suggestions on how to renovate the company's logo in a way that was recognizable but new, traditional yet cutting-edge. In 2007 Bierut created for the firm a new logo (**fig. 11.1**) that shattered the previous elements of the design. He took the familiar cursive script of the old logo, sliced it into 64 square pieces, and recombined them randomly. The logo is still recognizable to everyone who has ever taken home a Saks bag, but it also looks so innovative that it is even a little disorienting at first glance.

Bierut did what designers generally are supposed to do: at the invitation of a client, solve problems and offer solutions. Designers can work in a number of disciplines including interactive design, motion graphics, product design, textile design, clothing design, interior design, packaging design, and environmental design. In this chapter, we will consider several of these, beginning with graphic design, moving on to motion graphics and interactive design, and concluding with industrial product design.

Graphic Design

Of all artforms, we encounter graphic design most frequently in our daily life. We interact with graphic design almost constantly; most designers have chosen it as their profession because they relish that close interaction with people in all situations. Our encounters with graphic design are usually casual and unintended; we do not seek out design the way we might seek other artforms in a gallery or museum. This

11.2 Donald Meeker. Clearview Hwy typeface. 2004 to present.

a. Sample road sign using Clearview 5-w.

FHWA Series E   Original Sketch   Clearview Version 1   Clearview 5-W

FHWA Series E-m   ClearviewOne BD-55

b. Development of Clearview Hwy font from the Federal Highway font.

fact gives graphic designers an unequalled opportunity to attract, inform, persuade, delight, bore, offend, or repel us.

The term "graphic design" refers to the process of working with words and pictures to enhance visual communication. Much of graphic design involves designing materials to be printed or viewed on a screen, including books, magazines, posters, and imagery for electronic media. Such design ranges in scale and complexity from postage stamps and trademarks to magazine pages, film, video, personal digital screens, websites, and apps.

Graphic design is a creative process employing art and technology to communicate ideas. Using symbols, type, color, and illustration, the graphic designer produces visual compositions meant to attract, inform, and persuade a given audience. A good graphic designer can memorably arrange text and image for the benefit of both.

Typography

Typography is the art and technique of composing printed material from letterforms, or designing letterforms themselves. A complete set of letterforms, including all capitals, lower case, numerals, and accent marks is a **typeface**, also called a **font**. Designers, hired to meet clients' communication needs, frequently create designs that relate nonverbal images and printed words in complementary ways.

Just a few decades ago, when people committed words to paper, their efforts were handwritten or typewritten—and nearly all typewriters had the same typeface, the name

of which was unknown to most users. Now anyone who uses a computer can select fonts and create documents that look professional, producing desktop publications such as newsletters, brochures, and Web pages. But computer programs, like pencils, paintbrushes, and cameras, are simply tools: They can facilitate artistic aims if their operator has artistic sensibilities. Recording artist Kanye West recently underlined the importance of typography when he stated, "I get emotional with fonts, spacing, proportion."[1]

Since the Chinese invention of printing in the eleventh century, thousands of typefaces have been created—helped recently by digital technology. This text uses Adobe Garamond for its elegance and readability.

Many European-style typefaces are based on the capital letters carved in stone by early Romans. Roman letters are made with thick and thin strokes ending in **serifs**—short lines with pointed ends, at an angle to the main strokes. The capital letter H in a Roman type of font has four serifs, one at each extremity. In typesetting, the term "roman" is used to mean "not *italic*." **Sans serif** (without serifs) typefaces have a modern look thanks to their association with modernist designs. They are actually ancient in origin. 𝔅𝔩𝔞𝔠𝔨 𝔩𝔢𝔱𝔱𝔢𝔯 typefaces are based on Northern medieval manuscripts.

Today, many type designers are redesigning and updating old fonts, keeping in mind readability and contemporary preferences. We see the typographer's art in action with the Clearview Hwy typeface (**fig. 11.2**).

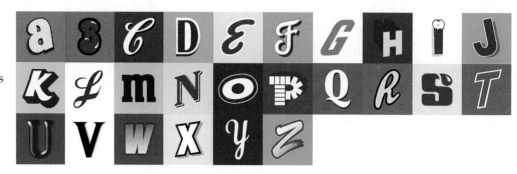

11.3 Heidi Cody. *American Alphabet*. 2000. A set of 26 aluminum light boxes which feature the isolated first letters of American grocery products. Lambda Duratrans print. Each box 28″ × 28″ × 9″.

© 2000 Heidi Cody.
www.heidicody.com

Donald Meeker and his associates designed this font because they thought they could improve the readability of white-on-green Interstate freeway signs. Using the existing font as a starting point, they expanded the hollow spaces in the lower-case letters, such as e's and a's, and they narrowed the size ratio between lower- and upper-case letters. They made many other more subtle changes, such as adding a base to the lower-case l. The Federal Highway Administration tested the new font in all kinds of weather and lighting conditions, with drivers of varying visual acuity, and they found that it was more quickly legible than the old typeface. They approved this new font for Interstate highway signs in 2004, and it is gradually replacing the old one across the United States, as new signs are required.

Heidi Cody took a more ironic stance with her 2000 work *American Alphabet* (**fig. 11.3**). She found all 26 alphabet letters in the initials of corporate logos. She said, "I try to get viewers to consciously acknowledge how indoctrinated, or 'branded' they are."[2]

Jonathan Cuervo Cisneros is another typographer who redesigns and updates old fonts. He recently created the new font Febrile (**fig. 11.4**), based on black letter typefaces found on documents in colonial Latin America. He slanted the letters backward and added frilly details to the capitals.

11.4 Jonathan Cuervo Cisneros. Febrile Type Font. 2014.
Courtesy of Jonathan Cuervo Cisneros.

11.5 Superflex. *Bankrupt Banks* series. 2012.
Acrylic on cotton. Each 79″ × 79″.
a. Sovereign Bank acquired by Banco Santander SA,
October 13, 2008.
Courtesy of the artist and Peter Blum Gallery, New York.

b. Colonial Bank acquired by BB&T, August 14, 2009.
Courtesy of the artist and Peter Blum Gallery, New York.

These changes reflect the nervous excitement or energy in the meaning of the word *febrile*. Like many typographers today, he created the font digitally and offers it for sale on his website.

Logos

In our age, when image seems to be everything, companies spend large sums on graphic design to present the best "identity package." A **logo** is an identifying mark, or trademark, based on letterforms combined with pictorial elements. Corporations finely calibrate such designs to present a distinctive and memorable appearance.

Let us examine logos from two banks to see the messages that they carry as simple symbols. The artist group Superflex recently appropriated the logos for artworks, stripping away their associated typography; this creates an opportunity to examine how logos themselves communicate. The Sovereign Bank logo (**fig. 11.5a**) is a lantern that sheds light. It looks radiant, but also prim and traditional, which is what many people imagine banks to be. The logo for Colonial Bank is based on the letter C, which is turned into a lighted orb like the sun (**fig. 11.5b**). The image of the eagle in the C suggests the bald eagle that symbolizes the United States; this eagle seems to stand

guard, peering off into the distance, as vigilant as one might hope for in a banker. The color blue is like the sky, reassuring and indicative of fair weather. The messages of these two logos could not, however, prevent the two banks from failing during the mortgage crisis of 2008; this made possible the action that Superflex took, turning the logos into artworks on banners.

Posters and Other Graphics

A poster combines type and images in a single panel designed to provide information. An effective poster will, in a flash, both attract attention and convey its message. The creativity of a poster designer is directed toward a specific purpose, which may be to advertise or to persuade.

The concept of the modern poster is more than 100 years old. In the nineteenth century, most posters were lithographs, and many artists made extra income by designing them. Henri de Toulouse-Lautrec was the most important of these (see fig. 8.17). Early lithographic posters were all hand-drawn; designers added color to their work by printing the same sheet with multiple stones, one for each color. In the 1920s and 1930s, advances in printing methods made high-quality mass production possible, including the printing of photographs at large scale with text. Since the 1950s,

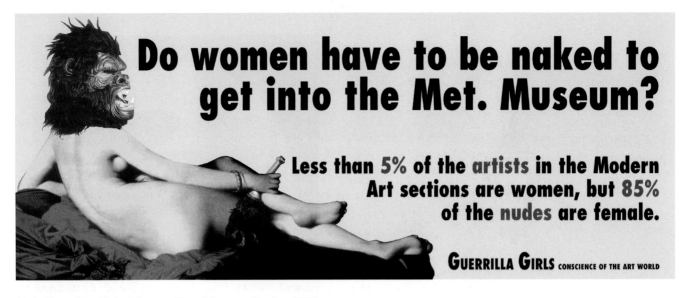

11.6 Guerrilla Girls. Metropolitan Museum Poster. 1989.
© Guerrilla Girls. Courtesy of guerrillagirls.com

radio, television, and print advertising have overshadowed posters. Although they now play a lesser role than they once did, well-designed posters can still fulfill needs for instant communication.

Many social causes find vivid expression in posters. The Black Panther Party, an African-American activist organization, made many creative (and militant) posters in the 1960s and 1970s. Near the same time, the Chicano movement commissioned many artists to make silkscreens promoting the causes of Mexican Americans. (An example of the latter is the poster by Jesús Barraza; see fig. 8.20). In the 1980s and 1990s, the Guerrilla Girls made activist posters protesting the inadequate representation of women in the art world. Their poster about the Metropolitan Museum of Art (**fig. 11.6**) uses a nude figure from a famous nineteenth-century painting. The oversized gorilla mask was the standard headgear for the group when they made public appearances. The bright yellow background with

11.7 Chaz Maviyane-Davies. *Seeking Asylum is a Human Right*. 2016. Poster.
Courtesy of the artist.

its sans serif font immediately draws attention as well. The Guerrilla Girls plastered these posters in many locations near the museum and in other parts of New York City where galleries were located.

Chaz Maviyane-Davies makes posters for both the Internet and street use. He often works without a commission, but rather for self-expression and from a desire to inform and arouse the public about urgent issues. His recent poster on the refugee problem (**fig. 11.7**) uses negative space to suggest the worldwide nature of the problem, while the type reminds us plainly of the human right to seek asylum. He distributed this poster electronically to his mailing list and sold the paper version on his website at a non-profit price.

Humor has great appeal in design. The advertising poster for the television show *Portlandia* (**fig. 11.8**) was based on a studio photo of two stars of the show dressed as urban hipsters posing stiffly next to clichés that refer to the northwestern city of Portland. The backdrop is obviously painted onto the wall, as we see from the window frame at the right. The format of this poster makes it appropriate for both outdoor and magazine use.

English designer Jonathan Barnbrook mocked the media overload that seems to accompany every renewal of the Olympic Games. For the 2010 Winter Games, Barnbrook and his firm Virus Fonts created a set of pictograms called *Olympukes*. One of the set was called *Drowning in Advertising* (**fig. 11.9**). In a sea of deep-red and wavy lines borrowed from the logo of a famous brand of soft drink, we see the head and arm of a submerged consumer calling for help. Barnbrook and Virus Fonts designed this *Olympuke* as iPhone wallpaper and made it available as a free download.

11.8 Cold Open. Poster for *Portlandia*. 2015.
Photo courtesy of The Broadway Video Group, Inc.

11.9 Virus Fonts. *Drowning in Advertising*.
From *Olympukes* set of pictograms. 2009.
iPhone wallpaper. 480 × 320 pixels.
Barnbrook.

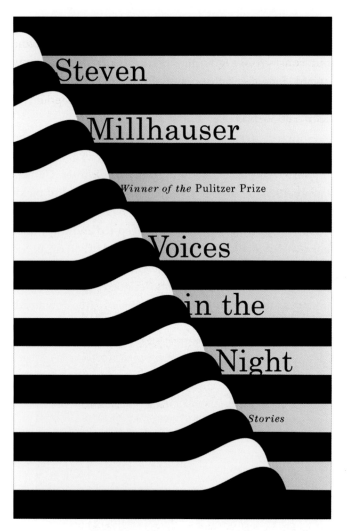

11.10 Janet Hansen. *Voices in the Night* by Steven Millhauser. Book cover. 2015.

Designer: Janet Hansen, Knopf.

Book covers function like corporate logos, uniting image and text to extend the message of a book and condense it into a single memorable page that shoppers will see online or in bookstores. Book cover design is a specialized field that has not gone out of style with the rise of digital books. Janet Hansen's cover for *Voices in the Night* (**fig. 11.10**) suggests a turned-down bedsheet. The curving black-and-white lines also recall lines of type on pages that we turn. Even digital reading devices simulate the turning of paper pages.

Motion Graphics

Logos, posters, and book covers are generally static objects, but today a growing design field is motion graphics, in which a designer uses visual effects, live action, and animation to create a two-dimensional project that moves. Designers combine these techniques in various ways for time-based sequences in websites, television commercials, public signage, and music videos.

Motion graphics as a discipline began with **title sequences** for Hollywood movies, the roll of credits at the beginning of a movie. Most title sequences were merely slow scrolls of names until the arrival of Saul Bass in the early 1960s. Bass said in an interview that an opening title sequence for a movie can "create a climate for the story that is to follow," because "the audience involvement with a film should really begin with the first frame."[3]

The arrival of advanced digital editing in the 1990s ensured the takeoff of motion graphics. The new computer applications enable designers to create each frame of a sequence with all the freedom that photo-editing allows. Thus, motion graphics designers are increasingly directors of short but intense projects that combine input from many sources.

The most original use of the new technologies came with Kyle Cooper's work on the title sequence for *Se7en* (**fig. 11.11**), a dramatic crime story. The title sequence has a plot of its own, as a man with bandaged fingers assembles and stitches together a booklet about murder and sexual deviance. Layered images, film clips, and spoiled type nervously twitch across the screen along with the hand-lettered credits, over a soundtrack by Nine Inch Nails. Most important, this haunting close-up sequence has a function in the script: It introduces the audience to the mind of the killer, who does not appear until 40 minutes into the film. Cooper said that his aptitude for vivid graphics came in part from his earlier study at Yale with Paul Rand, one of America's legendary designers.

Although title sequences are a digital medium, many motion graphics designers still crave the hand-drawn look. Karin Fong, for example, created a fast-moving and revealing sequence for the television series *Rubicon* (**fig. 11.12**). The main character of the series is an intelligence analyst who, as he investigates the suspicious death of his mentor, begins to uncover a wide-ranging conspiracy among a secret society of war profiteers. The title sequence follows a hand-drawn yellow chalk line through lists of data, pages of computer printouts, barcodes, maps, censored documents, aerial photographs, and short film clips. It hints at a person searching for connections among clues found in various kinds of evidence, just as the lead character of the series does. The clues and hunches that he follows in his investigation are foreshadowed in the opening title sequence, which combines still images, animations, live action, and sound. *Rubicon* lasted for just one season, but Fong's title sequence was nominated for an Emmy award. Fong also creates motion graphics for various other media, including video games and advertisements (see *Karin Fong: Animating New Narratives* on p. 184).

11.11 Kyle Cooper. Title Sequence for *Se7en*. 1995.
Film directed by David Fincher. A Time Warner Company, Inc.

11.12 Karin Fong. Trial frames for title sequence to *Rubicon*. 2010. Film stills.
Courtesy of the artist.

Karin Fong: Animating New Narratives

11.13 Karin Fong.
Courtesy of Imaginary Forces.

Karin Fong (b. 1971) began her design career at a very young age. She recalled, "I always was a designer before I knew what to call it. I spent my childhood making my own newspapers, books, and comics that my dad would take to work and 'publish' for me on a Xerox machine."[4] This led her to Yale University, where her senior project was an animated children's book. Animating graphics was a leading-edge idea at the time, as digital animation was still in its infancy. After graduation, she was among the founders of Imaginary Forces, one of the leading motion-graphics design firms.

Fong's specialty is title sequences for movies and television programs (see fig. 11.12). "I always think a great main title is a little bit like the curtain opening," she says. It invites the audience to "leave the real world and go into this other place."[5]

Creating a motion-graphics title sequence involves shaping many types of media into a cohesive whole. Fong describes the birth of a project: "The process usually begins with a conversation with the film's director. From there we bounce around ideas. Sometimes there's a concept outlined in the script, but often there are just some basic themes to explore. That's one of my favorite stages: the research and design phase where we try to learn all we can about the film and its world. From there many ideas can bloom, and we often work on a few storyboards to flush something out. We'll brainstorm different ways to enter into the story."[6]

Motion-graphics designers today create in a wide variety of media. Fong has also designed a trailer for the video game *God of War: Ascension*, and a television advertisement for Target stores that starred Christina Aguilera as a comic-book superhero. One project for the Lincoln Center for the Performing Arts in New York required the coining of a new name: an *Infopeel* (**fig. 11.14**), which is a template of moving shapes, with spaces for the insertion of dates of upcoming events and photos of the performers. The goal was to create a design that attracted the attention of moving viewers, while directing their eyes to the information. Pedestrians and motorists who cross that busy Broadway intersection can now inform themselves about Lincoln Center programming without stopping.

"I have always been interested in the relationship between image, story, and word," Fong says. Motion graphics today provides "opportunities for new narrative structures and new ways of telling a story," aided by the latest software and technology. "The world of filmmaking is opening up," she says, "because people are accepting—and expecting—the integration of animation and live action and type. So it's becoming a new language, and that's very exciting."[7]

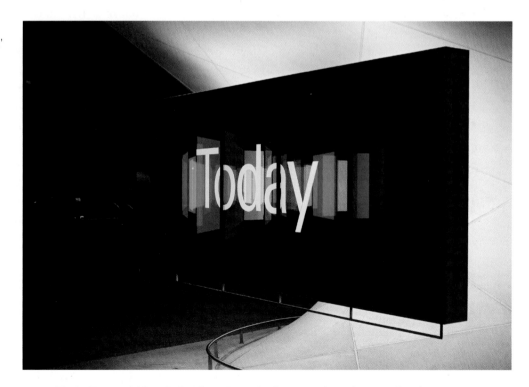

11.14 Karin Fong and Mark Gardner. Lincoln Center Infopeel. 2009. Outdoor motion graphics display at 65th Street and Broadway, New York.

Interactive Design

As more and more of our media become interactive, designers work to organize the information presented and keep the designs attractive. This is a relatively new area of design, but already there have been standout projects.

Across all of our media, the QR code (or Quick Response code) is increasingly a symbol of interactive potential. Scanning a QR code with an enabled device such as a smartphone brings up a website, a video, an application, or other information. A 2009 building in Japan broke new ground by building interactivity into its surface (**fig. 11.15**). Scanning the QR codes on the façade will show information about the building's hours of operation, sales that are taking place in the stores inside, and even recent tweets by users who walk its hallways. The designers of the building created an alternative to billboards; instead of pushing content on everyone as most outdoor displays do, the information in the N Building is accessible only if a consumer "asks" by activating its QR codes.

Websites are still a major source of information for all of us, and a well-designed site can make gathering information pleasurable. The website about the movie *The Sonic Sea* (**fig. 11.16**) presents information about the movie and the recently recognized problem of noise in the ocean. Slow-moving graphics and an overall blue color scheme make the site peaceful; voiceovers play out over background sounds of waves. Scrolling down in the learning section of the site brings well-proportioned words and

11.15 Terada Design Architects. N Building. 2009.
Tachikawa, Japan.
Interactive façade by Qosmo, Inc. Lighting by Izumi Okayasu Lighting Design.
Photograph by Yuki Omori.

text, along with clickable links to more information about how to take action. All of this information unfolds clearly, without overloading the user.

The smartphone app INKS (**fig. 11.17**) is an interactive game based on pinball but with an artistic component. Viewers shoot virtual pinballs that hit colored edge areas to release flowing digital paint that can be controlled. The colors flow and blend according to the speed of the ball and the degree of tilt that the user applies to the device. The ball takes on the color that it most recently struck, leaving a curving trail and adding a design element.

11.16 Imaginary Forces. Website
for *The Sonic Sea*. 2015.
Henry Chang, designer.

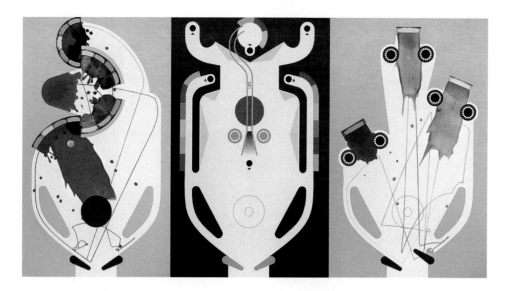

11.17 State of Play. INKS. 2016. Handheld device game app.
State of Play Games.

All handheld media devices, such as tablets and smartphones, have their origins in the transistor radio, which was first made practical by the Sony Corporation in 1957 (**fig. 11.18**). This new radio, the TR-610, fitted in the hand and had a small speaker and a built-in antenna. Buyers could also select the exterior color. A large loop at the back was extendable for setting the device on a table. During its two years of shelf life, this model sold more than two million units.

The app offers many tables with differing ball paths and colors, and the opportunity to save, print, or share results. It enables users to experiment with nonrepresentational painting and to amass a gallery of their own creations.

The name Sony was itself invented near the time of the release of the TR-610, in order to facilitate global sales. A custom-designed word, it was not tied to any nationality and was easy to read and say in many languages. In the 1970s, the company united miniature headphones with the new cassette technology and invented the Walkman. When compact-disc recordings became feasible in the 1980s, Sony developed a portable player, and the advent of computer-based digital audio at the beginning of the twenty-first century led to a proliferation of mp3 players.

Industrial Product Design

We all handle designed products every day, and industrial designers work to make these products more beautiful, useful, and sustainable. We close this chapter by examining objects that have made history by integrating utility, technology, and cutting-edge design.

11.18 Sony Corporation. TR-610 transistor radio. 1957.
INTERFOTO/Alamy Stock Photo.

11.19 New BMW Concept e Scooter on the IAA 2011 International Motor Show in Frankfurt am Main, Germany.
artpartner-images.com/Alamy Stock Photo.

11.20 Andrew Jones. The Battery Chair. 2014.
Battery Park Conservancy, NY. Maglin Site Furniture, Woodstock, Ontario.

The advent of lithium ion batteries in the new millennium broadened the uses of electricity for powering many kinds of devices, among them motorcycles such as the BMW Concept e Scooter (**fig 11.19**). The new electric motor in turn enabled new design solutions for two-wheeled transport. The first thing we may notice about this model is the lack of a gas tank and tailpipe. The structural elements in the design seem to lean forward, suggesting speed. And indeed, this model accelerates more quickly than a gasoline-powered motorcycle of similar size. It also runs nearly silently while producing zero emissions. This is one of many examples of products that designers are creating to help encourage green thinking.

A chair is a mundane device for sitting, but recently Andrew Jones rethought its parameters and came up with the Battery Chair (**fig. 11.20**). The overall shape suggests a flower, and the blue color refers to the blooms of the scilla plant, which flourishes locally in the northeastern United States. The lightweight stackable design and cartoony, flower-petal shape of the chair suggests informality and relaxation. This is appropriate because Jones designed it for the National Park Service to install in the grassy Battery Park at the southern tip of Manhattan, which also hosts an outdoor market, concerts, and movie screenings. The park service commissioned the chair from Jones after an open competition for a new chair design that drew 679 entries from around the world. Committees and the general public assessed and sifted the entries in a process that included sitting in prototypes to check comfort; they found that the Battery Chair encourages a relaxed posture and judged this entry the best for the setting.

As we have seen, we encounter graphic design and related design disciplines frequently in our daily lives. Design is a creative process that employs art and technology to produce visual compositions and objects that can attract, inform, persuade, delight, and assist us.

KEY TERMS

font – the name given to type in a particular size and weight; today often used interchangeably with typeface to indicate a complete set of letterforms, including all capitals, lower case, numerals, and accent marks in all sizes and weights

logo – a sign, name, or trademark of an institution, firm, or publication, consisting of letterforms or pictorial elements

sans serif – a typeface without a serif

serif – short lines that end the upper and lower strokes of a letter in some fonts

title sequence – the roll of credits at the beginning of a motion picture or television program

typeface – a complete set of letterforms, including all capitals, lower case, numerals, and accent marks in all sizes and weights; also called a font

typography – the art and technique of composing printed materials from type

12

SCULPTURE

LEARNING OBJECTIVES

12.1 Compare examples of freestanding, low-relief, and high-relief sculpture.

12.2 Describe modeling, casting, carving, and constructive techniques used to make sculpture.

12.3 Define and describe kinetic sculpture.

12.4 Explain the parameters and components of mixed media sculpture.

12.5 Discuss artists' use of installation and site-specific art to transform their surroundings.

Most viewers who approach Martin Puryear's work *C.F.A.O.* (**fig. 12.1,** opposite left) will first see a dizzying welter of wood pieces, stacked in a loose network and glued together, atop an old wheelbarrow. Mostly unpainted, the stack of pieces seems to have a rectilinear organization, but it is too dense to see through. It is also, at 8 feet 5 inches, rather tall. It looks as if someone may have thought of a unique way to bring home the day's purchases from the lumber yard.

But if we walk around it and look from the other side (**fig. 12.1,** opposite right), we see the reason for the apparent density of the work: a large, curving shape, based on an elongated African mask, that the artist painted white. Clearly, in order to see and grasp this work, we must walk around it and examine it from various angles.

Freestanding and Relief Sculpture

Sculpture meant to be seen from all sides is called in-the-round, or **freestanding**. As we move around it, our experience of a sculpture is the sum of its various aspects. A single photograph shows only one view of a sculpture under one kind of light; thus, we receive only a limited impression of a sculpture unless we can see many photographs or, better yet, a video; or, best of all, view the piece ourselves. *C.F.A.O.* is a freestanding sculpture that offers different characteristics and impressions depending on the position of the viewer.

A sculpture that is not freestanding but projects from a background surface is in **relief**. In **low-relief** (sometimes called **bas-relief**) sculpture, the projection from the surrounding surface is slight. As a result, shadows are minimal. Coins, for example, are works of low-relief sculpture stamped from molds. The Apollo coin (**fig. 12.2**), shown here, has a strong presence in spite of being in low relief and very small.

Some of the world's most finely crafted low-relief sculptures are found at the temple of Angkor Wat in Cambodia. This vast temple complex was the center of the Khmer empire in the twelfth century. Here Khmer kings sponsored an extensive program of sculpture and architecture. Within the chambers of the complex, carvings are in such delicate low relief that they barely rise above the background surface. One scene, *Army on the March* (**fig. 12.3**), depicts an army commanded by a prince. The rhythmic pattern of the spear-carrying soldiers contrasts with the curving patterns of the jungle foliage in the background. The soldiers and background provide a setting for the prince, who stands with bow and arrow poised in his carriage on the elephant's back. Intricate detail covers entire surfaces of the stone walls of the temple complex.

In **high-relief** sculpture, more than half of the natural circumference of the modeled form projects from the surrounding surface, and figures are often substantially undercut.

12.1 Martin Puryear. *C.F.A.O.* 2006–7. Painted and unpainted pine and found wheelbarrow. 8′5″ × 6′5½″ × 61″.

The Museum of Modern Art, New York. Photograph: Richard Goodbody. © Martin Puryear. Courtesy of Matthew Marks Gallery.

12.2 Silver Coin with Apollo. c.400 BCE.

British Museum 1896,0601.18. © The Trustees of the British Museum.

12.3 *Army on the March.* Relief from Angkor Wat, Cambodia. 1100–50. Sandstone.
Photographer: Eliot Elisofan. Time & Life Pictures/Getty Images.

This is the case with Robert Longo's *Corporate Wars: Wall of Influence* (**fig. 12.4**), where male and female figures convulse in painful conflict. Much of the composition is high relief with undercutting; in only a few areas are limbs and garments barely raised above the background surface. Dynamic gestures and the diagonal placement of torsos and limbs make the sculpture very active. The emotional charge of the piece suggests that Longo is horrified by the intense competition of corporate life.

12.4 Robert Longo. *Corporate Wars: Wall of Influence.* 1982. Middle portion. Cast aluminum. 7′ × 9′.
Courtesy of the artist and Metro Pictures.

Methods and Materials

Most sculpture is made by modeling, casting, carving, constructing, and assembling, or a combination of these processes.

Modeling

Modeling is usually an **additive** process. Artists work with their hands to model pliable material such as clay, wax, or plaster. They build up, remove, or push the material into a final form.

Cultures around the world have left us examples of their arts through modeled ceramics. Tool marks and fingerprint

12.5 *Ballplayer with Three-Part Yoke and Bird Headdress.* Maya Classic period. 600–800 CE. Ceramic with traces of blue pigment. 13$\frac{15}{32}$″ × 7″.
Princeton University Art Museum. Museum purchase, Fowler McCormick, Class of 1921 Fund, in honor of Gillett G. Griffin on his 70th birthday. 1998–36. Photograph by Bruce M. White. © 2018. Princeton University Art Museum/Art Resource NY/Scala, Florence.

impressions are visible on the surface as evidence of the modeling technique employed to make *Ballplayer with Three-Part Yoke and Bird Headdress* (**fig. 12.5**). Body volume, natural gesture, and costume detail are clearly defined. The ancient Maya, who lived in what are now parts of Mexico, Guatemala, and Honduras, used clay to create fine ceramic vessels and lively sculptures. This player wears a bright blue headdress that the sculptor added to the figure before firing. He also wears a wide yoke around his waist for protection, and wristbands and anklets for hitting the ball, because use of the hands was not allowed.

The working consistencies of clay, wax, and plaster are soft. To prevent sagging, sculptors usually start all but very small pieces with a rigid inner support called an **armature**. When clay is modeled to form large sculptures, the total piece can be built in relatively small, separately fired, structurally self-sufficient sections, thereby eliminating the need for an armature.

Auguste Rodin used a small armature to hold the plaster up as he worked on *Naked Balzac* (**fig. 12.6**). He created the sculpture by gradually adding plaster, working up from below; when the plaster dried, he removed the armature. Balzac was a well-known French author, and a literary society had commissioned Rodin to make an honorary statue. In preparation, the artist studied Balzac's novels and essays for several months. Rodin thought the nudity and decisively striding pose effectively captured Balzac's personality. When he presented this sculpture the society rejected it, so the artist kept it in his studio.

Artworks made through modeling need not be representational, as Ken Price's *Vink* (**fig. 12.7**) shows. He modeled this work out of clay, fired it, painted it with multiple layers of acrylic paint, and then sanded the surface to expose spots of the paint layers below. Although the title refers to a small European songbird, any resemblance is coincidental. Rather, this piece suggests body parts, undersea organisms yet undiscovered, or some kind of knobby plant life. The iridescent color adds to the mysteriousness of the shape.

12.6 Auguste Rodin. *Naked Balzac*. 1892–93. Plaster painted with varnish. Height 29¾″.
Rodin Museum, Philadelphia. 1971-142-1. Philadelphia Museum of Art, Pennsylvania, PA, USA/Bridgeman Images.

12.7 Ken Price. *Vink*. 2009. Acrylic on fired ceramic. 9″ × 20″ × 11″.
© Ken Price. Courtesy of L.A. Louver, Venice, CA.

Casting

Casting is a way of making three-dimensional works by pouring a liquid into a mold and allowing it to harden before removing the mold. This process makes it possible to execute a work in an easily handled medium (such as clay) and then to reproduce the results in a more permanent material (such as bronze). Because most casting involves the substitution of one material for another, casting is also called a **substitution** process. The process of bronze casting was highly developed in ancient China, Greece, Rome, and parts of Africa. It has been used extensively in the West for the last five centuries, and is the most common medium for memorial statues in public parks.

Casting requires several steps. First, a **mold** is made from the original work. The process of making the mold varies, depending on the material of the original and the material used in the casting. Materials that will harden can be used to make molds: clay, concrete, or a liquid plastic such as fiberglass. Whatever the material, the mold completely surrounds the original, leaving no gaps. Second, the original sculpture is removed from the mold; this may require disassembly of either the original or the mold. Next, the casting liquid (most often molten bronze) is poured into the resulting hollow cavity of the mold. Finally, when the casting liquid has hardened, the mold is removed.

Some casting processes use molds or flexible materials that allow many casts to be made from the same mold. One of these is the **lost-wax** process (**fig. 12.8**), one of several processes that preserve the mold for possible later use. In some other methods the mold must be destroyed to remove the hardened cast, thus permitting the creation of only a single cast.

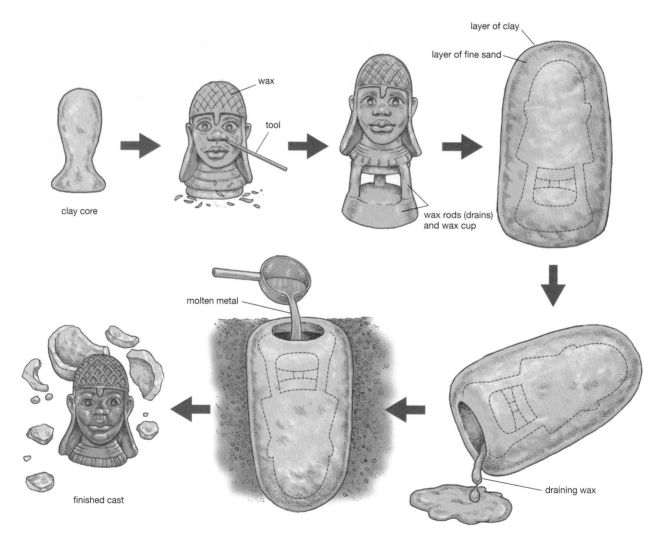

12.8 The Lost-Wax Casting Process.

12.9 Charles Ray. *Father Figure*. 2007. Painted steel.
93¾″ × 137¼″ × 71¾″.
© Charles Ray. Courtesy of Matthew Marks Gallery, New York.

Castings can be solid or hollow, depending on the casting method. The cost and the weight of the material often help to determine which casting method will be used for a specific work. The Statue of Liberty in New York harbor, for example, was cast in many pieces and reassembled into a hollow whole on site; an elaborate armature holds it up.

The process of casting a large object such as a bronze memorial statue can be extremely complicated. Except for small pieces that can be cast solid, most artists turn their originals over to foundry experts, who make the molds and do the casting. Most of our monuments in public parks were cast in bronze from artists' clay or wax models. Robert Longo's *Corporate Wars: Wall of Influence* (see fig. 12.4) is made from cast aluminum.

Many items are cast besides artworks, such as automobile engine parts, some dishes, and children's toys. Charles Ray made witty reference to the latter in his cast-steel work *Father Figure* (**fig. 12.9**). He based it on a green plastic toy tractor, which he enlarged to life-size in a plaster model before casting it in solid steel. The work weighs more than 18 tons, and its original toylike nature has vanished as the "father figure" looms, faintly menacing, at one with his machinery.

Duane Hanson, in contrast, cast actual people from life, using friends and relatives as models (**fig. 12.10**). After shaving all body hair, the models posed and were cast in segments applying silicone rubber directly onto their skin. After the rubber coating hardened, Hanson cut it away from the model and filled it with either polyester resin or auto body filler. He then painted the skin tones and added human hair before clothing them. Because the mold was ruined in the removal, the artist made only unique casts. As we see in *Man with Camera*, his models were generally posed in everyday postures and unremarkable clothing, which gave his sculpture a jolt of realism.

12.10 Duane Hanson. *Man with Camera*. 1991. Auto body filler polychromed in oil, mixed media, accessories. Life size.
Van de Weghe Fine Art, New York.
Photo by Tom Powel Imaging, Inc.
© Estate of Duane Hanson/Licensed by VAGA, New York, NY.

English artist Rachel Whiteread also uses new materials such as polyvinyl resin in fascinating cast pieces that turn empty spaces into solid volumes. To create *Untitled (Hive) I* (**fig. 12.11**), she filled a beehive with lustrous brown-orange resin and then took away the hive to leave only the interior, now rendered solid. In casting, artists make use of absence and presence, replacing one substance with another. By casting empty volumes, Whiteread gives absence a new kind of haunting presence.

Carving

Carving away unwanted material to form a sculpture is a **subtractive** process. Michelangelo preferred this method. Close observation of his chisel marks on the surfaces of the unfinished *Awakening Slave* (**fig. 12.12**) reveals the steps he took toward increasingly refined cutting, even before he had roughed out the figure from all sides. Because Michelangelo left this piece in an unfinished state, it seems as though we are looking over his shoulder midway through the

12.11 Rachel Whiteread. *Untitled (Hive) I*. 2007–8. Resin (two parts). 32⅛″ × 19¹⁵⁄₁₆″ × 25³⁄₁₆″.
© Rachel Whiteread. Courtesy of the Gagosian Gallery.

12.12 Michelangelo Buonarroti. *Awakening Slave.* 1530–34. Marble. Height 9´.

Galleria dell'Accademia, Florence. akg-image/Rabatti-Domingie.

carving process. For him, making sculpture was a process of releasing the form from within the block of stone. This is one of four figures, later called *Slaves*, that he abandoned in various stages of completion.

Carving is the most challenging of the three basic sculptural methods because it is a one-way process that provides little or no opportunity to correct errors. Before beginning to cut, the sculptor must visualize the finished form from every angle within the original block of material. (Another example of Michelangelo's carving is his *Pietà*; see fig. 4.21.)

The various types of stone with their different characteristics greatly influence the kind of carving that can be done with them. The marble that Michelangelo and many sculptors in the European tradition prefer is typically soft and workable enough that it can be cut with a chisel. Final polishing with a light abrasive yields a smooth and creamy surface not unlike human skin. Marble has been a preferred material in the West for outdoor sculpture for centuries, but modern air pollution and acid rain harm the stone, making it far less desirable today. Granite avoids these pitfalls, and thus is often used for outdoor monuments such as tombstones, but it is so hard that carving in detail is difficult. Sandstone and limestone are sedimentary materials that have also found wide use in many parts of the world. The Cambodian creators of *Army on the March* (see fig. 12.3) took advantage of the fine-grained qualities of sandstone when carving the intricate background foliage. Sedimentary stones are relatively soft, allowing much detail, and can be polished to a high gloss, although weather reduces this over time.

The ancient Egyptians used schist, a dense stone similar to slate. The jade that the Chinese favored is so hard and brittle that it can be ground down only by abrasion or filing; hence it is suitable only for small pieces. The disk, or *bi* (**fig. 12.13**), found in a Chinese royal tomb, is an exquisite example of carving using pale green nephrite, a rare type of jade. Chinese workers ground the stone nearly 2,000 years ago, using drills and quartz sand in a highly laborious process. The results of their work in this piece show a rare order of quality; the raised circles in the disk (called **bosses**) line up in perfectly even rows, and the feline monster above shows a rounded body and graceful, cat-like movement, amid a pattern that suggests clouds and wind.

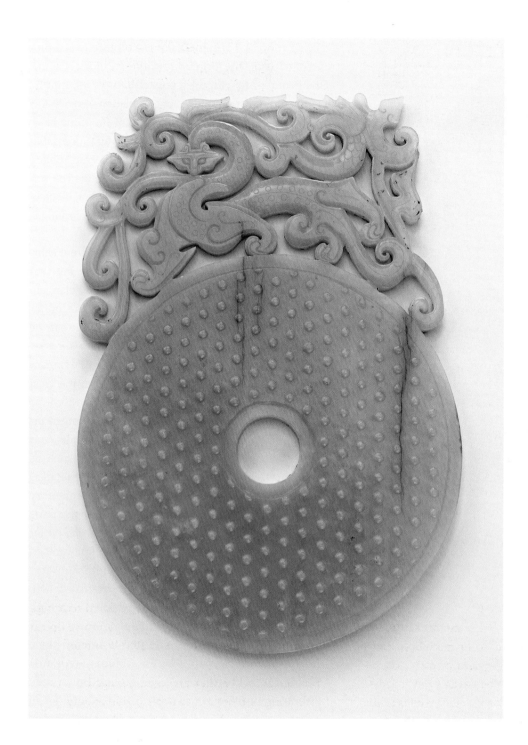

12.13 *Disk (bi).* China. Western Han dynasty, c.100–220 CE. Jade (nephrite). Diameter 7″.

Freer Gallery of Art and Arthur M.Sackler Gallery, Smithsonian Institution, Washington. D.C. Gift of Charles Lang Freer. F1916.155.

In wood carving, many sculptors prefer walnut and cypress because they combine strength and ease of working. The process begins with a block of wood, which the artist may draw on to help visualize the design. Carving is done with a variety of tools, such as gouges and chisels, subtracting material until the final form is reached. In Elizabeth Catlett's carved *Mother and Child #2* (**fig. 12.14**), the gesture of the mother suggests anguish, perhaps over the struggles all mothers know each child will face. Both figures have been abstracted in a composition of bold sweeping curves and essential shapes. Solidity of the mass is relieved by the open space between the uplifted chin and raised elbow and by the convex and concave surfaces. An engraved line indicating the mother's right hand accents the surface of the form. The smooth, highly polished wood invites the viewer to touch.

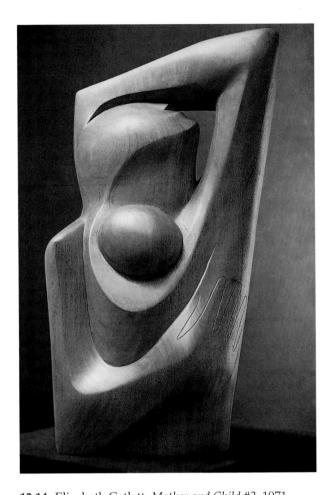

12.14 Elizabeth Catlett. *Mother and Child #2.* 1971. Walnut. Height 38″.

Photograph by Samella Lewis. © Catlett Mora Family Trust/Licensed by VAGA, New York, NY.

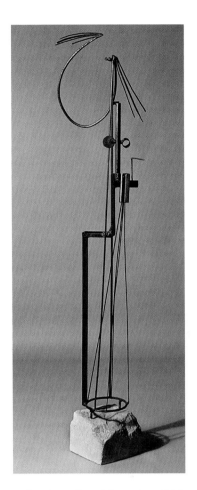

12.15 Julio González. *Maternity.* 1934. Steel and stone. Height 49⅞″.

© Tate, London 2018. © 2018 Artists Rights Society (ARS), New York.

Constructing and Assembling

For most of recorded history, the major sculpting techniques in the Western world were modeling, carving, and casting. Early in the twentieth century, assembling methods became popular. When artists put together pieces that they have shaped themselves, the result is called a **construction**. Sculpture built from found objects is called assemblage.

In the late 1920s, Spaniard Julio González pioneered the use of the welding torch for cutting and welding metal sculpture. The invention of oxyacetylene welding in 1895 had provided the necessary tool for welded metal sculpture, but it took three decades for artists to use the new tool's potential. González had learned welding while working briefly in an automobile factory. After several decades—and limited success—as a painter, he began

assisting Picasso with the construction of metal sculpture. Subsequently, González committed himself to sculpture and began to create constructions. In 1932 he wrote:

The Age of Iron began many centuries ago by producing very beautiful objects, unfortunately mostly weapons. Today it makes possible bridges and railroads as well. It is time that this material cease to be a murderer and the simple instrument of an overly mechanical science. The door is wide open, at last! for this material to be forged and hammered by the peaceful hands of artists.[1]

González welded flexed iron rods to create his construction *Maternity* (**fig. 12.15**). It is airy and playful as it suggests a feminine anatomy atop a stone base.

Some sculptors assemble found objects in ways that radically change the way we see familiar things. Yet we see enough of the objects' original characteristics that we can participate in their transformation. Such work requires metaphorical visual thinking by both artists and viewers.

Marc André Robinson shops in thrift stores for pieces of old used furniture and assembles new objects from them. *Throne for the Greatest Rapper of All Time* (**fig. 12.17**) is one such assemblage. We see at the lower center that the piece is based on found chairs, but he added a higher back and wings to the sides. If the purpose of a throne is to dignify whoever sits in it, this assemblage accomplishes that. This throne is a higher form of chair, made mostly from chairs.

Martin Puryear manipulates and shapes wood in several different ways. In *C.F.A.O.* (see fig. 12.1), he combined carving with construction in a work that includes a found wheelbarrow. His pieces also often involve carving, constructing, and then finishing the work into a finely crafted shape (see *Martin Puryear: Constructing Possibilities*, opposite).

12.16 Phyllida Barlow. *Untitled:stiltedcrates2015.* 2015. Timber, polyurethane foam, polystyrene, cement, steel, plywood, plastic fastenings, paint, hardboard, and PVA. Eight parts, each approx. 196⅞″ × 393¾″ × 472½″.
© Phyllida Barlow. Courtesy of the artist and Hauser & Wirth.

Phyllida Barlow uses carpentry techniques to create aggressively ungainly constructions that fill galleries to the point of obstruction. Her recent work *untitled:stiltedcrates2015* (**fig. 12.16**) at first seems dangerous to approach, as it consists of large wooden crates that she built, perched on pieces of lumber. The work delivers a visual jolt to viewers, who wonder how the teetering piece came into its present form. The disorder is apparent, however, only because Barlow carefully engineers her works for safety.

12.17 Marc André Robinson. *Throne for the Greatest Rapper of All Time.* 2005. Wood. 76″ × 69″ × 48″.
Private Collection.

CREATORS

Martin Puryear: Constructing Possibilities

Why become a sculptor? Martin Puryear (b. 1941) said, "The difference is so great when you go into the third dimension.... It's not simply a two-dimensional thing expanded. It's like an infinitely multiple view, an infinitely multiplied sense of possibilities, spatial possibilities. That's what interests me."[2]

The son of a self-taught woodworker, Puryear grew up attending segregated schools in Washington, D.C. He recalled an early electrifying experience that turned his mind toward art: "I was lucky enough as a really little kid to see a guy painting a portrait on my block, a black guy painting in oils a portrait of somebody right out on the street. And I was just transfixed to see in it an absolute likeness. I remember it was like grisaille [gray], it was black and white, it was like monochromatic.... I couldn't have been more than 6 years old, but I just couldn't believe it, it just . . . and it was a black guy, painting another black person, with his easel and paints and everything and a palette, right in front of the apartment. And it just blew something open in me."[3]

Puryear studied art at the Catholic University of America, before serving in the Peace Corps for two years in Sierra Leone. Here he came to admire the woodworkers he met for their resourcefulness and skill as they handcrafted objects for daily use. It seemed to him that many of the crafted objects that he saw in Africa seemed like works of art, although their makers regarded them only as

tools. Puryear then attended the Swedish Royal Academy of Art in Stockholm, where he studied printmaking. He also apprenticed himself in the private studio of a master woodworker.

Respect for craft has characterized Puryear's art ever since. We see this in the wood construction *Hominid* (**fig. 12.18**). A hominid is a pre-human primate, halfway between chimp and person. The work is an irregular polygonal block on wooden rollers that stands more than 6 feet tall. We may well imagine hominids pushing this piece along on its rollers, for reasons

that remain mysterious. Puryear finished the block using all the cabinet maker's traditional skills of sawing, joining, and finishing, but these only add to its enigmatic quality. In titling a work, Puryear tries to "juxtapose things in order to open up various possible meanings to the imagination."[4] In *Hominid*, as in many of his other works, his creation shows obvious craftsmanship, but its meaning is only suggested to the viewer.

Puryear prefers to leave any symbolism for the viewer to determine. His work does not generally allow easy correspondence between imagery and meaning. Rather,

he creates his work to only suggest shapes, which viewers will then complete in their minds. Some of his pieces may suggest various possible meanings through their shapes, but the artist regards such ambiguity as added interest. His thought process as he creates involves managing and distilling those possible meanings.

Puryear's sculptures create an absorbing mix of possibilities in the mind. The time that it takes for viewers to sense, and then weigh possible meanings is the key moment for appreciating his work. He says, "I think my work speaks to anybody who has the capacity to slow down."[5]

12.18 Martin Puryear. *Hominid*. 2007–11. Eastern white pine. 73″ x 77½″ x 57″. Currently located at Martin Puryear's studio.
Photograph: Christian Erroi. © Martin Puryear. Courtesy of Matthew Marks Gallery.

Kinetic Sculpture

Alexander Calder was among the first to explore the possibilities of **kinetic sculpture**, or sculpture that moves. Sculptors' traditional focus on mass is replaced in Calder's work by a focus on shape, space, and movement. Works such as his huge *Untitled* (see fig. 3.33) at the National Gallery of Art in Washington, D.C., are often called **mobiles** because the suspended parts move in response to small air currents.

If Calder's mobiles are massive and exuberant, far more delicate are the mobiles of Jesús Rafael Soto, such as *Escritura Hurtado* (**fig. 12.19**). Against a background of painted, thin vertical stripes, suspended curves of wire slowly sway in whatever air currents are present. These wire pieces resemble the strokes of handwriting; hence the title. Their motion makes the background seem to vibrate.

Some kinetic works move under human-made power rather than breezes. Jean Tinguely used electricity to power his large work *Méta-Harmonie II* (**fig. 12.20**). Viewers activate the work with the foot pedal on the floor; this starts the many rotors whirring slowly. They in turn hit gongs and

12.19 Jesús Rafael Soto. *Escritura Hurtado* (*Hurtado Writing*). 1975. Paint, wire, nylon cord, and wood. 40″ × 68″ × 18″.

Reprinted with permission from the General Secretariat of the OAS AMA. Art Museum of the Americas Collection. © 2018 Artists Rights Society (ARS), New York/ADAGP, Paris.

drums, rub against abrasive surfaces, and even bang on the piano to create a cacophony of sound. Most kinetic works need to be experienced in motion; this one should be heard as well. Several viewers who have seen this work in action have uploaded videos of it to sharing sites.

12.20 Jean Tinguely. *Méta-Harmonie II*. 1979. Mobile scrap-iron sculpture with musical instruments and other objects. Three parts; iron, sheet metal, brass, plastic, rubber, wood, leather, glass, electric motor. 149½″ x 271½″ x 63″.

Emanuel Hoffmann Foundation. Gift of Paul Sacher 1980, on permanent loan to the Öffentliche Kunstsammlung Basel. Photograph: Bisig & Bayer, Basel. © 2018 Artists Rights Society (ARS), New York/ADAGP, Paris.

Mixed Media

Today's artists frequently use a variety of media in a single work. Such works may be labeled with a long list of materials, or they may be identified only as **mixed media**. If a mixed media work includes only found objects, the work may also be called an assemblage. A mixed media work may include two- or three-dimensional elements, or a mixture. Often, the choice of media expresses some cultural or symbolic meaning.

The contemporary Chinese-born artist Cai Guo-Qiang created a huge and symbolic mixed media piece in 2004 with *Inopportune: Stage One* (**fig. 12.21**), now in the Seattle Art Museum. The work consists of nine automobiles perforated by light tubes. The cars are arrayed as if we are seeing momentary glimpses of one car flipping through the air as it explodes. Cai intended this work to refer both to contemporary action movies (where cars often explode and fly through the air) and to car bombings by terrorists. The work challenges us to consider if this is a thrilling scene, as in a movie, or a horrendous one, as in real life.

When Lara Schnitger drapes and stretches fabric over wooden armatures, she creates both a sculpture and a

12.21 Cai Guo-Qiang. *Inopportune: Stage One*. 2004. Nine cars and sequenced multichannel light tubes. Each car: 16′ x 6′.

12.22 Lara Schnitger. *Grim Boy*. 2005. Wood, fabric, and mixed media. 71″ × 59″ × 20″.
Anton Kern Gallery, New York.

12.23 Nick Cave. *Sculpture*. 2013. Mixed media, including ceramic birds, metal flowers, ceramic Doberman, vintage settee, and light fixture. 88″ × 72″ × 44″.
Photograph by James Prinz Photography. Courtesy of the artist and Jack Shainman Gallery, New York.

hollow interior space. The work of this Los Angeles-based artist straddles the boundary between sculpture and fashion design, just as the figures she creates hover nervously between human and some other living thing. In *Grim Boy* (**fig. 12.22**), for example, she used various dark-colored fabrics together with beads and fur to suggest a mannequin from hell. This tense, lurking figure seems to exude the nervous energy of an adolescent combined with the quick eye of a bird. But it stands almost 6 feet tall, like a gangling teenager, and the work's title may remind us of a brooding, trenchcoat-clad youth. There is an additional feminist message to most of Schnitger's work as well, because she is doing a sort of "dressmaking," a traditional women's artform. Rather than creating beautiful adornments, though, she fashions curious quasi-human beings.

Nick Cave frequently creates three-dimensional works using an extremely wide variety of media. His 2013 work titled simply *Sculpture* (**fig. 12.23**) includes an antique couch, a ceramic dog, metal flowers, and a light fixture, among other things. This work has a strong element of fantasy, as if the open-eyed dog is dreaming of a lush garden. The artist, who is not related to the Australian rock musician of the same name, does a lot of shopping at thrift stores and home-furnishing outlets. He may keep an object for years until, as he put it, "it finds its way into my work." He said that he wants to counteract a natural tendency humans have "to want to categorize things," so he creates sculptures in which recognizable things come into unfamiliar juxtapositions. He said of his work, "There's a sort of humanness to it, but yet it's not of this world."[6]

Installation and Site-Specific Art

Many artists now use the three-dimensional medium of **installation** to make their visual statements. In an installation, the artist treats an entire space as an artwork and transforms it.

Rafael Lozano-Hemmer used all of the walls in a gallery for his interactive installation *Airborne* (**fig. 12.24**). He projected regularly changing texts from news stories onto the walls. As viewers passed before them, they cast shadows that blocked the texts; standing farther away from the wall yielded a larger shadow. Many viewers danced or walked or pantomimed, making their moving shadows part of the news story. If viewers remained stationary, heat rising from their bodies took on a smoky appearance in the shadow, which further distorted and erased the news items on the walls behind. The installation afforded viewers a new and entertaining way to interact with the news of the day.

Airborne has been installed in several locations as a temporary exhibition, but some installations are intended only for particular locations. Such works are called **site-specific**.

The best-known work of site-specific art in the United States became famous because of a lawsuit that tested the limits of the artist's power. In 1981, the government installed Richard Serra's large work *Tilted Arc* (**fig. 12.25**) in the plaza adjoining a federal office building in New York City; it was a tilting, curving blade of steel 12 feet high. Soon the office workers began to complain about it: it blocked the view; it forced them to walk a detour around it; it became a

12.24 Rafael Lozano-Hemmer. *Airborne*. 2013. Installation.
As installed in the Museo de Arte Contemporáneo, Mexico City, 2015. Photograph: Oliver Santana.

12.26 Olafur Eliasson. *Waterfall.* 2016. Crane, water, stainless steel, pump system, hose, ballast.
Palace of Versailles.

homeless shelter; it collected graffiti. When the government announced plans to relocate the work, the artist filed a lawsuit, claiming that *Tilted Arc* was meant for that spot, and to relocate it would be to destroy it. The artist lost his case, but the matter did not turn on any legal requirement of site-specificity; rather, the court held that the government, as owner of the work, could dispose of it. After years of court cases, *Tilted Arc* was removed in 1989.

In 2016, Olafur Eliasson created a stunning site-specific work for the gardens of Versailles outside Paris. *Waterfall* (**fig. 12.26**) is a huge cascade that from some angles appears to emerge out of nowhere. This work is an extreme version of the waterfalls and fountains that have graced that formerly royal property since the sixteenth century. A metal scaffold and accompanying pumps carry the water from the lake to a height that the artist refused to divulge. He felt that keeping the height a secret helps to preserve the dramatic impact.

When an artist creates a work in three dimensions, the result is called sculpture. A sculptor may create an object using diverse materials and processes, or even alter an entire space, converting it into an artwork.

KEY TERMS

additive sculpture – sculptural form produced by adding, combining, or building up material from a core or (in some cases) an armature

armature – a rigid framework serving as a supporting inner core for clay or other soft sculpting material

assemblage – sculpture made by assembling found or cast-off objects

bas relief (also called **low relief**) – sculpture in relief in which the subjects emerge only slightly from the surface; no undercutting is present

boss – a circular, often dome-shaped, decoration that protrudes from a flat surface

carving – a subtractive process in which a sculpture is formed by removing material from a block or mass of wood, stone, or other material, with the use of sharpened tools

casting – a process that involves pouring liquid material such as molten metal, clay, wax, or plaster into a mold; when the liquid hardens, the mold is removed, and a form in the shape of the mold is left

construction – creating a work of sculpture by putting together pieces that are already formed by the artist

freestanding – any piece or type of sculpture that is meant to be seen from all sides

high relief – sculpture in relief in which more than half of a significant portion of the subject emerges from the background; high-relief sculpture thus requires undercutting, in contrast to low relief

installation – an art medium in which the artist arranges objects or artworks in a room, thinking of the entire space as the medium to be manipulated

kinetic sculpture – sculpture that incorporates actual movement as part of the design

lost wax – a casting method: First a model is made from wax and encased in clay or casting plaster; when the clay is fired to make a mold, the wax melts away, leaving a void that can be filled with molten metal or other self-hardening liquid to produce a cast

low relief (also called **bas relief**) – sculpture in relief in which the subjects emerge only slightly from the surface; no undercutting is present

mixed media – works of art made with more than one medium

mobile – a type of sculpture in which parts move, usually suspended parts activated by air currents

modeling – working pliable material such as clay or wax into three-dimensional forms

mold – a cavity usually created out of plaster, clay, or plastic for use in casting

relief – sculpture in which three-dimensional forms project from the flat background of which they are a part

site-specific – any work made for a certain place, which cannot be separated or exhibited apart from its intended environment

substitution – the process of making a work of art by casting, as opposed to additive or subtractive processes

subtractive sculpture – sculpture made by removing material from a larger block or form

13

CRAFT MEDIA IN USEFUL OBJECTS

LEARNING OBJECTIVES

13.1 Identify the three general categories of clay and describe their characteristics.

13.2 Discuss some of the techniques used by artists working with glass.

13.3 Describe metalworking techniques used in the creation of functional objects.

13.4 Identify crafting techniques associated with wood.

13.5 Describe three traditional methods used in textile works.

William Morris's *Windrush* (**fig. 13.1**) is an elegant and well-crafted woodblock print that fulfills a commonplace function with artistry. A design in several colors that is repeatable, it can serve as either a textile or a wallpaper pattern. Covering your table or your bedroom wall with *Windrush* can enrich your surroundings, so that it may seem as if you are living with an artwork.

In 1861 in England, Morris created an interior design company with the goal of helping people improve their lives by making them more artistic. In several books and hundreds of public lectures, he urged the creation of art for everyday use, affordable to buy and enjoyable to live with. "I do not want art for a few, any more than education for a few, or freedom for a few," he said. Artists, he believed, should devote their skills to creating useful objects for everyone. "Have nothing in your house that you do not know to be useful or believe to be beautiful," was the maxim he tried to live by. Thus in his workshop he made dishes, wallpaper, furniture, and textiles, all by hand. His workshop was so influential in the late nineteenth and early twentieth centuries that many craft media enjoyed a rebirth in Europe and the United States.

Many other artists before and since have found stimulation in making beautiful and useful objects. In the Western world, we have traditionally termed such objects "craft work," and ranked them below art in status. But in fact, most of the world's cultures have always regarded an excellent piece of pottery as highly as a painting, and a textile as equal in merit to a piece of sculpture.

In this chapter we will consider several art media generally employed in the creation of practical objects: clay, glass, metal, wood, and textiles. The subject is nearly as expansive as the world itself, but we will look at a few traditional and contemporary examples of works created from each of these media. In a previous era, we might have regarded the works illustrated here as crafts, but in this text they are all artforms.

Clay

Clay comes from soil with a heavily volcanic makeup, mixed with water. Since humans began to live in settled communities, clay has been a valuable art material. It is extremely flexible in the artist's hands, yet it hardens into a permanent shape when exposed to heat.

The art and science of making objects from clay is called **ceramics**. Any person who works with clay is a **ceramist**; a ceramist who specializes in making dishes is a **potter**. A wide range of objects, including tableware, dishes, sculpture, bricks, and many kinds of tile, are made from clay. Most of the basic ceramic techniques were discovered thousands of years ago. All clays are flexible until baked in a dedicated high-temperature oven called a **kiln**, a process known as **firing**.

13.1 William Morris. *Windrush*. 1892. Textile pattern, repeatable. Woodblock print on paper.
Victoria and Albert Museum, London. V&A Images, London/Art Resource, NY.

Clays are generally categorized in one of three broad types. **Earthenware** is typically fired at a relatively low temperature (approximately 800°C to 1,100°C) and is porous after firing. It may vary in color from red to brown to tan. Earthenware is the most common of the three types, and a great many of the world's pots have been made from it. **Stoneware** is heavier, is fired at a higher temperature (1,200°C to 1,300°C), and is not porous. It is usually grayish or brown. Combining strength with easy workability, stoneware is the preferred medium of most of today's ceramists and potters. **Porcelain** is the rarest and most expensive of the three types. Made from deposits of decomposed granite, it becomes white and nonporous after firing at a typically high temperature (1,300°C to 1,400°C). It is translucent and rings when struck, both signs of its unique

quality. Porcelain was first perfected in China, and even today in Britain and America the finest white dishes are called "china," no matter where they are made.

With any type of clay, the ceramic process is relatively simple. Ceramists work with soft, damp clay using hand-building methods such as modeling, or by **throwing**—that is, by shaping clay on a rapidly revolving wheel. Invented in Mesopotamia about 6,000 years ago, the potter's wheel allows potters to produce circular forms with great speed and uniformity. In the hands of a skilled worker, the process looks effortless, even magical, but it takes time and practice to perfect the technique. After shaping, a piece is air-dried before firing in a kiln.

Two kinds of liquid are commonly used to decorate ceramics, though rarely on the same piece. A **slip** is a mixture of clay and water about the consistency of cream, sometimes colored with earthen powders. With this relatively simple technique, only a limited range of colors is possible, but many ancient cultures made a specialty of this type of pottery decoration.

A **glaze** is a liquid paint with a silica base, specially formulated for clay. During firing, the glaze vitrifies (turns to a glasslike substance) and fuses with the clay body, creating a nonporous surface. Glazes can be colored or clear, translucent or opaque, glossy or dull, depending on their chemical composition. Firing changes the color of most glazes so radically that the liquid that the ceramist applies to the vessel comes out of the kiln an entirely different color.

Ancient Greece was a center of pottery production that supplied the entire Mediterranean world. Greek ceramics were generally made from terra cotta, a type of earthenware that can be fired at a low temperature. Making the vessels and decorating them were specialized tasks generally done by different people. The ceramist who shaped *Oil Jar with Man Holding a Lyre* (**fig. 13.2**) threw it on a wheel and added the base later; the thin neck helped to preserve the expensive oil that it held. The Eurcharides Painter, who decorated the jar, covered the body of the vessel with black slip, while the reddish figure, unpainted, shows the color of the underlying clay. The painter added a few strokes of black and rust to delineate the features.

13.2 Eucharides Painter. *Oil Jar with Man Holding a Lyre.* Greek Attic Period. c.500–470 BCE. Height 13⅚″.
J. Paul Getty Museum, 73.AE.23.

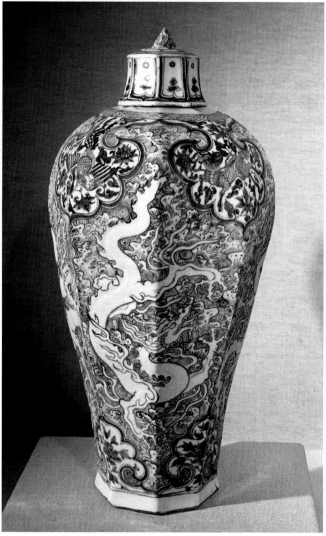

13.3 Octagonal P'ing Vase. China. Yuan Dynasty. 1179–1368. Blue and white porcelain.
People's Republic of China/Bridgeman Images.

13.4 Betty Woodman. *Divided Vases: Cubist.* 2004. Glazed earthenware, epoxy resin, lacquer, and paint. 34½″ × 39″ × 7″.
Salon 94, New York.

The Octagonal P'ing Vase from China (**fig. 13.3**) was made with fine white porcelain; it was likely used as a flower vase. This type of blue decoration on the white body was known nearly worldwide in the seventeenth and eighteenth centuries because Chinese ceramists were the first to perfect this technique. The vessels were blue because in the first few hundred years after the discovery of porcelain, blue was the only color of glaze that could withstand the high firing temperatures. The octagonal shape reveals that this vase was not thrown on a wheel but rather hand-built. The profile of this piece with its narrower base has a dignified look, as a person might if they inhaled deeply and stood at attention.

Ceramic processes evolved very slowly until the mid-twentieth century, when new formulations and even synthetic clays became available. Other changes have included more accurate methods of firing and less toxic techniques and equipment.

Betty Woodman's *Divided Vases: Cubist* (**fig. 13.4**) is a contemporary work that has an exuberant, free-form look that preserves the expressiveness of spontaneous glaze application. The handles are actually flat perforated panels that still show traces of the working process. The earthenware that she used is conducive to natural shapes like the bamboo segments that the vase bodies suggest. She threw each in three pieces on the wheel, and then joined them

13.5 Grayson Perry. *Quotes from the Internet*. 2005. Glazed ceramic. 25⅝″ × 17¾″ .

© Grayson Perry. Courtesy of the artist and Victoria Miro, London.

before adding the handles. The *Divided Vases* have a fresh look, as if they just came out of the firing kiln.

Grayson Perry shows a more ironic sensibility in his vessel (**fig. 13.5**). The shape of this piece is related to traditional jugs of whiskey, although this one lacks a handle. Like traditional crafters of such jugs, the artist used stoneware, throwing the piece on a wheel. Perry's painting style looks spontaneous, but he painted the glaze decorations slowly and painstakingly. Some of the imagery on this jug comes from folk art, and Perry said that he got all the text excerpts for this work from the Internet in web searches. His casual approach to creation parallels his down-to-earth views about art. He said, "People look at art and they find it very hard to just enjoy it; they have to kind of 'interpret' it or 'understand' it. They don't just ask themselves, 'Do I think it's beautiful?' I think there should be more of *that*."[1]

Glass

Glass has been used for about 3,000 years as a material for practical containers of all shapes and sizes. Stained glass has been a favorite in churches and cathedrals since the Middle Ages. Elaborate blown-glass pieces have been made in Venice since the fifteenth century. Glass is also a fine medium for decorative inlays in a variety of objects, including jewelry.

Chemically, glass is closely related to ceramic glaze. As a medium, however, it offers a wide range of unique possibilities. Hot or molten glass is a sensitive, amorphous material that is shaped by blowing, casting, or pressing into molds. As it cools, glass solidifies from its molten state without crystallizing. After it is blown or cast, glass may be cut, etched, fused, laminated, painted, polished, sandblasted, or slumped (softened for a controlled sag). The fluid nature of glass produces qualities of mass flowing into line, as well as translucent volumes of airy thinness.

The character of any material determines the character of the expression; this statement is particularly true of glass. Molten glass requires considerable speed and skill in handling as it cools.

Stained glass reached a peak of technical development in Europe in religious buildings of the Middle Ages (see fig. 16.26d), and the technique of producing stained glass is little changed since then. An artist creates a full-sized design of the subject (a cartoon), and this is transferred to pieces of colored glass of the appropriate sizes, which have been created in molds. Glass may be colored either during manufacture by adding material to the silica mix, or afterward by painting with glazes and firing. The colored pieces are embedded between thin strips of lead called cames and the whole is framed in the window opening. A practical need for shelter and light becomes a work of art.

As part of the crafts revival led by William Morris (see fig. 13.1), stained glass enjoyed a resurgence in Europe and the United States in the late nineteenth and early twentieth centuries. One of the leading artists in this medium was Mary Lowndes, who made over 100 windows, mostly in England and Wales, for churches, homes, and community buildings. She created the *Resurrection Window* (**fig. 13.6**) in 1901 for a church where her father had served as a priest. Lowndes painted liberally on the panes, evoking textures of garments and facial shadings. The composition is adventurous, as the deep reds and blues on the right are not balanced with similar shades on the left.

Christ dominates the central window; among the adorers of his resurrected body, women outnumber men, reflecting the fact that women were the first to visit and announce his empty tomb. This emphasis also likely reflects the artist's feminism, because she was active in the movement for women's suffrage, designing banners that women carried on the movement's marches. She also started a professional workshop for stained glass in London, admitting both men and women equally, an unusual stance for that time.

When Dale Chihuly first saw Native American baskets in a museum in the late 1970s, they gave him an idea for glass vessels. He noticed that the older baskets, made of woven fibers, tended to sag somewhat and were no longer perfectly round. Soon after, he began a long series of glass works in which he attempted to capture and reinterpret some of those shapes (**fig. 13.7**). Each element in the *Citron Basket Set* began with the artist blowing a round piece of molten glass out to the desired size, then spinning it so that it opened at one end and slumped slightly. Imperfections introduced during the spinning yielded the black lines. Gradually slowing the spinning as the molten glass cooled allowed final control of the shape.

13.6 Mary Lowndes. *Resurrection Window.* 1901. St. Mary's Church, Sturminster Newton, UK.
craft images/Alamy Stock Photo.

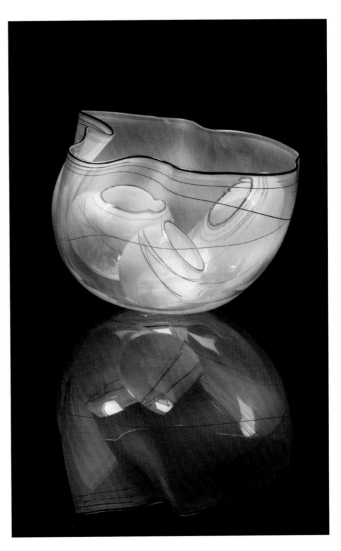

13.7 Dale Chihuly. *Citron Basket Set with Ebony Lip Wraps.* 2015. Blown glass. 11″ × 16″ × 16″.
Courtesy of the artist.

13.8 Mona Hatoum. *Nature morte aux grenades* (*Still Life with Hand Grenades*). 2006–7. Crystal, mild steel and rubber. 38⅜″ × 81⅞″ × 27½″.
Photograph: Marc Domage. Courtesy of Alexander and Bonin, New York.

Contemporary artist Mona Hatoum used both slumping and molding techniques in her provocative work *Nature morte aux grenades* (*Still Life with Hand Grenades*; **fig. 13.8**). She researched the design of various sorts of small explosive device that the world's armies use, and re-created them in colorful pieces of solid glass. She placed these precious-looking objects on a gurney as if they were specimens of some kind, which they are: specimens of humanity's tendency to violence. She used the beauty of glass to represent "useful" objects of a lethal sort.

Metal

Metal's primary characteristics include both strength and formability. The various types of metal most often used for crafts and sculpture can be hammered, cut, inlayed, drawn out, welded, joined with rivets, or cast. Early metalsmiths created coins, tools, vessels, armor, and weapons.

In Muslim regions of the Middle East in the thirteenth and fourteenth centuries, artists practiced shaping and **inlaying** with unparalleled sophistication. The d'Arenberg Basin (**fig. 13.9**), named after a French collector who owned it for many years, was made for the last ruler of the Ayyubid dynasty in Syria in the mid-thirteenth century. The body of the basin was first cast in brass; its extremely intricate

design included lowered areas into which precisely cut pieces of silver were placed. Although most of the silver pieces are only a fraction of an inch in size, they enliven a carefully patterned design that occupies several finely proportioned horizontal bands. The lowest band is a decorative pattern based on repeated plant shapes. Above is a row of real and imaginary animals that decorates a relatively narrow band. The next band depicts a scene of princely pleasure, as well-attired people play polo. The uppermost band contains more plant shapes between the uprights of highly stylized Arabic script that expresses good wishes to the owner of the piece. A central panel in this upper row depicts a scene from the life of Christ, who is regarded as an important teacher in Islam.

Besides creating intricate inlays, artists can also mold or hammer metal into elegant and useful shapes. Margaret De Patta, for example, handcrafted a flatware set (**fig. 13.10**) from copper, silver, and stainless steel in 1936. She had learned metalsmithing in 1929 in order to design her own wedding ring, because she was bored with the options available in stores and markets. De Patta believed that our daily objects should keep pace with the latest innovations in modern art, which at that time included abstract painting. So her flatware dispenses with decoration and curving surface treatments in favor of simple shapes that do not sacrifice utility. The copper handles for each piece end in scrollwork over a silver post, which provides a balanced feel in the hand. For the knife, she used a stainless-steel end for easier cutting, and she looped the copper strip over the post and fastened it back to the blade to give the piece greater stability under pressure.

13.9 The d'Arenberg Basin. Probably Damascus, Syria. 1247–49. Brass inlaid with silver. 8⅞″ × 19⅝″.
Freer Gallery of Art and Arthur M.Sackler Gallery, Smithsonian Institution, Washington D.C. Purchase – Charles Lang Freer Endowment, F1955.10.

Wood

The living spirit of wood is given a second life in handmade objects. Growth characteristics of individual trees remain visible in the grain of wood long after trees are cut, giving wood a vitality not found in other materials. Its abundance, versatility, and warm tactile qualities have made wood a favored material for common use as well as for art pieces. Like many natural products, wood can be harvested in a sustainable manner or a wasteful one. Many woodworkers today have moved toward sustainability by using wood that is already down, or harvested from certified forests.

Because various species of tree produce woods of many colors and textures, some woodworkers create works of **marquetry** that take advantage of this property. Marquetry resembles inlay in that multiple small pieces are laid down in a design, but with marquetry there is no bounding wall between the pieces of wood. To create a work, the artist first draws a cartoon, lays the paper on a prepared wood panel and pricks holes in it. The paper is then dusted, so that the particles show the design when the paper is removed. The artist then cuts wood pieces to fit the design and glues them all into place.

Marquetry was known to the ancient Egyptians, but it flourished especially in Northern Europe in the eighteenth century. A European immigrant who brought the artform to the United States in the nineteenth century was Peter Glass. His octagonal folding table (**fig. 13.11**) is a highly ornate work that includes various panels of twining vegetation, birds, plants in vases, and military heroes (George Washington is at the lower left). Among the 30,000 pieces of

13.11 Peter Glass. Marquetry Table. 1868. Wood. Height 41″.

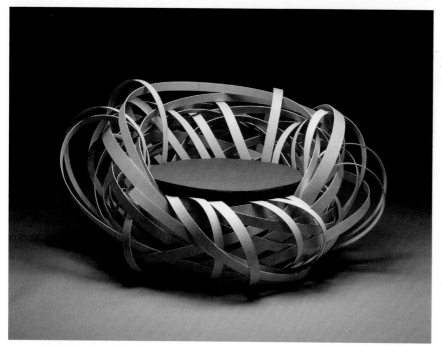

13.12 Nina Bruun. *Nest Chair*. 2010. Birchwood. Height 36″.
Courtesy of the artist.

wood that he used are two small oval panels at the bottom that carry his signature.

Most wood is flexible when wet, and retains its shape when dry. Nina Bruun used long, thin strips of flexed birch to craft the *Nest Chair* (**fig. 13.12**). Its central cushion has soft feather padding to recall the place where birds lay their eggs. This relatively plain chocolate-colored pad is supported by a custom-made low stool with four legs; the surrounding swirl of birch strips hides this. The strips are of different thicknesses, allowing varying degrees of flex. Once Bruun got the idea for this chair from looking at a bird's nest, she arrived at this design primarily by trial and error. "I had to do the chair over and over again before it was perfect," she said.[2]

Textiles

Textile arts include such processes as weaving, stitching, knitting, and looping. These processes use natural and synthetic fibers in both traditional and innovative ways. Artists working with fibers (like artists working in any medium) draw on the heritage of traditional practices and also explore new avenues of expression (one such artist is Faith Ringgold, as we see in *Faith Ringgold: Stitching History* on p. 218). Here we will consider weaving, embroidery, and quilt making.

Weaving

Weaving is an ancient artform. The oldest piece of woven fabric yet found was created in about 7000 BCE in south-

central Turkey. All weaving is based on the interlacing of fibers. Weavers generally begin with long fibers in place, called the **warp** fibers, which determine the length of the piece they will create. Often the warp fibers are installed on a **loom**, a device that holds them in place and may pull them apart for weaving. Mechanical looms use foot pedals, which pull strings to lift and separate the warps. **Weft** fibers (related to the word *weave*) cross the warps at right angles.

Weavers create patterns by changing the number and placements of interwoven weft threads, and they can choose from a variety of looms and techniques. Even simple hand looms can produce very sophisticated, complex weaves. Creating a sophisticated design often requires that the weaver visualize the entire composition before beginning work; this is usually accomplished by installing a cartoon nearby for reference. A large tapestry loom, capable of weaving hundreds of colors into intricate forms, may require several days of preparation before work begins. For several centuries in Europe, aristocrats valued **tapestries** as much as paintings for decorating and also insulating their stately homes and palaces.

Contemporary artists use looms in new ways. Egyptian artist Lara Baladi creates large-scale tapestries that combine hundreds of pictures. *Sandouk el Dounia* (*The World in a Box*) (**fig. 13.13**), for example, was titled after a type of ambulatory street theater practiced in Egypt in the early twentieth century. To form the work, she first created a huge collage of about 900 photographs of costumed and staged scenes that she shot in Cairo, as well as photographs drawn from her personal archive, taken in many parts of the world. She then photographed the collage and used this high-resolution reproduction to program a digitally operated loom at Flanders Tapestries in Belgium. The pixels of the photograph take on new life as vividly dyed strands of fabric. She attempts in this multilayered piece, she says, "to blur the boundary between the mundane and the sacred, the private and the public, the pharaonic and the contemporary."[3] Like most tapestries, this work also fulfills a need for insulation in a highly decorative way.

13.13 Lara Baladi. *Sandouk el Dounia (The World in a Box)*. 2007. 10′4″ × 8′2¹⁄₁₀″. Tapestry made with a digitally operated loom from the original photo-collage of 900 C41 3¹⁵⁄₁₆″ × 5²⁹⁄₃₂″ prints.

Cini Foundation, Venice, 2011.

a. Installation view at the exhibition *Penelope's Labour: Weaving Words and Images*.

b. Detail.

13.14 The Ardabil Carpet. Tabriz. 1540. Wool pile on silk warps and wefts. 34´ × 17´6″.
Victoria and Albert Museum, London. V&A Images, London/Art Resource, NY.

Most carpets are traditionally made by weaving, and some of the world's most spectacular carpets came from Islamic Persia during the Safavid dynasty in the sixteenth century. These rugs were made off-loom by weavers employed in royal workshops who knotted carefully dyed wool over the warps and among the wefts as the work progressed. The Ardabil Carpet (**fig. 13.14**), long recognized as one of the greatest Persian carpets, contains about 300 such knots, over fine silk threads, per square inch. Thus this carpet required approximately 25 million knots!

The design of the carpet is centered on a sunburst surrounded by 16 oval shapes. Two mosque lamps of unequal size share space with an intricate pattern of flowers. At the corners of the main field, quarters of the central design are repeated. A small panel near the bottom gives the date and the name of an artist, who must have been the designer. Another inscription is a couplet by Hafiz, the best-known lyrical poet in Iran: "I have no refuge in this world other than thy threshold. My head has no resting-place other than this doorway." The carpet originally covered the floor of a prayer chapel.

Embroidery and Quilt Making

In **embroidery**, artists stitch decorative colored threads into and over a base of woven fabric. Embroidery may be as ancient as weaving itself, but the oldest surviving embroideries date from the fourth century BCE. Some of the most sophisticated early embroideries come from the coastal region of Peru, especially the Paracas peninsula, where burials unearthed in the 1930s revealed well-preserved and impressive textiles. Artists created the cape pictured here (**fig. 13.15**) by embroidering vicuña and alpaca wool over a cotton cloth. We know frustratingly little about the Paracas culture, but hybrid human-animal forms, such as the ones

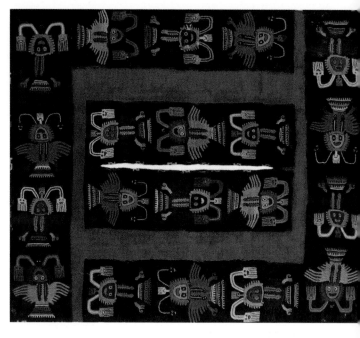

13.15 Funerary Cape. Paracas Culture, Peru. c.200 CE.
Museo Nacional de Antropologia y Arqueologia, Lima, Peru. Photograph: Jorge Provenza. © 2018. DeAgostini Picture Library/Scala, Florence.

seen here, populate many of its textiles. Art historians generally describe these particular figures as bird impersonators. The density of the stitching and the variety of design motifs are standout characteristics.

In some African-American communities, women have carried on a tradition of quilt making for generations. One of the most active groups has been meeting in Gees Bend, Alabama, for more than 100 years, where the quilters gather to share fabric, discuss neighborhood news, and encourage creativity. Jessie Pettway made *Bars and String-Piece Columns* (**fig. 13.16**) from leftover pieces of cloth. This quilt, like many produced at Gees Bend, resembles some kinds of African textiles (see Chapter 19). Many Gees Bend quilters create their work with only a minimum of advance planning, and this lends their work a look of spontaneity and exuberance. The coincidental resemblance to modern art also attracts the attention of collectors.

This has been a brief overview of a vast subject, but we have had some discussion of the techniques and possibilities that clay, glass, metal, wood, and textile bring to the embellishment of objects for use or for mere admiration. Most of the world's cultures do not distinguish between craft and art, and Western culture is gradually moving toward that view.

13.16 Jessie Pettway. *Bars and String-Piece Columns*. 1950s. Cotton quilt. 95″ × 76″.

Tinwood Alliance Collection. San Francisco MoMA. Photograph: Steve Pitking. © 2018 Jessie T. Pettway/Artists Rights Society (ARS), New York.

KEY TERMS

ceramics – clay hardened into a relatively permanent material by firing, and the artform that includes this procedure

ceramist – a practitioner of the art of ceramics

earthenware – a type of clay used for ceramics; it fires at 1,100–1,150°C and is porous after firing

embroidery – a technique in which decorative colored threads are stitched into and over a base of woven fabric

firing – baking clay in a special high-temperature oven to solidify it; secondary firings may also be done to fix finishing coats on fired pieces

glaze – a silica-based paint for clay that fuses with the clay body on firing; can be almost any color, or translucent

inlay – a type of decoration used in metalwork and some woodwork in which small pieces are fitted into carved recesses

kiln – a high-temperature oven in which pottery or ceramic ware is fired

loom – a device for producing cloth or fiber art by interweaving fibers at right angles

marquetry – a technique in which multiple small pieces of wood in different colors and textures are laid down in a design with no bounding wall between them

porcelain – a type of white or grayish clay for ceramics; it fires at 1,350–1,500°C, and after firing it is translucent and rings when struck

potter – a ceramist who specializes in making dishes

slip – clay that is thinned to the consistency of cream and used as paint on earthenware or stoneware ceramics

stoneware – a type of clay used for ceramics; it fires at 1,200–1,300°C and is nonporous when fired

tapestry – a loom weaving method in which colored weft fibers of irregular length are pulled through stable warps to create patterns or pictures

throwing – the process of forming clay objects on a potter's wheel

warp – in weaving, the threads that run length-wise in a fabric, crossed at right angles by the weft

weft – in weaving, the horizontal threads interlaced through the warp

Faith Ringgold: Stitching History

13.17 Faith Ringgold, with detail of *The Purple Quilt*. 1986.
Photograph: C'Love.

Most quilt makers have worked to create dazzling designs from fabric, but Faith Ringgold (b. 1930) innovated by using her own life and heritage to make quilts that tell stories. Brought up in Harlem in the 1930s, in 1972 she left a teaching position and began to devote herself full time to art. She also began a ten-year collaboration with her mother in the creation of works on cloth. Quilt making had been a family tradition as far back as her great-great-grandmother, who had made them as a slave in Florida. The mother–daughter team collaborated on a new type of textile art that included images and stories on the sewn fragments.

Ringgold said of quilt making: "It is an art form that slave women used, to embellish and beautify useful objects such as quilts. Because the African-American experience with quiltmaking was very much like the African who made the tools roughly, and then adorned them and made them skillfully, so that things were useful, but then they were beautified. So here's something: We're going to sew some cloth together to cover ourselves because we want to keep warm. And now we're going to beautify those pieces so that we sew them together and make them into quilts. So now it's an art piece, and it's useful. I really like that."[4]

A standout among the artist's story quilts is *Tar Beach* (**fig. 13.18**), which tells the story of the fictional Cassie, an 8-year-old character who is based on Ringgold's own childhood memories of growing up in New York City. She would go up to the asphalt roof of her apartment building ("Tar Beach") with her family on hot nights, because there was no air-conditioning in the home. Cassie describes Tar Beach as a magical place, with a 360-degree view of tall buildings and the George Washington Bridge in the distance. She dreams that she can fly, that she can do anything she imagines, as she lies on a blanket with her little brother. She dreams that she can give her father the union card that he has been denied because of his race. She dreams that she can let her mother sleep late, and eat ice cream every day for dessert. She even dreams that she can buy the building her father works in,

and that her mother will not cry when her father can't find work. The quilt depicts the two children on the blanket, and her parents playing cards with the neighbors next to a table set with snacks and drinks. We also see Cassie flying through the sky near the top center. *Tar Beach* was later made into a children's book, one of several that Ringgold has written.

Asked her view of the artist's function in society, Ringgold replied in a way that illuminates *Tar Beach*: "I think the artist's role is to, in some ways, document the times. Because we look at art through history. We can tell a lot about the time the artist lived by just looking at the pictures, or the sculpture that they did. And every group of people does this, every culture of people, every race of people does this. Those who have highly developed, fascinating cultures create artists who have the same, because they work together. So as a black woman, my role is to speak in my voice as to race and gender, about the times that I lived in. And I see that as a responsibility that I take on."[5]

13.18 Faith Ringgold. *Tar Beach*. (Part I from *The Women on a Bridge* series.) 1988. Acrylic on canvas, bordered with printed, painted, quilted, and pieced cloth. 74⅝″ × 68½″.

Guggenheim Museum, New York. Gift of Mr. and Mrs. Gus and Judith Lieber 1988. © 2018. The Solomon R. Guggenheim Foundation/Art Resource, NY/ Scala, Florence. © 2018 Faith Ringgold, member Artists Rights Society (ARS), New York.

ARCHITECTURE

LEARNING OBJECTIVES

14.1 Identify the characteristics of traditional architectural materials and methods.

14.2 Explain how modern materials such as concrete and steel have changed architecture.

14.3 Discuss how recent innovations in construction techniques and materials have led to the development of new architectural forms.

14.4 Recognize the impact of contemporary environmental concerns on architecture.

Among the world's oldest surviving structures are these dolmens in the Golan Heights (**fig. 14.1**), near the border between Syria and Israel. They were constructed from huge boulders, some set upright and another used as a roof to create a space large enough to serve as a tomb. These bulky structures resemble others in many parts of the world, including France, Jordan, India, and Korea. Although other dolmens have various functions, they all share a basic construction technique and a massive appearance.

For at least 5,000 years, people have built impressive structures, like these dolmens, that go beyond providing mere shelter. Architecture is the art and science of designing and constructing spaces not only for practical purposes but also for symbolic and aesthetic ones. It has great potential to express our values and to enhance many aspects of our daily lives, from the houses we live in to the places where we work, worship, or spend our leisure time.

No matter what sort of structure they are building, architects address and integrate three key issues: function (how a building is used); form (how it looks); and structure (how it stands up). The functions of buildings have changed little over many centuries; their form and structure have evolved almost constantly across cultures and time. When a building has a beautiful form or an innovative structure, it becomes important architecture.

In this chapter we will examine the art and craft of architecture, considering various engineering methods in turn from the most basic to today's high-tech creations. We will see that beyond meeting our need for shelter, architecture can make important expressive statements about architects and the cultures that they serve.

14.1 Dolmens. Golan Heights, Syria.
Photograph: akg-images/Erich Lessing.

Traditional Materials and Methods

Architecture is always in part an engineering project: How does a structure support its own weight and the loads placed on it? Buildings must be designed to withstand the forces of compression, or pushing (→ ←); tension, or stretching (← →); and bending, or flexing (( )); and combinations of these physical forces. Solving these problems will yield a stable structure.

There are only three ways of constructing almost any building: the load-bearing method of piling blocks or planks atop one another; the skeletal method, which involves erecting a framework and wrapping it in a skin of some kind; and the molding method, in which a liquid such as mud or concrete is poured into a mold and allowed to harden. Structural systems for buildings throughout the world are based on these, and they are as varied as the humans who use them.

The evolution of architectural methods and styles has been determined by the materials available and by the evolving needs and values of societies. In ancient times, when nomadic hunter-gatherers became farmers and village dwellers, housing evolved from caves, huts, and tents to more substantial structures.

Because early building designers (as well as those in nonindustrialized countries today) made structures only out of the materials at hand, regional styles developed that blended with their sites and climates. Modern transportation and the spread of advanced technologies now make it possible to build almost anything anywhere.

Traditional materials include wood, stone, earth, and brick. Each of these natural materials has its own strengths and weaknesses. For example, wood, which is light, can be used for roof beams. Stone, which is heavy, can be used for load-bearing walls but its weight limits its usefulness as a beam. Earth is abundant but lacks strength. Building with brick (pressed, baked earth) yields strong structures but is very labor-intensive. Much of the world's major architecture has been constructed of stone because of its permanence, availability, and beauty. In the past entire cities were slowly built by cutting and placing stone upon stone.

Dry Masonry

Probably the simplest building technique is to pile stones atop one another, as we saw with the dolmens opposite. The process has been used to make such rudimentary structures as markers, piles, and cairns throughout the world. When such piling is done with a consistent pattern, the result is called **masonry**. In dry masonry, where no mortar is used, the weight of the stones themselves holds the structure up. If the stones are cut or shaped before use, they are **dressed**.

Great Zimbabwe in East Africa (**fig. 14.2**) is an elliptical structure made of dressed local stone that gave its name to the country in which it is located. Probably built between 1350 and 1450 CE, it was used for about 300 years. Great Zimbabwe ("Great Stone House") is nearly round, with several conical structures inside whose original function is still unknown. Its stone walls are approximately 30 feet high and, for added stability, they were built up to 15 feet

14.2 Great Zimbabwe. Zimbabwe. Before 1450. Height of wall 30´.

a. Plan.

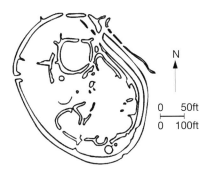

b. Interior.
Lynn Y/Shutterstock.

thick at the base, tapering slightly toward the top. Roofing was probably grass or thatch held together with sticks. The structure is the largest of a group of stone dwellings that formed a trading city of perhaps 20,000 people at its height. Although the outer walls of Great Zimbabwe have openings in selected locations for entry and exit, there are no windows; because these tend to weaken masonry walls, only structures that are considerably smaller can use them without external support.

Great Zimbabwe is the largest ancient stone structure in Africa south of the great pyramids of Egypt, which are also built of dry masonry (see fig. 15.16). Other notable examples of such buildings are Machu Picchu in Peru (see fig. 20.38) and the ancient pueblos in the southwestern United States, such as Mesa Verde.

Post and Beam

Much of the world's architecture has been built with **post-and-beam** construction, sometimes called **post-and-lintel** (**fig. 14.3**). Vertical posts or columns support horizontal beams and carry the weight of the entire structure to the ground.

The form of post-and-beam buildings is determined by the strengths and weaknesses of the materials used. Stone beam lengths must be short, and posts relatively thick to compensate for stone's weight and brittleness. Wood beams

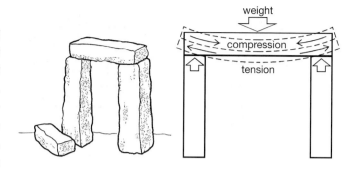

14.3 Post-and-Beam Construction.

may be longer, and posts thinner, because wood is lighter and more flexible.

Bundled reeds provided the model for the monumental post-and-beam Egyptian temples. A row of columns spanned, or connected, by beams is called a **colonnade**, as seen in the Colonnade and Court of Amenhotep III (**fig. 14.4**). Most ancient Egyptian temples were symmetrical, with aisles for processions that connected adjacent pavilions. Their massive appearance is partly a structural necessity for their height, and partly a design feature intended to create an awe-inspiring appearance of authority and power.

Following the lead of the Egyptians, the Greeks further refined stone post-and-beam construction. For more than 2,000 years, the magnificence of the Parthenon and other classical Greek architecture (see fig. 16.6) has influenced the designers of a great many later buildings.

14.4 Colonnade and Court of Amenhotep III. Temple of Amun-Mut-Khonsu. c.1300 BCE. View of the Great Court. 18th dynasty.
Fotolia.

14.5 Round Arch.

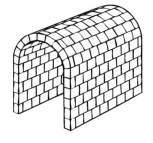

14.6 Barrel Vault.

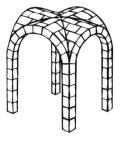

14.7 Groin Vault.

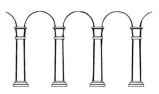

14.8 Arcade.

Round Arch and Vault

Both Egyptian and Greek builders had to place their columns relatively close together because stone is weak under the load-bearing stresses inherent in a beam. The invention of the round **arch** (**fig. 14.5**) allowed builders to transcend this limitation and create new architectural forms. An arch may be supported by either a column or a **pier**, a more massive version of a column. When extended in depth, the round arch creates a tunnel-like structure called a **barrel vault** (**fig. 14.6**). A **vault** is a curving ceiling or roof structure, traditionally made of bricks or blocks of stone tightly fitted to form a unified shell. Roman builders perfected the round arch and developed the **groin vault** (**fig. 14.7**), formed by the intersection of two barrel vaults.

Early civilizations of western Asia and the Mediterranean area built arches and vaults of brick, chiefly for underground drains and tomb chambers. But the Romans were the first to use the arch extensively in above-ground structures. They learned the technique of stone arch and vault construction from the Etruscans, who inhabited central Italy between 750 and 200 BCE.

A round stone arch can span a longer distance and support a heavier load than a stone beam because the arch transfers the load more efficiently. The Roman arch is a semicircle made from wedge-shaped stones fitted together with joints at right angles to the curve. During construction, temporary wooden supports carry the weight of the stones. The final stone that is set in place at the top is called the **keystone**. When the keystone is placed, a continuous arch with load-bearing capacity is created and the wood support is removed. A series of such arches supported by columns forms an **arcade** (**fig. 14.8**).

Roman builders used the arch and arcade to create structures of many types throughout their vast empire in most of Europe, the Near East, and North Africa. The aqueduct bridge called the Pont du Gard, near Nîmes, France (**fig. 14.9**), is one of the finest remaining examples of the functional beauty of Roman engineering. The combined height of the three levels of arches is 161 feet. Dry masonry blocks, weighing up to 2 tons each, make up the large arches of the two lower tiers. Water was once carried in a conduit at the top, with the first level serving as a bridge for traffic. The excellence of its design and construction has kept this aqueduct standing for 2,000 years.

14.9 Pont du Gard. Nîmes, France. 15 CE. Limestone. Height 161′; length 902′.
Filip Fuxa/Shutterstock.

14.10 Dome.

a. Dome (arch rotated 180°).

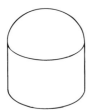

b. Dome on a cylinder.

c. Dome on pendentives.

14.11 *Hagia Sophia.* Istanbul, Turkey. 532–35 CE.
a. Exterior.

Roman architects borrowed Greek column design and combined it with the arch, enabling them to greatly increase the variety and size of their architectural spaces. The Romans also introduced liquid **concrete** as a material for architecture. Concrete is a mixture of water, sand, gravel, and a binder such as lime or gypsum. Liquid concrete is poured into wooden molds and allowed to harden, creating walls or vaults. Roman architects generally faced the outside of concrete buildings with stone or brick. Cheap, stone-like, versatile, and strong, concrete allowed the Romans to cut costs, speed construction, and build on a massive scale.

Dome

An arch rotated 180 degrees on its vertical axis creates a **dome** (**fig. 14.10**). Domes may be hemispherical or pointed. In general usage the word *dome* refers to a hemispherical vault built up from a circular or polygonal base. The weight of a dome pushes downward and outward all around its circumference. Therefore, the simplest support is a cylinder with walls thick enough to resist the downward and outward thrust.

One of the most magnificent domes in the world was designed for the Byzantine cathedral of Hagia Sophia ("Holy Wisdom") in Istanbul (**figs. 14.11a** and **14.11b**). It was built in the sixth century as the central sanctuary of the Eastern

b. Interior.

Photographs: Ayhan Altun.

Orthodox Christian Church. After the Islamic conquest of 1453, towers were added for its later use as a mosque. It is now a museum. The dome of Hagia Sophia rests on curving triangular sections called **pendentives** over a square base.

Hagia Sophia's distinctive dome appears to float on a halo of light—an effect produced by the row of windows encircling its base. Pendentives carry the enormous weight from the circular base of the upper dome downward to a square formed by supporting walls.

Pointed Arch and Vault

After the round arch, the pointed arch was the next important structural advance in the Western world. This new shape seems a small change, but it had a spectacular effect on the building of cathedrals. Vaults based on the pointed arch made it possible to build wider aisles and higher ceilings. We see the results of this new technology in the awesome height of the central aisle in the cathedral of Notre-Dame de Chartres, France (**fig. 14.12**).

14.12 Notre-Dame de Chartres. Chartres, France. 1145–1513. Interior, nave. Height 122'; width 53'; length 130'.
© 2018 Scala, Florence.

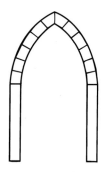

14.13 Gothic Arch.

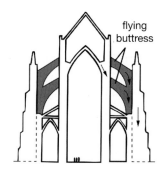

14.14 Flying Buttresses.

A pointed arch (or Gothic arch; **fig. 14.13**) is steeper than a round arch, and therefore sends its weight more directly downward, but a substantial sideways thrust must still be countered in tall buildings. Medieval builders accomplished this by constructing elaborate supports called **buttresses** at right angles to the outer walls. In the most developed Gothic cathedrals, the outward force of the arched vault is carried to large buttresses by stone half-arches called **flying buttresses (fig. 14.14)**.

By placing part of the structural skeleton on the outside, medieval builders were able to make their cathedrals higher and lighter in appearance. Because the added external support of the buttresses relieved the cathedral walls of much of their weight-bearing function, large parts of the wall could be replaced by enormous stained-glass windows (see fig. 16.26), allowing more light (a symbol of God's presence) to enter the sanctuary. From the floor of the sanctuary to the highest part of the interior above the main altar, the windows increase in size. Stones carved and assembled to form thin ribs and pillars make up the elongated columns along the nave walls, which emphasize verticality and give the cathedral its apparent upward thrust. (We will consider the stylistic features of Gothic architecture in more detail in Chapter 16.)

After the Gothic pointed arch and vault, no basic structural technique was added to the Western architectural vocabulary until the nineteenth century. Instead, architects designed a variety of structures—at times highly innovative—by combining elements from different periods. Forms and ornamentation from the classical and Gothic periods were revived again and again and given new life in different contexts.

Wooden Frameworks

Wood has a long history as a building material. Tree branches embedded in a skin of mud or animal hide have provided shelter for thousands of years; they are the ancestors of today's tents. A great deal of ancient wooden architecture, however, has unfortunately perished because it is not as durable as stone. Besides the expected post and beam, timbers or logs have been used for centuries in **trusses (fig. 14.15)**. A truss is a triangular framework used to span or to support.

The perfection of mass-produced nails and mechanical saws in the nineteenth century led to advances in wood construction; the most important of these was the **balloon frame (fig. 14.16)**. In balloon framing, heavy timbers are replaced with thin studs held together only with nails, leading to vastly reduced construction time and wood consumption. Because the studs bear the weight of the building, walls can be of light plasterboard. The method helped to make possible the rapid settlement of North America's western frontier and is still used in much new construction today.

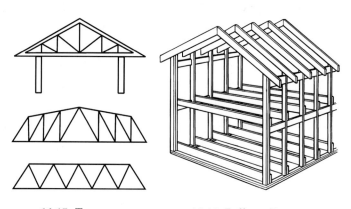

14.15 Trusses.   **14.16** Balloon Frame.

Modern Materials and Methods

Since about 1850, modern materials have revolutionized architecture. The techniques (post and beam, arch, vault, truss) have remained the same, but the arrival of cast iron, steel, and reinforced concrete has provided a wealth of new ways to create and organize spaces. More recently, some even newer materials, such as carbon fiber and cross-laminated timber, are shaping the buildings that we use.

Cast Iron

Iron has much greater strength than stone or wood and can span much larger distances. After the technology for uniform smelting was perfected in the nineteenth century, cast and wrought iron became important building materials. Iron supports made possible lighter exterior walls and more flexible interior spaces because walls no longer had to bear structural weight. Architects first used this new material in factories, bridges, and railway stations.

The Crystal Palace (**fig. 14.17**), designed by Joseph Paxton, was a spectacular demonstration of what cast iron could do. It was built for the Great Exhibition of the Works of Industry of All Nations, the first international exposition, held in London in 1851. Designed to show off the latest mechanical inventions, the Crystal Palace was built in six months and covered 19 acres of park land. This was the first time new industrial methods and materials were used on such a scale.

Paxton used relatively lightweight, factory-made modules (standard-size structural units) of cast iron and glass. By freeing himself from past styles and masonry construction, he created a whole new architectural vocabulary. The light, decorative quality of the glass and cast-iron units was created not by applied ornamentation, but by the structure itself. Paxton, inspired by leaf structures, said nature had given him the idea. The modular units provided enough flexibility for the entire structure to be assembled on the site, right over existing trees, and later disassembled and moved across town.

Unfortunately, the building also showed the great defect of early cast-iron buildings: The unprotected metal struts tend to buckle on exposure to heat, making such buildings very susceptible to destruction by fire. The Crystal Palace indeed burned in 1936 after a fire broke out in its interior.

Steel and Reinforced Concrete

The next breakthrough in construction methods for large structures came between about 1890 and 1910 with the development of high-strength structural steel, used by itself and as the reinforcing material in reinforced concrete. The extensive use of cast-iron skeletons in the mid-nineteenth century had prepared the way for multistory steel-frame construction in the late 1880s.

Steel frames and newly perfected elevators, together with rising urban land values, impelled a fresh approach to structure and form that culminated in the skyscraper. The movement began to take shape in commercial architecture in Chicago, where a destructive fire in 1871 had cleared the way for a building boom.

14.17 Joseph Paxton. Crystal Palace. London. 1850–1851. Cast iron and glass.
British Library.

Leading the Chicago school was Louis Sullivan, whom many regard as the first important modern architect. Sullivan's buildings made little reference to past architectural styles in their decoration as they sought to meet the needs of the time by using new methods and materials. He had a major influence on the early development of the skyscraper.

Among the first of these skyscrapers that survives in good condition is Sullivan's Wainwright Building (**fig. 14.18**) in St. Louis, Missouri. The building boldly breaks with nineteenth-century tradition. Its exterior design reflects its internal steel frame and emphasizes the height of the structure by underplaying horizontal elements in favor of tall vertical shafts. Sullivan demonstrated his sensitivity and adherence to the harmony of traditional architecture by dividing the building's façade into three distinct zones, reminiscent of the base, shaft, and capital of Greek columns (see fig. 16.5). These areas also reveal the various functions of the building, with shops at the base, offices in the central section, and utility rooms at the top. The heavily ornamented band at the top stops the vertical thrust of the piers located between the office windows.

Thus, the exterior form of the building shows its interior functions; this was a novel concept. Sullivan's observation that "form ever follows function"[1] eventually helped architects to break with their reliance on past styles and to rethink architecture from the inside out.

In this functional spirit, modern architecture arose in Europe between 1910 and 1930. Modern architects rejected decorative ornamentation and references to the past, as well as traditional stone and wood construction, and they began to think of a building as a useful arrangement of spaces rather than as a mass. The resulting International Style expressed the function of each building, its underlying structure, and a logical (usually asymmetrical) plan that used only modern materials such as concrete, glass, and steel.

The Swiss-French architect and planner Le Corbusier showed the basic components of steel columns and reinforced-concrete slabs in a system that he called the Domino Construction System (**fig. 14.19**). The six steel supports are placed in concrete slabs at the same approximate locations as the spots on a domino game piece. Le Corbusier's idea of supporting floors and roof on interior load-bearing columns instead of load-bearing walls made it possible to

14.18 Louis Sullivan. Wainwright Building. St. Louis, Missouri. 1890–91.
Getty Images.

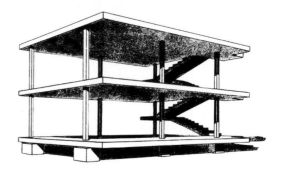

14.19 Le Corbusier. Domino Construction System. Perspective drawing for Domino Housing Project. 1914.
© F.L.C./ADAGP, Paris/Artists Rights Society (ARS), New York 2018.

vary the placement of interior walls according to how the various rooms were used. He called one of his homes a "machine for living in," but in fact its flexible spaces made it very comfortable. And because walls no longer bore any weight, they could become windows and let in a great deal of natural light.

Walter Gropius used the principles of the International Style in his new building for the Bauhaus when that design school moved to Dessau, Germany (**fig. 14.20**). The workshop wing, built between 1925 and 1926, follows the basic concept illustrated in Le Corbusier's drawing. Because the reinforced-concrete floors and roof were supported by steel columns set back from the outer edge of the building, exterior walls did not have to carry any weight: they could be **curtain walls** made of glass. Even interior walls were non-load-bearing and could be placed anywhere they were needed.

Most International Style architects did not consider a building in relation to its environment. An early exception to this trend was the American Frank Lloyd Wright, one of

the most important (and iconoclastic) architects of the era. Wright was among the first to use open planning in houses, even before the International Style took hold (see his Robie House; fig. 22.25). With a steel frame as a skeletal structure, Wright eliminated walls between rooms, enlarged windows, and discovered that one of the best ways to open a closed-in room was to place windows in corners. With these devices, he created flowing spaces that opened to the outdoors, welcomed natural light, and related houses to their sites and climates. Sliding glass doors were influenced by the sliding paper-covered doors in traditional Japanese architecture.

Wright also made extensive use of the **cantilever** to unite indoor and outdoor spaces. When a beam or slab is extended a substantial distance beyond a supporting column or wall, the overhanging portion is called a cantilever. Before the use of steel and reinforced concrete, cantilevers were not used to a significant degree because the available materials could not extend far enough to make the concept viable.

14.20 Walter Gropius. Bauhaus Building. Exterior. 1926–27.
LianeM/Shutterstock.

14.21 Frank Lloyd Wright. Fallingwater (Edgar Kaufmann Residence). Bear Run, Pennsylvania. 1936.
Library of Congress.

Steel-frame construction (**fig. 14.22**) came into wide use after 1945 as a simpler and more efficient version of the International Style. We see this in the Seagram Building (**fig. 14.23**). Non-load-bearing glass walls had been a major feature of plans for skyscrapers for years, but only in the 1950s, with greater public acceptance of modern architecture, could such structures be built. The Seagram Building created enough office space through sheer height that it allowed the architects to leave a large, open public area at the base. The vertical lines emphasize the height and provide a strong pattern that is capped by a top section designed to give a sense of completion. The austere and decoration-free design embodies architect Ludwig Mies van der Rohe's famous statement "Less is more."

One of the boldest and most elegant uses of the principle occurs in Wright's Edgar Kaufmann Residence (also known as Fallingwater) at Bear Run, Pennsylvania (**fig. 14.21**). Horizontal masses cantilevered from supporting piers echo the rock ledges on the site and seem almost to float above the waterfall. The steel frame is sheathed in local stone, visible at the structure's core. Vertical accents were influenced by surrounding tall, straight trees. The intrusion of a building on such a beautiful location seems justified by the harmony Wright achieved between the natural site and his equally inspiring architecture.

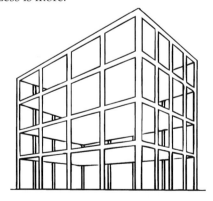

14.22 Steel-Frame Construction.

The International Style had an enormous, if sometimes negative, influence on world architecture. It often replaced unique, place-defining regional styles with standardized simplicity. By the mid-twentieth century, modern architecture had become synonymous with the style. The uniformity of glass-covered rectilinear grid structures was considered the appropriate formal dressing for the anonymity and efficiency of the modern corporation.

Recent Innovations

In the late twentieth century, improved construction techniques and materials, new theories regarding structural physics, and computer analyses of the strengths and weaknesses in complex structures led to the further development of fresh architectural forms.

Suspension structures were known for decades through their use in tents and bridges, but the most dramatic recent use of this technique in a major public building was in the Jeppesen Terminal Building at Denver International Airport (**fig. 14.24**). Its roof is a giant tent composed of 15 acres of woven fiberglass, making it one of the largest suspension buildings on Earth. This white roofing material lets in large amounts of natural light without conducting heat, and it is coated with Teflon for water resistance and easy cleaning. Its exterior design was inspired by the snow-capped Rocky Mountains, which are visible from inside.

14.23 Ludwig Mies van der Rohe and Philip Johnson. Seagram Building. New York. 1956–58.
Photograph: Andrew Garn.

14.24 Fentress-Bradburn Architects. Jeppesen Terminal Building. Denver International Airport. 1994.
Photograph provided courtesy of the Denver International Airport.

14.25 Frank O. Gehry. Guggenheim Museum Bilbao. Bilbao, Spain. 1997.
Photograph by Erika Barahona Ede.
© FMGB Guggenheim Bilbao Museo.

In recent years, art museums have become showplaces for cutting-edge architecture. Frank Gehry's Guggenheim Museum, Bilbao (**fig. 14.25**), is more like a piece of functional sculpture. The development of computer graphics and modeling applications in the 1980s made possible this design, which the architect called a "metallic flower." The museum's exterior is a dramatic limestone and titanium-clad cluster of soaring, nearly dancing volumes that climax in a gigantic, glass-enclosed atrium. These billowing forms completely conceal the steel structure beneath, with its blocks of rectangular galleries.

Architecture's first technical innovation of the twenty-first century is carbon fiber; although it is still rather expensive today, it may have an important impact on how we build in the future. Scientists found that heating carbon atoms in an oxygen-free environment fuses them into some of the lightest and strongest materials yet discovered. Certain aircraft parts, racing-car bodies, and bicycle frames already use carbon fiber. Shaping this fiber carefully and coating it with polyester or nylon yields a new material that can literally be woven to create a building.

The Tokyo firm Atelier Bow-Wow recently created a public seminar space using carbon fiber (**fig. 14.26**). All this building's components are light enough to be handled easily by one person. The BMW Guggenheim Lab can house talks, exhibitions, discussions, screenings, and workshops; all the implements for such functions are stored in the upper portion on pulleys, to be raised or lowered as needed. The building's lightness was advantageous, because it eventually housed seminars on three continents.

Some old materials are also getting new treatments in the twenty-first century. Cross-laminated timber (CLT) uses wood in a new way, by laminating slabs of wood with their grains at an angle. This makes wood as strong as concrete, but much lighter. CLT slabs can range up to 11 inches thick and 60 feet long, and their flexibility makes them more earthquake-resistant than concrete. The compression of the wood during CLT manufacture makes the material fire-resistant. Using trees harvested from sustainable forests also makes CLT a carbon-neutral building material.

The Radiator Building in Portland (**fig. 14.27**) is one of the largest structures created with this old-new material. The wood that makes up its structure was sustainably harvested nearby. The vertical accents in the design allude to the lumber that makes it up, while over the windows the angled slats are programmable to admit the most appropriate amount of natural sunlight. Although this building is already seismically safer than its steel-framed neighbors, it still has sensors embedded in the earth 12 feet underground. In the event of a temblor, all elevators go immediately to the ground floor, the gas is shut off, and all workers in the building who have registered their cell phones get a text message.

14.26 Atelier Bow-Wow. BMW Guggenheim Lab. 2011–12. Berlin, Germany. Open-air, carbon-fiber structure.

Photograph: Christian Richters. © 2012 Solomon R. Guggenheim Foundation.

14.27 PATH Architecture. The Radiator Building. Portland, Oregon. 2015.

Andrew Pogue Photography.

14.28 Michelle Kaufmann. mkSolaire Home. 2008. Prefabricated house.
As exhibited at the Museum of Science and Industry, Chicago. Photograph: John Swain Photography. Courtesy of Michelle Kaufmann.

Building Green

Across the world increasing numbers of architects in recent years are thinking of ways to reduce the impact of building on the environment, and to make the interiors more healthful. In the United States, the Green Building Council gives annual awards for leadership in environmentally sensitive design. Architects can submit their plans to the Council for rating, and the Council assigns points for such factors as harmony with prevailing wind or sunshine patterns, indoor energy efficiency, use of recycled water, and reduction of transportation costs for materials. The Council then makes annual awards for Leadership in Energy and Environmental Design (LEED), presenting Certified, Silver, Gold, and Platinum awards each year to projects that reach designated point levels.

The mkSolaire Home by Michelle Kaufmann (**fig. 14.28**) represents the leading edge in green single-family home design. This prefabricated house can be placed on a wide variety of sites in an orientation to maximize sunlight. It uses the most efficient insulation available, and window placements maximize cross-ventilation. On-demand water heaters, low-flow fixtures, and a green roof also

reduce energy demands. The architect certifies that this home, depending on where it is located, will earn either a Gold or a Platinum certification.

An important way for architects to earn green points for their designs is to rehabilitate old buildings rather than build new ones. (fer) studio did just that with a mixed-use commercial structure in 2009 that the Louisville, Kentucky, locals soon dubbed The Green Building (**fig. 14.29**). Re-adapting the disused 120-year-old dry-goods store began with the task of sandblasting it: not with sand but with corn husks. The original brick walls were then insulated with material from recycled blue jeans. New flooring in the building is 100 percent recycled as well. Insulated glass and an energy-recovery system that captures both hot and cold air also help to reduce energy use. During the planning process the architects discovered some geothermal wells below the building, which they tapped for heating both air and water. Solar panels on the roof shelter an open-air event space. The building's energy

14.29 (fer) studio. The Green Building. Louisville, Kentucky. 2009.
Douglas Pierson, pod architecture + design PLLC/Christopher Mercier, (fer) studio. Photograph © Ted Wathen/Quadrant.

14.30 Joe Shih Architects. Y. S. Sun Green Building Research Center. Taiwan. 2011.
National Cheng Kung University, Tainan, Taiwan.

use is so low compared to a conventional structure that the building comfortably offsets the carbon footprint of the cars of all employees who work there. Certified Platinum, the building now anchors a pedestrian-friendly arts district.

The LEED occasionally certifies buildings outside the United States; the first building in Asia to earn the highest Platinum rating was the Y. S. Sun Green Building Research Center, a university building in Taiwan (**fig. 14.30**). Half of the roof is covered with drought-tolerant plants; the other half collects solar energy. Fourteen small wind turbines around the exterior generate about 5 percent of the building's needs. Three vertical shafts inside the structure passively cool the interior by venting rising warm air upward and out above the roof. The sustainably produced concrete in the framework of the building was strengthened by the addition of metal slag leftover from smelting steel. Indoor carpets and curtains are made from corncobs and recycled plastic bottles. No construction materials were imported for this building, which uses only about 30 percent of the energy per square foot used by the average building of this type.

Most skyscrapers, with their heavy structural skeletons, sealed interior environments, and glassy exteriors, are very energy inefficient. But the Aqua Tower in Chicago (**fig. 14.31**) incorporates several green characteristics that emboldened the owner to seek LEED Certification. The curving and irregular balconies that give the residential

14.31 Jeanne Gang/Studio Gang Architects. Aqua Tower. Chicago, Illinois. 2010.
© Hedrich Blessing / Steve Hall.

CREATORS

Jeanne Gang: Rethinking the High-Rise

14.32 Jeanne Gang.
Photograph by Sally Ryan.
Courtesy of Studio Gang.

Most skyscrapers, with their heavy structural skeletons, sealed interior environments, and glassy exteriors, are energy inefficient and often lack potential for socialization among occupants. Jeanne Gang (b. 1964) has been working to change both of these disadvantages. Her visually striking tall buildings are forcing a reconsideration of what is possible.

Born in a town northwest of Chicago, Gang earned her Bachelor of Science in Architecture from the University of Illinois Urbana-Champaign and her Master of Architecture from the Harvard Graduate School of Design. Before founding her own firm in 1997, she worked in the office of Rem Koolhaas, a Dutch designer known for innovative buildings.

This background only partially explains Gang's use of the undulating balconies that jut out from the Aqua Tower (see fig. 14.31). Such radical shaping also makes possible socialization among people on different floors

14.33 Jeanne Gang. 40 Tenth Avenue, New York City, anticipated 2019. Night view.
Copyright and courtesy of Studio Gang.

because residents can see one another. Gang designed this feature into the structure in order to reduce the isolating quality of most tall buildings, where people generally interact only briefly and guardedly in elevators. She believes that a rising demographic tide of younger people are ready to attempt more personal urban encounters. She wrote, "Millennials, the current generation moving to cities, are highly social and desire opportunities for interactions that are both virtual and real. Comfortable with sharing, this generation is capable of transforming many established aspects of urban living."[2]

The rectangular bulk of most tall buildings gives them a forbidding appearance from the street as they block sunlight and throw public spaces into shadow. In colder climates, such shadowed spaces are especially unconducive to pausing and interacting. Gang worked to remedy this problem in the new 40 Tenth Avenue, an office tower in New York City (**fig. 14.33**). She designed the "solar carved" silhouette of this building to maximize solar exposure on the streets and park below to make them more people-friendly. The shaved and faceted surfaces of the building align with the sun's path in both winter and summer

(**fig. 14.34**), so that sunlight has sculpted its façade. The building rises alongside the High Line, a popular urban park on an elevated section of a former railroad. The design of 40 Tenth Avenue not only allows more sunlight onto the park, but also affords park users wider vistas of the nearby Hudson River. These features and others less visible, such as a green roof and frequent use of recycled materials inside, allow this building to target a LEED Gold sustainability rating.

Gang is now at work on the Vista Tower in Chicago, her tallest building at 95 stories.

On completion in 2019, it will offer public plazas, several amenity levels for residents and hotel guests, an undulating silhouette, and multiple shades of glass tinting to maximize solar efficiency. The world's steadily urbanizing population means that skyscrapers will likely remain a feature of life in cities. The task at hand becomes, she said, "continuing to make the vertical building more social, more green, and more habitable."[3]

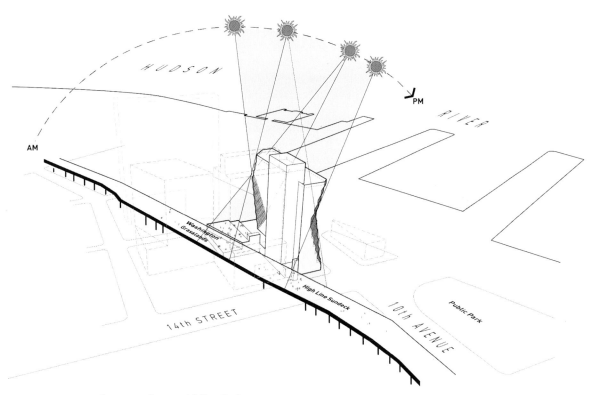

14.34 Diagram of sun angles on 40 Tenth Avenue.
Copyright and courtesy of Studio Gang.

tower such a striking appearance also have a practical function: They reduce the building's sway in Chicago's prevalent winds, so that the structural supports on the upper floors can use less material. Heat-resistant glass in the building reduces the need for air conditioning in summer. The three-story entrance pavilion at the base has an 80,000-square-foot garden on its roof, a literal "patch of green." Inside the building, the apartments have sustainable bamboo floors and energy-efficient appliances. A 24-car electric vehicle charging system awaits drivers in the basement. Aqua Tower architect Jeanne Gang has been working for several years to make tall buildings more sustainable and user-friendly (see *Jeanne Gang: Rethinking the High-Rise* on p. 236).

We all live with architecture every day. As we have seen in this chapter, architects can use engineering techniques and their sense of design to make buildings both useful and expressive.

KEY TERMS

arcade – a series of arches supported by columns or piers

arch – a curved structure designed to span an opening, usually made of stone or other masonry; Roman arches are semicircular, Islamic and Gothic arches come to a point at the top

balloon frame – a wooden structural support system developed in the United States in the mid-nineteenth century in which standardized, thin studs are held together with nails

barrel vault – a semicircular arch extended in depth; a continuous series of arches one behind the other

buttress – a support, usually exterior, for a wall, arch, or vault that opposes the lateral forces of these structures

cantilever – a beam or slab projecting a substantial distance beyond its supporting post or wall

colonnade – a row of columns usually spanned or connected by beams

concrete – a liquid building material invented by the Romans; made of water, sand, gravel, and a binder of gypsum, lime, or volcanic ash

curtain wall – a non-load-bearing wall, typical of the International Style; generally well-endowed with windows

dome – a generally hemispherical roof or vault

dressed stone – stone used for building that is cut, trimmed, or ground down to fit into a masonry wall

flying buttress – a strut or segment of an arch carrying the thrust of a vault to a vertical pier positioned away from the main portion of the building; an important element in Gothic cathedrals

groin vault – a vault formed by the intersection of two barrel vaults

International Style – an architectural style that emerged in several European countries between 1910 and 1920; characterized by the use of modern materials (concrete, glass, steel), avoidance of applied decoration, and focus on a building's inner uses

keystone – the stone at the central, highest point of a round arch, which holds the rest of the arch in place

masonry – building technique in which stones or bricks are laid atop one another in a pattern

pendentive – a curving triangle that points downward; a common support for domes in Byzantine architecture

pier – an upright support for an arch or arcade; fulfills the same function as a column, but is more massive and usually not tapered at the top

post-and-beam system (post and lintel) – structural system in which uprights or posts support a horizontal beam that spans the space between them

truss – a structural framework of wood or metal based on a triangular system, used to span, reinforce, or support walls, ceilings, piers, or beams

vault – a curving masonry roof or ceiling constructed on the principle of the arch

Part Three

ART AS CULTURAL HERITAGE

From the Earliest Art to the Bronze Age

The Classical and Medieval West

Renaissance and Baroque Europe

Traditional Arts of Asia

The Islamic World

Africa, Oceania, and the Americas

Fig. 16.12. National Gallery of Art, Washington, D.C., Samuel H. Kress Collection, 1939.1.24.

15 FROM THE EARLIEST ART TO THE BRONZE AGE

LEARNING OBJECTIVES

15.1 Trace the origins of early art in the Paleolithic period.

15.2 Identify the changes in Neolithic art that parallel the shift from Paleolithic society.

15.3 Discuss the style and functions of Bronze Age art of Mesopotamia.

15.4 Explain the stylistic and cultural features of art from ancient Egypt.

Art history makes history visible and accessible. It is a record of how the people of the past—our ancestors—lived, felt, and acted in widely separated parts of the world at different periods of time.

Art history differs from other kinds of history because works of art from the past are with us in the present. One-to-one communication still occurs, even when artist and viewer are separated by thousands of years. This communicative power of art makes it possible for us to glimpse some of the experiences of those whose lives preceded ours, to better understand societies other than our own, and to see beyond our own cultural boundaries. Although interesting, old science has little practical use; but old art can be as life-enriching as new art.

There is no "better" or "best" when we compare the art of different societies, or even the art of different times within the same society. Rather, differences in art reflect differences in points of view. Pablo Picasso put the subject of art history in perspective in this way:

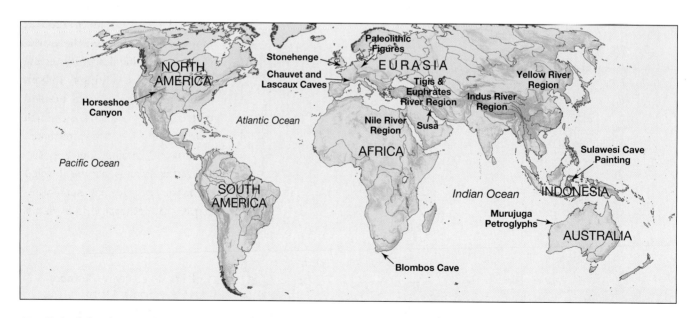

15.1 Paleolithic Sites and Early Centers of Civilization.

To me there is no past or future in art. If a work of art cannot live always in the present it must not be considered at all. The art of the Greeks, the Egyptians, the great painters who lived in other times, is not an art of the past; perhaps it is more alive today than it ever was.[1]

Among the earliest major civilizations were those in four fertile river valleys: the Tigris and Euphrates rivers in Iraq, the Nile River in Egypt, the Indus River in west Pakistan and India, and the Yellow River in northern China (**fig. 15.1**). Early civilizations in India and China are covered in Chapter 18. In this chapter, we will examine some of the earliest known artworks around the world, and then begin to trace a history across thousands of years to the Bronze Age civilizations in the Middle East and Egypt.

The Paleolithic Period

Roughly two million years ago, in east-central Africa, early hominids made crude stonecutting tools. The making of these tools enabled our predecessors to extend their skills and thereby gain a measure of control over their surroundings. From such beginnings, human beings developed the abilities to reason and to visualize: to imagine the need for a tool, to craft one from available materials, to use it, and later to improve it. As we became form-creating creatures, our ability to conceive mental images set us apart from other animals. Imagination is our special advantage.

About one million years ago in Africa, and more recently in Asia and Europe, people made more refined tools by chipping flakes from opposite sides of stones to create sharp cutting edges. It took another 250,000 years or so for human beings to develop choppers and hand axes that were symmetrical and refined in shape. An awareness of the relationship of form to function, and of form as enjoyable in itself, was the first step in the history of art.

Sprinkled powders and beads accompany many widely dispersed gravesites from about 100,000 years ago. These finds suggest to archaeologists that humans at that time practiced ritual burial, although the meaning of these decorative additions is unknown.

Recent discoveries have enlivened the debate about when art began. In 2002, archaeologists digging in the Blombos Cave in South Africa unearthed what may qualify as the earliest art that we know of. In a soil layer 77,000 years old, they found some pieces of engraved ochre (**fig. 15.2**) bearing marks that appear to be symbols. The marks form an abstract pattern of parallel diagonal lines between horizontal bars. Any practical use for the markings is highly unlikely; rather, they seem symbolic or at least decorative, making these ochres the oldest embellished objects yet found. In 2010, researchers at a nearby site found ostrich egg shells with similar parallel scratch marks. Many archaeologists concluded that these African sites contain the first known instances of artistic creativity.

More sophisticated examples of art have been discovered at many locations around the world. Current scientific dating places the earliest of these findings at about 40,000 years ago, toward the end of the last ice age. As the Earth warmed and ice slowly retreated northward, ancient peoples followed the animals that they hunted for food. They lived by such hunting, and by gathering edible plants.

15.2 Engraved ochre. Blombos Cave, South Africa. c.75,000 BCE. Length 4″.
Image courtesy of Christopher Henshilwood.

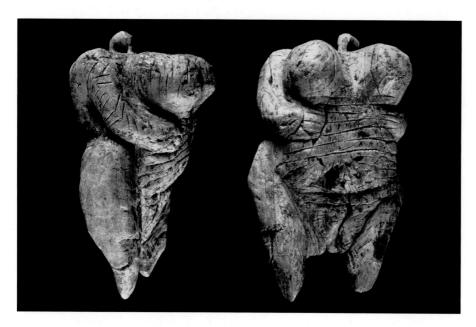

15.3 *Hohle Fels Figure.* c.35,000 BCE. Carved mammoth tusk. Front and side views of the recently discovered female figurine from the Aurignacian levels of Hohle Fels. Height 2½″.

Photograph: H. Jensen. © University of Tübingen.

15.4 *Woman of Willendorf.* Aurignacian (late Paleolithic). c.25,000–20,000 BCE. Limestone. Height 4½″.

Naturhistorisches Museum, Vienna. akg-image/Erich Lessing.

Because the tools that they used were made from stone, this period is called the **Paleolithic Age**, or Old Stone Age. They also carved and painted images of these animals on cave walls deep in the earth.

The oldest surviving carved human figure was found in southwestern Germany in 2008; the *Hohle Fels Figure* (**fig. 15.3**) is just over 2 inches high and at least 35,000 years old. Her female characteristics are highly exaggerated, and she shows carefully placed grooves at various points on her body. Her arms cling to her abdomen. In place of a head is a ring suitable for stringing the figure around a wearer's neck (the ring shows wearing marks).

A similar figure about 10,000 years younger is the *Woman of Willendorf* (**fig. 15.4**), which was found in northern Austria. In both of these figures, the pointy legs, lack of facial detail, and exaggerated emphasis on hips and breasts implies a specific purpose, which we can only guess at. These figures may be the earliest known works of religious art; some scholars believe that they depict the Paleolithic image of the Creator—the Great Mother Goddess. A more recent theory holds that these figures were signs of recognition, proffered when widely scattered groups of hunter-gatherers encountered one another. The *Hohle Fels Figure* was found near a three-hole flute carved of bone, indicating that music also existed in that remote era.

Painting

Paleolithic paintings have a different style from the copious bulges of the sculpture. Animal subjects predominate; humans that appear tend to be more simplified and abstract than the images of animals. Animals portrayed in sculpture and paintings of this period have an expressive naturalism.

The oldest known paintings were discovered in a cave in Indonesia decades ago, but only in 2014 were they convincingly dated to at least 39,900 years ago (**fig. 15.5**). This photo shows a handprint at the upper right, which an early human made by blowing dark red powder to leave a negative image. It is the oldest known representation created by a human. A four-legged animal occupies the central third of the picture, outlined in similar reddish powder applied at least 35,400 years ago; the subject is a now extinct species called a pig-deer.

Paintings in the Chauvet Cave in south-central France are more recent and better preserved. The wall painting of animals (**fig. 15.6**) is among dozens of 30,000-year-old images painted with charcoal and earthen pigments on the cave walls. The unknown artists depicted in a lifelike fashion horses, rhinoceroses, tigers, and other large animals, many of them now extinct. Explorers found a bear's skull in the middle of a flat stone slab nearby, which may have been an altar.

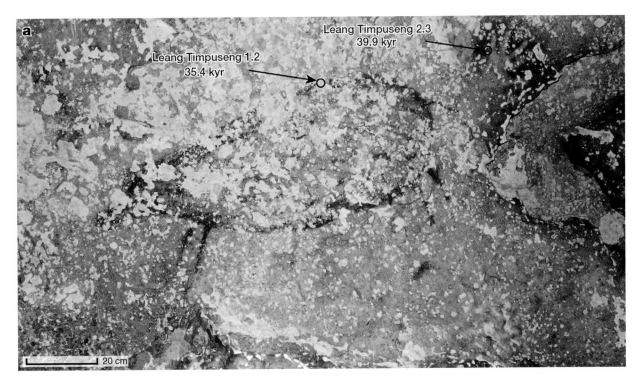

15.5 Pig-Deer and Hand. Cave painting in Sulawesi, Indonesia. 39,000–35,000 BCE. Length of animal 31½″.

Indonesian Heritage Deparment. Photograph: Maxime Aubert.

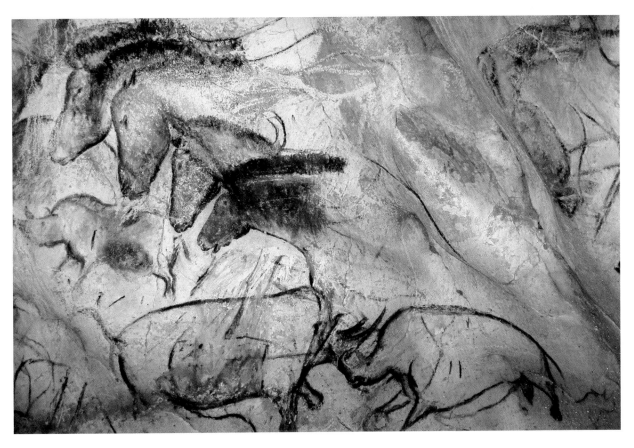

15.6 Wall painting of animals. Chauvet Cave, Pont d'Arc, France. c.28,000 BCE.

French Ministry of Culture and Communication, Regional Direction for Cultural Affairs—Rhône-Alpes region—Regional department of archaeology. Slide no. 10. Photograph: Jean Clottes.

15.7 Great Gallery. Horseshoe Canyon, Utah. c.7400–5200 BCE. Pictographs. Height of tallest figures 7´.
Photograph: Patrick Frank.

Scholars long believed that the purpose of **naturalistic** Paleolithic art was to bring the spirits of animals into rituals related to the hunt. Many scholars accept this theory. However, careful study of footprints and other archaeological remains has recently led some experts to theorize that Chauvet and similar sites were used as sanctuaries where youth were initiated in ceremonies based on symbolic or spiritual associations with the portrayed animals. Archaeologists cannot conclusively prove these theories, but either is plausible.

Much of the world's Paleolithic art is found in caves, but large parts of this heritage are above ground, painted or carved on stones in many locations around the world where people also lived by hunting and gathering.

15.8 Murujuga Petroglyphs. Northwest Australia. Up to 10,000 years old.
Photograph: Robert G. Bednarik.

Some of the oldest Paleolithic rock art in North America is found in Utah, where native peoples painted silhouette forms that resemble humans wrapped in symbolic garments (**fig. 15.7**). The meaning of these ghostly figures eludes us, but they were created with a high degree of detail using the same sort of earthen pigments that characterize Paleolithic art the world over. Unlike European Paleolithic paintings, which are much older, the North American artists rarely depicted animals. Many archaeologists speculate that shamanic rituals practiced in the region by successor peoples offer a clue to the meaning and function of these haunting works.

Rock art carvings, also known as **petroglyphs**, are made by scratching or pecking the surface of exposed stone. One of the largest petroglyph complexes is in the Dampier Archipelago off the northwest coast of Australia. There we see the Murujuga petroglyphs (**fig. 15.8**), thousands of carvings that depict humans, animals, and mythic beings. Like the cave paintings, the purpose of the petroglyphs is a matter of conjecture. Their age is also difficult to determine because they are in exposed locations apart from the soil sediments that help us to date paintings. A great deal of the world's rock art is also endangered for this reason; the Murujuga petroglyphs, for example, have been eroded by acid rain, and economic development in the area threatens their destruction.

The Neolithic Period

The transition from Old Stone Age to New Stone Age (Paleolithic to **Neolithic**) marked a major turning point in human history. The New Stone Age seems to have arisen first in what is now northwestern Iraq, between 9000 and 6000 BCE, when people made the gradual transition from the precarious existence of nomadic hunters and gatherers to the relatively stable life of village farmers and herders. The agricultural revolution—this major shift from nomadic groups to small agricultural communities—stabilized human life and produced early architecture and other technological developments. People learned new techniques for working with seasonal rhythms. Because food and seeds required storage, it is not surprising that clay storage pots are among the most significant artifacts of the period.

Neolithic art reflects the great shift in living patterns. The vigorous, naturalistic art of Paleolithic hunters was largely replaced by the geometric abstract art of Neolithic farmers. From about 10,000 to 3000 BCE, we see a fairly consistent style of abstract designs embellishing articles for daily use. The motifs, or dominant themes, used on clay pots were often derived from plant and animal forms.

We see some of these forms in the painted earthenware beaker (**fig. 15.9**) from Susa, the first developed city on the Iranian plateau. Solid bands define areas of compact decoration. The upper zone consists of a row of highly abstract long-necked birds, below which appears to

15.9 Earthenware Beaker with Ibexes. Susa, Iran. c.4000 BCE. Painted terra cotta. Height 11¼″.
Musée du Louvre. RMN-Grand Palais (Musée du Louvre)/Gérard Blot/ Christian Jean.

15.10 Burial Urn. Kansu type. China. Neolithic period. c.2200 BCE. Pottery with painted decoration. Height 14⅛″.

The Seattle Art Museum. Eugene Fuller Memorial Collection (51.194). Photograph: Paul Macapia.

15.11 Stonehenge. Wiltshire, UK. c.2000 BCE.

Skyscan Photolibrary/Alamy Stock Photo.

be a band of dogs running in the opposite direction. The dominant image is an ibex or goat abstracted into triangular and circular shapes. The significant difference between the naturalism of Paleolithic animal art and the abstraction of Neolithic art becomes clear when we compare this goat with the naturalistic bulls of Chauvet (see fig. 15.6).

Some of the finest Neolithic pottery was made in China. The well-preserved burial urn from Kansu Province (**fig. 15.10**) is decorated with a bold interlocking design, which may have been abstracted from spirals observed in nature. The design in the center of the spirals is probably derived from the bottoms of cowrie shells.

Most Neolithic structures are primitive (such as the dolmens pictured in fig. 14.1); one that shows real sophistication is Stonehenge in south-central England (**fig. 15.11**). Built in layers over more than a millennium, its oldest phase is the outermost circular ditch and bank; these date from about 3200 BCE. This bank is interrupted for a road (at lower right) that is aligned to the northernmost midwinter moonrise. Many archaeologists believe that this orientation was important in funeral rituals. Near the same time, wood structures were erected at the center of the circle.

Later phases involved replacing the wood structures with huge stones (weighing 25 tons) brought to the site from a quarry 19 miles away. These stones were fitted together using techniques borrowed from lumber construction; they form a semicircle surrounded by a ring of posts and lintels. Some of these stones have carvings of daggers and axes that resemble carvings found across the Channel

in France, which appear next to a female guardian of the afterlife. Many burials have been found near Stonehenge, with most of the dead showing some sort of trauma or wound. An upright "heel stone" was placed on the road at a point beyond our photo that aligns with the midsummer sunrise. These indications make the function of Stonehenge a matter of debate. The most current theory holds that it was a site for funerary rites, but it may have had various functions at different times in its lengthy evolution.

Bronze Age Mesopotamia

Artifacts indicate that early civilizations emerged independently, at different times, in many parts of the world. We use the term "civilization" to distinguish cultures, or composites of cultures, that have fairly complex social orders and relatively higher degrees of technical development. Key elements are food production through agriculture and animal husbandry, occupational specialization, writing, and production of bronze by smelting lead and tin. All these developments were made possible by the move to cooperative living in urban as well as agricultural communities. The rise of bronze also made possible better weapons, and thus larger empires.

The Greeks named the broad plain between the Tigris and Euphrates rivers Mesopotamia, "the land between the rivers" (**fig. 15.12**). Today, the heart of this plain is part of central and northern Iraq. The geography of Mesopotamia made it vulnerable to repeated invasion; thus, the area was ruled by a succession of different peoples.

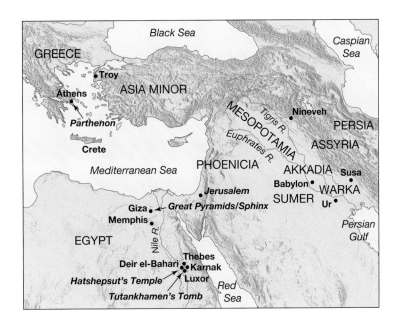

15.12 The Ancient Middle East.

The ancient civilizations of Mesopotamia and Egypt were almost parallel in time, arising in the fourth millennium BCE and lasting some 3,000 years. Yet urban civilization developed earlier in Mesopotamia than it did in Egypt. The first Mesopotamian civilization arose in the southernmost part of the plain in an area called Sumer. The Sumerian people developed the world's first writing, the wheel, and the plow.

In the city-states of Sumer, religion and government were one; authority rested with priests who claimed divine sanction as they elected their rulers. The Sumerians worshiped a hierarchy of nature gods in temples set on huge platforms called **ziggurats**, which stood at the center of each city-state. Ruins of many early Mesopotamian cities are still dominated by eroding ziggurats, such as the Ziggurat of Ur-Nammu (**fig. 15.13**). The Tower of Babel mentioned in the Bible was probably a ziggurat.

Ziggurats embodied the concept of the "sacred mountain" that links heaven and Earth. They were filled with sun-baked bricks, then faced with bricks colored with ceramic glazes and fired in kilns. Two or more successively smaller platforms stood on the solid base, with a shrine on the uppermost platform. On these heights, closer to heaven, the city's deities might dwell, and there the ruling priests and priestesses had their sanctuaries. A lack of stone led to the use of brick and wood for building; consequently, very little Mesopotamian architecture remains.

Much of the art of Sumer serves ritualistic needs; a well-crafted example is the vase from Warka (**fig. 15.14**). One of the earliest surviving examples of narrative relief sculpture, this vase is a celebration of fertility carved in fine white alabaster. At the lowest level, a wavy line represents the source of the organic growth, the waters of the Tigris and Euphrates rivers, flowing beneath a row of alternating grains and date palms. Above, rams and ewes march along. At the center, nude men in an orderly row bring baskets of food offerings. At the top is the culmination of the procession: A man brings an offering basket to a priestess representing Inanna, the goddess of fertility, who stands before the entrance to her temple. Inanna was one of the most important gods of Sumer and appears

15.13 Ziggurat of Ur-Nammu. Iraq. c.2100 BCE.
World Religions Photo Library/Alamy Stock Photo.

frequently in both art and literature. This vase depicts humans in harmony with the natural world in carvings of fine quality throughout.

Sumerian culture flourished among independent city-states in lower Mesopotamia. By about 2300 BCE, Sumer came under the authority of a single Akkadian king from the region just to the north. The serene head of an Akkadian ruler (**fig. 15.15**) portrays such an absolute monarch. Clearly, this sophisticated work evolved from a long tradition of creating representational art through lost-wax casting (see fig. 12.8). The elaborate hairstyle and rhythmic patterning show the influence of Sumerian stylization. The handsome face expresses calm inner strength. Such blending of formal design with carefully observed representation is a characteristic of both later Mesopotamian and Egyptian art.

15.14 Warka Vase. Alabaster. Height 36″. Iraq Museum, Baghdad.

15.15 Head of an Akkadian Ruler. Nineveh. c.2300–2200 BCE. Bronze. Height 12″.

Mesopotamia was an area of continual local rivalries, foreign invasions, and the rise and fall of military powers. Yet this disorder did not prevent the development and continuity of cultural traditions.

Ancient Egypt

Deserts on both sides of the Nile diminished outside influences (see fig. 15.12) and enabled Egypt to develop distinctive Bronze Age styles of architecture, painting, and sculpture that remained relatively unchanged for 2,500 years—longer than the time from the birth of Christ to today. In our age of rapid cultural and technological change, such artistic stability is difficult to imagine.

Architecture

Among the most impressive and memorable works of Egyptian civilization are the Great Pyramids (**fig. 15.16**), gigantic mountain-like structures built as burial vaults and commemorative monuments for pharaohs—rulers who were considered god-kings. Legions of workers cut huge stone blocks, moved them to the site, and stacked them, without mortar, to form the pyramidal structure. The interiors are mostly solid, with narrow passageways leading to small burial chambers.

Egyptian religious belief focused intently on life after death. Preservation of the body and care for the dead were considered essential for extending life beyond the grave.

15.16 The Great Pyramids. Giza, Egypt. Pyramid of Mycernius (Menkaura), c.2500 BCE; Pyramid of Chefren, 2650 BCE; Pyramid of Cheops, c.2570 BCE.
Pius Lee/Shutterstock.

15.17 Funerary Temple of Queen Hatshepsut. Deir el-Bahari, c.1490–1460 BCE.
Getty Images.

Upon death, bodies of royalty and nobility were embalmed. Together with accompanying artifacts, tools, and furniture, they were then buried in pyramids or in hidden underground tombs. Architects put great effort into preventing access to these funerary structures. As a result, most of what we know about ancient Egypt comes from such tombs.

Names of a few Egyptian architects are known in association with their buildings. A striking and well-preserved example is the Funerary Temple of Queen Hatshepsut (**fig. 15.17**), which may have been designed by Senenmut, the queen's chancellor and advisor (see *Senenmut: The Great Steward* on p. 252). Complementing the majestic cliffs of the site, the ramps and colonnades provide an elegant setting for ritual pageantry. Wall paintings and reliefs at the site tell of an expedition that Hatshepsut funded to explore the legendary birthplace of the gods, and her own birth from the sun god Amen. This grandiose temple, completed during her reign, aided her effort to be taken seriously as a ruler in her own right, and its narrative art tells the exploits of the first famous woman in the history of art.

CREATORS

Senenmut: The Great Steward

15.18 Artist's Gridded Sketch of Senenmut. 1479–1458 BCE. Ink on limestone. DT1534. 8⅞″ × 7⅛″.
Metropolitan Museum of Art. Acc. No. 36.3.252.

Ancient Egyptians regarded most artists on the same social level as manual laborers, who merely carried out the orders of overseers. Among the most powerful of such overseers was Senenmut, who supervised some of Queen Hatshepsut's most important building projects.

Senenmut (active c.1473–1458 BCE) was apparently born into a family of modest means in a small city not far from Luxor and Karnak, important ceremonial centers and the site of many temples. We can glimpse something of both Senenmut's physical appearance and the techniques of Egyptian artists from a portrait drawing on limestone (**fig. 15.18**) that was recovered near his tomb. It shows a man with a slightly hooked nose, ridges around his mouth, and a near-double chin.

The artist first sketched the portrait in red ink before adjusting it to its final version in black. The artist then drew a network of squares over it in order to facilitate its enlargement on other surfaces. This drawing was indeed enlarged to become a wall painting in Queen Hatshepsut's Funerary Temple.

Senenmut first appears in surviving inscriptions as the tutor to Neferure, Hatshepsut's daughter. This brought him close to the royal household where he quickly rose in power after the Queen took the Pharaoh's throne. She appointed him an administrator of the temple at Karnak, and when she commissioned her own funerary temple at nearby Deir el-Bahari (see fig. 15.17), she put Senenmut in charge of its construction with the title Great Steward of Amen. He may well have also served as architect.

Like most ancient Egyptians, Senenmut seems to have been concerned with the perpetuation of his spirit in the afterlife. He acted on this by commissioning a large tomb for himself along with more than 20 statues. Several of these show him in the company of his student Neferure (**fig. 15.19**). This particular work has an inscription by Senenmut that suggests he had a significant role in determining the work's appearance: "Images which I have made from the devising of my own heart and from my own labor; they have not been found in the writings of the ancients."[2] Other inscriptions on this work include prayers for himself and his student.

We know little about Senenmut's later life because he disappears from surviving inscriptions and documents before the end of Hatshepsut's reign. It is possible that he died young, or that he fell out of favor for some yet unknown reason. There is likewise no record of a wife or children which would normally accompany someone of his high position. The tomb that he built went unfinished and apparently unoccupied.

But Senenmut was allowed to build his funerary temple adjoining that of Hatshepsut herself, which speaks volumes about the close relationship the two of them shared.

15.19 Block Statue of Senenmut with Neferure. 40″ × 23½″ × 31″.
Werner Forman Archive/The Egyptian Museum, Cairo.

Sculpture and Wall Painting

Egyptians generally entombed portrait sculpture of the deceased person as an aid to his or her successful transition to the afterlife. Such statues were believed to serve as receptacles for the spirit of the deceased. The style of sculpture is characterized by compact, solidly structured figures that embody qualities of strength and clarity also found in Egyptian architecture. Egyptian sculptors worked by first sketching the outline of the figure onto the stone to be carved (in the manner of fig. 15.18 opposite), and then working inward. This triple figure sculpture (**fig. 15.20**) shows the Pharaoh Menkaura at the center wearing the crown of Upper Egypt. On the left is the goddess Hathor with her distinctive crown of a sun between bull's horns. One of the most important figures among Egyptian deities, she presided over natural cycles and fertility. She also wel-

15.21 Mask from Mummy Case. Tomb of Tutankhamen. c.1340 BCE. Gold inlaid with enamel and semiprecious stones. Height 21¼″.
Photograph: Jose Ignacio Soto/Shutterstock.

comed worthy souls into the afterlife, which she appears to be doing here by holding the king's hand. On the other side is a goddess local to the central Nile region where this group was recovered. The strength, clarity, and lasting stability expressed by the figures result from a union of portraiture and idealization. With formal austerity, all three figures stand in the frontal pose that had been established for royal portraits: the ruler stands with left foot forward, a false ceremonial beard, and the figures remain attached to the block of stone from which they were carved. Menkaura's face as he appears to stare off into eternity is a recognizable likeness similar to other known portraits. The inscription at the feet of the figures records the names of all three and lists the gifts presented at Menkaura's funeral.

Tutankhamen ("King Tut"), who died at age 18, is the best-known Egyptian ruler because his was the only Egyptian royal tomb discovered in modern times with most of its contents intact. The volume and value of the objects in the small tomb make it clear why grave robbers have been active in Egypt since the days of the first pharaohs. Tutankhamen's inlaid gold mask from his mummy case (**fig. 15.21**) is but one of hundreds of extraordinary artifacts from the tomb. Its formal blend of portraiture and idealism is distinctly Egyptian.

15.20 Group Statue of King Mycerinus (Menkaura).
Werner Forman Archive/The Egyptian Museum, Cairo.

15.22 Wall Painting from the Tomb of Nebamun. Thebes, Egypt. c.1450 BCE. Paint on dry plaster.

The British Museum © The Trustees of the British Museum.

Egyptian artists in all media generally depicted the human figure either in a completely frontal position or in profile. The artists portrayed each object and each part of the human body from what they identified as its most characteristic angle, thus avoiding the ambiguity caused by random or chance angles of view (see also *Pool in the Garden*, fig. 3.18).

In the wall painting from the tomb of Nebamun (**fig. 15.22**), the painter of the hunting scene presented a wealth of specific information without making the painting confusing. Flat shapes portray basic elements of each subject in the clearest, most identifiable way. The head, hips, legs, and feet of the nobleman who dominates this painting are shown from the side, while his eye and shoulders are shown from the front. Sizes of human figures are determined by social rank, a system known as **hierarchic scale**; the nobleman is the largest figure, his wife is smaller, his daughter smaller still.

The family stands on a boat made of papyrus reeds; plants grow on the left at the shore. The entire painting is teeming with life, and the artist has even taken great care to show life below the water's surface. Attention to accurate detail lets us identify species of insect, bird, and fish.

The hieroglyphs—the picture writing of ancient Egyptian priesthood—can be seen behind the figures.

Egyptian art greatly influenced that of early Greece, and the Greeks later developed one of the most important styles in Western art.

KEY TERMS

hierarchic scale – use of unnatural proportions or scale to show the relative importance of figures; most commonly practiced in ancient Near Eastern and Egyptian art

naturalistic – an art style in which the curves and contours of a subject are accurately portrayed

Neolithic – the period after the introduction of agriculture but before the invention of bronze

Paleolithic Age – a very ancient period coincident with the Old Stone Age, before the discovery of agriculture and animal herding

petroglyph – an image or a symbol carved in shallow relief on a rock surface, usually ancient

ziggurat – a rectangular or square stepped pyramid, often with a temple at its top

16

THE CLASSICAL AND MEDIEVAL WEST

LEARNING OBJECTIVES

16.1 Explain the artistic and architectural innovations of ancient Greece.

16.2 Relate the characteristics of ancient Roman art to Roman cultural values.

16.3 Summarize the characteristics of early Christian and Byzantine art.

16.4 Discuss the influence of Christianity on art and society in medieval Europe.

If your definition of the word "beautiful" includes something ideal or perfect, then you have probably been influenced by Classical Greece. Greece gave the West several concepts that we still value today. The Classical cultures of Greece and Rome dominated Western civilization from the fifth century BCE until the decline of Rome in the late fifth century CE. The later periods of Roman rule of Europe also saw the rise of Christianity, a faith that brought a wealth of new subjects to Western art.

The period between the fall of Rome and the beginning of the Renaissance in the fifteenth century is referred to as the Middle Ages or medieval period, a term that does little justice to the creativity of that era. If you attend a university,

then you are involved with an institution that had its birth during the medieval period. Meanwhile, Eastern Europe was dominated by the Byzantine Empire, headquartered in Constantinople (today's Istanbul). Byzantine Christianity is today known as the Orthodox Church. Hence, Christianity of one form or another was a major force in the art of both Eastern and Western Europe for 1,000 years.

Greece

The Greeks distinguished themselves from other peoples of Europe and Asia by their attitude toward being human. They came to regard humankind as the highest creation of nature—the closest thing to perfection in physical form, endowed with the power to reason. Greek deities had human weaknesses, and Greek mortals had godlike strengths.

With this attitude came a new concept of the importance of the individual. The Greek focus on human potential and achievement led to the development of democracy and to the perfection of naturalistic images of the human figure in art. The philosopher Plato taught that behind the imperfections of transitory reality was the permanent, ideal form. Thus, to create the ideal individual (the supreme work of nature) became the goal of Greek artists. Greek civilization passed through three broad stages: the Archaic period, the Classical period, and the Hellenistic period.

16.1 Europe from 117 to 1400 CE.

Archaic Period

In the art of the **Archaic period** (from the late seventh to the early fifth centuries BCE), the Greeks assimilated influences from Egypt and the Near East. Greek writers of the time tell us that Greek painters were often better known than Greek sculptors. Yet what we now see of Greek painting appears only on pottery, because very few wall paintings survive. The Euphronios Krater (**fig. 16.2**) shows the level of achievement of Greek potters and painters. It is in the Archaic "red-figure" style and depicts a scene from Homer's *Odyssey*: The dead Trojan warrior Sarpedon, wounds gushing blood, is carried off to eternity by the gods of Sleep and Death. The painter Euphronios signed the work; the word **krater** refers to the vessel's handled shape, traditionally used for mixing ceremonial beverages.

The Greeks honored individual achievement by creating numerous life-size, freestanding statues of nude male and clothed female figures. The Archaic-style *kouros* (**fig. 16.3**) has a rigid frontal position that is an adaptation from Egyptian sculpture. (*Kouros* is Greek for male youth; *kore* is the word for female youth.) The Egyptian figure of Menkaura (see fig. 15.20) and the *kouros* both stand with arms held straight at the sides, fingers drawn up, and left

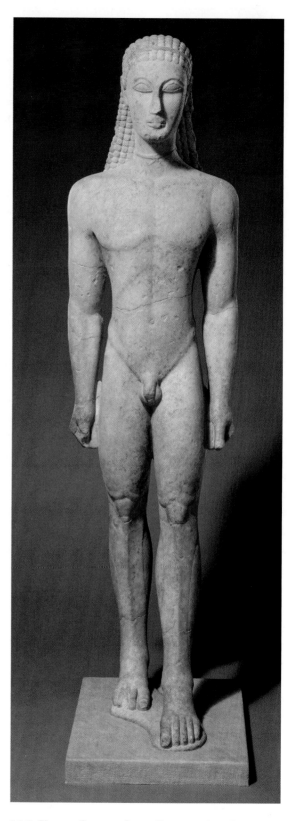

16.2 Euphronios Krater. c.515 BCE. Terra cotta. Height 18″, diameter 21¾″.

16.3 *Kouros.* Statue of standing youth. c.580 BCE. Marble. Height 76″.

leg forward with the weight evenly distributed on both feet as the figures stare off into space.

In spite of the similarity of stance, however, the character of Greek sculpture is already quite different from that of Egyptian. The *kouros* honors an individual who was not a supernatural ruler. The *kouros* thus adapted the Egyptian form to reflect Greek cultural values.

Classical Period

Within 100 years of the making of the *kouros* figure, Greek civilization entered its Classical phase (480–323 BCE). Greek aesthetic principles from this period provide the basis for the concept of Classicism. **Classical art** emphasizes rational simplicity, order, and restrained emotion. The rigid poses of Egyptian and early Greek figures gave way to a greater interest in anatomy and more relaxed poses. Classical Greek sculpture became increasingly naturalistic and began to show the body as alive and capable of movement, while maintaining an interest in portraying the ideal human anatomy.

The statue known as the *Spear Bearer (Doryphoros)* (**fig. 16.4**) is an excellent example of Greek classicism. Its sculptor, Polykleitos of Argos, wrote a treatise on the perfect proportions of the human form and created this statue as an example. Neither the book nor the original statue survives, but both are known from documents and later copies. Polykleitos envisioned the human body as a harmonious set of divinely inspired ratios. By studying numerous models and measuring key ratios such as the size of the head to the size of the body, he arrived at what he thought were the ideal proportions for a human. Hence the *Spear Bearer* combines actual observations with mathematical calculation.

The statue depicts an athlete who once held a spear on his left shoulder. Typical of Classical art, the figure is in the prime of life, and blemish-free. It is not a portrait of an individual but rather a vision of the ideal. He bears most of his weight on one leg in a pose known as **contrapposto**, meaning counterpoised. The Greeks and then the Romans used this pose to give a lifelike quality to figures at rest. Centuries later, their sculpture would inspire Renaissance artists to use the same technique.

Surviving Greek buildings are mostly religious, symmetrical, and based on a post-and-beam system, like the Egyptian buildings that influenced them (see fig. 14.4). However, Greek architects worked with a great deal more refinement to create more human-scaled structures.

16.4 Polykleitos of Argos. *Spear Bearer (Doryphoros)*. Roman copy of Greek original, c.440 BCE. Marble. Height 6′6″.

Museo Acheologico Nazionale, Naples, Italy. akg-images/Nimatallah.

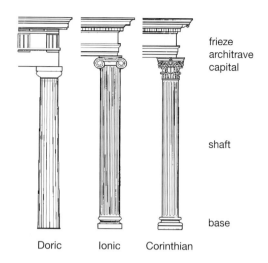

frieze
architrave
capital

shaft

base

Doric   Ionic   Corinthian

16.5 Architectural Orders.

The Greeks developed three architectural orders: Doric, Ionic, and Corinthian (**fig. 16.5**). Each order comprises a set of architectural elements and proportions. The most telling details for identification of the orders are the three types of **capital** used at the tops of columns. Doric is simple, geometric, and sturdy; Ionic is taller and more decorative than Doric; Corinthian is complex and organic. The Parthenon is in the Doric order, the first of the three to be developed.

The city-state of Athens was the artistic and philosophical center of Classical Greek civilization. Above the city, on a large rock outcropping called the Acropolis, the Athenians constructed the Parthenon (**fig. 16.6a**), one of the world's most admired structures. The largest of several sacred buildings on this site, the Parthenon was designed and built as a gift to Athena Parthenos, goddess of wisdom and prudent warfare, and protector of the Athenian navy. Even in its current ruined state, the temple continues to express the ideals of the people who created it.

When Ictinus and Callicrates designed the Parthenon (**fig. 16.6b**), they were following Egyptian tradition of temple design. Rites were performed on altars placed in front of the eastern entrance; the interior space held a 40-foot statue of Athena. The axis of the building was carefully calculated so that on Athena's birthday the rising sun coming through the east doorway would fully illuminate the towering (now lost) gold-covered statue. The entire exterior with its sculpture was originally painted in bright colors, which have worn off over time.

The Parthenon exhibits the refined clarity, harmony, and vigor that are the basis of the Greek tradition. The proportions of the Parthenon are based on harmonious ratios. The ratio of the height to the widths of the east and west

16.6 Ictinus and Callicrates. Parthenon. Acropolis, Athens. 448–432 BCE.
a. View from the southwest.
Photograph: Duane Preble.

b. View from the northwest.
Photograph: Duane Preble.

ends is approximately 4 to 9. The ratio of the width to the length of the building is also 4 to 9. The diameter of the columns relates to the space between the columns at a ratio of 4 to 9, and so on.

None of the major lines in the building is perfectly straight. The columns have an almost imperceptible bulge (called **entasis**) above the center, which causes them to appear straighter than if they were in fact straight-sided, and this gives the entire structure a tangible grace. Even the steps and tops of doorways rise slightly in perfect curves. Corner columns, seen against the light, are somewhat larger in diameter to counteract the diminishing effect of strong light in the background. The axis lines of the columns lean inward a little at the top. If extended into space, these lines would converge about a mile above the building. These unexpected variations are not consciously seen, but they are felt, and they help to make the building visually appealing and to correct optical illusions.

The sculptural program of the Parthenon shows specific aspects of the culture of that time. Athens had just concluded a successful war to resist a Persian invasion, and the costs of the Parthenon were paid from leftover war contributions collected from other Greek cities.

Surrounding the entire building just above the colonnade, the designers installed evenly spaced square panels called **metopes**; these, too, promote Greek culture. The theme of the metopes is the Battle of the Lapiths and Centaurs (**fig. 16.6c**): In an ancient myth, the Lapiths were ruled by reason, and the Centaurs were violent and unpredictable; when the Centaurs kidnapped the Queen of the Lapiths, the Lapiths went to war and defeated the Centaurs in battle. Just as order and reason triumphed in that ancient conflict, the democratic Greeks had defeated

the despotic Persians. Thus, recent events confirmed the ultimate triumph of the Greek worldview.

During the latter part of the Classical period (the late fourth century BCE), Greek sculpture took a turn away from the noble and serious idealism of the *Spear Bearer* toward a more sensuous vision. *Venus de' Medici* (**fig. 16.7**) is a Roman copy of a fourth-century BCE Greek original by Praxiteles, the best-known sculptor of this time. Nude goddesses were unknown in previous periods of Greek art. Its

c. *The Battle of the Lapiths and Centaurs*. Metope from the Parthenon. c.440 BCE. Marble. Height 67¾″.
The British Museum © The Trustees of the British Museum.

refined profile and modest pose are features of the Greek idealization of human figures. This figure came to represent a feminine ideal, and has strongly influenced many artworks since that time, down to the feminists of the twentieth century who rebelled against it.

Hellenistic Period

After the decline of the Greek city-states at the end of the fourth century BCE, the art of the Mediterranean changed. Although Greek art was still the strongest influence, the art was often produced for non-Greek patrons. Thus, Mediterranean art during this era is called **Hellenistic**, meaning Greek-like. The transition from Classical to Hellenistic coincided with the decline of Athens as a

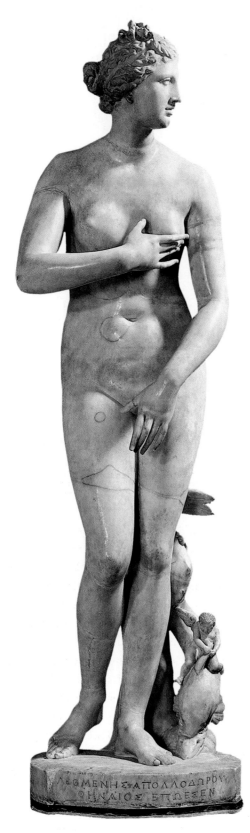

16.7 *Venus de' Medici.* 3rd century BCE. Marble. Height 5′.

Galleria degli Uffizi. © 2018. Photo Scala, Florence. Courtesy of the Ministero Beni e Att. Culturali e del Turismo.

16.8 *The Laocoön Group.* c.1st century CE. Roman copy of a 1st- or 2nd-century BCE Greek original, perhaps after Agesander, Athenodorus, and Polydorus of Rhodes. Marble. Height 95¼″.

Musei Vaticani, Rome. © 2018. Photo Scala, Florence.

city-state after it fought a useless war with the neighboring city of Sparta, and with the rise of an absolute monarchy in Macedonia that soon took over the entire peninsula. Most historians date the period from approximately the death of Alexander the Great (323 BCE) to the Roman conquest of Egypt (30 BCE).

In the Hellenistic period, Greek art became more dynamic and less idealized. Everyday activities, historical subjects, and portraiture became more common subjects for art. Hellenistic Greek art contrasts with Classical Greek art in that it is more expressive and frequently shows exaggerated movement.

The Laocoön Group (**fig. 16.8**) is a Roman copy of a Hellenistic work. In Greek mythology, Laocoön was the Trojan priest who warned against bringing the huge wooden horse into Troy during the Trojan War. He suspected that the horse, a gift from the Greeks, was a trick, as indeed it was: Greek soldiers emerged from it and opened the gates to let their compatriots in and attack. Later, Laocoön and his sons were attacked by serpents, an act the Trojans interpreted as a sign of the gods' disapproval of Laocoön's prophecy. Laocoön is shown in hierarchic proportion to his sons.

The rationalism, clarity, and restraint of Classical sculpture have given way to writhing movement, tortured facial expressions, and strained muscles expressing emotional and physical anguish. When this sculpture was unearthed in Italy in 1506, it had an immediate influence on the young Michelangelo.

Rome

The Hellenistic era saw the rise of Rome, a formidable new force in the Mediterranean. By the second century BCE, Rome had become the major power in the Western world. At its height near the end of that century, the Roman Empire would include Western Europe, North Africa, and the Near East, as well as the shores of the Mediterranean. Their governance of a multitude of unique peoples and cultures provides evidence of the Roman genius for order and practical politics. Roman culture has affected our lives in many areas: our systems of law and government, and our calendar, festivals, religions, and languages. Much Roman art, with its emphasis on public use, reflected the need to administer a huge empire.

The Romans were practical and less idealistic than the Greeks, and their art reflects these characteristics. Roman

16.9 *Bust of Emperor Vespasian.* Flavian Era. Marble. Height 21⅝".

Farnese Collection Inv. 6066. The National Archaeological Museum. Photograph: Raffaello Bencini. Reproduced with the permission of Ministero per i Beni e le Attività Culturali/Alinari Archives, Florence.

portraiture, such as the *Bust of Emperor Vespasian* (**fig. 16.9**), achieved a high degree of individuality rarely found in Greek sculpture. The emperor's wrinkled brow and forehead show that portraiture rather than idealization was the goal of the sculptor who made this work. The warts-and-all style probably grew out of the Roman custom of making wax death masks of ancestors for the family shrine or altar. Later, these images were re-created in marble to make them more durable. Roman sculptors observed and carefully recorded those physical details and imperfections that give character to each person's face. Even Roman civic monuments to its heroes were relatively realistic portraits.

The Romans' greatest artistic achievements were in civil engineering, town planning, and architecture. They created utilitarian and religious structures of impressive beauty and grandeur that had a major influence on later Western architecture. The outstanding feature of Roman architecture was the round arch, which the Romans utilized and refined in the construction of arcades, barrel vaults, and domes (see diagrams in figs. 14.5–14.8 and 14.10).

16.10 The Colosseum. Rome. 70–80 CE.
abadesign/Shutterstock.

16.11 Pantheon. Rome. 118–25 CE.
a. View of the entrance.
© Vincenzo Pirozzi, Rome.

An excellent example of a Roman public works project is the Colosseum (**fig. 16.10**). Built by the aristocratic Flavian family between 70 and 80 CE, it was originally known as the Flavian Amphitheater. The foundation of the Colosseum is an elliptical ring of concrete over 44 feet high. Brick, stone, and marble blocks complete the structure. The exterior is a three-story round-arch colonnade, with each level a different architectural order; each round arch on the lower floors opens to a concrete barrel vault. The principal use of the building was for amusements such as gladiatorial matches and wild game hunts. Its capacity was between 50,000 and 75,000 spectators, about as many as today's sports stadiums (a more accurate guess is impossible because much of the exterior marble was carried off during the Middle Ages). The Flavian family likely built the Colosseum to improve its public image and thus its legitimacy as rulers.

By developing the structural use of concrete combined with semicircular arch and vault construction, the Romans were also able to enclose large indoor spaces.

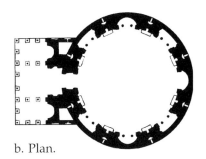

b. Plan.

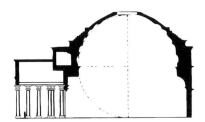

c. Section.

They erected many domed and vaulted buildings to provide spacious accommodation for large numbers of people. In the Pantheon (**fig. 16.11**), a major temple dedicated to all the gods, Roman builders created a domed interior space of immense scale. The building is essentially a cylinder, capped by a hemispherical dome, with a single entrance framed by a columned porch, or **portico**.

Because the interior of the Pantheon is dimly lit and difficult to photograph, we see it here in a famous 1734 painting (**fig. 16.12**).

16.12 Giovanni Paolo Panini. *The Interior of the Pantheon, Rome.* c.1734. Oil on canvas. 50½″ × 39″.

16.13 Roman Painting. 1st century BCE. Bedroom from the villa of P. Fannius Synistor at Boscoreale, Pompeii. Fresco on lime plaster. Height (average) 8´.
Metropolitan Museum of Art. Rogers Fund, 1903. N. inv.: 03.14.13a–g.

Whereas Greek temples, such as the Parthenon, were designed both as inner sanctuaries for priests and as focal points for outdoor religious ceremonies, the Pantheon was built as a magnificent, awe-inspiring interior space. The Pantheon's circular walls, which support the huge dome, are stone and concrete masonry, 20 feet thick and faced with brick. The dome diminishes in thickness toward the crown, and it is patterned on the interior surface with recessed squares called **coffers**, which both lighten and strengthen the structure. Originally covered with gold, the coffered ceiling symbolizes the dome of heaven. The distance from the summit to the floor is equal to the 143-foot diameter, making the Pantheon a virtual globe of space. At the dome's crown, an opening called an oculus, or eye, 30 feet in diameter, provides daylight and ventilation to the interior. Neither verbal description nor views of the exterior and interior can evoke the awe many visitors experience on entering the Pantheon.

Wall paintings show the Roman love of luxury. The majority of surviving Roman paintings come from Pompeii, Herculaneum, and other towns buried—and thus preserved—by the eruption of Mt. Vesuvius in 79 CE. In the first century, Roman artists continued the late Greek tradition of portraying depth in paintings of landscapes and urban views. The Roman painting from a villa near Naples (**fig. 16.13**) presents a complex urban scene painted with a form of perspective inherited from Hellenistic murals. As is typical of Roman painting, the receding lines are not systematically related to one another to create a sense of common space, nor is there controlled use of the effect of diminishing size relative to distance. (In other words, neither one-point perspective nor recession in space was practiced.) Perhaps the artist intended viewers simply to enjoy the pleasing inter-woven shapes, patterns, colors, and varied scale. After the collapse of the Roman Empire in the fifth century, representation of the third dimension ceased to be of interest, and the knowledge was forgotten until it was rediscovered and developed as a scientific system during the Renaissance, about 1,000 years later.

Early Christian and Byzantine Art

After the death of Jesus Christ in about 33 CE, his followers became convinced that he was the Son of God, who had physically resurrected from the grave. They began to collect and disseminate his teachings. From its beginnings in Palestine, the new Christian faith spread rapidly across the Mediterranean world and influenced the art of two empires: Roman and Byzantine.

Early Christian Art

The Romans at first regarded Christianity as a strange cult and attempted to suppress it through law. This forced the followers of Christ to worship and hide their art in private homes and underground burial chambers called **catacombs**. The earliest Christian art was a simplified interpretation of Roman figure painting, with a new emphasis on storytelling through images of Christ and other biblical figures, as well as through symbols. *Christ and the Apostles* (**fig. 16.14**) shows a beardless Christ, dressed like a Roman senator, only slightly larger than the faithful who surround him.

By the time Emperor Constantine acknowledged Christianity in 313, Roman attitudes had changed considerably. The grandeur of Rome was rapidly declining. As confidence in the stability of the material world fell, more people turned toward the spiritual values that Christianity offered. To reflect this change in orientation, Constantine pioneered a new type of imperial portrait, as we see in the *Head of Constantine* (**fig. 16.15**). Once part of an immense figure, the head is an image of imperial majesty, yet the large eyes and stiff features express an inner spiritual life. The late Roman style of the facial features, particularly the eyes, is very different from the naturalism of earlier Roman portraits, and Constantine's otherworldly gaze contrasts markedly with the realistic squint of the *Bust of Emperor Vespasian* (see fig. 16.9).

In 330, Constantine moved the capital of the Roman Empire east from Rome to the city of Byzantium, which he renamed and rebuilt as Constantinople (present-day Istanbul). Although he could not have known it, the move would effectively split the empire in two. In 395, the Roman Empire was officially divided, with one emperor in Rome and another in Constantinople. After Constantine's death the city again became known as Byzantium, capital of the Byzantine, or Eastern Empire. Over the course of the next century, the Western empire was infiltrated and attacked by nomadic Germanic tribes. They placed one of their own

16.14 *Christ and the Apostles.* Early Christian fresco. Catacomb of St. Domitilla, Rome, Italy. Mid-4th century CE.
© 2018. Photograph: Scala, Florence.

16.15 *Head of Constantine.* c.312 CE. Marble. Height 8´.
Museo dei Conservatori, Rome.

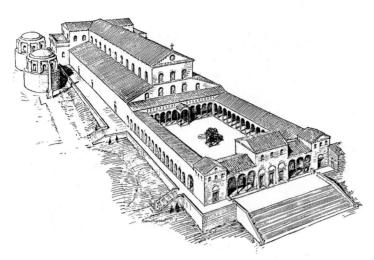

16.16 Old St. Peter's Basilica. Rome. c.320–35 CE.
a. Reconstruction drawing.

Kenneth J. Conant, Old St. Peter's Basilica, Rome. Restoration study.
Courtesy of the Frances Loeb Library, Harvard Graduate School of Design.

b. Interior view of basilica of Old Saint Peter's. Fresco.
S. Martino ai Monti, Rome, Italy.

© 2018. Photograph: Scala, Florence/Fondo Edifici di Culto—Min. dell'Interno.

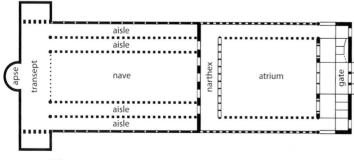

c. Plan.

on the imperial throne in 476, a convenient marker for the end of the Western Roman Empire. Under attack from the tribes, and weakened from within by military rebellions and civil wars, the political unity of the Western Roman Empire decayed, ushering in the era in Europe known as the Middle Ages.

The eastern portion of the empire, however, did not collapse. Indeed, the Byzantine Empire survived well into the fifteenth century. Founded as a Christian continuation of the Roman Empire, Byzantium developed a rich and distinctive artistic style that continues today in the mosaics, paintings, and architecture of the Orthodox churches of Eastern Europe.

Besides granting Christianity official recognition, Constantine also sponsored an extensive building program. Thus, in the late Roman and early Byzantine empires, we find the first flowering of Christian art and architecture. For example, Christians adapted the Roman **basilica**, or assembly hall, for use in public worship. The original Roman basilica was a long hall flanked by columns with a semicircular **apse** at each end where government bodies and law courts met. One of the earliest Christian churches was Old St. Peter's Basilica in Rome (**fig. 16.16**). Its long central aisle, now called the **nave**, ends in an apse, as in a Roman building. Here, Christians placed an altar.

In contrast to the external grandeur of Greek and Roman temples, early Christian churches were built with an inward focus. Their plain exteriors gave no hint of the light and beauty that lay inside.

The rapid construction of many large churches created a need for large paintings or other decorations to fill their walls. Mosaic technique was perfected and widely used in early Christian churches. Although other cultures knew the art of attaching pieces of colored glass and marble (**tesserae**) to walls and floors, early Christians used smaller tesserae, with a greater proportion of glass, in a wider range of colors. Thus they achieved a new level of brilliance and opulence.

Byzantine Art

We see the transition from Early Christian to Byzantine styles in the churches of Ravenna, an old Roman city about 80 miles south of Venice. Hoping to avoid the Germanic invasions, the Roman emperor moved his capital there in 404. When the Western empire fell in 476, Ravenna remained an important administrative center. However, Emperor

16.17 San Vitale.
Ravenna, Italy.
526–47 CE.
a. Exterior.

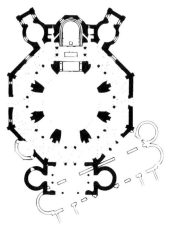

b. Plan.

Justinian sent an army from his capital of Constantinople and reconquered it in 540, turning it into a showplace of Byzantine culture on the Italian peninsula.

The most important sixth-century Byzantine church is San Vitale in Ravenna (**fig. 16.17a** and **b**). The octagonal plan below its round dome signals that this church lies over the tomb of a martyr, San Vitale. The exterior is plain, making the interior like an ornate jewel box.

The glittering mosaic compositions that cover most of the interior surfaces depict the figures of Emperor Justinian and Empress Theodora (**fig. 16.17c**) in addition to religious figures and events. In a blending of religious and political authority, Justinian and Theodora are shown with halos, analogous to Christ and Mary, yet both are royally attired and bejeweled.

The elongated, abstracted figures provide symbolic rather than naturalistic depictions of the Christian and royal figures. Emphasis on the eyes is a Byzantine refinement of the stylized focus seen in the *Head of Constantine*. (see fig. 16.15) Figures are depicted with heavy outline and stylized shading. The only suggestion of space has been made by overlap. Background and figures retain a flat, decorative richness typical of Byzantine art.

The arts of the Early Christian period were affected by an ongoing controversy between those who sought to follow the biblical prohibition against idolatry (the

c. *Empress Theodora* (detail). Mosaic.
© Cameraphoto Arte, Venice.

making and worshiping of sacred images) and those who wanted pictures to help tell the holy stories. The Byzantine style developed as a way of inspiring the illiterate while keeping the biblical commandment that forbids the making of images. Byzantine theory held that highly stylized

(abstract) and decorative images could never be confused with a real person, as a naturalistic work might be. As a result, the naturalism and sense of depth found in Roman painting gradually gave way to Byzantine stylization.

The apse mosaic in the interior of San Vitale (**fig. 16.17d**) shows Christ dressed in royal purple and seated on an orb that symbolizes the universe. He is beardless, in the fashion of Classical gods. With his right hand, he passes a crown to San Vitale, who stands in a depiction of the biblical paradise along with other saints and angels. The appearance of all these figures owes something to Roman art, but, in keeping with Byzantine style, they stand motionless and stare straight ahead. In their heavenly majesty, they seem to soar above human concerns.

In the eighth and ninth centuries, the Byzantine Empire was racked by the Iconoclastic Controversy, a debate over religious images that at times turned violent. In 726, Byzantine emperor Leo III ordered the destruction of all images of Christ, Mary, the saints, and the angels. He and his party believed that such images encouraged worship of the image rather than the divine being. They were soon termed **iconoclasts**, or image-breakers, and they punished persons who owned images by flogging or blinding them. (The iconoclasts did not resist all decoration; they permitted jeweled crosses and pictures of leafy paradises, for example.) Those who favored images (the iconophiles) argued that just as Christ was both god and human, an image of Christ combines the spiritual and the physical.

Although the emperor's decree was not uniformly enforced, the controversy lasted for more than 100 years, and it contributed to the split between the Roman Catholic and the Eastern Orthodox churches. There was a political struggle as well: The iconoclasts favored the emperor's power over that of local monasteries, which were wealthy with sumptuous images. The dispute finally came to an end in 843, when a church council officially overturned Leo's decree.

As the controversy subsided, the inside of the dome of Hagia Sophia was adorned with a new kind of image, Christ as ruler of the universe, or **Pantocrator**. This mosaic (now destroyed) became the inspiration for similar portrayals in smaller Byzantine churches such as the cathedral of Monreale, Sicily, where the mosaic of *Christ as Pantocrator with Mary and Saints* (**fig. 16.18**) shows the typical Byzantine style employing hierarchic scale to express the greater magnitude of Christ relative to Mary, the saints, and angels portrayed in rows below him.

By the tenth and eleventh centuries, Byzantine artists had created a distinct style that expressed Eastern Orthodox Christianity and also met the needs of a lavish court. The style had its roots in the Early Christian art of the late Roman Empire, as we have seen. But it also absorbed Eastern influences, particularly the flat patterns

16.18 *Christ as Pantocrator with Mary and Saints.*
Apse mosaic. Cathedral of Monreale, Sicily.
Late 12th century.
© 2018. Photograph: Scala, Florence.

and nonrepresentational designs of Islam. Eastern influence continued with the hierarchical sizing and placement of subject matter in Byzantine church decoration.

The Byzantine style is still followed by painters and others working within the tradition of the Eastern Orthodox Church. Clergy closely supervise the iconography and permit little room for individual interpretation. Artists of the

Eastern Orthodox faith seek to portray the symbolic or mystical aspects of religious figures rather than their physical qualities. The figures are painted in conformity to a precise formula. Small paintings, referred to as **icons** (from the Greek *eikon*, meaning image or picture), are holy images that inspire devotion but are not worshiped in themselves. The making of portable icon paintings grew out of mosaic and fresco traditions.

Even within the relatively tight stylistic confines of the Orthodox style, occasionally an artist is able to make icons that not only have the required easy readability but also communicate powerful feeling. Such an artist was Andrei Rublev, one of the most highly regarded painters in Russian history. His *Icon of the Old Testament Trinity* (**fig. 16.19**) depicts a story in which Jewish patriarch Abraham entertained three strangers who later turned out to be angels: Christians have seen this story as foreshadowing their doctrine of the Trinity. Rublev gave the scene a sweetness and tenderness through subtle facial expressions and elongation of bodies. The bright colors add intensity to the work, even in its present poor state of preservation.

16.19 Andrei Rublev. *Icon of the Old Testament Trinity.*
c.1410. Tempera on panel. 55½″ × 44½″.
Moscow, Tretyakov State Gallery. © 2018. Photograph: Scala, Florence.

The Middle Ages in Europe

The 1,000 years that followed the fall of the Western Roman Empire have been called the medieval period, or the Middle Ages, because they came between the fall of the Roman Empire and the rebirth, or renaissance, of Greek and Roman ideas in the fifteenth century. The age that gave us transcendent cathedrals also gave birth to memorable artworks in many media.

Early Medieval Art

The art of the early Middle Ages took shape as Early Christian art absorbed a new influence: the art of the invaders. Many nomadic peoples traveled across the Eurasian grasslands, which extend from northwest China to central Europe. Their migrations occurred over a long period that began in the second millennium BCE and lasted well into the Middle Ages. Our knowledge of them is derived from artifacts and records of literate cultures of the Mediterranean, the Near East, and China, to whom the nomads were a menace. Both the Great Wall of China and Hadrian's Wall in Britain were built to keep out such invaders.

Nomadic metalwork often exhibits exceptional skill. Because of frequent migrations and the durability and value of portable art objects, the style was diffused over large geographic areas. The gold and enamel purse cover (**fig. 16.20**) found in a grave at Sutton Hoo in Suffolk, England, belonged to a seventh-century East Anglian king. The distinct variations of its motifs indicate that they are derived from several sources. The motif of a man standing between confronting animals likely came to East Anglia via nomadic cultures.

The meeting of decorative nomadic styles with Christianity can be seen most clearly in the illustrated holy books created in Ireland. The Irish had never been part of the Roman Empire, and in the fifth century they were Christianized without first becoming Romanized. During the first chaotic centuries that followed the fall of Rome, Irish monasteries became the major centers of learning and the arts in Europe, and they produced numerous hand-lettered copies of religious manuscripts.

The initial letters in these manuscripts were increasingly embellished over time, moving first into the margin and then onto a separate page. This splendid initial page is the opening of Saint Matthew's account of the Nativity in the *Book of Kells* (**fig. 16.21**), which contains the four Gospels in Latin. It is known as the "Chi-Rho monogram" because it is composed of the first two letters of Christ in Greek (*XP*) and is used to represent Christ or Christianity. Except for *XP* and two Latin words beginning the story of Christ's birth, most of the page is filled with a rich complexity of spirals and tiny interlacings. If we look closely at the knots and scrolls, we see angels to the left of the X, a man's head in the P, and cats and mice at the base.

16.20 Purse cover. From the Sutton Hoo Ship Burial, Suffolk, England. Before 655. Gold and enamel. Length 7½″.

16.21 Chi-Rho Monogram (XP). Page from the *Book of Kells*. Late 8th century. Inks and pigments on vellum. 12¾″ × 9½″.
Trinity College Library. Dublin. Ireland. Photo © Tarker/Bridgeman Images.

Romanesque

The stylistic term **Romanesque** was first used to designate European Christian architecture of the eleventh and twelfth centuries, which revived Roman principles of stone construction, especially the round arch and the barrel vault. This term is now applied to all medieval art of Western Europe during that period.

Romanesque art developed in a Western Europe dominated by feudalism and monasticism. Feudalism involved a complex system of obligations to provide services through personal agreements among local leaders of varying ranks. In addition to accommodating religious practices, monasteries provided shelter from a hostile world and served as cultural centers and sources of education.

Monasteries and churches were also destinations for pilgrimages, a popular phenomenon throughout the entire Middle Ages. During this period believers undertook pilgrimages to mark important life events or to seek religious solace. The ideal pilgrimage was to the Holy Land itself, but because the region was under control of Muslims, this was difficult. Instead, most pilgrims went to places in Europe where important relics of saints were kept and venerated.

Visual artists aided pilgrimages by decorating churches and by creating splendid **reliquaries** to hold the sacred objects. One of the latter is the reliquary of Sainte Foy (**fig. 16.22**). The subject is a young Christian girl of the late third century who refused on penalty of torture to recant her faith. Her relics, reportedly including her skull and several bones, are housed in this portrait statue. The artist hammered gold sheets over a hollow wood sculpture before encrusting the exterior with precious stones. The head itself is not modeled on the saint, but rather on a late Roman portrait. The saint's remains arrived at Conques in southern France in the ninth century; his reliquary was created soon afterward, with later additions.

16.22 Majesty of Sainte Foy, statue reliquary in gold and precious stones. Conques, Trésor De L'Eglise Sainte-Foy (Sacred Art Museum). Height 33½″.
Photograph: akg-images/De Agostini Picture Lib./A. Dagli Orti.

16.23 *Christ of the Pentecost.* Saint Madeleine Cathedral, Vézelay, France. 1125–50. Stone. Height of tympanum 35½″.

Granger Historical Picture Archive/Alamy Stock Photo.

Religious pilgrimages brought large groups of Christians to remote places, creating the need for larger churches. Romanesque architecture made liberal use of round arches and vaults, creating a feeling of solid stability. Churches continued to have wooden roofs, but stone vaults gradually replaced fire-prone wooden ceilings, giving the new structures a close resemblance to Roman interiors. Consistent throughout the variety of regional styles was a common feeling of security provided by massive, fortress-like walls.

Romanesque churches feature imaginative stone carvings that are an integral part of the architecture. Subjects and models came from miniature paintings in illuminated texts, but sculptors gradually added a degree of naturalism not found in earlier medieval work. In addition to stylized figures from biblical stories, relief carvings include strange beasts and decorative plant forms. The largest and most elaborate figures were placed over the central doorways of churches. Such figures were the first large sculpture since Roman times.

Deviation from standard human proportions enabled sculptors to give appropriately symbolic form to figures such as *Christ of the Pentecost* (**fig. 16.23**). The mystical energy

and compassion of Christ are expressed in this relief carving above the doorway of the Church of Saint Madeleine at Vézelay, France. As worshipers enter the nave, the image above them depicts Christ at the time he asked the apostles and all Christians to take his message to the world. The image of Christ is larger in scale than the other figures, showing his relative importance. The sculptor achieved a monumental quality by making the head smaller than normal and by elongating the entire figure. Swirling folds of drapery are indicated with precise curves, and spirals show an imaginative linear energy. Surrounding Christ and the apostles are depictions of the peoples of the world; in the round medallions we see the signs of the zodiac and the monthly tasks associated with each.

At monasteries under the Benedictine rule—such as Saint Madeleine was during the Romanesque period—many monks and nuns regarded copying Christian books as a sacred duty. Secular rulers frequently funded such books as an act of piety, and regional styles of illustration developed. This led to a flowering of the arts of book illustration across Europe (see *Hildegard of Bingen: Visionary*, opposite).

CREATORS

Hildegard of Bingen: Visionary

16.24 "Inspired by heavenly fire, the 43-year-old nun begins to write down her visions." From *Scivias*.
Photograph: akg-images/Erich Lessing.

Born into the lower nobility, Hildegard of Bingen (1098–1179) began seeing visions while still a child. Her parents gave her a basic education before she joined an abbey of Benedictine nuns at the age of 14. In the monastery she led a life of achievement, composing liturgical music and writing books about botany and medicine. She was widely known as a healer who used herbs and potions, accompanied by prayers, at the appropriate phases of the moon.

Elected leader of her monastery in 1136, Hildegard went on to found two others in western Germany. The most distinctive of these was the one established in 1150 in Rupertsberg. Here Hildegard and the nuns under her direction produced many books, among them *Scivias* (*Know the Ways*), a record of her visions. She was at first reluctant to share or publicize her spiritual experiences, until the Pope learned of them in 1147 and granted her permission to do so. In this illustration (**fig. 16.24**), we see Hildegard receiving a vision from above, which she transcribes on a tablet as she dictates it to an assistant. She sits in a round-arched structure with a high ceiling and scant exterior windows, all characteristics of Romanesque architecture. (The original version of *Scivias* was lost during World War II. These pages are from a copy made in the early twentieth century.)

One of the most remarkable visions in *Scivias* illustrates Hildegard's vision of the cosmos as a whole (**fig. 16.25**). It is egg-shaped with an outer layer of flame. Near the top we see the red star of the sun with three planets above, which to her symbolized God and the Christian Trinity. Just inside this outer ring is another of hail and lightning.

The third ring is the sky, which Hildegard described as follows: "Beneath that zone was purest ether, with no zone beneath it, and in it I saw a globe of white fire and great magnitude over which two little torches were placed, holding the globe so that it would not exceed the measure of its course." This probably refers to the moon and the planets Venus and Mercury, which she thought symbolized the Catholic Church and the Old and New Testaments. The stars in the sky are "many bright spheres, into which the white globe from time to time poured itself out and emitted its brightness."[1] She thought that the phases of the moon were caused by the exhaustion and regeneration of its light as it fed the stars. Again, the moon symbolized the Catholic Church, which spent itself in deeds of mercy (the stars) and regenerated itself with divine light from God. All these layers illustrate a typical characteristic of medieval thought: to find in the natural world evidence of God's revelation that parallel the scriptures and church teachings.

The top of the oval is east, with west at the bottom. Each layer has a group of heads which we see at three cardinal points, giving off energizing winds. The innermost layer is the Earth, at the center of the universe, surrounded by clouds, sky, and water.

We cannot say that *Scivias* was a bestseller in its day, because all books were copied by hand and very rarely sold. But Hildegard was widely renowned across Europe. She went on four preaching tours, a most unusual thing for a woman to do at that time. At her death she left behind more than 400 letters, testifying to her communication with bishops, monarchs, emperors, and popes.

16.25 Hildegard of Bingen. *The Cosmos.*
Photograph: akg-images/Erich Lessing.

Gothic Art

The Romanesque style had lasted barely 100 years when the **Gothic** style began to replace it in about 1145. The shift is seen most clearly in architecture, as the Romanesque round arch was superseded by the Gothic pointed arch (see fig. 14.13). This new advance, coupled with the flying buttress, a support at right angles to an outer wall (see fig. 14.14), made possible some of the most spectacular religious buildings ever seen.

Gothic cathedrals were expressions of a new age of faith that grew out of medieval Christian theology and mysticism. The light-filled, upward-reaching structures symbolize the triumph of the spirit over the bonds of earthly life, evoking a sense of joyous spiritual elation. Inside, the faithful must have felt that they had actually arrived at the splendid Heavenly City.

Gothic cathedrals such as Notre-Dame de Chartres (Our Lady of Chartres; **fig. 16.26a**) were the center of community life. In many cases they were the only indoor space that could hold all the townspeople at once; thus they were used for meetings, concerts, and religious plays. But, most of all, they were places of worship and pilgrimage. Above the town of Chartres the cathedral rises, its spires visible for miles around.

The entire community cooperated in the building of Notre-Dame de Chartres, although those who began its construction never saw its final form. The cathedral continued to grow and change for more than 300 years. Although the basic plan is symmetrical and logically organized (**fig. 16.26b**), the architecture of Chartres has a rich, enigmatic complexity that is quite different from the easily grasped totality of the classical Parthenon.

16.26 Notre-Dame de Chartres. Chartres, France. 1145–1513. Cathedral length 427′; facade height 157′; south tower height 344′; north tower height 377′.
a. View from the southeast.
Gautier Willaume/Shutterstock.

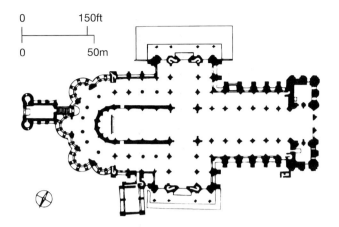

0   150ft

0   50m

b. Plan based on Latin cross.

c. West façade.

Photograph: Duane Preble.

One of the first cathedrals based on the full Gothic system of pointed arches and flying buttresses, it helped to set the standard for Gothic architecture in Europe. In its west façade (**fig. 16.26c**), Chartres reveals the transition between the early and late phases of Gothic architecture. The massive lower walls and round-arch portals were built in the mid-twelfth century. The north tower (on the left) was rebuilt with the intricate flamelike curves of the late Gothic style early in the sixteenth century, after the original tower collapsed in 1506. These flamelike decorations in the upper tower influenced late Gothic architecture elsewhere in Europe, so that the style was called **flamboyant**, or flaming. The word has other meanings nowadays.

The principal goal of the Gothic structural advances was to fill churches with light, a metaphor for the presence of God. Stained-glass windows fulfill this transcendent function in a specifically Christian fashion, in imagery that transforms the nave with showers of color, changing hour by hour. At Chartres, the brilliant north rose window (**fig. 16.26d**), known as the "Rose de France," is dedicated to the Virgin Mary, who sits in majesty, surrounded by doves, angels, and royal figures of the celestial hierarchy. Placing Mary and the infant Jesus in such a central and prominent place would help to instruct the illiterate about the importance of Mary for this church and for Christianity in general.

Like most medieval cathedrals, Notre-Dame de Chartres was also an active pilgrimage site. Pilgrims typically entered through the west doors and proceeded along the side aisles (see fig. 16.26b). They passed along the walls behind the altar, where smaller round chapels held relics of saints. The most notable relic here was a piece of cloth reputed to be the veil that Mary wore the night she gave birth to Christ.

The statues of the Old Testament prophet, kings, and queen (**fig. 16.26e**) to the right of the central doorway at the west entrance of Chartres are among the most impressive remaining examples of early Gothic sculpture. The kings and queen suggest Christ's royal heritage and also honor French monarchs of the time. The prophet on the left depicts Christ's mission as an apostle of God. In contrast to active, emotional Romanesque sculpture, these figures are passive and serene. Their elongated forms allow them to blend readily with the vertical emphasis of the architecture.

d. "Rose de France" window. c.1233.
Patrick Forget/SAGAPHOTO.COM/Alamy Stock Photo.

Whoever you may be, if you are minded to praise this door,

Wonder not at the gold, nor at the cost, but at the work.

The work shines in its nobility; by shining nobly,

May it illumine the spirit, so that, through its trusty lights,

The spirit may reach the true Light in which Christ is the Door.

The golden door proclaims the nature of the Inward:

Through sensible things, the heavy spirit is raised to the truth;

From the depths, it rises to the light.[2]

e. Old Testament prophet, kings, and queen. c.1145–70. Doorjamb statues from west (or royal) portal.
Photograph: Duane Preble.

Although they are part of the total scheme, the figures stand out from the columns behind them. Their draped bodies, and especially their heads, reveal a developing interest in portraying human features. Such interest eventually led again to full portraiture and freestanding figures.

The cathedral expresses an idea of Abbot Suger, who is generally credited with starting the Gothic style. At the abbey church of St. Denis, where Suger first united pointed arches and flying buttresses into the Gothic style, he had an inscription placed on the entrance door stating his idea of the church's spiritual purpose:

KEY TERMS

apse – a semicircular end to an aisle in a basilica or a Christian church; usually placed at the eastern end of the central aisle in Christian churches

Archaic period – the art of ancient Greece from the late seventh to the early fifth centuries BCE that assimilated influences from Egypt and the Near East

basilica – a Roman town hall, with three aisles and an apse at one or both ends; Christians appropriated this form for their churches

capital – in architecture, the top part or head of a column or pile

catacomb – underground burial places in ancient Rome

Classical art – the art of ancient Greece and Rome, particularly the style of Greek art that flourished during the fifth century BCE; emphasizes rational simplicity, order, and restrained emotion

coffer – in architecture, a decorative sunken panel on the underside of a ceiling

contrapposto – the counterpositioning of parts of the human figure about a central vertical axis, as when the weight is placed on one foot causing the hip and shoulder lines to counterbalance each other

entasis – a slight swelling or bulge in the center of a column, which corrects the illusion of concave tapering produced by parallel straight lines

flamboyant – a style of flamelike decorations used in late Gothic architecture

Gothic – primarily an architectural style that prevailed in Western Europe from the twelfth through the fifteenth centuries; characterized by pointed arches, ribbed vaults, and flying buttresses

Hellenistic – style of the later phase of ancient Greek art (300–100 BCE), characterized by emotion, drama, and interaction of sculptural forms with the surrounding space

icon – an image or symbolic representation, often with sacred significance

iconoclast – in Byzantine art, one who opposes the creation of images of holy persons, believing that they promote idolatry

kouros – an Archaic Greek statue of a standing nude young male

krater – in Classical Greek art, a wide-mouthed vessel with handles, used for mixing wine and water for ceremonial drinking

metope – a square panel, often decorated with relief sculpture, placed at regular intervals above the colonnade of a Classical Greek building

nave – the tall central space of a church or cathedral, usually flanked by side aisles

Pantocrator – literally, "ruler of everything;" a title for Christ, especially as he is depicted in Byzantine art

portico – a porch attached to a building, supported with columns; usually surmounted by a triangular pediment under a gable roof

reliquary – a container for holy relics

Romanesque – a style of European architecture prevalent from the ninth to the twelfth centuries with round arches and barrel vaults

tessera (plural tesserae) – a piece of colored glass, ceramic tile, or stone used in a mosaic

17

RENAISSANCE AND BAROQUE EUROPE

LEARNING OBJECTIVES

17.1 Describe how artists in the Early Renaissance were influenced by Classical art.

17.2 Discuss humanism as interpreted by High Renaissance artists.

17.3 Explain how Renaissance art in Northern Europe diverged from that of Italy.

17.4 Contrast the stylistic characteristics of Mannerist art with that of the High Renaissance.

17.5 Describe how social and religious events of the seventeenth century shaped Baroque art.

17.6 Explain the ways in which the Rococo style continued and broke away from the Baroque style.

The Renaissance was foreshadowed in the fourteenth century, reached its clear beginning in the early fifteenth century, and came to an end in the early seventeenth century. However, Renaissance thinking continues to influence our lives today, not only in Western countries but in all parts of the world where individualism, modern science, and technological progress influence the way people live. In art, new and more scientific approaches were brought to the quest for representational accuracy. The resulting naturalism defined the Western tradition for more than 400 years. In the succeeding Baroque period, which lasted into the early eighteenth century, artists expanded on Renaissance techniques to take art in a more dramatic direction, fueled in part by religious controversies that arose out of the Protestant Reformation and the Roman Catholic Church's response. Artists generally treated light, space, and action in a more dynamic fashion. Secular patronage also grew during this period, among both aristocrats and merchant class collectors.

The **Rococo** period that followed, centered in France in the mid-eighteenth century, was a more decorative and playful elaboration of the Baroque style. As with the Renaissance, techniques and attitudes developed during the Baroque and Rococo periods remained in force until the twentieth century.

The Renaissance

A shift in attitude occurred in Europe as the religious fervor of the Middle Ages was increasingly challenged by logical thought and the new philosophical, literary, and artistic movement called **humanism**. Leading humanist scholars did not discard theological concerns, yet they supported the secular dimensions of life, pursued intellectual and scientific inquiry, and rediscovered the classical culture of Greece and Rome. Humanist thought gives most importance to human questions, rather than to divine or supernatural matters. Humanists stress the potential value and ability of humans, using their God-given wisdom, to solve problems, and they seek rational solutions rather than divinely inspired ones. The cultural focus thus gradually shifted from God and the hereafter to humankind and the here and now.

The intellectuals of the time were the first in European history to give their own era an identifying name. They named their period the **Renaissance**—literally, *rebirth*—an apt description for the period of revived interest in the art and ideas of classical Greece and Rome. Fifteenth-century Italians believed they were responsible for the rebirth of "the glory of ancient Greece," which they considered the high point of Western civilization. Yet Classical culture was not totally reborn, because this heritage had never truly disappeared from the medieval West. Muslim scholars in Spain, Egypt, and Iraq maintained respect for the Greeks and translated their works into Arabic for their libraries. Muslim and European scholars of the thirteenth and fourteenth centuries then recovered these works and made them available in Latin. In essence, the Renaissance was a period of new and renewed understanding that transformed the medieval European world, and laid the foundation for modern society.

New values combined with technological advances brought forth a new style of art in the fourteenth century. Painting and sculpture were liberated from their medieval roles as supplements to architecture. Artists, who considered themselves anonymous workers in the Middle Ages, began to be seen as individuals of creative genius.

The art of the Renaissance evolved in different ways in northern and southern Europe because the people of the two regions had different backgrounds, attitudes, and experiences. The Gothic style reached its high point in the north, while Byzantine and Classical influences remained strong in the south. Italian Renaissance art grew from Classical Mediterranean traditions that were human-centered and often emphasized the ideal. In contrast, the art of the Northern Renaissance evolved out of pre-Christian, nature-centered religions that had become God-centered through conversion to Christianity.

We see the beginnings of the new humanistic art in the work of Italian painter Giotto di Bondone, known as Giotto. He departed from the abstract Byzantine style by portraying the feelings and physical nature of human beings. His innovative depictions of light, space, and mass gave a new sense of emotional immediacy to painting. In *Lamentation* (**fig. 17.1**), Giotto depicted physical as well as spiritual reality. His figures stand out as individuals within a shallow, stagelike space, and their expressions portray personal feelings of grief rarely seen in medieval art. These are real people who feel a loss, and even the angels in the sky underline the emotion of the moment.

In retrospect, Giotto is considered not only a precursor of the Renaissance, but also the reinventor of naturalistic painting, which had not been seen in Europe since the decline of Rome 1,000 years earlier. This human-centered realism is still an important current in Western painting.

The ancient Greeks had been concerned with idealized physical form; Roman artists had emphasized physical accuracy; and artists of the Middle Ages had focused

17.1 Giotto di Bondone. *Lamentation*. Scrovegni Chapel, Padua, Italy. c.1305. Fresco. 72″ × 78″.
© Studio Fotografico Quattrone, Florence.

on spiritual concerns rather than physical existence. In the Renaissance, as attention shifted from heaven to Earth, artists portrayed Christian subjects in human terms. Italian civic leaders expressed a desire to equal or surpass the glory of ancient Greece and Rome and to imbue their achievements with the light of Christian understanding.

Italy was the principal homeland of the Renaissance. In time the movement spread northward, but it did not flourish everywhere in Europe; it came late to Spain and Portugal, and it barely touched Scandinavia.

Early Renaissance in Italy

Artistic and intellectual developments in the Italian city-states were aided by a flourishing economy set against a chaotic political background. The wealth of Italian merchants enabled them to compete with one another, and with church officials and nobility, for the recognition and power that came with art patronage.

Italian architects, sculptors, and painters sought to integrate Christian spiritual traditions with the rational ordering of physical life in earthly space. Artists began an intense study of anatomy and light, and they applied geometry to the logical construction of implied space through the use of **linear perspective**. In turn, the careful observation of nature initiated by Renaissance artists aided the growth of science.

About 100 years after Giotto, Masaccio became the first major painter of the Italian Renaissance. In his fresco *The Holy Trinity* (**fig. 17.2**), the composition is centered on an open chapel in which we see the Trinity: God the father, Christ the son, and between their heads a white dove symbolizing the Holy Spirit. Within the niche stands Mary, the mother of Jesus, gesturing to Christ; opposite her is Saint John. Kneeling outside are the donors who paid for the painting, a husband and wife who headed a powerful banking family of that time. He is wearing the red robe that marks him as a member of the Florence city council. Below, a skeleton lies on a sarcophagus beneath the inscription, "I was what you are, and what I am, you shall become." If we view the painting from top to bottom, we move from the spiritual to the physical.

The Holy Trinity was the first painting to be based on the systematic use of linear perspective. Although perspective was known to the Romans in a limited way, it did not become a consistent science until architect Filippo Brunelleschi rediscovered and developed it in Florence early in the fifteenth century. Masaccio used perspective to construct an illusion of figures in three-dimensional space. The single vanishing point is below the base of the cross, about 5 feet above ground, near the viewer's eye level. Masaccio's perspective is so precise that we can see the interior of the illusionary chapel as a believable extension of the space we occupy. The setting also reveals Masaccio's knowledge of the new Renaissance architecture developed by Brunelleschi, which he based on Roman examples.

The figures in *The Holy Trinity* each have a physical and emotional presence that shows what Masaccio learned from the work of Giotto. In Giotto's paintings, however, body and drapery still appear as one; Masaccio's figures are clothed nudes, with garments draped like real fabric.

During the Italian Renaissance, the nude became a major subject for art, as it had been in Greece and Rome. The few nudes that appeared in medieval art showed little sensual appeal and often portrayed shame and lust. Under the influence of humanist scholars who sought to surpass the Greeks and Romans in the nobility of form,

17.2 Masaccio. *The Holy Trinity.* Santa Maria Novella, Florence, Italy. 1425. Fresco. 21′10½″ × 10′5″.
© Studio Fotografico Quattrone, Florence.

the nude became a symbol of human worth and divine perfection, a representation of the "immortal soul."

As Masaccio innovated in painting, Donatello did in sculpture. Donatello brought the Greek ideal of what it means to be human into the Christian context. As a young adult, he made two trips to Rome, where he studied medieval and Roman art.

Donatello shows himself as an ambitious artist even in his early work. His bronze figure *David* (**fig. 17.3**) was the first life-size, freestanding nude statue since ancient Roman times. In Florence, where the work was located, David was not only a biblical figure; his resistance to foreign domination of the Jews inspired the Florentines, who were surrounded by stronger enemy cities.

Although he was greatly attracted to the classical ideal in art, Donatello's sculpture was less idealized and more naturalistic than that of ancient Greece. He chose to portray the biblical shepherd David—slayer of the giant Goliath and later king of the Jews—as an adolescent youth rather than as a robust young man. The sculptor celebrated the sensuality of the boy's body by clothing him only in hat and boots. Every shift in the figure's weight and pose is expressive. The youth's position is derived from Classical **contrapposto**.

During the Renaissance, artists received growing support from the new class of wealthy merchants and bankers, such as the Medici family, who, with great political skill and a certain ruthlessness, dominated life in Florence and Tuscany. It is likely that Donatello created his bronze *David* as a private commission for Cosimo de' Medici, for the courtyard of the Medici palace.

A major influence on Donatello and other Renaissance artists was the renewal of Neoplatonist philosophy, embraced by the Medici family and their circle of humanist philosophers, artists, and historians. These intellectuals believed that all sources of inspiration or revelation, whether from the Bible or Classical mythology, are a means of ascending from earthly existence to mystical union with the divine. In this context Donatello's *David* was intended to be a symbol of divine beauty.

Another Medici commission is Sandro Botticelli's *Birth of Venus* (**fig. 17.4**), the first large mythological painting since Classical antiquity. Completed about 1480, this work depicts the Roman goddess of love just after she was born from the sea. She is blown to shore by a couple symbolizing the wind. As she arrives Venus is greeted by

a young woman who represents Spring. The lyric grace of Botticelli's lines shows Byzantine influence. The background is decorative and flat, giving almost no illusion of deep space. The figures appear to be in relief, not fully three-dimensional. Botticelli and his Medici patrons believed that an artwork need not have a Christian subject to be uplifting and beautiful.

17.3 Donatello. *David.* c.1425–30. Bronze. Height 62¼".
Museo Nazionale del Bargello, Florence. © Studio Fotografico Quattrone, Florence.

17.4 Sandro Botticelli. *Birth of Venus*. c.1480. Tempera on canvas. 5′8⅞″ × 9′1⅞″.
Uffizi Gallery, Florence, Italy. © Studio Fotografico Quattrone, Florence.

The posture and gestures of modesty were probably inspired by the classical Venus statue that Botticelli must have seen in the Medici family collection (see fig. 16.7). In her posture of introspection and repose, Botticelli's Venus combines the Classical Greek idealized human figure with a Renaissance concern for thought and feeling.

To place a nude non-Christian goddess at the center of a large painting, in a position previously reserved for Mary or for Christ, was novel. Botticelli's focus on Classical mythology was, like Donatello's, based on Neoplatonist philosophy, a central preoccupation of the business-oriented, secular art patrons, who commissioned most early Renaissance art.

The High Renaissance

Between about 1490 and 1525—the period known as the High Renaissance—Italian art reached a peak of accomplishment in the cities of Florence, Rome, and Venice. The three artists who epitomized the period were Leonardo da Vinci, Michelangelo Buonarroti, and Raffaello Sanzio (Raphael). They developed a style of art that was calm, balanced, and idealized, combining Christian theology with Greek philosophy and the science of the day.

Leonardo da Vinci

Leonardo was motivated by strong curiosity and belief in the human ability to understand the fascinating phenomena of the physical world. He believed that art and science are two means to the same end: knowledge.

Leonardo showed his investigative and creative mind in his journals, where he documented his research in notes and drawings (see fig. 6.2). His notebooks are filled with studies of anatomy and ideas for mechanical devices, explorations that put him at the forefront of the scientific development of his time. His study *The Fetus in the Womb*

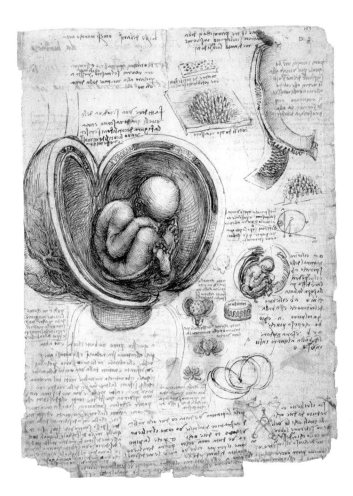

17.5 Leonardo da Vinci. *The Fetus in the Womb.* c.1510.
Pen and ink. 11⅞″ × 8⅜″.

17.6 Leonardo da Vinci. *Mona Lisa.* c.1503–6.
Oil on wood. 30¼″ × 21″.

(**fig. 17.5**) has a few errors, yet much of the drawing is so accurate that it could serve as an example in one of today's medical textbooks.

So frequently has Leonardo's world-famous portrait *Mona Lisa* (**fig. 17.6**) been reproduced that it has become a cliché and the source of innumerable spoofs. Despite this overexposure, it still merits our attention as an expression of Renaissance ideas. We can still be intrigued by the mysterious mood evoked by the faint smile and the strange, otherworldly landscape. The ambiguity is heightened by the hazy light quality that gives a sense of atmosphere around the figure. This soft blurring of the edges—in Leonardo's words, "without lines or borders in the manner of smoke"[1]— achieved through subtle value gradations, is a special type of **chiaroscuro** invented by Leonardo. Most important for the history of art, this work is a portrait of an individual, a type of art fairly common in ancient Rome and almost

unknown in the medieval period. Humanism influenced the belief that an individual could be worthy of a portrait.

The impact of Renaissance humanism becomes apparent when we compare *The Last Supper* by Leonardo (**fig. 17.7a**) with the Byzantine mosaic *Christ as Pantocrator with Mary and Saints* (see fig. 16.18). In the Byzantine work, Christ is portrayed as a lofty being of infinite power, the King of Heaven. In Leonardo's painting, Jesus sits across the table from us—an accessible person who reveals his divinity in an earthly setting, among disciples who look like us. Leonardo depicted a moment of human tension during the supper: Christ has just announced that one of the 12 disciples would betray him to the authorities. We see the various responses to this surprising statement in the bodies and expressions of the gathered disciples. Judas, the eventual betrayer, recoils in shock; he is the third figure counting leftward from Christ.

17.7 a. Leonardo da Vinci. *The Last Supper.* Santa Maria delle Grazie, Milan, Italy. c.1495–98. Experimental paint on plaster. 14´5″ × 28´¼″.

© Studio Fotografico Quattrone, Florence.

b. Perspective lines as both organizing structure and symbol of content.

© Studio Fotografico Quattrone, Florence.

c. Christ's figure as stable triangle, contrasting with active turmoil of the disciples.

© Studio Fotografico Quattrone, Florence.

The composition of the work contains a hidden geometry, which structures the design and strengthens the painting's symbolic content. There are three windows at the back and four at each side; the three symbolizes the trinity and three multiplied by four yields twelve, the number of apostles. The interior is based on a one-point linear perspective system, with a single vanishing point in the middle of the composition, behind the head of Christ (**fig. 17.7b**).

Leonardo placed Christ in the center, at the point of greatest implied depth, associating him with infinity. Over Christ's head an architectural pediment suggests a halo, further setting him off from the irregular shapes and movements of the surprised disciples on either side. In contrast to the anguished figures surrounding him, Christ is shown with his arms outstretched in a gesture of acceptance, his pose forming a stable triangle (**fig. 17.7c**).

Michelangelo Buonarroti

Like *The Last Supper*, Michelangelo's *David* (**fig. 17.8**) is an important work that expresses many Renaissance ideas. The biblical hero David was a symbol of freedom from tyranny for Florence, which had just become a republic. Other Renaissance artists such as Donatello had already given the city images of the young David, but Michelangelo's figure gave the most powerful expression to the idea of David as hero, the defender of a just cause.

Michelangelo took *David*'s stance, with the weight of the body on one foot, from the contrapposto of Greek sculpture. But the positions of the hands and the tense frown indicate anxiety and readiness for conflict. David's torso is slightly bent in an active posture that contributes to the drama. Through changes in proportion and the depiction of inner feeling, Michelangelo humanized, then made monumental, the Classical Greek athlete.

Michelangelo worked for three years on this sculpture. When it was finished and placed in the town square, most citizens of Florence greeted it with approval. *David* made Michelangelo one of the most important artists of that time, an artist who also produced significant works in painting and architecture (see *Michelangelo Buonarroti: Moody Virtuoso* on p. 288).

When Pope Julius II decided to redecorate the ceiling of his private prayer chapel, he begged, cajoled, and eventually ordered the unwilling sculptor to take on the painting commission. Michelangelo began work on the Sistine Chapel ceiling (**fig. 17.9a**) in 1508 and finished it four years later. The true fresco surface is divided into three zones (**fig. 17.9b**). In the highest are nine panels of scenes of the creation of the world from Genesis, including *The Creation of Adam* (**fig. 17.9c**). The next level contains prophets and sibyls (female prophets). The lowest level consists of groups of Old Testament figures, some of them Christ's biblical ancestors. *The Last Judgment*, painted later, fills the end wall above the altar. The most admired composition on the ceiling is the majestic *The Creation of Adam*, in which God reaches out to give life to the first man. Eve, not yet mortal, stares at Adam from behind God's left arm.

The work powerfully expresses the Renaissance humanist concept of God: an idealized, rational man who actively tends every aspect of creation, and has a special interest in humans. Michelangelo invented this powerful image, which does not exist in the Bible, to tell the story of the relationship between God and humanity from a Renaissance point of view.

17.8 Michelangelo Buonarroti. *David*. 1501–4. Marble. Height of figure 14′3″.

Accademia, Florence. Photograph © Studio Fotografico Quattrone, Florence.

17.9 Michelangelo Buonarroti. Frescoes in the Sistine Chapel. Vatican, Rome. Ceiling, 1508–12; end wall, 1536–41.
  a. The Sistine Chapel.

Vatican Museums, Rome, Italy. Photo Adam Eastland / Alamy Stock Photo.

b. Diagram of the Sistine Chapel ceiling.

c. *The Creation of Adam.*
Vatican Museums, Rome, Italy. Michele Falzone / Alamy Stock Photo.

CREATORS

Michelangelo Buonarroti: Moody Virtuoso

17.10 Daniele da Volterra. *Bust of Michelangelo.* 1565. Bronze. Height 32".

Florence, Bargello National Museum. Reproduced with the permission of Ministero per i Beni e le Attività Culturali/Raffaello Bencini/Alinari Archives, Florence.

Michelangelo (1475–1564) probably fits the stereotype of the temperamental but innovative artist. Over a long lifetime he created important works in sculpture, painting, and architecture.

Born in Florence, Michelangelo showed artistic talent from an early age. This disappointed his father, who, like most people at that time, regarded artists as on the level of manual laborers. Nevertheless, the young artist served apprenticeships with both a painter and a sculptor in his teenage years before his father sent him to the school run by the Medici family. There he learned of the humanist ideas that were brewing, and was exposed to important examples of earlier Renaissance art. He also made sketches of ancient buildings and studied human anatomy in the morgue of a charity hospital.

Although he excelled in many artforms, Michelangelo always preferred sculpture. He drew incessantly and often made wax or clay models of his projects. The models determined the size and shape of marble blocks to be cut from quarries. Fortunately, excellent marble was available only about 60 miles from Florence at the Carrara quarry; the artist was a frequent visitor and often supervised the selection of blocks for carving.

At the age of 24, Michelangelo achieved fame for his large *Pietà* (see fig. 4.21), which was put on public display in Rome soon after its creation. Breaking with the medieval tradition of artistic anonymity, he signed the work on the strap across Mary's chest, its most prominent possible location. Five years later came *David* (see fig. 17.8), made for a public square in Florence. These works created demand for his art among important patrons.

The first of two biographies written about Michelangelo during his lifetime came out in 1527. We know from these books and others that many of his contemporaries regarded him as a difficult person. He was at times contemptuous of fellow artists, and behaved in a fickle fashion with some clients. Even after he signed a contract, if a better job came along he sometimes slighted the first task. He never took on students or apprentices, and he never married, although he wrote erotic poetry to both men and women. Those verses have generated debate about his sexual orientation, but it is likely that he was celibate and solitary for all of his life.

Michelangelo created many of his most important works for the most prominent patron of that day, the Papacy. He painted both the ceiling and the end wall of the Sistine Chapel (see fig. 17.9a), works that have influenced artists for centuries. He also designed the eastern end of St. Peter's Cathedral, still in use today. In 1535, the Pope named him his chief architect, sculptor, and painter.

We see Michelangelo as architect in his design for the Campidoglio in Rome (**fig. 17.11**). The Pope commissioned him to create a suite of buildings surrounding an ancient Roman statue of Emperor Marcus Aurelius on horseback (visible at the center). The plaza is not rectangular; Michelangelo dealt with this by setting the symmetrical flanking buildings at an angle to each other. These show his complex design based on Roman buildings, with flat columns marking off bays holding decorated windows above and Ionic columns below. The pavement surrounding the central statue is also Michelangelo's design, a dramatic 12-pointed star in an irregular oval shape that compensates for the site by bulging further at the near end of this view. The compound as a whole is both striking and noble.

During Michelangelo's life, the common conception of artists changed from day laborer to cultured and educated person; he influenced this evolution more than anyone, as he was welcomed into the higher social circles. He was a devout but somewhat tormented Catholic, and doubts regularly plagued him; on his deathbed he said, "I regret that I have not done enough for the salvation of my soul and that I am dying just as I am beginning to learn the alphabet of my profession."[2]

17.11 Michelangelo. The Campidoglio at night. Rome. Begun 1536.

Susana Guzman/Alamy Stock Photo.

Raphael

Raphael was the third major artist of the High Renaissance. His warmth and gentleness were in sharp contrast to Leonardo's solitary, intellectual nature and Michelangelo's formidable moodiness. Of these three major creators, Raphael's work most frequently embodied the clarity and balance that marked the art of the period. His paintings present his awareness of the divine in human beings, the insight that was the driving enthusiasm of the Italian Renaissance.

In *The School of Athens* (see fig. 3.22), we see one of the clearest summations of Renaissance beliefs. Raphael organized the complex composition into symmetrical subgroups, all revolving around the central figures of Plato and Aristotle under the arch. Perspective lines help to frame our focus on them. Most of the figure poses in this work are based in Classical antiquity. More important, *The School of Athens* elevates human reason by presenting a philosophical discussion among learned people as an ideal. The Pope commissioned this work for the wall of a meeting room, so that those discussing Church business could be inspired by an ideal meeting of great people from the past. Rarely has humanism been so clearly expressed.

For Pope Leo X (a Medici descendant), Raphael made a series of cartoons for tapestries that would decorate the walls of the Sistine Chapel, below Michelangelo's ceiling. The tapestries have faded, but the cartoons retain most of the original vivid colors (**fig. 17.12**). Leo wished to glorify the early Church by commissioning illustrations of important events in the Acts of the Apostles, and Raphael responded by creating memorable and dramatic works. *Paul Preaching at Athens* is a diverse yet well-organized composition, as Paul preaches to the philosophically inclined Athenians. Among the audience is Pope Leo, just to the left of Paul. The message of this work, that reason can transmit religious truth, perfectly expresses Renaissance beliefs.

The Renaissance in Northern Europe

As the Early Renaissance was unfolding in Italy, a parallel new interest in realism arose in northern Europe, where artists were even more concerned than the Italians with depicting life in the real world. Jan van Eyck was a leading painter in Flanders, the region of present-day Belgium and adjacent parts of France and the Netherlands. He was one of the first to use oil as a painting medium. The fine consistency and flexibility of the new oil medium made possible a brilliance and transparency of color that were previously unattainable. His oil paintings remain in almost perfect condition, attesting to his skill and knowledge of materials. Later Italian artists admired and imitated the innovations of van Eyck and other Flemish artists.

On the same type of small wooden panel previously used for tempera painting, van Eyck painted in minute detail, achieving an illusion of depth, directional light, mass, rich implied textures, and the physical likenesses of particular people. Human figures and their interior settings took on a new, believable presence.

17.12 Raphael. *Paul Preaching at Athens*. 1515–16. Watercolor on paper mounted on canvas. 11′5½″ × 14′6¾″

Victoria and Albert Museum, London.
© V&A Images/Alamy Stock Photos/The Royal Collection, on loan from HM The Queen.

17.13 Jan van Eyck. *The Arnolfini Portrait.* 1434. Oil on panel. 33½″ × 23½″.
© 2018 The National Gallery, London/Scala, Florence.

event, Jan van Eyck placed his signature and the date, 1434, directly above the mirror—and he himself appears reflected in the mirror. What makes this a Renaissance work is the fact that it seems to take place in the next room, the figures and the space are so accurately captured. The concept of a painting as a window into a world similar to ours originated with works such as this.

In the early sixteenth century in Germany, Albrecht Dürer further developed the practice of combining instructive symbolism with detailed realism. His engraving *The Knight, Death, and the Devil* (see fig. 8.9) combines Christian symbols with familiar subjects in the Flemish tradition of van Eyck. Dürer practiced nearly every form of printmaking with a high degree of skill and dedication.

Dürer's two trips to Italy enabled him to bring back knowledge of Italian techniques of perspective and figure drawing, which he wrote about in several widely studied treatises. Also among the ideas that he gleaned in Italy was the increasing belief in the artist as a uniquely creative individual rather than a wage worker. He embodied this belief in several self-portraits, most especially in the one he completed in 1500 (**fig. 17.14**). He posed himself face-to-face with the viewer using a position and otherworldly gaze generally reserved for Jesus Christ. He appears thoughtful, confident, and perhaps even spiritual as he emerges from darkness. Dürer indicated his profession with his right hand (which held the brush) fingering a collar of marten fur, the material used for most paintbrushes at the time. At the left is his monogram and the date; at the right this ambitious-sounding inscription: "Thus I, Albrecht Dürer from Nuremburg, painted myself with indelible colors at the age of 28 years." The renown

Van Eyck's most famous work, *The Arnolfini Portrait* (**fig. 17.13**), is also among the most puzzling. It likely commemorates a wedding or a betrothal, although because the identity of the people is in question, we may never know. Many of the ordinary objects portrayed with great care have sacred significance, indicating the artist's skillful use of iconography. The single lighted candle in the chandelier symbolizes the presence of Christ; the amber beads and the sunlight shining through them are symbols of purity; the dog indicates marital fidelity. The bride holding up her skirt suggestively in front of her stomach may indicate her willingness to bear children. Green, a symbol of fertility, was often worn at weddings. As witness to the

17.14 Albrecht Dürer (1471–1528). *Self-Portrait with Fur Coat*. 1500. Limewood panel (Tilia sp.), 26″ x 19″.

Alte Pinakothek, Munich. Bayerische Staatsgemäldesammlungen. Inv: 537. © 2018. Photo: Scala, Florence/bpk, Bildagentur fuer Kunst, Kultur und Geschicte, Berlin.

that he achieved during his life in Northern Europe indeed approached that of Michelangelo in the South.

A major factor that conditioned art production in Northern Europe was the Protestant Reformation, which began in about 1521 when Pope Leo X excommunicated the rebellious monk Martin Luther from the Roman Catholic Church. Clergy allied with the burgeoning Protestant movement discouraged elaborate church interiors, and this led to a sharp drop in commissions for altarpieces and religious decorations. Therefore, a great deal of Renaissance art in the North was destined for private possession in homes.

Pieter Bruegel developed a new artistic vision of the Northern European landscape. As a young man he traveled extensively in France and Italy. Under the influence of Italian Renaissance painting, Bruegel developed a broad sense of composition and spatial depth. The special focus of his paintings was the lives and surroundings of common people. Such works that depict everyday life are still beloved today and are called **genre paintings**.

Toward the end of his life, Bruegel did a series of paintings representing the activities of the 12 months of the year. The work corresponding to January, *Hunters in the Snow* (**fig. 17.15**), is among the most highly regarded. Following the precedent set by manuscript painters of medieval calendars, who depicted each month according to the agricultural labor appropriate to it, Bruegel shows peasants augmenting their winter diet by hunting. New here is the emphasis on nature's winter mood as a backdrop for human activity. The heavy steps of the hunters are extended in the row of trees and the frozen ponds in the distance. The illusion of deep space, so important to this image, came from the innovations of the Italians and was also inspired by Bruegel's journey over the Alps.

17.15 Pieter Bruegel. *Hunters in the Snow (Jager im Schnee)*. 1565. Oil on panel. 46½″ × 63¾″.

Kunsthistorisches Museum, Vienna, Austria. akg images/Erich Lessing.

Late Renaissance and Mannerism in Italy

During the later sixteenth century, architects made a deliberate effort to rethink and extend Classical rules even as they used Classical forms. The most learned and influential architect was the Venetian Andrea Palladio. His famous Villa Rotonda (**fig. 17.16**) is a free reinterpretation of the Roman Pantheon (see fig. 16.11). It has four identical sides, complete with porches resembling ancient temple façades, built around a central domed hall. The villa's design hardly satisfies the architectural goal of livability, but it was not intended for family living; it was designed for a retired nobleman as a kind of open summer house for social occasions. From its hilltop site, visitors standing in the central rotunda could enjoy four different views of the countryside.

Palladio's designs were published in books that were widely circulated throughout the Western world. For the next two centuries, architects and builders from Russia to Pennsylvania often used motifs that he developed, and his designs have even reappeared on contemporary buildings.

Palladio's Venice became the scene of the last great flowering of Renaissance art. Using the newly developed oil paints on canvas supports, Venetian painters experimented with figure poses, compositions, and subjects. Responding to a clientele made wealthy from trading across the Mediterranean world, Venetian painting was rich and lavish, less idealized than the work of central Italian artists such as Raphael and Michelangelo.

We see an example of Venetian opulence in one of its most celebrated paintings, *Feast in the House of Levi* (**fig. 17.17**) by Paolo Veronese. This large work depicts a sumptuous banquet described in the New Testament that Jesus attended (we see him seated at the center). The artist set the scene under a Venetian arcade, using features borrowed from Palladio's buildings. Servants rush about, waiting on persons of various nationalities (including a German butcher in stripes at the right center). Not everyone in the work is sober. The atmosphere is one of elegant yet boisterous wealth.

Although today the work is called *Feast in the House of Levi*, it was commissioned by the monks of a monastery for their dining hall as a Last Supper. Veronese took such liberties with the traditional subject of Christ's bidding farewell to his disciples (compare to Leonardo's *Last Supper*; see fig. 17.7), that the religious authorities suspected the artist of impiety or heresy. They called him before the Inquisition, the tribunal where such cases were heard. This led to one of the first important trials of artistic freedom in the Western world.

Why, the inquisitors asked Veronese, did he include depictions of "buffoons, drunkards, Germans, dwarfs, and similar vulgarities" when none were present at the actual Last Supper? The artist's defense was one that most Western artists have eagerly embraced ever since: The artist should be free to interpret subjects as he wishes. Or, as Veronese said: "I paint pictures as I see fit and as well as my talent permits."[3] The Inquisitors ordered him to alter the painting and bring it more in line with what viewers of a Last Supper could expect. But instead of changing the work, the artist merely retitled it to reflect the lively party in the house of Levi. The controversy had no discernible impact on Veronese's reputation in otherwise liberal-minded Venice.

17.16 Andrea Palladio. *Villa Rotonda*. Vicenza, Italy. 1567–70.
© Boerescu/Shutterstock.

17.17 Paolo Veronese. *Feast in the House of Levi.* 1573. Oil on canvas. 18´4˝ × 16´7˝. Louvre, Paris.
© Cameraphoto Arte, Venice.

Meanwhile, in the former heartland of the Renaissance in central Italy, artists in the mid-sixteenth century both extended and questioned the heritage of Raphael and Michelangelo. Already during their lifetimes, those masters were celebrated for seemingly reaching a perfection of art. What to do afterward became a problem for younger painters. Some of them created works "in the manner of" the preceding generation. Others rebelled against the order and serenity of the High Renaissance and cultivated personal, idiosyncratic, "mannered" styles; thus their style is called **Mannerism**, even when they rejected some of the older artists' stylistic traits.

One of the most radical Mannerists was Rosso Fiorentino ("Red the Florentine"), who was born and trained in that center of the Renaissance. He knew well the works of Masaccio and Michelangelo, but developed instead a more tangled and problematic style. We see this in his painting *Moses Defending the Daughters of Jethro* (**fig. 17.18**). The Old Testament story tells of Jethro's daughters attempting to get water from a well but falling victim to some shepherds who abusively shove them aside in order to water their sheep; Moses happens by and forcibly evicts them.

Rosso created a highly confused composition of layered figures. A nude Moses is at the center, physically roughing up the also nude shepherds, who tumble into the foreground as one of Jethro's daughters expresses surprise. The artist drastically compressed the space, as we see in the well

17.18 Rosso Fiorentino. *Moses Defending the Daughters of Jethro.* 1523. Oil on canvas. 63˝ x 46˝.
The Uffizi Gallery. Florence. Reproduced with the permission of Ministero per i Beni e le Attività Culturali/Raffaello Bencini/Alinari Archives, Florence.

at the top against the sky and the daughters' faces in the upper right. Rosso also used **foreshortening**, or the depiction of an object in space so that it recedes from the viewer. We see this in the torsos of Moses and the fallen shepherd at the lower right. The well-muscled figures in this work show influence from Michelangelo, but the elder's Renaissance clarity and balance gives way here to Rosso's heaving energies and tangled limbs. The drama in this work is intense, but also somewhat contrived. Such pictorial strangeness is typical of central Italian Mannerism.

Baroque

During the **Baroque** period, which ran from about 1600 to about 1750, artists used Renaissance techniques to move art in the direction of drama, emotion, and splendor. The Baroque period had more varied styles than the Renaissance, yet much of the art shows great energy and feeling, and a dramatic use of light, scale, and composition. Partly under the influence of the Mannerists, Baroque artists set aside the balanced harmony achieved by Renaissance artists such as Raphael in his *School of Athens* (see fig. 3.22) and Michelangelo in his *David* (see fig. 17.8), as they explored more innovative uses of space and more intense ranges of light and shadow. Their art, with its frequent use of curves and countercurves, often appeals to the emotions first. Also, we can see a new degree of vivid realism in compositions using sharp diagonals and extreme foreshortening.

Many of the characteristics of the Baroque style were spawned and promoted by the Counter-Reformation, the Roman Catholic Church's response to the Protestant Reformation. In a series of decrees that emanated from the Council of Trent, the Church reaffirmed the mysteries of the sacraments, glorified the saints, and encouraged the arts as aids to prayer. Much Baroque religious art places a new emphasis on personal and mystical types of faith.

Italian Baroque

Michelangelo Merisi da Caravaggio's down-to-earth realism and dramatic use of light broke from Renaissance idealism and became the leading influences on other Baroque painters, north and south. Caravaggio created the most vivid and dramatic paintings of his time, using directed light and strong contrasts to guide the attention of the viewer and intensify the subject matter.

In *The Conversion of Saint Paul* (**fig. 17.19**), Caravaggio used light to imply a blinding flash, symbolizing the

17.19 Michelangelo Merisi da Caravaggio. *The Conversion of Saint Paul.* 1600–1. Oil on canvas. 100½″ × 69″.
Santa Maria del Popolo, Rome, Italy. © Vincenzo Pirozzi, Rome.

evangelist's sudden and soul-shattering conversion. The figure of Paul, in Roman dress, is foreshortened and pushed into the foreground, presenting such a close view that we feel we are right there. In keeping with the supernatural character of the spiritual events he portrayed, Caravaggio evoked a feeling for the mystical dimension within the ordinary world. Here we see a Baroque figure far removed from Raphael's logical, reasonable Paul who preached at Athens (see fig. 17.12). Some of the Roman clergy rejected Caravaggio's style; his emotional realism was too strong for people accustomed to idealized aristocratic images that demonstrated little more than gestures of piety.

Emotional realism and use of extreme chiaroscuro, especially in Caravaggio's night effects, influenced later

Baroque painters. Displayed in a dark chapel, Caravaggio's paintings take on a vivid, lifelike quality intended to heighten the religious experience.

We see an example of Caravaggio's influence in the work of Artemisia Gentileschi, who turned the style toward depiction of female religious heroes. *Judith and the Maidservant with the Head of Holofernes* (**fig. 17.20**) is a scene from the Old Testament story of Judith, who helped to liberate the Jews from foreign domination by visiting the Assyrian general Holofernes in his tent, getting him drunk, and then beheading him. This work shows Judith and her servant cleaning up the scene as they wrap their victim's severed head in a towel. According to the story, they then carried the head back to their people and displayed it as a symbol of resistance. The dramatic lighting, off-balance composition, and sweeping curves in bodies and draperies mark this as a particularly dramatic,

17.21 Gianlorenzo Bernini. *David*. 1623. Marble. Life-size.
Galleria Borghese, Rome. Photograph: dpa picture alliance/Alamy Stock Photo.

17.20 Artemisia Gentileschi. *Judith and the Maidservant with the Head of Holofernes*. c.1625. Oil on canvas. 6′½″ × 4′7¾″.
Photograph: Detroit Institute of Arts, USA/Gift of Mr Leslie H. Green/Bridgeman Images.

even lurid, example of the Baroque style. The artist portrayed Judith with many of her own features, showing that she identified with the heroine.

Gianlorenzo Bernini was as influential in sculpture as Caravaggio was in painting. Because Bernini's *David* (**fig. 17.21**) is life-size rather than monumental, viewers become engaged in the action. Rather than capture an introspective moment before the battle, as Michelangelo did, Bernini depicted David in the midst of his backswing, as he prepares to fling the stone at Goliath. *David*'s splayed limbs, twisting torso, and intent face underline the drama of the struggle.

Bernini's elaborate orchestrations of the visual arts are the climax of Italian Baroque expression. The emotional

17.22 Gianlorenzo Bernini. *The Ecstasy of Saint Teresa.* 1645–52. Marble. Life-size.

Cornaro Chapel, Santa Maria della Vittoria, Rome, Italy. Photograph: Stefano Ravera/Alamy Stock Photo.

intensity of his art is vividly apparent in his major work *The Ecstasy of Saint Teresa* (**fig. 17.22**), which features a life-size marble figure of the saint and depicts one of her visions as she recorded it in her diary. In this vision, she saw an angel who seemed to pierce her heart with a flaming arrow of gold, giving her great pain as well as pleasure and leaving her "all on fire with a great love of God,"[4] as she wrote in her autobiography. Bernini made the visionary experience vivid by portraying the moment of greatest feeling, revealing spiritual passion through physical expression. A skylight above provides dramatic lighting for the sculpture, and turbulent drapery heightens the emotional impact. Bernini's departure from the balanced, classical norm soon influenced sculptors throughout Europe.

The Baroque in Flanders and the Netherlands

The painter Peter Paul Rubens, a renowned diplomat and humanist, was the most influential Baroque artist in Northern Europe. Although he was Flemish, he worked for aristocratic and Church patrons across Europe. He studied painting in Antwerp, then traveled to Italy in 1600. During a stay of several years, he carefully studied the work of Michelangelo and the Venetians. When Rubens returned north, he won increasing acclaim and patronage; being a sophisticated businessman, he enjoyed an aristocratic lifestyle. His work came to be in such demand by the nobility and royalty of Europe that he established a large studio with many assistants. Rubens was noted for the exuberant quality of his nudes, and his paintings take on a similar sensuality. His free brushwork influenced many painters.

In *The Raising of the Cross* (**fig. 17.23**), we see Rubens's interpretation of a religious subject, painted for an important Roman Catholic cathedral in his homeland. The composition is arranged along a diagonal anchored at the bottom right by the well-muscled figure. This and other taut bodies in the work show the results of the artist's recent visit to Italy, where he saw works by Michelangelo and Caravaggio. At the same time there is a high degree of realistic detail in the foliage and the dog at the bottom left that show Rubens's Flemish heritage from Jan van Eyck and others. The action and drama in the work seem to burst out of the frame, led by the upward glance of Christ and the base of the cross, which seems to extend downward into our space. This visual dynamism, extending the action of the work toward the viewer, marks this work as a Baroque painting.

In the Netherlands a new type of art patron emerged in the seventeenth century as a result of recently won independence and booming international trade: wealthy middle-class merchants and bankers, most of them Protestants. These new patrons enjoyed and invested in contemporary art. Favored subjects were the same ones preferred to this day: landscape, still life, genre scenes, and portraits. Through Dutch painters, art became accessible and understandable in everyday terms.

We can see why Rembrandt remains one of the Western world's most revered artists in his large work *Return of the Prodigal Son* (**fig. 17.24**). The story comes from the Bible: A disobedient son cuts himself off from his family, demands his inheritance early, wastes it in disorderly living, and ends up in dire poverty. When he reaches the end of his rope, he returns to his wealthy father and asks for a job feeding the hogs. The father is not scornful or judgmental, rather the opposite. He tenderly welcomes the haggard and forlorn young man. Rembrandt portrays this touching scene with great reserve and economy. We see the prodigal son's ragged clothing, and the father's gentle embrace. We also see standing at the right, hanging back guardedly, the father's other son.

Rembrandt's composition shows the influence of the Italian Baroque painters in its dramatic contrasts of light

17.24 Rembrandt van Rijn. *Return of the Prodigal Son.* c.1668–69. Oil on canvas. 8′8″ × 6′8″.
The State Hermitage Museum, St. Petersburg.

and dark. The story, however, is not of the miraculous vision of a saint, as in Caravaggio's *Conversion of Saint Paul*, but rather a miraculous restoration of affection between estranged people.

Rembrandt was also a printmaker of considerable reputation. His many etchings show him putting the Baroque language of light and dark to good use in framing religious subjects, a common theme of his.

Jan Vermeer, another seventeenth-century Dutch painter, created genre paintings that raise daily life to a level of great solemnity. Unlike Caravaggio and Rembrandt, who used light for dramatic emphasis, Vermeer concentrated on the way light reveals each color, texture, and detail of the physical world. He showed immense passion for seeing, and apparent love for the visual qualities of the physical world.

17.23 Peter Paul Rubens. *The Raising of the Cross.* 1610–11. Oil on panel. One part of a three-part work. 15′2″ × 11′2″.
Onze Lieve Vrouwkerk, Antwerp Cathedral, Belgium. © Lukas—Art in Flanders VZW/Bridgeman Images.

17.25 Jan Vermeer. *The Kitchen Maid.* c.1658.
Oil on canvas. 18″ × 16⅛″.
Rijksmuseum, Amsterdam.

Vermeer's understanding of the way light defines form enabled him to give his images a clear, luminous vitality. Much of the strength of *The Kitchen Maid* (**fig. 17.25**) comes from a limited use of color: yellow and blue accented by red-orange, surrounded by neutral tones. The light has a mystical quality in this work; the act of pouring milk takes on the air of solemn ritual.

The Baroque in Spain and France

Many artists worked on behalf of the Church during the Baroque period; some worked in the service of the nobility. The most innovative of the latter was the Spaniard Diego Velázquez, who spent most of his career in the court of Philip IV, King of Spain. Philip was a broad-minded monarch who took delight in his chief painter's sometimes adventurous works. Such a painting is *Las Meninas* (*The Maids of Honor*; **fig. 17.26**), in which Velázquez plays an elaborate game. At first it is unclear who the subject is, because the artist himself stares out from behind a canvas, brush in hand. The maids of honor surround the king's daughter, who stares coquettishly at us, as if expecting something. She seems to be the center of the composition,

as she stands in the brightest light. Another courtier stands in an illuminated doorway in the background. Only when we see the mirror on the far wall, with the faces of the royal couple reflected in it, do we realize that this is a court portrait changed into a visual riddle. Velázquez painted a portrait of himself making a royal portrait! Like other Baroque works, this painting reaches out beyond its frame in a subtle dynamism of glance and image in which light and shadow play a major role.

Still-life painting enjoyed a new vogue during the Baroque period as well. A **still life** is a painting in which the subject is arranged by the artist on a tabletop, generally beginning with fruits or flowers, and often including other food items and domestic utensils. The term originated in the Netherlands, and Dutch artists were leaders in this field during the sixteenth and seventeenth centuries, as they painted elaborate still lifes celebrating the bounty of nature. Another important center was in Spain, where artists often isolated just a few items in dramatic light.

17.26 Diego Velázquez. *Las Meninas (The Maids of Honor).*
1665. Oil on canvas. 10′5″ × 9′.
Museo del Prado, Madrid, Spain. Photograph: akg-images/Erich Lessing.

17.27 Juan van der Hamen. *Still Life with Sweets and Pottery.* 1627. Oil on canvas. 33¼″ × 44⅜″.
National Gallery of Art, Washington, D.C. Samuel H. Kress Collection. 1961.9.75.

In the work of Juan van der Hamen we see influences from both schools. In *Still Life with Sweets and Pottery* (**fig. 17.27**), the stark lighting and bare setting are typically Spanish, but the rich bowls of fruit and pastries show northern influence. The artist here captured various textures of baskets, clay pots, and wood boxes along with the edible items. This work is also an interesting exercise in composition, as the artist created a rhythm of circular forms seen from various angles on the plain gray shelves.

During the Baroque period, French artists adopted Italian Renaissance ideas but made them their own. We can glimpse a clear view of Baroque aristocratic splendor in the architecture of the French royal palace of Versailles, built for King Louis XIV. The main palace and its gardens exemplify French Baroque architecture and landscape design. The Hall of Mirrors (**fig. 17.28**), at the heart of the palace, functioned like a stage set for the king's entrances and exits. The hall appears doubled in width by the nearly solid wall

17.28 Jules Hardouin-Mansart. *The Hall of Mirrors.* Versailles. Begun 1678. Length approx. 240′.
Hemis/Alamy Stock Photo.

of mirrors opposite the glass windows. Such glassworks were very expensive in that era, making the hall a display of opulence unique in Europe. Almost lost in the reflected splendor is the classical detailing in the pilasters and round arches. The ceiling is covered with paintings that depict the recent exploits of Louis XIV. At Versailles, Louis and his successors created a visual spectacle that supported their belief in the monarchy as the source of all power.

Rococo

By the 1730s in France, the heavy, theatrical qualities of Italian Baroque art gradually gave way to the decorative Rococo style, a light, playful version of the Baroque. Designers copied the curved shapes of shells for elegantly paneled interiors and furniture, and they influenced the billowing shapes later found in paintings. The arts moved out of the marble halls of palaces such as Versailles and into fashionable town houses (called *hôtels*) such as the

Hôtel de Soubise (**fig. 17.29**). Comparing this interior with that of the Hall of Mirrors at Versailles (see fig. 17.28) shows the delicacy of detail that exemplifies Rococo. Also, where the Versailles hall has a steady march of classically inspired round arches, the Rococo room is irregular, with organically shaped panels between the arches for a more fanciful effect.

The enthusiastic sensuality of the Rococo style was particularly suited to the extravagant and often frivolous life of the French court and aristocracy. Some of the movement, light, and gesture of the Baroque remained, but now the effect was one of lighthearted abandon rather than dramatic action or quiet repose. Rococo paintings provided romantic visions of life free from hardship, in which courtship, music, and festive picnics filled the days.

We clearly see the aristocratic life of ease and dalliance in Jean-Honoré Fragonard's painting *Happy Accidents of the Swing* (**fig. 17.30**). A well-dressed and idle young woman,

17.29 Germain Boffrand. Salon de la Princesse. Hôtel de Soubise, Paris. Begun 1732.
Photo 12/Alamy Stock Photo.

attended by a dimly visible bishop, swings in a garden. At the lower left, a youth hides in the bushes and admires her. The story line of the work is provided by her flying shoe, which has come off and will soon land in the young man's lap. Fragonard learned the lessons of the Baroque well, as we can see in the off-balance composition arranged along the diagonal, and the contrasts of light and dark visible in the lush garden. But Baroque drama gives way here to the sensual abandon and light-as-air subject matter of the Rococo at its best.

Or worst. The next generation of French artists and intellectuals would rebel against the social irresponsibility portrayed in this type of art, which they saw as merely fluffy. The Enlightenment was already breaking out across Western Europe, and its new ideas of social equality and scientific inquiry would soon shake European culture to its core.

17.30 Jean-Honoré Fragonard. *Happy Accidents of the Swing.* 1767. Oil on canvas. 31⅞″ × 25¼″.
Wallace Collection, London/Bridgeman Images.

KEY TERMS

Baroque – the seventeenth-century period in Europe characterized in the visual arts by dramatic light and shade, turbulent composition, and pronounced emotional expression

chiaroscuro – Italian word meaning "light dark;" the gradations of light and dark values in two-dimensional imagery, especially the illusion of rounded, three-dimensional form created through gradations of light and shade rather than line

contrapposto – Italian for "counterpose;" the counterpositioning of parts of the human figure about a central vertical axis, as when the weight is placed on one foot causing the hip and shoulder lines to counterbalance each other – often in a graceful S-curve

foreshortening – the representation of forms on a two-dimensional surface by shortening the length in such a way that the long axis appears to project toward or recede away from the viewer

genre painting – a type of art that takes as its subject everyday life, rather than civic leaders, religious figures, or mythological heroes

humanism – a cultural and intellectual movement during the Renaissance, following the rediscovery of the art and literature of ancient Greece and Rome

linear perspective – used to create an illusion of depth or three-dimensional space on a two-dimensional surface, it is based on the fact that parallel lines or edges appear to converge and objects appear smaller as the distance between them and the viewer increases

Mannerism – a style that arose in central Italy in the mid-sixteenth century, characterized by stylized and mannered expressions, often revolting against the balanced Classicism of the High Renaissance

Renaissance – the period in Europe from the late fourteenth through the sixteenth centuries, characterized by a renewed interest in human-centered classical art, literature, and learning

Rococo – a style used in interior decoration and painting in France and southern Germany in the eighteenth century, characterized by small-scale and ornate decoration, pastel colors, and organic arrangement of curves

still life – a painting of inanimate objects, such as flowers, fruit, other food items, and domestic utensils

18 TRADITIONAL ARTS OF ASIA

LEARNING OBJECTIVES

18.1   Demonstrate how key aspects of Buddhism and Hinduism are reflected in their art.

18.2   Explain how Southeast Asian art both absorbed and expanded upon influences from India.

18.3   Describe how Buddhism, Daoism, and Confucianism influenced Chinese and Korean art.

18.4   Discuss how Japanese art reflected both indigenous and external influences.

Human presence in Asia dates back to the Paleolithic period. Asia experienced a development of ancient cultures similar to that of Europe and Africa, from hunting and gathering to agricultural village societies, to Bronze Age kingdoms. (For examples of ancient Asian art, see Chapter 15.) Culturally as well as geographically, India is at the core of the continent (**fig. 18.1**). Many ideas that later permeated Asian societies originated in India and radiated outward. However, because each region of Asia also had its own local culture, outright borrowing was rare. Rather, we can trace the passage of ideas and art styles across the continent as they were adapted and modified in various locations.

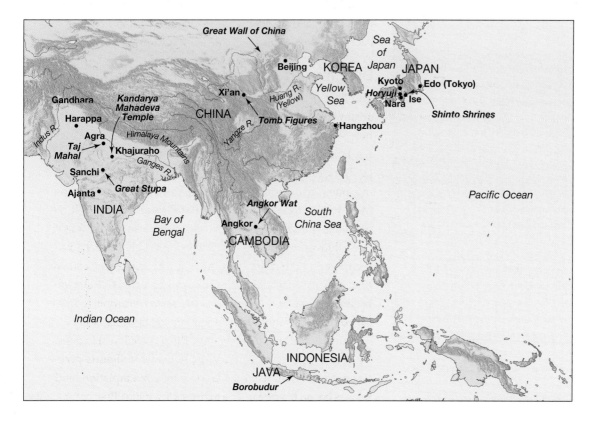

18.1 Historical Map of Asia.

India

Excavations at the sites of the ancient city of Harappa have revealed the remains of a well-organized society with advanced city planning and a high level of artistic production. The city was the focal point for a civilization that extended for 1,000 miles along the fertile Indus Valley between 3,000 and 5,000 years ago. (Most of this valley, where Indian culture began, became part of Pakistan after Indian independence in 1947.)

Ancient Indus Valley sculpture already shows the particularly sensual naturalism that characterizes much of later Indian art. This quality enlivens the small, masterfully carved male torso from Harappa (**fig. 18.2**). Comparing this figure with the classical Greek *Spear Bearer* (see fig. 16.4) is highly instructive. The male torso seems fleshy; the

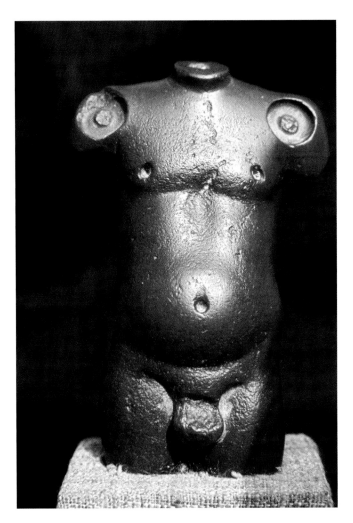

18.2 Male Torso. Harappa, Indus Valley. c.2400–2000 BCE. Limestone. Height 3½″.

National Museum of India, New Delhi. Photograph: akg-images/Jean-Louis Nou.

underlying bone structure difficult to see. *Spear Bearer,* in contrast, seems to have flesh integrated with a skeleton.

Very few works of art survive from the period between 1800 BCE, when the Indus Valley Civilization declined, and 300 BCE, when the first Buddhist art appeared. Nevertheless, the years in that interval were important for the development of Indian culture, as the set of beliefs known as Hinduism took form at that time.

Because a great deal of our knowledge of Indian culture from this era comes from hymns called Vedas, it is called the Vedic Period. Hindu culture and belief arose over a period of more than 1,000 years, during which time Indo-Aryan migrants from the northwest mingled with indigenous peoples. Vedic Period beliefs that influenced later Indian thought include the idea that the universe evolves in repeated cycles of creation and destruction; that individuals are reincarnated after death; and that there is one supreme form of wisdom. The Vedas and the related Upanishads (philosophical works) that state these beliefs are still regarded as sacred by many Indians.

In the sixth century BCE, two influential spiritual leaders preached variations on Hindu beliefs. They were Siddhartha Gautama (563–483 BCE), founder of Buddhism, and Mahavira (599–527 BCE), founder of Jainism. Although most Indians today are Hindus, Buddhism dominated the formative years of the development of Indian art, and it became a major cultural factor elsewhere in Asia.

Buddhist Art

The Buddhist religion began when Siddhartha Gautama achieved enlightenment. Seeking an answer to the question of human suffering, he arrived at what Buddhists call the Four Noble Truths: (1) Existence is full of suffering. (2) The cause of suffering is desire. (3) To eliminate suffering, one must eliminate desire. (4) To eliminate desire, one must follow the moral code of the Eightfold Path, which regulates speech, thought, and action. He also taught that if one achieves enlightenment, the endless cycle of death and rebirth will be broken, and the believer will experience a final rebirth (Nirvana) in a pure spiritual realm. Siddhartha began to attract followers in the late sixth century BCE; they called him the "Enlightened One," or the Buddha.

Early Buddhism did not allow the production of images. By about the second century CE, however, religious practice needed visual icons as support for contemplation, and images began to appear. The many styles of Buddhist art and

18.3 The Great Stupa. Sanchi, India. 10 BCE–15 CE.
   a. Exterior
      Photograph: veice/Shutterstock.

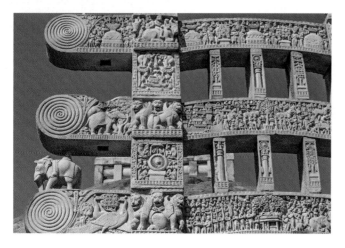

b. A view of the buddhist sculpture in Sanchi temple.
   © Andrzej Rostek/Shutterstock.

architecture vary according to the cultures that produced them. As Buddhism spread from India to Southeast Asia and across central Asia to China, Korea, and Japan, it interacted fruitfully with native religious and aesthetic traditions.

An excellent example of early Indian Buddhist art is the domelike structure called the **stupa**, which evolved from earlier burial mounds. The Great Stupa at Sanchi (**fig. 18.3a** and **b**) was built over a period of about 200 years.

Four gates, the last additions to the structure, are oriented to the four cardinal directions. The devout walk around the stupa in a ritual path, symbolically taking the Path of Life around the World Mountain. Such stupas were erected at sacred locations, and relics (items belonging to a holy person) were usually buried in their core.

The four gateways to the Great Stupa include layers of sculpture in relief. These tell the story of the Buddha's life, but without depicting him directly. The characteristic sensuousness that we observed in the male torso from Harappa still enlivens these early monuments.

We can trace the evolution of Buddhist architecture (**fig. 18.4**) from its origin in India to its later manifestations in other parts of Asia. Buddhist pagodas developed from a merging of the Indian stupa and the traditional Chinese watchtower. The resulting stepped tower structure was in turn adopted and changed by the Japanese.

Alexander the Great's conquest of large parts of West Asia in the fourth century BCE caused one of the world's great artistic fusions. This region of today's Afghanistan and Pakistan, then called Gandhara, continued its contacts with the West during the peak years of the Roman Empire. Buddhist sculptors in Gandhara developed a distinctive style that owes about equal amounts to East

18.4 Evolution of Buddhist Architecture.

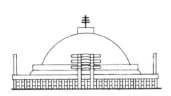

a. Early Indian stupa.
3rd century to early
1st century BCE.

b. Later Indian stupa.
2nd century CE.

c. Chinese pagoda.
5th to 7th centuries CE.

d. Japanese pagoda.
7th century CE.

and West; the Bodhisattva from Gandhara (**fig. 18.5**) is an excellent example. Here the sculptor shows a knowledge of the realism of Roman portraiture, as well as the classical Greek method of revealing a subject's body beneath the folds of the drapery in the legs. The figure's pose, with the weight borne mostly on one leg, owes a great deal to the contrapposto of Classical art. The subject, however, is Buddhist. A **bodhisattva** is a person who is on the point of achieving enlightenment, but delays it in order to remain on Earth and teach others. Bodhisattvas are usually depicted wearing rich garments and jewels.

The Indian Gupta dynasty (c.320–540 CE) is notable for major developments in politics, law, mathematics, and the arts. In the visual arts, the Gupta style combines native Indian ways of seeing with the naturalism of the Gandhara. Although slightly damaged, the carved stone Standing Buddha (**fig. 18.6**) is a fine example of Gupta sculpture. In its cool, idealized perfection, the refined Gupta style marks a period of high achievement in Indian art. The simplified mass of the figure seems to push out from within as though the body were inflated with breath. The rounded form is enhanced by curves repeated rhythmically down the figure. The drapery seems wet as it clings to and accentuates the softness of the body.

18.5 Bodhisattva. 2nd–3rd centuries. N.W. Pakistan, Gandhara region.
Photograph: akg-images/Jean-Louis Nou.

18.6 Standing Buddha. 5th century. Red Sandstone. Height 5'3".
Photograph: akg-images/De Agostini Picture Lib./G. Nimatallah.

18.7 "Beautiful Bodhisattva" Padmapani (detail).
Fresco from Cave 1. Ajanta, India. c.600–50.
Photograph: Duane Preble.

The Standing Buddha shows several conventions in representing the Buddha that remained in force for centuries. He wears the simple garment of a monk. His earlobes are long, referring to his earlier life as a wealthy prince who wore expensive earrings. The topknot on his head symbolizes his enlightenment. He is also shown in meditation; this latter characteristic contrasts vividly with Western depictions of God and Christ as active beings.

We can see similar elegance and linear refinement in the noble figure known as the "Beautiful Bodhisattva" Padmapani (**fig. 18.7**), part of a series of elaborate paintings in the Ajanta Caves in central India. The fine linear definition of the figure accents full, rounded shapes, exemplifying the relaxed opulence of the Gupta style. When Buddhism began to spread to China and Southeast Asia, this was the style that came with it.

Hindu Art

Hinduism recognizes three principal gods: Brahma, the creator of all things; Vishnu, the sustainer; and Shiva, the destroyer. These three gods intervene in human affairs at appropriate moments, either to guarantee the continuing evolution of the cosmos, or to restore the proper balance of good and evil forces in the world. Most Hindu devotional practices are done individually (rather than in a group, as is common in Christian worship), and Shiva is the god most often venerated in architecture and sculpture.

The Hindu temple is a major architectural form of India, and one of the world's most distinctive. It typically comprises two parts: a porch, for the preparation and purification of the worshiper, and the Womb Chamber, called in Sanskrit the *garba griha*, the sacred room where an image of the god is kept.

The Kandarya Mahadeva Temple at Khajuraho in north-central India (**fig. 18.8a**) is one of the most spectacular and best preserved. A stairway leads to not one, but several porches, which allow access to the *garba griha*. The sacred chamber is marked on the outside by a tall tower that has replicas of itself on its sides. The rounded projecting forms, symbolizing both male and female sexuality, seem to celebrate the procreative energy existing in nature and within ourselves.

Shown in figure **18.8b** is one of hundreds of erotic scenes from the abundant sculpture on the outside of Kandarya Mahadeva Temple. To the Hindu worshiper, union with God is filled with a joy analogous to the sensual pleasure of erotic love. The natural beauty and fullness of the human figures emphasize maleness and femaleness. Fullness seems to come from within the rounded forms, as we saw in the more ancient male torso from Harappa (see fig. 18.2). The intertwining figures symbolize divine love in human form, an allegory of ultimate spiritual unity.

In Hindu belief Shiva encompasses in cyclic time the creation, preservation, dissolution, and re-creation of the universe. Shiva shows these roles in sculptures that are as rich in iconography as any in the world. An eleventh-century bronze from South India, *Shiva as Lord of the Dance* (**fig. 18.9**), shows Shiva performing the cosmic dance within the orb of the sun. He tramples on the monster of ignorance within the encircling flame, which is the purifying fire of destruction and creation. He taps on a small drum (upper left) to mark the cosmic rhythm of death and rebirth; at the upper right, the opposite hand holds the consuming fire.

18.8 Kandarya Mahadeva Temple. Khajuraho, India.
10th–11th centuries.
a. Exterior
© Zzvet/Shutterstock.

b. Scene from Kandarya Mahadeva Temple, Khajuraho,
Madhya Pradesh, India. Erotic reliefs. Chandella
dynasty. 1025–50.
© hecke/123RF.

As he moves, the universe is reflected as light from his
limbs. The sculpture implies movement so thoroughly that
motion seems contained in every aspect of the piece. Each
part is alive with the rhythms of an ancient ritual dance.
His heavily ornamented hair flies outward. Multiple arms

18.9 *Shiva as Lord of the Dance.* India (Tamil Nadu) Late
12th–early 13th centuries. Copper Alloy. Height 24¾".
The Metropolitan Museum of Art/Rogers Fund/Harris Brisbane Dick Fund, 1964
(64.251).

increase the sense of movement, while his face is composed
and impassive, indicating that there is nothing to fear.

Most of India was conquered by Islamic Mughal rulers in the early sixteenth century. Several local Indian art
styles soon arose in the foothills of the Himalayas, as artists
influenced by Muslim techniques began to render Hindu
subjects. We see the Basohli style to good advantage in *The
Approach of Krishna* (**fig. 18.10**). A woman waits breathlessly
for her lover, the blue-skinned god Krishna. Like many
other Indian works, this painting uses erotic desire as a
symbol for the spiritual longing for union with the divine.
The inscription reads, "Friend, give up your waywardness
of mind." The bright red and blue colors symbolize the
emotional states of expectancy and desire for the crowned
and bejeweled Krishna, who brings a fragrant flower.
The use of color to depict emotional states is a technique
that modern artists in the West would take up in the late
nineteenth and early twentieth centuries, though without
knowing these early examples.

18.10 *The Approach of Krishna.* Pahari region, India. c.1660–70. Basohli style. Color, silver, and beetle wings on paper. 6⅞″ × 10¼″.
The Cleveland Museum of Art, OH, USA/The Cleveland Museum of Art, Edward L. Whittemore Fund/Bridgeman Images.

Southeast Asia

The Bronze Age in Southeast Asia began when that metal was first imported into the region, in about 800 BCE. Soon after, the major cultural division of the region appeared: The eastern coast, encompassing most of what is now Vietnam, fell under Chinese influence; most of the remainder willingly adopted and transformed cultural influences from India.

Buddhism and Hinduism both spread southward and eastward from India with traders and merchants. Early Southeast Asian art is primarily Buddhist; later monuments combine motifs, gods, and figures from both religions, as each region of Southeast Asia developed its own interpretation of the major Indian styles.

By any standard, Borobudur (**fig. 18.11a**) must rank among the major works of world art. Built about 800 CE on the island of Java (now part of Indonesia), it is an extremely elaborate version of an Indian stupa, or sacred mountain. Rising from a relatively flat plain, it stands above the local surroundings, measuring 105 feet high and 408 feet on a side. It is oriented to the four cardinal directions, with stairways at the four midpoints.

Pilgrims who come for spiritual refreshment may enter at any opening and then walk around and climb the various terraces in a clockwise direction, as at the Great Stupa at Sanchi. More than 10 miles of relief sculpture adorn the various corridors (**fig. 18.11b**), telling stories that duplicate the journey to enlightenment. On the lower levels, the reliefs deal with the struggle of existence and the cycle of death and rebirth. Then come reliefs depicting the life of the Buddha. As pilgrims walk in these corridors, the high walls prevent them from seeing out, and the curves in the path limit the view ahead. Upper terrace reliefs depict the ideal world of paradise. However, there is still more to come.

18.11 Borobudur. c.800. Java, Indonesia.

  a. Aerial view.

b. Borobudur Buddhist
temple. Stonework
reliefs in lower galleries.

18.12 Angkor Wat. Cambodia. c.1120–50. West entrance.
Vladimir Korostyshevskiy/Shutterstock.

The final four circular levels permit the pilgrim to look out over the landscape and take in the broad view, suggesting enlightenment. Each of the 72 small, hollow stupas contains a statue of a seated Buddha that is only dimly visible from the outside. At the very top is a sealed stupa whose contents the pilgrim can only guess at. Thus, Borobudur presents the Buddhist conception of the pathway through the cycles of birth and death, which culminates in enlightenment.

The sacred mountain of Borobudur was a principal influence on the Cambodian temple of Angkor Wat (**fig. 18.12**), which was erected in the twelfth century near the capital of the Khmer empire. This was the most prosperous period in Cambodia's history, as the rulers mastered the science of irrigation and were able to make the jungles produce abundant crops. The people at that time seemed to accord their rulers near-divine status, because the many stone carvings of Buddhas, bodhisattvas, and Hindu gods appear also to be portraits of real rulers. The two religions were apparently considered compatible.

Angkor Wat, which faces due west, was originally surrounded by moats, as if to remind everyone that management of water was the source of wealth. The many corridors are decorated with low-relief sculpture depicting primarily Hindu myths about the god Vishnu. One of the best of these was *Army on the March* (see fig. 12.3). The ruler of Cambodia thought of himself as a descendant of Vishnu, guarding the fertility of his domain. This emphasis on fertility in the design of Angkor Wat extends to the tops of the towers, which resemble sprouting buds.

China and Korea

Chinese civilization up to the modern period was characterized by the interaction of three traditions: Confucianism, Daoism, and Buddhism. The first two are Chinese creations, while Buddhism came from India. All three have interacted with and influenced one another, imparting richness and variety to Chinese culture. Before these traditions developed, however, distinctive Chinese arts were already flourishing, and were further adapted and altered in Korea.

Art of Ancient China

Some of the world's finest cast-bronze objects were produced in China during the Shang dynasty (sixteenth to eleventh centuries BCE). The ritual vessel (**fig. 18.13**) is covered with an intricate composite of animal forms: The handles are animals with piglike faces and winged backs, pointing downward. The entire side of the vessel is a face, its large round eyes and symmetrical brows prominent. This central face is a **taotie mask**, a composite monster with wings, claws, and horns whose meaning is unfortunately lost to us, but which appears on a great many Chinese bronze vessels. The lowest ring likewise has a procession of stylized monsters.

Most bronze vessels were used in rituals in honor of ancestors. The Chinese believed that one's ancestors lived eternally in the spiritual realm, and that they could influence worldly affairs for better or worse. These beliefs evolved into Confucianism, a moral and ethical system developed by Confucius (Kong Fuzi, 551–479 BCE). Confucius was no mystic; asked once about the proper way to honor the spirits, he replied, "You do not even honor man; how can you honor the spirits!" Cautious innovation and respect for tradition characterize much traditional Chinese art because of his influence.

In the hope of improving their afterlife, many people were buried with most of their possessions. No one, however, was more vain in collecting objects for their burial than the emperor Qin Shihuangdi, who at the time of his death in 210 BCE had unified China in something like its present form. (His dynastic name, Qin—pronounced *chin*—is the root of the word *China*.) So intent was he on guarding his afterlife that he ordered a massive army of life-size clay

18.13 Ritual Vessel. China. 12th century BCE. Cast bronze. Height 7⅛".
Freer Gallery of Art and Arthur M. Sackler Gallery, Smithsonian Institution, Washington, D.C. Gift of Eugene and Agnes E. Meyer. F1968.29.

18.14 Terra Cotta Warriors. Pit No. 1, Museum of the First Emperor of Qin. Shaanxi Province, China. Qin dynasty. c.210 BCE.

Jarno Gonzalez/Getty Images.

18.15 Stone Tomb Relief. Wu Family Shrine, Shandong Province, China. 2nd century CE. Rubbing; ink on paper. 28¼″ × 81¾″.

Far Eastern Seminar Collection, 2002-307.19. © 2018. Princeton University Art Museum/Art Resource NY/Scala, Florence.

soldiers made for his protection. The Terra Cotta Warriors (**fig. 18.14**) number about 6,000 in all, among them cavalrymen, archers, and foot soldiers. These lifelike figures in their huge tomb were discovered in 1974, an extraordinary archaeological find.

The Chinese empire during the Han dynasty (206 BCE–221 CE) was contemporary with the Roman Empire, but much larger. Grave goods have yielded most of the surviving artwork from that period, and from these remains we can learn a great deal about life in China.

The Wu Family Shrine in northeast China shows elaborate relief sculpture; some of this is captured in the stone tomb relief (**fig. 18.15**). (This illustration was made by laying paper over the relief and rubbing with graphite to show the imagery more clearly.) In the lowest register at the right, diggers open a mound and find ancient bronze objects. One of these is a disk that a nobleman presents as an offering to a ruler immediately above. In the top register at the left, we see a horse and chariot, among other scenes of vivid interaction.

None of the scenes in the Wu Family Shrine has much detail, but all are full of energy. Capturing

18.16 Mirror with Xiwangmu. China. Six Dynasties period, 317–581. Bronze. Diameter 7¼″.

Cleveland Museum of Art, OH, USA/The Severance and Greta Millikin Purchase Fund 1983.213/Bridgeman Images.

this inner life force, or *qi* in Chinese, animates a great deal of art production through the centuries in that culture.

The concept of *qi* derives from Daoist beliefs. For Daoists, the best life is one of harmony with the force that animates all created beings. According to traditional Daoism, achieving this harmony will make one immortal; the mirror with Xiwangmu (**fig. 18.16**) honors such a person. Also known as the Queen Mother of the West, she understood the harmony of the Dao and dispensed immortality from her home on faraway Jade Mountain.

The mirror (which is shiny on the other side) depicts Xiwangmu seated at the left of the mirror's central bulb. Opposite her is the Lord Duke of the East; according to Daoist mythology, the two meet each year on the seventh day of the seventh month, a lucky day on the calendar. Just outside their circle, an inscription wishes good fortune to the mirror's owner. In the outer bands are other heavenly beings and circles of clouds, which symbolize the endless cycle of time.

The Chinese Painting Tradition

Traditional Chinese painting revolves around two focal points: **calligraphy** and landscape. Chinese leaders of all kinds were expected to express the strength of their character through elegant writing (see fig. 2.7). By introducing calligraphic brush techniques for expressive purposes, painters sought to elevate painting to the levels that calligraphy and poetry had already attained. In China, painting and writing are closely related, and Chinese artists often include poems within their paintings. The same brushes and ink are used for both, and in both each brushstroke is important in the total design.

Contemporaries of the court painter Fan Kuan regarded him as the greatest landscape painter of the Song dynasty (960–1279). In his large hanging scroll *Travelers Among Mountains and Streams* (**fig. 18.17**), intricate brushwork captures the spirit of trees and rocks. Like most Chinese landscape paintings, this work renders no specific place; rather, it is an imaginative creation intended to capture some aspect of the energy of nature. Artists used many kinds of brushstroke, each identified by a descriptive name such as "raveled rope," "raindrops," "ax cuts," "nailhead," and "wrinkles on a devil's face." Here "raindrop" and other types of brushstroke suggest the textures of the vertical face of the cliff. Men and donkeys, shown in minute scale in the road at the lower right, travel a horizontal path dwarfed by high cliffs rising sharply behind them. To highlight the stylized waterfall as the major accent in the design, Fan Kuan painted the crevice behind the waterfall in a dark wash, and left the off-white silk unpainted to suggest the falling water. The vertical emphasis of the composition is offset by the almost horizontal shape of the light area behind the rocks in the lower foreground. The massive centrality of the composition is typical of the efforts of Northern Song artists to capture the more powerful aspects of nature.

When a vertical line intersects a horizontal line, the opposing forces generate a strong center of interest. Fan Kuan took advantage of this phenomenon by extending the implied vertical line of the falls to direct the viewer's attention to the travelers. Figures give human significance to the painting and, by their small scale, indicate the vastness of nature. Fan Kuan achieved his monumental landscape in part by grouping the fine details into a balanced design of light and dark areas.

A Mongol invasion from the north dislocated China's Song dynasty rulers in 1125. (These were the same Mongols

18.17 Fan Kuan. *Travelers Among Mountains and Streams.* Song dynasty. Early 11th century. Hanging scroll. Ink on silk. Height 81¼″.

National Palace Museum, Taipei, Taiwan, Republic of China. VCG Wilson/Corbis via Getty Images.

18.18 Ma Yuan. *Watching the Deer by a Pine-Shaded Stream.* Southern Song dynasty. Album leaf. Ink on silk. 9½″ × 10″.
© Cleveland Museum of Art, OH, USA/Gift of Mrs. A. Dean Perry 1997.88/ Bridgeman Images.

a fifth-generation descendant of academy teachers who was a favorite of the emperor. Ma's painting *Watching the Deer by a Pine-Shaded Stream* (**fig. 18.18**) captures a contemplative moment in which a scholar or official enjoys a respite on a wooded path. Ma's way of depicting pine branches gives the work an ethereal calm. The brushwork is as meticulous as in the preceding Northern Song, but the composition is relatively adventurous as it fades away into mist at the upper left. This composition is so off-balance that the artist's contemporaries referred to him as "one-corner Ma" because of his tendency to leave large areas of his works unpainted. Such boldness responds to Daoist beliefs, however, because without the voids we would not appreciate the fullness.

Most of the important painters of the Song dynasty were associated with official art academies or government service. During the following Yuan dynasty (1279–1368), the final conquest of China by Mongols radically altered this scenario. The most innovative artists refused to paint or teach for the foreign government; rather, they lived outside official sponsorship. Devoting themselves to a life of art and poetry, they flaunted their amateur status and created a new style called **literati painting**.

The Yuan dynasty literati painters made many innovations in brushwork and subject matter. One of the most important was to give paintings a more spontaneous look. A leader in this trend was Huang Gongwang, who worked briefly in the Yuan administration before suffering false imprisonment in a corruption scandal. On his release he gave up government service and devoted himself to the literati life of painting and literature.

who under Genghis Khan eventually occupied an empire stretching from Korea to eastern Poland and Baghdad to Siberia.) The Song court and art academy moved south to Hangzhou, where a new painting style arose.

If the earlier Northern Song style was monumental and philosophical, the later Southern Song was intimate and personal, emphasizing poetic views of relatively smaller landscapes. One of the leaders in the new style was Ma Yuan,

Huang's large work *Dwelling in the Fuchun Mountains* (**fig. 18.19**) is one of the most revered literati paintings. It is a **handscroll**, meaning that it is a long painting on paper, meant to

18.19 Huang Gongwang. *Dwelling in the Fuchun Mountains* (detail). Yuan dynasty. Handscroll. Ink on paper. 13″ × 252″.
Press Association/Zuma.

18.20 Qiu Ying. *Fisherman's Flute Heard Over the Lake.*
c.1547. Hanging scroll. Ink and color on paper.
62⅞″ × 33⅛″.

The Nelson-Atkins Museum of Art, Kansas City, Missouri.
Gift of John M. Crawford Jr., in honor of the Fiftieth Anniversary of the
Nelson-Atkins Museum of Art. F82-34.

techniques. These range from dots to dark dabs with a laden brush to dry strokes with little ink. Although he worked on this painting for more than three years, it has the look of a spontaneous creation. We also see red ownership stamps that later collectors applied to the work, an acceptable practice in traditional China.

Chinese painters often copied (with personal variations) the works of earlier artists. Even fully mature painters often produced a work in the style of an older master they particularly admired. This tendency reveals one of the basic precepts of Confucianism: respect for the past. The idea that a painter must fully comprehend tradition before expressing individuality was a hallmark of the artists who worked for the imperial court in the sixteenth and seventeenth centuries, and they produced many works in which this homage is clear.

For example, in Qiu Ying's work *Fisherman's Flute Heard Over the Lake* (**fig. 18.20**), a looming cliff at the upper right echoes the massive but meticulous landforms in Fan Kuan's *Travelers Among Mountains and Streams*, painted over three centuries earlier (see fig. 18.17). The human presence in both works is quite small, but Qiu included a scholar standing in his pavilion at the lower center. This motif of the scholar finding refreshment in nature is also common in Chinese landscape paintings (see fig. 18.18). The scholar in Qiu's work has taken a break from his studies, because he hears the fisherman at the left edge playing a haunting tune on his flute. This music was most likely "The Fisherman's Song," a famous Daoist hymn about the harmony of land and water. After Qiu's death, later artists made so many copies of his paintings, out of a similar respect for the past, that determining the authenticity of his works is often difficult.

Chinese painting in the Ming dynasty (1368–1644) and later dynasties evolved down two parallel paths. Within the academies, artists copied old masters and innovated cautiously; outside academies, the literati took a bolder and freer approach. One of the boldest of the latter was Bada Shanren, a descendant of Ming dynasty royalty who lived in the early part of the succeeding Qing dynasty (1644–1912). The Qing, like the Yuan, were foreign. Because the Qing persecuted descendants of the Ming, Bada lived the life of a recluse, taking refuge in a monastery and later faking madness. On the door of the abandoned building where he lived, he scrawled the word "dumb" (mute), and when visitors came he would laugh and drink with them

be viewed by slowly scrolling from the right hand to the left. This work is nearly 21 feet long, so that seeing it all at once is nearly impossible in any case. The part of the work illustrated here, near the beginning of the second section, shows Huang's varied and expressive brushwork

18.21 Bada Shanren. *Cicada on a Banana Leaf.* Qing dynasty. 1688–1689. Leaf "f" from the album *Flowers and Birds*. Ink on paper.
Freer Gallery of Art and Arthur M.Sackler Gallery, Smithsonian Institution, Washington D.C. Gift of Charles Lang Freer. F1955.21e.

but would not talk. This behavior lasted about five years. In 1684, he gave up his faked insanity and lived in his provincial capital, trading paintings for food. His works, such as *Cicada on a Banana Leaf* (**fig. 18.21**), combine free execution with subtle political comments. The cicada is a symbol of rebirth in Chinese mythology, and in Bada's painting it signifies a hope for the resurrection of the failed Ming.

Bada's art remained almost unknown until the twentieth century. Then, as Chinese artists began to radically question their tradition, they found in Bada's wildness an important precursor.

18.22 Porcelain Plate. Mid-14th century. China, Late Yuan dynasty. Painted in underglaze blue. Diameter 18˝.
Metropolitan Museum of Art. Purchase, Mrs. Richard E. Linburn Gift, 1987. Acc.n.: 1987.10.

Chinese Ceramics

The Chinese have traditionally held ceramic arts in high regard, and the history of pottery in China is primarily the story of imperial sponsorship and nearly continuous technical advances. Probably the best-known type of Chinese ceramic is porcelain, made from a rare type of clay that when fired becomes pure white (see Chapter 13 for a more technical discussion of porcelain). Early porcelains, such as the porcelain plate pictured (**fig. 18.22**), were decorated with blue because that was the only color that could withstand the high temperatures necessary to fire porcelain correctly. The Chinese were the first to develop this type of pottery. Porcelain emerges translucent from the oven, and it rings when struck; from this the Chinese concluded that their best dishes contained music. After it was first imported into the Western world, European workshops tried for generations to duplicate its translucency and deep blue colors. In the Ming dynasty in the fifteenth century, potters discovered how to glaze porcelain in almost any color through multiple firings.

Korean Art

Throughout Asia, potters in different provinces and countries produced their own variations on Chinese ceramic styles. This pitcher (**fig. 18.23**) is an exquisite example of a Korean adaptation of the Chinese greenish celadon glaze, with the addition of a new style of decoration. After applying and firing the green glaze, the potter etched lines in the surface that describe the willow trees, birds, and other motifs on the body of the vessel. The potter then filled these lowered areas with white and black slip before firing the vessel for the final time. This slip-inlay technique, a method of painting fine lines on ceramics without the risk of glazes running, is a Korean invention.

Korea developed some of its own artforms despite the influential presence of nearby China and Japan. We see one of these in the *Lotus Sutra* (**fig. 18.24**), a book page produced in the mid-fourteenth century. A sutra is a book of Buddhist teachings, and this one includes a large number of parables and teachings attributed to the historical Buddha. This illustration shows him teaching a group of disciples on the right, with illustrations of two parables at the left. The artists who illustrated it used fine strands of gold and silver, a uniquely Korean method.

18.23 Gourd-shaped Ewer with Inlaid Willow and Bird Design. Korea. Goryeo dynasty (918–1392). 13th–14th centuries. Wheel-thrown stoneware with incised and slip-filled decoration and green glaze. 12⅜″ × 8¼″ × 5⅞″.

Los Angeles County Museum of Art. Anonymous gift (55.13.2).

18.24 *Lotus Sutra*. Illustrated manuscript. Korea, Goryeo Dynasty. c.1340. Gold and silver on indigo-dyed mulberry paper. 9″ x 4 ½″.

Metropolitan Museum. Section 1, Acc. No. 1994.207.

Japan

Throughout its history, Japanese culture has been marked by periods of nationalism, in which typically Japanese forms have prospered, alternating with periods of eager borrowing of foreign influences.

Architecture

The indigenous religion of Japan is an ancient form of nature and ancestor worship called Shinto. In this religion forests, fields, waterfalls, and huge stones are considered holy places where gods dwell. The Shinto shrines at Ise occupy a sacred site within a forest. With only a few lapses, the present Main Hall of the inner Shrine at Ise (**fig. 18.25**) has been completely and exactly rebuilt every 20 years since the late seventh century. Builders take wood for the shrine from the forest with gratitude and ceremonial care. As a tree is cut into boards, the boards are numbered so that the wood that was joined in the tree is reunited in the shrine. No nails are used; the wood is fitted and pegged. In keeping with the Shinto concept of purity, surfaces are left unpainted and the roof is natural thatch. The shrines at Ise combine simplicity with subtlety. Refined craftsmanship, sculptural proportions, and spatial harmonies express the ancient religious and aesthetic values of Shinto.

The first major wave of cultural borrowing took place in the seventh century, when Japanese emperor Shotoku sent emissaries to China to study that civilization. They returned very impressed with many aspects of Chinese culture. For example, the emperor enthusiastically adopted Buddhism, making it the official religion. (Many Shinto gods became sacred beings in Japanese Buddhism.) Japanese Buddhist sculpture from this period was heavily influenced by Chinese sculpture, which the Japanese reinterpreted with subtle changes. Shotoku also encouraged the Japanese aristocracy to learn Chinese and use Chinese script. Confucian teachings about social order and respect for tradition were also adopted, along with many aspects of Chinese art and architecture. In fact, much of Chinese ancient architecture has not survived, because of warfare and fragile wood materials; thus, the best place to study it is in Japan on the Yamato plain near Kyoto, where Shotoku set up his capital and the emperors lived for centuries after.

18.25 Main Shrine. Ise, Japan. c.685. Rebuilt every 20 years.
Photograph: Kyodo News.

The temple complex of Horyuji (**fig. 18.26a**) exemplifies the Buddhist monastery as it existed in both China and Japan. In the center of the courtyard, we can see the many-storied pagoda, which has a symbolic function relating to its descent from Chinese watchtowers and Indian stupas (see fig. 18.4). Next to it is the *kondo*, or Golden Hall, a meditation hall where Buddha statues are kept. In the center of one wall is a gatehouse; opposite it along the back wall is a larger lecture hall, where monks hear religious teaching. The oldest parts of Horyuji date from the late seventh century, and are among the world's oldest surviving wooden buildings.

To hold up a two-story structure with a heavy tile roof, Japanese architects (influenced by Chinese predecessors) developed an elaborate bracketing system (**fig. 18.26b**) for the *kondo* at Horyuji. The empty second story is merely an accent to show the importance of the building, but it also demonstrates the skill of the architect.

Later architecture partakes of a distinctly Japanese pursuit of asymmetry, casualness, and surprise. Katsura Detached Palace (**fig. 18.27a**), a Japanese imperial villa, was built in Kyoto beside the Katsura River, whose waters were diverted into the garden to form ponds. All elements—land, water, rocks, and plants—were integrated in a garden design that blends human-made and natural elements. Because many of the palace walls are sliding screens, they provide flexible interconnections between interior and exterior spaces.

In contrast to a Chinese or European royal palace, Katsura seems humble. The complex was planned with no grand entrance either to the grounds or to the buildings. Instead, one approaches the palace along garden paths, watching unexpected views open up. Earth contours, stones, and waterways are combined to symbolize—on a small scale—mountains, rivers, fields, inlets, and beaches. The tea house (**fig. 18.27b**), which borrows from modest country dwellings, is constructed of common natural materials. It provides the appropriate setting for informal hospitality accompanied by tea drinking. The tea house embodies the attitudes of simplicity, naturalness, and humility that permeate the entire palace grounds.

18.26 Horyuji Temple. Nara, Japan. c.690.
    a. Aerial view.
        Photograph: Kazuyoshi Miyoshi/Pacific Press Service.

b. *Kondo*. Structural diagram.
  From *The Art and Architecture of Japan*, Robert Treat Paine and Alexander Coburn
  Soper. Reproduced courtesy of Yale University Press, London.

18.27 Katsura Detached
Palace. Kyoto, Japan.
17th century.
a. Gardens and
tea house.

b. Imperial villa and gardens.

18.28 Unkei. *Muchaku* (detail). c.1208.
Wood. Height 75˝.

Kofuku-ji Temple, Nara, Japan. 1212 National Treasure. Photograph
courtesy of Duane Preble.

Traditional Japanese houses, such as those at Katsura, are built of wood using post-and-beam construction. Posts bear most of the weight, allowing walls to be sliding screens rather than supports. The Japanese use of unpainted wood and the concept of spatial flow between indoors and outdoors influenced many modern architects in the West. The massing and rooflines of Katsura resemble those of many suburban "ranch-style" houses in the United States.

Sculpture, Painting, and Prints

Japan has the oldest surviving royal family of any society. This longevity has been made possible by frequent military interventions in which the generals ruled on behalf of the emperors, as in the Kamakura period (1185–1333). The dominant taste of the leaders at that time favored a locally based and vigorous realism in art, and we see this in the wood portrait statue of the detail of *Muchaku* (**fig. 18.28**). Unkei, one of the greatest sculptors of Japan, created this life-size work depicting a legendary Buddhist priest from India holding a cloth-covered, round offering box. The vividness of the facial expression and the delicacy of the hand gesture belie the wooden material from which he carved it.

Japanese painters of this period found the handscroll particularly effective for long narrative compositions that depict the passage of time. Like the sculptors, Kamakura period painters depicted their subjects with vividness, as we see in the scroll *Illustrated Legends of the Kitano Shrine*

18.29 *The Thunder God,* from *Illustrated Legends of the Kitano Shrine*. Japan. Second half of the 13th century. Kamakura period. Handscroll. Ink and colors on paper.

Private Collection. Photo © Boltin Picture Library/ Bridgeman Images.

18.30 Sesshu Toyo. *Haboku, Splashed Ink Landscape.* 1400s–early 1500s. Hanging scroll. Ink on paper. 28¼″ × 10½″.
Cleveland Museum of Art, OH, USA/Gift of the Norweb Foundation 1955.43/Bridgeman Images.

scatter before the wrath of the deity, one black-clad lord futilely raises his sword in the lower left center. According to the story, the thunder god came avenging the death of that lord's political rival who had been murdered years before. Note also how the artist captured the wind-blown gown of the figure to the left of the sword-wielder. Because nature plays such a strong role in Shinto beliefs, this scroll has many other depictions of floods, storms, and other natural phenomena.

Zen Buddhism, which came to Japan from China in the thirteenth century, was adapted and transformed in Japan, where it strongly influenced many Japanese artists. Zen teaches that enlightenment can be attained through meditation, and that enlightenment can come at any time. Zen influenced Japanese expressions in several artforms, including poetry, calligraphy, painting, gardens, and flower arranging.

Zen Buddhist priest Sesshu is considered the foremost Japanese master of ink painting. In 1467, he traveled to China, where he studied the works of Southern Song masters and saw the countryside that inspired them. Sesshu adapted the Chinese style and set the standard in ink painting for later Japanese artists. He was most influential when he painted in a simplified, somewhat explosive style, later called *haboku*, meaning "flung ink." *Haboku, Splashed Ink Landscape* (**fig. 18.30**) is abstract in its simplification of forms and freedom of brushwork. Sesshu suggested mountains and trees with single, soft brushstrokes. The sharp lines in the center foreground indicating a fisherman, and the vertical line above the rooftops representing the staff of a wine shop, contrast with the thin washes and darker accents of the suggested landscape.

(**fig. 18.29**). This scroll narrates the early history of the Kitano Shrine, one of the more important Shinto sites. In this segment the thunder god arrives to wreak havoc on a courtly gathering. We see the multi-armed monster at the top center dispensing catastrophes. As the aristocrats

18.31 Tawaraya Sotatsu. *Waves at Matsushima*. Japan. Edo period. 17th century. Folding screen. Ink, color, gold, and silver on paper. 59⅞″ × 145½″.

Freer Gallery of Art and Arthur M. Sackler Gallery, Smithsonian Institution, Washington D.C. Gift of Charles Lang Freer. F1906.231.

In traditional Japan, folding screens provided privacy by separating areas within rooms. Artists have used the unique spatial properties of the screen format in highly original ways. In contrast to the European easel paintings that function like a window in the wall, a painted screen within the living space of a home becomes a major element in the interior.

Tawaraya Sotatsu's large screen *Waves at Matsushima* (**fig. 18.31**) is one of a pair of six-panel folding screens. The screens are designed so that together or separately they form complete compositions. The subject is a pair of islands where there were ancient Shinto shrines. The degree of abstraction present in the ocean waves and the gold background landscape are typically Japanese.

In keeping with well-established Japanese artistic practices, Sotatsu created a composition charged with the churning action of waves, yet as solid and permanent in its design as the rocky crags. He translated his awareness of natural phenomena into a decorative, abstract design. Spatial ambiguity in the sky and water areas suggests an interaction that the viewer should feel, rather than read as a literal transcription of nature. In addition to rhythmic patterns that fill much of the surface, boldly simplified shapes and lines are contrasted with highly refined details and eye-catching surprises. The strongly asymmetrical design,

emphasis on repeated patterns, and relatively flat spatial quality were all often used in Japanese painting from the sixteenth to the nineteenth centuries.

By the mid-seventeenth century, the art of woodcut printing had developed to meet the demand for pictures by the newly prosperous middle class in the capital city of Edo (now known as Tokyo). Japanese artists took the Chinese woodcut technique and turned it into a popular art form. For the next 200 years, hundreds of thousands of these prints were produced. The prints are called **ukiyo-e**, meaning "pictures of the floating world," because they depict scenes of daily life, including landscapes, popular entertainments, and portraits of theater actors—the impermanent, pleasurable aspects of life known as the "floating world."

Kitagawa Utamaro's woodcut print *Reflected Beauty* (**fig. 18.32**) transforms the ordinary subject into a memorable image consisting of bold, curving outlines and clear, unmodeled shapes. As with many Japanese paintings and prints, flat shapes are emphasized by the absence of shading. The center of interest is the reflected face of the woman, set off by the strong curve representing the mirror's edge. In contrast to Western composition with its typically centered balance and subjects well within the frame, here the figure is thrust in from the right and cut off abruptly by

18.32 Kitagawa Utamaro. *Reflected Beauty, Seven Beauties Applying Make-Up: Okita.* c.1790. Woodblock print. 14¼″ × 9½″.
Honolulu Museum of Art. Gift of James A. Michener, 1969. (15490).

the edge of the picture plane, rather than presented completely within the frame. This type of radically cropped composition was one of the elements of Japanese art that influenced European artists in the nineteenth century.

European commerce and missionary work began to have a decisive impact across Asia in the nineteenth century. Various parts of Asia reacted differently to this new influence. India submitted, not always willingly, to colonial

18.33 Yoshitoshi. *The Battle of Sanno Shrine.* 1874. Triptych of woodblock prints. 14¹⁄₁₆″ × 28³⁄₁₆″.
Los Angeles County Museum of Art (LACMA), Herbert R. Cole Collection (M.84.31.142a-c). Digital Image: Museum Associates/LACMA.

status under Britain. The Chinese tried to severely limit foreign influence on their culture, leading to conflicts that lasted into the twentieth century. Commodore Perry's 1854 mission to Japan caused debate and turmoil among the aristocracy. A revolt in 1868 restored the emperor to power, and he began a vigorous program of cultural importation from the West.

Prints created by Yoshitoshi illustrate some of the turbulence of the period. *The Battle of Sanno Shrine* (**fig. 18.33**) depicts a turning point in the conflict that restored the emperor's power. We see soldiers fighting at the far left; in the corner a dead body lies, foreshortened in a way that shows the influence of Western art. At the right, a general and a soldier converse about how to resist the attack of the emperor's forces. The rightmost figure is the general who will soon lose this battle, which Yoshitoshi witnessed firsthand. The degree of journalistic accuracy and Western influence in this work is unprecedented, but it merely foreshadows the degree of cultural interchange between East and West that continues into the present. Yoshitoshi's art also evolved, but toward more gentle subjects (see *Yoshitoshi: From Violence to Folklore*, opposite).

KEY TERMS

bodhisattva – a Buddhist holy person who is about to achieve enlightenment but postpones it to remain on earth to teach others

calligraphy – the art of beautiful writing; broadly, a flowing use of line, often varying from thick to thin

garba griha – the sacred room of a Hindu temple, where rituals are performed and the image of the god is kept

handscroll – a long painting in ink on paper, which viewers contemplate by scrolling from hand to hand

literati painting – most commonly used to describe the work of painters not attached to the royal courts of the Yuan, Ming, and Qing dynasties in China

qi – "life force" in Chinese. The vibrant spirit that animates all things

stupa – a domelike structure probably derived from Indian funeral mounds

taotie mask – a mask of abstracted shapes commonly found on ancient Chinese bronze vessels

ukiyo-e – Japanese prints that depict scenes of the "floating world," including landscapes, popular entertainments, and theater scenes or actors

CREATORS

Yoshitoshi: From Violence to Folklore

The career of Yoshitoshi (1839–1892) tracks a tumultuous period of Japanese history. Born in the capital Edo into a lower-middle-class family, he showed talent for drawing at an early age. His family sent him as an apprentice to a printmaker, and he created his first prints as a teenager. His teacher's collection of foreign books showing Western art techniques influenced the younger artist.

In the 1860s, Yoshitoshi began to attract renown as a creator of violent and lurid prints. There was significant demand for such art, just as violent movies are popular today. Yoshitoshi satisfied this by creating works in series such as *28 Famous Murders with Verse*, which showed an unprecedented amount of blood for that time; the accompanying poems told the stories in a clumsy effort to give the sensational events a literary gloss.

After Commodore Perry's 1854 visit to Japan, the military government was thrown into turmoil about how to deal with the new influences and military threats from the technologically more advanced West. Instability among the upper classes, combined with popular uprisings and crop failures, created widespread unrest until a revolt in 1868 restored the emperor to power. Yoshitoshi lost some of the audience for his prints at about that time, so took various jobs illustrating crime stories in newspapers. He also experienced problems with his mental health that limited his creativity into the 1870s.

In the last decade of his life, Yoshitoshi's fortunes revived considerably. He adopted a new surname, Taiso ("great resurrection"), and established a large workshop to carve blocks under his direct supervision. His prints during this period showed a high level of technical accomplishment, and they also took up more gentle or folkloric subjects.

The Enlightenment of Jigoku-Dayu (**fig. 18.34**) is a good example of Yoshitoshi's late style. The main character is known in Japanese art and folklore as a prostitute who called herself Jigoku ("hell") because she had been sold into a life of prostitution as a youth. An encounter with a Buddhist monk led her to adopt a religious life of contemplation in accordance with Zen principles, and soon she achieved enlightenment, escaping and transcending her previous life, so that she was given the added title Dayu ("respected"). Her kimono shows the Buddhist heaven on the front and the corresponding hell on the back with its monsters and flames. Thus she sits between heaven and hell, reflecting on the passing world in the manner of classic ukiyo-e.

Yoshitoshi's print is a relatively simple composition that shows very skillful printmaking. Here we see Jigoku-Dayu in a thoughtful state of mind (if she were meditating, her eyes would be closed). The figure is posed in a three-quarter view, and it creates space for itself in a Western-influenced way. The panel at the upper right shows the title in two shaded colors, an effect that is difficult to achieve in woodblock printmaking. The backdrop is a group of skeletons, reminding her of mortality and the transitory quality of life; Yoshitoshi portrayed them as ghostlike, visible through a thin silk curtain. Their subtle and barely there appearance is likewise difficult to achieve in woodcut, which is more conducive to straight black and white. Finally, the meandering border of the work, which is both unnecessary and unusual, mimics the appearance of a worn plank of wood. It refers back to the matrix source of this work, which required printing by five separate blocks, one for each color.

This print comes from the final series that Yoshitoshi made, *New Views of 36 Ghosts*. His assistants had to finish the last few works because the artist died of a stroke at age 53. The ukiyo-e style also mostly perished with him, a victim of changing times and photographic reproduction techniques.

18.34 Yoshitoshi. *The Enlightenment of Jigoku-Dayu.* 1890. Woodblock print. 13⅜″ x 9″.
Photograph: akg-images/Pictures From History.

19

THE ISLAMIC WORLD

LEARNING OBJECTIVES

19.1 Describe the architecture and ceramic arts developed in Arab lands following the spread of Islam.

19.2 Explain the importance and use of calligraphy in Islamic art in Spain.

19.3 Discuss the use of decoration and detail in Persian architecture and painting.

19.4 Discuss the significance of art and architecture in the Mughal Empire.

19.5 Describe how modern innovations and art movements influenced Islamic architecture and art in Egypt and Sudan.

Islam is one of the three major world religions built on the teachings of the religious seers of the Middle East. Although based on the revelations to the prophet Muhammad, Islam shares some fundamental beliefs and religious history with its predecessors Judaism and Christianity. An adherent of Islam is called a Muslim—Arabic for "one who submits to God." Art produced in Muslim cultures is among the world's most beautiful and finely crafted.

Muhammad was born around 570 CE in the city of Mecca in today's western Saudi Arabia. The angel Gabriel transmitted to him that became the Qur'an, Islam's holy book. During his lifetime, the Five Pillars of Islam began to take shape. These are basic tenets that all branches of Islam observe: (1) to proclaim the belief that there is one God and that Muhammad is God's messenger; (2) to pray five times each day, facing in the direction of Mecca; (3) to give alms

19.1 The Islamic World.

to the poor; (4) to fast during the holy month of Ramadan; and (5) to make a pilgrimage to Mecca once in a lifetime.

The Islamic calendar begins in 622 CE with the Hijra, Muhammad's emigration from Mecca to the city of Medina about 280 miles north. The new religion spread quickly into much of what was once the Eastern Roman or Byzantine Empire, to Persia, then fanned out to include North Africa, Spain, and parts of Europe (**fig. 19.1**). Within 100 years of the Prophet's death in 632 CE, Christian armies were repelling Muslim troops from Tours in central France. Islam is now the principal religion in the Middle East, North Africa, and some parts of Southeast Asia.

The Muslims facilitated their rule by allowing the peoples of conquered lands to retain their own religions and cultures, as the Romans had done. This strategy enabled the Muslims, who had little art of their own in their early history, to adapt earlier artistic traditions. At its height, from the ninth through the fourteenth centuries, Islamic culture synthesized the artistic and literary traditions and scientific knowledge of the entire ancient world.

Unlike the medieval Christians, who mostly rejected pre-Christian civilization and scholarship, Muslims adapted and built on the achievements of their predecessors. Muslim scholars translated the legacy of Greek, Syrian, and Hindu knowledge into Arabic, and Arabic became the language of scholarship from the eighth through the eleventh centuries for Muslims as well as many Christians and Jews. During the European Middle Ages, Islamic civilization flourished, producing outstanding achievements in the arts, sciences, administration, and commerce that were not attained in Europe until the height of the Renaissance, in the late fifteenth century.

Traditional Muslims disapprove of the representation of human figures in any art that will be used in a religious context. Many Muslims believe that if an artist were to try to re-create the living forms of humans, he or she would be competing with Allah (God), who created everything. Muhammad also prohibited any pictures of himself while he was alive, claiming that he was not in any way exceptional—he was only a messenger. Thus the human form is rare in Islamic religious art, where more attention is given to geometry, to forms of vegetation, and to writing.

Arab Lands

When Islam first began to spread, local rulers took responsibility for building houses of worship in their territories.

19.2 Great Mosque. Kairouan, Tunisia. 836–75.
Photograph: © Roger Wood/CORBIS/VCG via Getty Images.

Early rulers often adapted abandoned buildings, converting them into mosques. (The word is based on the Arabic *masjid*, which means "place of prostration.") The typical mosque must be big enough to accommodate all male worshipers for Friday prayers, during which they hear a sermon, pray, and bow down in the direction of Mecca. The basic plan of a mosque is based on the design of the Prophet's house, which had an open courtyard bordered by colonnades. Most mosques include one or more **minarets** (towers), which mark the building's location and are used by chanters who ascend and call the faithful to prayer five times daily.

An early mosque that still stands in something resembling its original condition is the Great Mosque in Kairouan, Tunisia (**fig. 19.2**). The open courtyard is surrounded by porches, with a minaret over the main entrance in the center of one short side. The deeper covered area opposite the minaret shelters the **mihrab**, the niche in the end wall that points the way to Mecca.

The ceramic arts are highly valued in Islam, and Arab potters in Iraq made a major advance when they perfected the **lusterware** technique, probably in the ninth century.

19.3 Pitcher (Spouted Ewer). Kashan. Early 13th century. Luster over tin glaze. Height 6⅛″.

Lusterware requires an oily glaze that includes metallic oxides. Firing at a low temperature allows the metal to form a sheen on the surface of a vessel; it is one of the most difficult effects to control in ceramics. Ancient potters equated the luster technique with alchemy, the effort to convert simple materials into gold. Most luster pottery

was for the exclusive use of nobles and rulers. The pitcher shown here (**fig. 19.3**) has a very thin body, indicating that it was probably intended for decorative purposes rather than practical use. The script on this piece expresses praise and good wishes to the owner.

Spain

Muslims first conquered Spain for Islam in the eighth century, but soon the region (together with bordering North Africa) became a distinct Muslim culture with important scientists, poets, philosophers, architects, and artists. Some of Europe's largest libraries were in the Spanish Muslim cities of Córdoba and Granada, and respect for books and learning was higher here than in most other areas of the continent.

Calligraphy is an important Islamic art because it is used to enhance the beauty of the word of God. The most respected practice for a calligrapher is the art of writing the words of the Qur'an. In the Islamic world, the written text of the Qur'an (**fig. 19.4**) is the divine word in visible form. According to Islamic tradition, God's first creation was a reed pen for writing his words.

The decorative qualities of Arabic scripts combine well with both geometric and floral design motifs. We saw them combined in the pitcher, but they work together with unforgettable effect in the Court of the Lions at the Alhambra palace (**fig. 19.5**), which contains elaborate stucco arches resting on 124 white marble columns. Many of the walls seem to consist entirely of translucent webs of intricate decoration in marble, alabaster, glazed tile, and cast plaster. Light coming through the small openings in the decoration

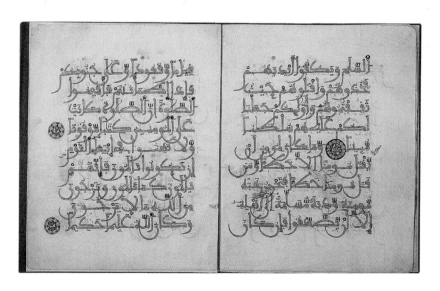

19.4 Text of the Qur'an. North Africa or Spain. 11th century. Colors on paper.

19.5 Court of the Lions, Alhambra. Granada, Spain. 1309–54.
© Rafael Ramirez/Fotolia.

of the most impressive). Carpets were not only prized possessions; they were also important to the history of Islamic arts as a means of spreading design ideas. Relatively portable, a carpet is a repository of motifs and compositions. Many decorative schemes on buildings or pottery were influenced by carpet design from distant regions.

Decorating architecture with tiles is an important offshoot of the ceramic arts, and this technique reached a peak of achievement in Persia. The mihrab shown here (**fig. 19.6**) was taken from a mosque, where it pointed the way to Mecca for worshipers. The disavowal of images in the religious context means that the art cannot tell a story with human figures, as is common in the West. Instead, Islamic

gives many of the rooms and courtyards a luminous splendor. Just above the columns is a horizontal band of calligraphy that says, "There is no victor except God."

The Court of the Lions is part of the much larger Alhambra, the royal palace and fort of the Muslim rulers in Granada. Occupying a commanding hill, the Alhambra was a self-contained city, with meeting rooms, royal residences, gardens, and housing for workers of various kinds. This was one of the last strongholds of Muslim rule in Spain, and when the last ruler abandoned it in 1492, the Spanish rulers kept it intact.

Persia

Now known as Iran, Persia has a lengthy cultural history that included an attempted invasion of Greece, as represented on the metopes of the Parthenon (see fig. 16.6c). After centuries as a secular monarchy, Persia submitted to Muslim rule in the seventh century CE.

Probably the best-known item of Persian art in the West is the carpet (see fig. 13.14 for the Ardabil Carpet, one

19.6 Mihrab. Iran. c.1354. Composite body, glazed, sawed to shape and assembled in mosaic. Height 11′3″.
The Metropolitan Museum of Art, Harris Brisbane Dick Fund, 1939 (39.20).

19.7 Mir-i-Arab Madrasa. Bukhara, Uzbekistan. 1535–1536. Façade.
INTERFOTO/Alamy Stock Photo.

art uses extremely intricate designs that satisfy the sensuous urge for beauty while also engaging the mind's desire for order and pattern. The writing on this mihrab contains well-known verses from the Qur'an about the value of building mosques. In this way a work such as this one can be absorbing to look at, spiritually uplifting, and aesthetically pleasing.

The mihrab has been separated from its original site, but it provides an example of the richness of Persian decorative arts. Such techniques were often applied to entire buildings, as we see at the Mir-i-Arab Madrasa in Uzbekistan (**fig. 19.7**). A **madrasa** is a Muslim theological school where the history of Islam and the interpretation of the Qur'an are taught. This one was named for its founder, a member of the philosophical Muslim sect known as Sufism.

The well-proportioned array of openings in two stories provides a counterpoint to the **iwan**, the large covered porch at the center. Behind are two domes, one marking the lecture hall, and the other the founder's tomb. Most surfaces are dazzling with tiles in floral, geometric, and epigraphic patterns, showing how color is often integral to Islamic architecture.

Persian painters rank among the world's great illustrators, as they made pictures to accompany handwritten copies of their major literary works. Such illustrated books were prized possessions of the aristocracy. One of the finest illustrations is *Sultan Sanjar and the Old Woman* (**fig. 19.8**), from the *Khamseh*, or *Five Poems*, by Nizami. Because this is a secular work, representation of the human form is acceptable.

19.8 Attributed to Sultan-Muhammad. *Sultan Sanjar and the Old Woman*. From the *Khamseh* (*Five Poems*) of Nizami, folio 181. 1539–43. Gouache on paper. 14½″ × 10″.
British Library, London, UK. © British Library Board. All Rights Reserved/ Bridgeman Images.

The story is an allegory on vanity: The sultan was out riding with his courtiers one day when an old woman approached him, complaining that one of his soldiers had robbed her. Sanjar dismissed her, saying that her troubles were nothing compared to his with his military campaigns. The woman then confronted him, saying, "What good is conquering foreign armies when you can't make your own behave?"

The work is a careful composition with luxurious details in the fabrics, vegetation, and clouds. Subtle gestures help to tell the story, which takes place in the center. The method of rendering rocks in Persian painting owes a great deal to Chinese art, which the Persians knew, but the Persian artist made some of these resemble faces. These paintings were most often produced in workshops, so that we do not generally know the artists' names, but in this case it seems fairly certain that the work is by Sultan-Muhammad, one of the two or three most highly regarded painters of Safavid Persia.

India: the Mughal Empire

The Mughal rulers of the Indian subcontinent were descended originally from Mongols, a relationship reflected in the name. The Mughals governed a wide mix of cultures in India during their period of dominance in the sixteenth and seventeenth centuries. Their subjects practiced a variety of Indian and Persian religions; a small number were Christian. Only a minority (the rulers and upper classes) were Muslim. This meant that in the Mughal Empire, Islam evolved further from its Arab roots than anywhere up to that time.

Governing such a diverse people led the Mughal rulers to a level of tolerance unknown elsewhere in the world. Akbar, for example, who ruled from 1556 to 1605, ordered his ministers to learn about the various religions practiced in his realm, and he hired tutors to teach them. He also established a new religion that combined elements of all, and made himself the head of it, the better to resolve disputes. When Jesuit missionaries from Baroque Rome visited him, he entertained them lavishly and bought Western religious prints from them for his art collection. He encouraged figural representation in art, saying that trying to copy God's handiwork by making pictures would lead artists to a deeper respect for divine creativity.

Akbar embodied his novel precepts in architecture, as we see in his throne room, the Divan-i-Khas (**fig. 19.9**). The room is dominated by an ornate pillar with four

19.9 Divan-i-Khas. Interior. Fatehpur Sikri, Uttar Pradesh, India. 1570–80.
Photograph: Jonathan M. Bloom and Sheila S. Blair. © mrpeak/Fotolia.

passageways that lead to it. The stone used for building was soft, making possible the carving of the numerous openwork grilles. Akbar sat at the center, atop the pillar, his position symbolizing the intersection of the religious systems in his realm. The English word *mogul*, with its connotations of wealth and power, derives from Mughal rulers such as Akbar.

The last Mughal ruler to hold the realm together was Shah Jahan, who also created the most memorable piece of Mughal art, the Taj Mahal in Agra (see fig. 2.14). Jahan erected this unforgettable building beside a river as a memorial to his favorite wife after she died in childbirth. There is no similar architectural testament to romantic love in all the world. Its white marble surfaces show different colors throughout the day, as the building catches sunlight from various angles. The bulb-shaped dome seems light in weight. The walls look paper-thin, with arch openings in a graceful rhythm. The building appears to hover above a garden, the design of which is based on the description of paradise in the Qur'an.

19.10 Taj Mahal (detail). Agra, India. 1632–48.
© pjhpix/Shutterstock.

Modern Expressions

In the mid-twentieth century, some creators in the Islamic world sought to adapt modern innovations from Europe and harmonize them with their own cultural traditions. In the 1940s, the Egyptian government needed to relocate some settlements in the upper Nile Valley in order to aid conservation of the ancient temples of Luxor and Karnak. Architect Hassan Fathy developed a novel method to tempt the people to move: He designed new houses and civic buildings for a planned community nearby that the displaced people would build and acquire at no cost. Mud-brick was abundantly available in the region; with advice from an architect, and following Fathy's designs, the people could provide new buildings for themselves. They erected the village of New Gourna in 1948.

The roof of the mosque (**fig. 19.11**) shows the results of their labors. We see many small domes over the prayer hall, and one dome with component bricks exposed in the lower right. The largest dome shelters the mihrab. These features are traditional in most mosques. The novelty of this project, besides its handmade construction, is its basic and clear shapes. The buildings of New Gourna are modern in that their plans and exteriors respond simply to the needs of the users, without decoration. Fathy wrote and lectured extensively about this village, and his ethic of self-help for the poor and the displaced has influenced many architects around the world since.

The central iwan is fronted with a pointed arch; just above the opening is a decoration of twining vegetation (**fig. 19.10**). The beauty of this building comes not from decorations, but rather from expensive materials and poetic arrangement of masses. The paradise motif of the garden is continued in the long inscription surrounding the doorway arch, which contains the most important chapter from the Qur'an describing the afterlife. Tombs for both Shah Jahan and his wife are at the center on a lower floor. Jahan expressed his vision for the building in a written note: "Like the garden of heaven a brilliant spot, full of fragrance like paradise fraught with perfume."[1] The Taj Mahal's central dome and high iwan show influence from earlier Mughal tombs, but here the rich marble and perfectly balanced masses create an otherworldly building.

19.11 Hassan Fathy. New Gourna Village Mosque, Egypt. 1948.
B.O'Kane/Alamy Stock Photo.

19.12 Ibrahim el-Salahi. *The Mosque.* 1964. Oil on canvas. 12⅛″ × 18⅛″.

New York Museum of Modern Art (MoMA), Elizabeth Bliss Parkinson Fund, Acc n.: 7.2965. © 2018. Digital image: The Museum of Modern Art, New York/Scala, Florence. © 2018 Artists Rights Society (ARS), New York/DACS, London.

In neighboring Sudan, a movement arose in the 1960s among painters who combined traditional calligraphy with abstract painting. The leader of the group was Ibrahim el-Salahi, who had studied in London (see *Ibrahim el-Salahi: Muslim Modernist* on p. 336). Salahi combined Muslim motifs with modern abstraction in oil paintings such as *The Mosque* (**fig. 19.12**). Dark brown shapes hover in a shallow pictorial space over a shaded white background. The shapes are abstract forms based on what one would see inside a mosque: calligraphic inscriptions, carpets, and people. The curving edges of many shapes are based on the strokes that Arabic calligraphers practice daily. Colored blocks at the right center suggest carpet weaving. At the lower far right is an abstracted human form. The artist textured the large shape next to it with paint strokes that sketch a mask-like face that confronts the viewer. Several of the round shapes in the work are partially eclipsed, especially at the top left center and left center; these shapes suggest the crescent moon that is the symbol of Islam.

Salahi described his work from that period in spiritual terms: "It is a kind of prayer, too, because you are appreciating God's creation and trying to think about it and meditate on his creativity."[2]

KEY TERMS

calligraphy – the art of beautiful writing; broadly, a flowing use of line, often varying from thick to thin

iwan – a high vaulted porch to mark an important building or entrance

lusterware – a ceramic glaze effect that imparts a metallic sheen to the surface of a vessel

madrasa – a building that combines a school, prayer hall, and lodging for students

mihrab – a niche in the end wall of a mosque that points the way to Mecca

minaret – a tower outside a mosque where chanters stand to call the faithful to prayer

CREATORS

Ibrahim el-Salahi: Muslim Modernist

19.13 Ibrahim el-Salahi. 2013.

Photograph: Nick Harvey/Wire Images/Getty Images.

In the twentieth century, increasing interaction among the world's cultures has caused some Muslim artists to find ways of taking advantage of the stylistic innovations of modern art. An early leader in this tendency is Ibrahim el-Salahi (b. 1930) of Sudan. His life and work have also been at times linked importantly with politics.

Salahi's father was a Muslim cleric who taught at a Qur'an School in the capital city of Khartoum; this gave the future artist early exposure to calligraphic techniques. Salahi studied art for three years at a local technical college before earning a scholarship to the Slade School of Art in London in the late 1950s. This made him one of the most highly trained artists in Sudan on his return, and led to his appointment as chair of the painting faculty at the School of Fine and Applied Arts in Khartoum.

Salahi combined his teaching duties with several trips around the country in which he observed the objects that everyday people used. He said, "I have always been fascinated with patterns in local Sudanese handicrafts and what simple peasants were doing and carving and decorating and painting. And suddenly I think the beauty of it came to me and hit me—it's so strong."[3]

In an interview, Salahi described his evolution toward a calligraphic style: "I started to write small Arabic inscriptions in the corners of my paintings, almost like postage stamps, and people started to come towards me," meaning that he began to build an audience. "I spread the words over the canvas, and they came a bit closer. Then I began to break down the letters to find what gave them meaning, and a Pandora's box opened. Animal forms, human forms and plant forms began to emerge from these once-abstract symbols. That was when I really started working. Images just came, as though I was doing it with a spirit I didn't know I had."[4]

In 1972 Salahi was appointed Vice Minister of Culture in the national government, but three years later he was falsely implicated in a military revolt led by a distant cousin. The national police arrested Salahi and held him in prison for six months without a hearing, before higher authorities realized that the artist had no involvement in the plot and released him without charge. He left Sudan for Qatar, where he served in the Ministry of Culture.

After working in Qatar for many years, Salahi moved to England in 1998. When agitation for democracy began in late 2010 in Tunisia and soon spread to other countries, Salahi was keenly interested. When the protests broke out in Libya, Syria, Egypt, and elsewhere, earning the nickname "Arab Spring," he hoped that some of the more autocratic regimes might evolve or even collapse. Not knowing that such hopes would eventually prove mostly illusory, he began making daily sketches of his interpretation of events, such as *Arab Spring* (**fig. 19.14**). Here we see vegetal shapes rising above roots in the soil. These are the energies of the protestors, but they are surrounded on either side by opposing shapes that limit growth. He said of that period, "I found it most exciting . . . I started with the pen just to draw what I saw in this beginning of a revolution in the Arab world . . . I was feeling so hopeful that sooner or later democracy could really come and become the dominant way of our lives and give us hope for the future."[5]

In 2015, Tate Modern, the largest modern art gallery in the United Kingdom, staged a solo exhibition of Salahi's work, its first such show accorded to a Muslim artist.

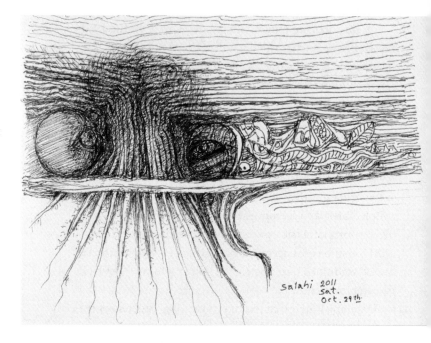

19.14 Ibrahim el-Salahi. *Arab Spring*. 2011. Ink on paper. 4¼″ × 5¾″.

Vigo Gallery, London. © 2018 Artists Rights Society (ARS), New York/DACS, London.

20

AFRICA, OCEANIA, AND THE AMERICAS

LEARNING OBJECTIVES

20.1   Identify the variety of materials, styles, and cultural purposes that characterize traditional African art.

20.2   Analyze the range of visual characteristics and meaning found in Oceanic and Australian art.

20.3   Examine the continuation of artistic traditions in native North American cultures.

20.4   Describe media and functions of art in Mesoamerica and South America.

Most of us in the West tend to think of art as something to go and see in a museum; that is where most art is kept, after all. Or perhaps we believe that art is something that decorates our homes. Most of us arrange paintings or sculptures (or reproductions of them) as embellishments of our personal spaces.

In this chapter we will consider traditional arts from regions where art is not created solely for visual pleasure or embellishment. These cultures did not set aside places for the care and enjoyment of art. Rather, the cultures we consider here found uses for art in religious ritual, civic life, and community functions. During the twentieth century, many modern artists looked to art from these regions for inspiration.

Africa

The arts of the African continent are extremely varied, and the diversity of style reflects the variety of cultures on the continent (**fig. 20.1**). Africa is larger than China, the United States, and Europe combined. North of the Sahara, the artforms of Africa generally fall under the influence of Egyptian (see Chapter 15), Roman (see Chapter 16), or Islamic traditions (see Chapter 19). Here we will focus on sub-Saharan Africa.

Humanity originated in Africa. But because most ancient African art was made from perishable materials, little remains from before the thirteenth century. Tin miners digging in central Nigeria in 1928 accidentally unearthed

the oldest surviving examples of sub-Saharan art, such as the figure from the Nok culture shown here (**fig. 20.2**). Archaeological evidence indicates that these works, of which hundreds have been found, date from the time of the ancient Greeks and the Romans. Made in **terra cotta** (unglazed reddish earthenware), they range from a few inches high to nearly life-size. Their finely carved hair

20.1   Africa.

Yoruba and Benin

Concurrent with the Gothic era in twelfth-century Europe, a naturalistic style of court portraiture was developed for the royal court of Ife, a sacred Yoruba city in southwestern Nigeria. The male portrait head (**fig. 20.3**) demonstrates the Ife skill in bronze lost-wax casting (see fig. 12.8). Such thin-walled, hollow metal casting probably represents the culmination of generations of technical progress. Grooved lines emphasize facial contours; rows of small holes probably held a beaded veil.

Ife influenced the sculptural arts of neighboring Benin. The royal head (**fig. 20.4**) exemplifies another court style, developed in Benin, which was somewhat abstract in comparison to the naturalism of Ife portrait sculpture.

20.2 Male Figure. Nok culture. c.195 BCE–205 CE. Terra cotta. 19½″ × 8¾″ × 6⅝″.

AP 1996.03. © 2018. Kimbell Art Museum, Fort Worth, Texas/Art Resource, NY/Scala, Florence.

ornaments and facial features show that these figures were worked with the clay in a semi-hard state, through carving and subtraction rather than modeling. This suggests that there may have been wood carving in that region which influenced the style. The vivid facial expression of the head makes it seem like a portrait of an individual, but at the same time there is a degree of abstraction in the treatment of the eyes and nose. Little else has survived from the Nok culture. Although not much is known about it, its art seems to have heavily influenced other cultures of West Africa, as the figures were traded across a wide area.

20.3 Male Portrait Head. Ife, Nigeria. 13th century. Bronze. Height 11⅞″.

Nigerian. Private Collection. Photo © Dirk Bakker/Bridgeman Images.

Bronze casting in Benin was an artform devoted exclusively to glorifying the king (or *oba*). The technology was a closely guarded secret, which only licensed royal artisans could practice. Most of the Benin heads are portraits of royalty or other distinguished ancestors. The heads were generally placed in altars that successive generations tended.

When sixteenth-century Europeans first arrived in the kingdom of Benin, they were impressed by cast-bronze sculptures, palaces, and a city that compared favorably to their own capital cities. The ivory pendant mask from Benin (**fig. 20.5**) was carved in the sixteenth century, and modern versions are still worn on the *oba*'s chest, or at his waist, during ceremonies. This pendant mask portrays a queen mother who gazes out with a serene expression. She wears a crown that depicts alternating human heads and mudfish. The human heads are meant to represent Portuguese traders and sailors who regularly visited Benin and, at times, helped the king to resolve diplomatic disputes with neighboring peoples. A close examination of the figures reveals that they wear round caps and have long mustaches. The mudfish symbolize immortality because they seem to rise up alive from the mud each year. The two vertical marks in the queen mother's brow are shallow slots that held inlaid pieces of iron.

The Yoruba peoples of Nigeria also have a tradition of figural wood carving that makes use of diminutive proportions and almond-shaped parts. The house post (**fig. 20.6**) by Olembe Alaye is not only a literal support for a roof; it is also a meditation on the idea of support. Stacked in this

20.4 Head of an Oba. Nigeria. c.1550. Metalwork-bronze. 91¼″ × 8⅝″ × 9″.

The Metropolitan Museum of Art, New York. The Michael C. Rockefeller Memorial Collection. Bequest of Nelson A. Rockefeller, 1979. (1979.206.86).

20.5 Pendant Mask. Court of Benin, Nigeria. Early 16th century. Ivory, iron, copper. Height 9⅜″.

Metropolitan Museum of Art, New York. The Michael C. Rockefeller Memorial Collection. Gift of Nelson A. Rockefeller (1978.412.323).

20.6 Olembe Alaye. House Post. Yoruba, Nigeria. Mid-20th century. Wood and paint. Height 83″.
Fowler Museum at UCLA. Photograph by Don Cole.

20.7 *Tomb of Former Chief Lisa.* Ondo, Nigeria. House Post in fig. 20.6 is third from left.
Photograph: W. Fagg, 1959. William B. Fagg Archive. Fowler Museum at UCLA.

composition are (from the top) a community elder seated in a folding chair, a woman holding a baby on her back, and a second woman holding her breasts in a traditional gesture of respectful welcoming. All three of these people are important to the maintenance of the society, as they represent wisdom, nurturing, and hospitality. All three personify characteristics that support the community.

The house post takes on added meaning when we see it on location in a 1959 photograph, *Tomb of Former Chief Lisa* (**fig. 20.7**). The chief was the "pillar of the community"; placing these posts at the front of his tomb added significance and honor to his memory. He is buried among other emblems of support that, all together, symbolize important aspects of tribal life.

Mali, Cameroon, and Congo

The Bamana people of Mali are renowned for their carved wooden antelope figure headdresses, which young men attach to basketry caps and wear atop their heads during agricultural ceremonies. When a new

20.8 Bamana *Chi Wara* (Antelope) headdresses. Near Bamako, Mali.
Photograph: Eliot Elisofon, 1971. Image no. EEPA EECL 3366. Eliot Elisofon Photographic Archives, National Museum of African Art, Smithsonian Institution.

20.9 Mask. Bamileke peoples, Bamendjo, Cameroon. Late 19th century. Wood, paint, iron dowel, plant fiber, plant gum. Height 21″; width 18½″; depth 12″.
Fowler Museum at UCLA. Photograph by Don Cole.

20.10 Mangaaka Power Figure (Nkondi tatu oath-taking figure). Yombe people, Democratic Republic of the Congo. 19th century. Wooden figure with iron nails. Height 34⅝″.
Photograph: Claudia Obrocki. Ethnologisches Museum, Staatliche Museen, Berlin, Germany. From the Richard Buettner collection. © 2017. Photograph: Scala, Florence/bpk, Bildagentur für Kunst, Kultur und Geschichte, Berlin.

field is cleared, the most diligent male workers are selected to perform a dance of leaps in imitation of the mythical *Chi Wara* (**fig. 20.8**), who taught human beings how to cultivate crops. The dance always represents both male and female *chi wara* figures: The female is identified by a baby on her back, the male by a stylized mane. Abstracted antelope bodies become energized, almost linear forms. Rhythmic curves are accented by a few straight lines in designs that emphasize an interplay of solid mass and penetrating space.

The bold, uninhibited style of art of the grasslands region of Cameroon looks far removed from the aristocratic styles of Ife and Benin, even though it was also developed for royal courts. The separate areas of the large dance headdress (**fig. 20.9**) are clearly defined by different patterns and textures. This heavy sculpture, worn by court officials during royal festivals, does not copy the human head but reinterprets it.

Not all African art has been made for royal or honorific uses. As with the *chi wara* antelope figures, much art is intended to influence future events for the better, or to secure the social order. An example is the Mangaaka power figure (**fig. 20.10**) from Congo. This figure was created to personify the force of justice (or Mangaaka). The carver endowed it with an honorary headdress and posed it leaning forward in an assertive manner to suggest decisiveness. In the abdominal cavity, tribal authorities placed medicinal matter (now lost) intended to strengthen the statue's function. Then, whenever a civil case was concluded, a treaty ratified, a promise made, a dispute settled, or a law enacted in the presence of the statue, tribal members affected by the decision symbolized their agreement by driving a metal piece into the statue's surface. More than 400 such pieces adorn this work, testifying to its use over many decades.

20.11 Kente Cloth. "Mmeeda" ("Something that has
not happened before"). Ghana. 20th century.
Cloth (strip weave). 92½″ × 59¹⁄₁₆″.

Seattle Art Museum. Gift of Katherine White and the Boeing Company. 81.17.434.
Photograph: Paul Macapia.

20.12 Kuba Cut-Pile Embroidery. Raffia. Democratic
Republic of the Congo. 20th century.

Werner Forman Archive/Anspach Collection, New York.

Ghana and Angola

The textile arts are highly developed in Africa, and many
cloth styles have specific uses. The Ashanti peoples of
Ghana use looms to weave narrow cloth strips, which they
then sew together into patterns that symbolize important proverbs or ideas. Weaving becomes a sort of public
art for instant communication. For example, the Kente
cloth pattern called "Mmeeda" (**fig. 20.11**) is worn when
something unprecedented happens. The most famous
instance of the use of this pattern came when Ghana was
still a colony and the political party of jailed independence leader Kwame Nkrumah won national elections.
He wore this Mmeeda pattern in public appearances
when the British released him from prison three days after
the balloting. Later, when announcing Ghana's independence on March 6, 1957, Nkrumah (by then Ghana's first

president) wore a different cloth with the pattern that said,
"I have done my best."

Cut-pile embroidery is one of the continent's oldest textile traditions (**fig. 20.12**). After men have woven a
stretch of cloth using raffia fibers, women embroider it by
lacing dyed strips through the warps and wefts. Without
knotting, they loop a strand behind the weaving and back
out to the top side before trimming it to approximately the
pile height of modern velvet. The texture of these fabrics is
indeed velvety, and the patterns of embroidery are vibrant,
as we see in this example. The diagonals in this work gather
strength and eventually overlay the square pattern. The
first of these fabrics came to Europe from today's Angola
in the seventeenth century and have been highly prized
since. In their indigenous territory they are used as skirts
for women in ceremonial dances.

Oceania and Australia

Oceania is the collective name for the thousands of Pacific islands that comprise Melanesia, Micronesia, and Polynesia (including New Zealand; **fig. 20.13**). These islands were settled by migrants from Southeast Asia over a very long period, lasting from about 26,000 BCE, when western New Guinea was populated, until about 800 CE, when migrants reached New Zealand.

Although it is difficult to generalize about Oceanic art, because the cultures, physical environments, and raw materials vary greatly over an enormous area, a few traditional beliefs seem to have been held in common across the Pacific, and these have influenced the creation of art.

First is the belief that the world as we know it was created by the union of the Earth Mother and the Sky Father. Their contact created life forms on the planet's surface. The Oceanic traditions view ancestors as intermediaries between people and the gods. Because ancestors who now live in the spirit world can intercede and influence future events, Oceanic artists have created many objects to honor or placate them.

Another widely shared concept is **mana**, or spiritual power. Mana may reside in persons, places, or things. Many artforms of Oceania were intended to possess this power, which can keep adversity at bay, promote community well-being, and enhance personal power and wisdom.

Oceanic peoples developed very little pottery because of a shortage of clay, and they were not acquainted with metal until traders introduced it in the eighteenth century. For tools, they used stone, bone, or shell; they made houses, canoes, mats, and cloth with wood, bark, and small plants. Feathers, bone, and shells were employed not only for utensils and sculpture, but also for personal adornment.

Melanesia

In the Solomon Islands and New Ireland (part of Melanesia), woodcarvings and masks are designed to serve ritual purposes. In the art of many Melanesian societies, birds appear with human figures to act as guides or messengers between the physical world of the living and the spiritual world of deceased ancestors. The bird held by the protective prow figure from a war canoe (**fig. 20.14**) from the Solomon Islands guides voyagers by acting as a protective spirit that watches out for shoals and reefs. Although the carving is only the size of a hand, it looks much larger because of the boldness of its form. The exaggerated nose and jaw help to give the head its forward thrust. Against the blackened wood, inlaid mother-of-pearl provides strongly contrasting white eyes and rhythmically curving linear bands of Zs.

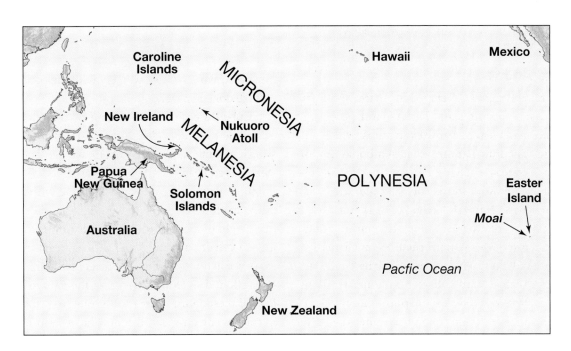

20.13 Oceania and Australia.

20.14 Protective Prow Figure from a War Canoe. New Georgia Island, Solomon Islands. 19th century. Wood, inlaid with mother-of-pearl. Height 6½″.

Werner Forman Archive/Museum fur Volkerkunde, Basle, Switzerland. Location: 03.

A bird also plays a prominent role in the New Ireland mask (**fig. 20.15**). The elaborately carved openwork panels are painted in strong patterns that accent and at times oppose the dynamic forms of the carving. Snail-shell eyes give the mask an intense expression. In the wings of this mask, chickens hold snakes in their mouths, a reference to the opposition of sky and Earth. Anthropologists believe that this piece was used to remove bad influences from a new ceremonial house. Once it had fulfilled its function, it was regarded as "used up," and discarded.

Micronesia and Polynesia

Carvings made in Micronesia and in much of Polynesia are streamlined and highly finished. The female figure from Nukuoro Atoll (**fig. 20.16**) has a distinctive spare quality. This figure is one of about 30 similar sculptures that were collected in the nineteenth century. All show similar bodily proportions, which suggests that the carvers followed a set of traditional customs. The degree of abstraction in these pieces is unusual. Most anthropologists believe that

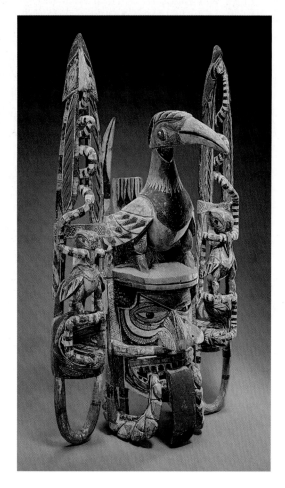

20.15 Mask. New Ireland. c.1920. Painted wood, vegetable fiber, shell. 37½″ × 21⅓″.

Fowler Museum at UCLA. Photograph by Don Cole.

20.16 Female Figure. Nukuoro Atoll, Central Carolines. 19th century. Wood. Height 15⁹⁄₁₆″.

Honolulu Museum of Art, by exchange, 1943 (4752).

20.17 Moai. Easter Island. c.1000–1500. Volcanic rock.
Height 12′.

the figures represent gods, but the local religion died out under the impact of missionaries and population shifts. Although Nukuoro is in the southern part of Micronesia, the culture is Polynesian.

Polynesia covers a large, triangular section of the Pacific, from New Zealand to Hawaii to Easter Island. Widely separated Polynesian islands and island groups developed greatly varied arts that include both delicate and boldly patterned bark cloth, featherwork, shellwork, wood carvings, and huge rock carvings.

The original inhabitants of Easter Island left more than 600 carved moai (**fig. 20.17**) before European explorers first visited the island in the 1770s. These stone figures, which are up to 32 feet tall, are statues of torsos and heads; some have a topknot made from stone of a different color, as we see here. These figures represent ancestors who have taken on spiritual power; they were placed on raised platforms overlooking small settlements along the coastline, as if protecting and overseeing the activities below. Many Polynesian cultures accord similar homage to ancestors, but none on the scale we see here.

An outstanding example of semi-abstract Hawaiian sculpture is the forceful aumakua (ancestral deity; **fig. 20.18**) found in the burial cave of a chief or high priest. By eliminating extraneous details and carefully articulating the parts of the body, the sculptor increased the impact of the female figure's bold stance. Its power is enhanced by the attached reddish human hair, shell eyes, and open mouth with bone teeth. The arms-out, knees-bent, feet-apart position gives the figure a strong presence. Full upper arms taper to small forearms and even smaller hands. There is consistent use of full, rounded, almost inflated mass. The well-polished dark wood and inset material show a high degree of craftsmanship.

20.18 Human Figure (kiʻi ʻaumakua). Forbes Cave,
Hawaii. Koa wood. Height 29″.

20.19 Waitangi Meeting House. Bay of Islands, North Island, New Zealand. 1934–1940.
   a. Front view.

eye35 stock/Alamy Stock Photo.

b. Waitangi Treaty Grounds. Maori Meeting House Interior.

Charles O. Cecil/Alamy Stock Photo.

Many artforms come together in the Maori meeting house (**fig. 20.19a**), which is a typical structure of traditional New Zealand. Such houses are used for extended family gatherings and rituals in honor of ancestors. The house pictured is a twentieth-century creation intended to commemorate the 1840 treaty between British settlers and native Maoris, which led to the founding of New Zealand.

Most meeting houses are named for specific ancestors and symbolize their presence. An ancestor's face and body is at the top of the gable; the ridge represents his back; the rafters are his ribs; the outer upright posts symbolize his arms, as if he is on all fours, looking straight ahead. The front gable boards are richly carved with abstract figures that represent other ancestors. The slightly ferocious aspect of these figures indicates that they inhabit the spirit world, and this carving attempts to communicate some of their mana.

The inside of the house (**fig. 20.19b**) is even more ornate. The ribs of the roof (which represent the ribs of ancestors) are painted in curving nonrepresentational patterns. On the walls, relief carvings alternate with abstract patterns in woven dyed flax. Most meeting houses represent only one ancestor, but because this one commemorates an important historical event, it represents ancestors of all of the Maori clan groups in today's New Zealand.

Australia

The human presence in Australia dates back 40,000 years. For tens of thousands of years before the invention of writing, Native Australians (called Aboriginals) maintained an intimate bond with nature, as demonstrated by their art. While most other human groups gradually changed from wandering food foragers to settled farmers, manufacturers, and merchants, Aboriginals continued to live as semi-nomadic hunter-gatherers with little clothing or permanent shelters and with only a few simple but highly effective tools.

The recognition of their dependence on nature is evident in nearly all Aboriginal art. They see the bond between themselves and nature as a close relationship established by creative beings in the remote past, a period that they call **Dreamtime**. The many disciplines and practices related to spiritual life vary from clan to clan and region to region, but Dreamtime spirits are prominent in nearly all Aboriginal groups.

The bark painting *The Myth of the Wawilak Sisters* (**fig. 20.20**) tells a story that is often illustrated in Aboriginal art. The sisters wandered across the land in Dreamtime, singing as they traveled and naming many features of the landscape. They created ceremonies to influence nature, and they also created many community rules and laws still observed today.

20.20 Dawarangulili. *The Myth of the Wawilak Sisters*. Eucalyptus bark painting. 34¾″ × 17½″.

This painting tells of the sisters' fateful encounter with a giant snake. The right vertical edge is a groundline, and the semicircular protuberance is a pond from which the snake emerged twice. The first time he emerged very large and swallowed the sisters and their children, as we see them surrounded by the snake's body in the center. Their dog escaped, as we see from his footprints leading to his image just below and to the left. The snake unleashed a powerful storm that caused a flood before he released the sisters near an anthill, visible in the lower right center near the two standing figures. The large lozenge shapes are sticks that the sisters used to dig yams, two of which lie along the top edge. The cylinder with black ends is a didjeridoo, a large musical pipe that plays deep bass notes, which the sisters used to make music that stopped the storm. The artist produced this work as an aid to memory about an important story, so that everything in it has meaning. He created it using earthen ochers in a naturally limited color palette; some Aboriginal artists began using paint and canvas in the 1970s, but their imagery has remained relatively constant for hundreds of years.

Native North America

Native peoples lived in North America for thousands of years before Europeans arrived on the continent. The oldest human-made artifacts—stone hearths and simple tools—may be 20,000 to 30,000 years old. Some carved bone tools and spear points are about 10,000 years old.

The Hopewell culture flourished in what is now Ohio from the second century BCE to the sixth century CE. Large Hopewell burial mounds contained rich offerings placed in elaborate log tombs. The later Adena culture built the Great Serpent Mound (**fig. 20.22**) in about 1070 CE near some of these early burials. The mound-builders first outlined the writhing design with rows of stones and then piled dirt between them. The serpent has a spiral tail, and its curving body ends with open jaws holding a large oval object. If it were extended, it would stretch more than 1,300 feet in length. Its meaning is a matter of debate, but the serpent's head and mouth point to the sunset at every summer solstice.

Native Americans today produce an astonishing variety of artworks, depending on their cultural tradition and the materials available in their region. In most cases native artforms that are now practiced vigorously went through a period of disuse in the late nineteenth century, when Indian

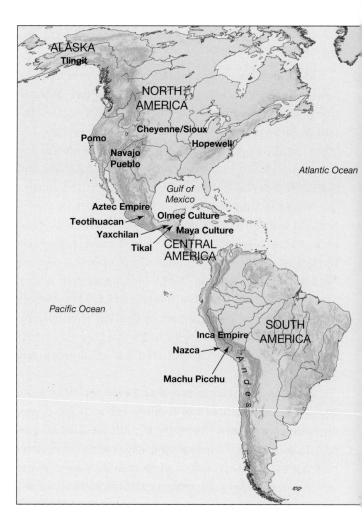

20.21 Americas.

reservations were first established. Today many Native American artists are making traditional works, and many more are working in contemporary styles.

Plains

Plains Indians practiced the traditional art of painting on buffalo hides. Men traditionally made representational paintings of their deeds in battle, as we see in the hide robe showing Mato Tope's exploits (**fig. 20.23**). Mato Tope (Four Bears) stretched this hide in the sun to dry and then painted it with organic pigments in a water-based solution. Exploit paintings are typically full of action, with the moving figures seen in profile views with no horizon line. The best examples date from before European contact, but they are very rare. Our example was collected by a fur trader and sent to Switzerland.

The nineteenth-century arrival of white settlers in the Plains had a twofold impact on hide painting. First, the decline of the buffalo led warriors to seek other surfaces

20.22 Great Serpent Mound. Ohio. Adena culture. c.1070 CE. Uncoiled length 1,370´.
Photograph: Mark Burnett/Alamy Stock Photo.

on which to depict their events and exploits. Second, the subject matter changed to include battles with United States military forces. We see both of these in *At the Sand Creek Massacre* by Howling Wolf (**fig. 20.24**). He painted the work in a ledger book, a support that became increasingly common for such exploit paintings. This work is based on an event the artist witnessed in 1864 as a teenager and painted about ten years later: Military troops surrounded an encampment and opened fire, bringing death to between 70 and 163 surprised Native Americans. The work depicts a confused scene, with warriors on horseback fleeing and rifle fire coming in from the left. Howling Wolf signed the work with a small wolf in the upper right (he was illiterate at the time of painting it); the writing on the work was made by the first collector who owned it. Howling Wolf's later art veered further from the profile views of classic exploit paintings (see *Howling Wolf: Warrior and Artist* on p. 350).

20.23 Mato Tope (Four Bears). Robe with Mato Tope's Exploits. c.1835. Buffalo hide; red wool cloth; sinew; dyed porcupine quills; horsehair and human hair; brown, yellow, and black pigment. 63″ × 83¾″.
Ethnographic Collection at the Bernisches Historisches Museum, Bern. Photograph: S. Rebsamen.

20.24 Howling Wolf. *At the Sand Creek Massacre.* 1874–75. Pen, ink, and watercolor on ledger paper.
Allen Memorial Art Museum, Oberlin College, Ohio, USA/Gift of Mrs. Jacob D. Cox/Bridgeman Images.

CREATORS

Howling Wolf: Warrior and Artist

20.25 Chief Howling Wolf, Cheyenne Indian.
Photograph: Kansas State Historical Society.

Little is known about the early life of Howling Wolf (1849–1927), except that he and his father were both members of the Bowstring Society, one of four warrior groups of the Cheyenne. After the Sand Creek Massacre (see fig. 20.24), father and son moved northward into central Wyoming, where they participated in other military activities with the intention of removing white people from their lands. However, after the Battle of Adobe Walls in northern Texas in 1875, Howling Wolf sensed the futility of further attacks and surrendered to the United States government, marking a drastic turn in his life.

Howling Wolf was imprisoned at Fort Marion, Florida, along with several hundred other formerly militant warriors, as part of a social experiment. The government cut the warriors' hair, gave them Christian names and Western clothing, and attempted to change them into upstanding citizens through education and religious training. Howling Wolf at first accepted this; he became literate and learned to speak both English and Spanish. When he developed problems with his vision, the government sent him to Boston for treatment, after which he returned voluntarily to the fort.

He also continued to draw regularly in government-issued notebooks. The drawings show him grappling with the new way of life, as we see in *Classroom at Fort Marion* (**fig. 20.26**). Twelve former warriors are seated at desks as a teacher attempts to show them how to hold a pen. Above the teacher's head is a chalkboard and a religious picture of Jesus with his disciples.

Howling Wolf here experiments with Western perspective.

Most Plains artists depict their subjects only in profile; Howling Wolf uses various viewpoints such as from above and from behind. In the lower right corner of the work, a student seems to remonstrate with a military officer seated at a desk, a combination of top and side views.

The government experiment at Fort Marion ended after three years, and Howling Wolf was released to the Cheyenne Reservation in Oklahoma. There he attempted to practice what he had learned about agriculture and trading, but by 1881 he became disillusioned with the effort to adopt foreign ways. He wrote to the Captain who had formerly supervised him at Fort Marion (all spelling from the original): "You gave me the white man's road and it is very good. At the fort you gave us cloths but we have been here for one year and they are about all gone.... When I hunted the Bufalo I was not poor; when I was with you I did not want for eney thing but here I am poor I would like to go out on the planes a gane whare I could rome at will and not come back a gain."[1] He resumed wearing traditional Cheyenne clothing and abandoned Christianity.

Howling Wolf made fewer drawings in succeeding years. Instead, he devoted himself to attempts to improve his people's lot on the reservation by legal means, through advocacy and food distribution. In an attempt to earn money for the reservation, he started a Wild West show in Houston, which included a mock Cheyenne village. On a journey back to the reservation after a set of performances, an auto accident on a highway took his life.

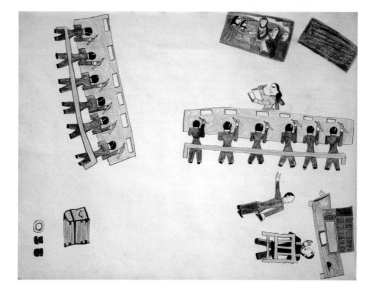

20.26 Howling Wolf. *Classroom at Fort Marion.* 1876. Colored pencil on paper. 8½″ × 11″.
New York State Library, Manuscript and Special Collections section, Albany, NY.

Southwest

The Navajo of Arizona have been resourceful weavers for more than two centuries. While many men weave blankets today, the artform was traditionally a woman's province. The Second Phase Chief Blanket (**fig. 20.27**) comes from an early period, before the Navajo were exiled to eastern New Mexico in 1863–68. Like most Navajo weavings, it was created on a loom with warps spaced close together, yielding a dense fabric that is nearly waterproof. The design of this blanket has an austere, symmetrical geometric pattern that includes some subtle touches, such as the thin blue lines, and the continuous red border around the four central bars. This style is called a Chief Blanket not because it was reserved for high officials, but because its quality made it so expensive that few could afford to own one.

The Pueblo peoples of the Southwest are best known for pottery, which is traditionally done by women. Each Pueblo has its own style; the jar (**fig. 20.28**) that we see here is from Ácoma. These pots are made from local earthenware and shaped without a wheel. The artists fire them in open fires and decorate them with pigments made from earthen powders. The abstract symbols in Pueblo pots generally do not have a fixed meaning, but refer to the forces of nature or to community life.

20.28 Jar. Ácoma Pueblo. 1870–1880. Earthenware and pigments. Height 8¾″; diameter 10½″.
LACMA. Gift of Camilla Chandler Frost (M.2008.113.6).

20.27 Second Phase Chief Blanket. Navajo. c.1830–50. Handspun wool with natural dyes. 74″ × 60″.

Private Collection.
Photograph: Tony Berlant.

and painted kachinas, such as the Hopi kachina shown here (**fig. 20.29**), are made by Hopi and Zuni fathers and uncles as a means of teaching children their sacred traditions. This is a Hemis Kachina, associated with prayers for a bountiful harvest. His headdress is a stepped pattern that symbolizes rain clouds; the blue bars are corn stalks.

Pacific and Northwest Coast

Native Americans of the Pacific Coast region produce fine baskets. In northern California, Pomo artists made baskets with such tight weaving that they can hold water. They vary greatly in size, shape, and decoration, from large containers up to 4 feet in diameter to tiny gift baskets less than a quarter of an inch across. Pomos wove strong geometric designs into many of their baskets and used ornaments such as feathers and shells to embellish others. The highest artistic achievements in Pomo culture are brightly colored feather baskets (**fig. 20.30**). As with Pueblo pottery, the art of basketmaking was traditionally passed down in families from mother to daughter and aunt to niece. The instruction was frequently accompanied by training in other tribal

20.29 Marshall Lomakema. Hopi Kachina. 1971. Shungopovi, Arizona. Painted wood. Height: 34″.
Courtesy of the National Museum of the American Indian, Smithsonian Institution. (24/7577). Photograph: Carmelo Guadagno.

Most Pueblo peoples recognize the spirits of invisible life forces. These spirits, known in Zuni Pueblo and neighboring Hopi areas as **kachinas**, are impersonated by masked and costumed male members of the tribes, who visit the villages in a variety of forms, including birds, animals, clowns, and demons. During ceremonies they dance, present kachina figures to delighted children, provide humor, and occasionally give public scoldings. The carved

20.30 Pomo Feather Basket. California. Before 1920. Feathers, abalone and shell beads. 4″ × 13″ × 13″.
Southwest Museum of the American Indian Collection, Autry Museum, Los Angeles. 811.G.1683. Photograph: Larry Reynolds.

20.31 Tlingit Community House. Ketchikan, Alaska.
Doug Wilson/Alamy Stock Photo.

traditions. Treasured pieces were made as gifts, designed solely to delight the eye.

Northwest Coast peoples developed highly imaginative arts to depict their mythology. Elegant abstractions of animal subjects typify the painting and sculpture of the Tlingit and other groups that inhabit the coastline from Seattle to Alaska. On house walls, boxes, blankets, and even dishes, major features of a symbolic animal form are laid out in two-dimensional abstract patterns. With its wide, gently sloping roof, elaborately painted façade, and totem poles, the Tlingit Community House (**fig. 20.31**) is characteristic of the art and architecture of the region. A **totem** is an object such as an animal or plant that serves as an emblem of a family or clan; it often symbolizes original, prehuman ancestors. The word itself, from a Native

American language of the Upper Midwest, means "he is related to me."

The flat surfaces of the Tlingit Community House show abstract shapes of beavers, bears, whales, and ravens. The totem pole at the center consists of such stacked symbols, which help a family clan to remember its history back to mythological times, much like a family crest.

Mesoamerica and South America

Here we consider Latin America before the Spanish conquest, which began in 1492, when Christopher Columbus landed in the Caribbean. It is a vast region covering all of South America and including today's Mexico, which anthropologists call Mesoamerica because it includes parts of both North and Central America. Among the pre-conquest cultures we agricultural communities, cities, and even empires.

Mesoamerica

A variety of agricultural civilizations flourished in Mexico from about the time of Christ until the Spanish conquest of the 1520s. These cultures influenced one another through trade and conquest, and as a result they share many cultural forms, among them pyramids, calendars, and some important gods and myths. The earliest was the Olmec, who inhabited the Gulf Coast near what is now Veracruz. Probably more influential were the people who built the city of Teotihuacan, in the central valley about 40 miles north of where Mexico City is today.

The Pyramid of the Sun (**fig. 20.32**) in Teotihuacan is among the largest pyramids in the world, covering slightly more ground than the largest of the pyramids of Egypt. It rises only about half as high, and it imitates the shape of the surrounding mountains. Many ancient Mexican cultures believed that humanity first emerged from a hole in the ground, and this pyramid may mark the spot: It sits over a deep cave. The pyramid is aligned to face the sunset on August 12, the date corresponding to the beginning of time in the Maya calendar. As we can see in the photograph, the Pyramid of the Sun was at the center of a large city, which archaeologists calculate was the world's sixth largest at its peak in 600 CE.

At one end of the central avenue of Teotihuacan lies the Temple of the Feathered Serpent (**fig. 20.33**), which has sculptural decorations that influenced several other cultures. Alternating on the layers of the temple are relief

20.32 Pyramid of the Sun. Teotihuacan, Mexico. 1st–7th century CE. 700´ wide, 200´ high.
Kate Connes/Shutterstock.

heads of the storm god, with its goggle eyes and scaly face, and the feathered serpent, its fanged head emerging from a plumed wreath. Teotihuacan itself was abandoned after burning in a mysterious fire in about 750 CE. However, both of these gods were widely adopted by later cultures in ancient Mexico.

The Maya, whose descendants still live in what are now parts of Mexico, Guatemala, and Honduras, developed a

20.33 Temple of the Feathered Serpent (detail). Teotihuacan, Mexico. 150–200 CE.
© Vladimir Korostyshevskiy/ Shutterstock.

20.34 Temple I. Tikal, Guatemala. Maya. c.300–900 CE.
© Daniel Loncarevic/Shutterstock.

have rendered effortlessly the casual fall of the feathers in his headdress. His wife, Lady Xoc, kneels before him performing a ritual. She draws blood from her pierced tongue, which she will blot with the pieces of paper in the basket in front of her. She wears richly patterned clothing that hints at highly developed textile arts of that time (none of which survive, unfortunately). Her elaborate headdress is crowned with the goggle-eyed storm god, who looks almost directly upward from the back of Lady Xoc's head. Especially noteworthy are the sculptor's evocation of the fleshiness of the figures, their subtle interaction, and the rich textures of their clothing. The writing on the work describes the action and even gives its date: October 28, 709.

written language, an elaborate calendar, advanced mathematics, and large temple complexes of stone.

The hundreds of stone temples at Tikal suggest that Maya priests had great power. Temple I (**fig. 20.34**), built during the classical Maya period (300–900 CE), rises over a spacious plaza in a Guatemalan rainforest. The 200-foot-high pyramid has a temple at the top, which priests used on ceremonial occasions; they emerged onto the high platform to perform dances as worshipers watched below.

Walls and roofs of Maya stone temples were richly carved and painted. An excellent example of Maya sculpture from one such temple is Lintel 24 (**fig. 20.35**) from Yaxchilan, a site on the border between Mexico and Guatemala. This stone relief is best understood with the help of the written symbols along its edges, which have recently been decoded. Standing is the king, Lord Shield Jaguar, holding a flaming torch. The sculptor seems to

20.35 Lintel 24. Yaxchilan, Mexico/Guatemala.
Maya. 709 CE. Limestone. Height 43″.
British Museum, London. Am1923,Maud.4. © The Trustees of the British Museum.

20.36 Chacmool. 10th–12th century. Toltec. Stone. Length 42″.
akg-images/François Guénet.

The Toltec civilization that developed in central Mexico between the ninth and thirteenth centuries forms a bridge between the decline of the Maya and the rise of the Aztecs. During a time of conflict and change, the Toltecs initiated a major new era in the highlands of central Mexico, distinguished by architectural innovations and massive carved figures. A Toltec form that also occurs in Aztec and Maya art is the recumbent figure from Chichén Itzá known by the Maya name "Chacmool" (**fig. 20.36**). The bowl at the figure's waist held sacrificial offerings.

The Aztecs were the most powerful kingdom in Mexico at the time of the Spanish conquest; their art is in many respects a summation of preceding styles. The Aztecs (who called themselves the Mexica) settled in the early fourteenth century in the area where Mexico City now stands. Their principal temple was a dual pyramid in honor of the storm god and a war god, and there they made human sacrifices of the prisoners they had taken in warfare with neighboring peoples. The Aztecs believed that such sacrifices were necessary in order to honor and re-create the self-sacrifice that the feathered serpent had performed in ancient times to ensure the continuation of the world. They believed that this original sacrifice had occurred at Teotihuacan, which they regarded as a holy place.

The feathered serpent, sometimes called by his Aztec name, Quetzalcoatl (**fig. 20.37**), is the patron of the priests who carried out human sacrifices. This finely carved

20.37 The Feathered Serpent Quetzalcoatl. Mexico. Aztec, 1450–1521. Stone.
Museo Nacional de Antropología, Mexico City/Bridgeman Images.

20.38 Machu Picchu. Peru. Inca. Early 16th century.
ckchiu/Shutterstock.

example shows the feathers that make up the serpent's skin; these refer to airborne birds just as the serpent's body alludes to the earth. Quetzalcoatl thus unites Earth and sky. The human personification of the god emerges from the serpent's mouth, above an ornate tongue decorated with symbols of conch shells that represent winds, dangling below. Like many Aztec works, this piece has a somewhat monstrous or menacing aspect, but Quetzalcoatl was also the bringer of knowledge. When the Spanish first visited the Aztec capital, they found the city cleaner and better governed than most European cities. The Aztec also had highly developed arts of poetry and literature.

South America

In the Andes of South America, Inca culture flourished for several centuries prior to the Spanish conquest of 1532. Spanish reports from the time tell of the magnificence of Inca art, but most of the culture's exquisite gold objects were melted down soon after the conquest, and all but a few of the refined fabrics have perished with age and neglect.

The Inca are perhaps best known for their skillful shaping and fitting of stones. Their masonry is characterized by mortarless joints and the "soft" rounded faces of granite blocks. The royal retreat center of Machu Picchu (**fig. 20.38**) was built on a ridge in the eastern Andes, in what is now Peru, at an elevation of 8,000 feet. The city, which escaped Spanish detection, was planned and constructed in such a way that it seems to be part of the mountain. Respect for stones was an integral part of Inca culture. According to the Inca creation myth, two of their early ancestors who emerged from the earth immediately turned themselves into stones. Some stone shrines were regarded as living things requiring offerings and care.

20.39 *Hummingbird.*
Nazca Valley, Peru.
Tomaz Kunst/Getty Images.

On a desert plateau overlooking Nazca Valley, ancient Nazca peoples created a network of geometric lines and patterns in the dry land across a wide swath of coastal southwestern Peru. There are perfectly straight lines, some almost 5 miles long, and geometric patterns such as spirals, trapezoids, and triangles, as well as abstracted images of various known and unknown birds and animals, including the hummingbird (**fig. 20.39**) shown here, which is about 310 feet long. The lines are similar to ancient roads in size and construction. Many of the animal shapes also exist on Nazca pottery, a fact that only deepens the mystery of their function.

One of the few Inca art forms to survive the Spanish conquest intact was the carving and painting of kero cups such as the one seen here (**fig. 20.40**). Kero cups held beverages for ancient rituals that the Inca performed in secret for many generations. The flat patterns in the decoration are stylistic descendants of both pottery and textile design.

20.40 Kero Cup. Peru. Late 16th–17th century. Wood with pigment inlay. 7⅜″ × 6¹⁵⁄₁₆″.
Brooklyn Museum of Art, Museum Expedition 1941,
Frank L. Babbott Fund. 41.1275.5.

KEY TERMS

cut-pile embroidery – a type of African textile in which a stretch of cloth is woven using raffia fibers and then embroidered by lacing dyed strips through the warps and wefts

Dreamtime – in Aboriginal culture, a period in the remote past when the close relationship with nature was established by creative beings

kachina – one of many deified ancestral spirits honored by the Hopi and other Pueblo Indian peoples; usually depicted in doll-like form

mana – in Oceania, spiritual power that may reside in persons, places, or things

terra cotta – a type of earthenware that contains enough iron oxide to impart a reddish tone when fired

totem – an object such as an animal or plant that serves as an emblem of a family or clan

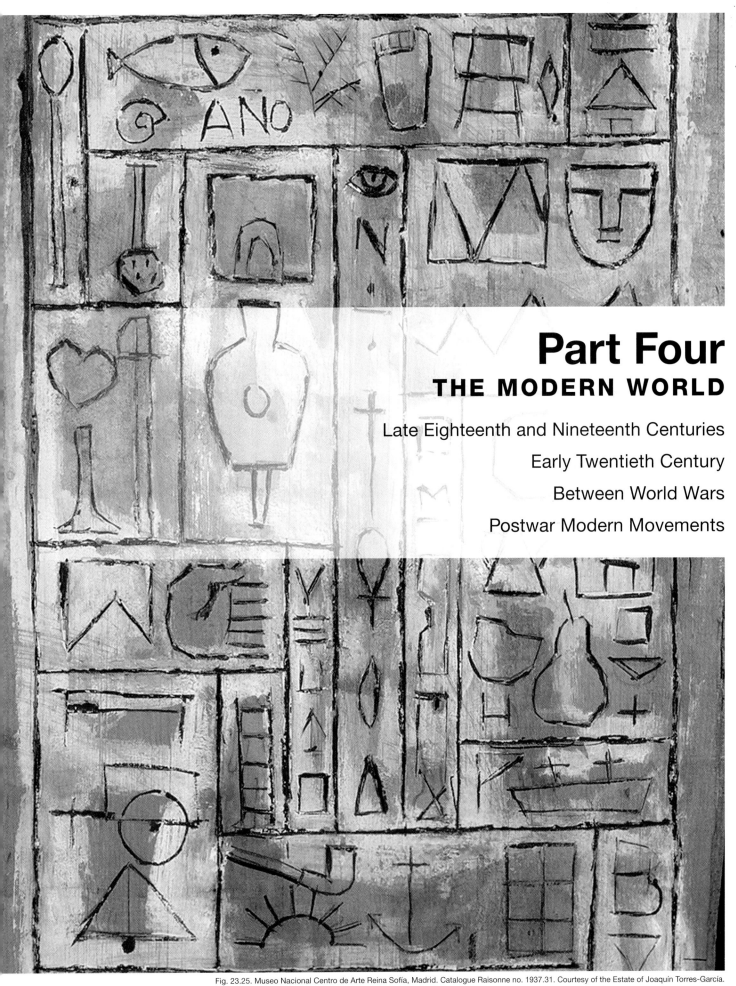

Part Four
THE MODERN WORLD

Late Eighteenth and Nineteenth Centuries

Early Twentieth Century

Between World Wars

Postwar Modern Movements

Fig. 23.25. Museo Nacional Centro de Arte Reina Sofía, Madrid. Catalogue Raisonne no. 1937.31. Courtesy of the Estate of Joaquín Torres-García.

21

LATE EIGHTEENTH AND NINETEENTH CENTURIES

LEARNING OBJECTIVES

21.1 Explain the social and political ideas that gave rise to Neoclassical art and architecture.

21.2 Identify the visual characteristics and themes in Romanticism.

21.3 Discuss the developments in photography and the medium's relationship to painting in the nineteenth century.

21.4 Describe the stylistic features and artistic concerns characterizing Realism.

21.5 Explain the principal characteristics of Impressionist painting.

21.6 Distinguish the various trends in the Post-Impressionist period.

The period of great social and technological change we call the modern age was launched by three revolutions: the Industrial Revolution, which began in Britain about 1760; the American Revolution of 1776; and the French Revolution of 1789. The Industrial Revolution caused the most significant shift in the way people lived since the Neolithic agricultural revolution 10,000 years earlier. Among the first businesses to be industrialized in the late eighteenth century was textile manufacture. Weaving mills were at first powered by flowing rivers; steam power took over in the 1820s. Iron and steel manufacture revolutionized building in the later nineteenth century, making possible the first skyscrapers. The American and French revolutions implanted the ideas of the Enlightenment in government and public life.

The Enlightenment, or Age of Reason, as the late eighteenth century has been called, was characterized by a shift to a more rational and scientific approach to religious, political, social, and economic issues. Belief in the importance of individual liberty, self-determination, and progress caused renewed interest in democracy and secular concerns. The consistent belief systems that tended to unify earlier societies, revolving mostly around religion, became increasingly fragmented. Traditional values were challenged by the new atmosphere of independent investigation, by technological changes, and by increased contact between peoples and cultures. Artists both expressed and abetted these changes.

A new stylistic pluralism began to grow. In earlier periods, artists generally adhered to a dominant style. Following the French Revolution and the subsequent breakdown of traditional art patronage in France, a variety of styles developed simultaneously. The traditional sources of art patronage (royalty, aristocracy, the Church) gradually withered away, leaving artists to hope for commercial galleries and business-class collectors to fill the gap.

Neoclassicism

With the beginning of the French Revolution in 1789, the luxurious life that centered on the French court ended abruptly, and French society was disrupted and transformed. As the social structure and values changed, so tastes also changed.

One of the artists who led the way to revolutions in both art and politics was painter Jacques-Louis David. Believing that the arts should serve a beneficial social purpose in a time of social and governmental reform, he rejected what he saw as the frivolous immorality of the aristocratic Rococo style. When he painted *The Oath of the Horatii* (**fig. 21.1**), David pioneered an austere style called **Neoclassicism**. The term refers to the emulation of

21.1 Jacques-Louis David.
The Oath of the Horatii. 1784.
Oil on canvas. 10′10″ × 14′.
Musée du Louvre, Paris, France. RMN-Grand
Palais/Gérard Blot/Christian Jean.

most professions was also true of the art world, where women were banned from academy classes in which unclothed models were used. If a woman did succeed as an artist, it was because she either could afford private study or came from an artistic family.

In the works of the Neoclassicist Angelica Kauffmann, who overcame such obstacles, we see a different vision of woman's abilities. Born in Switzerland and trained by her father, Kauffmann spent six years in Italy before settling in London in 1768. She was elected a full member of the British Royal Academy two years later, the last woman to be so honored until the 1920s. The Academy members commissioned her to create four oval paintings on the theme of the four basic skills of art, to decorate the ceiling of its home gallery. One of these is *Design* (**fig. 21.2**). As in the other three works of this series (*Invention*, *Composition*, and

Classical Greek and Roman art; much of the subject matter in Neoclassical art was Roman because Rome represented a republican, or non-hereditary, government.

The subject of *The Oath of the Horatii* is a story of virtue and readiness to die for liberty: The three brothers pledge to take the swords their father offers in order to defend Rome. With such paintings, David gave revolutionary leaders an inspiring image of themselves rooted in history. "Take courage," was the painting's message, "your cause is a noble one, and it has inspired heroes of the past."

David's Neoclassicism, seen in the rational, geometric structure of his composition, provides strong contrast to the lyrical softness of Rococo designs (see *Happy Accidents of the Swing*, fig. 17.30). *The Oath of the Horatii* has the quality of Classical relief sculpture, with strong side light emphasizing the figures in the foreground. Even the folds in the garments are more like carved marble than soft cloth. The background arcade gives strength to the design and provides a historically appropriate setting for the Roman figures. The two center columns separate the three major parts of the subject. Vertical and horizontal lines parallel the edges of the picture plane, forming a stable composition that resembles a stage set.

The women at the right of *The Oath of the Horatii* seem overcome by emotion, unable to participate in the serious decisions required of men who would defend their homeland. This painting reflects the common belief at that time that women were unfit for public life. Their exclusion from

21.2 Angelica Kauffmann (1740–1807). *Design.* 1778–80.
Oil on canvas. 4′4″ × 5′.
© Royal Academy of Arts, London. Photographer: John Hammond.

21.3 Thomas Jefferson. Monticello. Charlottesville, Virginia. 1793–1806.
Monticello/Thomas Jefferson Foundation, Inc. Ffooter © Shutterstock.

Color), the person practicing the skill is a woman. Seated between two Roman columns, she sketches a plaster cast of a Hellenistic torso. Academy painters regarded such sketching after antique statues as a key part of any artist's training. The title of the work is a translation of *disegno*, the Italian word for drawing.

The Neoclassical spirit also infected architecture. After the American statesman-architect Thomas Jefferson spent five years in Europe as minister to France (1784–89), he redesigned his home, Monticello (**fig. 21.3**), in accordance with Classical ideals. Monticello is based on Andrea Palladio's Renaissance reinterpretation of Roman country-style houses (see fig. 17.16). The Roman portico, topped by a dome, makes the entire design reminiscent of the Pantheon (see fig. 16.11) by way of contemporary French Neoclassical architecture.

Both Monticello and Jefferson's designs for the University of Virginia show the Roman phase of Neoclassical American architecture, often called the Federal Style. Jefferson advocated this Neoclassical style as an embodiment of the values of the new American republic, where Roman civic virtues of courage and patriotism would be reborn. Jefferson's Neoclassical style is reflected in much of American architecture before the Civil War. Neoclassical architecture can be found in practically every city in the United States, and it dominated government buildings in Washington, D.C. into the twentieth century.

Romanticism

The Enlightenment celebrated the power of reason; however, an opposite reaction, **Romanticism**, soon followed. This new wave of emotional expression motivated the most creative artists in Europe from about 1820 to 1850. The word Romanticism comes from *romances*, popular medieval tales of adventure.

Neoclassicism and Romanticism agree on the importance of individual liberty, but little else. Romantic artists, musicians, and writers believed that imagination and emotion are more valuable than reason, that nature is

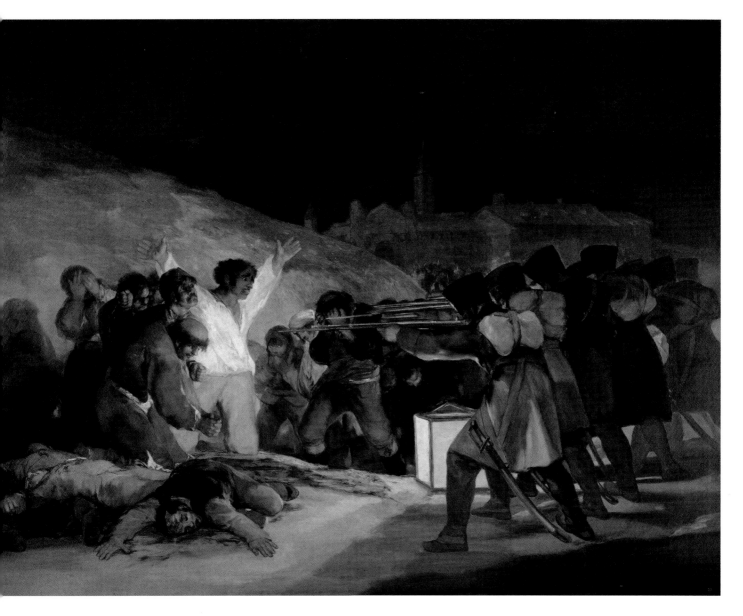

21.4 Francisco Goya. *The Third of May, 1808.* 1814. Oil on canvas. 8´9˝ × 3´4˝.
Museo Nacional del Prado, Madrid. © Photograph: MNP/Scala, Florence.

less corrupt than human society, and that human beings are essentially good. Romantics celebrated nature, rural life, common people, and exotic subjects in art and literature. They asserted the validity of subjective experience and sought to escape Neoclassicism's fixation on Classical forms.

Spanish artist Francisco Goya was a groundbreaking Romantic painter and printmaker. A contemporary of David, he was aware of the French Revolution, and he personally experienced some of the worst aspects of the ensuing Napoleonic era, when French armies invaded Spain and much of the rest of Europe. Goya at first welcomed

Napoleon's invading army because his sympathies lay with the French Revolution and its democratic values. But he soon discovered that the occupying army was destroying rather than defending the Revolution's best ideals. Napoleon's troops occupied Madrid in 1808; on May 2, a riot broke out against the French in the central square. Officers fired from a nearby hill, and the cavalry was ordered to cut down the crowds. The following night firing squads were set up to shoot anyone suspected of causing the disturbance. Later, Goya vividly and bitterly depicted these brutalities in his powerful indictment of organized murder, *The Third of May, 1808* (**fig. 21.4**).

The Third of May is enormous, yet so well-conceived in every detail that it delivers its message instantly. A structured pattern of light and dark areas organizes the scene, giving it impact and underscoring its meaning. Mechanical uniformity marks the faceless firing squad, in contrast to the ragged group that is the target. From the soldiers' dark shapes, we are led by the light and the lines of the rifles to the central figure in white. The focal point is this man, raising his arms in a gesture of helpless defiance. This work is more than a mere reconstruction of history; it is a universal protest against the brutality of tyrannical governments.

Goya's painting deals with events that took place only six years before the artist took up the brush; a preoccupation with current events (rather than a mythological past)

is an important characteristic of the Romantic movement. When the British Houses of Parliament burned in a disastrous fire one night in 1834, Joseph Mallord William Turner witnessed the event and made several sketches that soon became paintings. His work *The Burning of the Houses of Lords and Commons* (**fig. 21.5**) typifies the Romantic movement in several ways.

The brushwork is loose and expressive, as if Turner created the painting in a storm of passion. The colors are bright and vivid. Although the work depicts an event that happened only a few months before, the artist introduced distortions and exaggerations. According to contemporary reports, the flames did not leap up into the night as the artist shows them. Moreover, the Thames River has a

21.5 Joseph Mallord William Turner. *The Burning of the Houses of Lords and Commons.*
1834. Oil on canvas. 36¼″ × 48½″.
© Cleveland Museum of Art, OH, USA/Bequest of John L. Severance/Bridgeman Images.

21.6 Thomas Cole. *The Oxbow*. 1836. Oil on canvas. 51½″ × 76″.
The Metropolitan Museum of Art, New York. Gift of Mrs. Russell Sage, 1908 (08.228).

curve that would partially block the view; Turner "straightened" the river to afford a wide horizon. Turner made these departures from factual accuracy in order to convey the feeling of the event, as a British national symbol burned. This emphasis on feeling over fact is Romantic. Turner's loose painting style influenced the later Impressionist movement, but there are important differences between them, as we shall see.

Many Romantic artists also painted the landscape, finding there a reflection of their own emotional state. Romantic landscape painting flourished especially in the United States, where Thomas Cole founded the Hudson River School in the 1830s. Like Turner, Cole began with on-site oil and pencil sketches, then made his large paintings in his studio. The broad, panoramic view, carefully rendered details, and light-filled atmosphere of paintings such as

The Oxbow (**fig. 21.6**) became the inspiration for American landscape painting for several generations. (See also Asher Brown Durand's *Kindred Spirits*, fig. 3.24).

In nineteenth-century America it was difficult to obtain the education necessary to become a professional artist; for an African American it was almost impossible. Nevertheless, with the help of antislavery sponsors, a few succeeded.

Robert S. Duncanson was one of the first African-American artists to earn an international reputation. As the son of a Scots-Canadian father and an African-American mother, he may have had an easier time gaining recognition as an artist than those who did not straddle the color line. Prior to settling in Cincinnati, he studied in Italy, France, and England, and he was heavily influenced by European Romanticism. With *Blue Hole, Little Miami River*

21.7 Robert S. Duncanson. *Blue Hole, Little Miami River.* 1851. Oil on canvas. 29¼″ × 42¼″.

Cincinnati Art Museum, Ohio, USA. Gift of Norbert Heerman and Arthur Helbig 1926.18/ Bridgeman Images.

21.8 Eugène Delacroix. *The Death of Sardanapalus.* 1827. Oil on canvas. 12′1½″ × 16′2⅞″.
© 2018. DeAgostini Picture Library/Scala, Florence.

(**fig. 21.7**), Duncanson reached artistic maturity. He modified the precise realism of the Hudson River School with an original, poetic softening. He orchestrated light, color, and detail to create an intimate and engaging reverie of a person in nature.

In France, the leading Romantic painter was Eugène Delacroix. His painting *The Death of Sardanapalus* (**fig. 21.8**) is based on the life of a literary character, an ancient Assyrian king who may or may not have existed. In the play *Sardanapalus* by Lord Byron, the title character leads a decadent and wasteful life, and ends it in a hopeless military situation, surrounded by enemies. Rather than surrender, he takes poison and orders all his favorite possessions brought before him and destroyed in an orgy of violence. Delacroix composed this writhing work along a diagonal and lit it using strong chiaroscuro in a way that recalls certain Baroque paintings (see fig. 17.23). His brushwork is loose and open, or **painterly**, not at all like the cool precision of Neoclassicism. Delacroix used all these devices in order to enhance the viewer's emotional response to a horrifying, if imagined, event. The Romantic painters in general stressed strong viewer involvement, use of color in painterly strokes, and dramatic movement, in contrast to the detached rationality and clear idealism of the Neoclassicists.

Photography

Landscape and portrait painters initially saw photography as a threat to their livelihood. In fact the camera freed painters from the roles of narrator and illustrator, allowing them to explore dimensions of visual experience that were largely out of reach in Western art since the Renaissance. At the same time photography offered new opportunities to infuse images of objective reality with personal visions.

In its first two generations, the new medium was put to many uses. (See fig. 9.3 for an early example of a daguerreotype.) The perfection of glass-plate negatives in the 1850s made printed reproductions of photographs possible, although the technology was still quite cumbersome to use. Photographers had to smear a glass plate with just the right amount of toxic chemicals, insert it into a camera, expose the plate for the correct number of seconds, and develop the image almost immediately by applying more toxic chemicals in complete darkness.

If we transfer those operations to a small covered wagon in the trackless Western wilderness, we get a sense of the practical challenges of early landscape photography, as executed by Timothy O'Sullivan and others. Between 1867 and 1874, O'Sullivan traveled with several mapping expeditions that explored the more barren regions of the West. His stark and austere photographs show careful compositional balance, high resolution for that time, and well-crafted contrasts of light and dark. The "sitter" in this photo (**fig. 21.9**) is unknown—O'Sullivan himself was behind the camera—but he is perfectly positioned in this lunar-looking, rocky region. The publication in books of photos such as this helped Americans to learn about their new territories, and exposed alert viewers to the eye of an artist.

21.9 Timothy O'Sullivan. *Iceberg Canyon, Colorado River, Looking Above*. 1871. Albumen print. 8″ × 11″.
National Gallery of Art, Washington, D.C. Diana and Mallory Walker Fund and Horace W. Goldsmith Foundation through Robert and Joyce Menschel. 2005.10.1.

21.10 Nadar (Félix Tournachon). *Sarah Bernhardt.*
1855. Photograph.
Courtesy of the George Eastman Museum.

Delacroix was one of the first to recognize the difference between camera vision and human vision. He believed that photography was potentially of great benefit to art and artists. In an essay for students, Delacroix wrote:

> A daguerreotype is a mirror of the object; certain details almost always overlooked in drawing from nature take on in it characteristic importance, and thus introduce the artist to complete knowledge of construction as light and shade are found in their true character.[1]

Photographer Félix Tournachon, known as Nadar, first gained fame as a balloonist, and from a hot air balloon he made the first aerial photographs. He even took the first underground photographs in the sewers and catacombs of Paris, using artificial lighting techniques and long exposures.

Nadar recognized that photography was primarily a mechanical process, and that the photographer had to be intelligent and creative in order to make significant works of art with a camera. The most notable artists, writers, and intellectuals of Paris went to him to have their portraits made. His photograph of French actress Sarah Bernhardt (**fig. 21.10**) is an evolutionary link between Romantic painted portraits and today's celebrity photography. Through pose, drapery, and finely adjusted lighting, Nadar captured an expressive likeness. Another pioneer portrait photographer was Julia Margaret Cameron, who began photographing at age 48 and created an impassioned body of work (see fig. 9.5). As both a tool and a way of seeing, photography influenced **Realism**, the next major stylistic development.

Realism

Both Neoclassicism and Romanticism had their beginnings in rebellion. But by mid-century each had become institutionalized, functioning as a conservative force in French artistic life. At the state-sponsored Ecole des Beaux Arts, or School of Fine Arts, students were taught by members of the Academy of Fine Arts (an organization of government-approved artists) that "great painting" demanded "classical" technique and the "elevated" subject matter found in history, mythology, literature, or exotic locations.

Delacroix accused Academy members of teaching beauty as though it were algebra. Today, the term **academic art** describes generally tradition-minded works that follow overused formulas laid down by an academy or school, especially the French Academy of the nineteenth century.

French Academy members played a major role in selecting artists for a huge annual exhibition known as the **Salon**. Participating in the Salon was virtually the only way an artist might become known to the public in those days. The art history of the rest of the nineteenth century is largely one of rebellion against such institutions and authority figures. Vast changes in art and the artist's role in society were about to topple the dominance of the French Academy.

Realism describes a style of art and literature that depicts ordinary existence without idealism, exoticism, or nostalgia. We have seen it before the nineteenth century,

21.11 Gustave Courbet. *The Stone Breakers.* 1849 (destroyed in 1945). Oil on canvas. 5′5″ × 7′10″.
The Artchives/Alamy Stock Photo.

notably in Roman portrait sculpture (see Chapter 16) and Flemish and Dutch painting (see Chapter 17). By mid-century, a growing number of artists were dissatisfied with both the Neoclassicists' and the Romantics' attachment to mythical, exotic, extraordinary, and historical subjects. They believed that art should deal with human experience and observation. They knew that people in the nineteenth century were living a new kind of life, and they wanted art to show this.

In the 1850s, French painter Gustave Courbet revived Realism with new vigor by employing a direct, painterly technique for the portrayal of the dignity of ordinary things and common life. In doing so he laid the foundation for a rediscovery of the extraordinary visual qualities of everyday experience.

The Stone Breakers (**fig. 21.11**) shows Courbet's rejection of Romantic and Neoclassical formulas. His subject is neither historical nor allegorical, neither religious nor heroic. The men breaking stones are ordinary road workers,

presented almost life-size. Courbet did not idealize the work of breaking stones or dramatize the struggle for existence; he simply said, "Look at this."

Courbet's detractors were sure that he was causing artistic and moral decline by painting what they considered unpleasant and trivial subjects on a grand scale. They accused him of raising "a cult of ugliness" against cherished academic concepts of Beauty and the Ideal. He reportedly replied to his critics, "Show me an angel, and I'll paint one."[2] Conservative critics and most of the public saw Realism as nothing less than the enemy of art, and many believed that photography was the source and the sponsor of this disaster. When *The Stone Breakers* was exhibited in Paris at the Salon of 1850, it was attacked as inartistic, crude, and socialistic. The latter charge actually had some validity: Courbet was in fact a lifelong radical who espoused anarchist philosophies. He believed that most governments were oppressive institutions that served only the wealthy, and that average people could better meet their needs by

21.12 Rosa Bonheur. *The Horse Fair*. 1853–55. Oil on canvas. 96¼″ × 199½″.
The Metropolitan Museum of Art, New York. Gift of Cornelius Vanderbilt, 1887. (87.25).

banding together in voluntary associations for such functions as public works, banking, and policing. Beginning in 1855, Courbet practiced what he preached and set up his own exhibitions.

Courbet was one of the first to finish his paintings outdoors, working directly from nature. Previously, most landscape painting had been done in the artist's studio from memory, sketches, and reference materials such as rocks and plants brought in from outside. When portable tubes of oil paint became available in 1841, oil painting outdoors became practical. By working directly from subjects outdoors, painters were able to capture first impressions. This shift in practice opened up whole new ways of seeing and painting.

Of his own work, Courbet said: "To be able to represent the customs, the ideas, the appearance of my own era . . . to create living art; that is my aim."[3]

Realism of a more popular sort was practiced by Rosa Bonheur, who specialized in painting rural scenes with animals. In *The Horse Fair* (**fig. 21.12**), she captured the surging energy of a group of horses offered for sale, some of them

untamed. Many scholars believe that the riding figure in the blue-green coat near the center of the picture is a portrait of the artist wearing men's clothing.

The Realist paintings of American artist Thomas Eakins are remarkable for their humanity and insight into the everyday world. A comparison of the paintings of Eakins and those of his teacher, Jean-Léon Gérôme, shows the contrast between Realism and officially sanctioned academic art. Both *Pygmalion and Galatea* (**fig. 21.13**) by Gérôme and *William Rush Carving His Allegorical Figure* (**fig. 21.14**) take up the theme of the sculptor and his model; Gérôme created his painting based on classical and academic teachings, choosing a story from mythology, idealizing the figures, and painting it in a controlled fashion. Gérôme placed the woman, Galatea, on a pedestal, both literally and figuratively. The Greek myth of Pygmalion tells of a sculptor who carved a statue of a woman so beautiful that he fell in love with it. Pygmalion prayed to Aphrodite, goddess of love, who responded by making the figure come to life. The sentimental approach (note the cupid at right), smooth finish, and mild eroticism are typical of academic art.

21.13 Jean-Léon Gérôme. *Pygmalion and Galatea.* c.1860. Oil on canvas. 35″ × 27″.

The Metropolitan Museum of Art, New York. Gift of Louis C. Raegner, 1927. (27.200).

In contrast, Eakins presented a Realist view of the sculptor's trade, as he showed respect for the beauty of the ordinary human being. The somewhat lumpy model stands holding a dictionary as the carver works at the left, and the chaperone tends to her knitting. The painting style is also far looser, especially in the background. Eakins's insistence on painting people the way they actually look led him to escape the bondage of stylization imposed by the rules of the Academy; it also led to shock and rejection by the public and much of the art world. Eakins selected this subject because William Rush was the first American artist to use nude models, bringing controversy on himself in the 1820s, much as Eakins did 50 years later. Eakins himself lost his position as director of the Pennsylvania Academy of the Fine Arts because he allowed women students to see a live nude model.

We can see Eakins's influence in the work of his student and friend Henry Ossawa Tanner, who was the best-known African-American painter before the twentieth century. At the age of 13, Tanner watched a landscape painter at work and decided to become an artist. While studying with Eakins at the Academy of Fine Arts in Philadelphia, Tanner changed his subject matter from landscapes to scenes of daily life. In 1891, after an exhibition of his work was largely ignored, Tanner moved to France, where he remained for most of the rest of his life. He found less racial prejudice in Paris than in the United States. His paper "The American Negro in Art," presented at the

21.14 Thomas Eakins. *William Rush Carving His Allegorical Figure of the Schuylkill River.* 1876–77. Oil on canvas on masonite. 20⅛″ × 26⅛″.

21.15 Henry Ossawa Tanner.
The Banjo Lesson. 1893.
Oil on canvas. 49″ × 35½″.
Hampton University Museum, Virginia.

1893 World's Columbian Exhibition in Chicago, voiced the need for dignified portrayals of blacks, and he offered his painting *The Banjo Lesson* as a model (**fig. 21.15**).

The lively realism of *The Banjo Lesson* reveals Tanner's considerable insight into the feelings of his subjects, yet he avoids the sentimentality that was common in many late nineteenth-century American paintings. This painting shows the influence of Eakins in its detail and its humanistic content.

The most important predecessor of **Impressionism** in French art is without a doubt Edouard Manet, who

was the most controversial artist in Paris in the 1860s. He studied with an academic master, but soon broke away from traditional teaching in an effort to update the art of the Old Masters (Veronese, Velázquez, and Rembrandt, for example) by infusing painting with a dose of realism inherited from Gustave Courbet. In addition, Manet often flattened out the figures in his paintings under the influence of the Japanese prints that he knew and admired. His loose, open brushwork and sometimes commonplace subjects were an inspiration to younger painters who led the Impressionist movement.

21.16 Edouard Manet. *Le Déjeuner sur l'herbe* (*Luncheon on the Grass*). 1863. Oil on canvas. 7′ × 8′10″.
Musée d'Orsay, Paris. classicpaintings/Alamy Stock Photo.

Manet's painting *Luncheon on the Grass* (**fig. 21.16**) scandalized French critics and the public—because of the way it was painted as well as the subject matter. Manet painted the female figure without shading, employed flat patches of color throughout the painting, and left bare canvas in some places. He concentrated on the interplay among the elements of form that make up the composition: light shapes against dark, cool colors accented by warm colors, directional forces, and active balance. Manet's concern with visual issues over content or storytelling was revolutionary.

The juxtaposition of a female nude with males dressed in clothing of the time shocked viewers, but such a combination was not new. Nude and clothed figures were combined in landscape paintings going back to the Renaissance and

even Roman compositions that depicted ancient myths or stories from the Bible. However, in Manet's painting, there is no allegory, no history, no mythology, and not even a significant title to suggest morally redeeming values. Manet based his composition (but not his meaning) on the figures in an engraving of a Renaissance drawing by Raphael, who in turn had been influenced by Roman relief sculpture.

It is ironic that Manet, who had such reverence for the art of the past, would be attacked by the public and the critics for his radical innovations. Simultaneously, he was championed by other artists as a leader of the **avant-garde**. Manet became the reluctant leader of an enthusiastic group of young painters who later formed the group known as the Impressionists.

Impressionism

In 1874, a group of painters who had been denied the right to show at the Salon of 1873 organized an independent exhibition of their work. These artists, opposing academic doctrines and Romantic ideals, turned instead to the portrayal of contemporary life. They took their canvases outdoors and sought to paint "impressions" of what the eye actually sees, rather than what the mind knows or interprets from a scene. This is no simple goal; we usually generalize what we think we see from the most obvious fragments. A river may become a uniform blue-green in our mind, whereas direct, unconditioned seeing shows a rich diversity of colors.

Painting

Landscape and ordinary scenes painted outdoors in varied atmospheric conditions, seasons, and times of day were among the main subjects of these artists. For example, in 1877 Claude Monet took his easel to the St.-Lazare railroad station in Paris and painted a series of works in the train shed, among them *La Gare Saint-Lazare* (**fig. 21.17**). Rather than focus on the human drama of arrival and departure, he was fascinated by the play of light amid the steam of the locomotives and the clouds glimpsed through the glass roof above its cast-iron support. He made a series of paintings there under the constantly shifting conditions, creating them almost as quickly as traditional artists might make sketches.

21.17 Claude Monet. *La Gare Saint-Lazare* (*St. Lazare Station*). 1877. Oil on canvas. 30¼″ × 41½″.
Musée d'Orsay, Paris. Inv. No. RF 2775. akg-images/Laurent Lecat.

Monet and his colleagues were dubbed Impressionists by a critic who objected to the sketchy quality of their paintings. The term arose from one of Monet's versions of *Impression: Sunrise* (**fig. 21.18**). Although the critic's label was intended to be derogatory, the artists adopted the term as a fitting description of their work. Monet had seen the extremely fluid paintings of Turner (see fig. 21.5), but he used Turner's techniques in a more objective and less emotional manner.

From direct observation and from studies in physics, the Impressionists learned that we see light as a complex of reflections received by the eye and reassembled by the mind during the process of perception. Therefore, they used small dabs of color that appear merely as separate strokes of paint when seen close up, yet become lively depictions of subjects when seen at a distance. Monet often applied strokes of pure color placed next to one another, rather than colors premixed or blended on the palette. The viewer perceives a vibrancy that cannot be achieved with mixed color alone. The effect was startling to eyes accustomed to the muted, continuous tones of academic painting.

The Impressionists enthusiastically affirmed modern life, as Monet's paintings in the railroad station show. They saw the beauty of the world as a gift and the forces of nature as aids to human progress. Although misunderstood by their public, the Impressionists made visible a widely held optimism about the promise of the new technology. Impressionism was at its most creative between about 1870 and 1880. After 1880, Claude Monet continued for more than 40 years to advance Impressionism's original premise.

21.18 Claude Monet. *Impression: Sunrise.* 1872. Oil on canvas. 19½″ × 25½″.
Musée Marmottan Monet, Paris/Bridgeman Images.

21.19 Pierre-Auguste Renoir. *Le Moulin de la Galette* (*The Pancake Mill*). 1876. Oil on canvas. 51½″ × 68⅞″.
Musée d'Orsay, Paris. RMN-Grand Palais (Musee d'Orsay)/Hervé Lewandowski.

Pierre-Auguste Renoir's *Le Moulin de la Galette* (*The Pancake Mill*; **fig. 21.19**) depicts a popular Impressionist theme: contemporary middle-class people enjoying outdoor leisure activities. The young men and women depicted are conversing, sipping wine, and generally enjoying the moment at the popular outdoor café that served up pancakes and dance music with equal liberality. The Industrial Revolution had created an urban middle class with leisure, respect for the new technology, and a taste for fashion, and the Impressionists chronicled their lives. Renoir was more interested in the human drama than Monet—we sense the mood of some of the people in this work—but he was also very interested in how the light, filtered by the leaves of the trees, hits the bodies and clothing in the crowd.

Edgar Degas exhibited with the Impressionists, although his approach differed somewhat from theirs. He shared with the Impressionists a directness of expression and an interest in portraying contemporary life, but he combined the immediacy of Impressionism with a highly inventive approach to pictorial composition. Degas, along with the Impressionists, was influenced by the new ways of seeing and composing that he saw in Japanese prints and in unposed, street-scene photography.

Conventional European compositions placed subjects within a central zone. Degas, however, used surprising, lifelike compositions and effects that often cut figures at the edge. The tipped-up ground planes and bold asymmetry found in Japanese prints inspired Degas to create paintings

21.20 Edgar Degas. *The Ballet Class*. c.1879–80. Oil on canvas. 32⅜″ × 30¼″.

Philadelphia Museum of Art. Purchased with the W. P. Wilstach Fund. W1937-2-1. © 2018. Photograph: The Philadelphia Museum of Art/Art Resource/Scala, Florence.

of her prints (see *The Letter*, fig. 8.12) and paintings, such as *The Boating Party* (**fig. 21.21**), show the influence of the strong, flat shapes and sweeping curves of Japanese woodblock prints (see fig. 18.32).

The Boating Party also shows subtle feminist content. The difference in clothing styles between the woman and the man indicates that she has hired him to take her and the child out for a boat ride. This was an unusually assertive thing for a woman to do for herself in those days, and the glances between all three persons in the painting show some of the social tension that would have accompanied this event. The work is typical of Cassatt in its focus on the world of women and their concerns (see *Mary Cassatt: American Impressionist*, opposite).

The Impressionist group disbanded after its eighth exhibition, in 1886, but its influence was immeasurable—in spite of the fact that Impressionist paintings were looked upon with indifference or hostility by most of the public until the turn of the twentieth century.

filled with intriguing visual tensions, such as those in *The Ballet Class* (**fig. 21.20**), in which two diagonal groups of figures appear on opposite sides of an empty center.

Degas depicted ballet classes in ways that showed their unglamorous character. Often, as here, he was able to turn his ability to the task of defining human character and mood. The painting builds from the quiet, uninterested woman in the foreground, up to the right, then across to the cluster of dancing girls, following the implied sightline of the ballet master.

The American painter Mary Cassatt was another Impressionist who was influenced by Japanese prints, as well as by the casual compositions of late nineteenth-century do-it-yourself photography. Many

21.21 Mary Cassatt. *The Boating Party*. 1893–94. Oil on canvas. 35⅞″ × 46⅜″.

National Gallery of Art, Washington, D.C. 1963.10.94. Chester Dale Collection.

CREATORS

Mary Cassatt: American Impressionist

21.22 Mary Cassatt. *Self-Portrait.* c.1880. Gouache and watercolor over graphite on paper. 13″ × 9⅞″.
National Portrait Gallery, Washington, D.C. NPG.76.33. © 2018. Photo National Portrait Gallery Smithsonian/Art Resource/Scala, Florence.

If a forthright and rebellious temperament is required for success, Mary Cassatt (1844–1926) certainly had both. The daughter of a successful stockbroker and a well-educated mother, she knew from a very young age that she wanted to be an artist. She enrolled at age 15 in the Pennsylvania Academy of the Fine Arts. One of her fellow students there was the future rebel Thomas Eakins, but they could not undertake identical courses because, in those days, female students were not allowed to draw from live nude models.

Cassatt left for Paris in 1866 in search of better training. At first she studied privately with academic masters, including Jean-Léon Gérôme (see fig. 21.13). This gave her the skills that enabled her acceptance into several annual Salons between 1868 and 1874. Trips to Italy and Spain soon followed, and viewing works by the old masters convinced her that most of the contemporary academic artists of her day were unoriginal.

Not surprisingly, Cassatt began to bridle against the unspoken rules that governed Salon acceptance. She showed some of her rebellious side in 1875, when her work was rejected by the jury. The next year she merely repainted the background of one rejected work a darker shade, and the jury accepted it. This puzzled her.

In late 1877, Cassatt had a life-changing encounter when Edgar Degas visited her studio. She recalled the meeting:

> Degas asked me not to send to the Salon again but to exhibit instead with his friends in the Impressionist group. I accepted with joy. Finally I could work with an absolute independence without being concerned with the ultimate opinion of a jury. I already knew who my masters were: I admired Manet, Courbet, and Degas. I hated conventional art. I began to live.[4]

Degas and Cassatt became lifelong friends. Because they were both well-mannered aristocrats who never married and held themselves somewhat aloof, they got along well. Besides, Cassatt regarded marriage as an impediment to what mattered most: painting. She exhibited with the Impressionists four times, including their last exhibition in 1886. Through this association she developed her personal style, which was based far less than the other Impressionists on painting outdoors.

Painting modern women in their own situations became Cassatt's specialty. We see this with *The Boating Party* (see fig. 21.21), and also with *Young Mother Sewing* (**fig. 21.23**). This painting shows the mother and child theme that became Cassatt's dominant subject in later life. Her paintings are not sentimental, nor do they idealize motherhood. No one seems to be posing; rather, she approached the subject in a down-to-earth fashion. For the 1893 World's Columbian Exposition in Chicago, she painted a mural titled *Young Women Plucking the Fruits of Knowledge or Science.* Unfortunately, it does not survive. After about 1911 she painted less frequently because of declining health.

Cassatt never took on students, but she did have an important influence in another respect: When wealthy friends of her family came over to Paris to visit, Cassatt introduced them to the work of the Impressionists. Through her influence, several of these Americans became the earliest serious collectors of Impressionism, and many museums in the United States now proudly hang these works.

21.23 Mary Cassatt. *Young Mother Sewing.* 1900. Oil on canvas. 36⅜″ × 29″.
Metropolitan Museum of Art. H.O. Havemeyer Collection. Bequest of Mrs. H.O. Havemeyer, 1929. (29.100.48).

Sculpture

French artist Auguste Rodin was at least as innovative in sculpture as his contemporaries were in painting; he instituted a level of innovation not seen since Bernini (see fig. 17.21).

In 1875, after training as a sculptor's helper, Rodin traveled to Italy, where he carefully studied the work of the Renaissance masters Donatello and Michelangelo. Rodin was the first to use Michelangelo's unfinished pieces (see fig. 12.12) as an inspiration for making rough finish an expressive quality. In contrast to Michelangelo, however, Rodin was primarily a modeler in plaster and clay, rather than a carver in stone.

Rodin's best-known work, *The Thinker* (**fig. 21.24**), shows his expressive style to good advantage. He wrote that at first he was inspired by a figure of the medieval poet Dante, but he rejected the idea of a thin, ascetic figure:

21.24 Auguste Rodin. *The Thinker.* c.1910.
Bronze. Life-size.
Photograph: Christie's Images Ltd./SuperStock.

Guided by my first inspiration I conceived another thinker, a naked man, seated upon a rock, his feet drawn under him, his fist against his teeth, he dreams. The fertile thought slowly elaborates itself within his brain. He is no longer dreamer, he is creator.[5]

In *The Thinker*, Rodin projected the universal artist/poet as creator, judge, and witness, brooding over the human condition. Rodin combined a superb knowledge of anatomy with modeling skill to create the fluid, tactile quality of hand-shaped clay. He restored sculpture as a vehicle for personal expression after it had lapsed into mere decoration and heroic monuments.

The Post-Impressionist Period

Post-Impressionism refers to trends in painting starting in about 1885 that followed Impressionism. The Post-Impressionist painters did not share a single style; rather, they built on or reacted to Impressionism in different ways. Some felt that the Impressionists' focus on sketchy immediacy had sacrificed solidity of form and composition. Others felt that Impressionism's emphasis on objective observation did not leave enough room for personal expression or spiritual content. Thus, Post-Impressionist artists went in two different directions: some toward clearer formal organization, and some toward greater personal expression.

Formal Organization

French artists Georges Seurat and Paul Cézanne were interested in developing formal structure in their paintings. Each in his own way organized visual form to achieve structured clarity of design, and their paintings influenced twentieth-century formalist styles.

Seurat's large painting *A Sunday on La Grande Jatte* (**fig. 21.25**) has the subject matter, light, and color qualities of Impressionism, but this is not a painting of a fleeting moment; it is a carefully constructed composition of lasting impact. Seurat set out to systematize the optical color mixing of Impressionism and to create a more solid, formal organization with simplified shapes. He called his method divisionism, but it is more popularly known as **pointillism**. With it, Seurat tried to develop and apply a "scientific" technique. He arrived at his method by studying the principles of color optics that were being formulated at the time. Through the application of tiny

21.25 Georges Seurat. *A Sunday on La Grande Jatte.* 1884–86. Oil on canvas. 81¾″ × 121¼″.
The Art Institute of Chicago, IL, USA/Helen Birch Bartlett Memorial Collection 1926.22./Bridgeman Images.

dots of color, Seurat achieved a vibrant surface based on **optical color mixture**.

Seurat preceded *A Sunday on La Grande Jatte* with more than 50 drawn and painted preliminary studies in which he explored the horizontal and vertical relationships, the character of each shape, and the patterns of light, shade, and color. The final painting shows the total control that Seurat sought through the application of his method. The frozen formality of the figures seems surprising, considering the casual nature of the subject matter; yet it is precisely this calm, formal grandeur that gives the painting its strength and enduring appeal.

Like Seurat, Cézanne sought to achieve strength in the formal structure of his paintings. "My aim," he said, "was to make Impressionism into something solid and enduring like the art of the museums."[6]

Cézanne saw the planar surfaces of his subjects in terms of color modulation. Instead of using light and

shadow in a conventional way, he relied on carefully developed relationships between adjoining strokes of color to show solidity of form and receding space. He questioned, then abandoned, linear and atmospheric perspective and went beyond the appearance of nature, to reconstruct it according to his own interpretation.

Landscape was one of Cézanne's main interests. In *Mont Sainte-Victoire* (**fig. 21.26**), we can see how he flattened space, yet gave an impression of air and depth with some atmospheric perspective and the use of warm (advancing) and cool (receding) colors. The dark edge lines around the distant mountain help to counter the illusion of depth. Cézanne simplified the houses and trees into patches of color that suggest almost geometric planes and masses. This entire composition uses color and brushstroke to orchestrate nature to a degree that was unprecedented in Western art at the time. His rhythm of parallel brushstrokes and his

21.26 Paul Cézanne. *Mont Sainte-Victoire*. 1902–4. Oil on canvas. 27½″ × 35¼″.

Philadelphia Museum of Art. The George W. Elkins Collection, 1936. © 2018. Photograph: The Philadelphia Museum of Art/Art Resource/Scala, Florence.

concept of a geometric substructure in nature offered a new range of possibilities to later artists.

Personal Expression

Among Post-Impressionists of an expressive bent, Vincent van Gogh and Paul Gauguin brought to their work emotional intensity and a desire to make their thoughts and feelings visible. They often used strong color contrasts, shapes with clear contours, bold brushwork, and, in van Gogh's case, vigorous paint textures. Their art greatly influenced twentieth-century **Expressionist** styles.

With the Dutch artist Vincent van Gogh, late nineteenth-century painting moved from an outer impression of what the eye sees to an inner expression of what the heart feels.

From Impressionism, van Gogh learned the expressive potential of open brushwork and relatively pure color, but the style did not provide him enough freedom of expression. He intensified the surfaces of his paintings with textural brushwork that recorded each gesture of his hand and gave an overall rhythmic movement to his paintings. He also began to use strong color in an effort to express his emotions more clearly. In letters to his brother Theo, he wrote, "instead of trying to reproduce exactly what I have before my eyes, I use color more arbitrarily so as to express myself forcibly."[7]

As did other artists of the period, van Gogh developed a new sense of design from studying Japanese prints, as we see in *Japonaiserie: Flowering Plum Tree* (**fig. 21.27**). Van Gogh owned many Japanese prints, and he frequently praised

21.27 Vincent van Gogh. *Japonaiserie: Flowering Plum Tree.* 1887. After Hiroshige. Oil on canvas. 21½″ × 18″.
Van Gogh Museum, Amsterdam (Vincent van Gogh Foundation).

them in letters. He created the composition of this work by tracing a print by Hiroshige.

In *The Sower* (**fig. 21.28**) the Japanese influence led van Gogh to adopt bold, simplified shapes and flat areas of color. The wide band of a tree trunk cuts diagonally across the composition; its strength balances the sun and its energy coming toward us with the movement of the sower.

Van Gogh had a strong desire to share personal feelings and insights. In *The Starry Night* (**fig. 21.29**), a view of a town at night became the point of departure for a powerful symbolic image. Hills seem to undulate, echoing tremendous cosmic forces in the sky. The small town nestled into the dark forms of the ground plane suggests the small scale of human life. The church's spire reaches toward the heavens, echoed by the larger, more dynamic upward thrust of the cypress trees in the left foreground. (The evergreen cypress is traditionally planted beside graveyards in Europe as a symbol of eternal life.) All these elements are united by the surging rhythm of lines that express van Gogh's passionate spirit and mystical vision. Many know of van Gogh's bouts of mental illness, but few realize that he did his paintings between seizures, in moments of clarity.

21.28 Vincent van Gogh. *The Sower.* 1888. Oil on canvas. 12⅜″ × 15¾″.
Van Gogh Museum, Amsterdam (Vincent van Gogh Foundation).

21.29 Vincent van Gogh. *The Starry Night.* 1889. Oil on canvas. 29″ × 36¼″.
The Museum of Modern Art, New York. Acquired through the Lillie P. Bliss Bequest (472.1941).
© 2018. Digital image: The Museum of Modern Art, New York/Scala, Florence.

French artist Paul Gauguin was highly critical of the materialism of industrial society. He experienced that business world firsthand during the several years that he worked as a stockbroker to support his family, painting on the weekends. He exhibited occasionally with the Impressionists, but he longed to escape what he called the European struggle for money. This attitude led Gauguin to admire the honest life of the Brittany peasants of western France. In 1888, he completed *The Vision After the Sermon* (**fig. 21.30**), the first major work in his new, expressive version of Post-Impressionism. The large, carefully designed painting shows Jacob and the angel as they appear to a group of Brittany peasants in a vision inspired by the sermon in their village church.

The symbolic representation of unquestioning faith is an image that originated in Gauguin's mind rather than in his eye. With it, Gauguin took a major step toward personal expression. In order to avoid what he considered the distraction of implied deep space, he tipped up the simplified background plane and painted it an intense vermilion. The entire composition is divided diagonally by the trunk of the apple tree, in the manner of Japanese prints. Shapes have been reduced to flat curvilinear areas outlined in black, with shadows minimized or eliminated.

Both van Gogh's and Gauguin's uses of color were important influences on twentieth-century painting. Their views on color were prophetic. The subject of a painting, Gauguin wrote, was only a pretext for symphonies of line and color.

> In painting, one must search rather for suggestion than for description, as is done in music…. Think of the highly important musical role which color will play henceforth in modern painting.[8]

Gauguin retained memories of his childhood in Peru that persuaded him that the art of ancient and non-Western cultures had a spiritual strength that was lacking in the European art of his time. He wrote:

> Keep the Persians, the Cambodians, and a bit of the Egyptians always in mind. The great error is the Greek, however beautiful it may be…. A great thought system is written in gold in Far Eastern art.[9]

Gauguin's desire to rejuvenate European art and civilization with insights from non-Western traditions would be continued in the early twentieth century by Matisse, Picasso, and the German Expressionists. They adopted Gauguin's vision

21.30 Paul Gauguin. *The Vision After the Sermon (Jacob Wrestling with the Angel)*. 1888.
Oil on canvas. 28¾″ × 36½″.
National Galleries of Scotland.

of the artist as a spiritual leader who could select from the past, and from various world cultures, anything capable of releasing the power of self-knowledge and inner life.

At the age of 43, Gauguin tried to break completely with European civilization by going to Tahiti, leaving behind his wife and their five children. In *Mahana no Atua* (*Day of the God*; **fig. 21.31**), he summarized the results of several years of painting. At the top center of this beach scene is a god figure from a book about Southeast Asia (not Tahiti). The women at the left bring offerings as the two on the right dance. In the foreground, three other women sit or lie on the edge of the sea, but the colors of this body of water are nothing like reality; rather, Gauguin here used colors as "the language of dreams," as he put it.[10] Where we might expect to see the statue reflected, we get a mysterious ooze of organic shapes in acidic hues. The seated figure just above stares back at us with a mysterious look.

Henri de Toulouse-Lautrec painted the gaslit interiors of Parisian nightclubs and brothels. His quick, long strokes of color define a world of sordid gaiety. Toulouse-Lautrec was influenced by Degas, but he plunged more deeply into nightlife. In *At the Moulin Rouge* (**fig. 21.32**), he used unusual angles, cropped images (such as the face on the right), and expressive, unnatural color to heighten feelings about the people and the world he painted. His paintings, drawings, and prints of Parisian nightlife influenced twentieth-century Expressionist painters, just as his posters influenced graphic designers (see fig. 8.17).

21.31 Paul Gauguin. *Mahana no Atua* (*Day of the God*). 1894. Oil on canvas. 26⅞″ × 36″.
The Art Institute of Chicago, IL, USA/Bridgeman Images.

21.32 Henri de Toulouse-Lautrec. *At the Moulin Rouge.* 1893–95. Oil on canvas. 48⅜″ × 55¼″.
The Art Institute of Chicago, Helen Birch Bartlett Memorial Collection. 1928.610. Shawshots/Alamy Stock Photo.

Symbolism

For Paul Gauguin, art had become above all a means of communicating through symbols, a synthesis of visual form carrying memory, feelings, and ideas. These beliefs link him to **Symbolism**, a movement in literature and the visual arts that developed around 1885.

Reacting against both Realism and Impressionism, Symbolist poets and painters sought to lift the mind from the mundane and the practical. They employed decorative forms and symbols that were intentionally vague or open-ended in order to create imaginative suggestions. The poets held that the sounds and rhythms of words were part of their poems' deeper meaning; the painters recognized that line, color, and other visual elements were expressive in themselves. Symbolism, a trend rather than a specific style, provided the ideological background for twentieth-century abstraction; it has been seen as an outgrowth of Romanticism and a forerunner of Surrealism.

As the century closed, Norwegian artist Edvard Munch articulated some of its darkest nightmares. He had traveled to Paris to study the works of his contemporaries, especially Gauguin, van Gogh, and Toulouse-Lautrec. What

21.33 Edvard Munch. *The Scream.* 1893. Tempera and crayon on cardboard. 36″ × 28⁹⁄₁₀″.

National Gallery, Oslo. Photograph: Jacques Lathion/Nasjonalmuseet. © 2018 Artists Rights Society (ARS), New York.

Art Nouveau

In the last decade of the nineteenth century and the first decade of the twentieth, some artists' explorations of line and color were transplanted into architecture and interior design. This yielded an abstract style called **Art Nouveau**, meaning "new art." Using ideas gleaned from Paul Gauguin, Japanese prints, and the decorative schemes of William Morris (see fig. 13.1), architects and designers created projects that brought nature into art in new ways.

An early leader in this trend was French designer Hector Guimard. In 1897, he designed the first Parisian Art Nouveau house, Castel Beranger. Guimard designed not only the exterior of this building, but also its wallpaper, door handles, carpets, and light fixtures. The lobby (**fig. 21.34**) strongly exploits the motif of organic growth as abstracted plant forms populate layered compartments on the walls before climbing up onto the ceiling. The novelty of this style is not in its coverage of the available space; it is rather in the fact that this scheme makes no reference to past styles.

he learned from them, particularly from Gauguin's works, enabled him to carry Symbolism to a new level of expressive intensity. Munch's powerful paintings and prints explore depths of emotion: grief, loneliness, fear, love, sexual passion, jealousy, and death.

In *The Scream* (**fig. 21.33**), Munch takes the viewer far from the pleasures of Impressionism and extends considerably van Gogh's expressive vision. In this powerful image of anxiety, the dominant figure is caught in isolation, fear, and loneliness. Despair reverberates in continuous linear rhythms. Munch's image has been called the soul-cry of the age.

21.34 Hector Guimard. Lobby of Castel Beranger. Paris. 1897–98.
B.O'Kane/Alamy Stock Photo.

21.35 Antoni Gaudí. Casa Milà, Barcelona. 1906–12. View of the Facade (photograph).
La Pedrera (Casa Mila) Barcelona, Spain/Bridgeman Images.

Castel Beranger is a town house, which limited the scope for invention in the structure of the building. But when the Milà family presented Spanish architect Antoni Gaudí with a vacant lot in Barcelona in 1906, he took Art Nouveau ideas into the framework of the design (**fig. 21.35**). Gaudí used limestone carved into wildly curving blocks for the façade; behind it is a network of steel posts and undulating, flexed beams that support the building. This metal skeleton affords ample space for window openings, which the architect shaped organically. The upper utility floor is similarly sculptural but with fewer openings, below chimneys in fanciful shapes. The Casa Milà overall resembles a weatherworn natural cliff; the locals call it La Pedrera, or The Quarry. The Art Nouveau style soon spread across Europe and the United States, where it also influenced graphic design and product design.

The Impressionists had staged their own exhibitions that competed with the official Salons; the following generation of Post-Impressionists and Symbolists gave up on even that level of recognition. The most creative artists worked outside the normal channels of advancement in the art world, giving rise to the term avant-garde to describe their social group. The term comes from military theory: It describes the foremost soldiers who attack in advance of the main body of troops—literally, the "advance guard." The analogy held that the most creative artists similarly work well ahead of the general public's ability to comprehend, pioneering new ideas in taste and thought that will eventually take hold in society at large. This model aptly symbolized the social structure of artistic innovation far into the twentieth century.

KEY TERMS

academic art – art governed by rules, especially works sanctioned by an official institution, academy, or school

Art Nouveau – a style of decorative art and architecture characterized by curving shapes abstracted from nature

avant-garde – artists who work in an experimental or innovative way, often opposing mainstream standards

Expressionism – refers to individual and group styles originating in Europe in the late nineteenth and early twentieth centuries

Impressionism – a style of painting executed outdoors, aiming to capture the light and mood of a particular moment and the transitory effects of light and color

Neoclassicism – a revival of Classical Greek and Roman forms in art, music, and literature

optical color mixture – apparent rather than actual color mixture, produced by interspersing brushstrokes or dots of color instead of physically mixing them

painterly – painting characterized by openness of form, in which shapes are defined by loose brushwork in light and dark color areas rather than by outline or contour

pointillism – a system of painting using tiny dots or "points" of color, developed by French artist Georges Seurat in the 1880s; Seurat systematized the divided brushwork

and optical color mixture of the Impressionists and called his technique "divisionism"

Post-Impressionism – a general term applied to various personal styles of painting by French artists (or artists living in France) that developed from about 1885 to 1900 in reaction to what artists saw as the somewhat formless and aloof quality of Impressionist painting; Post-Impressionist painters were concerned with the significance of form, symbols, expressiveness, and psychological intensity

Realism – the mid-nineteenth-century style of Gustave Courbet and others, based on the idea that ordinary people and everyday activities are worthy subjects of art

Romanticism – a literary and artistic movement aimed at asserting the validity of subjective experience; characterized by intense emotional excitement, and depictions of powerful forces in nature, exotic lifestyles, danger, suffering, and nostalgia

Salon – an official art exhibition in France, judged by members of the official French Academy

Symbolism – a movement in late nineteenth-century Europe (c.1885–1900) concerned with communication of inner emotional states through forms and colors that may not copy nature directly

22 EARLY TWENTIETH CENTURY

LEARNING OBJECTIVES

22.1 Identify how Fauves and Expressionists extended the innovations of the Post-Impressionists.

22.2 Describe the artistic goals and development of Cubism.

22.3 Trace the shift toward abstraction in sculpture in the work of Brancusi.

22.4 Describe modern art in the United States in the early twentieth century.

22.5 Explain the goals and stylistic forebears of the Futurists.

During the first decade of the last century, Western views of the nature of reality changed radically. This upheaval was driven by new findings in psychology, technology, and physics. In 1900, Sigmund Freud published *The Interpretation of Dreams*, a vast work that explored the power and influence of the subconscious mind on all of us. He argued that we are often driven by psychic forces that we do not well understand. In 1903, the Wright brothers flew the first self-propelled aircraft, and Marie and Pierre Curie isolated the radioactive element radium for the first time. In 1905, Albert Einstein changed our conception of time, space, and substance with his theory of relativity. Matter could no longer be considered solid; rather, it was a form of energy.

The Industrial Revolution had changed life in myriad ways. Thousands of new jobs opened in city-based factories, drawing rural people into a new, crowded, and impersonal urban environment. Business-oriented capitalism moved the workplace farther from family life than it had ever been before, and most wage work became much more unpleasant. The most violent revolutions of the century—in Russia, Mexico, and China—sprang from class tensions. At the same time, the industrial system created vast amounts of wealth that engendered a middle class and gave millions a financial floor. Better vaccines and public health led to longer life expectancies and a lower birth rate. A steady stream of inventions made business more productive and made

scientists into heroes. Government functions expanded into new areas such as factory inspection, education, regulation of currency, and product safety.

Simultaneously, great changes occurred in art, and some of them were inspired by scientific discoveries. In 1913, Russian artist Wassily Kandinsky described how deeply he was affected by the discovery of subatomic particles:

> A scientific event cleared my way of one of the greatest impediments. This was the further division of the atom. The crumbling of the atom was to my soul like the crumbling of the whole world.[1]

The art of the twentieth century thus came from a series of revolutions in thinking and seeing. Its characteristics are those of the century itself: rapid change, diversity, individualism, and exploration—always accompanied by abundant discoveries. Twentieth-century artists, as well as scientists, have helped us to see the world in new ways and revealed new levels of consciousness.

The explosion of new styles of art at the beginning of this century grew from Impressionist and Post-Impressionist innovations. In their search for forms to express the new age, European artists often looked to ancient and non-Western cultures for inspiration and renewal. In so doing, they completed the breakaway from Renaissance techniques, which had dominated Western artistic thought for 500 years.

22.1 Henri Matisse. *Harmony in Red
(The Red Room).* 1948. Oil on canvas.
70⅞″ × 86⅝″.

The merest glance at *Harmony in Red* (**fig. 22.1**) by
Henri Matisse reveals that a new world is dawning in art.
The rich maroon of the tablecloth shows a deep-blue vine
pattern that also claws its way up the wall. The colors of the
fruit are bold and flat. The window with its bright golden
edge looks out to a radically simplified, yet intensely colored scene. Matisse was a leader in the early twentieth-
century movement known as **Fauvism,** which expanded on
the innovations of the Post-Impressionists.

The Fauves and Expressionism

At the turn of the century, the most creative young
painters in France carefully studied Post-Impressionist
works. Some drew inspiration from the rationalizing tendencies of Cézanne; others wanted to move farther down
the expressive path that Vincent van Gogh and Paul
Gauguin had charted.

Fauvism

Matisse was in the latter camp. He saw a large collection of
Gauguin's Tahitian works in 1905 and soon he extended the
older artist's expressive color choices. He also led a faction
of painters who experimented with vigorous brushwork
and large, flat areas of bright color. Their first group exhibition shocked the public. A critic of that show derisively
called them *les fauves* ("the wild beasts"); this became the
group's nickname.

However, Matisse was not as rebellious as his detractors claimed; rather, he was a thoughtful person who simply tried to express his enthusiasm for life. Every part of a
painting by Matisse is expressive: the lines, the colors, the
subject, and the composition itself. He frequently reduced
his subjects to a few outlines, rather than fill in all their
details. He did this to better preserve the original impulse
of feeling. More detail in a work would merely overburden
the viewer and distract attention from the immediate burst
of emotion.

Matisse's painting *Le Bonheur de vivre* (*The Joy of Life*;
fig. 22.2) is a more radical Fauvist work that shows the artist's degree of enthusiasm. Pure hues vibrate across the surface; lines, largely freed from descriptive roles, align with
simplified shapes to provide a lively rhythm in the composition. The seemingly careless depiction of the figures
is based on Matisse's knowledge of human anatomy and
drawing. The intentionally direct, childlike quality of the
form serves to heighten the joyful content. Matisse defined
his aim: "What I am after, above all, is expression."[2]

Matisse had befriended fellow Fauve member André
Derain while the two were still in art school. In Derain's
London Bridge (**fig. 22.3**), brilliant, invented color is balanced by some use of traditional composition and perspective. Derain spoke of intentionally using discordant color.
His use of strong color in this painting probably does not
appear disharmonious today, an indication of changing

22.2 Henri Matisse. *Le Bonheur de vivre* (*The Joy of Life*). 1905–6. Oil on canvas. 69⅛″ × 94⅞″.
The Barnes Foundation, Merion, Pennsylvania/Bridgeman Images. © 2018 Succession H. Matisse/Artists Rights Society (ARS), New York.

22.3 André Derain. *London Bridge*. 1906. Oil on canvas. 26″ × 39″.
The Museum of Modern Art (MoMA). Gift of Mr. and Mrs. Charles Zadok. 195.1952. © 2018. Digital image: The Museum of Modern Art, New York/Scala, Florence. © 2018 Artists Rights Society (ARS), New York/ADAGP, Paris.

tastes. Note also the pure touches of yellow, blue, and green in the lower left; these are expanded versions of the pointillist dots of Georges Seurat (see fig. 21.25).

The Fauve movement lasted little more than two years, from 1905 to 1907, yet it was one of the most influential developments in early twentieth-century painting. The Fauves took color farther from its traditional role of describing the natural appearance of an object. In this way their work led to an increasing use of color as an independent expressive element.

Expressionism

We can categorize Fauvism as an expressive style. **Expressionism** is a general term for art that emphasizes inner feelings and emotions over objective depiction. (Expressionism has also enlivened works of music and literature.) In Europe, romantic or expressive tendencies can be traced from seventeenth-century Baroque art (see figs. 17.20 and 17.23) to the early nineteenth-century painting of Eugène Delacroix (see fig. 21.8), who in turn influenced the expressive side of Post-Impressionism (particularly van Gogh).

A few German artists at the beginning of the century shared the expressionist goals of the Fauves. Their desire to express attitudes and emotions was so pronounced and sustained that we call their art German Expressionism. They developed imagery characterized by vivid, often angular simplifications of their subjects and dramatic color contrasts, with bold, at times crude finish. These techniques added emotional intensity to their works. Like their Fauve counterparts, the German Expressionists built on the achievements of Gauguin and van Gogh and the soul-searching paintings of Edvard Munch. They felt compelled to use the power of Expressionism to address the human condition, often exploring such themes as natural life, sorrow, passion, spirituality, and mysticism. As their art developed, it absorbed formal influences from medieval German art and some non-Western art from Africa and Oceania.

Two groups typified the German Expressionist movement of the early twentieth century: The Bridge (*Die Brücke*) and The Blue Rider (*Der Blaue Reiter*). Ernst Ludwig

22.4 Ernst Ludwig Kirchner. *Street, Berlin*. 1913. Oil on canvas. 47½″ × 35⅞″.

The Museum of Modern Art (MoMA). Purchase. 274.1939. © 2018. Digital image: The Museum of Modern Art, New York/Scala, Florence.

Kirchner, architecture student turned painter, was one of the founders of The Bridge. These groups appealed to artists to revolt against academic painting and establish a new, vigorous aesthetic that would form a bridge between the Germanic past and modern experience. They first exhibited as a group in 1905, the year of the first Fauve exhibition.

Kirchner's early paintings employed the flat color areas of Fauvism; by 1913, he had developed a style that incorporated the angularities of **Cubism** (see pp. 398–402). In *Street, Berlin* (**fig. 22.4**), elongated figures are crowded together. Repeated diagonal lines create an urban atmosphere charged with energy. Dissonant colors, chopped-out shapes, and rough, almost crude brushwork heighten the emotional impact.

22.5 Paula Modersohn-Becker. *Self-Portrait with an Amber Necklace*. 1906. Oil on canvas. 24″ × 19¾″.

Kunstmuseum Basel. Photograph: akg-images.

Paula Modersohn-Becker developed an Expressionist language apart from the organized groups. Trips to Paris in 1903 and 1905 exposed her to the art of Cézanne and Gauguin, and she combined their influences in self-revealing paintings such as *Self-Portrait with an Amber Necklace* (**fig. 22.5**). She reduced the curves of her head to flat regions, and used color for expressive rather than representational purposes. The oversized eyes seem to tell us something, but they remain mysterious.

The Blue Rider group was led by Kandinsky, who lived in Munich between 1908 and 1914. In contrast to other German Expressionists, Kandinsky hoped to lead viewers toward spiritual rejuvenation through introspection. In *Blue Mountain* (**fig. 22.6**), he created what he called a choir of colors, influenced by the vivid, freely expressive color of the Fauves.

Kandinsky's paintings evolved steadily away from straightforward representation. In *Blue Mountain*, subject matter is secondary to the powerful effect of the visual elements released from merely descriptive roles. Influenced by the vivid expressive color of the Fauves, Kandinsky uses colors that are heightened to a peak of intensity; the horsemen riding across seem more dreamlike than real.

By 1910, Kandinsky overturned one of the most important rules of Western art. He made the shift to totally nonrepresentational imagery in order to concentrate on the expressive potential of pure form, freed from the need to depict anything. A person of mystical inclinations, he hoped to create art only in response to what he called "inner necessity," or the emotional stirrings of the soul, rather than in response to what he saw in the world. He said that art should transcend physical reality and speak directly to the emotions of viewers without intervening subject matter. He sought a language of visual form comparable to the sound language we experience in music. The rhythms, melodies, and harmonies of music please or displease us because of the way they affect us. To exploit this relationship between painting and music, Kandinsky often gave his paintings musical titles, such as *Composition IV* (**fig. 22.7**). Here we see colors and shapes that only vaguely correspond to things in the world. Rather, the artist painted out of inner necessity to make visible his personal mood at that time. Just as a composer uses harmony and melody, Kandinsky used color and form to (as he put it) "set the soul vibrating."

Kandinsky said that the content of his paintings was "what the spectator *lives* or *feels* while under the effect of the *form and color combinations* of the picture."[3] He was an important innovator in the history of art, and his revolutionary nonrepresentational works played a key role in the development of later styles. His purpose was not simply aesthetic novelty. By turning away from the material world of subject matter, he hoped that his paintings would lead the way to a great new era of spirituality. Kandinsky hoped that nonrepresentational art could provide spiritual nourishment for the modern world.

22.6 Wassily Kandinsky. *Blue Mountain* (*Der Blaue Berg*). 1908–9. Oil on canvas. 41¾″ × 38″.

The Solomon R. Guggenheim Museum, New York. Gift of Solomon R. Guggenheim, 1941. 41.505. Photograph by David Heald. © 2018 Artists Rights Society (ARS), New York.

22.7 Wassily Kandinsky. *Composition IV*. 1911. Oil on canvas. 62¹³⁄₁₆″ × 98⅝″.

Kunstsammlung Nordrhein-Westfalen, Düsseldorf. Photograph: Peter Willi/Bridgeman Images. © 2018 Artists Rights Society (ARS), New York.

Cubism

While living in Paris, Spanish artist Pablo Picasso shared ideas and influences with French artist Georges Braque. Together they pursued investigations that led to Cubism, another principal innovation in painting before World War I. Generally speaking, Cubist painters emphasized pictorial composition over personal expression. Cubism heavily influenced the basic visual structure of many of the notable paintings and sculptures of the century. Through its indirect influence on architecture and the arts, Cubism has become part of our daily lives.

Picasso absorbed influences quickly, keeping only what he needed to achieve his objectives. His breakthrough painting, *Les Demoiselles d'Avignon* (*Young Ladies of Avignon*; **fig. 22.8**), shows a radical departure from traditional composition.

Picasso created a new vocabulary of form influenced by Cézanne's faceted reconstructions of nature, and by the inventive abstraction and power he admired in African sculpture such as the Kota reliquary figure (**fig. 22.9**) and the mask from Ivory Coast (**fig. 22.10**). While the meanings and uses of African sculpture held little interest for him, their form revitalized his art.

In *Les Demoiselles d'Avignon*, the fractured, angular figures intermingle with the sharp triangular shapes of the background, activating the entire picture surface. This reconstruction of image and ground, with its fractured triangulation of forms and its merging of figure and ground,

22.8 Pablo Picasso. *Les Demoiselles d'Avignon* (*Young Ladies of Avignon*). 1907. Oil on canvas. 8′ × 7′8″.

The Museum of Modern Art, New York. Acquired through the Lillie P. Bliss Bequest (333.1939). © 2018. Digital image: The Museum of Modern Art, New York/Scala, Florence. © 2018 Estate of Pablo Picasso/Artists Rights Society (ARS), New York.

22.9 Reliquary Figure. Gabon. Kota peoples, 19th–20th centuries. Wood, copper, brass. 28⅞″ x 15⅝″ x 3″.

The Metropolitan Museum of Art, New York. Purchase. The Michael C. Rockefeller Memorial Collection. Bequest of Nelson A. Rockefeller, by exchange, 1983 (1983.18). © 2018. The Metropolitan Museum of Art/Art Resource/Scala, Florence.

22.10 Mask. Ivory Coast. Wood. 9¾″ × 6½″.

Musee du Quai Branly. 71.1952.59.1. © Musée du Quai Branly - Jacques Chirac, Dist. RMN-Grand Palais/Patrick Gries/Bruno Descoings.

22.11 Paul Cézanne. *Gardanne*. 1885–1886. Oil on canvas. 31½″ × 25¼″.

The Metropolitan Museum of Art. Gift of Sr. and Mrs. Franz H. Hirschland, 1957. (57.181).

was the turning point. With this painting, Picasso shattered the measured regularity of Renaissance perspective. Doing away with vanishing points, uniform lighting, and academic figure drawing, he overturned some important traditions of Western art. *Les Demoiselles* thus set the stage and provided the impetus for the development of Cubism. Although some art historians decry this work's negative depiction of women, viewers are challenged by the painting's hacked-out shapes and overall intensity.

While Picasso made the first breakthrough with *Les Demoiselles d'Avignon*, Braque did more to develop the vocabulary of Cubism. A comparison of two paintings— Cézanne's *Gardanne*, completed in 1886 (**fig. 22.11**) and Braque's *Houses at l'Estaque* (**fig. 22.12**), completed in 1908— shows the beginning of the progression from Cézanne's Post-Impressionist style to the new Cubist approach.

22.12 Georges Braque. *Houses at l'Estaque.* 1908.
Oil on canvas. 28½″ × 23″.

Rupf Foundation, Bern, Switzerland. Photograph: Giraudon/Bridgeman Images.
© 2018 Artists Rights Society (ARS), New York/ADAGP, Paris.

In a series of landscapes painted in the South of France (where Cézanne had worked), Braque took Cézanne's faceted planar constructions a step further. Instead of the regular perspective that had been common in European painting since the Renaissance, Braque's shapes define a rush of forms that pile up rhythmically in shallow, ambiguous space. Buildings and trees seem interlocked in a heaving array that pushes and pulls across the picture surface.

Houses at l'Estaque provided the occasion for the movement's name: When Matisse saw this painting, he declared it to be nothing but a bunch of little cubes. (His somewhat dismissive attitude indicates the widely varying goals of the Cubists and the Expressionistic Fauves.) From 1908 to 1914, Braque and Picasso were jointly responsible for inventing and developing Cubism. Braque later described their working relationship as resembling mountain climbers roped together. They worked for a time in relatively neutral tones, to explore formal structure without the emotional distractions of color.

Analytical Cubism

During the phase of **Analytical Cubism** (1910 to 1911), Picasso, Braque, and others analyzed their subjects from various angles, then painted abstract, geometric references to these views. This is how we see, after all: by building up a mental image through brief, focused glances at a subject rather than a long, centered look. Because mental concepts of familiar objects are based on experiences of seeing many sides, the artists aimed to show objects as the mind, rather than the eye, perceives them. Braque's *The Portuguese* (**fig. 22.13**) is a portrait of a man sitting at a café table strumming a guitar. The subject is broken

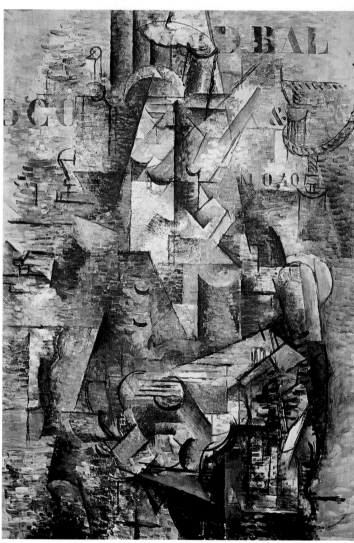

22.13 Georges Braque. *The Portuguese.* 1911.
Oil on canvas. 46″ × 32″.

Offentliche Kunstsammlung, Basel, Switzerland/Bridgeman Images.
© 2018 Artists Rights Society (ARS), New York/ADAGP, Paris.

down into facets and recombined with the background. Figure and ground thus collapse into a shallow and jagged pictorial space.

Cubism was a rational, formalist counterpart to the personal emphasis of the Fauves and other Expressionists. Above all, it was a reinvention of pictorial space. The Cubists realized that the two-dimensional space of the picture plane was quite different from the three-dimensional space we occupy. Natural objects were points of departure for abstract images, demonstrating the essential equality of forms within the spaces that surround and penetrate them. Cubism is thus a reconstruction of objects based on geometric simplification. By looking first at Cézanne's *Gardanne*, then at Braque's *Houses at l'Estaque*, and finally at *The Portuguese*, we see a progression in which forms seem to build and then spread across the surface in overlapping planes.

Synthetic Cubism

In 1912, Picasso and Braque modified Analytical Cubism with color, textured and patterned surfaces, and the use of cutout shapes. The resulting style came to be called **Synthetic Cubism**. Artists used pieces of newspaper, sheet music, wallpaper, and similar items, not represented but actually *presented* in a new way. The newspaper in *Violin, Fruit and Wineglass* (**fig. 22.14**) is part of a real Paris newspaper. The shapes that in earlier naturalistic, representational paintings would have been "background" have been made equal in importance to foreground shapes. Picasso chose traditional still-life objects; but rather than paint the fruit, he cut out and pasted printed images of fruit. Such compositions, called *papier collé* in French, or pasted paper, became known as **collage** in English. Analytical Cubism involved taking apart, or breaking down, the subject into its various aspects; Synthetic Cubism was a process of building up or combining bits and pieces of material.

22.14 Pablo Picasso. *Violin, Fruit and Wineglass*. 1913. Charcoal, colored papers, gouache, and painted paper collage. 25¼″ × 19½″.

Philadelphia Museum of Art. A.E. Gallatin Collection, 1952-61-106. © 2018 The Philadelphia Museum of Art/Art Resource/ Scala, Florence. RMN-Grand Palais/Béatrice Hatala. © 2018 Estate of Pablo Picasso/ Artists Rights Society (ARS), New York.

22.15 Pablo Picasso. *Guitar.* 1914. Construction of sheet metal and wire. 30½″ × 13¾″ × 7⅝″.

The Museum of Modern Art. Gift of the artist. 94.1971. © 2018. Digital image: The Museum of Modern Art, New York/Scala, Florence. © 2018 Estate of Pablo Picasso/Artists Rights Society (ARS), New York.

22.16 Constantin Brancusi. *Sleep.* 1908. White marble. 10¼″ × 17⅜″ × 11⅞″.

National Art Museum of Bucharest. Photograph: Adam Woolfitt/Robert Harding. © Succession Brancusi—All rights reserved (ARS) 2018.

22.17 Constantin Brancusi. *Sleeping Muse I.* 1909–11. Marble. 6¾″ × 10⅝″ × 8⅜″.

Hirschhorn Museum and Sculpture Garden, Smithsonian Institution. Gift of Joseph H. Hirschhorn (1966). © Succession Brancusi—All rights reserved (ARS) 2018.

Picasso extended the Cubist revolution to sculpture when he assembled his *Guitar* (**fig. 22.15**) from pieces of sheet metal; the flat pieces in this work overlap in a way similar to a Cubist painting. This work began a dominant trend toward sculptural construction: Before *Guitar*, most sculpture was carved or modeled. Since *Guitar*, a great deal of contemporary sculpture has been constructed.

Toward Abstract Sculpture

At the beginning of the twentieth century, the most influential sculptor was Auguste Rodin (see fig. 21.24), who had brought a new expressiveness to the medium. The Romanian Constantin Brancusi started sculpting under Rodin's influence, but later his work moved toward abstraction.

A sequence of Brancusi's early work shows his radical, yet gradual, break with the past. *Sleep* (**fig. 22.16**) of 1908 appears similar to Rodin's romantic naturalism. With *Sleeping Muse I* (**fig. 22.17**) in 1911, Brancusi simplified

the subject as he moved from naturalism to abstraction. *Newborn [I]* (**fig. 22.18**) of 1915 is stripped to essentials. Brancusi said, "Simplicity is not an end in art, but one arrives at simplicity in spite of oneself, in approaching the real sense of things."[4]

Brancusi's journey toward abstraction was also a journey back to a pre-Classical style of carving. Ancient sculpture from the Cyclades (islands of the Aegean Sea) has a distinctive, highly abstract elegance similar to Brancusi's, as the *Cycladic II* head (**fig. 22.19**) shows. Just as the Cubists studied African sculpture, Brancusi spent time sketching works in the ancient Mediterranean section of the Louvre. Brancusi gradually eliminated the surface embellishments that had dominated European sculpture since the Gothic

22.18 Constantin Brancusi. *Newborn [I]*. 1915.
White marble. 5¾″ × 8¼″ × 5⅞″.

22.19 *Cycladic II.* Naxos, Greece. 2700–2300 BCE. Marble. Height 10½″.

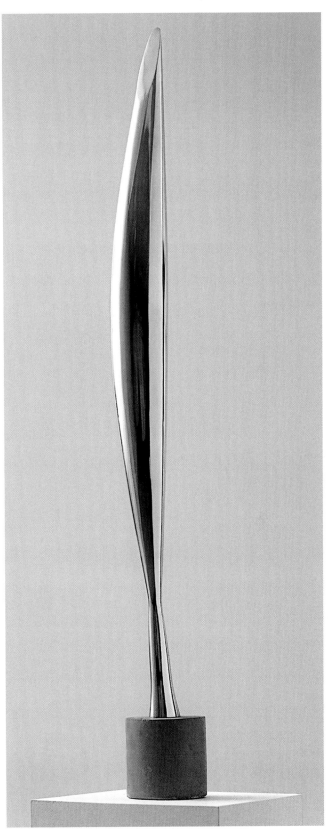

period, instead creating shapes that were recognizable but simplified. He achieved expressive strength by carefully abstracting and reducing forms to their essence. As a result his sculpture invites contemplation.

With *Bird in Space* (**fig. 22.20**), Brancusi used cast bronze to create an elegant, uplifting form. The implied soaring motion of the "bird" embodies the idea of flight. The highly reflective polish Brancusi applied to the bronze surface contributes to the form's weightless quality. Brancusi started working on this visual concept about a decade after the Wright brothers initiated the age of human flight, but long before the world was filled with streamlined consumer goods. Brancusi said, "All my life I have sought the essence of flight."[5]

22.20 Constantin Brancusi. *Bird in Space*. 1928.
Bronze (unique cast). 54″ × 8½″ × 6½″.

Early Modern Art in the United States

The American public had its first extensive look at leading developments in European art during the Armory Show, which opened in New York in 1913 before traveling to Boston and Chicago. In this show of over 1,300 works, the organizers attempted to demonstrate that modern art was not revolutionary, but rather had evolved from movements in the mid-nineteenth century. Most of the public missed this lesson, however, in the shock of seeing Cubism and Expressionism for the first time. Although the show was controversial, it was also extremely popular, drawing over 300,000 visitors. American artists were able to see key works by Impressionists, Post-Impressionists, and Fauves—particularly Matisse, who was much maligned by critics. Also shown were paintings by Picasso and Braque, and sculpture by Brancusi. As a result, Cubism and other forms of abstract art spread to the United States.

22.21 Alfred Stieglitz. *The Steerage*. 1907. From *Camera Work, No. 34*. New York. Published October 1911. Photogravure. 12⅝″ × 10³⁄₁₆″.
The J. Paul Getty Museum, Los Angeles. 84.XM.695.19.

Photography and Painting

As Picasso and Braque took the steps that led to Cubism, Alfred Stieglitz was turning photography into an artform. When Picasso saw Stieglitz's photograph *The Steerage* (**fig. 22.21**), he said, "This photographer is working in the same spirit as I am."[6] By that he meant that Stieglitz had a similar eye for abstract composition.

Stieglitz saw the complex scene as an array of interacting forces of light, shade, shape, and directional force. Aboard a ship headed for Europe, he saw the composition of this photograph as "a round straw hat, the funnel leaning left, the stairway leaning right, the white drawbridge with its railings made of circular chains, white suspenders crossing on the back of a man on the steerage below, round shapes of iron machinery, a mast cutting into the sky, making a triangular shape.... I saw a picture of shapes and underlying that, the feeling I had about life."[7] He rushed to his cabin to get his camera, and he made the photograph he considered his best.

Even before the Armory Show, Stieglitz played a key role in introducing the new European painting and sculpture to Americans. In 1905, he opened a gallery in New York and began showing the work of the most progressive European artists, including photographers. The gallery was known as 291 after its address on Fifth Avenue. Although it had few visitors except those in the know, its influence was immense. The gallery was the first in America to show works by Cézanne, Matisse, Brancusi, Picasso, and Braque. Stieglitz also published a highly influential magazine, *Camera Work*, that featured essays on photography and modern aesthetics. 291 also exhibited children's art and African art.

Following the exhibition of art by the European pioneers, Stieglitz began to show work by the first American modernists, including Georgia O'Keeffe (see *Georgia O'Keeffe and Alfred Stieglitz: Art and Lives Intertwined* on p. 406). Her work from the time of World War I was innovative, consisting mostly of loosely brushed abstractions based on nature. In 1917, while teaching in the Texas Panhandle, she took frequent walks in the lonely, windswept prairie. Finding its emptiness immensely stimulating, she made a series of expressive abstract watercolors titled *Evening Star* (**fig. 22.22**), based on her sightings of the planet Venus in the darkening sky. Venus is the small unpainted circle that the yellow orb encloses, and this empty spot seems to radiate ever wider sweeps of rich, saturated color. The grandiosity of the Texas landscape inspired O'Keeffe; she wrote to a friend, "It is absurd how much I love this country."[8]

22.22 Georgia O'Keeffe. *Evening Star No. VI.* 1917. Watercolor on paper. 8⅞″ × 12″.

The Georgia O'Keeffe Museum. Gift of the Burnett Foundation 1997.18.03. Photograph: Malcolm Varon 2001/Art Resource/Scala, Florence. © 2018 Georgia O'Keeffe Museum / Artists Rights Society (ARS), New York.

CREATORS

Georgia O'Keeffe and Alfred Stieglitz: Art and Lives Intertwined

Two of the most important early modern artists in the United States were Georgia O'Keeffe (1887–1986) and Alfred Stieglitz (1864–1946); their nearly lifelong relationship evolved from admiration to marriage to mutual influence to separation to respect.

Stieglitz first showed O'Keeffe's art at his gallery before the two even met, and they began a passionate correspondence while she was still living in North Texas. Shortly after she moved to New York City in 1919 they became a couple, even though he was still married. After his divorce became final in 1924, the two married and took an apartment.

O'Keefe's new environment and Stieglitz's urban-focused photography caused her to shift her painting style toward tighter brushwork and city subjects. We see this in *The Radiator Building—Night, New York* (**fig. 22.23**). She portrayed the skyscraper as an awesome presence, looming upward from the low vantage point. The steam rising at the right hints at her previous style. At the center left she painted Stieglitz's name in bright red neon; an invention because his gallery had no such sign. The Radiator Building had opened in 1924, and its nocturnal illumination made it "one of the sights of the city," according to a leading architectural magazine.[9]

A few years later, however, O'Keeffe was beginning to chafe in the relationship with Stieglitz, who was 23 years older, somewhat controlling, and apparently infatuated with a still younger woman. After 1929 O'Keeffe began spending increasing amounts of time in New Mexico, back in the rural dry landscapes that she had loved as a teacher in neighboring Texas. Stieglitz complained in a letter, "Without you I am nothing. Without me, you go right ahead—will be Georgia O'Keeffe. The fact is, you really do not need me anymore." She replied, "I chose coming away because at least here I feel good—and it makes me feel I am growing very tall and straight inside—and very still.... I have not wanted anything but to be kind to you—but there is nothing to be kind to you if I cannot be me—and me is something that reaches very far out into the world, and all around."[10] She bought a remote ranch and resumed painting southwestern landscapes beneath expansive skies, along with tightly focused views of flowers (see fig. 1.21).

Stieglitz, meanwhile, had begun taking an interest in the sky himself. In 1925, he began a lengthy series of nearly abstract photographs that he titled *Equivalents* (**fig. 22.24**). In these works, he sought to

22.23 Georgia O'Keeffe. *The Radiator Building—Night, New York*. 1927. Oil on canvas. 48″ x 30″.

Alfred Stieglitz Collection. Co-owned by Fisk University, Nashville, Tennessee, and Crystal Bridges Museum of American Art, Bentonville, Arkansas. Photography by Edward C. Robison III. © 2018 Georgia O'Keeffe Museum/Artists Rights Society (ARS), New York.

express an inner feeling through the arrangement and lighting alone. In this work the darkness and diagonal orientation of the clouds reinforces the off-balance composition with the moon in the corner. He hoped that the mysterious and haunted mood of this work came only from its design elements rather than from its subject. The work's aerial subject, off-balance quality, and degree of abstraction parallel O'Keefe's *Evening Star No. VI* (see fig. 22.22).

In late 1929, Stieglitz opened a new gallery called An American Place, devoted only to American artists. Although he and O'Keeffe were separated for all practical purposes, he exhibited her most recent paintings there every year for the rest of his life; she eventually lived long enough to experience recognition as a legendary American creator.

22.24 Alfred Stieglitz. *Equivalents*. 1927. Gelatin silver print. 3¹¹⁄₁₆″ x 4⅝″.

The Georgia O'Keeffe Museum. Gift of the Georgia O'Keeffe Foundation. © 2018. Photograph: Georgia O'Keeffe Museum, Santa Fe/ Art Resource/Scala, Florence.

22.25 Frank Lloyd Wright. Robie House. Chicago, Illinois. 1909.

Architecture

Between 1905 and 1910, architects began to challenge traditional concepts of form in space just as painters and sculptors had done. While Cubism was developing in painting, leading American architect Frank Lloyd Wright was designing what he called prairie houses, in which he often omitted or minimized walls between living and dining rooms, and between interior and exterior spaces. Wright's concept of open plans changed the way people design living spaces. In many present-day homes, kitchen, dining room, and living room now join in one continuous space, and indoors often intermingles with outdoors.

In the Robie House (**fig. 22.25**) of 1909, a striking cantilevered roof reaches out and unifies a fluid design of asymmetrically interconnected spaces. To get a feeling of how far ahead of his time Wright was, imagine the incongruity of a new 1909 automobile that could have been parked in front of the Robie House the year it was completed. Wright's designs were soon published in Europe, and influenced the course of modern architecture there.

Futurism and the Celebration of Motion

The Italian **Futurists** were among the many artists who gained their initial inspiration from Cubism, but they used it to different ends. To the shifting planes and multiple vantage points of Cubism, Futurists such as Giacomo Balla and Umberto Boccioni added a sense of speed and motion and a celebration of the machine.

By multiplying the image of a moving object, Futurists expanded the Cubist concept of simultaneity of vision. In 1909, the poet Filippo Tommaso Marinetti proclaimed in the *Initial Manifesto of Futurism*: "the world's splendor has been enriched by a new beauty; the beauty of speed . . . a roaring motorcar . . . is more beautiful than the [classical] Victory of Samothrace."[11]

The Futurists translated the speed of modern life into works that captured the dynamic energy of the new century. Giacomo Balla intended his work *Abstract Speed— The Car Has Passed* (**fig. 22.26**) to depict the rushing air and dynamic feeling of a vehicle passing. We do not know exactly which type of automobile Balla was observing, but the fastest racing cars in 1913 reached speeds of 100 miles per hour, faster than both trains and airplanes at the time.

An abstract sculpture of a striding figure climaxed a series of Umberto Boccioni's drawings, paintings, and sculpture. Boccioni insisted that sculpture should be released from its usual confining outer surfaces in order to open up and fuse the work with the space surrounding it. In *Unique Forms of Continuity in Space* (**fig. 22.27**), muscular forms seem to leap outward in flamelike bursts of energy. During this period the human experience of motion, time,

and space was transformed by the development of the automobile, the airplane, and the movies. Futurist imagery reflects this exciting period of change.

French artist Marcel Duchamp, working independently of the Futurists, brought the dimension of motion to Cubism. His *Nude Descending a Staircase, No. 2* (**fig. 22.28**) was influenced by stroboscopic photography, in which sequential camera images show movement by freezing successive instants (see fig. 10.2). Through

22.27 Umberto Boccioni. *Unique Forms of Continuity in Space.* 1913. Bronze (cast in 1931). 43⅞″ × 34⅞″ × 15¾.

22.28 Marcel Duchamp. *Nude Descending a Staircase, No. 2.*
1912. Oil on canvas. 58″ x 35″.

22.29 Sonia Delaunay-Terk. *Le Bal Bullier.* 1913. Oil on mattress ticking. 3′2¾₆″ × 12′9½″.
Musée National d'Art Moderne, Centre Pompidou. White Images © 2018. Photograph: Josse/Scala, Florence. © Pracusa 2017637.

sequential, diagonally placed, abstract references to the figure, the painting presents the movement of a body through space, seen all at once, in a single rhythmic progression. Our sense of gravity intensifies the overall feeling of motion. When the painting was displayed at the Armory Show in New York in 1913, it caused cries of dismay and was seen as an exercise in madness. The painting, once described as "an explosion in a shingle factory,"[12] has remained an inspiration to artists who use rhythmic repetition to express motion.

Sonia Delaunay-Terk expressed motion in her paintings through color contrasts. Her large work *Le Bal Bullier* (**fig. 22.29**) is an interpretation of couples moving about on the floor of one of Paris's leading nightclubs

of the time. We see Cubist influence in the work, as it is composed of flat shapes that overlap in shallow space. But the added push and pull of contrasting color contributes both depth and motion to the composition. Stretching a canvas 12 feet across proved difficult, so the artist used mattress ticking. Delaunay-Terk was an early crusader for the integration of modern art into everyday things. Even as she painted, she made book bindings, embroideries, textiles, and fashions that included ideas from the latest modern art movements. In 1922, she started her own clothing design studio, where she specialized in what she called *Simultaneous Dresses* (see fig. 5.6). Not for many years would such ideas take hold in the mass market.

KEY TERMS

Analytical Cubism – the style of Cubism developed by Picasso and Braque from 1910 to 1911 in which they analyzed their subjects from various angles, then painted abstract, geometric references to these views

collage – a work made by gluing various materials, such as paper scraps, photographs, and cloth, on a flat surface

Cubism – an art style developed in Paris by Picasso and Braque, beginning in 1908 based on the simultaneous presentation of multiple views, disintegration, and geometric reconstructions of subjects in flattened, ambiguous pictorial space

Expressionism – refers to individual and group styles originating in Europe in the late nineteenth and early twentieth centuries, characterized by bold execution and free use of distortion and symbolic or invented color

Fauvism – a style of painting introduced in Paris in the early twentieth century, characterized by areas of bright, contrasting color and simplified shapes

Futurism – a group movement originating in Italy in 1909 that celebrated both natural and mechanical motion and speed

Synthetic Cubism – a modification of Analytical Cubism with color, textured and patterned surfaces, and the use of cutout shapes

23

BETWEEN WORLD WARS

LEARNING OBJECTIVES

23.1 Explain Dada's use of the readymade and photomontage as forms for social critique.

23.2 Identify the interests, visual characteristics, and techniques associated with Surrealism.

23.3 Recognize how artists after World War I took Cubism in new directions.

23.4 Compare the social interests of Constructivism, De Stijl, Bauhaus, and International Style architecture.

23.5 Discuss how art was used as a means of political expression in the 1930s.

23.6 Summarize the distinctive characteristics of Latin American modernism.

23.7 Identify the principal characteristics of American regionalism.

23.8 Discuss some of the distinctive concerns of African-American artists.

23.9 Explain how organic abstract art can be seen as an anti-Fascist statement.

In 1914, enthusiasm for grand, patriotic solutions to international tensions led citizens of many countries into World War I, an intense and protracted conflict that involved most European countries and eventually the United States. But the war turned out to be far more devastating than the people of the time expected: More than ten million were killed and twice that number wounded. The promise of an entire generation was lost in the world's first experience of mechanized mass killing.

The war changed the political and cultural landscape forever. It set the stage for the Russian Revolution, and sowed grievances that the Nazis of Germany and the Fascists of Italy later exploited. Governments assumed new powers to mobilize people and material, to dictate economic life, to censor public expression, and, by controlling information, to manipulate the way people thought. Dissent was denounced as unpatriotic.

Many artists in the interwar period consciously linked their creations to their hopes for a better world. Some expressed those hopes by angrily denouncing present conditions; others offered utopian visions. This tendency to use art as a tool for social betterment is a prominent marker for this period. Another marker is the spread of modernist innovations to non-European populations, as variations on modern styles arose in many places.

Dada

Dada began in protest against the horrors of World War I. The artists and writers who began the movement in Zurich chose the ambiguous word Dada as their rallying cry. According to some accounts, they arrived at the name by randomly sticking a knife into a dictionary. The two-syllable word expressed the essence of what was more a rebellious attitude than a cohesive style. In the eyes of the Dadaists, the causes of the war were embedded in European traditional values, which they set out to overturn. According to artist Marcel Janco:

Dada was not a school of artists, but an alarm signal against declining values, routine, and speculation, a desperate appeal on behalf of all forms of art, for a creative basis on which to build a new and universal consciousness of art.[1]

French artist and poet Jean Arp said:

> While the thunder of guns rolled in the distance, we sang, painted, glued, and composed for all our worth. We were seeking an art that would heal mankind from the madness of the age.[2]

The insanity of the war proved to Dadaists that European culture had lost its way. To make a new beginning, the Dadaists rejected most moral, social, political, and aesthetic values. They thought it pointless to try to find order and meaning in a world in which so-called rational behavior had produced only chaos and destruction. They aimed to shock viewers into seeing the absurdity of the Western world's social and political situation.

The Dadaists often protested through play and spontaneity. Chance rather than premeditation often guided their literature, art, and staged events. Poets shouted nonsense words at random; artists joined diverse elements into startling and irrational combinations.

Marcel Duchamp was the most radical of the Dadaists, and perhaps the most radical artist of the twentieth century. He had the audacity to offer mass-produced objects as artworks, calling them **readymades**. For example, he once signed a snow shovel and titled it *In Advance of the Broken Arm*. In 1917, he signed a urinal with someone else's name and called it *Fountain*.

In a purposeful slap at traditional standards of beauty, Duchamp bought a picture postcard reproduction of Leonardo da Vinci's *Mona Lisa*, and drew a mustache and beard on her face. He signed the work with his own name and titled it *L.H.O.O.Q.* (**fig. 23.1**). The title is a vulgar pun, comprehensible to those who can read the letters aloud quickly in French. Roughly translated into English it means, "She's hot in the tail." By showing outrageous irreverence toward a deeply treasured painting, Duchamp tried to shake people out of their unthinking acceptance of dominant values.

The American artist Man Ray, a friend of Duchamp, was a leader of Dada in the United States. His Dada works include

23.1 Marcel Duchamp. *L.H.O.O.Q.* Paris. 1919. Pencil on reproduction of Leonardo's *Mona Lisa*. 7¾″ × 4¾″.
Philadelphia Museum of Art, Pennsylvania. Louise and Walter Arensberg Collection, 1950. © 2018. Photograph: The Philadelphia Museum of Art/Art Resource/Scala, Florence. © Association Marcel Duchamp/ADAGP, Paris/Artists Rights Society (ARS), New York 2018.

paintings, photographs, and assembled objects. In 1921, he visited a housewares shop and purchased a clothes iron, a box of tacks, and a tube of glue. After gluing a row of tacks to the smooth surface of the iron, he titled his assemblage *Gift* (**fig. 23.2**), thus creating a useless and dangerous object.

Dadaists expanded on the Cubist idea of collage with **photomontage**, in which parts of photographs are combined in thought-provoking ways. In *The Multi-Millionaire* (**fig. 23.3**), by Dadaist Hannah Höch, industrial-age man stands as a fractured giant among the things he has produced. At the time she created this work, the artist was attacked for lacking originality, because she merely combined already existing things. But now we see how her unorthodox methods of composition can yield a powerful statement.

23.2 Man Ray. *Cadeau (Gift).* c.1958. Replica of 1921 original. Painted flatiron, with row of 13 tacks, heads glued to the bottom. 6⅛″ × 3⅝″ × 4½″.

Museum of Modern Art (MoMA) James Thrall Soby Fund. 1966. © 2018. Digital image: The Museum of Modern Art, New York/Scala, Florence. © Man Ray Trust/Artists Rights Society (ARS), NY/ADAGP, Paris 2018.

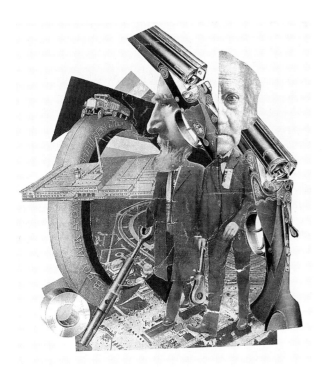

23.3 Hannah Höch. *The Multi-Millionaire.* 1923. Photomontage. 14″ × 12″.
© 2018 Artists Rights Society (ARS), New York/VG Bild-Kunst, Bonn.

Some Dadaists maintained that art was dead. By this they meant that it was useless to try to create beauty in a world that could destroy itself. They often intended to be anti-aesthetic but, ironically, they created a new aesthetic of lasting influence.

Surrealism

In the mid-1920s, a group of writers and painters gathered to protest the direction of European culture. They thought that the modern emphasis on science, rationality, and progress was throwing the consciousness of Europeans out of

balance. In response, they proclaimed the importance of the unconscious mind, of dreams, fantasies, and hallucinations. They held that these illogical aspects of human consciousness ought to be given equal status with reason and logic. They were indebted to the irrationality of Dadaism, and they also drew heavily on the new psychology of Sigmund Freud.

The new movement, **Surrealism**, was officially launched in Paris in 1924 with the publication of its first manifesto, written by poet-painter André Breton. He defined the movement's purpose as:

> the future resolution of these two states, dream and reality, which are seemingly so contradictory, into a kind of absolute reality, a surreality, if one may so speak.[3]

One of the first converts to the movement was the former Dadaist Max Ernst, who had fought in the war and was still haunted by its nightmares. To allow freer play to fantasy, he laid his canvases over textured surfaces such as asphalt pavement, and rubbed the canvas with pencils and crayons. In this way he could be surprised by the patterns that emerged for fertilization in his paintings. This technique is called **frottage**, the French word for "rubbing." In the 1927 work *The Horde* (**fig. 23.4**), we see a gaggle of silhouetted monsters tumbling over one

23.4 Max Ernst. *The Horde.* 1927. Oil on canvas. 44⅞″ × 57½″.
Stedelijk Museum, Amsterdam, The Netherlands/De Agostini Picture Library/ Bridgeman Images. © 2018 Artists Rights Society (ARS), New York/ADAGP, Paris.

23.5 René Magritte. *The Lovers.* 1928. Oil on canvas. 21⅜″ × 28⅞″.

Museum of Modern Art, (MoMA). Gift of Richard S. Zeisler. Acc. n.: 530.1998. © 2018 Digital Image: The Museum of Modern Art, New York/Scala, Florence. © 2018 C. Herscovici, London/Artists Rights Society (ARS), New York.

23.6 Joan Miró. *Woman Haunted by the Passage of the Bird-Dragonfly Omen of Bad News.* 1938. Oil on canvas. 31½″ × 10′4″.

Toledo Museum of Art. Purchased with funds from the Libbey Endowment. Gift of Edward Drummond Libbey. 1986.25. © Successió Miró/Artists Rights Society (ARS), New York/ADAGP, Paris 2018.

another in a violent scene. The artist's combat experience in World War I most likely influenced the chaotic nature of this work.

Belgian Surrealist painter René Magritte used an illogical form of realism to engage the viewer in mind-teasing mystery and playful humor. *The Lovers* (**fig. 23.5**) depicts a couple in an impossible kiss. If we imagine ourselves in that scene, we get the jolt that the Surrealists wanted to induce. (Perhaps his best-known work is *La Trahison des Images;* see fig. 1.10.)

In contrast, Joan Miró's **Abstract Surrealism** provides suggestive elements that give wide play to the viewer's imagination, and emphasize color and design rather than storytelling content.

To probe the unconscious, Miró and others used automatic processes, sometimes called **automatism**, in which chance was a key factor. They scribbled, doodled, and poured paint in order to cultivate the chance accident that might prove revealing. With the adoption of such spontaneous and "automatic" methods, the Surrealists sought to expand consciousness by throwing out the sort of rational planning that frequently accompanies art creation.

Miró's evocative paintings often depict imaginary creatures. He made them by scribbling or doodling on the canvas and then examining the results to see what the shapes suggested. The bold, organic shapes in *Woman Haunted by the Passage of the Bird-Dragonfly Omen of Bad News* (**fig. 23.6**) are typical of his mature work. The wild, tormented quality, however, is unusual for Miró and reflects his reaction to the times. Miró pointed out that this painting was done at the time of the Munich crisis, in which Hitler was allowed to take over part of Czechoslovakia, a prelude to World War II. Even though there is a sense of terror here, Miró's underlying playful optimism is apparent. He loved the art of children so much that he tried to paint like a child.

Miró took Surrealism into the third dimension in works such as *Object* (**fig. 23.7**). Like a Surrealist movie, it is a union of seemingly random visual material. However, the themes that it broaches touch on our deep fears, such as death (the stuffed parrot and the orange fish), dismemberment (the stuffed silk stocking in the paper shoe), and disorientation (the map). The artist hoped that these irrational juxtapositions would jolt viewers

23.7 Joan Miró. *Object.* 1936. Stuffed parrot on wood perch, stuffed silk stocking with velvet garter and doll's paper shoe suspended in hollow wood frame, derby hat, hanging cork ball, celluloid fish, and engraved map. 31⅞″ × 11⅞″ × 10¼″.

23.8 Salvador Dalí. *The Persistence of Memory.* 1931. Oil on canvas. 9½″ × 13″.

The Museum of Modern Art (MoMA). Given anonymously. Acc. n.: 162.1934. © 2018. Digital image: The Museum of Modern Art, New York/Scala, Florence. © 2018 Salvador Dalí, Fundació Gala-Salvador Dalí/Artists Rights Society (ARS), New York.

out of their normal modes of thinking and open them to fresh possibilities.

Spanish painter Salvador Dalí made his nightmares into his principal subjects, which he re-created in a highly illusionistic fashion based on academic techniques. *The Persistence of Memory* (**fig. 23.8**) evokes the eerie quality of some dreams. Mechanical time wilts in a deserted landscape of infinite space. A blasted miniature tree grows out of the tabletop as ants crawl over a watch. The warped,

headlike image in the foreground may be the last remnant of a vanished humanity; the artist called it a self-portrait.

Dalí's illusionary deep space and representational techniques create near-photographic dream images that make the impossible seem believable (see *Salvador Dalí: Confusion and Creativity,* opposite). The startling juxtaposition of unrelated objects creates a hallucinatory sense of a superreality beyond the everyday world. This approach has been called **Representational Surrealism**.

CREATORS

Salvador Dalí: Confusion and Creativity

23.9 Salvador Dalí with one of his pieces used for a benefit for refugee artists in California, 1941.

Everett Collection Inc/Alamy Stock Photo. © 2018 Salvador Dalí, Fundació Gala-Salvador Dalí/Artists Rights Society (ARS), New York.

Salvador Dalí (1904–1989) practiced a distinctive version of Surrealism based on paranoia. He was also the first modern artist to become a celebrity outside the art world. Combining noteworthy creativity with canny personal image management, he blazed a trail that later celebrities would follow.

Dalí's birth was unusual, coming nine months and ten days after the death of his brother, also named Salvador, at age 2. His parents told Dalí that he was a replacement. Beginning in childhood, he suffered lurid nightmares that later provided subject matter for many paintings. His family supported his early artistic proclivities by enrolling him in Spain's national fine arts academy. There he showed exceptional skill, but was thrown out of the school twice: once for political activities,

and the second time for refusing to take the art history exam because he felt his teachers were not qualified to judge his knowledge. He was already showing the daring and thirst for notoriety that later propelled him.

Settling in Paris in 1928, Dalí gravitated to the Surrealist movement, which he found congenial because the Surrealist style provided an outlet for his vivid inner life. The next year he made the film *Un Chien Andalou* (*An Andalusian Dog*) with former academy classmate Luis Buñuel. This nightmarish mash-up of hallucinatory scenes (see fig. 10.6) is one of the most commented-upon movies in cinema history.

Dalí called his approach the paranoiac-critical method. This means that he cultivated a paranoid state of mind in which the sufferer confuses everyday perception with hallucinations of threat or danger. Something seen (such as a pocket watch) becomes repulsive or bizarre (by melting; see fig. 23.8). Such irrational moments received realistic treatment in his highly polished painting style. In an essay Dalí proclaimed a wish to "systematize confusion and thus help to discredit completely the world of reality."[4] Such beliefs harmonized well with the Surrealist manifesto, which announced the hope of fusing logic and illogic, reason and unreason.

When the Surrealist group staged its exhibitions, Dalí participated with flamboyant actions. In London in 1936, he gave a lecture while sealed

inside a full-body deep-sea diving suit. Of course no one could hear him, and soon he began to suffocate and required rescue by a fellow Surrealist.

Surrealist art was supposed to be distasteful and challenging, but Dalí noticed that the public loved his provocations. His wife, Gala Éluard, took up the task of manager, coordinating his appearances and overseeing sales of his work. He set up his own pavilion in the 1939 World's Fair in New York, a hallucinated, walk-in version of the Renaissance painting *Birth of Venus* by Botticelli. In 1941, he staged a benefit banquet in California for war refugees, decorating the hall with fancifully clothed mannequins (**fig. 23.9**). Guests were asked to attend dressed as their worst nightmares.

Dalí's urge for fame led him to Hollywood, where he collaborated with director Alfred Hitchcock by creating a dream sequence for the movie *Spellbound* (**fig. 23.10**) in 1945.

In true paranoid fashion, normal things become something else: A shadowy figure lurks behind a chimney that becomes tree roots, observed from above by a stone outcrop that assumes the shape of a human head.

In the 1950s, Dalí enlarged his commercial activities to a scope previously unknown for a modern artist. He appeared in television ads endorsing chocolates, autos, airlines, and Alka Seltzer. (Some of these are viewable today on video-sharing websites.) Surrealist founder André Breton denounced Dalí's commercialism, rearranging the letters of his name to Avida Dollars.

In his last years Dalí signed hundreds of blank sheets of paper, which his assistants populated with lithographs that the artist may or may not have created or even seen. Confronted with this violation of art-world ethics, he replied that he was merely sowing confusion as he had always done: "The more confusion the better.... Confusion frees creativity."[5]

23.10 Still from *Spellbound*. 1945. Dream sequence by Salvador Dalí from film by Alfred Hitchcock.

Collection Christophel/Alamy Stock Photo. © 2018 Salvador Dalí, Fundació Gala-Salvador Dalí/Artists Rights Society (ARS), New York.

Expanding on Cubism

Cubism makes possible many ambiguities between presence and absence, representation and abstraction, figure and ground. Far from presenting the world as stable and predictable, Cubism suggests constant change and evolution. An art historian wrote, "By devaluing subject matter, or by monumentalizing simple, personal themes, and by allowing mass and void to elide, the Cubists gave effect to the flux and paradox of modern life and the relativity of its values."[6] Thus, Cubism makes visible some important characteristics of modern life.

23.11 Kazimir Malevich. *Suprematist Composition: Airplane Flying.* 1915. Oil on canvas. 22⅞″ × 19″.

The Museum of Modern Art (MoMA) Purchase. Acquisition confirmed in 1999 by agreement with the Estate of Kazimir Malevich and made possible with funds from the Mrs. John Hay Whitney Bequest (by exchange). 248.1935. © 2018. Digital image: The Museum of Modern Art, New York/Scala, Florence.

23.12 Fernand Léger. *The City.* 1919. Oil on canvas. 91″ × 177½″.

Philadelphia Museum of Art. Gallatin Collection, 1952-61-58. © 2018. Photograph: The Philadelphia Museum of Art/Art Resource/Scala, Florence. © 2018 Artists Rights Society (ARS), New York/ADAGP, Paris.

Russian artists took Cubism in a more abstract direction. A leader there was Kazimir Malevich, who branded his style Suprematism. His painting *Suprematist Composition: Airplane Flying* (**fig. 23.11**) shows in its title that the artist was familiar with Futurism: Its subject is a speeding modern airplane. Yet Malevich so simplified the Cubist pictorial language that we are left with a succession of flat, irregular rectangles against a pure background.

Malevich believed that shapes and colors in a painting always communicate, no matter what the subject of the work. Ideally, he thought, art should not need subject matter. This is why he named his movement Suprematism, because he wanted to focus on the supremacy of shape and color in art over representation or narrative. He shared some points of view with his fellow Russian Wassily Kandinsky, whom he knew. But while Kandinsky (who worked in Germany) painted brash, expressive works (see fig. 22.6), Malevich's constant urge to simplify makes him a more radical painter.

French artist Fernand Léger brought new shapes and a more dynamic style to Cubism. In his large painting *The City* (**fig. 23.12**), he crushed jagged shapes together, collapsing space in a composition reminiscent of a Cubist portrait or still life. The forms in his paintings look machine-made, rounded and tubular; this is in keeping with the urban bustle that is the work's subject.

Léger soon took Cubist composition into film when he made *Ballet Mécanique* (**fig. 23.13**), a 17-minute cinematic collage in which churning machines alternate with a swinging pendulum, a smiling woman, and shifting geometric shapes. Sometimes these forms are distorted with a kaleidoscopic mirror, which mashes them up and flattens them in the manner of a Cubist still life. Léger intended the film to have

23.13 Fernand Léger. *Ballet Mécanique*. 1924. Film.
© 2018 Artists Rights Society (ARS), New York/ADAGP, Paris.

a score by the American George Antheil, but practicalities prevented this. Antheil composed an unforgettably riotous work for 17 player pianos, percussion, and a siren, but because it ran twice as long as the film, the two could not be synchronized. Léger's film follows no obvious logic, but it seems to argue that machines and humans are about equally rhythmic if not equally graceful.

Building a New Society

Several art movements that emerged between the wars had the goal of improving the world somehow. Surrealists, for example, hoped to liberate human consciousness. Pioneer abstractionists felt that the nonrepresentational language they were creating would provide an ideal basis for the utopian society they sought. Constructivism, in Russia, focused on developing a new visual language for a new industrial age. De Stijl, in Holland, advocated the use of basic forms, particularly rectangles, horizontals, and verticals. Both movements spread throughout Europe and strongly influenced many artforms.

Constructivism

Constructivism was a revolutionary movement that began in Russia, inspired in part by the Suprematism of Malevich and others. Seeking to create art that was relevant to modern life in form, materials, and content, Constructivists made the first nonrepresentational constructions out of such modern materials as plastic and electroplated metal.

The Constructivists agreed with the Cubists in rejecting the traditional view of space as regular and static. The name of the movement came from their preference for constructing planar and linear forms that suggested a dynamic quality and, whenever possible, contained moving elements.

23.14 Lyubov Popova.
Painterly Architectonic.
1917. Oil on burlap.
27¾″ × 27¾″.

Museo Thyssen-Bornemisza,
Madrid. Inv. 716 (1977.52).
© 2018. Museo Thyssen-
Bornemisza/Scala, Florence.

23.15 Aleksandr Rodchenko.
View of *The Workers'
Club.* Reconstruction
exhibited at the
International Exposition
of Modern Decorative
and Industrial Arts,
Paris. 1925.

© Estate of Alexander Rodchenko/
RAO, Moscow/VAGA, New York.

The painter Lyubov Popova pioneered many of these effects in nonrepresentational works that she called *Painterly Architectonic* (**fig. 23.14**). Planes intersect in a shallow space that derives from Cubism. Although the work seems to resemble a mechanical contrivance of unknowable function, nothing is pictured here except forms and colors. Popova combined her painting with teaching in workers' schools, and she helped to found the First Working Group of Constructivists in 1921.

One of Popova's Constructivist colleagues was Aleksandr Rodchenko, one of the century's most innovative multimedia artists. He began as a painter, working with compasses and ruler in true Constructivist fashion. Soon he renounced painting in favor of more useful arts: He designed posters for public display, as he also worked on furniture, photography, and stage sets. He created *The Workers' Club* (**fig. 23.15**) as a training ground for the new Soviet mind. Rodchenko envisioned every aspect of this installation to educate workers in the new historical dynamic that would lead to a future classless society. The chairs, shelves, and desks are all made of simple, mass-produced parts, and they are designed to facilitate sitting upright.

De Stijl

A group of Dutch artists took Cubism toward utopian speculation when they formed the movement called **De Stijl** (meaning "The Style"). Led by painter Piet Mondrian, this group began to employ nonrepresentational geometric elements in a group style that involved both two- and three-dimensional artforms. Their goal was the creation of a world of universal harmony. Using the new vocabulary of abstract art, they created an inventive body of work in painting, architecture, furniture, and graphic design.

Mondrian's evolution as an artist represents the origin and essence of De Stijl. Working to free painting completely from both the depiction of real objects and the expression of personal feelings, he developed an austere style based on the expressive potential of simple visual elements and their relationships. He created a new aesthetic that would provide a poetic vitality capable of setting standards of harmony for the new technological age.

From 1917 until his death in 1944, Mondrian was the leading spokesperson for an art reflecting universal order. In his mind these universal elements were straight lines, the three primary colors, and rectangular shapes. He reduced painting to four elements: line, shape, color, and space. His painting *Tableau 3* (**fig. 23.16**) exemplifies his nonrepresentational work. Mondrian hoped that the rhythms and forms of his works paralleled those of nature itself, which he viewed as rational and orderly.

23.16 Piet Mondrian. *Tableau 3, with Orange-Red, Yellow, Black, Blue, and Gray.* 1921. Oil on canvas. 19¼" × 16⅜".
Emanuel Hoffmann Foundation, on permanent loan to the Öffentliche Kunstsammlung Basel. Photograph: Öffentliche Kunstsammlung Basel, Martin P. Bühler.

International Style Architecture

The search for a new visual language engaged architects as well as painters. Ideas about form developed by the Constructivists, the De Stijl artists, and previously by American architect Frank Lloyd Wright (see Chapter 22) were carried further by architects stimulated by the structural possibilities of modern materials including steel, plate glass, and reinforced concrete.

About 1918, a new style of architecture emerged simultaneously in Germany, France, and the Netherlands and came to be called the **International Style**. Steel-frame, curtain-wall construction methods made it possible to build structures with undecorated rectilinear planes. The steel frame freed the exterior walls from bearing weight, which brought abundant light and flexible space to interiors. In many International Style buildings, asymmetrical designs created dynamic balances of voids and solids, always without decoration of any kind. Unlike Wright, who blended his houses with their natural surroundings (see Fallingwater; fig. 14.21), architects working in the International Style deliberately created a visual contrast between the manufactured-looking house and its natural environment.

Probably the best-known International Style house is the Villa Savoye in the western suburbs of Paris (**fig. 23.17**). This modern classic was designed by Le Corbusier as a country house for the Savoye family; they placed few restrictions on the architect. Steel stilts bear the weight of the building,

permitting an open plan with ample windows. The location of the stilts follows the architect's Domino Construction System (see fig. 14.19). The ground floor is devoted mostly to garage space, with a small entry hall. The living areas on the two upper floors include outdoor terraces joined by ramps and spiral staircases. Le Corbusier included space for all the latest domestic appliances (such as a trash compactor) because he thought a house should be a "machine for living in." The house has all the characteristics of the International Style: It plainly shows its structure, it uses modern materials—concrete, glass, and steel—and it lacks decoration.

The International Style buildings designed by Walter Gropius for the Bauhaus Building (see fig. 14.20) clearly reflect the concepts of both De Stijl and Constructivism. Today, the spare style that Mondrian and the Bauhaus Building helped to initiate can be seen in the design not only of buildings, but also of books, interiors, clothing, furnishings, and many other articles of daily life.

Architect and designer Ludwig Mies van der Rohe was one of the most influential figures associated with the Bauhaus and the International Style. For the Barcelona World's Fair in 1929, he designed the German Pavilion in marble, glass, and steel (**fig. 23.18**). Mies designed the pavilion with flowing spaces so that the visitor never feels "boxed in." An attached rectangular pool on the left reflects the elegant design on the water's surface. In 1938, Mies emigrated to the United States. There, his

23.17 Le Corbusier. Villa Savoye, Poissy, France. 1929–31.
Photograph: akg-images/Bildarchiv Monheim. © F.L.C./ADAGP, Paris/Artists Rights Society (ARS), New York 2018.

ideas and works potently influenced the post-World War II development of the skyscraper.

Political Expressions

Many artists in the interwar period focused their art on political life. Protesting against fascism and dictatorship was a dominant theme.

Throughout the 1920s and into the 1930s, Spanish-born Pablo Picasso continued to produce innovative drawings, paintings, prints, posters, and sculptures. In 1937, while the Spanish Civil War was in progress, Picasso was commissioned by the doomed Spanish democratic government to paint a mural for the Paris International Exposition. On April 26 of that year he was shocked into action by the "experimental" mass bombing of the defenseless Basque town of Guernica. To aid his bid for power, General Franco had allowed Hitler to use his bombers on the town as a demonstration of military power. The bombardment, which leveled the 15 blocks of the city center, was the first incidence of saturation bombing in the history of warfare. Hundreds died, and more were strafed with machine-gun fire from German aircraft as they fled the city into neighboring fields.

Appalled by this brutality against the people of his native country, Picasso responded by creating the mural-size painting *Guernica* (**fig. 23.19**). Although this work stems from a specific incident, it is a statement of protest against the brutality of all war.

23.19 Pablo Picasso. *Guernica.* 1937. Oil on canvas. 11′5½″ × 25′5¼″.
Museo Nacional Centro de Arte Reina Sofía. Photograph: The Bridgeman Art Library. © 2018 Estate of Pablo Picasso/Artists Rights Society (ARS), New York.

Guernica covers a huge canvas more than 25 feet long. It is painted mostly in the somber blacks, whites, and grays of newspapers before the days of color printing. A large triangle embedded under the smaller shapes holds the whole scene of chaotic destruction together as a unified composition. *Guernica* combines Cubism's intellectual restructuring of form with the emotional intensity of earlier forms of Expressionism and Abstract Surrealism. In dream symbolism, a horse often represents a dreamer's creativity. Here the horse is speared and is dying in anguish. Beneath the horse's feet a soldier lies in pieces; near his broken sword a faint flower suggests hope. Above, a woman reaches out from an open window, an oil lamp in hand. Near the old-fashioned lamp and above the horse's head is an eyelike

shape with an electric light bulb at the center: Jagged rays of light radiate out from the bottom edge. Sometimes an eye representing the eye of God was painted on the ceiling of medieval churches. The juxtaposition between old and new sources of illumination could be a metaphor relating to enlightenment.

Interviewed during the war, Picasso remarked that "painting is not done to decorate apartments. It is an instrument of war for attack and defense against the enemy."[7] Unfortunately, the type of aerial bombardment that he decried in *Guernica* soon became a common strategy that all sides adopted.

Between the world wars, a socially and politically committed form of art called **social realism** became common in many countries. This style took many forms, but they all include a retreat from the radical innovations of modern art and a desire to communicate more readily with the public about social causes and issues. In Nazi Germany and in Communist Russia, this style became an officially sponsored "norm" for art, which artists could ignore only if they did not care to have a successful career. A good example of Russian social realism is Vera Mukhina's *Monument to the Proletariat and Agriculture* (**fig. 23.20**). Her huge statue, which depicts a male factory worker and a female farm worker in stainless steel 78 feet high, was first exhibited at the Paris International Exposition of 1937. The work expresses the Communist vision of the Soviet state, where rural and urban workers would happily unite in a choreographed dance of praise to the regime. It still stands in Moscow, celebrating the system that came crashing down in 1991 with the fall of the Communist regime.

Mexican social realism took the form of mural paintings that embodied the ideals of the revolution of 1910–17, when a popular uprising overthrew a long-entrenched dictatorship. The Mexican government in 1921 embarked on

23.20 Vera Mukhina. *Monument to the Proletariat and Agriculture.* 1937. Stainless steel. Height 78´.

© Estate of Vera Mukhina/RAO, Moscow/VAGA, New York.
Photograph: akg-images/Sputnik.

23.21 Diego Rivera. *The Liberation of the Peon*. 1931. Fresco. 73″ × 94¼″.

Philadelphia Museum of Art. Gift of Mr. and Mrs. Herbert Cameron Morris. 1943–46–1. © 2017. Photograph: The Philadelphia Museum of Art/Art Resource/Scala, Florence. © 2018 Banco de México Diego Rivera Frida Kahlo Museums Trust, Mexico, D.F./Artists Rights Society (ARS), New York.

a program to pay artists an hourly wage to decorate public buildings with murals that spoke to the people about their long history and recent revolution. Inspired by the murals of the Italian Renaissance and by pre-Columbian wall paintings of ancient Mexican cultures, the muralists envisioned a national art that would glorify the traditional Mexican heritage and promote the new post-revolutionary government. Diego Rivera's fresco *The Liberation of the Peon* (**fig. 23.21**) is a good example that deals with a common event of the revolution: The landlord's house burns in the background, while revolutionary soldiers untie the peon from a stake and cover his naked body, which is scarred by repeated lashings. This work is a variation of

a large painting on a wall of the Ministry of Education in Mexico City. Both Diego Rivera and fellow muralist José Clemente Orozco visited the United States, where they influenced American art.

During the Depression years of the 1930s, the United States government maintained an active program of subsidy for the arts. The Works Progress Administration (WPA) commissioned painters to paint murals in public buildings, and the Farm Security Administration (FSA) hired photographers and filmmakers to record the drought-stricken Dust Bowl and its workworn inhabitants. With government support, the art of documentary photography reached a peak of achievement.

23.22 Dorothea Lange. *Three Families Camped on the Plains along U.S. 99 in California.* 1938. Photograph. 4″ × 5″.
Library of Congress, Washington, D.C.

Brancusi (see fig. 22.18). But the composition has "tropical" clichés, such as the lemon-slice sun and the cactus. Thus she slyly affirmed Brazilian culture. The solitary figure is the cannibal, or, translating the title from the indigenous Brazilian language, "the one who eats." One of the poets of that period wrote in a *Cannibalistic Manifesto* that Brazilians have a dual heritage: the jungle and the school. Tarsila's art shows both of these.

When photographer Dorothea Lange received a commission from the FSA to document poverty in agricultural areas, she directed her lens toward the thousands of migrants who fled the parched Midwest in search of agricultural work in California. In late 1938, for example, she found and photographed three families camping behind a billboard that advertised train travel (**fig. 23.22**). Apparently they found the sign to be a convenient windbreak, but it promotes a luxury that they may never experience. Photos such as this both made people more aware of current needs and built sympathy for those most affected by the Depression.

Latin American Modernism

Modern art showed distinctive characteristics when it bloomed across Latin America in the 1920s. Art movements were often interdisciplinary, allying painters with poets or composers. A case in point was Modern Art Week in São Paulo, Brazil, in 1922: Artists showed works influenced by Cubism and abstraction, poets read lyrics denouncing their elders, and musicians played new work that reflected Afro-Brazilian traditions. The crucial question that they all faced was how to relate to European culture, and Brazilian modernists came up with a perfectly logical, but also rebellious answer: cannibalism. Brazilians would "ingest" European culture and let it nourish their own self-expression.

Tarsila do Amaral embodied this cannibalism in her painting *Abaporu* (**fig. 23.23**). The style shows her study of Fernand Léger's Cubism and the abstract sculpture of

In Argentina, visual artists and poets of the 1920s banded together around the journal *Martin Fierro* to struggle against the public's ignorance about modern

23.23 Tarsila do Amaral. *Abaporu.* 1928.
Oil on canvas. 34″ × 29″.
Museo de Arte Latinoamericano, Buenos Aires (Malba). Courtesy of Guilherme Augusto do Amaral.

23.24 Pedro Figari. *Candombe o Candombe bajo la luna.* 1922. Oil on cardboard. 18¾″ × 22¾″.

Museo Nacional de Bellas Artes (National Museum of Fine Arts) Argentina. INV 9234.

23.25 Joaquín Torres-García. *Universal Constructivism.* 1930. Oil on wood. 23¼″ × 11⅜″.

Museo Nacional Centro de Arte Reina Sofía, Madrid. Catalogue Raisonne no. 1937.31. Courtesy of the Estate of Joaquín Torres-García.

art. A 1924 manifesto announced support for artists who "believe in the importance of the intellectual contribution of Latin America, after snipping off all umbilical cords."[8] One of the artists that the magazine regularly featured was the Uruguayan painter Pedro Figari, who had settled in Buenos Aires in 1921. He made many paintings depicting a typical Afro-Uruguayan cultural event called Candombe (**fig. 23.24**), in which urban black domestic servants gathered on religious holidays for dances. Two seated figures in the right foreground play drums in African-derived rhythms that activate the moving dancers in the center and left. On a white table in the background are small statues of two saints; one of these is the black San Benito de Palermo. Figari hoped to honor and perpetuate such Latin American expressions as Candombe and folk dances, which he also frequently painted.

Uruguayan artist Joaquín Torres-García developed a uniquely American version of Constructivism (and here we refer to all of the Americas, as the artist did). The rectangular blocks in his work *Universal Constructivism* (**fig. 23.25**) refer both to Mondrian's paintings and to the stone architecture of pre-conquest indigenous Peru. Over that framework, he drew symbols that refer both to modern life and to the pottery designs of ancient Americans. Thus, he aimed at a cross-cultural synthesis of modern and ancient that he hoped would have universal appeal. A few words in Spanish (year, light, world) also mark this as a specifically Latin American work.

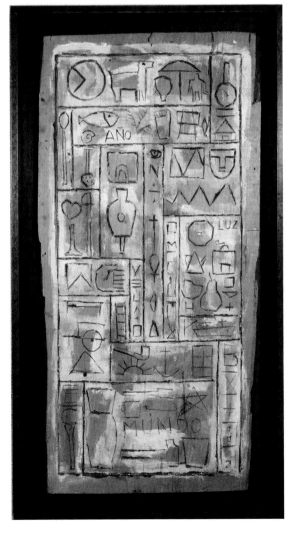

23.26 Frida Kahlo. *The Two Fridas.* 1939.
Oil on canvas. 5′8½″ × 5′8½″.

Museo de Arte Moderno, Instituto Nacional de Bellas Artes, Mexico City.
© 2017. Photograph: Art Resource/Bob Schalkwijk/Scala, Florence. © 2018
Banco de México Diego Rivera Frida Kahlo Museums Trust, Mexico, D.F./Artists
Rights Society (ARS), New York.

The Surrealists claimed Mexican painter Frida Kahlo as one of their own, even though her sources were closer to the folk arts of her native country. Her painting *The Two Fridas* (**fig. 23.26**) shows herself as a split personality, divided between her European and Mexican heritage.

As each stares back at us, we see their hearts plainly visible, joined by blood vessels. This is an allusion both to ancient Aztec human sacrifice and to the artist's own surgical traumas. Her many self-portraits provide insight into an exceptional person who lived life with passionate intensity.

American Regionalism

In the 1930s, the spread of the Depression, along with political upheaval, helped to motivate artists in America (and here we mean the United States) to search for both national and personal identity. American artists were caught between a public largely indifferent to art and a feeling, both at home and abroad, that American art was merely provincial. In this atmosphere of relative cultural isolation, an American **Regionalism** developed, based on the idea that artists in the United States could find their identity by focusing attention on the subject matter that was local and American.

Edward Hopper made several trips to Europe between 1906 and 1910, but he mostly ignored European avant-garde movements as he portrayed the loneliness of much of American urban life. *Nighthawks* (**fig. 23.27**) shows Hopper's fascination with the mood of people in a particular place and time. The haunting effect of his paintings comes largely from his carefully organized compositions and his controlled use of light and shadow. Both Hopper and the Impressionists were interested in light, but for different purposes: Hopper employed it to clarify and organize the structure of a composition, whereas the Impressionists used light in ways that dissolved structure.

Regional painter Grant Wood studied art in Paris in the early 1920s. Although he never worked with Cubist or Expressionist ideas, he did identify with modern trends and began making freely brushed paintings derived from Impressionism. After years of little success, Wood

23.27 Edward Hopper.
Nighthawks. 1942. Oil
on canvas. 33⅛″ × 60″.
The Art Institute of Chicago, IL,
USA/Friends of American Art
Collection 1942.51/Bridgeman
Images.

23.28 Grant Wood. *American Gothic*. 1930.
Oil on beaverboard. 29¼″ × 24½″.

returned to his birthplace in rural Midwestern America and dedicated himself to memorializing the unique character of the land, the people, and their way of life.

Wood's personal style of crisp realism was inspired by the paintings of the northern Renaissance masters such as van Eyck (see fig. 17.13) and Dürer (see fig. 17.14). He also drew on American folk painting and the characteristically stiff, long-exposure portraits taken by late nineteenth-century photographers. Wood, like van Eyck, calculated every aspect of design and all details of the subject matter to enhance the content of his paintings.

The idea for the famous painting *American Gothic* (**fig. 23.28**) came to Wood when he saw a modest farmhouse built in a local carpenter's version of the Gothic style. The restrained color, the simplification of round masses such as trees and people, and the high detail are typical of Wood's paintings. The two figures (the artist's sister and his dentist) are echoed in the pointed-arch window shapes. Vertical lines and paired elements dominate. For example, the lines of the pitchfork are repeated in the man's overalls and shirt front. The upright tines of the fork seem to symbolize the

pair's firm, traditional stance and hard-won virtue. Wood's *American Gothic* has become a national icon that speaks clearly to many; it continues to spark a wealth of responses.

The most forceful spokesperson for American regional art was Thomas Hart Benton, son of a Missouri United States senator. Benton worked to create a style that was American in both form and content—a realistic style that would be easily understood by all, based on the depiction of American themes. Some of the strength in his figures came from the influence of Michelangelo's muscular bodies. But Benton transformed Renaissance and modern influences into a highly personal style in which all forms are conditioned by strong curvilinear rhythms. The push and pull of shapes in shallow space, emphasized by contrasting light and dark edges, shows what Benton learned from Cubism.

Palisades (**fig. 23.29**) was part of a series of paintings titled *American Historical Epic*. In contrast to conventional histories that feature great men, Benton wanted to create a people's history, one that depicted the actions of ordinary people on the land. Here, the European colonizers are staking out and dividing up the land; while the Indians, in contrast, are sharing their knowledge of growing corn, which the newcomers will need for survival.

23.29 Thomas Hart Benton. *Palisades*. From the series *American Historical Epic*. c.1919–24. Oil on cotton duck on aluminum honeycomb panel. 66⅛″ × 72″.

African-American Modernists

Philosopher Alain Locke wrote in the 1925 book *The New Negro* that African-American artists should reconnect with their roots in the "ancestral arts of Africa." They should not seek to paint or sculpt in highly polished academic styles; neither should they explore Parisian modern movements. Rather, they should attune themselves to their own cultural heritage and express themselves through recognizably African-based styles.

This book was a major force behind the cultural flowering known as the Harlem Renaissance, which included poets, musicians, and novelists along with visual artists. Important figures associated with the Renaissance include Langston Hughes, Paul Robeson, Zora Neale Hurston, and many others both in Harlem and elsewhere in the United

23.31 Jacob Lawrence. *General Toussaint l'Ouverture Defeats the English at Saline.* 1937–38. Gouache on paper. 19″ × 11″.

Aaron Douglas Collection. Photograph courtesy of Amistad Research Center. © 2018 The Jacob and Gwendolyn Knight Lawrence Foundation, Seattle/ Artists Rights Society (ARS), New York.

23.30 Sargent Johnson. *Forever Free.* 1933. Wood with lacquer on cloth. 36″ × 11½″ × 9½″.

San Francisco Museum of Modern Art. Gift of Mrs. E. D. Lederman. © Estate of Sargent Johnson. Photograph: Don Ross.

States. Visual artists were an integral part of the movement; they illustrated books, designed interior spaces, and photographed the teeming life around them.

The principal vehicle for displaying the painting and sculpture of African Americans at that time was the annual traveling exhibition sponsored by the Harmon Foundation; one artist who often won prizes in that show was Sargent Johnson. A resident of California, he produced painted wood sculptures such as *Forever Free* (**fig. 23.30**) that expressed his view of the black identity. A motherly woman shelters two smaller figures, all of whom show pronounced African characteristics. The title of the work comes from the Emancipation Proclamation of 1863, which ended slavery in the Confederate states. Johnson wrote of this expression of cultural roots: "I am producing strictly a Negro Art, studying not the culturally mixed Negro of the cities, but the more primitive slave type as existed in this country during the period of slave importation."[9]

During the Depression of the 1930s, the Works Progress Administration (WPA) set up community art centers in 100 cities. Jacob Lawrence was a product of one of these centers in Harlem, where he met most of the leaders of the Renaissance. In 1938, he made a series of 41 paintings on the life of Toussaint l'Ouverture, the black leader of the revolt that made Haiti the first independent nation in Latin America in 1804. *General Toussaint l'Ouverture Defeats the English at Saline* (**fig. 23.31**) shows his style, which he called "dynamic Cubism." Lawrence was not practicing the French Cubism of Braque and Picasso, however; he made his own investigation of African art and reinterpreted it in his own way.

Archibald Motley of Chicago took a realist view of African-American culture. His painting *Barbeque* of 1934 (**fig. 23.32**) is ebullient and full of motion, and also shows an interest in how figures look under artificial light. Motley specialized in depicting all aspects of the urban black experience, including on occasion gamblers and drinkers during Prohibition. Such subject matter did not endear him to pretentious art patrons, but Motley replied, "I have tried to paint the Negro as I have seen him and as I feel him, in my self without adding or detracting, just being frankly honest."[10]

Organic Abstraction

The Fascist and Communist regimes in Germany and Russia suppressed most modern art, especially abstract art; European artists in opposition to this stance reaffirmed abstract art by forming the group Abstraction-Creation in 1931. Their second manifesto proclaimed "total opposition to all oppression, of whatever kind it may be." Abstract art thus became a statement on behalf of personal and political freedom. Moreover, because it was not obviously tied to any one nationality, abstract art also stood apart from the intent nationalist focus of Fascist regimes. Many 1930s abstract artists adopted organic shapes that resembled life forms.

An early member of Abstraction-Creation was the English sculptor Barbara Hepworth. Her *Forms in Echelon* (**fig. 23.33**) consists of two pieces of tulip wood, carved into shapes that suggest growing plant forms. She was the first to put holes in her sculpted works, opening the shape to light and air. Viewers who apply a little imagination to the arrangement of *Forms in Echelon* can visualize a conversation, or perhaps mutual nurturing, between the two forms.

Hepworth's colleague and friend Henry Moore took her invention in a more figural direction. After serving in World War I, Moore used a veteran's grant to study art in London. While there, he spent long hours studying the

23.32 Archibald Motley Jr. *Barbeque.* 1934.
Oil on canvas. 36¼″ × 40⅛″.
Howard University Gallery of Art, Washington D.C. © Valerie Gerrard Browne/
Chicago History Museum/Bridgeman Images.

23.33 Barbara Hepworth. *Forms in Echelon.*
1938. Wood. Height 42½″.
© Tate, London 2018. Presented by the artist, 1964.
© Bowness.

an organic abstract shape that suggests the human form without exactly depicting it. Moore's carving of the stone also preserves its origins in sedimentary geological deposits, and the label (Green Hornton stone), specified at Moore's insistence, identifies where he quarried it.

The outbreak of World War II in Europe in 1939 took humanity to the brink of destruction yet again. Besides the suffering that it created, the war also redrew the world map of artistic innovation. Many European artists migrated to the Americas and fertilized modern movements there.

collections of non-Western arts in the British Museum and the Victoria and Albert Museum. His *Recumbent Figure* from 1938 (**fig. 23.34**) is an elaboration of the reclining Toltec Chacmool (see fig. 20.36). Moore smoothed the stone into

KEY TERMS

Abstract Surrealism – a form of Surrealism that uses abstract shapes and which emphasizes color and design rather than storytelling content

automatism – action without conscious control, as employed by Surrealist writers and artists to allow unconscious ideas and feelings to be expressed

Constructivism – art movement that originated in Russia at the time of the Soviet Revolution of 1917, which emphasized abstract art, modern materials, and useful arts such as set design, furniture, and graphics

Dada – a movement in art and literature, founded in Switzerland in the early twentieth century, which ridiculed contemporary culture and conventional art

De Stijl – a Dutch purist art movement begun during World War I by Mondrian and others; involved painters, sculptors, designers, and architects whose works and ideas were expressed in *De Stijl* magazine; De Stijl, Dutch for "The Style," was aimed at creating a universal language of form that would be independent of individual emotion; visual form was pared down to primary hues plus black and white, and rectangular shapes

frottage – a technique in which a canvas is laid over a textured surface and rubbed with crayons and pencils

International Style – an architectural style that emerged in several European countries between 1910 and 1920; International Style architects avoided applied decoration, used only modern materials (concrete, glass, steel), and arranged the masses of a building according to its inner uses

photomontage – the process of combining parts of various photographs in one photograph

readymade – a concept pioneered by Dadaist Marcel Duchamp in which a common manufactured object is signed by an artist and thereby turned into an artwork

Regionalism – an art movement developed in the United States in the 1930s, based on the idea that artists could find their identity by focusing attention on the subject matter that was local and American

Representational Surrealism – a type of Surrealism that depicts objects in realistic detail

social realism – a socially and politically committed form of art that became common in many countries between the two world wars and which included a retreat from the radical innovations of modern art, and the desire to communicate more readily with the public about social causes and issues

Surrealism – a movement in literature and the visual arts that developed in the mid-1920s, based on revealing the unconscious mind in dream images and the fantastic

24 POSTWAR MODERN MOVEMENTS

LEARNING OBJECTIVES

24.1 Discuss the New York School and distinguish examples of Abstract Expressionist and color field painting.

24.2 Describe the evolution of International Style architecture in the postwar years.

24.3 Identify the key influences on Assemblage artists.

24.4 Explain happenings as efforts to blend art and life.

24.5 Describe common techniques and themes characteristic of Pop Art.

24.6 Explain the goals and stylistic features of Minimalism.

24.7 Express the importance of the artist's idea in Conceptual art.

24.8 Discuss the aims and characteristics of site-specific works and earthworks.

24.9 Demonstrate how installations can transform gallery and exterior spaces.

24.10 Summarize the influence of feminism on art in the early 1970s.

24.11 Discuss performance art as an attempt to banish the art object.

In the years following World War II, modern artists made a frontal assault on the rules of art. The conventions and customs that had governed artistic creation since the Renaissance were gradually but thoroughly overturned, rejected, or ignored. In 1945, even the most innovative artists still worked in traditional media; but 30 years later they were also erecting poles in the desert, copying news photographs, gluing themselves to trees, and selling kisses for money. Whatever an artist did, or whatever a gallery exhibited, became art. It was a restless and wildly creative period.

At the end of World War II, Europe lay in ruins—financially, emotionally, and physically. The war took the lives of a 250,000 British people, 600,000 French, 5 million Germans, and 20 million Russians. The Nazi Holocaust accounted for 6 million of these deaths. Refugees and displaced persons numbered 40 million. Britain's wartime prime minister, Winston Churchill, in 1947 described Europe as "a rubble heap, a charnel house, a breeding ground for pestilence and hate."[1] Many prominent European artists had fled from Nazi oppression to the United States, which emerged from the war economically strong and optimistic.

Among the artists who settled in New York were Piet Mondrian, Fernand Léger, Marcel Duchamp, Salvador Dalí, and André Breton. They worked, taught, exhibited, and brought new ideas, opening new possibilities for American artists. This immigration made modernism no longer a distant, European phenomenon; many of its leading practitioners came to the United States. Mexican muralists Diego Rivera and David Siqueiros also exhibited and taught in New York during the 1930s, encouraging artists away from traditional easel painting.

War had altered the consciousness of the developed world in subtle but profound ways. The Nazi genocide machine had taken human cruelty to a new low, and the atomic bomb gave humankind terrifying new powers: People were now living in a world they had the power to destroy in minutes. These conditions formed the background for art and life in Europe and the United States at the close of the war.

The New York School

The new émigrés to the United States influenced many American painters to move away from the realist styles dominant in the 1930s, and to experiment with more expressive and inventive ways of creating. The unparalleled crisis of the world war also led artists to move away from public issues of history, community, and social comment that Depression-era painting emphasized. As a result, they began to paint in styles that were both stylistically innovative and personal.

In the first ten years after the end of the war, much of this innovation was centered in New York, giving rise to the term New York School; it consisted of two movements, Abstract Expressionism and color field.

24.1 Rudolph Burckhardt. *Jackson Pollock Painting in East Hampton, Long Island.* 1950.
Photograph. © 2018 Estate of Rudy Burckhardt and The Pollock-Krasner Foundation / Artists Rights Society (ARS), New York.

24.2 Jackson Pollock. *Autumn Rhythm (Number 30).* 1950. Oil on canvas. 105″ × 207″.
The Metropolitan Museum of Art. George A. Hearn Fund, 1957. Acc.n.: 57.92. © 2018. Image copyright: The Metropolitan Museum of Art/Art Resource/Scala, Florence. © 2018 The Pollock-Krasner Foundation/Artists Rights Society (ARS), New York.

Abstract Expressionism

The horrors of World War II impelled artists to rethink the relationship between art and life. The dislocations caused by war led them to explore visual realms beyond the representational and narrative. One result was **Abstract Expressionism**, a culmination of the expressive tendencies in painting from Fauvism, German Expressionism (see Chapter 22), and the automatic methods of Surrealism (see Chapter 23).

Jackson Pollock, the leading innovator of Abstract Expressionism, studied in the 1930s with both Thomas Hart Benton and the Mexican muralist David Siqueiros. The rhythmic structure of Benton's style and the mural-scale art of the Mexicans influenced Pollock's poured paintings of the late 1940s and early 1950s. Searching for ways to express primal human nature, Pollock also studied Navajo sand painting and psychologist Carl Jung's theories of the unconscious. His belief that he was painting for the age of the "atom bomb and the radio" led Pollock to innovative techniques (**fig. 24.1**). He created *Autumn Rhythm (Number 30)* (**fig. 24.2**) by dripping thin paint onto the canvas rather than brushing it on. Working on huge canvases placed on the floor, Pollock was able to enter the space of the painting physically and psychologically. The huge format allowed ample room for his sweeping gestural lines. Pollock dripped, poured, and flung paint, yet he exercised control and selection by the rhythmical, dancing movements of his body. A similar approach in the work of many of his colleagues led some to call this movement **action painting**.

The influence of Expressionist and Surrealist attitudes on Willem de Kooning's work is evident in his spontaneous, emotionally charged brushwork and provocative use of shapes. Throughout his career, de Kooning emphasized abstract imagery, yet the human figure underlies many of his paintings. After several years of working without subjects, he began a series of large paintings in which ferocious female figures appear. These canvases, painted with slashing attacks of the brush, have an overwhelming presence. In *Woman and Bicycle* (**fig. 24.3**), the toothy smile is repeated in a savage necklace that caps tremendous breasts. While it explodes with the energies of Abstract Expressionism, this work is controversial for the monstrous image of women that it presents.

Like many New York School painters, Lee Krasner participated in the Depression-era programs that gave employment to artists. Shortly after 1945, impelled by an urge for

24.3 Willem de Kooning. *Woman and Bicycle*. 1952–53. Oil, enamel, and charcoal on linen. 76½″ × 49⅛″
Whitney Museum of American Art, New York. Purchase 55.35 2018. © 2018 The Willem de Kooning Foundation/Artists Rights Society (ARS), New York.

more personal expression, she moved into abstraction, as we see with her work from 1949 (**fig. 24.4**). Every part of this canvas is equally energized without a foreground, background, or point of emphasis or subordination. She filled the picture space with quick, textured strokes that define the shapes of some mysterious sort of handwriting, as if this work is an urgent message from a culture yet unknown. By leaving the work untitled she declined to direct the viewer's imagination; rather, this work explores abstract symbols and how they may create meaning.

24.4 Lee Krasner. *Untitled.* 1949. Oil on composition board. 48″ x 37″.

Museum of Modern Art, New York. 500.1969. Gift of Alfonso A. Ossorio. 500.1969.
© 2018 Digital image, The Museum of Modern Art, New York/Scala, Florence.
© 2018 The Pollock-Krasner Foundation/Artists Rights Society (ARS), New York.

David Smith, for many critics the most important American sculptor of the postwar period, was strongly influenced by action painting. His assembled metal sculpture began with a Cubist framework of overlapping jagged shapes, and added the elemental energy of Abstract Expressionism. His use of factory methods and materials provided new options for the next generation of sculptors. Smith's late work included the stainless-steel *Cubi* series (**fig. 24.5**), based on cubic masses and planes balanced dynamically above the viewer's eye level. He scoured the steel surfaces with energetic curving motions as an Abstract Expressionist might, creating reflective exteriors that seem to dissolve their solidity. Smith intended the sculpture to be viewed outdoors in strong light, set off by green landscape.

24.5 David Smith. *Cubi XVII.* 1963. Polished stainless steel. 107¾″ × 64⅜″ × 38⅛″.

Dallas Museum of Art. The Eugene and Margaret McDermott Art Fund, Inc.
© Estate of David Smith/Licensed by VAGA, New York, NY.

Color Field Painting

A related painting style that evolved at about the same time was **color field**, a term for painting that consists of large areas of color, with no obvious structure, central focus, or dynamic balance. The canvases of color field painters are dominated by unified images, often so huge that they engulf the viewer.

Mark Rothko is now best known as a pioneer of color field painting, although his early works of the 1930s were urban scenes. By the 1940s, influenced by Surrealism, he began producing paintings inspired by myths and rituals. In the late 1940s, he gave up the figure and began to focus primarily on color. In works such as *Blue, Orange, Red* (**fig. 24.6**), Rothko used color to evoke moods ranging from joy and serenity to melancholy and despair. By superimposing thin layers of paint, he achieved a variety of qualities from dense to atmospheric to luminous. Rothko's paintings have sensuous appeal and monumental presence.

24.7 Helen Frankenthaler. *Mountains and Sea*. 1952.
Oil and charcoal on canvas. 86⅜″ × 117¼″.

Collection Helen Frankenthaler Foundation (on extended loan to the National
Gallery of Art, Washington, D.C.) © 2018 Helen Frankenthaler Foundation,
Inc./Artists Rights Society (ARS), New York.

24.6 Mark Rothko. *Blue, Orange, Red*. 1961.
Oil on canvas. 90¼″ × 81¼″.

Hirshhorn Museum and Sculpture Garden, Smithsonian Institution. Gift of
the Joseph H. Hirshhorn Foundation. 1966. HMSG 66.4420. Photograph: Lee
Stalsworth. © 1998 Kate Rothko Prizel & Christopher Rothko/Artists Rights Society
(ARS), New York.

Helen Frankenthaler's work also evolved during the
height of Abstract Expressionism. In 1952, she pioneered
staining techniques as an extension of Jackson Pollock's
poured paint and Mark Rothko's fields of color.
Brushstrokes and paint texture were eliminated
as she spread liquid colors across a horizontal,
unprimed canvas. As the thin pigment soaked
into the raw fabric, she coaxed it into fluid,
organic shapes. Pale, subtle, and spontaneous,
Mountains and Sea (**fig. 24.7**) marked the beginning of a series of paintings that emphasize softness and openness and the expressive power of
color. Frankenthaler painted it in one day, after
a trip to Nova Scotia; as in many of her works,
landscape is faintly suggested.

Robert Motherwell's series of paintings titled *Elegy
to the Spanish Republic* is permeated with a tragic sense of
history. His elegies brood over the destruction of the fragile Spanish democracy by General Franco in the bloody
Spanish Civil War of the 1930s. Heavy black shapes crush
and obliterate the lighter passages behind them (**fig. 24.8**).
Motherwell began with a specific subject as his starting
point and expressed its inner mood through abstract means.

24.8 Robert Motherwell. *Elegy to the Spanish
Republic, No. 34*. 1953–54. Oil on canvas.
80″ × 100″.

Albright Knox Art Gallery/Art Resource, NY/Scala, Florence. Art
© Dedalus Foundation, Inc./Licensed by VAGA, New York, NY.

Architecture at Mid-Century

In the immediate postwar years, the International Style (see fig. 14.20) represented the leading edge of architecture. Its clean masses and sleek exteriors spoke across the Western world of efficiency, cosmopolitanism, and future-oriented thinking.

Most American architects at mid-century also used the International Style, but in simpler, more boxlike shapes.

Lever House in New York City (**fig. 24.9**) heralded the future of office buildings for the next 25 years: It is a steel-and-glass box that looks slick, convenient, and modern. Most American cities have such buildings. Later architects would revolt against it, but for a generation this ultra-clean look represented the image of the American corporation. Following the words of American architect Louis Sullivan ("Form ever follows function"), International Style architects built practical buildings that clearly showed structural supports and banished all ornament.

While many such buildings looked elegant and distinguished, the glass-box regularity of the style began to seem limiting. For example, Brazilian architect Oscar Niemeyer seized the opportunity that his country presented when it commissioned a new capital city to open in 1960. His Planalto Palace (**fig. 24.10**) participates in the glass-box style yet departs from it in important ways. The entrance ramp hardly looks practical, and the sweeping, curved struts of the external skeleton take on a decorative life of their own. Such imaginative building soon became a hallmark of the postmodern movement (see Chapter 25).

Le Corbusier, one of the founders of the International Style, also departed from it in the postwar years. He began to use concrete as a more prominent feature of building exteriors, taking advantage of its potential for casting. Influenced in part by the curves in some of Niemeyer's early work, Le Corbusier used large expanses

24.9 Skidmore, Owings, and Merrill. Lever House. 1952. New York City.
Photograph: Howard Architectural Models Inc.

24.10 Oscar Niemeyer. Planalto Palace. Presidential Residence, Brasília, Brazil. 1960.
© ostill/Shutterstock.

of curving unpainted concrete in the buildings for the new provincial capital of Chandigarh in northern India. The Assembly Building (**fig. 24.11**) has a rectangular block with prominent concrete exterior, behind a massive porch with deep bays under a flying curved canopy. Such assertive use of cast concrete soon earned this building the label brutalist, after the French phrase *béton brut*, or raw concrete. **Brutalism** became a dominant trend in architecture across the world in the 1960s and 1970s, especially in government and university buildings.

24.11 Le Corbusier. Assembly Building. Chandigarh, India. 1953.
Bjanka Kadic/Alamy Stock Photo. © 2018 F.L.C./ADAGP, Paris/Artists Rights Society (ARS), New York.

Assemblage

Most leading artists of the 1940s and early 1950s chose not to deal with recognizable subject matter; they mostly avoided referring to the world in which they lived. In the mid-1950s, a few young artists began to acknowledge, confront, and even celebrate the visual diversity of the urban scene; they wanted to move beyond the exclusive, personal nature of Abstract Expressionism. In their effort to re-engage art with ordinary life, these artists created **assemblages,** loose conglomerations of seemingly random objects. The art of assemblage took the Dada collage of Hannah Höch (see fig. 23.3) into three dimensions.

Under the influence of avant-garde composer John Cage, who urged artists to make art from the lives they were living, Robert Rauschenberg began combining ordinary objects and collage materials with Abstract Expressionistic brushwork in what he called "combine-paintings." If creative thinking involves combining elements of the world in order to make an unexpected, previously unthinkable new thing, this is what Rauschenberg achieved with *Monogram* (**fig. 24.12**). What is a stuffed, long-haired Angora goat with a tire around its middle doing, standing in the middle of a collage-painting?

This strange assemblage offers glimpses of seemingly unrelated objects and events, and acts as a symbol for the jarring juxtapositions of modern life. Rauschenberg used

24.13 Jasper Johns. *Target with Four Faces.* 1955. Assemblage: encaustic on newspaper and collage on canvas with objects, surmounted by four tinted plaster faces in wood box with hinged front. Overall dimensions with box open: 33⅝″ × 26″ × 3″.
Museum of Modern Art (MoMA). Gift of Mr. and Mrs. Robert C. Scull. © 2018. Digital image: The Museum of Modern Art, New York/Scala, Florence. © Jasper Johns/Licensed by VAGA, New York, NY.

24.12 Robert Rauschenberg. *Monogram.* 1955–59. Freestanding combine. 42″ × 64″ × 64½″.
Moderna Museet, Stockholm. © Robert Rauschenberg Foundation/Licensed by VAGA, New York, NY.

whatever was available in the run-down urban neighborhood where he worked. (He found the goat in a second-hand store.) Instead of blocking out the chaotic messages of city streets, T.V., and magazines, Rauschenberg incorporated the disorder of urban civilization into his art.

Rauschenberg often discussed art making with Jasper Johns during their formative years in the 1950s. Whereas Rauschenberg's work is filled with visual complexity, Johns's work is deceptively simple. His large early paintings were based on common graphic forms such as targets, maps, flags, and numbers. He was interested in the difference between signs (emblems that carry meaning) and art. In Johns's work, common signs play a dual role: They have the power of Abstract Expressionist forms in their size, bold design, and painterly surface qualities, yet they represent familiar objects and thus bring art back to everyday life. In his *Target with Four Faces* (**fig. 24.13**), a canvas target becomes a painting, while the sculpted faces are perceived as a sign.

Johns's common subjects are now objects of contemplation. His irony relates back to Dada and forward to **Pop Art** (discussed later in this chapter). The Neo-Dada works of Johns and Rauschenberg provided a bridge between Abstract Expressionism and later Pop Art.

The Neo-Dada spirit also broke out in Europe, where in 1958 Yves Klein greeted visitors at an empty gallery, in a show he called "The Void." Niki de Saint Phalle made paintings and collages and then symbolically killed them by piercing them with nails, darts, or even gunshots. In *Saint Sebastian, or the Portrait of My Love* (**fig. 24.14**), we see one of her husband's shirts and neckties below a dartboard.

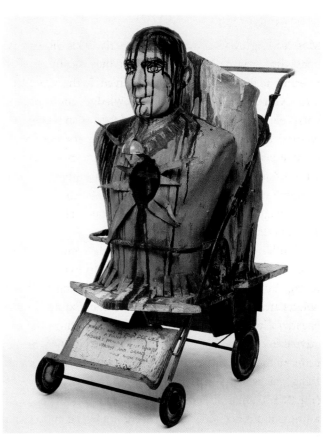

24.15 Edward Kienholz. *John Doe.* 1959. Oil, metallic paint, resin, plaster, and graphite on mannequin parts with wood, metal, plastic, paper, rubber, and stroller. 39½″ × 19″ × 31¼″.
The Menil Collection, Houston. Photograph: George Hixson. © Kienholz. Courtesy of L.A. Louver, Venice, CA.

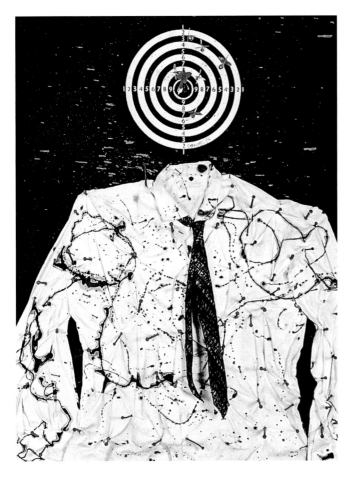

24.14 Niki de Saint Phalle. *Saint Sebastian, or the Portrait of My Love.* 1960. Oil, fabric, darts, and nails on wood and dartboard. 28½″ × 21¾″ × 2¾″.
Collection of the artist. © 2018 Niki Charitable Art Foundation. All rights reserved/ARS, NY/ADAGP, Paris.

The artist drove dozens of nails into the shirt, and then threw darts at the board. These works by Saint Phalle and others continue the irreverent aspects of the spirit of Dada. Saint Phalle's target carries a far more direct meaning than that of Jasper Johns in his *Target with Four Faces.*

Assemblage artists on the West Coast made more direct social comments. For example, *John Doe* by Edward Kienholz (**fig. 24.15**) makes the average American into an outrageous caricature. Half of a store mannequin rides on a baby stroller with his chest blown out (revealing a cross). Paint drips add to the ridiculous effect. An inscription below adapts a sarcastic riddle: "How is John Doe like a piano? Because he is square, upright, and grand." Kienholz was friendly with many writers of the Beat movement, who similarly despaired over the blandness of middle-class life.

When protests against aggressive policing in Los Angeles escalated into the Watts Riots in the summer of

Events and Happenings

Artists have continued to extend the boundaries of the visual arts until they can no longer simply be defined as stable aesthetic objects. Some artists in the late 1950s and early 1960s began to create living, moving art events. In part, they were responding to the new phenomenon of the media event, in which an unusual occurrence gets seemingly constant news coverage for a brief period. In this new environment, some artists attempted to create their own events.

Japanese artists were important in developing the idea that a work of art could be an event, rather than an object. The most radical Japanese artists joined a group called Gutai (Embodiment), which functioned from 1954 to 1972. One artist made paintings with his feet; another shot pigment-filled bullets at his canvases. The Gutai manifesto proclaimed the end of traditional art making, and the members "decided to pursue the possibilities of pure and creative activity with great energy." Saburo Murakami

24.16 Noah Purifoy. *Watts Riot.* 1966. Assemblage. 46″ x 61″ x 9″.

California African American Museum, Catalog Number AF19933.7.20. Noah Purifoy Foundation. Photo Bob Carey/Los Angeles Times via Getty.

1965, many local African-American artists mobilized in their own way. Noah Purifoy was working in a community art center at the Watts Towers (see fig. 1.4), a few blocks from the epicenter of the disturbance. He and several other artists collected debris from the burned-out buildings and used this material in assemblages. One of the most explicit of these works is Purifoy's *Watts Riot* (**fig. 24.16**). This work is essentially a layered composition in three zones in which we see red, tan, and green colors, all made from ruined building parts, plaster, and signage. A round sign near the lower edge reads "Always be careful" in relief. The work memorializes the violent uprising without glorifying it. Although Purifoy was nearly 50 years of age when he made this work, it gave him a new set of themes and materials. "I wasn't an artist yet until Watts. That made me an artist," he told an interviewer.[2]

24.17 Saburo Murakami. *Passing Through.* 1956. Performance.

© Makiko Murakami. Courtesy of the Estate of Saburo Murakami, Osaka City Museum of Modern Art and ARTCOURT Gallery.

24.18 Jean Tinguely. *Homage to New York: A Self-Constructing, Self-Destructing Work of Art.* 1960.

mounted blank sheets of paper in frames and destroyed them in performances that he called *Passing Through* (**fig. 24.17**). Because paper is a treasured material in Japan, traditionally thought to manifest a sacred spirit, Murakami's performance symbolized the rebellious, questioning attitude of the postwar period. Performances like his by other members of the Gutai group also anticipated several aspects of **happenings** and **performance art** that emerged later in the West.

For Swiss sculptor Jean Tinguely, life was play, movement, and perpetual change. Tinguely made machines that do just about everything except work in the manner we expect. Although much kinetic art has celebrated science and technology, he enjoyed a mocking yet sympathetic relationship to machines and machine fallibility. He said, "I try to distill the frenzy I see in the world, the mechanical frenzy of our joyful, industrial confusion."[3]

In 1960, Tinguely built a large piece of mechanized sculpture that he put together from materials gathered from junkyards and stores in and around New York City (**fig. 24.18**). The result was a giant assemblage designed to destroy itself at the turn of a switch—which it did in the courtyard of the Museum of Modern Art in New York City on March 17, 1960. The environmental sculpture was titled *Homage to New York: A Self-Constructing, Self-Destructing Work of Art.* This work was an event, similar in its effect to a happening.

Happenings are cooperative events in which viewers become active participants in partly planned, partly spontaneous performances that combine scripted scenarios with considerable improvisation. One critic defined happenings as drama with "structure but no plot, words but no dialogue, actors but no characters, and above all, nothing logical or continuous."[4]

24.19 Allan Kaprow. *Household*. City dump, Ithaca, New York. 1964. Happening presented for the Festival of Contemporary Arts.

Getty Research Institute, Los Angeles (980063). © J. Paul Getty Trust. Courtesy of Allan Kaprow Estate and Hauser & Wirth. Photograph: Sol Goldberg.

The term "happening" was first used by Allan Kaprow in the late 1950s. There were no spectators at Kaprow's happening, *Household* (**fig. 24.19**). At a preliminary meeting, participants were given parts. The action took place at an isolated rural dump, amid smoldering piles of refuse. The men built a wooden tower on a trash pile while the women constructed a nest on another mound. During the course of a series of interrelated events, the men destroyed the nest and the women retaliated by pulling down the men's tower. In the process, participants gained a new perspective on the theater of life in our time.

Pop Art

Advertising and mass culture became much more prominent across the Western world in the increasingly affluent 1960s. People were exposed to unprecedented amounts of commercial appeals and entertaining popular culture through magazines and television. These media encroached on what art had traditionally done: tell engaging stories, present beauty, and comment on life. In response, Pop artists made their own comments on mass culture by using real objects or mass-production techniques in their art. Like the Dadaists before them, Pop artists wanted to challenge cultural assumptions about the definition of art; they also made ironic comments on contemporary life.

Design and commercial art, long denigrated by painters and sculptors, became a source of inspiration. Pop painters used photographic screenprinting and airbrush techniques to achieve the surface characteristics of such anonymous mass-produced imagery as advertising, food labels, and comic books. The resulting slick look and ironic attitude separates Pop Art works from assemblages.

Pop Art flowered most brilliantly in the United States, but it first appeared in London, where a group of young artists made collages with images cut from popular magazines. In 1957, English artist Richard Hamilton published a list of characteristics of Pop Art for the London artists who were beginning to work in this vein. The list includes qualities of contemporary mass culture that these artists addressed. Hamilton wrote that Pop Art should be:

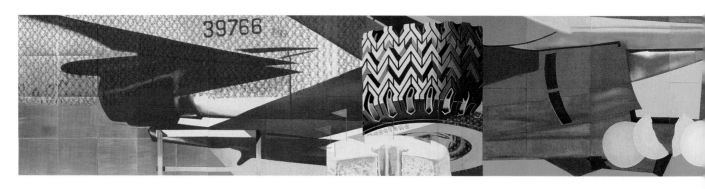

Popular (designed for a mass audience)

Transient (short-term solution)

Expendable (easily forgotten)

Low-cost

Mass-produced

Young (aimed at youth)

Witty

Sexy

Gimmicky

Glamorous

Big business[5]

Pop Art's media sources include the comic strip, the advertising layout, the famous-name-brand package, and the visual clichés of billboard, newspaper, movie theater, and television. Elements from all these mass media are included in Hamilton's collage *Just What Is It That Makes Today's Homes So Different, So Appealing?* (**fig. 24.20**). The word "pop" on the giant lollipop gave the movement its name.

American artist James Rosenquist worked as a billboard painter after attending art school. Later, he incorporated his billboard experience in a mature style that presents impersonally rendered imagery from contemporary American popular culture. He drew on the techniques and imagery of sign painting, rendering outsized close-up details of faces, natural forms, and industrial objects with a mechanical airbrush.

Rosenquist's huge mural *F-111* (**fig. 24.21**) filled all four walls of the Leo Castelli Gallery in New York City when it was first presented in 1965. The image of an F-111 fighter jet sweeps across his wall-to-wall environment of 1960s Americana. Rosenquist mixed symbols of affluence and destruction in his billboard-size painting, which includes—in addition to a jet fighter plane—a chain-link fence, a child under a hair dryer, a tire, light bulbs, a beach umbrella, and a mushroom cloud from a nuclear bomb.

24.20 Richard Hamilton. *Just What Is It That Makes Today's Homes So Different, So Appealing?* 1956. Collage. 10¼″ × 9¾″.
Kunsthalle, Tubingen, Germany/flab/Alamy Stock Photo. © R. Hamilton. All Rights Reserved, DACS and ARS 2018.

No American artist in the 1960s sparked more public indignation than Andy Warhol. He did not invent Pop Art, but he was its most visible and controversial exponent. Like Rosenquist, Warhol began his career as a commercial artist. Warhol's art shows us, in new ways, the effect of mass media and mass marketing on all of us.

24.21 James Rosenquist. *F-111.* 1965. Oil on canvas with aluminum. Four parts. 10′ × 86′.
Private collection. © Estate of James Rosenquist/Licensed by VAGA, New York.

Among his most common subjects were consumer products such as Coca-Cola and Campbell's soup. He blew up images of these products, silkscreened them onto new surfaces, and presented them as art. He made these works at a time when nationally standardized brands were just becoming the norm, as Americans began to prefer them to locally produced goods. If multiple rows of identical cans in a store make us happy, then why not make them into art?

This is precisely what Warhol did in *Kellogg's Corn Flakes Boxes* (**fig. 24.22**). The cereal company spent millions on advertisements promoting this product so that it was known to nearly every American, whether they ate it regularly or not. Television made such unprecedented nationwide mass marketing possible for the first time in the postwar period. The artist's repackaging of this product in a new context, as with his other images of consumer products, enabled the public to assess its omnipresent impact and to take a deeper look at just what they were buying.

Celebrities are also consumer products, and Warhol's *Marilyn Diptych* (**fig. 24.23**) is his meditation on celebrity status. The work gives us the actress's face 50 times over, in smudged black-and-white and garish color. The work seems to be telling us that a celebrity is a packaged commodity. This was news in the 1960s; today most people seem to realize it. When the diptych was created, in 1962, the actress had only recently been found dead in her home from an overdose of sleeping pills; she seemed like a martyr, sacrificed on the altar of stardom. Warhol's work called attention to the pervasive and insistent character of our commercial environment. The repetition of mass imagery has become our cultural landscape and our mythology.

24.22 Andy Warhol. *Kellogg's Corn Flakes Boxes*. 1971. Silkscreen painted wood. 27″ x 24″ x 19″.

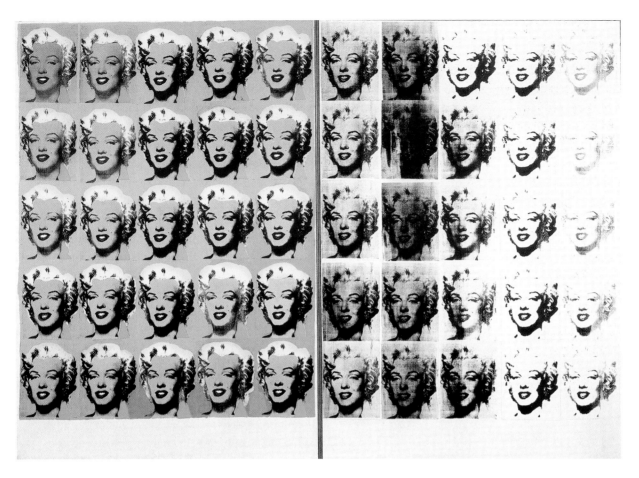

24.23 Andy Warhol. *Marilyn Diptych.* 1962. Synthetic polymer paint and silkscreen ink on canvas. 6′10″ × 57″.

In *Drowning Girl* (**fig. 24.24**) and other paintings, Roy Lichtenstein used comic-book images with their bright primary colors, impersonal surfaces, and characteristic printing dots. He borrowed panels from comic books of the day, but he usually altered them to enhance their drama. He then painted them by hand with the aid of a stencil, using the colored dots of contemporary mass printing. His work is a commentary on a world obsessed with consumer goods and spectacles. He saw Pop Art as "involvement with what I think to be the most brazen and threatening characteristics of our culture, things we hate, but which are also powerful in their impingement on us."[6]

24.24 Roy Lichtenstein. *Drowning Girl.* 1963.
Oil and magna on canvas. 67⅝″ × 66¾″.

24.25 Donald Judd. *Untitled.* 1967.
Stainless steel and Plexiglas, 10 units.
9½′ × 40″ × 31″.

Minimal Art

In the late 1950s and early 1960s, a number of artists aimed to create art that would exclude subject matter, symbolic meanings, personal content, and hidden messages of any kind. Was it possible to have art that referred to nothing outside itself, told no story except for its own shapes and colors? The artists who went on this quest were called **Minimalists**. They saw themselves as continuing a long-term modernist quest to throw out rules and conventions that governed art. The movement ran in parallel to other movements of the 1960s that questioned norms and conventions of society as a whole.

Among the leaders of this movement was Donald Judd. He worked with industrial materials such as sheet metal, aluminum, and molded plastics, which had not previously been used for art. Judd was the major spokesman for the Minimalist movement. In his essay "Specific Objects," he wrote about the aims of his art:

> It isn't necessary for a work to have a lot of things to look at, to compare, to analyze one by one, to contemplate. The thing as a whole, its quality as a whole, is what is interesting…. In the new work the shape, image, color, and surface are single, and not partial and scattered.[7]

Judd never titled his works, because he did not want viewers to infer any meaning beyond the colors and shapes that he used. His 1967 work *Untitled* (**fig. 24.25**) tells no story, has no personal expression, no symbolic content; he wants us to see it as only color and form.

Some painters had a parallel interest in what they saw as the essence of painting: a flat surface covered with colors. Quick-drying acrylic paints, which were developed at this time, lend themselves to uniform application and to the use of tape to obtain shapes with precise edges. Brushstrokes were suppressed, because they told a story of the work's creation or the artist's emotional state. Minimalist painters urged viewers to see their paintings as objects, not as pictures.

Ellsworth Kelly's bold paintings are richly hued studies in color and form. *Blue Green Yellow Orange Red* (**fig. 24.26**) is self-explanatory in at least a superficial sense. At a deeper level, Minimalism is a quest to see if art can still be art without representation, storytelling, or personal feeling. If the work had curved lines, modeled color, or paint strokes, it would not be as pure. Rather, the subject seems

24.26 ELLSWORTH KELLY. *Blue Green Yellow Orange Red.* 1966. Oil on canvas, five joined panels. 60″ × 240″.
Solomon R. Guggenheim Museum. © Ellsworth Kelly Foundation EK 360.

to be color itself: how we respond to it, and how different colors interact with one another in our field of view. It is an optical experiment that throws away a great many of the traditional rules. Such quests for the essence of art motivated many in those years.

Frank Stella's paintings of the 1960s emphasize the flatness of the picture plane and its boundaries. He used shaped canvases because a rectangular work might still be seen as a picture of something. In *Agbatana III* (**fig. 24.27**),

Stella used a distinctive outer profile to further extend the concept of the painting as an object in its own right rather than as a field for pictorial allusions. External boundaries of the overall shape are arrived at from the internal shapes. There is no figure–ground relationship; within the painting, everything is figure. Interwoven bands of both muted and intense colors pull together in a tight spatial weave. He summarized the Minimal movement with this statement: "What you see is what you see."[8]

24.27 Frank Stella. *Agbatana III.* 1968. Fluorescent acrylic on canvas. 120″ × 180″.
Allen Memorial Art Museum, Oberlin College, Ohio. Ruth C. Roush Fund for Contemporary Art and National Foundation for the Arts and Humanities Grant, 1968.37/Bridgeman Images. © 2018 Frank Stella/Artists Rights Society (ARS), New York.

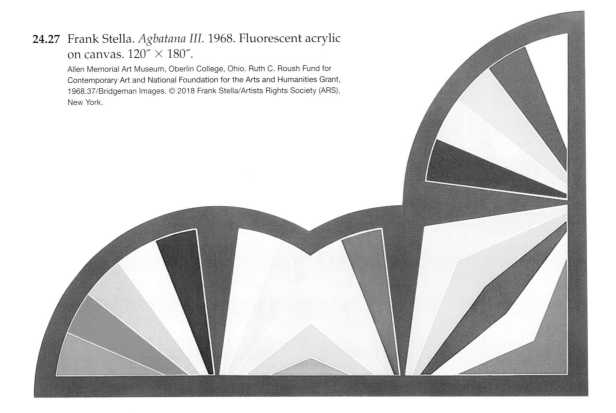

Conceptual Art

During the 1960s and 1970s, artists reacted ever more quickly to each successive aesthetic movement. Pushing back the limits, the next step after Minimalism became art about only an idea. **Conceptual art**, in which an idea takes the place of the art object, was an outgrowth of Minimalism. The Conceptual movement was also indebted to Marcel Duchamp, the first champion of an art of ideas (see Chapter 23).

Joseph Kosuth, the most rigorous early Conceptualist, was perplexed by the materialism of the art market and Pop Art's embrace of commercialism. In 1965, he produced *One and Three Chairs* (**fig. 24.28**), which consisted of a wooden chair, a photograph of the same chair, and a photographic enlargement of a dictionary definition of the word "chair." The work is about how we apprehend things, images, and words; it shows that we take in and process each version of the chair differently.

Creativity in any field begins when someone gets an idea. In the 1960s, this could have been for a new type of razor blade or a new government social program.

Consumers in advanced societies were for the first time constantly exposed to such novelties in the mass media. Conceptual art is related to this phenomenon; it is based on the fact that a work of art usually begins as an idea in the artist's mind. A great work of art is a great idea first, and its creator merely carries out the idea. If we "get the idea," then we have understood the piece. Creativity is, after all, a mental process. If this is true, then art can still be art without a unique, artist-made object.

Rather than making things, Conceptual artists present us with enough information so that we grasp the concept they have in mind. Joseph Kosuth wondered how a real chair differed from a photo and a verbal description of one, so he set up those items for us to consider. Another early leader in the movement was Yoko Ono, whose pieces are generally instructions to viewers. She questioned how sounds create meaning, so she created a piece with this instruction: Take 15 minutes to pronounce the word *south*. The best way to illustrate this work is to try it yourself and see what happens.

Site-Specific Works and Earthworks

Minimal and Conceptual works are radical, but they are still seen in art galleries. Several artists in the late 1960s and 1970s began creating works for display elsewhere, in specific sites other than the normal art venues. In such **site-specific** works, the artist's response to the location determines the composition, the scale, the medium, and even the content of each piece. (See fig. 12.25 for a site-specific work by Richard Serra.)

Some artists who created works were protesting against the materialism of the art world, which is based on buying and selling precious things. These site-specific works and earthworks thus make an anti-capitalist statement because they are generally outside the marketplace.

Bulgarian-born artist Christo, a leader in the site-specific movement, was well-trained enough to earn his living at first as a portrait painter. Later, he exhibited in Paris with the New Realists, a group of French and Swiss artists in the early 1960s who were presenting common objects as art rather than making painted or sculpted representations of objects. Christo often used fabric in his early works at this time and, in 1961, he and his wife and artistic collaborator, Jeanne-Claude, began creating temporary works of art, often using fabric as well. They began wrapping objects ranging in size from a motorcycle to a mile of Australian sea cliffs.

24.28 Joseph Kosuth. *One and Three Chairs*. 1965. Wooden folding chair, photographic copy of a chair, and photographic enlargement of dictionary definition of a chair. Chair 32⅜″ × 14⅞″ × 20⅞″; photo panel 36″ × 24⅛″; text panel 24″ × 24⅛″.

One of Christo and Jeanne-Claude's most ambitious projects was *Running Fence* (**fig. 24.29**), a temporary environmental artwork that was as much a process and an event as it was sculpture. The 18-foot-high white nylon fence ran from the ocean at Bodega Bay in Sonoma County, California, through 24½ miles of agricultural and dairy land. *Running Fence* stood for two weeks and ultimately involved thousands of people. The project required 18 public hearings, the agreement of landowners, and the help of hundreds of workers. The artists paid the workers and raised the funds for this project by selling early works, preparatory drawings, and collages.

The seemingly endless ribbon of white cloth made the wind visible and caught the changing light as it stretched across the gently rolling hills, appearing and disappearing on the horizon. The simplicity of *Running Fence* relates it to Minimalist art, but the fence itself was not presented as an art object. It also differs from a traditional artwork in that it is temporary. Rather, it was the focal point for a work that involved people, process, object, and place.

Walter De Maria's *The Lightning Field* (**fig. 24.30**) consists of 400 stainless-steel poles arranged in a rectangular

24.29 Christo and Jeanne-Claude. *Running Fence.*
Sonoma and Marin Counties, California. 1972–76.
Nylon fabric and steel poles. 18′ × 24½ miles.
© Volz/laif/Camera Press.

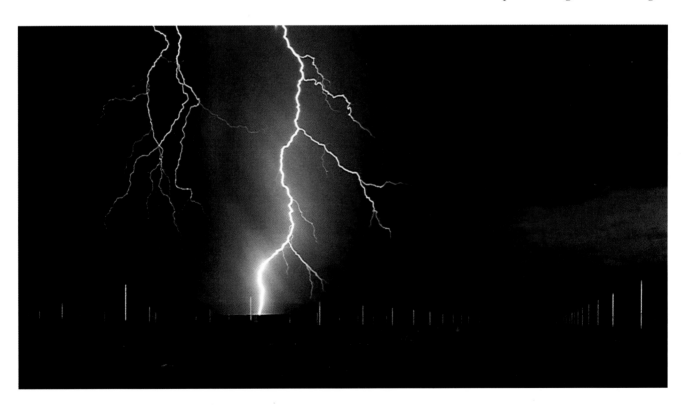

24.30 Walter De Maria. *The Lightning Field.* 1977. Quemado, New Mexico. 400 stainless-steel poles.
Average pole height 20′7″; land area 1 mile × 1 kilometer.
© The Estate of Walter De Maria. Photograph: John Cliett. Courtesy Dia Art Foundation, New York.

24.31 Robert Smithson. *Spiral Jetty*. Great Salt Lake, Utah. 1970. Earthwork. Length 1,500´; width 15´.

Photograph: Gianfranco Gorgoni. © Holt-Smithson Foundation/Licensed by VAGA, New York, NY.

grid over an area measuring 1 mile by 1 kilometer (⅝ mile) in west-central New Mexico. The sharpened tips of the poles form a level plane, a kind of monumental bed of nails. Each of the poles can act as a lightning conductor during the electrical storms that occur occasionally over the desert. Early and late in the day, the poles reflect the sun, creating accents of technological precision in sharp contrast to the otherwise natural landscape. Deliberately isolated from the art-viewing public, *The Lightning Field* combines aspects of both Conceptual and Minimalist art. Viewers must arrange their visits through the Dia Art Foundation, which commissioned the piece. Once there, they are left to study the work and make their own interpretations.

Site-specific works are environmental constructions, frequently made of sculptural materials, designed to interact with, but not permanently alter, the environment. **Earthworks** are sculptural forms made of materials such as earth, rocks, and sometimes plants. They are often very large, and they may be executed in remote locations. Earthworks are usually designed to merge with or complement the landscape. Many site-specific works and earthworks show their creators' interest in ecology and in the earthworks of ancient America.

Robert Smithson was one of the founders of the earthworks movement. His *Spiral Jetty* (**fig. 24.31**), at Great Salt Lake, Utah, was installed by hauling several thousand tons of basalt rock to the site to create the 1,500-foot long spiral. It has since gone in and out of view several times with changes in the water level. Its natural surroundings contrast with its form as a willful human design. Although our society has little agreed-upon symbolism or iconography, we instinctively respond to universal signs such as the spiral, which are found in nature and in ancient art.

Although site-specific works can be commissioned, they are almost never resold unless someone buys the land they occupy. Artists who create Conceptual art, earthworks, site-specific works, and performance art share a desire to subvert the gallery-museum-collector syndrome, to present art as an experience rather than as a commodity.

Installations

While some artists were creating outdoor earthworks and site-specific works, others were moving beyond the traditional concepts of indoor painting and sculpture. Since the mid-1960s, artists from diverse backgrounds and points of view have created interior **installations** rather than portable works of art (see *Yayoi Kusama: Obsessive Installations* on p. 454). Some installations alter the entire spaces they occupy (see fig. 12.25); others are experienced as large sculpture; most of them assume that the viewer will enter the piece.

The walls of a gallery need not limit an artist's installations. Outside the principal hall of the 1977 Documenta art exhibition in Kassel, Germany, Alice Aycock installed *The Beginnings of a Complex . . .* (**fig. 24.32**). Viewers who approached the work first saw a group of irregular wooden structures, some with porches or ladders. These five

buildings concealed a narrow underground passageway, which viewers could access one at a time by climbing a ladder, then descending a shaft. Once a viewer had entered the passageway there was just one route through the tunnel. Towers were accessible only from underground, and the artist provided no maps.

Aycock wrote of the work, "The complex is designed so that as one emerges from the underground labyrinth, one is contained within a well/shaft or tower. When access to the outside or open air is finally gained, one is so high up that the ground level is inaccessible. One is therefore lost when underground, and imprisoned in towers or stranded on platforms/ledges when above ground."[9] She intended the work to instill fear, claustrophobia, or disorientation in the viewer, upsetting or transforming the normal states of mind. This set of feelings diverges radically from what we might normally hope for in a work of art.

24.32 Alice Aycock. *The Beginnings of a Complex. . .* 1977. Wood and concrete.
Wall façade: length 40´ × heights 8´, 12´, 16´, 20´, 24´ respectively. Square tower: 24´ × 8´ × 8´.
Tall tower group: height 32´. Executed for Documenta 6, Kassel, Germany.
Photograph courtesy of the artist.

CREATORS

Yayoi Kusama: Obsessive Installations

An early leader in installations, Yayoi Kusama (b. 1929) has had a long and varied career. Through it all she remained focused on just a few aesthetic concepts, among them multiplicity and repetition.

Kusama was born in Nagano prefecture, a rural and mountainous area west of Tokyo, where her parents owned a large plant nursery. During World War II the future artist sewed parachutes. In 1948, she began studies at the Kyoto Municipal School of Arts and Crafts, but her art training was sporadic and incomplete. She began to feel an urge to go to the United States in search

of opportunity, so she found Georgia O'Keeffe's address and wrote to her, seeking advice from an established woman artist. To Kusama's great surprise, O'Keeffe responded favorably.

Encouraged, Kusama migrated in 1957 to Seattle, then to New York. By 1961 she had a studio in the same building as the future Minimalist Donald Judd, a friend. Her first solo show in New York consisted of large paintings covered with pea-sized, curving, monochromatic brushstrokes. These works used the allover compositional method of Abstract Expressionism, but more intimately and obsessively.

When Kusama took her compulsive urge for repetition into the third dimension, recognition began to come her way. She created tremendous accumulations of polka dots on all sorts of surfaces, from walls to furniture to stuffed shapes. With the *Infinity Mirror Room: Phalli's Field* (**fig. 24.33**), she reached an endpoint, installing mirrors on the walls of a room filled with hundreds of hand-sewn wormy creatures, all dotted in bright red. The mirrors gave visitors a vision of infinity, which usually included the artist herself. The installation did not survive, but Kusama's reputation as a radical creator did.

Where most of us might see the dots as a mere decorative pattern or perhaps as holes, Kusama intended deeper meanings, as she told an interviewer: "Our earth is only one polka dot among a million stars in the cosmos. Polka dots are a way to infinity."[10] In other words, dots suggest the expanse of interstellar space in the gallery, and perhaps give viewers a renewed sense of their own smallness.

In the high-energy New York art culture of the 1960s, Kusama stood out even more when she began creating controversial *Body Festivals* in the street. At an announced place and

24.33 Yayoi Kusama. *Infinity Mirror Room: Phalli's Field*. 1965. Installation. 98½″ × 197″ × 197″.
© Yayoi Kusama.

24.34 Yayoi Kusama. *Infinity Mirror Room—Filled with the Brilliance of Life*. 2011.
Wood, mirrors, plastic, acrylic, LED lights, water and aluminum. 116½″ x 245⅛″ x 245⅛″.
© Yayoi Kusama.

time, usually at a well-known location such as the Stock Exchange or Central Park, she would paint polka dots on the bodies of whoever showed up. Kusama said that the goal was helping people to join the infinite universe. This being the 1960s, often visitors wanted Kusama's polka dots over their entire expanse of skin, and that naturally attracted the police. These events evolved into anti-tax rallies and political protests against the war in Vietnam.

All involved protest signs, nudity, and polka dots, and they continued at each location until the authorities broke them up. Such daring made the artist more notorious than even Andy Warhol at the time.

As the 1960s faded into the 1970s, however, Kusama's fortunes ebbed as well. The happenings became predictable. Demand for polka dots proved finite. She retreated to her native Japan in 1973

as her mental health began to deteriorate, and in 1977 she was admitted to a psychiatric hospital, where she still lives.

Kusama's institutional regime allows ample scope for creativity, and she soon diverged into creative writing along with painting dots on canvas. She wrote 19 novels and short stories, several books of poetry, and an autobiography. In the latter, she stated, "I fight pain, anxiety, and fear every day, and the only

method I have found that relieves my illness is to keep creating art."[11]

In recent years, Kusama's installations have become more immersive, as we see in *Infinity Mirror Room—Filled with the Brilliance of Life* (**fig. 24.34**). The addition of darkness, LED lights, and pools of water has made these environments into major attractions, and has driven a worldwide renewal of interest in her art at this stage in her long career.

Early Feminism

The decade of the 1960s saw new demands for equality by members of many ethnic groups, such as African Americans, Native Americans, Latinos, and by people of various sexual orientations. In the late 1960s, many women artists began to speak out against the discrimination they faced in their careers. It was rare for women to be taken seriously in artists' groups; galleries were more willing to exhibit the work of men than of women; and museums collected the work of men far more often than that of women. Moreover, it seemed to the early **feminists** that making art about their experience as women might doom them to obscurity in a male-dominated art world. In the early 1970s in New York and California, they began to take action as part of a larger feminist movement.

Lucy Lippard, an art critic and feminist, wrote, "The overwhelming fact remains that a woman's experience in this society—social and biological—is simply not like that of a man. If art comes from the inside, as it must, then the art of men and women must be different, too."[12] The work of some women artists definitely is influenced by their gender and their interest in feminist issues.

California feminists tended to work collaboratively, and to make use of media that have been traditionally associated with craft work and with women: ceramics and textiles. *The Dinner Party* (**fig. 24.35**) was a collaboration of many women (and a few men), organized and directed by Judy Chicago over a period of five years. This cooperative venture was in itself a political statement about the supportive nature of female experience, as opposed to the frequently competitive nature of the male.

A large triangular table contains place settings for 39 women who made important contributions to world history. These run a wide gamut, from Egyptian queen Hatshepsut to Georgia O'Keeffe. The names of 999 additional women of achievement are inscribed on ceramic tiles below the table. Each place setting includes a hand-embroidered fabric runner and a porcelain plate designed in honor of that woman. Some of the plates are painted with flat designs; others have modeled and painted relief motifs; many are explicitly sexual, embellished with flower-like female genitalia.

East Coast feminists were more pointed in their protests. Some of them formed the group Women Artists in

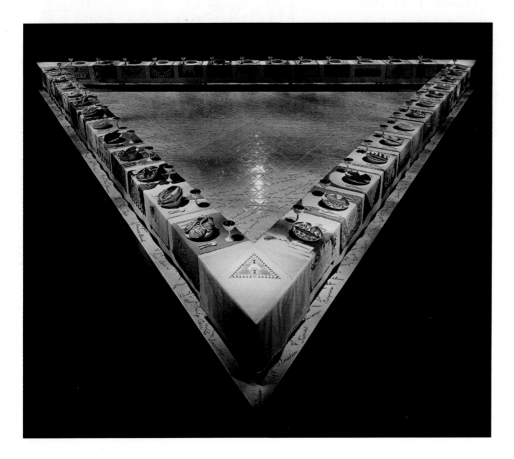

24.35 Judy Chicago.
The Dinner Party.
1979. Mixed media.
48′ × 42′ × 3′.

Collection of The Brooklyn Museum of Art. Gift of the Elizabeth A. Sackler Foundation. Photograph © Donald Woodman/Through the Flower. © 2018 Judy Chicago/Artists Rights Society (ARS), New York.

24.36 Nancy Spero. *Rebirth of Venus* (detail). 1984. Handprinting on paper. 12″ × 62′.

Courtesy of the artist. Photograph: David Reynolds. © The Nancy Spero and Leon Golub Foundation for the Arts/Licensed by VAGA, New York, NY.

Revolution (WAR), which picketed museums. In response to private dealers who were reluctant to show work by women, they formed their own collaborative gallery, Artists in Residence (AIR). Nancy Spero, a leader in East Coast feminist circles, participated in both groups. Her work from the late 1960s and early 1970s used unusual media such as paper scrolls, stencils, and printing to document subjects such as the torture and abuse of women. Her later scrolls, such as *Rebirth of Venus* (**fig. 24.36**), attempt to present images of women different from those commonly seen in art. In the segment illustrated here, an ancient statue of the love goddess Venus is split open to reveal a woman sprinter, who runs directly toward the viewer. The contrast between the two images is difficult to miss. Woman as love object gives way to woman as achiever.

One of the most radical feminists in Europe was Orlan, who, like Judy Chicago, rejected her birth name. Orlan's persistent theme has been the woman's body as the site of cultural debate and struggle. In 1974, she donned a nun's costume based on Bernini's *Ecstasy of Saint Teresa* (see fig. 17.22) and performed a striptease that she documented in a series of photographs. Thus, she passed between the two poles of identity (virgin and whore) that she saw the culture allotting to women.

Orlan's most controversial work came in 1977, when she crashed a contemporary art exhibition in Paris with *Le Baiser de l'artiste* (*The Artist's Kiss*; **fig. 24.37**). She was not invited to this show, but rather she set up her exhibit at the staircase leading to it. On a large black pedestal, viewers approached either Orlan the Saint (a photo from the earlier striptease act) or Orlan the Body (the artist herself sitting behind an invented vending machine). A soundtrack invited viewers either to bring a candle to the virgin, or to insert a coin in the slot below the artist's chin. As the coin ran down to its receptacle, the artist dispensed kisses. This rather scandalous performance forcefully raised the issue of woman as virginal ideal or as marketable commodity; it also cost the artist her teaching position.

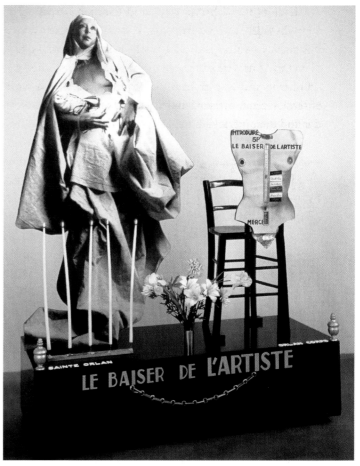

24.37 Orlan. *Le Baiser de l'artiste* (*The Artist's Kiss*). 1976–77. Mixed media with paint, metal chain, photographs, wood, blinking diode, artificial candles, artificial flowers, and CD. 86½″ × 67″ × 23½″.

In the collection of the Fonds Regional d'art Contemporain, Pays de la Loire, France. © 2018 Artists Rights Society (ARS), New York/ADAGP, Paris.

Performance Art

The works that artists create exist in the space between artist and viewer, carrying the artist's ideas to the public. In the 1970s, some artists began to wonder if they could do without artworks and address the audience directly. In performance art, artists do not create anything durable. Rather, they perform actions before an audience or in nature. Thus, this artform contains both visual art and drama, and has historical antecedents in Dada performances of the early twentieth century as well as in Expressionist painting. The happenings movement is another important antecedent. Performance artists eliminate the object and concentrate on the event itself. The only record is in the remembered experience of the participants or in a few photographs.

One of the most influential performance artists of the 1960s and 1970s was German-born Joseph Beuys. He carried out actions that resonated with deep symbolic significance, as if he were a healer or shaman. For one 1965 piece, he swathed his head in honey and gold leaf, and carried a dead rabbit around an art gallery explaining to it the paintings on view, touching the rabbit's lifeless paw to each. Some people, he later said, were as insensitive in their daily lives as the rabbit was in the art gallery. Arriving in New

24.39 Ana Mendieta. *Tree of Life.* 1976. Lifetime color photograph. 20″ × 13¼″.

Collection of Raquelin Mendieta, Family Trust [GL2225-B]. © The Estate of Ana Mendieta Collection. Courtesy Galerie Lelong, New York.

24.40 Asco (Willie Herrón III, Humberto Sandoval, Gronk, Patssi Valdez, Harry Gamboa Jr.).
Decoy Gang War Victim. 1975.
Photograph: © Harry Gamboa Jr.

York for the first time in 1974, he immediately plunged into a work called *I Like America and America Likes Me* (**fig. 24.38**). Met at the airport by an ambulance, he was wrapped in felt and taken to a gallery, where he lived for a week with a coyote. The animal symbolized the Wild West; copies of *The Wall Street Journal* were delivered daily to represent contemporary, business-oriented culture. He meant to heal the breach between the two.

Cuban émigré Ana Mendieta used her own body in several works as a symbol of the Earth and natural cycles. In the *Tree of Life series* (**fig. 24.39**), she coated her body with mud and grasses and stood against ancient tree trunks. She intended to show the essential equivalence between femaleness and natural processes such as birth and growth. For her, as for many early feminists, biology accounted for most of the differences between women and men. Through the natural cycles of their bodies, she seems to be saying, women are closer to the rhythms of the Earth.

Some performance artists engaged the most urgent contemporary issues. The art collective Asco in 1975 laid one of their members down in the street and set out cautionary flares, titling the event *Decoy Gang War Victim* (**fig. 24.40**). The event took place in a strife-torn zone of east Los Angeles where gangs had indeed recently been in conflict. The collective photographed the event and presented it to the media as the last victim of a gang war. Not realizing that it was a hoax, television news channels broadcast the image as another example of gang violence. The work drew attention to an urban social problem as it also pushed out the boundaries of art.

KEY TERMS

Abstract Expressionism – an art movement, primarily in painting, that originated in the United States in the 1940s, in which artists worked in many different styles that emphasized spontaneous personal expression

action painting – a style of nonrepresentational painting that relies on the physical movement of the artist by using such gestural techniques as vigorous brushwork, dripping, and pouring

assemblage – sculpture made by assembling found or cast-off objects that may or may not contribute their original identities to the total content of the work

Brutalism – movement in post-World War II architecture characterized by prominent use of unpainted exterior concrete, often cast into curving shapes

color field painting – a movement that grew out of Abstract Expressionism, in which large stained or painted areas, or "fields," of color evoke aesthetic and emotional responses

Conceptual art – a trend developed in the late 1960s; an artform in which the originating idea and the process by which it is presented take precedence over a tangible product

earthwork – a sculptural form made from earth, rocks, or sometimes plants, often on a vast scale and in a remote location

feminism – in art, a movement among artists, critics, and art historians that began in an organized fashion in the 1970s; feminists seek to validate and promote artforms that express the unique experience of women, and to redress oppression by men

happening – a usually unrehearsed event conceived by artists and performed by artists and others, who may include viewers

installation – an art medium in which the artist arranges objects or artworks in a room, thinking of the entire space as the medium to be manipulated; some installations are site-specific

Minimalism – a nonrepresentational style of sculpture and painting that came to prominence in the middle and late 1960s; usually severely restricted in the use of visual elements and often consisting of simple geometric shapes or masses

performance art – dramatic presentation by visual artists (as distinguished from theater artists) in front of an audience, usually not in a formal theatrical setting

Pop Art – a style of painting and sculpture that developed in the late 1950s and early 1960s in Britain and the United States, using mass-production techniques (such as silkscreen) or real objects in works that are generally more polished and ironic than assemblages

site-specific art – any work made for a certain place, which cannot be separated or exhibited apart from its intended environment

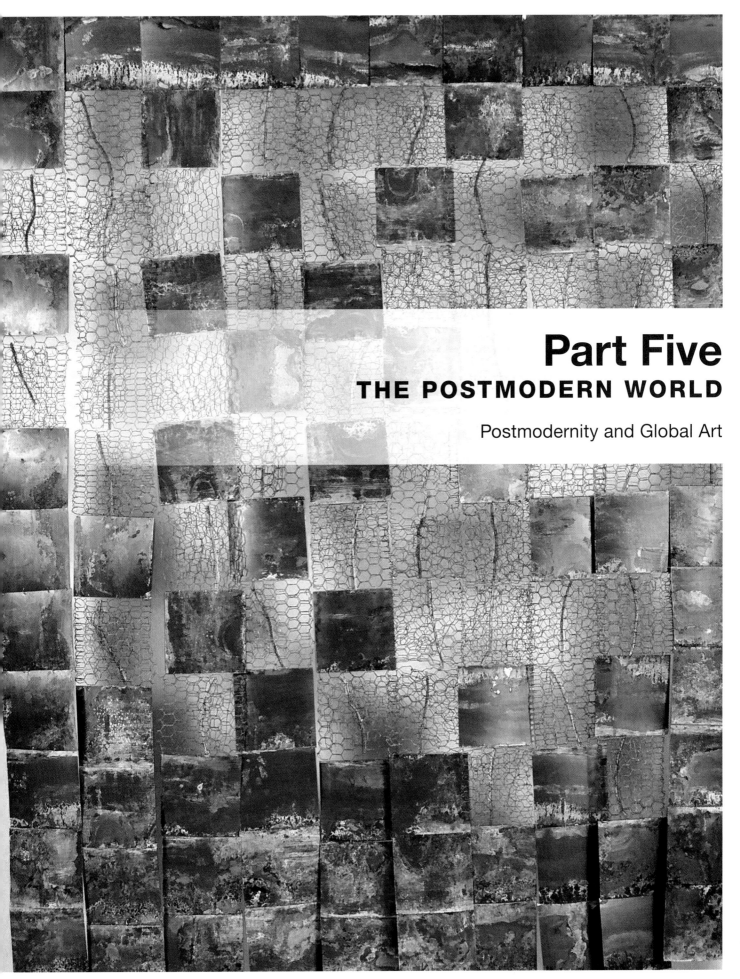

Part Five
THE POSTMODERN WORLD

Postmodernity and Global Art

Fig. 25.25. Photograph: N. Wanjiku Gakunga. Courtesy October Gallery, London.

25 POSTMODERNITY AND GLOBAL ART

By the late 1970s or early 1980s, the impulses and drives that caused modern art seemed spent. Modern art was based on rejecting tradition and breaking rules. Each new movement found some rule to break: regular perspective, recognizable subject matter, location in a gallery, and creation by hand are only a few of the rules that modern artists cast aside.

In the wider culture, the urge to rebel against the norm lost its impact when such rebellion became the norm in most Western cultures. We now look intently forward: to the next medical advance, to the next presidential term, or to the next digital innovation; not backward to the wisdom of our elders, ancient rituals, or eternal principles. Departing from the norm is widely seen as healthy. In fact, this was the slogan of a chain of fast-food restaurants in the early 1990s: "Sometimes you just gotta break the rules."

Artists today are left with few rules to break. While it is still possible to create art that offends people, it is difficult to invent a new style such as Cubism, Expressionism, Constructivism, or Minimalism. Most artists today are not striving for this.

In general, artists of the present generation prefer to comment on life, rather than focusing on perfecting form, creating beauty, or fine-tuning their sense of sight. They want to create work that illuminates the relationships between what we see and how we think. Rather than objects of timeless beauty or shocking novelty, most artists since the 1980s create objects laden with information about the period in which we live. This chapter will present some movements of the current generation, beginning with postmodernism and proceeding to recent developments in several media. Summarizing our own times is difficult, like catching a waterfall. Many of the artists discussed in this chapter could be placed in more than one category, but most would prefer not to be categorized at all.

Architecture

Modern architecture rejected tradition, ornament, and references to the past, and embraced modern materials and a utilitarian look. The modern movement culminated in the International Style, a glass-box look that swept most Western cities in the years after World War II. However, a growing discontent with the sterile anonymity of the

International Style (see the Lever House, fig. 24.9) led many architects to look once again at meaning, history, and context. Their departure from architectural modernism was dubbed **postmodern** in the late 1970s.

Postmodernists thought that the unadorned functional purity of the International Style made all buildings look the same, offering no identity relative to purpose, no symbolism, no sense of local meaning, no excitement. Postmodern architects celebrate the very qualities of modern life that modern architects rejected: complexity, ambiguity, nostalgia, and popular taste.

Among the first architects to rebel against the International Style were Robert Venturi and his partner Denise Scott-Brown, and they did it by writing a book in 1976: *Learning from Las Vegas*. They urged architects to study what is local, vernacular, and even tacky. They realized that even if Las Vegas was tasteless, people loved it, and architects who refuse to recognize that fact turn the public off. The book brought the entire profession to attention.

The postmodern style of Michael Graves uses **classical** architecture in knowing and even humorous ways. His Public Services Building (**fig. 25.1**) is both formal and playful. The exterior is dominated by a pair of fluted classical columns. They are red-brown, a color that the Greeks would never have used. They also share a single huge capital. These off-color vertical elements have no structural function, and Graves underlined this by setting them in a reflecting pool of mirrored glass. The remainder of the façade consists of featureless rows of square openings, an ironic reference to the bureaucrats inside.

25.1 Michael Graves. Public Services Building. Portland, Oregon. 1980–82.
Photograph: Nikreates/Alamy.

25.2 Thom Mayne and Morphosis. Gates Hall, Cornell University. 2014–15.
Photograph: Roland Halbe.

If postmodernism freed architects from the rigid ideas of modernism, the development of computer graphics and three-dimensional computer modeling in the 1980s made new shapes possible. Frank Gehry has mastered these techniques more than most architects, as his Guggenheim Museum Bilbao, built in 1997, shows (see fig. 14.25). The museum's exterior is a dramatic limestone and titanium-clad cluster of soaring, nearly dancing volumes that climax in a gigantic, glass-enclosed atrium.

The most creative architects today neither rebel against modernism nor quote tradition whimsically as postmodernists do. Rather, they try to make visually stunning buildings that fulfill their functions with ease. Californian Thom Mayne is a leader in this new trend in combining aesthetics and utility. The new Gates Hall at Cornell University (**fig. 25.2**) houses the Computing and Information Science Faculty in a striking building that is barely contained within its rectangular lot. The dramatic entrance has abstract

25.3 Kunlé Adeyemi. Chicoco Radio Station, Port Harcourt, Nigeria. 2014.
Courtesy of NLÉ, the architects.

sculptural shapes on a slope before the curving orange hood that shelters students from the storms of upstate New York. This entrance leads to an open, four-story atrium with glass exterior walls, as we see in the near corner. Exterior panels are perforated stainless steel, protruding at various angles to filter sunlight while promoting views both outward and inward. "We told the architects we needed light, light, light," said one of the faculty members. "I work in computer graphics, and it's important to have bright, open spaces where ideas can flow."[1] Every floor has a naturally lit sociability zone to tempt students and faculty away from their computer screens.

Gates Hall is by necessity a high-tech building, but many architects today are finding low-tech solutions to local problems. An example is African-born architect Kunlé Adeyemi, who designed a community radio station for an impoverished waterside settlement in Nigeria (**fig. 25.3**). The Chicoco Radio Station sits in the midst of the community that it serves in the Niger River delta. It has a welcoming dock at the end of a long, sloping deck that doubles as an amphitheater for public functions. The angled tower both broadcasts the station's signal and anchors the cantilevered boat ramp, which rises and falls with the tide. Many of the surrounding houses are shanties, built by local residents themselves using improvised materials. Those same people joined the work force that is building the station, which will give the neighborhood a powerful new voice.

Painting

At various times in recent decades, critics and curators have wondered whether painting might have come to an end, given the decline of modernism and the proliferation of other media. Yet painting survives, partly because it is attractive to collectors and partly because artists still find new things to do with it.

As modernism came to an end, many painters in America and Europe began to revive expressive, personal styles in a movement known as **Neo-Expressionism**. This was partly in response to the impersonality of movements such as Conceptual art and Minimalism, and to the ironic, tongue-in-cheek quality of Pop Art and related trends.

One of the first Neo-Expressionists was Susan Rothenberg, who in the 1970s began making symbolic, heavily brushed works in which subject matter teeters on the brink of being recognizable. After the cleansing blankness of Minimalism, Rothenberg could return to figurative images with original vision; what emerges is almost ethereal.

Rothenberg works in a narrow range of tones, using a muted palette of white, beige, and silvery or dark gray, with a bit of color. *Juggler with Shadows* (**fig. 25.4**) seems to show a moving figure emerging from thick darkness. She painted this work with shimmering strokes that enliven the entire surface and suggest a mysterious deep space. The figure hovers above, just recognizable enough to stimulate the imagination.

25.4 Susan Rothenberg. *Juggler with Shadows*. 1987. Oil on canvas. 72¼″ × 124¼″.

The Eli and Edythe L. Broad Collection. © 2018 Susan Rothenberg/Artists Rights Society (ARS), New York.

25.5 Anselm Kiefer. *Osiris and Isis*. 1985–87. Oil, acrylic, emulsion, clay, porcelain, lead, copper wire, and circuit board on canvas. 150″ × 220½″ × 6½″.

San Francisco Museum of Modern Art. Purchased through a gift of Jean Stein, by exchange; the Mrs. Paul L. Wattis Fund; and the Doris and Donald Fisher Fund. Photograph by Ben Blackwell. © Anselm Kiefer.

German painter Anselm Kiefer combines expressive paint application with nineteenth-century feelings for history and mythology. He gives equal attention to moral and aesthetic issues. His paintings, loaded with symbolism, mythology, and religion, speak to us through powerful stories in dramatic compositions.

Osiris and Isis (**fig. 25.5**) retells the ancient Egyptian myth of the cycle of death and rebirth. Osiris symbolized the indestructible creative forces of nature; according to legend, the god was slain and cut into pieces by his evil brother. Isis, sister (and wife) of Osiris, collected the pieces and brought him back to life. In Kiefer's huge painting, a network of wires

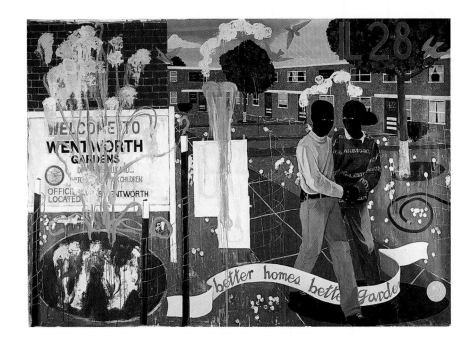

25.6 Kerry James Marshall. *Better Homes Better Gardens*. 1994. Acrylic and collage on canvas. 8′4″ × 12′.

Denver Art Museum Collection: Funds from Polly and Mark Addison, the Alliance for Contemporary Art, Caroline Morgan, and Colorado Contemporary Collectors: Suzanne Farver, Linda and Ken Heller, Jan and Frederick Mayer, Beverly and Bernard Rosen, Annalee and Wagner Schorr, and anonymous donors, 1995.77. Photograph © Denver Art Museum. Courtesy Jack Shainman Gallery, New York.

attached to fragments of the dismembered Osiris connects to the goddess Isis in the form of a T.V. circuit board atop a pyramid. The heavily textured surface of paint, mud, rock, tar, ceramic, and metal intensifies the image's epic treatment of the afterlife theme.

The Neo-Expressionists tended to favor painting because a seemingly infinite variety of surface textures and colors is possible. Every creative decision can leave a trace on the finished work, registering every twitch in sensibility. Other artists use painting media because they facilitate storytelling, allowing the artist to create a two-dimensional world with the utmost freedom.

Kerry James Marshall investigates African-American life in richly textured paintings. His 1994 work *Better Homes Better Gardens* (**fig. 25.6**) is part of a series of paintings that he made about Chicago housing projects that contain the word "garden" in their names. This one is obviously set in Wentworth Gardens, and it depicts a couple walking down a flowered pathway in a low-rise setting. At the left is a fenced area enclosing a communal flower garden. Three bluebirds fly across the upper portion of the scene, and all seems peaceful. Whatever else happens in housing projects, they are places of community and neighborhood feeling, he seems to be telling us.

Yet for all its apparent optimism, there are ironic touches in this work. The perfectly spiraled garden hose, the white blotches over the heads of the couple, and the flowered entry with the "Welcome" sign add a note of complexity to the mood, casting a flickering shadow over its sweetness. The inscription "IL 2-8" in the upper right reminds us that this is both an illustration and a painting that is in fact rigorously composed. It is based on a solid grid of horizontals, verticals, and a few diagonals. Although the work is optimistic, Marshall is not merely painting an idealistic scene. Because his work is often closely connected to African-American life, Marshall's paintings are often acquired by museums, as this one was.

In the 1990s, a new movement called **Relational Aesthetics** arose across various media. Rather than creating stable objects, artists created situations that depended on the presence of the viewer for their realization. For example, for a work called *This Progress*, Berlin-based artist Tino Sehgal stationed trained guides in a series of empty galleries. These guides engaged in conversation with visitors as they walked through; the interaction became the art experience, which was different for each viewer.

British artist Angela Bulloch made a relational painting in her 1994 work *Betaville* (**fig. 25.7**). It consists of a motion sensor attached to a machine that paints lines on the wall in response to viewer movements. If no one is present the machine paints vertical lines in random spacings; when a viewer sits on the bench, the direction changes to horizontal; sitting and standing motions generate diagonal lines. Over the course of an exhibition, the work will evolve depending on how many visitors see it and how they behave, and the work will look different at the end of each installation. In relational aesthetics, the artist renounces control over the development and final appearance of the work. Bulloch said, "It was interesting to me that the person looking at the piece was involved in a level of power given to them unexpectedly or that they could take it upon themselves to use. This renegotiation of power interested me."[2]

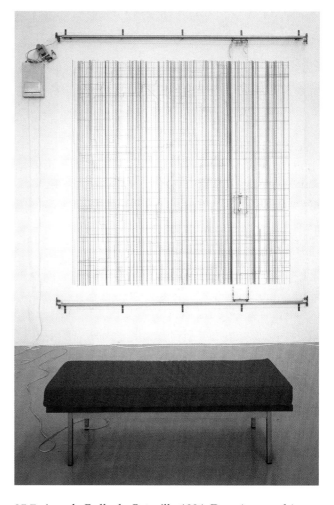

25.7 Angela Bulloch. *Betaville.* 1994. Drawing machine with switch bench. Drawing approx. 10′ × 10′.
Photograph © Fredrik Nilsen. Courtesy of Esther Schipper, Berlin.

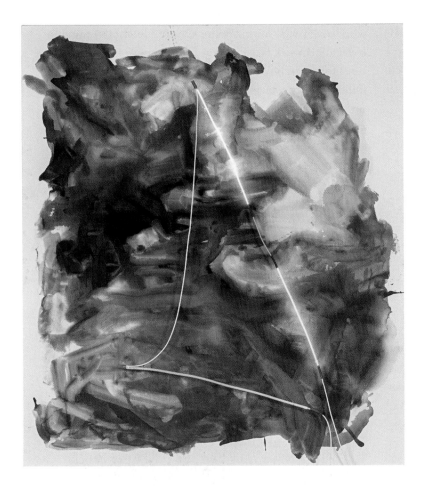

25.8 Mary Weatherford. *Oxnard Ventura*. 2014. Flashe and neon on linen. 112½″ × 100″ × 4⅜″.
Photograph: Frederik Nilsen. Courtesy of David Kordansky Gallery, Los Angeles, CA.

In recent years, nonrepresentational art has made a comeback, as we see in *Oxnard Ventura* (**fig. 25.8**). Mary Weatherford uses Flashe, a new type of acrylic paint, in a style that owes something to the thin washes of color field painters such as Helen Frankenthaler (see fig. 24.7). Weatherford also names her works after places, as Frankenthaler often did, but the younger artist paints more emphatically; she also embeds handmade neon tubes in her works. These tubes coordinate with the masses and directional forces in the painted surface, shedding light and adding a dimension. They suggest neon signs glimpsed through fog, or perhaps thunderbolts in the sky.

Photography

The postmodern movement has been a primary influence on recent photography. The principal new insight that postmodernists brought to the medium was the perhaps unsurprising notion that a photograph is not merely a "straight" record of fact. There are ways of composing, taking, developing, and printing pictures that serve to encode information and influence viewers. Postmodern photographers show through their pictures that they know their medium is not an objective one, and that today's cameras can easily lie. Even the most straightforward scenes can have hidden meanings. Postmodernists want to show us that the camera can influence us in ways we may not suspect, and the camera itself has a certain way of seeing.

Cindy Sherman's photographs of the late 1970s were among the first to be called postmodern. She took black-and-white photos of herself, posing with props in scenes that corresponded to stereotyped female characters from popular culture. In *Untitled Film Still #48* (**fig. 25.9**), for example, she stands on a deserted road at dusk, her back to us, hastily packed suitcase at her side. As in many "teen movies" of the 1950s and 1960s, she is the misunderstood daughter running away from home. Other photos from the series depict the girl next door, daddy's little girl, the anxious young career woman, the oppressed housewife. Without referring to specific movies, Sherman's photos are imagined stills from

25.9 Cindy Sherman. *Untitled Film Still #48*. 1979. Black and white photograph.
Courtesy of the artist and Metro Pictures.

25.10 Vik Muniz. *Atlas (Carlão)*. 2008. From the series *Pictures of Garbage*. Photograph.

Photograph: Vik Muniz Studio. © Vik Muniz/Licensed by VAGA, New York, NY.

popular film types that have helped to form stereotypical images of women. She knowingly imitates these stereotypes as if to satirize them; this strategy of ironic recycling is some of the purest postmodernism. Sherman's work is influenced about equally by Pop Art, performance art, and feminism. She differs from early feminists, though, in presenting women as a product of the culture and not of biology. In her eyes culture has a much larger role than nature in forming women's identities.

Many photographers today do not "find" their subjects; they set them up, as Sherman does. Brazilian-born Vik Muniz works hardest at this task, as we see in his work *Atlas (Carlão)* from the series *Pictures of Garbage* (**fig. 25.10**). The artist guided the arrangement of huge amounts of trash on his studio floor, thereby "painting" a picture, which he then photographed. This work took up a large expanse of the floor space, as we see from the small green spots along the upper right edge; most of these are flattened 2-liter plastic soft-drink bottles. A dirty pair of blue jeans is visible at the lower right, waist downward. Muniz used garbage to create a noble image of a garbage collector, and he used that person's materials to make it. Proceeds from the sale of

works from this series went to the aid fund of the garbage collectors' union.

Moroccan-born Hassan Hajjaj uses photography to undermine stereotypes. For a series called *Kesh Angels*, he posed and photographed women on motorcycles, wearing Muslim veils of his design which are emblazoned with corporate logos (**fig. 25.11**). *Khadija* sits jauntily astride her scooter, defiant, audacious, and dressed like a conservative Muslim. Colors in her outfit and the backdrop clash knowingly, and all have a near-complementary relationship to the frame of the photograph constructed by the artist. Hajjaj painted it bright yellow and included shelves for about four dozen cans of the orange soft drink Fanta. The artist's exercise in branding both the costume and the cans is so obvious that it becomes an ironic version of product placement. Such overt game-playing with stereotypes and image uses is essentially postmodern.

25.11 Hassan Hajjaj. *Khadija*. 2010. Metallic Lambda print on 3mm white Dibond. 53½″ × 36¾″.

Taymour Grahne Gallery, New York.

Sculpture

The range of options available to sculptors spreads out beyond traditional carving and casting to include assemblage and new media. Partly in reaction to the simplicity of Minimal and Conceptual art, sculptors today draw on a range of techniques and materials. Many contemporary sculptors are exploring the symbolic value of shapes. How can a shape "mean something"? What range of memories and feelings are viewers likely to attach to a given figure? At what point does a form "take shape" so that a viewer can recognize it? Are viewers likely to see what the creator had in mind? These are some of the questions that sculptors have posed in recent years.

Indian-born British sculptor Anish Kapoor takes such explorations in a ritualistic direction in his work *To Reflect an Intimate Part of the Red* (**fig. 25.12**). He deployed across a gallery floor several shapes that allude to ancient religious structures such as Mayan pyramids, Indian stupas, and onion-shaped domes. Kapoor sprinkled his sculpture with powder, an action that also seems ritualistic. The translation of these shapes into an art gallery makes us wonder how their spiritual meanings come about, and how much of that meaning persists in the new context.

25.12 Anish Kapoor. *To Reflect an Intimate Part of the Red.* 1981. Pigment and mixed media. Installation 78″ × 314″ × 314″.
Photograph: Andrew Penketh, London. Courtesy of Barbara Gladstone.

As some sculptors investigate the meaning of shapes, so others question the meanings of materials. They use almost any substance or object as an experiment, to see what might be said with it. One of these is Rachel Harrison,

25.13 Rachel Harrison. *This Is Not an Artwork.* 2006. Wood, polystyrene, cement, acrylic, table, fake vegetables, plastic surveillance camera, mannequin, wig, cowboy hat, stickers, and plastic KISS figure with drum. 59″ × 22″ × 22″.
Courtesy of the artist and Greene Naftali, New York. Photograph: Jean Vong.

who brought together an amazing array of things and titled it *This Is Not an Artwork* (**fig. 25.13**). Fake vegetables, a wig model, and a cheap table only begin the list of this work's components. It also includes an action figure of the famous classic rock drummer Peter Criss, and a surveillance camera. The piece as a whole seems to be a meditation on what is real and what is a representation, a crucial question in today's culture.

Some sculptors have begun using 3-D printers, the newest piece of technology available to them. Josh Kline begins with high-resolution photos, then creates 3-D models from them using software on his computer; this allows for adjustments in size, color, and texture. The output, as we see in *Tastemaker's Choice* (**fig. 25.14**), looks ghostly on its industrial shelving. These are hands holding bottles in a way that recalls magazine advertisements. He told an interviewer, "I'm interested in any kind of tool that can be used for sampling, and also in tools that can alter, composite, and export sampled content and subjects."[3]

25.14 Josh Kline. *Tastemaker's Choice*. 2012. Six 3-D printed sculptures in acrylic-based photopolymer, various liquids, commercial shelving with LED lights. 36½″ × 26⅛″ × 15½″.
Courtesy of the artists and 47 Canal, New York. Photograph: Joerg Lohse.

Public Art

Public art is art that you might encounter without intending to; it exists in a public place, accessible to everyone. The idea of public art originated in ancient times, as government and religious leaders commissioned artists to create works for public spaces. In our time artists still make public art that responds to the needs and hopes of broad masses of people.

The Vietnam Veterans Memorial, by Maya Lin, located on the Mall in Washington, D.C., is probably America's best-known public art piece (see fig. 2.16). The almost 250-foot-long, V-shaped black granite wall bears the names of the nearly 60,000 American servicemen and women who died or are missing in Southeast Asia.

Lin's bold, eloquently simple design creates a memorial park within a larger park. It shows the influence of Minimalism and site-specific works of the 1960s and 1970s. The polished black surface reflects the surrounding trees and lawn, and the tapering segments point to the Washington Monument in one direction and the Lincoln Memorial in the other. Names are inscribed in chronological order by date of death, each name given a place in history. As visitors walk toward the center, the wall becomes higher and the names pile up inexorably. The monument's thousands of visitors seem to testify to its power to console and heal.

A great deal of public art in the United States is created under a mandate that one-half of 1 percent of the cost of public buildings be spent on art to embellish them. When a community-minded artist works with the local people, the results can be quite successful, as in the following case.

Seattle-based Buster Simpson specializes in public art, and one of his recent commissions embodies the environmental concerns of an eastern Washington agricultural community. *Instrument Implement: Walla Walla Campanile* (**fig. 25.15**) begins with a core of metal farmers' disks arranged in a repeating bell-shape pattern. Sensors track environmental conditions in nearby Mill Creek: water temperature, flow level, and amount of dissolved gases. All three of these measures are critical for the annual salmon migration, which has been diminishing in recent years. The data are processed by a computer that encodes them into musical notes. Hammers on the piece then strike the relevant disks to ring a chime, which becomes an hourly auditory update on the condition of the river. The health of the local salmon is a "canary in the coal mine," an early warning of other environmental problems. Simpson included a yellow effigy of a salmon as an indicator of this. The entire piece is powered by an attached solar collector. *Instrument Implement* is located at Walla Walla Community College, within sight and earshot of hundreds of people each day.

Public art can be made in almost any medium, depending on the needs of the commissioning body. Catherine Opie installed a series of photographs of Lake Erie, titled *Somewhere in the Middle*, in the main corridor of a public hospital in Cleveland (**fig. 25.16**). The photographs were taken from the same spot during all seasons of the year. After making several visits to the hospital site, Opie selected four photos each for spring, summer, and fall, but five for winter because, as she said, it lasts a long time there. The horizon exactly bisects each photo, establishing a visual rhythm across the images that the artist hoped would contribute to a sense of tranquility. Walking down the corridor also gives a sense of the slow passage of time in a familiar place, which Opie hoped would comfort both patients and visitors.

When artists take the initiative themselves to create works for public view, without waiting for a commission, the result is street art. Often this type of art is created or installed illegally, but some street art works are executed with permission of the owner of the property.

Street art as we know it today began in the 1960s with tagging, a customary way for local gangs to mark out their

25.15 Buster Simpson. *Instrument Implement: Walla Walla Campanile*. 2008. William A. Grant Water & Environmental Center, Walla Walla Community College, Walla Walla, WA. Height 25′6″.
Courtesy of the artist.

25.16 Catherine Opie. *Untitled #8*. From series *Somewhere in the Middle*. 2011. Inkjet print. 50″ × 37½″.
© Catherine Opie. Courtesy of Regen Projects, Los Angeles.

25.17 Banksy. *Stone Age Waiter*. Los Angeles. 2006. Spray paint and stencils. Height 5´6˝.
Photograph: Patrick Frank.

territory with names or initials. An increase in the availability of spray paint in a wide array of colors fueled an upsurge of creativity in the 1970s. Some street artists became so well-known for their illegal work that they moved indoors and became gallery artists. Two notable creators who began in that decade and moved indoors in the 1980s were Jean-Michel Basquiat (see fig. 5.5) and Keith Haring (see fig. 3.50).

Probably the most famous street creator today is the English artist Banksy, who has been active since the 1990s and still shields his identity with a pseudonym. His street art is generally witty, as we see in *Stone Age Waiter* (**fig. 25.17**). This piece, which was done with permission, adorns an outdoor location in a Los Angeles neighborhood with many restaurants; a cave man has apparently joined the ranks of the pleasure-seekers. Well-heeled Angelenos who walk the (always short) distance from their cars to their favorite restaurants will pass this

stencil-and-spray-paint creation. Banksy is also one of the most popular artists in his homeland, and many of his outdoor works have been preserved. In 2015, he rented an abandoned amusement park on the English seacoast and converted it into a street art festival with 58 other creators. With typical wit, he called it Dismaland Bemusement Park; it drew more than 150,000 visitors during its five-week run.

Socially Conscious Art

Many artists of recent generations have sought to link their art to current social questions. These artists believe that if they limit their art to aesthetic matters, then their work will be only a distraction from pressing problems. Furthermore, they recognize that what we see influences how we think, and they do not want to miss an opportunity to influence both. Some public art is also socially conscious, as we saw with Simpson's *Instrument Implement*.

25.18 Barbara Kruger. *Untitled (I Shop Therefore I Am)*. 1987. Photographic silkscreen/vinyl. 111″ × 113″.
© Barbara Kruger. Courtesy Mary Boone Gallery, New York. MBG 4057.

Barbara Kruger was trained as a magazine designer, which shows in her piece *Untitled (I Shop Therefore I Am)* (**fig. 25.18**). She invented the slogan, which sounds as though it came from advertising. The position of the hand, too, seems to come from an ad for aspirin or sleeping medication. Do our products define us? Are we indeed what we shop for? Often we buy a product because of what it will say about us, and not for the thing itself. These are some of the messages present in this simple yet fascinating work. Perhaps its ultimate irony is that the artist later silkscreened it onto a shopping bag.

Kruger's piece is confrontational and ironic, but some socially conscious art transforms social problems into attractive artworks that pull us in and beguile us into learning more. Tiffany Chung's works such as *UNHCR Red Dot Series* (**fig. 25.19**) often resemble handmade maps with their seductive bright colors, but the information they contain is ripped from the news headlines. This work depicts the flow of Syrian refugees over an eight-month period in 2012. Chung researched statistics

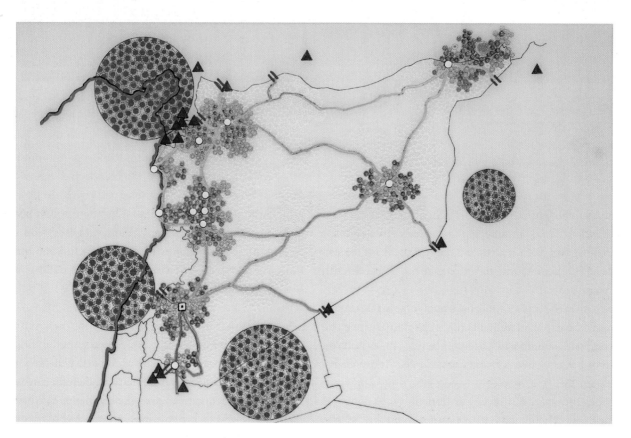

25.19 Tiffany Chung. *UNHCR Red Dot Series—Tracking the Syrian Humanitarian Crisis: April-Dec 2012* (detail). 2014–15. Oil and ink on vellum and paper. 8¼″ × 11¾″.
Courtesy of the Artist and Tyler Rollins Fine Art, NY.

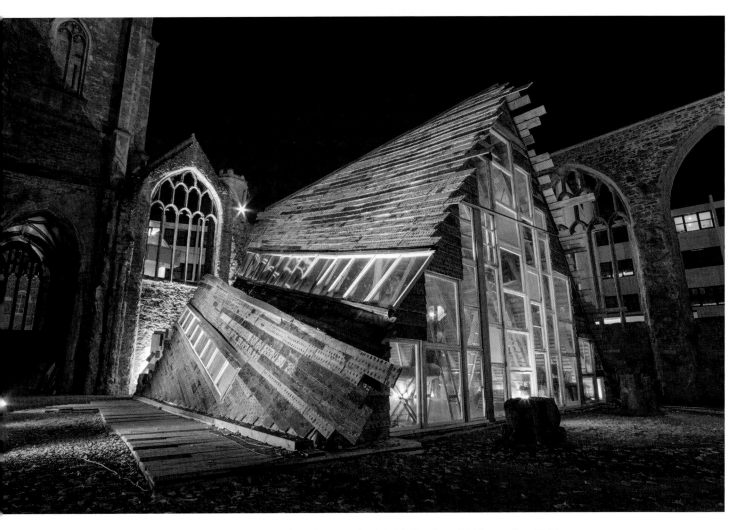

25.20 Theaster Gates. *Sanctum*. 2015. Temple Church, Bristol, UK. 29 October–21 November 2015.
© Theaster Gates. Photo © Max McClure. Courtesy Situations.

gathered by the United Nations High Commissioner for Refugees (UNHCR) on internal displacement and foreign exodus, and then translated the numbers into dots. The smaller dots surround zones of military engagements inside the country, with resulting internal migrants; the huge red spots are the much heavier cross-border refugee flows in each direction. The artist has an affinity for this issue because she was born in Vietnam in 1969, during the war, and was a refugee herself from that conflict with her family.

Influenced by relational aesthetics (see fig. 25.7), Chicago-based Theaster Gates creates spaces for experiences that he hopes will help to improve communities. In a ruined church in Bristol, England, he gathered disused and cast-off building materials from run-down local neighborhoods and carpentered them into a performance space (**fig. 25.20**). *Sanctum* hosted events for 24 days, 24 hours a day in late 2015, but the schedule was not announced ahead of time, so that viewers did not know what they might see there when they visited. The list of performers, all locally based, included choirs, spoken-word artists, historians, poets, political speakers, and musicians of all kinds from punk to opera. Gates described the work as "a collaboration with the city's materials, the city's administrators, the city's artists and musicians to engage in quietly restorative work and to amplify the city's unheard voices."[4] Completing the picture of regeneration, the surrounding church building is a fourteenth-century Gothic structure that was bombed by the Nazis in World War II, a historical monument that got a surprising new use.

Post-Internet Art

Many artists today base their work on an issue or a question, and then create using whatever media seem necessary or appropriate to the investigation. Moreover, we live in a time in which there is not one dominant style in art, as was true during, say, the Renaissance or Romanticism; rather, today there are several that draw attention.

Post-Internet Art is one example of a cross-media movement that has arisen lately. The term does not mean that the Internet is over; rather, it designates art that responds to our current networked condition. These works may or may not use the Internet itself, but they show awareness of, or comment on, the Internet and social media, which have an increasingly important role in our lives. The movement was defined by a pair of art critics for a 2014 exhibition by that name, and it continues to grow.

Rafael Rozendaal is one of the artists mentioned most often under this rubric; his art is among the most closely tied to the Web. *15 05 10 IMDb* (**fig. 25.21**) is a weaving that he commissioned from a tapestry factory, one of a series of works titled *Abstract Browsing*. Rozendaal wrote a software program that works with a web browser to convert any web page into an abstract composition. This particular work is based on what his browser found at the popular movie database website imdb.com on

October 5, 2015. The type of abstraction that the program does is based on that of the de Stijl painter Theo van Doesburg (see fig. 1.13), reducing the input to brightly colored rectangles. The similarity that Rozendaal saw between pixels on a screen and stitches in a piece of fabric led him to the weaving medium. To complete the work, he made the Abstract Browsing application into a free extension for Google Chrome browsers. The curious can download it to their own browsers and put websites they visit through it, so that they can curate their own screen-based abstract art shows.

One artist who exhibited in the 2014 exhibition was sculptor Artie Vierkant, although he prefers to call his works *Image Objects* rather than sculptures (**fig. 25.22**). He creates irregular metal constructions and decorates them with computer-generated imagery. The works have a playful, even exuberant quality that owes something to earlier abstract work by Julio González (see fig. 12.15) or David Smith (see fig. 24.5), but painted. What makes Vierkant's work Post-Internet is that he creates the imagery out of installation shots of his own previous exhibitions. He downloads those images from the Internet and then mashes them up to fit onto his metal sculptures. The work thus collapses past and present into a literal compendium of his other work that leads up to it.

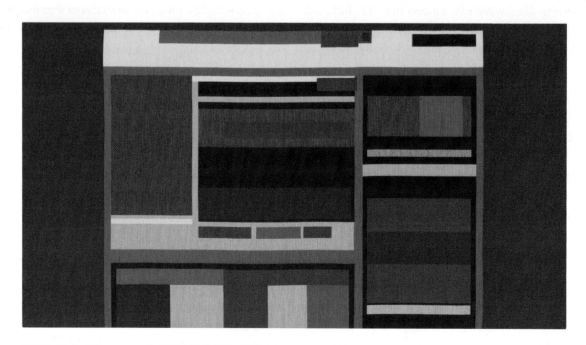

25.21 Rafael Rozendaal. *15 05 10 IMDb*. 2015. From series *Abstract Browsing*. Jacquard weaving. 56¾″ × 104¾″.
Image courtesy of the artist and Steve Turner.

25.22 Artie Vierkant, *Image Object Thursday 4 June 2015 12:53PM*. 2015. Aluminum and vinyl. 49″ × 49″ × 38″.
Courtesy of the artist.

Postmodern artists often quote other artists, but Post-Internet artist Vierkant quotes himself.

Surveillance and sharing are two aspects of the same hyper-connected environment that we inhabit. The former is done to us; the latter we do with others. German artist Hito Steyerl's video installation *Factory of the Sun* (**fig. 25.23**) is a disjointed meditation on both. A banking company has discovered how to increase the speed of light, and thus of stock trading. It recruits dancers from YouTube videos to dance in a motion-capture studio to create more light energy. One of the dancers escapes and is killed by a drone,

an event that a bank official narrates in a news broadcast near the beginning of the movie. What follows is a collage of news reportage, documentary film, video games, and Internet dance videos that portrays a near-future world in which surveillance is monetized and sharing is co-opted for corporate use. The artist included a video game that her assistant invented. The movie implicates viewers as well, as the theater's blue lines mimic a motion-capture studio. The movie ends with an announcement that the projection has been hacked. We are left wondering what is real and what is in the movie.

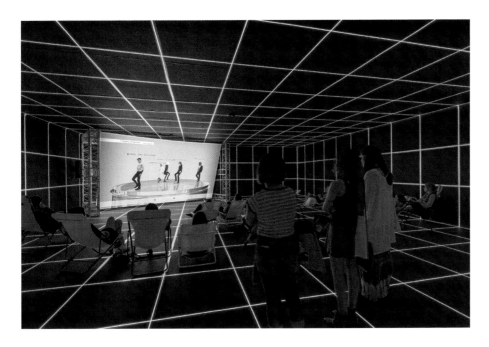

25.23 Hito Steyerl. *Factory of the Sun*. 2015. Single-channel high-definition video, environment, luminescent LE grid, bear chains. 23 minutes.
Image courtesy of the artist and Andrew Kreps Gallery, New York. © 2018 Artists Rights Society (ARS), New York/SABAM, Brussels.

The Global Present

Communication and travel technologies are making the world ever smaller. The Internet, air travel, mobile phones, cable television, social media, and international migration are bringing us all into ever closer proximity.

This globalization of culture has had a profound impact on art. Contemporary artforms such as installation and performance art have spread around the world. Innovative work is emerging in formerly unexpected places, as artists in many countries use increasingly international modes of expression to interpret the contemporary world in the light of their own traditions. This union of the cosmopolitan and the local is a major inspiration of the new creative effort that has always fertilized art. A few examples from disparate continents will have to suffice to indicate the directions that art is taking. All these works examine our global condition today through the lens of local traditions or events.

Pakistani artist Imran Qureshi was trained in the traditional art of manuscript illustration, but he turns it to commentaries on violence in works such as *You Who Are My Love and My Life's Enemy Too* (**fig. 25.24**). This work, which extends more than 15 feet across, seems at first like darkened puddles of blood from an extremely gory massacre. Closer looking reveals that the splashes are also flowers and petals, rendered in a representational style. The title is a line of poetry from ancient Pakistani literature. Both aspects of this work reflect Qureshi's life in Lahore, a city frequently rocked by terrorist violence but also sprinkled with hope. "There's the idea of life, beauty and death working together," he said. "There is an element of violence in the work. At the same time, when you come close to it and start looking at it carefully, it becomes poetic as well."[5] Such polarities of cruelty and optimism characterize many parts of the world today.

25.24 Imran Qureshi. *You Who Are My Love and My Life's Enemy Too*. 2015. Acrylic paint on canvas. 83″ × 185″.
Courtesy Galerie Thaddaeus Ropac, London · Paris · Salzburg. © Imran Qureshi. Photograph: Charles Duprat.

25.25 Naomi Wanjiku Gakunga. *Routes of Migration*. 2015. Sheet metal, steel wire, poultry wire and fabric. 96″ × 96″.
Photograph: N. Wanjiku Gakunga. Courtesy October Gallery, London.

Because human creativity is spread about equally around the globe, a good idea can emerge from almost anywhere. Growing up in Kenya, Naomi Wanjiku Gakunga noticed the many shades and colors that appear when tin roofs corrode under the impact of repeated storms. She now corrodes pieces sheet metal in her studio and combines them with other non-art material to create non-representational wall hangings that resemble textiles (**fig. 25.25**). This work, titled *Routes of Migration*, alludes to the migrant crisis affecting many regions of Africa, and also to the evolution of her materials under the impact of oxidation.

25.26 Doris Salcedo. *Plegaria Muda* (*Silent Prayer*). 2008–10. Wood, mineral compound, metal and grass. 166 units as installed at CAM, Fundação Calouste Gulbenkian, Lisbon, November 12, 2011–January 22, 2012.

Photograph: Patrizia Tocci. Image courtesy Alexander and Bonin, New York.

Colombian artist Doris Salcedo creates poignant monuments that channel mourning and hope. Her installation *Plegaria Muda* (**fig. 25.26**) begins with a multitude of empty tables, stacked in pairs with one table upended atop another. These give the appearance of an abandoned space, of a once-busy, occupied zone now gone silent. She created this work as a memorial to the innocent victims of civil strife in her country; each table is approximately the size and shape of a coffin, and their upturned legs seem at first to suggest a forest of futility. But between the top and bottom of each pair of tables Salcedo embeds masses of soil, so that during exhibitions, thin shoots of grass spring up between the wooden boards of each upended table. The work is thus a "silent prayer" (the meaning of the title) of mourning for the dead, as well as an expression of hope in the fertility of the soil. Although Salcedo created the installation in response to the story of Colombia, the work's evocation of bereavement and tender hope could also speak about many of the world's wounded places.

Like *Plegaria Muda*, much of the best contemporary art is multi-leveled: not necessarily difficult to understand, in media that we can all respond to. In 2010 Chinese artist Ai Weiwei unveiled a similarly layered series of bronze sculptures titled *Circle of Animals/Zodiac Heads* (**fig. 25.27**). He modeled the heads on the 12 imaginary creatures that populate the Chinese zodiac. The slightly monstrous aspect of the work appeals to children, yet the piece has deeper, subtle meanings that address some tense moments in East–West relations. The heads are based on the remnants of an eighteenth-century fountain in a former imperial retreat outside Beijing, where each spouted water at two-hour intervals. This building was at first a sign of international cooperation, as it was designed by European Jesuit architects for the emperor. When this splendid palace was sacked and destroyed by French and British troops in 1860, the majority of the heads vanished, and the Chinese government soon declared the remainder national treasures. Ai alluded to the ancient fountain by placing each head atop a column that resembles a spout of gushing water. He created the piece, in part, in response to a 2000 art auction at which three of the formerly lost heads appeared for sale, causing protests from many Chinese cultural officials. Soon after its creation, *Circle of Animals/Zodiac Heads* went on a tour of several world cities, where it was displayed over fountains or pools. More recently, Ai has created films and installations highlighting suffering and injustice (see *Ai Weiwei: Global Visual Activist* on p. 482).

25.27 Ai Weiwei. *Circle of Animals / Zodiac Heads*. 2010. Bronze. 12 units, average height 10′.
Grand Army Plaza, New York City.
Private Collection. Image courtesy of the artist and AW Asia. Photograph: Adam Reich.

CREATORS

Ai Weiwei: Global Visual Activist

25.28 Ai Weiwei at the Royal Academy of Arts.

Guy Corbishley/Alamy Live News

Ai Weiwei (b. 1957) achieved his celebrity status in the old-fashioned way, by risking his personal safety and freedom. His activities involve many different media on several continents, and sometimes stray beyond art itself.

The artist's family already knew the risks of dissent in China's restrictive artistic environment: Ai's father, Ai Qing, was a dissident poet who was sent to a labor camp for five years. The young Ai studied animation techniques at the Beijing Film Academy, but was too distracted by other art media to finish the degree. He lived in the United States from 1981 to 1993, taking further art courses in New York City as he pursued photography.

Back in China, Ai devoted himself to performance art, which was then practically unknown there. He also organized collaborative art studios and dabbled in architecture. His career as an activist began in earnest in 2008, after an earthquake in Sichuan province leveled nearly all its school buildings. Ai learned that thousands of children had died in the buildings because of flimsy government-funded construction, so he assembled an investigative team to interview the parents, most of whom lost their only children because of China's one-child policy. Such investigations by citizens are unheard of in China. Ai also pestered the authorities to release more information while he searched for a count of the dead students. After he found and listed more than 5,000 names on his blog, the government Internet authority not only shut it down but blocked his name from any Internet search.

In late 2010, after making several films documenting the plight of other dissidents who were imprisoned or harassed, Ai was banned from all foreign travel and his passport confiscated. In early 2011, the authorities demolished his studio and arrested him for tax evasion. Protests in Europe and the United States drew 60,000 signatures on a petition to free him. He was released after 81 days, his brain injured from a concussion he suffered during an interrogation.

Since then, Ai has played a cat-and-mouse game with the government. The police installed surveillance cameras outside his rebuilt studio, so Ai hung brightly colored traditional lanterns next to them. He took a nude photo of himself with a surveillance camera, ensuring his modesty by hiding his private parts behind a goat; the police charged him with pornography. International publicity keeps the government from imprisoning him, but his freedom is always at risk. In 2012, he created a 96-ton sculpture with iron bars salvaged from the collapsed schools, but he has never exhibited it in China.

International issues have drawn Ai's attention in recent years. In 2014, he had a solo exhibition at the former federal penitentiary at Alcatraz in San Francisco Bay, which is now a park. He made for this show a traditional long paper dragon, and inscribed among its colorful patterns quotations from civil rights heroes Nelson Mandela and Edward Snowden. He arranged this exhibition by teleconference because he was still banned from travel. After the government returned his passport in 2015, he opened a studio in Berlin and increased his social media presence on Twitter and Instagram. On the island of Lesbos in Greece, he documented with photos in an Instagram feed the difficult situation of the flood of refugees then arriving there from conflicts in Syria and Afghanistan.

In late 2015, Ai created a room-sized installation out of plastic bricks for an exhibition in Australia; he used the Lego-style blocks to create portraits of activists and civil rights campaigners from that country. At the time of writing, he is working on a documentary titled *Human Flow* about the wartime migrants from Iraq, Syria, and Afghanistan who faced an uncertain fate after they arrived in Greece. In mid-2017, a television reporter asked Ai if he was an artist or an activist. He replied that it amounts to the same thing to him: to be an artist is to be an activist.

Conclusion

The examples in this chapter show that art comes from basic feelings that we all share. Through their work, artists interact with life, to find purpose and meaning in it. Human life varies considerably across time and space, but the art endures. Creative expression is a response to being alive, and artists' creativity can activate the artist within us.

We will close with Renzo Piano's new building for the Whitney Museum of American Art because it embodies ideas that motivate many museums today. The urban location of this structure makes photographing the whole difficult, but just from the view of the entrance (**fig. 25.29a**) we can see that one of the architect's principal goals was openness to the outside. He wanted the museum to be nested in its environment, with free exchange across the doorway. He said, "When you go underneath, it's partially open; it's so transparent that you don't even understand where you are at first. Are you in the street or are you in the building?"

25.29 Whitney Museum of American Art, New York. 2015.
a. Entrance.
Architect: Renzo Piano Building Workshop.
VIEW Pictures Ltd/Alamy Stock Photo.

b. Gallery and exterior wall.

VIEW Pictures Ltd/Alamy Stock Photo.

That openness extends to the galleries on the upper floors, where many exterior walls are also of glass (**fig. 25.29b**). The purpose of the building, then, is to encourage people to interact with art, to make it easy and comfortable for viewers to explore what artists have to offer. As the architect put it:

> When you are in front of a piece of art, it's about the untold; it's about something almost mysterious. There is something coming out, something that causes you to dream or think in a different way. Art and beauty switches on a special light in your eyes. You think differently, almost meandering. This is why art makes people better.[6]

TIMELINE

| | 30,000 | 20,000 | 10,000 | 5,000 | 3,000 | 2,000 | 1,000 | 500 | 250 | BCE 0 CE | 200 | 400 | 600 | 800 | 1,000 |

AMERICAS

OLMECS

NAZCA

MAYA
Temple I

Pyramid of
the Sun

TOLTECS

Rock Art, Australia

RUSSIA

**NORTHERN
EUROPE**

VIKINGS

Book of
Kells

Purse Cover

Woman of
Willendorf

Stonehenge

Bison

**SOUTHERN
EUROPE**

Chauvet Cave Paintings

Euphronios Krater

CHRISTIAN ERA
BEGINS

POMPEII
BURIED

ROMAN EMPIRE

San Vitale

CLASSICAL
Parthenon
Spear Bearer

Pantheon

DIVISION
OF EMPIRE

FALL OF WESTERN EMPIRE

ARCHAIC
Kouros

HELLENISTIC
Laocoön

Head of
Constantine

BYZANTIUM

**MIDDLE
EAST**

Earthenware Beaker

SUMERIAN CITIES
Bull-headed Lyre
Ziggurats

BRONZE AGE
BEGINS

AKKADIANS
Head of Ruler

BIRTH OF
CHRIST 4 BCE

BIRTH OF
MUHAMMAD 570

NEOLITHIC
REVOLUTION
BEGINS

OLD KINGDOM
Mycerinus
Pyramids

NEW KINGDOM
Tomb Paintings

Mummy Portraits

Great Mosque,
Kairouan

AFRICA

Blombos Cave

NOK CULTURE
Head

INDIA

Engraved
Ochre

INDUS VALLEY
CIVILIZATION
Harappa Torso

BIRTH OF
BUDDHA 563 BCE

Great
Stupa

GUPTA
DYNASTY

Standing Buddha

CHINA

Burial
Urn

SHANG DYNASTY

Ritual
Vessel

Great Wall

BUDDHISM SPREAD TO CHINA

Terra cotta
Warriors

CHAN (LATER ZEN)
BUDDHISM

PAPER INVENTED

PRINTING
DEVELOPED

JAPAN

BUDDHISM
SPREAD TO JAPAN

Ise Shrine

Horyuji
Temple

TIMELINE

1000 1100 1200 1300 1400 1450 1500 1550 1600 1650 1700 1750 1800 1850 1870 1880 1890 190

Machu Picchu

HUDSON RIVER SCHOOL
Durand
Cole

Cassatt
The Letter

Kero Cup

CIVIL WAR

INCA

AZTEC
Chacmool

Vessel of the Feathered
Serpent Quetzalcoatl

■ DECLARATION
OF INDEPENDENCE

TOLTECS

VIKINGS

GOTHIC
Chartres Cathedral

van Eyck

REFORMATION

Vermeer
The Kitchen Maid

NEOCLASSICISM   Manet **IMPRESSIONISM**
David   Monet
Kauffman   Renoir
                              Degas
ROMANTICISM   Rodin
Delacroix
Turner   Crystal Palace   **POST-IMPRESSION**
                              Cézanne
REALISM   Gauguin
Courbet   van Gogh

"Rose de France"
window

■ FRENCH
REVOLUTION

BAROQUE
Rubens

Versailles

■ INVENTION OF
PHOTOGRAPHY

ROMANESQUE

Dürer

Rembrandt   **ROCOCO**
            Fragonard

Daguerre
Nadar

Cézanne
Mont Sainte-Victoire

Raphael

Palladio

Giotto

Michelangelo
David

Goya
The Third of May, 1808

Carriera

BYZANTIUM

Alhambra

Titian

Ardabil Carpet

D'Arenberg Basin

IFE

Male Portrait Head
Great Zimbabwe

Congo
Power
Figure

Benin Head

Taj Mahal

MUGHAL EMPIRE

NOTE: In presenting the
Artforms Timeline, it has
been necessary to use
several different scales
to indicate both long and
short spans of years on a
few pages. If a ten-year
scale were used to cover
the entire 32,000-year
period presented, the
timeline would be more
than a hundred feet long.

**MONGOL
INVASION**

Qiu Ying

■ GUNPOWDER
INVENTED

Ma Yuan
Watching the Deer

Bada Shanren

Katsura
Palace

Utamaro

Burning of the
Sanjo Palace

Sotatsu

UKIYO-E

Hiroshige

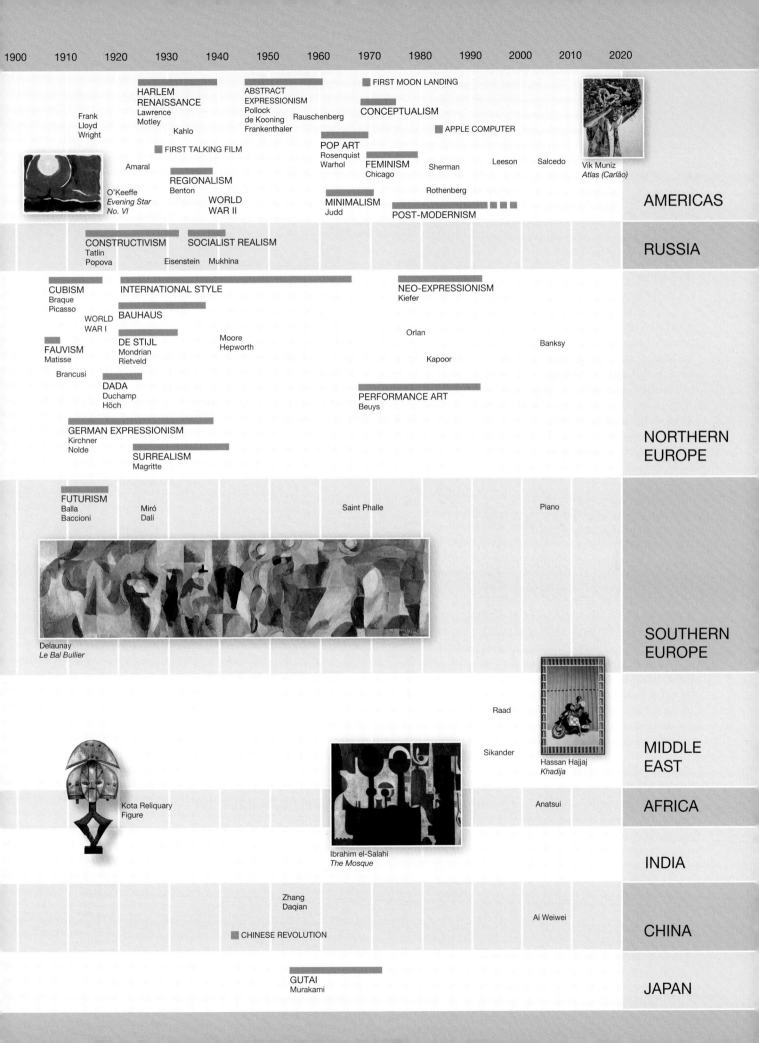

1900   1910   1920   1930   1940   1950   1960   1970   1980   1990   2000   2010   2020

AMERICAS

HARLEM RENAISSANCE
Lawrence
Motley
Kahlo

Frank Lloyd Wright

FIRST TALKING FILM

Amaral

REGIONALISM
Benton

O'Keeffe
Evening Star No. VI

WORLD WAR II

ABSTRACT EXPRESSIONISM
Pollock
de Kooning
Frankenthaler
Rauschenberg

FIRST MOON LANDING

CONCEPTUALISM

APPLE COMPUTER

POP ART
Rosenquist
Warhol

FEMINISM
Chicago

Sherman

Leeson

Salcedo

Rothenberg

MINIMALISM
Judd

POST-MODERNISM

Vik Muniz
Atlas (Carlão)

RUSSIA

CONSTRUCTIVISM
Tatlin
Popova

SOCIALIST REALISM
Eisenstein   Mukhina

NORTHERN EUROPE

CUBISM
Braque
Picasso

WORLD WAR I

FAUVISM
Matisse

Brancusi

INTERNATIONAL STYLE

BAUHAUS

DE STIJL
Mondrian
Rietveld

DADA
Duchamp
Höch

Moore
Hepworth

NEO-EXPRESSIONISM
Kiefer

Orlan

Kapoor

PERFORMANCE ART
Beuys

Banksy

GERMAN EXPRESSIONISM
Kirchner
Nolde

SURREALISM
Magritte

SOUTHERN EUROPE

FUTURISM
Balla
Baccioni

Miró
Dalí

Saint Phalle

Piano

Delaunay
Le Bal Bullier

MIDDLE EAST

Raad

Sikander

Hassan Hajjaj
Khadija

AFRICA

Kota Reliquary Figure

Anatsui

Ibrahim el-Salahi
The Mosque

INDIA

CHINA

Zhang Daqian

CHINESE REVOLUTION

Ai Weiwei

JAPAN

GUTAI
Murakami

GLOSSARY

3-D printing – printing in three dimensions from a design created using modeling software

abstract art – art that depicts natural objects in simplified or exaggerated ways which may not be recognizable at first

Abstract Expressionism – an art movement, primarily in painting, that originated in the United States in the 1940s, in which artists worked in many different styles that emphasized spontaneous personal expression

Abstract Surrealism – a form of Surrealism that uses abstract shapes and which emphasizes color and design rather than storytelling content

academic art – art governed by rules, especially works sanctioned by an official institution, academy, or school

achromatic – having no color (or hue)

acrylic – paint that uses an acrylic polymer (a synthetic resin that provides a fast-drying, flexible film) as the binder and water as the vehicle

action painting – a style of nonrepresentational painting that relies on the physical movement of the artist by using such gestural techniques as vigorous brushwork, dripping, and pouring

additive color mixture – the mixture of colored light

additive sculpture – sculptural form produced by adding, combining, or building up material from a core or (in some cases) an armature

aesthetics – the philosophy of art focusing on questions regarding what art is, how it is evaluated, the concept of beauty, and the relationship between the idea of beauty and the concept of art

airbrush – a small-scale paint sprayer that allows the artist to control a fine mist of paint

analogous colors – colors that are adjacent to each other on the color wheel, such as blue, blue-green, and green

Analytical Cubism – the style of Cubism developed by Picasso and Braque from 1910 to 1911 in which they analyzed their subjects from various angles, then painted abstract, geometric references to these views

animation – the technique of photographing a series of hand-drawn or computer-generated frames of a movie to create the illusion of motion

aperture – the width of the opening that admits light into a camera; a narrow aperture that lets in little light might be used in bright light and a wider aperture for lower-light conditions

apse – a semicircular end to an aisle in a basilica or a Christian church; usually placed at the eastern end of the central aisle in Christian churches

aquatint – an intaglio printmaking process in which value areas rather than lines are etched on the printing plate; powdered resin is sprinkled on the plate, which is then immersed in an acid bath, and the acid bites around the resin particles, creating a rough surface that holds ink; also a print made using this process

arcade – a series of arches supported by columns or piers

arch – a curved structure designed to span an opening, usually made of stone or other masonry; Roman arches are semicircular, Islamic and Gothic arches come to a point at the top

Archaic period – the art of ancient Greece from the late seventh to the early fifth centuries bce that assimilated influences from Egypt and the Near East

armature – a rigid framework serving as a supporting inner core for clay or other soft sculpting material

art criticism – the process of using formal analysis, description, and interpretation to evaluate or explain the quality and meanings of art

Art Nouveau – a style of decorative art and architecture characterized by curving shapes abstracted from nature

artist's proof – a trial print, usually made as an artist works on a plate or block, to check the progress of a work

assemblage – sculpture made by assembling found or cast-off objects that may or may not contribute their original identities to the total content of the work

asymmetrical balance – the various elements of a work are balanced but not symmetrical

asymmetry – lack of symmetry

atmospheric (aerial) perspective – a type of perspective in which the illusion of depth is created by changing color, value, and detail

automatism – action without conscious control, as employed by Surrealist writers and artists to allow unconscious ideas and feelings to be expressed

avant-garde – artists who work in an experimental or innovative way, often opposing mainstream standards

balance – an arrangement of parts achieving a state of equilibrium between opposing forces or influences

balloon frame – a wooden structural support system developed in the United States in the mid-nineteenth century in which standardized, thin studs are held together with nails

Baroque – the seventeenth-century period in Europe characterized in the visual arts by dramatic light and shade, turbulent composition, and pronounced emotional expression

barrel vault – a semicircular arch extended in depth; a continuous series of arches one behind the other

bas relief (also called **low relief**) – sculpture in relief in which the subjects emerge only slightly from the surface; no undercutting is present

basilica – a Roman town hall, with three aisles and an apse at one or both ends; Christians appropriated this form for their churches

binder – the material used in paint that causes pigment particles to adhere to one another

biomorphic shape – a shape in a work of art that resembles a living organism or an organic shape

blaxploitation movement – a cinema movement of the 1970s in which studios employed African-American directors and actors in action-adventure movies that were set mostly in urban neighborhoods

bodhisattva – a Buddhist holy person who is about to achieve enlightenment but postpones it to remain on earth to teach others

boss – a circular, often dome-shaped, decoration that protrudes from a flat surface

Brutalism – movement in post-World War II architecture characterized by prominent use of unpainted exterior concrete, often cast into curving shapes

burin – a tool used in engraving

burr – the ridge left by scratching a drypoint line in a copper plate; the burr holds ink for printing

buttress – a support, usually exterior, for a wall, arch, or vault that opposes the lateral forces of these structures

calligraphy – the art of beautiful writing; broadly, a flowing use of line, often varying from thick to thin

camera obscura – the forerunner of the modern camera, a dark room (or box) with a small hole in one side, through which an inverted image of the view outside is projected onto the opposite wall, screen, or mirror, and then traced

cantilever – a beam or slab projecting a substantial distance beyond its supporting post or wall

capital – in architecture, the top part or head of a column or pile

cartoon – a full-size drawing made as a guide for a large work in another medium, particularly a fresco painting, mosaic, or tapestry; a humorous or satirical drawing

carving – a subtractive process in which a sculpture is formed by removing material from a block or mass of wood, stone, or other material, with the use of sharpened tools

casting – a process that involves pouring liquid material such as molten metal, clay, wax, or plaster into a mold; when the liquid hardens, the mold is removed, and a form in the shape of the mold is left

catacomb – underground burial places in ancient Rome

censorship – the alteration of works of art, or their removal from public view

ceramics – clay hardened into a relatively permanent material by firing, and the artform that includes this procedure

ceramist – a practitioner of the art of ceramics

charcoal – a dry drawing medium made from charred twigs, usually vine or willow

chiaroscuro – Italian word meaning "light dark;" the gradations of light and dark values in two-dimensional imagery, especially the illusion of rounded, three-dimensional form created through gradations of light and shade rather than line

cinema – the production of movies as an art or industry

cinematography – the art of camerawork and photography in making movies

Classical art – the art of ancient Greece and Rome, particularly the style of Greek art that flourished during the fifth-century bce; emphasizes rational simplicity, order, and restrained emotion

close-up – a shot taken when the camera is so close to a subject that it fills the frame

closed form – a self-contained or explicitly limited form that has a resolved balance of tensions

coffer – in architecture, a decorative sunken panel on the underside of a ceiling

collage – a work made by gluing various materials, such as paper scraps, photographs, and cloth, on a flat surface

colonnade – a row of columns usually spanned or connected by beams

color field painting – a movement that grew out of Abstract Expressionism, in which large stained or painted areas, or "fields," of color evoke aesthetic and emotional responses

color scheme – a set of colors chosen for a work of art in order to promote a specific mood or effect

complementary colors – two hues directly opposite one another on a color wheel, such as red and green, that, when mixed together in proper proportions, produce a neutral gray

composition – the organization of visual elements in an artwork

Conceptual art – a trend developed in the late 1960s; an artform in which the originating idea and the process by which it is presented take precedence over a tangible product

concrete – a liquid building material invented by the Romans; made of water, sand, gravel, and a binder of gypsum, lime, or volcanic ash

construction – creating a work of sculpture by putting together pieces that are already formed by the artist

Constructivism – art movement that originated in Russia at the time of the Soviet Revolution of 1917, which emphasized abstract art, modern materials, and useful arts such as set design, furniture, and graphics

Conté crayon – a drawing medium developed in the late eighteenth century; similar to pencil in its graphic content, includes clay and small amounts of wax

content – the meaning or message communicated by a work of art, including its emotional, intellectual, symbolic, thematic, and narrative connotations

contextual theory – a method of art criticism that focuses on the cultural systems behind works of art; these may be economic, racial, political, or social

contour hatching – a set of parallel curved lines that suggest a volume in space

contrapposto – Italian for "counterpose;" the counterpositioning of parts of the human figure about a central vertical axis, as when the weight is placed on one foot causing the hip and shoulder lines to counterbalance each other – often in a graceful S-curve

contrast – the juxtaposition of strongly dissimilar elements; dramatic effects can be produced when dark is set against light, large against small, bright colors against dull

cool colors – colors whose relative visual temperatures make them seem cool

cross-hatching – drawing one set of hatchings over another in a different direction so that the lines cross

Cubism – an art style developed in Paris by Picasso and Braque, beginning in 1908 based on the simultaneous presentation of multiple views, disintegration, and geometric reconstructions of subjects in flattened, ambiguous pictorial space

curtain wall – a non-load-bearing wall, typical of the International Style; generally well-endowed with windows

cut-pile embroidery – a type of African textile in which a stretch of cloth is woven using raffia fibers and then embroidered by lacing dyed strips through the warps and wefts

Dada – a movement in art and literature, founded in Switzerland in the early twentieth century, which ridiculed contemporary culture and conventional art

daguerreotype – a photograph taken by an early photographic process developed in the 1830s, in which a treated metal plate was exposed to light, and the chemical reactions on the plate created the first satisfactory photographic images

De Stijl – a Dutch purist art movement begun during World War I by Mondrian and others; involved painters, sculptors, designers, and architects whose works and ideas were expressed in *De Stijl* magazine; De Stijl, Dutch for "The Style," was aimed at creating a universal language of form that would be independent of individual emotion; visual form was pared down to primary hues plus black and white, and rectangular shapes

depth of field – the depth of the area before the camera that will be in sharp focus in a photo

design – the process of organizing visual elements and the product of that process

direct painting – execution of a painting in one sitting, applying wet over wet colors

directional forces – pathways that the artist embeds in a work for the viewer's eye to follow

dome – a generally hemispherical roof or vault

Dreamtime – in Aboriginal culture, a period in the remote past when the close relationship with nature was established by creative beings

dressed stone – stone used for building that is cut, trimmed, or ground down to fit into a masonry wall

drypoint – an intaglio printmaking process in which lines are scratched directly into a metal plate with a steel needle; the scratch raises a ridge (burr) that takes the ink

earthenware – a type of clay used for ceramics; it fires at 1,100–1,150°C and is porous after firing

earthwork – a sculptural form made from earth, rocks, or sometimes plants, often on a vast scale and in a remote location

edition – the total number of prints made and approved by the artist, usually numbered consecutively

editioned work – any work produced in an edition, such as a print; not unique as in the case of a painting

embroidery – a technique in which decorative colored threads are stitched into and over a base of woven fabric

emphasis – a method an artist uses to draw attention to an area; may be done with central placement, large size, bright color, or high contrast

encaustic – a type of painting in which pigment is suspended in a binder of hot wax

engraving – an intaglio printmaking process in which grooves are cut into a metal or wood surface with a sharp cutting tool called a burin or graver; also the resulting print

entasis – a slight swelling or bulge in the center of a column, which corrects the illusion of concave tapering produced by parallel straight lines

etching – an intaglio printmaking process in which a metal plate is first coated with acid-resistant wax or varnish, then scratched to expose the metal to the bit of nitric acid where lines are desired; also the resulting print

Expressionism – refers to individual and group styles originating in Europe in the late nineteenth and early twentieth centuries, characterized by bold execution and free use of distortion and symbolic or invented color

expressive theory – a method of art criticism that attempts to discern personal elements in works of art, as opposed to formal strategies or cultural influences

eye level – in linear perspective, the presumed height of the artist's eyes; this becomes the presumed height of the viewer standing in front of the finished work

f-stop – the ratio of the focal length to the size of the opening (aperture); low f-stops give a shallower field of focused material and higher ones can bring everything, near and far, into focus

Fauvism – a style of painting introduced in Paris in the early twentieth century, characterized by areas of bright, contrasting color and simplified shapes

feminism – in art, a movement among artists, critics, and art historians that began in an organized fashion in the 1970s; feminists seek to validate and promote artforms that express the unique experience of women, and to redress oppression by men

figurative art – representational art in which the human form (rather than the natural world) plays a principal role

figure – separate shape(s) that seem to lie above a background or ground

film – spooled photographic stock for the recording of movies

film editing – the process by which an editor compiles shots into scenes and into a movie

film noir – a genre of dark and brooding black-and-white movies originating in Hollywood in the 1940s

firing – baking clay in a special high-temperature oven to solidify it; secondary firings may also be done to fix finishing coats on fired pieces

fixative – a light, liquid varnish sprayed over finished charcoal or pastel drawings to prevent smudging

flamboyant – a style of flamelike decorations used in late Gothic architecture

flying buttress – a strut or segment of an arch carrying the thrust of a vault to a vertical pier positioned away from the main portion of the building; an important element in Gothic cathedrals

focal length – the distance between the lens and the image sensor

focal point – the principal area of emphasis in a work of art; the place to which the artist directs the most attention through composition

folk art – art of people who have had no formal, academic training, but whose works are part of an established tradition of style and craftsmanship

font – the name given to type in a particular size and weight; today often used interchangeably with typeface to indicate a complete set of letterforms, including all capitals, lower case, numerals, and accent marks in all sizes and weights

foreshortening – the representation of forms on a two-dimensional surface by shortening the length in such a way that the long axis appears to project toward or recede away from the viewer

form – the total effect of the combined visual qualities within a work, including such components as materials, color, shape, line, and design

formal theory – a method of art criticism that values stylistic innovation over personal expression or cultural communication

format – the shape or proportions of a picture plane

freestanding – any piece or type of sculpture that is meant to be seen from all sides

fresco – a technique in which pigments suspended in water are applied to a damp lime-plaster surface

fresco secco – a technique in which tempera paint is applied to a dried lime-plaster surface or over an already dried true fresco to achieve greater color intensity

frottage – a technique in which a canvas is laid over a textured surface and rubbed with crayons and pencils

Futurism – a group movement originating in Italy in 1909 that celebrated both natural and mechanical motion and speed

garba griha – the sacred room of a Hindu temple, where rituals are performed and the image of the god is kept

genre painting – a type of art that takes as its subject everyday life, rather than civic leaders, religious figures, or mythological heroes

geometric shape – any shape enclosed by square or straight or perfectly circular lines

gesso – a mixture of glue and chalk, thinned with water and applied as a ground before painting with oil or egg tempera

glaze – a thin transparent or translucent layer brushed over another layer of paint, allowing the first layer to show through but enriching its color slightly

Gothic – primarily an architectural style that prevailed in Western Europe from the twelfth through the fifteenth centuries; characterized by pointed arches, ribbed vaults, and flying buttresses

gouache – an opaque, water-soluble paint

groin vault – a vault formed by the intersection of two barrel vaults

ground – the background in a two-dimensional work; the area around and between figure(s)

handscroll – a long painting in ink on paper, which viewers contemplate by scrolling from hand to hand

happening – a usually unrehearsed event conceived by artists and performed by artists and others, who may include viewers

hatching – a technique in which lines are placed in parallel series to darken the value of an area

Hellenistic – style of the later phase of ancient Greek art (300–100 bce), characterized by emotion, drama, and interaction of sculptural forms with the surrounding space

hierarchic scale – use of unnatural proportions or scale to show the relative importance of figures; most commonly practiced in ancient Near Eastern and Egyptian art

high relief – sculpture in relief in which more than half of a significant portion of the subject emerges from the background; high-relief sculpture thus requires undercutting, in contrast to low relief

horizon line – in linear perspective, the implied or actual line or edge placed on a two-dimensional surface to represent the place in nature where the sky meets the horizontal land or water plane

hue – that property of a color identifying a specific, named wavelength of light such as green, red, blue, and so on

humanism – a cultural and intellectual movement during the Renaissance, following the rediscovery of the art and literature of ancient Greece and Rome

icon – an image or symbolic representation, often with sacred significance

iconoclast – in Byzantine art, one who opposes the creation of images of holy persons, believing that they promote idolatry

iconography – the symbolic meanings of subjects and signs used to convey ideas important to particular cultures or religions

image sensor – the surface inside a camera where the image is collected, upside down; in traditional cameras the sensor was photographic film, but in digital cameras the sensor converts the light into an electric charge, which the camera's software reconstitutes as a photograph for display on the camera's screen

impasto – thick paint applied to a surface in a heavy manner, having the appearance and consistency of buttery paste or of cake frosting

implied line – a line in a composition that is not actually drawn; it may be a sight line of a figure in a composition, or a line along which two shapes align with each other

Impressionism – a style of painting executed outdoors, aiming to capture the light and mood of a particular moment and the transitory effects of light and color

inlay – a type of decoration used in metalwork and some woodwork in which small pieces are fitted into carved recesses

installation – an art medium in which the artist arranges objects or artworks in a room, thinking of the entire space as the medium to be manipulated; some installations are site-specific

intaglio – any printmaking technique in which lines and areas to be inked are recessed below the surface of the printing plate

intensity – the relative purity or saturation of a hue (color), on a scale from bright (pure) to dull

International Style – an architectural style that emerged in several European countries between 1910 and 1920; International Style architects avoided applied decoration, used only modern materials (concrete, glass, steel), and arranged the masses of a building according to its inner uses

iwan – a high vaulted porch to mark an important building or entrance

kachina – one of many deified ancestral spirits honored by the Hopi and other Pueblo Indian peoples; usually depicted in doll-like form

keystone – the stone at the central, highest point of a round arch, which holds the rest of the arch in place

kiln – a high-temperature oven in which pottery or ceramic ware is fired

kinetic art – art that incorporates actual movement as part of the design

kinetic sculpture – sculpture that incorporates actual movement as part of the design

kouros – an Archaic Greek statue of a standing nude young male

krater – in Classical Greek art, a wide-mouthed vessel with handles, used for mixing wine and water for ceremonial drinking

Kuleshov effect – an editing technique that takes advantage of the fact that viewers' emotional responses to one shot are transferred to the next

line – a long, narrow mark; usually made by drawing with a tool or a brush, but may be created by placing two forms next to each other

linear perspective – used to create an illusion of depth or three-dimensional space on a two-dimensional surface, it is based on the fact that

parallel lines or edges appear to converge and objects appear smaller as the distance between them and the viewer increases

linoleum cut (or **linocut**) – a relief printmaking process in which an artist cuts away negative spaces from a block of linoleum, leaving raised areas to take ink for printing

literati painting – most commonly used to describe the work of painters not attached to the royal courts of the Yuan, Ming, and Qing dynasties in China

lithography – a planographic printmaking technique based on the antipathy of oil and water; the image is drawn with a grease crayon or painted with tusche on a stone or grained aluminum plate; the surface is then chemically treated and dampened so that it will accept ink only where the crayon or tusche has been used

local color – the color of an object as we experience it, without shadows or reflections

logo – a sign, name, or trademark of an institution, firm, or publication, consisting of letterforms or pictorial elements

long shot – a camera shot taken at a distance from the subject; used to emphasize groups of people or a panoramic setting

loom – a device for producing cloth or fiber art by interweaving fibers at right angles

lost wax – a casting method: First a model is made from wax and encased in clay or casting plaster; when the clay is fired to make a mold, the wax melts away, leaving a void that can be filled with molten metal or other self-hardening liquid to produce a cast

low relief (also called **bas relief**) – sculpture in relief in which the subjects emerge only slightly from the surface; no undercutting is present

lusterware – a ceramic glaze effect that imparts a metallic sheen to the surface of a vessel

madrasa – a building that combines a school, prayer hall, and lodging for students

mana – in Oceania, spiritual power that may reside in persons, places, or things

Mannerism – a style that arose in central Italy in the mid-sixteenth century, characterized by stylized and mannered expressions, often revolting against the balanced Classicism of the High Renaissance

marquetry – a technique in which multiple small pieces of wood in different colors and textures are laid down in a design with no bounding wall between them

masonry – building technique in which stones or bricks are laid atop one another in a pattern

mass – the physical bulk of a solid body of material

matrix – the block of metal, wood, stone, or other material that an artist works to create a print

matte – a dull finish or surface

medium (plural: media) – a particular material along with its accompanying technique

metope – a square panel, often decorated with relief sculpture, placed at regular intervals above the colonnade of a Classical Greek building

mihrab – a niche in the end wall of a mosque that points the way to Mecca

minaret – a tower outside a mosque where chanters stand to call the faithful to prayer

Minimalism – a nonrepresentational style of sculpture and painting that came to prominence in the middle and late 1960s; usually severely restricted in the use of visual elements and often consisting of simple geometric shapes or masses

mixed media – works of art made with more than one medium

mobile – a type of sculpture in which parts move, usually suspended parts activated by air currents

modeling – working pliable material such as clay or wax into three-dimensional forms

mold – a cavity usually created out of plaster, clay, or plastic for use in casting

monochromatic – a color scheme limited to variations of one hue

montage – in motion pictures, the combining of shots into a sequence to portray the character of a single event through multiple views

motion capture – the process of digitally recording movements of actors for animation

mural – any wall-size painting; fresco is one possible medium for such a work

naturalistic – an art style in which the curves and contours of a subject are accurately portrayed

nave – the tall central space of a church or cathedral, usually flanked by side aisles

negative shape – a background or ground shape seen in relation to foreground or figure shapes

Neo-Expressionism – a movement in the late 1970s and 1980s in America and Europe that revived expressive, personal styles, partly in response to the impersonality of movements such as Conceptual art and Minimalism

Neoclassicism – a revival of Classical Greek and Roman forms in art, music, and literature

Neolithic – the period after the introduction of agriculture but before the invention of bronze

neutrals – not associated with any single hue; can be made by mixing complementary hues

nonrepresentational art – art without reference to anything outside itself (also called "nonobjective")

offset lithography – lithographic printing by indirect image transfer from photomechanical plates; the plate transfers ink to a rubber-covered cylinder, which "offsets" the ink to the paper

one-point perspective – a perspective system in which all parallel lines converge at a single vanishing point

open form – a form whose exterior is irregular and which has a sense of growth, change, or unresolved tension

optical color mixture – apparent rather than actual color mixture, produced by interspersing brushstrokes or dots of color instead of physically mixing them

organic shape – an irregular, non-geometric shape

outsider art – art produced by those with no formal training, outside the established channels of art exhibition

painterly – painting characterized by openness of form, in which shapes are defined by loose brushwork in light and dark color areas rather than by outline or contour

Paleolithic Age – a very ancient period coincident with the Old Stone Age, before the discovery of agriculture and animal herding

Pantocrator – literally, "ruler of everything;" a title for Christ, especially as he is depicted in Byzantine art

pastels – sticks of powdered pigment held together with a gum binding agent

pattern – all-over design created by the repetitive ordering of design elements

pendentive – a curving triangle that points downward; a common support for domes in Byzantine architecture

performance art – dramatic presentation by visual artists (as distinguished from theater artists) in front of an audience, usually not in a formal theatrical setting

persistence of vision – an optical illusion that makes cinema possible; the eye and mind tend to hold images in the brain for a fraction of a second after they disappear from view

perspective – a system for creating an illusion of depth or three-dimensional space on a two-dimensional surface

petroglyph – an image or a symbol carved in shallow relief on a rock surface, usually ancient

photo screen – a variation of a silkscreen in which the stencil is prepared by transferring a photograph to the stencil

photomontage – the process of combining parts of various photographs in one photograph

picture plane – the two-dimensional picture surface

picturesque – used to describe natural landscapes that are attractively poetic, rather than dramatic; original meaning is traced to the paintings of Claude Lorrain and other landscape painters

pier – an upright support for an arch or arcade; fulfills the same function as a column, but is more massive and usually not tapered at the top

pigment – any coloring agent, made from natural or synthetic substances, used in paints or drawing materials

plate mark – an impression made on a piece of paper by pressing a printing plate onto it; usually a sign of an original print

pointillism – a system of painting using tiny dots or "points" of color, developed by French artist Georges Seurat in the 1880s; Seurat systematized the divided brushwork and optical color mixture of the Impressionists and called his technique "divisionism"

Pop Art – a style of painting and sculpture that developed in the late 1950s and early 1960s in Britain and the United States, using mass-production techniques (such as silkscreen) or real objects in works that are generally more polished and ironic than assemblages

porcelain – a type of white or grayish clay for ceramics; it fires at 1,350–1,500°C, and after firing it is translucent and rings when struck

portico – a porch attached to a building, supported with columns; usually surmounted by a triangular pediment under a gable roof

positive shape – a figure or foreground shape, as opposed to a negative ground or background shape

post-and-beam system (post and lintel) – structural system in which uprights or posts support a horizontal beam that spans the space between them

Post-Impressionism – a general term applied to various personal styles of painting by French artists (or artists living in France) that developed from about 1885 to 1900 in reaction to what artists saw as the somewhat formless and aloof quality of Impressionist painting; Post-Impressionist painters were concerned with the significance of form, symbols, expressiveness, and psychological intensity

Post-Internet Art – a movement defined by a pair of art critics for an exhibition of that name first shown in Beijing in 2014; works may or may not use the Internet itself, but they show awareness of, or comment on, the Internet and social media

postmodern – an attitude or trend of the late 1970s, 1980s, and 1990s; characterized in architecture by a move away from the International Style in favor of an imaginative, eclectic approach, and in the other visual arts by influence from all periods and styles and a willingness to combine elements of all

potter – a ceramist who specializes in making dishes

primary hues (also referred to as primary colors) – red, yellow, and blue; these pigment hues cannot be produced by an intermixing of other hues

primer – a primary layer of paint applied to a surface that is to be painted

print – a multiple original impression made from a plate, stone, woodblock, or screen by an artist or made under the artist's supervision; usually made in editions, with each print numbered and signed by the artist

proportion – the size relationship of parts to a whole and to one another

qi – "life force" in Chinese. The vibrant spirit that animates all things

readymade – a concept pioneered by Dadaist Marcel Duchamp in which a common manufactured object is signed by an artist and thereby turned into an artwork

Realism – the mid-nineteenth-century style of Gustave Courbet and others, based on the idea that ordinary people and everyday activities are worthy subjects of art

Regionalism – an art movement developed in the United States in the 1930s, based on the idea that artists could find their identity by focusing attention on the subject matter that was local and American

registration – in color printmaking or machine printing, the process of aligning the impressions of blocks or plates on the same sheet of paper

Relational Aesthetics – a movement that began in the 1990s in which artists create situations that depend on viewer presence or interaction for their form

relief – sculpture in which three-dimensional forms project from the flat background of which they are a part

relief printmaking – a technique in which the parts of the printing surface that carry ink are left raised, while remaining areas are cut away

reliquary – a container for holy relics

Renaissance – the period in Europe from the late fourteenth through the sixteenth centuries, characterized by a renewed interest in human-centered classical art, literature, and learning

repetition – the recurrence of visual elements

representational art – art that recognizably represents or depicts a particular subject

Representational Surrealism – a type of Surrealism that depicts objects in realistic detail

rhythm – the regular or ordered repetition of dominant and subordinate elements or units within a design with related variations

Rococo – a style used in interior decoration and painting in France and southern Germany in the eighteenth century, characterized by small-scale and ornate decoration, pastel colors, and organic arrangement of curves

Romanesque – a style of European architecture prevalent from the ninth to the twelfth centuries with round arches and barrel vaults

Romanticism – a literary and artistic movement aimed at asserting the validity of subjective experience; characterized by intense emotional excitement, and depictions of powerful forces in nature, exotic lifestyles, danger, suffering, and nostalgia

Salon – an official art exhibition in France, judged by members of the official French Academy

sans serif – a typeface without a serif

scale – the size relation of one thing to another

screenprinting (silkscreen, serigraphy) – a technique in which stencils are applied to fabric stretched across a frame, and paint or ink is forced through the unblocked portions of the screen onto paper or another surface beneath

secondary hues – orange, green, and violet; the mixture of two primaries produces a secondary hue

serif – short lines that end the upper and lower strokes of a letter in some fonts

shade – a hue with black added

shape – a two-dimensional or implied two-dimensional area defined by line or changes in color

shot – any uninterrupted run of a movie camera; shots are compiled into scenes, then into movies

shutter speed – the length of time the camera shutter is open; this determines the brightness of the resulting photo

site-specific art – any work made for a certain place, which cannot be separated or exhibited apart from its intended environment

sizing – any of several substances made from glue, wax, or clay, used as a filler for porous material such as paper, canvas, or other cloth, or wall surfaces

slip – clay that is thinned to the consistency of cream and used as paint on earthenware or stoneware ceramics

social realism – a socially and politically committed form of art that became common in many countries between the two world wars and which included a retreat from the radical innovations of modern art, and the desire to communicate more readily with the public about social causes and issues

special effects – the creation of illusions in cinema through the use of camerawork, models, animation, computer graphics, or other means

stencil – a sheet of paper, cardboard, or metal with a design cut out; painting or stamping over the sheet prints the design on a surface

still life – a painting of inanimate objects, such as flowers, fruit, other food items, and domestic utensils

stoneware – a type of clay used for ceramics; it fires at 1,200–1,300°C and is nonporous when fired

storyboard – a sequence of drawings prepared to guide camera shots in motion picture production

stupa – a domelike structure probably derived from Indian funeral mounds

subject – in representational art, what the artist chooses to depict

subordination – technique by which an artist ranks certain areas of a work as of lesser importance; areas are generally subordinated through placement, color, or size

substitution – the process of making a work of art by casting, as opposed to additive or subtractive processes

subtractive color mixture – mixture of colored pigments in the forms of paints, inks, pastels, and so on

subtractive sculpture – sculpture made by removing material from a larger block or form

support – the physical material that provides the base for and sustains a two-dimensional work of art; canvas and panels are common supports for paintings

Surrealism – a movement in literature and the visual arts that developed in the mid-1920s, based on revealing the unconscious mind in dream images and the fantastic

Symbolism – a movement in late nineteenth-century Europe (c.1885–1900) concerned with communication of inner emotional states through forms and colors that may not copy nature directly

symmetrical balance – the near or exact matching of left and right sides of a three-dimensional form or a two-dimensional composition

symmetry – a design (or composition) with nearly identical form on opposite sides of a dividing line or central axis

Synthetic Cubism – a modification of Analytical Cubism with color, textured and patterned surfaces, and the use of cutout shapes

taotie mask – a mask of abstracted shapes commonly found on ancient Chinese bronze vessels

tapestry – a loom weaving method in which colored weft fibers of irregular length are pulled through stable warps to create patterns or pictures

tempera – a water-based paint that uses egg yolk as a binder

terra cotta – a type of earthenware that contains enough iron oxide to impart a reddish tone when fired

tertiary hues – red-orange, yellow-orange, yellow-green, blue-green, blue-violet, and red-violet; each hue is located between the primary and the secondary hue of which it is composed

tessera (plural tesserae) – a piece of colored glass, ceramic tile, or stone used in a mosaic

texture – the tactile qualities of surfaces, or the visual representation of those qualities

three-dimensional – having height, width, and depth

throwing – the process of forming clay objects on a potter's wheel

tint – a hue with white added

title sequence – the roll of credits at the beginning of a motion picture or television program

tooth – a quality of roughness or surface grain in paper that gives texture to a drawing

totem – an object such as an animal or plant that serves as an emblem of a family or clan

truss – a structural framework of wood or metal based on a triangular system, used to span, reinforce, or support walls, ceilings, piers, or beams

two-dimensional – having the dimensions of height and width only

two-point perspective – a perspective system in which two sets of parallel lines appear to converge at two points on the horizon line

typeface – a complete set of letterforms, including all capitals, lower case, numerals, and accent marks in all sizes and weights; also called a font

typography – the art and technique of composing printed materials from type

ukiyo-e – Japanese prints that depict scenes of the "floating world," including landscapes, popular entertainments, and theater scenes or actors

unity – the appearance of similarity, consistency, or oneness

value – the relative lightness and darkness of surfaces

vanishing point – in linear perspective, the point on the horizon line at which lines or edges that are parallel appear to converge

vantage point – the position from which the viewer looks at an object or visual field

variety – the opposite of unity; diverse elements in the composition of a work of art

vault – a curving masonry roof or ceiling constructed on the principle of the arch

vehicle – liquid emulsion used as a carrier or spreading agent in paints

vertical placement – a method for suggesting the third dimension of depth in a two-dimensional work by placing an object above another in the composition

virtual reality – an immersive form of cinema in which viewers don headsets that allow them to move their heads or bodies to see the action unfold around them in a complete panorama

volume – the space enclosed or filled by a three-dimensional object or figure

warm colors – colors whose relative visual temperature makes them seem warm

warp – in weaving, the threads that run lengthwise in a fabric, crossed at right angles by the weft

wash – a thin, transparent layer of paint or ink

watercolor – paint that uses water-soluble gum as the binder and water as the vehicle; characterized by transparency

weft – in weaving, the horizontal threads interlaced through the warp

wood engraving – a method of relief printing in wood; made with denser wood, cutting into the end of the grain rather than the side

woodcut, woodblock – a type of relief print made from a plank of relatively soft wood; the artist carves away the negative spaces, leaving the image in relief to take the ink for printing

work of art – what the artist makes or puts in front of us for viewing

ziggurat – a rectangular or square stepped pyramid, often with a temple at its top

Alê Abreu (ah-lay ob-*bray*-oo)

Ácoma (*ah*-co-mah)

Kunlé Adeyemi (koon-*lay* ah-deh-*yeh*-mee)

Ai Weiwei (eye way-way)

Alhambra (al-*am*-bra)

Tarsila do Amaral (tar-*see*-lah doo ah-mah-*rahl*)

El Anatsui (ell ah-naht-sway)

Angkor Wat (*ang*-kohr waht)

Ardabil (ar-*dah*-bil)

Aumakua (ow-mah-*koo*-ah)

avant-garde (ah-vahn *gard*)

Giacomo Balla (*jah*-koh-moh *bahl*-la)

Jean-Michel Basquait (jawn mee-*shell* boss-kee-*ah*)

Bauhaus (*bow*-house)

Bayeux (buy-yuh)

Benin (ben-*een*)

Gianlorenzo Bernini (jahn-low-*ren*-tsoh ber-*nee*-nee)

Joseph Beuys (*yo*-sef boyce)

Umberto Boccioni (oom-*bair*-toh boh-*choh*-nee)

Bodhisattva (boh-dee-*saht*-vah)

Germain Boffrand (zher-*main* bof-*frohn*)

Rosa Bonheur (buhn-*er*)

Borobudur (boh-roh-boo-*duhr*)

Sandro Botticelli (bought-tee-*chel*-lee)

Constantin Brancusi (*kahn*-stuhn-teen brahn-*koo*-see)

Georges Braque (zhorzh brahk)

Pieter Bruegel (*pee*-ter *broy*-guhl)

Michelangelo Buonarroti see *Michelangelo*

Cai Guo-Qiang (tseye gwoh *chyahng*)

Callicrates (kah-*lik*-rah-teez)

Michelangelo da Caravaggio (mee-kel-*an*-jeh-loe da car-ah-*vah*-jyoh)

Rosalba Carriera (roh-*sal*-bah car-*yair*-ah)

Henri Cartier-Bresson (on-*ree* car-tee-*ay* bruh-*sohn*)

casein (cass-*seen*)

Mary Cassatt (cah-*sat*)

Paul Cézanne (say-*zahn*)

chacmool (chalk-mole)

Marc Chagall (shah-*gahl*)

Chartres (*shahr*-truh)

Chauvet (show-*vay*)

Dale Chihuly (chi-*hoo*-lee)

chola (*choh*-lah)

Christo (*kree*-stoh)

Constantine (*kahn*-stuhn-teen)

Conté (kahn-tay)

contrapposto (kohn-trah-*poh*-stoh)

Gustave Courbet (*goos*-tahv koor-*bay*)

Cycladic (sik-*lad*-ik)

Louis-Jacques-Mandé Daguerre (loo-*ee* zhahk mahn-*day* dah-*gair*)

Honoré Daumier (awn-ohr-*ay* doh-mee-ay)

Jacques-Louis David (*zhahk* loo-ee dah-*veed*)

Dawarangulili (dwah-rahng-goo-*lee*-lee)

Edgar Degas (ed-gahr deh-*gah*)

Willem de Kooning (*vill*-em duh *koe*-ning)

Eugène Delacroix (oo-*zhen* duh-lah-*kwah*)

André Derain (on-*dray* duh-ran)

de Stijl (duh steel)

Donatello (dohn-ah-*tell*-loh)

Marcel Duchamp (mahr-*sell* doo-*shahm*)

Albrecht Dürer (*ahl*-brekht *duh*-ruhr)

Thomas Eakins (*ay*-kins)

Sergei Eisenstein (sair-gay *eye*-zen-schtine)

Olafur Eliasson (o-la-fur ee-*lie*-ah-sun)

Fan Kuan (fahn kwahn)

Jean-Honoré Fragonard (zhon oh-no-*ray* fra-go-*nahr*)

Helen Frankenthaler (*frank*-en-thahl-er)

fresco (*fres*-coh)

Ganges (*gan*-jeez)

Paul Gauguin (go-*gan*)

Frank Gehry (*ger*-ree)

genre (*zhan*-ruh)

Artemisia Gentileschi (ahr-tuh-*mee*-zhyuh jen-till-*ess*-kee)

Théodore Géricault (*zhair*-ee-koh)

Jean-Léon Gérôme (zhon *lay*-on zhay-*roam*)

Alberto Giacometti (ahl-*bair*-toh jah-ko-*met*-tee)

Giotto di Bondone (*joht*-toe dee bone-*doe*-nay)

Francisco Goya (fran-*sis*-coe go-yah)

Walter Gropius (*val*-tuhr *grow*-pee-us)

Guo Xi (gwo shr)

Guernica (*ger*-nih-kah)

Hector Guimard (gi-*mahr*)

Zaha Hadid (*zah*-hah hah-*deed*)

Hagia Sophia (hah-zhah so-*fee*-ah)

Hangzhou (hung-joe)

Hatshepsut (hah-*shep*-soot)

Heiji Monogatari (hay-jee mo-no-gah-*tah*-ree)

Ando Hiroshige (ahn-doh he-*roh*-shee-gay)

Hannah Höch (*hahn*-nuh *hohk*)

Hokusai (hohk-*sy*)

Pieter de Hooch (*pee*-tuhr duh *hohk*)

Horyuji (hohr-*yoo*-jee)

Shirazeh Houshiary (*sheer*-ah-zey hoosh-*yahr*-ee)

Ictinus (ick-*tee*-nuhs)

Inca (*eenk*-ah)

Ise (*ee*-say)

kachina (kah-*chee*-nah)

Frida Kahlo (*free*-dah *kah*-loh)
Kandarya Mahadeva (Kan-*dahr*-ya mah-hah-*day*-vuh)
Wassily Kandinsky (vass-see-lee can-*din*-skee)
Anish Kapoor (ah-*neesh* kah-*puhr*)
Katsura (kah-*tsoo*-rah)
Khamerernebty (kahm-er-er-*neb*-tee)
Anselm Kiefer (*ahn*-sehlm *kee*-fuhr)
Ernst Ludwig Kirchner (airnst *loot*-vik *keerkh*-ner)
Torii Kiyonobu (*tor*-ee key-yoh-*noh*-boo)
Torii Kiyotada (*tor*-ee key-yoh-*tah*-da)
Krishna (*krish*-nuh)
Laocoön (lay-*oh*-koh-on)
Le Corbusier (luh core-boo-zee-ay)
Fernand Léger (fair-*non* lay-*zhay*)
Emanuel Leutze (*loyts*-uh)
Roy Lichtenstein (*lick*-ten-stine)
Maya Lin (*my*-uh *lin*)
Machu Picchu (*mah*-choo *peek*-choo)
René Magritte (reh-*nay* mah-*greet*)
Edouard Manet (ed-*wahr* mah-*nay*)
Maori (*mow*-ree)
Masaccio (mah-*sach*-chyo)
Henri Matisse (on-*ree* mah-*tees*)
Mato Tope (*mah*-toh *toh*-pay)
Chaz Maviyane-Davies (mah-vee-*yah*-neh)
Maya (*my*-uh)
de Medici (deh *meh*-dee-chee)
Cildo Meireles (*seal*-doh may-*rell*-ess)
Mende (men-day)
Ana Mendieta (*ah*-nah men-*dyet*-ah)
metope (*meh*-toe-pee)
Michelangelo Buonarroti (mee-kel-*an*-jeh-loe bwoh-nah-*roe*-tee)
Ludwig Mies van der Rohe (*loot*-vig *mees* vahn dair *roh*-eh)
mihrab (*mee*-rahb)
Mimbres (*mim*-brace)
Moai (*mo*-eye)
Piet Mondrian (*peet mohn*-dree-ahn)
Claude Monet (*klohd* moh-*nay*)
Berthe Morisot (*bairt* moh-ree-*zoh*)
mosque (mahsk)
Vera Mukhina (*vir*-ah moo-*kee*-nah)
Edvard Munch (*ed*-vard *moonk*)
Murujuga (mu-ru-*ju*-ga)
Eadweard Muybridge (*ed*-wurd *moy*-brij)
Nadar (Félix Tournachon) (nah-*dar fay*-leeks toor-nah-*shohn*)
Emil Nolde (*ay*-meal *nohl*-duh)
Notre-Dame de Chartres (*noh*-truh dahm duh *shahr*-truh)
Claes Oldenburg (klahs *ol*-den-burg)
Ken Okiishi (oh-*kee*-shee)
Olmec (*ohl*-mek)
José Clemente Orozco (ho-*say* cleh-*men*-tay oh-*rohs*-coh)
Nam June Paik (nahm joon pike)
Andrea Palladio (ahn-*dray*-uh pahl-*lah*-dyo)
Giovanni Paolo Panini (jyo-*vahn*-nee *pow*-lo pah-*nee*-nee)
Pablo Picasso (pab-lo pee-*cah*-so)
pietá (pee-ay-*tah*)

Jackson Pollock (*pah*-lock)
Pompeii (pahm-*pay*)
Pont du Gard (pohn duh *gahr*)
Praxiteles (prak-*sit*-el-eez)
qi (chee)
Qiu Ying (choo ying)
Quetzalcoatl (kets-ahl-*kwah*-til)
Robert Rauschenberg (*row*-shen-buhrg)
Gerrit Rietveld (*gair*-it *reet*-velt)
Rembrandt van Rijn (*rem*-brant van *ryne*)
Pierre-August Renoir (pee-*err* oh-*goost* ren-*wahr*)
Gerhard Richter (*gair*-hart *rick*-ter)
Diego Rivera (dee-*ay*-goh ri-*ver*-ah)
Sabatino Rodia (roh-*dee*-uh)
François Auguste Rodin (frahn-*swah* oh-*goost* roh-*dan*)
Andrei Rublev (*ahn*-dray *ru*-blof)
Saint Foy (sanh fwah)
Niki de Saint Phalle (*nee*-kee duh san *fall*)
Doris Salcedo (sal-*say*-doh)
Sanchi (*sahn*-chee)
Sassetta (suh-*set*-tuh)
Scythian (*sith*-ee-ahn)
Sesshu (seh-shoo)
Georges Seurat (zhorzh sur-*ah*)
Bada Shanren (*bah*-dah *shan*-ren)
Shiva Nataraja (*shih*-vuh nah-tah-*rah*-jah)
Tawaraya Sotatsu (tah-wa-*rah*-ya *soh*-taht-soo)
Hito Steyerl (hee-toh sterile)
Alfred Stieglitz (*steeg*-lits)
stupa (*stoo*-pah)
Sulawesi (soo-la-way-zee)
Sarah Sze (zee)
taotie (taow tyeh)
Teotihuacan (tay-oh-tee-wah-*cahn*)
Jean Tinguely (zhon tan-*glee*)
Tlingit (*kling*-git)
Henri de Toulouse-Lautrec (on-*ree* duh too-*looz* low-*trek*)
tusche (too-*shay*)
Tutankhamen (too-tahn-*kahm*-uhn)
Unkei (*un*-kay)
Ur (er)
Kitagawa Utamaro (kit-ah-*gah*-wah ut-ah-*mah*-roh)
Theo van Doesburg (*tay*-oh van dohz-*buhrg*)
Jan van Eyck (*yahn* van *ike*)
Vincent van Gogh (*vin*-sent van goe; also, van *gawk*)
Diego Velázquez (dee-*ay*-goh behl-*ahth*-kehth; also, veh-*las*-kes)
Robert Venturi (ven-*tuhr*-ee)
Jan Vermeer (*yahn* ver-*mir*)
Versailles (vair-*sigh*)
Elisabeth Vigée-LeBrun (vee-*zhay* leh-*broon*)
Leonardo da Vinci (lay-oh-*nahr*-doh dah *veen*-chi)
Andy Warhol (*wohr*-hohl)
Willendorf (*vill*-en-dohrf)
Xiwangmu (shee-wang-moo)
Yaxchilan (yash-chee-*lahn*)
ziggurat (*zig*-uh-raht)

NOTES

Chapter 1

1. Janet Echelman quoted in "Dust Swirls and Cloud Shadows", http://landscapeonline.com/research/article.php/12361, accessed Nov. 27, 2012. Reproduced with permission of Janet Echelman, Inc. (Studio Echelman).

2. "Park's Details, Sculpture a Nod to City's Future," *Arizona Republic*, April 20, 2009, B-6.

3. Georgia O'Keeffe, *Georgia O'Keeffe* (New York: Viking, 1976), opposite plate 13.

4. Jeff Dyer et al, *Innovator's DNA: Mastering the Five Skills of Disruptive Innovators* (Cambridge, MA: Harvard Business Review Press, 2011).

5. History of the Watts Towers, www.wattstowers.us/history.htm, accessed November 17, 2012.

6. Alma Thomas, quoted in Ken Johnson, "Alma Thomas, an Incandescent Pioneer," *New York Times*, August 5, 2016, C17.

7. Quoted in Eleanor Munro, "Late Springtime of Alma Thomas," *Washington Post Magazine*, April 7, 1979, 23.

8. Ibid.

9. Quoted in Adolphus Ealey, "Remembering Alma," in Merry Foresta, *A Life in Art: Alma Thomas 1891–1978* (Washington, D.C.: National Museum of American Art, 1982), 12.

10. Henri Matisse, "The Nature of Creative Activity" *Education and Art a Symposium*, edited by Edwin Ziegfeld (New York: UNESCO, 1953), 21. Copyright © 2017, Succession H. Matisse.

11. Edward Weston, *The Daybooks of Edward Weston*, edited by Nancy Newhall (Millerton, NY: Aperture, 1973), Vol 2, 2004, p.181. Copyright © 1981 Center for Creative Photography, Arizona Board of Regents.

12. Georgia O'Keeffe, *Georgia O'Keeffe* (New York: Viking, 1976), opposite plate 23.

Chapter 2

1. Eva Zeisel, "The Playful Search for Beauty," TED Conference Talk, Monterey, California, February 2001, www.ted.com/talks/eva_zeisel_on_the_playful_search_for_beauty, accessed September 9, 2016.

2. George Nakashima Woodworker, "Interview with George Nakashima", http://www.nakashimawoodworker.com/philosophy/9, accessed Nov. 18, 2016. Courtesy of Jim Bunn, with assistance from John Nakashima. Reproduced by permission of Nakashima Foundation for Peace.

3. Clive Bell, "The Aesthetic Hypothesis," Art (New York: Frederick A. Stokes, 1913), 30.

4. Abraham Cruzvillegas, "*Autoconstrucción,* or Self-Construction," in *Autoconstrucción: The Book* (Los Angeles: REDCAT, 2009), n.p.

5. Quoted in James Estrin, "The 'Genius' of Carrie Mae Weems," *New York Times*, September 25, 2013.

6. Wassily Kandinsky, *Concerning the Spiritual in Art*, Chapter 5.

7. Bill Reid, "Out of the Silence," in *Solitary Raven: The Essential Writings of Bill Reid*, ed. Robert Bringhurst (Vancouver: Douglas & McIntyre, 2000), 109–10.

8. Quoted in Anne Morgan, "From Form to Formlessness: A Conversation with Shirazeh Houshiary," Sculpture, vol. 19 (July 2000), 25.

9. Quoted in Sean P. Means, "UMFA Exhibit Looks through Nancy Holt's Viewfinder," *Salt Lake Tribune*, October 3, 2012.

10. Quoted in Thomas Fecht, *Käthe Kollwitz: Works in Color* (New York: Schocken, 1988), 6.

11. Kollwitz to Romain Rolland, October 23, 1922, in Kollwitz, *Briefe der Freundschaft und Begegnungen* (Munich: List, 1966), 84; translated by Hans Kollwitz.

12. Diary entry, October 1920, in *The Diary and Letters of Kaethe Kollwitz* (Evanston: Northwestern University Press, 1988), 483; translated by Richard and Clara Winston (emphasis in the original).

Chapter 3

1. Quoted in "National Airport: A New Terminal Takes Flight," *Washington Post*, July 16, 1997, www.washingtonpost.com/wp-srv/local/longterm/library/airport/architect.

2. Quoted in Faber Birren, *Color Psychology and Color Theory* (New Hyde Park, NY: University Books, 1961), 20.

3. Keith Sonnier, Interview with the author, New York, Apr. 16, 2008. Reproduced with permission of the Keith Sonnier Studio.

4. Keith Sonnier, *Interview Magazine* by Max Blagg, Nov. 30, 2008, http://www.interviewmagazine.com/art/keith-sonnier/. Reproduced with permission of the Keith Sonnier Studio.

5, 6 and 7. Keith Sonnier, quotations. Reproduced with permission of the Keith Sonnier Studio.

Chapter 4

1. Quoted in Elizabeth McCausland, "Jacob Lawrence," *Magazine of Art* (November 1945), 254.

2 and 3. Henri Matisse, *Matisse on Art* edited by Jack Flam (New York: Dutton, 1978), p.36; originally in "Notes d'un peintre," *La Grande Revue* (Paris, 1908). Copyright © 1995 by Jack Flam. English translation copyright © 1995 by Jack Flam. Underlying text and illustrations by Henri Matisse. Copyright © 1995, 1973 by Succession H. Matisse. Reprinted by permission of Georges Borchardt, Inc. on behalf of Jack Flam.

Chapter 6

1. Quoted in Ellen Gamerman, "Sculpting on Paper," *Wall Street Journal*, April 15, 2011, d4.

2. Keith Haring, *Keith Haring Journals* (New York: Viking, 1996), entry for Mar. 18, 1982. Copyright © 1996, Keith Haring Foundation. Used by permission of The Wylie Agency (UK) Limited.

3. Vincent to Theo van Gogh, April 1882, Letter 184. Translated by Mrs. Johanna van Gogh-Bonger, edited by Robert Harrison. http://www.webexhibits.org/vangogh/letter/11/184.htm?qp=feelings.ambition.

4. Josef Pilhofer, "Searching for the Synthesis," www.lifeart.net/articles/pillhofer/ripillhofer.htm, accessed November 19, 2012.

5. Vincent to Theo van Gogh, April 1882, Letter 219, *Vincent van Gogh: The Complete Letters*, accessed Sept. 7, 2012. Copyright © 2009 Van Gogh Museum, Enterprises B.V.

6. Ibid., June 2, 1885, Letter 506;

7. Ibid., May 22, 1885, Letter 502;

8. Ibid., Sept. 24, 1888, Letter 776;

9. Ibid., Sept. 23-24, 1888, Letter 686;

10. Ibid., May 26, 1888. Letter 613.

11. Quoted in Anthony Blunt, *Picasso's Guernica* (New York: Oxford University Press, 1969), 28.

Chapter 7

1. Quoted in Deborah Solomon, "Celebrating Paint," *New York Times Magazine*, March 31, 1991, 24.

2. Ibid.

3. Quoted in Michael Brenson, "A Look at a Decade of Elizabeth Murray's Works," *New York Times*, April 22, 1988, D1.

4. Quoted in Michael Kimmelman, "At the Met with Elizabeth Murray," *New York Times*, October 21, 1994, C28.

5. Ibid.

6. Quoted in Solomon, "Celebrating Paint," 24.

7. Quoted in "Jason Stopa Interviews Keltie Ferris," *NY Arts Magazine*, www.nyartsmagazine.com/conversations/in-conversation-jason-stopa-interviews-keltie-ferris, accessed November 20, 2012.

Chapter 8

1. Quoted in Barbara Isenberg, "Prices of Prints," *Los Angeles Times*, May 14, 2006, E27.

2. Kiki Smith quoted in Crown Point Press, Biographical Summary by Rachel Lyon, http://www.crownpoint.com/artists/211/biographical-summary, accessed Jan. 15, 2013. Reproduced with permission of Kiki Smith.

3. Quoted in Mary Weaver Chapin, "The Chat Noir & The Cabarets," in *Toulouse-Lautrec and Montmartre* (Washington, D.C.: National Gallery of Art, 2005), 91.

Chapter 9

1. Henri Cartier-Bresson, *The Decisive Moment* (New York: Simon & Schuster, 1952), 14.

2. Binh Danh, "Faces Fleshed in Green" by Robert Schultz, *Virginia Quarterly Review Online*, Winter 2009, Vol 85 (1)m http://www.vqronline.org/vqr-gallery/faces-fleshed-green, accessed Nov. 21, 2012. Reproduced with permission of Binh Danh.

3 and 5. Binh Danh, "Images Make Faces of War Victims Grow" by Bob Keefer, Register-Guard (Eugene, OR), June 4, 2009, p.D1. Reproduced with permission of Binh Danh.

4. Binh Danh, Binh Danh: Life, Times and *Matters of the Swamp*, http://www.youtube.com/watch?v=3wKPYiVdAy4, accessed Nov. 21, 2012. Reproduced with permission of Binh Danh.

6. Binh Danh, "Binh Danh's Yosemite Daguerreotypes" by Sam Whiting, *San Francisco Chronicle*, Sept. 24, 2012. Republished with permission of the author and San Francisco Chronicle. Permission conveyed through Copyright Clearance Center, Inc.

7. Binh Danh, "World Documents" by Anthony W. Lee (South Hadley, MA: Hadley House Press, 2011), n.p. Reproduced with kind permission of Binh Danh.

Chapter 10

1. The "Agent Ruby" campaign slogan for San Francisco Museum of Modern Art by Lynn Hershman Leeson, http://www.lynnhershman.com. Reproduced with permission.

Chapter 11

1. Kanye West, Commencement Speech, School of the Art Institute of Chicago, May 10, 2015, transcribed at www.complex.com/style/2015/05/kanye-west-saic-lecture-transcript, accessed January 17, 2017.

2. "Do You Know Your ABCs?", *Advertising Age*, June 19, 2000.

3. Saul Bass, interviewed for the film *Bass on Titles* (Pyramid Films, 1977).

4. Quoted in Holly Wills, "Biography," www.aiga.org/design-journeys-karin-fong, accessed November 23, 2012.

5. Quoted in Mark Blankenship, "You Are Now Exiting the Real World," *Yale Alumni Magazine*, November 2011, www.yalealumnimagazine.com/issues/2011_11/arts_karinfong.html.

6. Karin Fong, interview with Remco Vlaanderen, Submarine Channel, http://mmbase.submarinechannel.com/interviews/index.jsp?id=24451, accessed Nov. 23, 2012. Reproduced with permission of Karin Fong.

7. Karin Fong, telephone interview with the author, April 30, 2012.

Chapter 12

1. Josephine Withers, *Julio González, Sculpture in Iron*, New York University Press, 1978. Reproduced with permission of Josephine Withers.

2 and 3. Quoted in Michael Brenson, "Maverick Sculptor Makes Good," *New York Times*, November 1, 1987.

4. Martin Puryear interviewed by David Levi Strauss, *Brooklyn Rail*, November 2007, www.brooklynrail.org/2007/11/art/martin-puryear-with-david-levi-strauss, accessed November 23, 2012.

5. Quoted in Michael Kimmelman, "Art View," *New York Times*, March 1, 1992.

6. Quoted in Sarah Rose Sharp, "Nick Cave on Tackling Really Hard Issues with Art," *Hyperallergic*, July 31, 2015, www.hyperallergic.com/226206/nick-cave-on-tackling-really-hard-issues-with-art.

Chapter 13

1. Grayson Perry, "Pottery Is My Gimmick," TateShots, Grayson Perry Studio visit, accessed Jan. 4, 2016. Reproduced with permission of Grayson Perry.

2. Nina Bruun, "The Nest Chair by Nina Bruun," *Contemporist*, Mar. 17, 2010, accessed Jan. 14, 2016. Reproduced with permission of Nina Bruun.

3. Quoted in Roderick Morris, "Show Highlights Return of the Loom," *International Herald Tribune*, June 13, 2011.

4. Faith Ringgold, *Faith Ringgold: Quilting as an Art Form*, http://www.youtube.com/watch?v=lia6SFTOeu8, accessed Nov. 24, 2012. Copyright © 2017 Faith Ringgold, member Artists Rights Society (ARS), New York.

5. Faith Ringgold, interview with Ben Portis, New York, Mar. 18, 2008, http://faithringgold.blogspot.com/2007/11/welcome.html, accessed Nov. 24, 2012. Copyright © 2017 Faith Ringgold, member Artists Rights Society (ARS), New York.

Chapter 14

1. Louis Sullivan, "The Tall Office Building Artistically Considered," *Lippincott Monthly Magazine*, March 1986, 408.

2. Jeanne Gang, "Three Points for the Residential High-Rise: Designing for Social Connectivity" *International Journal of High-Rise Buildings* Vol 5 (2), June 2016. http://studiogang.com/publications, accessed Jan. 14, 2016. Reproduced by permission of Studio Gang.

3. Quoted in Philip Stevens, "Interview with Architect Jeanne Gang," *Designboom*, February 4, 2016.

Chapter 15

1. "Picasso Speaks," *The Arts*, May 1923, 319.

2. Cathleen A. Keller, "The Statuary of Senenmut," in *Hatshepsut from Queen to Pharaoh*, ed. Catharine H. Roehrig (New York: Metropolitan Museum of Art and Yale University Press, 2005), 117.

Chapter 16

1. Hildegard of Bingen, *Scivias*, Book 1, Vision 3: "The Universe and its Symbolism," translated by Columba Hart and Jane Bishop (Mahwah, NJ: Paulist Press, 1990), 93.

2. Abbot Suger, adapted from *Chartres and the Birth of the Cathedral*, Second Edition by Titus Burckhardt (Bloomington, IN: World Wisdom, 2010, p.47). Reproduced with permission.

Chapter 17

1. Leonardo da Vinci, *Treatise on Painting*, quoted in Irene Earls, *Renaissance Art: A Topical Dictionary* (Boulder, CO: Greenwood, 1987), 263.

2. Quoted in Robert Coughlan, *The World of Michelangelo* (New York: Time-Life Books, 1972), 192.

3. For a transcript of the entire hearing before the Inquisition, see Philipp Fehl, "Veronese and the Inquisition: A Study of the So-called *Feast in the House of Levi*," *Gazette des Beaux-Arts*, series 6, vol. 43 (1961), 325–54.

4. Saint Teresa of Jesus, *The Life of Saint Teresa of Jesus*, translated by David Lewis, edited by Benedict Zimmerman (Westminster, MD: Newman, 1947), 266.

Chapter 19

1. Quoted in John Hoag, *Islamic Architecture* (New York: Abrams, 1975), 383.

2. Quoted in Salah M. Hassan, "Khartoum Connections: The Sudanese Story," in *Seven Stories About Modern Art in Africa*, ed. Clementine Deliss (Paris: Flammarion, 1995), 114.

3. Ibrahim el-Salahi, "El-Salahi: A Painter from the Sudan," *African Arts* 1 (Autumn 1967), 17.

4. Quoted in Mark Hudson, "Ibrahim el-Salahi: From Sudanese Prison to Tate Modern," *The Guardian*, July 3, 2013.

5. Ibrahim el-Salahi, "Ibrahim el-Salahi on The Arab Spring Notebook" Interview by Nick Hackworth, *1:54 Contemporary African Art Fair*, Oct. 14, 2016, https://www.artsy.net/article/1-54-contemporary-african-art-fair-interview-with-ibrahim-el-salahi, accessed Nov. 1, 2016. Video produced by Modern Forms. Reproduced by permission of the El-Salahi Studio and Modern Forms.

Chapter 20

1. Quoted in *Our Hearts Fell to the Ground: Plains Indian Views of How the West Was Lost*, ed. Colin G. Calloway (New York: Bedford St. Martin's, 1996), 124.

Chapter 21

1. Quoted in Beaumont Newhall, "Delacroix and Photography," *Magazine of Art* (November 1952), 300.

2. Quoted by Vincent van Gogh in a letter to Theo van Gogh, July 1885, *The Letters of Vincent van Gogh*, translated by Ronald de Leeuw (New York: Penguin, 1996), 302.

3. Quoted in Margaretta Salinger, *Gustave Courbet, 1819–1877, Miniature Album XH* (New York: Metropolitan Museum of Art, 1955), 24.

4. Mary Cassatt to Achille Segard, quoted in Nancy Mathews, *Mary Cassatt: A Life* (New Haven: Yale University Press, 1998), 342 n. 19.

5. Quoted in Albert E. Elsen, *Rodin* (New York: Museum of Modern Art, 1963), 53; from a letter to critic Marcel Adam, published in an article in *Gil Blas* (Paris: July 7, 1904).

6. Quoted in John Rewald, *Cézanne: A Biography* (New York: Abrams, 1986), 208.

7. Vincent van Gogh, *Further Letters of Vincent van Gogh to His Brother, 1886–1889* (London: Constable, 1929), 139.

8. Quoted in Ronald Alley, *Gauguin* (Middlesex, England: Hamlyn, 1968), 8.

9. Paul Gauguin, *Lettres de Paul Gauguin à Georges-Daniel de Monfried* (Paris: Georges Cres, 1918), 89.

10. Quoted in John Russell, *The Meanings of Modern Art* (New York: HarperCollins, 1974), 35.

Chapter 22

1. Wassily Kandinsky, "Reminiscences," in Robert L. Herbert, ed., *Modern Artists on Art* (Englewood Cliffs, NJ: Prentice Hall, 1964), 27.

2. Henri Matisse, *Matisse on Art* edited by Jack Flam (New York: Dutton, 1978), p.36; originally in "Notes d'un peintre," *La Grande Revue* (Paris, 1908). Copyright © 1995 by Jack Flam. English translation copyright © 1995 by Jack Flam. Underlying text and illustrations by Henri Matisse. Copyright © 1995, 1973 by Succession H. Matisse. Reprinted by permission of Georges Borchardt, Inc. on behalf of Jack Flam.

3. Quoted in William Fleming, Art, *Music and Ideas* (New York: Holt, 1970), 342.

4. Quoted in Alfred H. Barr, Jr., ed., *Masters of Modern Art* (New York: Museum of Modern Art, 1955), 124.

5. Quoted in H. H. Arnason, *History of Modern Art*, rev. ed. (New York: Abrams, 1977), 146.

6. Quoted in Nathan Lyons, ed., *Photographers on Photography* (Englewood Cliffs, NJ: Prentice Hall, 1966), 133.

7. Quoted in Beaumont Newhall, *The History of Photography* (New York: Museum of Modern Art, 1964), 111.

8. Quoted in Dan Flores, *Caprock Canyonlands* (Austin: University of Texas Press, 1990), 129.

9. From *American Architect*, quoted in Christopher Gray, "Streetscapes: The American Radiator Building," *New York Times*, February 20, 1994.

10. A letter from Alfred Stieglitz to Georgia O'Keeffe, July 6, 1929, *My Faraway One: Selected Letters of Georgia O'Keeffe and Alfred Stieglitz, Volume One*, ed. Sarah Greenough (New Haven: Yale University Press, 2011), pp.460, 471. Georgia O'Keefe letters and Alfred Stieglitz letters copyright © 2011 by Yale University. Text and compilation copyright © 2011 by Sarah Greenough. Reproduced with permission of Yale Rep. Ltd. On behalf of Yale University Press.

11. Quoted in Joshua C. Taylor, *Futurism* (New York: Museum of Modern Art, 1961), 124.

12. Julian Street, *New York Times* art critic, quoted in Calvin Tomkins, *Duchamp: A Biography* (New York: Henry Holt, 1996), 78.

Chapter 23

1. Quoted in Hans Richter, *Dada 1916–1966* (Munich: Goethe Institut, 1966), 22.

2. Quoted in Paride Accetti, Raffaele De Grada, and Arturo Schwarz, *Cinquant'annia Dada—Dada in Italia 1916–1966* (Milan: Galleria Schwarz, 1966), 39.

3. André Breton, *Manifestos of Surrealism*, translated by Richard Seaver and Helen R. Lane (Ann Arbor: University of Michigan Press, 1972), 14.

4. Salvador Dalí, "The Stinking Ass," translated by J. Bronowski, *This Quarter*, Vol. 5, No. 2, September 1932, 49.

5. Quoted in Stan Lauryssens, *Dalí and I: The Surreal Story* (New York: Thomas Dunne, 2008), 75.

6. Sam Hunter and John Jacobus, *Modern Art* (New York: Harry N. Abrams, 1985), 148.

7. Quoted in Herbert Read, *A Concise History of Modern Painting* (New York: Praeger, 1959), 160.

8. Oliverio Girondo, "Manifiesto," *Martin Fierro*, No. 4, May 15, 1924, n.p.

9. San Francisco Chronicle, October 6, 1935, quoted in Evangeline Montgomery, "Sargent Claude Johnson," *Ijele: Art Journal of the African World* (2002), 1–2.

10. Quoted in Romare Bearden and Harry Henderson, *A History of African American Artists from 1792 to the Present* (New York: Pantheon Books, 1993), 152.

Chapter 24

1. Winston Churchill, "United Europe" lecture delivered at Royal Albert Hall, London, May 14, 1947. Copyright © The Estate of Winston S. Churchill. Reproduced with permission of Curtis Brown, London on behalf of The Estate of Winston S. Churchill.

2. Noah Purifoy interviewed by Karen A. Mason, 1992, UCLA Oral History Collection, African-American Artists of Los Angeles, http://digital2.library.ucla.edu/viewFile.do?contentFileId=1701834, accessed July 12, 2016.

3. Quoted in Edward Lucie-Smith, *Sculpture Since 1945* (London: Phaidon, 1987), 77.

4. Calvin Tomkins, *The World of Marcel Duchamp* (New York: Time-Life Books, 1966), 162.

5. Richard Hamilton, *Catalogue of an Exhibition at the Tate Gallery*, Mar. 12 to Apr. 19, 1970 (London: Tate Gallery) p.31. Copyright © The Estate of Richard Hamilton.

6. Quoted in R. G. Swenson, "What Is Pop Art?," *Art News*, November 1963, 25.

7. Donald Judd, "Specific Objects," *Arts Yearbook 8* (1965), 78.

8. Quoted in Museum of Modern Art, *MoMA Highlights* (New York: Museum of Modern Art, 2004), 233.

9. Alice Aycock, *A Project Entitled "The Beginnings of a Complex:" Notes, Drawings, Photographs* (New York: Lapp Princess Press, 1977), n.p.

10. Yayoi Kusama, *Into Performance: Japanese Women Artists in New York* by Midori Yoshimoto (New Brunswick, NJ: Rutgers University Press, 2005), p.72, https://hirshhorn.si.edu/kusama/yayoi-kusama/. Reproduced by permission of Yayoi Kusama Inc.

11. Yayoi Kusama, *Infinity Net: The Autobiography of Yayoi Kusama* (London: Tate Publishing, 2011), n.p.

12. Lucy R. Lippard, *From the Center: Feminist Essays on Women's Art* (New York: Dutton, 1976), 48.

Chapter 25

1. Kavita Bala, quoted in Michael Webb, "Bill and Melinda Gates Hall," *The Architect's Newspaper*, January 15, 2015, 1.

2. Quoted in *Performance Anxiety* (Chicago: Museum of Contemporary Art, 1997), n.p.

3. Josh Kline, "Critic's Page," *Brooklyn Rail*, March 5, 2015.

4. Theaster Gates, "Announcing the Sanctum Programme," accessed Nov. 24, 2015. Reproduced with permission of White Cube.

5. Quoted in David Shariatmadari, "'Violence is All Around Me:' Imran Qureshi on his disturbing miniatures," *Guardian*, February 18, 2016.

6. Mark di Suvero, "Interview with Renzo Piano," *Interview*, May 2015, www.interviewmagazine.com/art/renzo-piano.

Closer Videos

Jackson Pollock, radio interview with William Wright, 1951, *In Pollock: A Catalogue Raisonné*, ed. Eugene Thaw and Francis O'Connor, Yale Press 1978, pp.248–251. Copyright © 1978 by Yale University.

James Welling, *Choreograph* exhibition press release, Regen Projects, Los Angeles, http://www.regenprojects.com/exhibitions/james-welling9/press-release, Feb. 2016. Copyright © James Welling. Courtesy of Regen Projects, Los Angeles.

Figures in *italics* refer to illustrations.

Kaufmann, Michelle: mkSolaire Home 234, *234*
Kaufmann Residence (Wright) *see* Fallingwater
Kellogg's Corn Flakes Boxes (Warhol) 446, *446*
Kelly, Ellsworth 448
    Blue Green Yellow Orange Red 448, *449*
Kente cloth, Ashanti 342, *342*
Kentridge, William 102
    Drawing for "Lulu" 108, *109*
Kero cups, Inca 358, *358*
keystones 223, *223*, 238
Khadija (Hajjaj) 469, *469*
Khajuraho, India: Kandarya Mahadeva Temple
    306, *307*
Khamseh (Nizami) 332, *332–3*
Khmer empire 189, 310
Khmer Rouge 154, 155
Kiefer, Anselm 466
    Osiris and Isis 466, *466–7*
Kienholz, Edward: *John Doe* 441, *441*
kilns 206, 217
Kindred Spirits (Durand) 49, *49*, 50
kinetic art 53, *53*, 67
    sculpture 53, 200, *200*, 205
Kirchner, Ernst Ludwig 395
    Port Scene 130–31, *131*
    Street, Berlin 395, *395*
Kiss, The (Brancusi) 15, *15*
Kiss, The (Rodin) 15, *15*
Kitagawa Utamaro: *Reflected Beauty...*
    324–5, *325*
Kitchen Maid, The (Vermeer) 298, *298*
Kitchen Table Series, The (Weems) 26–7
Kiyonobu, Torii, I: *Kabuki Actor* 38, *38*
Kiyotada, Torii: *An Actor of the Ichikawa Clan...*
    38, *38*, 41
Klein, Yves 441
Kline, Josh 471
Knight, Death, and the Devil, The (Dürer) 133, *133*
Kodachrome film 152
Kollwitz, Käthe 35
    The Outbreak (from *The Peasants' War*) 35, *35*
    Self-Portrait 35
Korea
    Lotus Sutra 318, *318*
    stoneware pitcher 318, *318*
Korin, Ogata: *Cranes* 78–9, *79*
Kosuth, Joseph 450
    One and Three Chairs 450, *450*
Kota reliquary figure 398, *399*
kouros/kouroi 256, *256–7*, 277
Krasner, Lee 435
    Untitled 435, *436*
kraters 256, *256*, 277
Krazy Kat (Herriman) 51, *51*
Kruger, Barbara 474
    Untitled (I Shop Therefore I Am) 474, *474*
Kuba peoples: Royal Portrait figure 28, *29*

Kuleshov, Lev 160–61
Kuleshov effect 161, 174
Kurosawa, Akira 163–4
    Throne of Blood 164, *164*
Kusama, Yayoi 454–5
    Body Festivals 454–5
    Infinity Mirror Room—Filled with the Brilliance of Life
    455, *455*
    Infinity Mirror Room: Phalli's Field 454, *454*
Kyoto, Japan: Katsura Detached Palace 320,
    321, 322

L

Lamentation (Giotto) 279, *279*
landscape painting
    American 49, 365, 367
    Chinese 49–50, 314–16
    French 23–4, 381–2, 400
    Japanese 323
Lange, Dorothea 426
    Three Families Camped on the Plains along U.S.99...
    426, *426*
Laocoön Group 260, *261*
Large Reclining Nude (Matisse) 83–4, *84*, *85*
Last Judgment, The (Michelangelo) 92–3
Last Supper, The (Leonardo) 283–4, *284*, 285, 292
Latinos 456
Lawrence, Jacob 431
    General Toussaint l'Ouverture Defeats the English at
    Saline 430, 431
    Going Home 70, *70*, 77
Leadership in Energy and Environmental Design (LEED)
    234, 235
Learning from Las Vegas (Venturi and Scott-Brown) 463
LEED *see* Leadership in Energy and Environmental
    Design
Leeson, Lynn Hershman 175, *175*
    DiNA 173–4, *174*
    Lorna 175
    Teknolust 175, *175*
Léger, Fernand 419, 426, 433
    Ballet Mécanique 419, *419*
    The City 418, *419*
Leigh, Vivien 162
Leo III, Emperor 268
Leo X, Pope 289, 291
Leonardo da Vinci 56, 88, 92, 145, 282, 289
    Facial Proportions of a Man in Profile 97, *97*
    The Fetus in the Womb 282–3, *283*
    The Last Supper 283–4, *284*, 285, 292
    Mona Lisa 283, *283*, 412
Letter, The (Cassatt) 135, *135*
L.H.O.O.Q. (Duchamp) 412, *412*
Li Shida: *Five Deer Hermitage* 117, *117*
Liberation of the Peon, The (Rivera) 425, *425*
Lichtenstein, Roy 447
    Drowning Girl 447, *447*

Rome 261, 282
    Campidoglio (Michelangelo) 288, *288*
    Catacomb of St. Domitilla fresco 265, *265*
    Colosseum *262*, 263
    Old St. Peter's Basilica 266, *266*
    Pantheon *262*, *263*, 263–4, 292
    St. Peter's Cathedral (Michelangelo) 288
    Sistine Chapel 92–3, 285, *286*, *287*, 289
Romero, Betsabeé 132
    Ciudades que se van (*Cities on the Move*) 132, *132*
Rosenquist, James 445
    F-111 444–5, *445*,
Rosso Fiorentino 293
    Moses Defending the Daughters of Jethro 293, 293–4
Rothenberg, Susan 465
    Juggler with Shadows 465, *465*
Rothko, Mark 435
    Blue, Orange, Red 436, *437*
Routes of Migration (Gakunga) 497, *479*
Royal Academy, London 361, *362*
Rozendaal, Rafael 476
    15 05 10 IMDb (from *Abstract Browsing*) 476, *476*
Rubens, Peter Paul 296
    The Raising of the Cross 296, *297*
Rubicon: title sequence (Fong) 182–3, *183*
Rublev, Andrei 269
    Old Testament Trinity 269, *269*
Rue Transnonain, April 15, 1834 (Daumier) 136, *137*
rugs *see* carpets
Running Fence (Christo and Jeanne-Claude) 451, *451*
Rush, William 372
Russia
    Constructivism 419, 421, 422, 432
    painting 269, 419; *see also* Kandinsky, Wassily
    sculpture 424
    silent movies/film 160–62
Russian Revolution 382

S

SA MI 75 DZ NY 12 (Wheeler) *44*, 45
Sabraw, John 126
    Chroma S1 13 126, *126*
Safavid rugs 216
Sainte-Chapelle, Paris *31*, 31–2
St. Louis, Missouri: Wainwright Building (Sullivan)
    228, *228*
Saint Phalle, Niki de 441
    Saint Sebastian, or the Portrait of My Love 441, *441*
Saint Sebastian, or the Portrait of My Love (de Saint Phalle)
    441, *441*
Saks Fifth Avenue logo (Bierut) 176, *176*
el-Salahi, Ibrahim 336, *336*
    Arab Spring 336, *336*
    The Mosque 335, *335*
Salcedo, Doris 480
    Plegaria Muda (*Silent Prayer*) 480, *480*
Saltire Compton (Newsome) 18–19, *19*

Sanchi, India: Great Stupa 304, *304*, 308
Sanctum (Gates) 475, *475*
Sandback, Fred: *Untitled* (*Sculptural Study, Six-Part
    Construction*) 39, *39*
Sandouk el Dounia (Baladi) 214, *215*
Sandoval, Humberto *see* Asco
sandstone 195
Sassetta, Il (Stefano di Giovane): *The Meeting of Saint
    Anthony and Saint Paul* 50, *50*
satellite transmission 168
saturation *see* intensity
Sauce Boat with ladle (Zeisel) 20–21, *21*
scale (of design) 69, 79–80, 81, 85
    relationships 79, *79*
Schnitger, Lara 201–2
    Grim Boy 202, *202*
School of Athens, The (Raphael) 47, *48*, 49, 118, 289, 294
Science, Fiction (Thater) 171, *171*
Scivias (Hildegard) 273, *273*
Scorpio Rising (Anger) 165, *165*
Scorsese, Martin 165
Scott, Ridley: *Prometheus* 168, *168*
Scott-Brown, Denis *see* Venturi, Robert
Scream, The (Munch) 388, *388*
screenprinting *139*, 139–40, 143
sculpture (*see also* relief sculpture)
    abstract 10, 402–3, 431–2
    Abstract Expressionist 436
    additive 402–3
    Aztec 356–7
    Baroque 295–6
    Buddhist 304–6
    Cameroon 10, 341
    carving 190, 194–6, 205
    casting 190, 192–4, 205
    Colombian 42–3
    Congo 28, 341
    early Christian 265
    Easter Island 345
    Gandhara 304–5
    Gothic 275–6
    Gupta 305
    Harappan 303, 304
    Hawaiian 345
    Hellenistic 261
    Hindu 306
    in-the-round/freestanding 188, 205
    kinetic 53, 200, 205
    Kota 398
    Maori 347
    Maya 355
    Melanesian 343–4
    Micronesian 344
    mixed media 201–2
    modeling 190–91, 205
    Nok 337–8
    Paleolithic 242

Taylor, Judy: *History of Labor in Maine* 94, *94*
Teflon 231
Teknolust (Leeson) 175, *175*
television 51, 82, 127
tempera painting 50, *50*, 115, 120–21, *121*, 127
temples
    ancient Egyptian 222, *222*
    ancient Greek *258*, 258–9, *259*, 264
    Maya 355, *355*
    Roman *262*, *263*, 263–4
    Teotihuacan 353–4, *354*
Teotihuacan 353, 356
    Pyramid of the Sun 353, *354*
    Temple of the Feathered Serpent 353–4, *354*
Terada Design Architects: N Building 185, *185*
Teresa of Ávila, Saint 296
terra cotta 358
    Chinese Warriors 311, *312*, 313
    Greek krater 256, *256*
    Neolithic beaker (from Susa) 245, *245*, 247
    Nok figures 337, 338, *338*
tertiary colors/hues 61, 67
tessera/tesserae 266, 277
textiles 214
    Afghan carpets/rugs 77, *77*
    Kente cloth 342, *342*
    Navajo 12, 351, *351*
    Windrush (Morris) 206, *207*
    Yoruba 21, *22*
texture 64–5, 67
    digital simulation 66
Thater, Diana: *Science, Fiction* 171, *171*
Theodora, Empress 267, *267*
Thinker, The (Rodin) 380, *380*
Third of May, 1808, The (Goya) 363, 363–4
This Is Definitely Not a Pipe (Beldner) 9, *9*
This Is Not an Artwork (Harrison) 470, 470–71
This Progress (Sehgal) 467
Thomas, Alma 11, *11*
    White Roses Sing and Sing 11, *11*
3-D modeling, computer 172, 464
3-D printing 142–3, 471
Three Families Camped on the Plains along U.S.99... (Lange) 426, *426*
Three Flags (Johns) 120, *121*
Throne for the Greatest Rapper of All Time (Robinson) 198, *198*
Throne of Blood (Kurosawa) 164, *164*
throwing (ceramics) 207, 208, 217
Tigris River 241, 247, 248
Tikal, Guatemala: Maya Temple 355, *355*
Tilt brush (drawing system) 112
Tilted Arc (Serra) 203, *204*, 205
timber
    cross-laminated (CLT) 226, 232
    see also wood
time and motion 50–51

Tinguely, Jean 443
    Homage to New York: A Self-Constructing, Self-Destructing Work of Art 443, *443*
    Méta-harmonie II 200, *200*
tints 58, 61, 67
Titian
    Bacchus and Ariadne 25, *25*
    Noli Me Tangere 73, 73–4, 75, 76
    Pietà 88, *88*, 89, 90
title sequences (movies) 182–3, 184
Tlingit people 353
    Community House 353, *353*
    totem pole 353, *353*
To Reflect an Intimate Part of the Red (Kapoor) 470, *470*
Tobit Burying the Dead (Andrea di Lione) 40, 40–41
Today's Ideology (Reas) 173, *173*
Toland, Gregg 163
Toltecs 86, 356
    Chacmool 356, *356*
tones 54
Tooker, George 121
    The Waiting Room 121, *121*
tools, Paleolithic 241, 242
tooth (of papers) 104, 113
Torres-García. Joaquín 427
    Universal Constructivism 427, *427*
Totem Pole (Reid) 30–31, *31*
totems, Native American 353, *353*, 358
Toulouse-Lautrec, Henri de 137, 138, *138*, 179, 386
    Ambassadeurs: Aristide Bruant 138, *138*
    Aristide Bruant 137, *137*
    At the Moulin Rouge 386, *387*
Trahison des Images, La (Magritte) 9, *9*
Travelers Among Mountains and Streams (Fan Kuan) 314, *314*
Treachery of Images, The (Magritte) 9, *9*
Tree of Life (Mendieta) 458, *459*
Trees with Ivy in the Asylum Garden (van Gogh) 100, *100*
Trent, Council of (1545–63) 294
Triple Point (*Gleaner*) (Sze) 69, *69*
Trojan War 261
trompe l'oeil 9
trusses 226, *226*, 238
Tuning the Samisen (Hokusai) 107, *107*
Turner, Joseph Mallord William: *The Burning of the Houses of Lords and Commons* 364, 364–5
tusche 136, 137, 138, 143
Tutankhamen 253
    mask 253, *253*
Two Fridas, The (Kahlo) 428, *428*
Two Pairs of Legs (Álvarez Bravo) 149, *149*
two-point perspective 47, *47*, *48*, 67
typefaces 177, 187
    Adobe Garamond 177
    black letter 177
    Clearview Hwy (Meeker) 177, 177–8
    Febrile (Cuervo Cisneros) *178*, 178–9

Warka Vase 248–9, *249*
warp fibers 214, 217
washes *see* ink washes
Washington, D.C.
    government buildings 362
    Lincoln Memorial (French) 54
    Ronald Reagan Washington National Airport (Pelli) 44, *44*
    U.S. Supreme Court Building 33–4, *34*
    Vietnam Veterans Memorial (Lin) 28–9, *29*, 471
    The White House (Hoban) 71, *71*
Watching the Deer by a Pine-Shaded Stream (Ma Yuan) 315, *315*
watercolor painting 115–17, 127
Waterfall (Eliasson) 204, 205
Watts Riot (Purifoy) 441–2, *442*
Waves at Matsushima (Sotatsu) 324, *324*
Wayne, June 129
We Are Fighting! (Barraza) 140, *140*, 180
Weatherford, Mary 468
    Oxnard Ventura 468, *468*
weaving 214
    see also carpets; tapestries
Web #5 (Celmins) 104, *105*, 106
webcomics *110*, 111
websites 185
Weems, Carrie Mae
    The Kitchen Table Series 26, 26–7
weft fibers 214, 217
Welles, Orson: *Citizen Kane* 162, 163
Welling, James 156
    9812 156, *157*
West, Kanye 177
Weston, Edward: *Pepper #30* 14, *14*, 15
Wheeler, Doug: *SA MI 75 DZ NY 12* 44, 45
White House, The (Hoban) 71, *71*
Whiteread, Rachel 194
    Untitled (Hive) I 194, *194*
White Roses Sing and Sing (Thomas) 11, *11*
Whitney Museum of American Art, New York (Piano) 11, *483*, 483–4, *484*
William Rush Carving His Allegorical Figure (Eakins) 370, 372, *372*
Williams, William Carlos 68
Wilson, Jane and Louise: *The Silence is Twice as Fast Backwards I* 144, 144–5
Windrush (Morris) 206, *207*
Woman and Bicycle (de Kooning) 435, *435*
Woman Haunted by the Passage of the Bird-Dragonfly Omen of Bad News (Miró) *414*, 415
Woman of Willendorf 242, *242*
women artists (pre-20th century) 6, 72–3, 75, 87, 295, 361–2
Women Artists in Revolution (WAR) 456–7
wood
    as building material 221, 222, 226, *226*, 232
    carving 196, *197*
    engraving(s) 131, *131*, 143

Wood, Grant 428–9
    American Gothic 429, *429*
woodblock/woodcut prints 129–30, 143
    German 130–31, *131*
    Japanese 38, *38*, 41, 130, *130*, 324–6, *325*, *326*, 327, *327*
Woodman, Betty: *Divided Vases: Cubist 209*, 209–10
woodworking 213–14
Workers' Club, The (Rodchenko) 420, 421
works of art: definition 3, 19
Works Progress Administration 425, 431
World in a Box, The (Baladi) 214, *215*
World War I 411, 415
World War II 415, 432, 433, 435
Wright, Frank Lloyd 229, 422
    Barnsdall House, Los Angeles 22, *22*
    Fallingwater (Kaufmann Residence) 230, *230*, 422
    prairie houses 408
    Robie House, Chicago 229, 408, *408*
Wright, Orville and Wilbur 392
writing
    Sumerian 248
    see also calligraphy
Wudl, Tom: *Rembrandt's Indulgence was Van Gogh's Dilemma* 123, *123*

X

Xiwangmu 313
Xoc, Lady 355

Y

Yaxchilan, Mexico/Guatemala: Maya lintel 355, *355*
Yellow and Black (Herrera) 12, *13*
Yellow River valley 241
Yombe people: Magaaka power figures 341, *341*
Yoruba peoples 339
    house post 339–40, *340*
    textiles 21, *22*
Yoshitoshi 325, 327
    The Battle of Sanno Shrine 326, *326*
    The Enlightenment of Jigoku-Dayu 327, *327*
You and I, Horizontal (III) 37, *37*
You Who Are My Love and My Life's Enemy Too (Qureshi) 478, *478*
Young Ladies of Avignon (Picasso) *398*, 398–9
Young Mother Sewing (Cassatt) 379, *379*
Yuan dynasty (China) 315, 316
    literati painting 315–16
    porcelain plate 317, *317*

Z

Zeisel, Eva 21
    Sauce Boat with ladle 20–21, *21*
Zen Buddhism 323
ziggurats 248, 254
    Ur-Nammu, Iraq 248, *248*
Zimbabwe: Great Zimbabwe *221*, 221–2
Zuni Pueblo people 352